Hula shows are performed everywhere. Wasn't it King David Kalakaua who said "Hula is the language of the heart and therefore the heartbeat of the Hawaiian people"?
- *Tibor Bognàr*

The first Polynesians came upon the archipelago's shores aboard double-hulled canoes.
- *Claude Hervé-Bazin*

Some of the islands' coasts, such as Na Pali, north of Kaua'i, are chiselled by many deep valleys. - *Claude Hervé-Bazin*

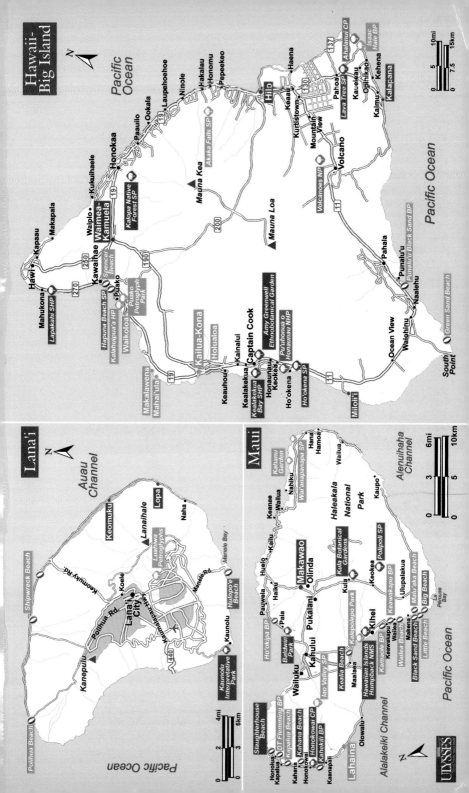

In the Hanapepe Valley, a rainbow pierces the sky above a steep cliff.
- *Claude Hervé-Bazin*

Hawaii

Claude Hervé-Bazin
Sophie Czaplejewicz

Travel better, enjoy more

Authors
Claude Hervé-Bazin
Sophie Czaplejewicz

Publisher
Pascale Couture

Editor
Stéphane G. Marceau

Project Coordinators
Jacqueline Grekin
Cindy Garayt

Copy Editing
Cindy Garayt
Jacqueline Grekin
Editing Assistance
Dena Duijkers

Translation
Danielle Gauthier
Stephanie Heidenreich
Renata Isajlovic
Myles McKelvey
Suzanne Murray

Page Layout
Typesetting
Dena Duijkers
Visuals
Isabelle Lalonde

Cartographers
Bradley Fenton
Yanik Landreville
Patrick Thivierge
Isabelle Lalonde

Computer Graphics
Stéphanie Routhier
Illustrations
Sophie Czaplejewicz

Photography
Cover Page
Don King (The
Image Bank)
Inside Pages
Claude Hervé-Bazin
Tibor Bognàr
M. Ragert (Megapress)

Artistic Director
Patrick Farei (Atoll)

Special thanks: Laura Aquino, Current Events, Heidi Auman, Midway Phoenix, Ruth Ann Becker, Becker Communications, Donovan DeLacruz, Stryker Weiner Associates Rob Deveraturda, Stryker Weiner Associates Michelle Kalama, McNeil Wilson Communications Charlene Kauhane, Maui Visitors Bureau Charles Kauluwehi Maxwell Sr., " Uncle Charlie " Gale Mejia, McNeil Wilson Communications Kammy Purdy and Maria, Moloka'i Visitors Association Alain Sacasas et Laure Simoes, Clipper House, Midway, for the delicious cuisine and great memories, Bob Tracey, Midway Phoenix, Gigi Valley, Lana'i Company.

OFFICES
CANADA: Ulysses Travel Guides, 4176 Rue St-Denis, Montréal, Québec, H2W 2M5,
☎ (514) 843-9447 or 1-877-542-7247, ≈(514) 843-9448, info@ulysses.ca, www.ulyssesguides.com

EUROPE: Les Guides de Voyage Ulysse SARL, BP 159, 75523 Paris Cedex 11, France,
☎ 01 43 38 89 50, ≈01 43 38 89 52, voyage@ulysse.ca, www.ulyssesguides.com

U.S.A.: Ulysses Travel Guides, 305 Madison Avenue, Suite 1166, New York, NY 10165,
☎ 1-877-542-7247, info@ulysses.ca, www.ulyssesguides.com

DISTRIBUTORS
CANADA: Ulysses Books & Maps, 4176 Saint-Denis, Montréal, Québec, H2W 2M5,
☎ (514) 843-9882, ext.2232, 800-748-9171, Fax: 514-843-9448, info@ulysses.ca,
www.ulyssesguides.com

GREAT BRITAIN AND IRELAND: World Leisure Marketing, Unit 11, Newmarket Court, Newmarket Drive, Derby DE24 8NW, ☎ 1 332 57 37 37, Fax: 1 332 57 33 99
office@wlmsales.co.uk

SCANDINAVIA: Scanvik, Esplanaden 8B, 1263 Copenhagen K, DK, ☎ (45) 33.12.77.66,
Fax: (45) 33.91.28.82

SPAIN: Altaïr, Balmes 69, E-08007 Barcelona, ☎ 454 29 66, Fax: 451 25 59,
altair@globalcom.es

SWITZERLAND: OLF, P.O. Box 1061, CH-1701 Fribourg, ☎ (026) 467.51.11,
Fax: (026) 467.54.66

U.S.A.: The Globe Pequot Press, 246 Goose Lane, Guilford, CT 06437 - 0480,
☎1-800-243-0495, Fax: 800-820-2329, sales@globe-pequot.com

Other countries, contact Ulysses Books & Maps, 4176 Rue Saint-Denis, Montréal, Québec, H2W 2M5,
☎ (514) 843-9882, ext.2232, 800-748-9171, Fax: 514-843-9448, info@ulysses.ca, www.ulyssesguides.com

Canadian Cataloguing in Publication Data (see page 4)
© September 2000, Ulysses Travel Guides.
All rights reserved
Printed in Canada
ISBN 2-89464-313-6

How shall we account for this nation having spread itself to so many detached islands so widely disjoined from each other in every quarter of the Pacific Ocean? What we know already in consequence of this voyage warrants our pronouncing it to be, by far, the most extensive nation on Earth.

Captain Cook, 1778

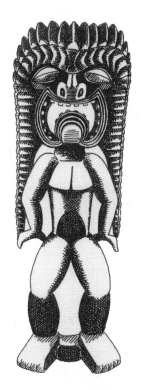

Canadian Cataloguing in Publication Data

Hervé-Bazin, Claude

    Hawaii

    (Ulysses travel guide)
    Translation of: Hawaii.
    Includes index.

    ISBN 2-89464-313-6

    1. Hawaii - Guidebooks   I. Title   II. Series.

DU622.H4713 2000   919.6904'42   C00-941172-0

Table of Contents

List of Maps

Map Symbols

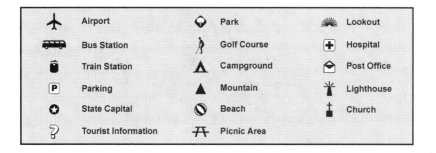

✈ Airport	⚲ Park	� Lookout
🚌 Bus Station	🏌 Golf Course	✚ Hospital
🛄 Train Station	⛰ Campground	✉ Post Office
P Parking	▲ Mountain	🗼 Lighthouse
★ State Capital	Ø Beach	✝ Church
? Tourist Information	⊼ Picnic Area	

Symbols

(ship symbol)	Ulysses's Favourite
☎	Telephone Number
⇄	Fax Number
≡	Air Conditioning
⊗	Fan
≈	Pool
ℜ	Restaurant
ℝ	Refrigerator
K	Kitchenette
△	Sauna
⊖	Exercise Room
tv	Television
ctv	Cable Television
pb	Private Bathroom
sb	Shared Bathroom
bkfst incl	Breakfast Included
♉	Lanai
Ⅱ	Minibar
◙	In-room Safe

ATTRACTION CLASSIFICATION

★	Interesting
★★	Worth a visit
★★★	Not to be missed

The prices listed in this guide are for the admission of one adult,
unless otherwise indicated.

HOTEL CLASSIFICATION

The prices in this guide are for one room, double occupancy
in high season.

RESTAURANT CLASSIFICATION

The prices in the guide are for a meal for one person,
not including drinks and tip.

All prices in this guide are in U.S. dollars.

Write to Us

We acknowledge the financial support of the Government of Canada through the Book Publishing Industry Development Program (BPIDP) for our publishing activities.

We would also like to thank SODEC (Québec) for its financial support.

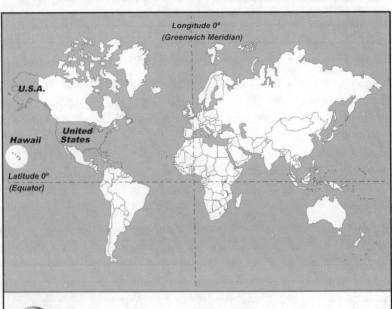

 Where is Hawaii?

Hawaii

Population : 1,186,815 inhab.
Capital : Honolulu
Area : 6,424 mi² (16,638 km²)
Currency : US dollar

©ULYSSES

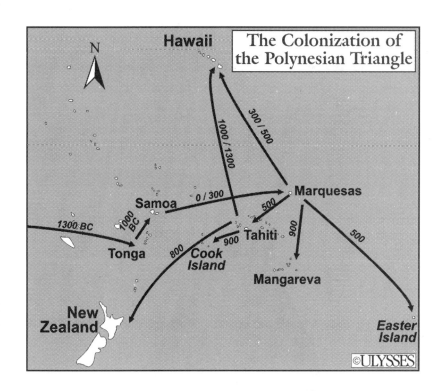

The Colonization of the Polynesian Triangle

Hawaii

N

300 / 500

1000 / 1300

Marquesas

0 / 300

Samoa

500

1300 BC

1000 BC

Tahiti

900

Tonga

800

Cook Island

900

500

Mangareva

New Zealand

Easter Island

©ULYSSES

When European

explorers stumbled upon the Pacific islands in the 18th century, they thought they had found heaven on earth.

In this Age of Enlightenment, society, beyond romanticism and a taste for the exotic, was still profoundly religious, and this discovery was a true revelation: life could be happy, carefree, blessed by the gods and blessed by nature. The last Polynesian archipelago to be discovered since it was so far from land, Hawaii, despite the tragic fate of its discoverer, Captain Cook, would eventually welcome its fair share of sailors smitten by lovely *wahine*, of dreamers and of unconditional enthusiasts. From Mark Twain to Robert Louis Stevenson, from Herman Melville to Jack London, the archipelago would cast its spell on generations of artists and adventurers. And who could ever blame them?

Here, forces of nature seem to have

banded together to create the most beautiful decor in the world: dishevelled mountains shrouded in lush vegetation and billowy clouds, deep valleys moistened by abundant waterfalls, incessant rainbows, powerful volcanoes spewing streams of lava all the way to the ocean, and the world's most magnificent waves, a surfer's dreams come true, beating on the shores of perfect beaches lined with coconut trees. Through the course of genera-

tions, these merry islands have been inhabited by people from the four corners of the globe: first came the Polynesians, whose culture is presently going through a rebirth that is beyond all expectations, followed by the Europeans and then the Asians. First divided, now united, the various cultures have embraced one another to bring forth a kaleidoscopic people thriving in the tropical heat.

Geography

Situated approximately 2,480mi (4,000km) from the closest continent (North America) and 1,240mi (2,000km) from the nearest populated island, Hawaii is the most isolated archipelago in the world. Right in the middle of the North Pacific, its 132 islands and islets are spread over 1,550mi (2,500km) across the Tropic of Cancer. The eight main islands, seven of which are populated, cover 95% of the southeastern surface area of the archipelago (6,422.3 sq mi or 16,638km²). They include, from east to west: Hawaii, Maui, Kaho'olawe, Lana'i, Moloka'i, O'ahu, Kaua'i and Ni'ihau. Although archeological findings show that they were populated a long time ago, the northwestern islands beyond Kaua'i and Ni'ihau now form an immense wildlife reserve, forbidden to visitors, and are home to seabirds and monk seals. Only Midway Island, formerly populated by military personnel but recently returned to civilians, can be visited; about 100 people live there year-round.

The Islands

O'ahu

With a surface area of 608 sq mi (1,574km²), O'ahu is the third largest island in Hawaii. As the intersection of the archipelago, it includes three quarters of the population, the capital city of Honolulu, .as well as the Pearl Harbor military base. A stone's throw away, the world-famous Waikiki beach resort area is where tourism in the islands all began. Most of the northern coast is still preserved from development and is renowned for its winter rollers that make it a favorite site for international surfing competitions.

Hawaii

Nicknamed the Big Island because of its size (4,038 sq mi or 10,461km²), Hawaii covers nearly two thirds of the archipelago, giving it its name, and is more to the east. Located right over the hot spot that gave birth to all of the islands, Hawaii features the archipelago's only remaining active volcanoes, such as the capacious Kilauea. Much of this young island (only 800,000 years old) is covered with moon-like landscapes still unconquered by nature. The sunnier and greener western coast features the Kona seaside resort.

Maui

Floating in the centre of the archipelago, Maui is the second most visited island after O'ahu. Its name, "Island of the Valley," refers to the plain in the middle of the island that was formed by the lava flows of two volcanoes. Silent since 1790, the majestic Hale'a'kala and its immense caldera rise over 9,840ft (3,000m). The western side of Maui is the most developed and is overrun with sugar-cane and pineapple plantations. It also features the old whaling port of Lahaina, now a tourist attraction. The eastern side of the island, crossed by a winding road, is far more luxuriant.

Lana'i

Formerly known as the "Island of Pineapples" (140 sq mi or 362km²) and transformed into an immense plantation by the Dole company, Lana'i now focuses on a quiet and luxurious type of tourism. Paths, rather than roads, twist and turn across the island, leading to extensive deserted beaches.

Moloka'i

Closest to O'ahu, the quiet island of Moloka'i is the least visited of all the islands and is mostly populated with Hawaiians. On the north shore, inaccessible for the greater part, tremendous cliffs plunge straight into the ocean. As for the Kalaupapa Peninsula, it is the remnant of an old lava flow and was once inhabited by exiled lepers. On the

western side of the
island, ranches extend
as far as the eye can
see, as well as magnifi-
cent deserted beaches
that have strong ocean
currents to thank for
their tranquillity.

Kaho'olawe

The smallest of the
eight main islands
(45 sq mi or 116km²),
Kaho'olawe has known
a rather tragic fate: for
years, this ancient sa-
cred site was used to
train American marine
bombardiers. Finally
returned to the state of
Hawaii in 1995 after 30
years of controversy, it
still remains closed to
most visitors.

Kaua'i

The most occidental of
the main islands
(553 sq mi or
1,432km²), Kaua'i is
known as the "Garden
Island" and is reputed
for its unbridled vegeta-
tion and preserved
wilderness. Waterfalls,
high-mountain forests
and sculpted cliffs
along the Na Pali coast-
line create the perfect
image of a tropical
paradise. The culminat-
ing point of the island,
Mount Wai'ale'ale, ri-
vals with one or two
other areas in the world
for the privilege of be-
ing the most rained-on
place on earth. Kaua'i
also features the superb
Waimea canyon,
known as the "Pacific
Grand Canyon."

Ni'ihau

Located next to Kaua'i,
the small island of
Ni'ihau (73 sq mi or
189km²) is entirely
owned by none other
than the Robinson fam-
ily, who came to the
islands in the 19th cen-
tury. This island shel-
ters a small community
of less than 200 people
who have maintained a
lifestyle that has disap-
peared from every-
where else. Access is
denied even to resi-
dents of the other is-
lands.

Geological Origins

The Hawaiian Islands
are the summits of
towering volcanoes
rising from the depths
of the Pacific Ocean.
Plate tectonics, a theory
that was adopted in the
early 20th century by
the scientific commu-
nity, plate tectonics
help understand this
phenomenon: the
envelope of the earth is
made up of approxi-
mately 15 independent
plates that continuously
slide in different and
sometimes opposite
directions on a bed of
molten lava. These
plates vary in size and
support continents or
oceans, often both.
Fracture lines appear
where they split apart
or come together, and
it is along these fracture
lines that volcanoes
appear.

Birth

Sometimes volcanoes
are created right on a
plate over a crack in
the earth's crust that
geologists call "hot
spot." This is how they
explain the phenome-
non in Hawaii: gener-
ally 22mi (35km) thick
under the continents
and 6mi (10km) under
the oceans, the earth's
crust sometimes be-
comes much finer,
allowing magma to
infiltrate. In Hawaii,
magma escaped from
one hot spot for 70
million years. As it
encountered the cold
waters of the Pacific
Ocean, it coagulated
into "basalt cushions"
that piled up like can-
non balls. For as long
as the lava flow did not
dry up because of plate
movement, the pile
ended up reaching the
surface, giving birth to
an island; otherwise, it
formed an underwater
mountain. The entire
archipelago was cre-
ated in this manner
starting with the great
Kure, born 35 million
years ago. Between
90% and 99% of the
volcano constituting
each of the islands is in
fact under water.

Adulthood

Because the ocean
bottom drifts along
with the Pacific plate to
which it belongs, only
hot spots remain sta-
tionary. Transported by
this movement, the
islands move towards

Japan at an average speed of 3.4 to 3.5in (8.5 to 9cm) per year. First visible consequence of this movement: the Hawaiian Islands are aligned over 1,550mi (2,500km) on a southeast-northwest axis which corresponds to the direction taken by the Pacific plate. Second sign: as it progressively moves further away from the source hot spot, the volcano forming the island eventually dries up and coagulates. Then begins a long period of wearing away at the base.

Old Age

As soon as the flow of magma ceases, the island is exposed to the wind, rain and waves and even frost at higher altitudes. Little by little, it burns away despite its efficient passive resistance: built by an accumulation of lava layers, the shield volcano has relatively symmetric and soft slopes and provides less resistance to the effects of air and water than the majestic and proud explosive cones found on other shorelines. But time, with regards to geology, is not of the essence, and day after day the island imperceptibly melts. Attacked from all sides, it regularly collapses into gigantic landslides.

From the southeast to the northwest, each island thus represents a

march in time. Several thousands of kilometres away from their birthplace, the very eroded northwest islands are now mere atolls, formed by the accumulation of coral on the sunken shores that once rose in the centre of lagoons. Still more to the west, the 50-million-year-old mountains of the Emperor Seamount Chain have returned to the sea, eroded by natural forces. Their highest point is located 958ft (292m) "under" sea level.

The Future

The Big Island's proximity to the source hot spot makes it home to the only two remaining volcanoes in activity in the archipelago: the Mauna Loa and the Kilauea. Although it is presently dormant, the nearby Mauna Kea, with its snow-covered slopes, is the highest mountain in the world: measured from its oceanic base, it reaches 33,413.4ft (10,187m), of which 13,792.4ft (4,205m) are above sea level. The caldera of the Mauna Loa, the largest volcano in activity and 70 times greater than the Etna, is the place of origin of most lava flows that have shaped the island. Its last eruption in 1984 lasted three weeks. Since then, the activity has shifted to the Kilauea, one of the most active volcanoes

on the planet, which has been in constant eruption since 1983. But soon, it too will also cease to be fed, and calm will return to Hawaii until the day of a new birth. Twenty-five miles (40km) southeast of the Big Island, a mountain is already in the making: Lo'ihi, whose summit reaches, for the time being, 3,178.3ft (969m) below the ocean's surface. The big day of its revelation to the world is predicted in 10,000 to 100,000 years from now. It is highly likely that, should it remain nourished by the hot spot, this new island will end up joining Hawaii.

Fauna and Flora

Located far from any existing life, Hawaii has given birth to flora and fauna that are unique in the world, with close to 90% of endemic species (far more than the Galapagós Islands made famous by Charles Darwin). As a great outdoor laboratory, the islands of all different ages provide direct observation of the evolution of species. This is made all the more interesting by the fact that the archipelago, on account of great variations in altitude and pluviometry, is home to 11 of the 13 great biotopes of the world, leading to a rare biological diversity. Surprisingly, before Darwin had his say, the ancient Hawaiians, great observers of nature, developed their own theory on the evolution of the species. In the creation myth called *Kumulipo*, it is stated that the most complex animals descend from the most primitive forms of life.

Colonization of the Lands

The great distance between Hawaii and the closest continent made its colonization by nature very difficult. Since the ocean prevented land mammals, reptiles and amphibians from reaching the islands, the land was conquered by insects and birds alone whose legs, wings and feces served as vehicles for plant seeds. The currents and winds also pushed crabs, shells and other small marine animals who were attached to floating tree trunks or vegetation debris. Small insects were carried in by the jet stream, a high-altitude aerial current. Studies show it is that way that every 35,000 to 70,000 years, a new species succeeded in integrating itself to the archipelago. Each new species adapted itself to the environment, sometimes evolving into 10 subspecies, successively populating all the available ecological niches: from alpine tundra on the highest volcanoes to dried-up lava flows and swamps

to rainforests in the coastal areas.

Biogeographers refer to this process of colonization and evolution as "adaptive radiation." Facing few predators, many species abandoned their defence mechanisms: certain birds lost the capacity to fly; the Hawaiian raspberry, *'akala*, lost its thorns, and the *ko'oko'olau* lost its barbs. If this faculty of nature is the reason for the great biotic wealth of Hawaii, it is also responsible for the disappearance of many endemic plants and animals who were no longer able to defend themselves against foreign species more accustomed to fighting for survival.

The Human Impact

Humans are the source of all the misfortunes suffered by the Hawaiian species, many of which have now disappeared. The Polynesians were the first to interfere with the ecosystem, dispersing livestock, food crops and ornamental plants, and competing with or destroying the endemic vegetation. But it was mostly the colonization of the islands by the Occidentals that made the situation much worse. Despite a continually enforced sanitary system, insects, weeds and diverse bacteria are continuously unfurled on the

archipelago through visitors' luggage, in freighter cargoes or by sticking to the hulls and anchors of ships. New species colonize the island two million times faster than its natural biological rhythm. However, the worst results are perhaps direct consequences of human activity, such as the draining of humid zones and the increase of homesteads and pastures to the detriment of forests.

Introducing New Animals

Let loose in the wilderness, goats devour rare and fragile plants without distinction, and very nearly caused the extinction of the emblematic silversword plant which grew on the Hale'a'kaka, on Maui. Everywhere, birds' eggs are attacked by rats as well as mongooses, who were introduced in the 19th century to sugar-cane plantations in an attempt to exterminate those very rats. But since the mongoose hunts during the day and the rat has nocturnal habits, he shouldn't have anything to worry about.

Some "pet" snakes and alligators have also been imported, right under the noses of sanitary control services, and either managed to escape their owners or were set free when they became too "greedy." Pigs, intro duced by the Polynesians, also represent a major problem. Not only do they uproot many plants but they also create pools of briny water by taking mud baths in the forest, leading to the development of malaria-carrying mosquito larvae. To control their presence, searches are organized and zones entirely surrounded with wire netting. But how can they ensure their total eradication? This dispersion-control problem is similar to Argentinean-ants problem: having colonized the higher slopes of the Hale'a'kala, they invade the land at a rate of 426ft (130m) per year, supplanting in that region all other insects on which depend many species of endemic plants for pollination.

Alien Plants

Plants from tropical America, Asia and even Africa, some brought to embellish gardens and others as clandestine passengers, have spread without much difficulty throughout the islands. Among the more dangerous invaders are three important species of invasive lianas: passionflower, honeysuckle and mulberry. Entire forests of *ohi'a* or of *koa* (Hawaiian acacia), Hawaii's two emblematic trees, are dying of asphyxiation as a result. Lianas create a screen that stops all light from reaching the ground, thus preventing the growth of seeds of endemic species. The *Coccinia grandis*, an Asian cucurbitaceae introduced to Hawaii in 1968, is now out of the

control on O'ahu and the western coast of the Big Island. A biological control program (introducing African insects that are natural predators) was initiated on Kaua'i and Maui, still relatively unaffected, at the risk of once again spreading a new species and creating more uncontrollable interactions. Then there is the *Miconia calvescens*, an ornamental tree from South America that eats away natural spaces at a surprising speed, especially the forests of *o'hia* on which a large number of endemic species depend. In Tahiti, where it appeared earlier, it already takes up 60% of all wooded surfaces. It is for this reason that strict control methods are practiced by agricultural services in Hawaiian airports.

Disappearing Species

The situation is alarming: the archipelago, which barely represents 0.3% of the total surface area of the United States, was once home to 75% of all extinct species and 27% of currently endangered species. Of the 2,000 endemic plants that were inventoried, one third is in more or less imminent danger of disappearing. Below 3,936ft (1,200m), alien plants have taken over most of the land; only half of the original ecosystems remain. Since Cook's discovery of the

Humuhumunukunukuapua'a
(*Rhinecantus rectangulus*)

What in the world does this long word mean? It is the name of Hawaii's official fish, more precisely, a species of triggerfish that lives on the reef. "Humuhumunukunuk uapu'a" actually means "pig's nose," which probably refers to the strange spur

located behind its head. The head is striped with a black mask and its body is mostly orange and white, with geometrical patterns. Its high-set eyes allow it to safely attack long-spine sea urchins with its powerful mouth.

islands, hundreds of species have forever disappeared: at least 70 bird species, snails, insects and over 100 kinds of plants. Surely many more never-repertoried species existed and died even before the arrival of Occidentals.

The Future

Fortunately, some natural areas still remain intact in the forests of eastern Maui, on the northern coast of Moloka'i and in the high plateaus of Kaua'i. There has been a notable increase in the number of protected areas in the archipelago thanks to private conservation groups such as Nature Conservancy. After much hesitation, Hawaiian authorities and wildlife-protection groups have finally begun waging a real war against alien species.

Under the auspices of the Bishop Museum of Honolulu, which has been involved in the study of Hawaiian biotopes since the 19th century, the Hawai'i Botanical Survey is performing an exhaustive inventory of the ecosystems, of the fauna and flora and of the endemic and introduced species to study their dispersion across the archipelago. Another program, HEAR (Hawaiian Ecosystems at Risk), jointly launched by the Natural Parks Services and

the University of Hawai'i, studies the secrets of the colonization of invasive plants and their consequences on the environment. A model of climatic dispersal has been created in an attempt to predict and control their extension.

Mammals

Being so far away from any continent, the Hawaiian archipelago was colonized by a very limited number of mammals, not including those that were introduced by man (pigs, goats, dogs, cats, rats and antelopes). In fact, only one land mammal arrived on its own: the **Hawaiian Hoary Bat** (*Lasiurus cinereus hawaiiensis*). This small animal with a reddish-brown coat measures between 5 to 6in (12 to 15cm) with its wings fully spread out, and weighs 0.7oz (20g) at most. This insectivore bat is perched in trees or lives in caves. Although it is nocturnal, it can sometimes be seen during the day. Having suffered from deforestation and human installations, it lives mostly on the Big Island.

No doubt, you will get to see one of the many **mongooses** that scurry across the streets. Yet despite their cute little faces, mongooses are quite detrimental to endemic bird species. If the Big Island is where you will see the most,

Kaua'i is the only island that managed to escape their raids. Legend has it that the longshoreman who was supposed to offload the first couple of mongooses there was bitten by one of them and dropped the crate in the water.

Birds

Some 296 species of birds of all origins inhabit Hawaii and fall under several categories: the brightly coloured forest birds, usually Hawaiian and quite rare; the seabirds that inhabit or visit the islands, such as the Laysan albatross which occupies every square inch of Midway Island from winter to summer; the water birds, either endemic or not, populating the preserved humid zones; and the many migratory birds including, among others, the *kolea*, or Pacific plover, which summers in Alaska.

It is impossible to know exactly how many species inhabited the islands before the arrival of humans, but the number is estimated at between 70 and 140. Among these, approximately two thirds are thought to have belonged to the Drepanididae family (forest birds), and researchers at the University of Hawai'i estimate that many descended from a unique type of Fringillidae (goldfinch).

Based on estimates, one third to one half of Hawaiian bird species have disappeared over the last two centuries and nearly 40% of the remaining species are in immediate danger of extinction.

The following list describes the most typical species you are likely to see. Since this list is far from exhaustive, certain feathered species that are endemic to the northwestern islands have not been included.

Forest Birds

Among all the life forms populating the archipelago, the brightly coloured forest birds are certainly the most remarkable. Living proof of Darwin's theory, in red, yellow and olive shades, some have long bills, others short, either large or very curved, which have specifically adapted to their environment and to the kinds of plants on which they subsist. Three types can easily be spotted: the 'amakihi, the 'i'iwi and the 'apapane. Others are more discrete, sometimes quite rare. For instance, the two beautiful kinds of mamo have not been seen since the early 20th century. As for the o'o, it was seen for the last time in 1989. One of the reasons for its scarcity is quite extraordinary: its feathers were used to make capes for Polynesian chiefs, some of which required the primaries of over 8,000 birds!

Despite constantly increasing human presence, researchers sometimes have pleasant surprises: in 1973, a new species called po'ouli was discovered on Maui. And about 10 years ago, a Nature Conservancy team found, again on Maui, not one but six 'akohekohe nests, reported disappeared since 1860.

'Akepa (Loxops coccineus)

This small Fringillidae includes several subspecies, some of which have died out. It lives at fairly high altitudes, between 4,920ft (1,500m) and 6,888ft (2,100m), in forests of 'ohi'a or koa on the Big Island. The male is easily recognizable by its scarlet colour and rather long tail. The female is greyish-green with yellow specks on the belly.

'Akiapola'au (Hemignathus munroi)

The remaining 1,500 'akiapola'au live on the windy slopes of the Big Island, between 4,264ft (1,300m) and 6,560ft (2,000m) in altitude. A superb bird, the sparkling greenish-yellow male has a pointed beak which is hooked on the upper side, allowing it to pick larva and spiders under tree bark. The female is not as colourful and has a shorter beak.

'Akohekohe or Crested Honeycreeper (Palmeria dolei)

Certainly the strangest of all the birds in Hawaii, the 'akohekohe (crested honeycreeper) has a tuft of yellowish feathers at the front of its head. Mostly black and grey, its plumage has yellow streaks and a large orange spot on the back of the head. Long thought to have disappeared, the 'akohekohe was rediscovered in the depths of the Maui rainforests (in the Waikamoi Reserve).

'Alala or Hawaiian Crow (Corvus hawaiiensis)

The Hawaiian crow was widespread in the archipelago until the end of the 19th century when it was mercilessly hunted down by generations of pioneers because of its nasty habit of pecking at hens. Even though it is not one of the loveliest birds, it is indisputably one of the more endangered species. Recent numbers show that no more than a few dozen birds remain, only four of which are not in captivity, on the western coast of the Big Island.

'Amakihi (Hemignathus)

Nesting on all the islands of the archipelago (with three subspecies) except Lana'i, the 'amakihi is sometimes called the Zorro bird because of the black mask on the male's face which contrasts with its yellow and greenish plumage. Known for its rapid flight, it feeds on insects and nectar. If the flower is too deep, it perforates it at the base to collect the nectar using its black, lightly curved beak.

'Anianiau (*Hemignathus parvus*)
Smallest member of the Drepanididae family, the *'anianiau* feeds exclusively on nectar thanks to its small hooked beak. It lives on Kaua'i where it is commonly sighted above 3,936ft (1,200m). Adult birds have greenish-yellow feathers on their back and a yellow breast.

'Apapane (*Himatione sanguinea*)
The *'apapane* is one of the most common forest birds in Hawaii. It prefers forests of *'ohia* where, in former times, it flocked by the hundreds. It feeds on flower and *mamane* nectar in addition to berries and insects. It is easily recognizable by its dark-red plumage, black wings and tail, and black, slightly hooked beak. Feathers under the tail are white.

Cardinal (*Cardinalis cardinalis* and *Paroaria*)
Common throughout North America, this small passerine that was introduced to Hawaii, where it is often spotted, must not be confused with the rarer endemic species. There are three types: the most common is grey with a vermilion head; the other has a yellow beak; and the third is completely red. The name of the species refers to the colour of its plumage which resembles the robes of a cardinal. To make sure you are not mistaken, look at the beak: the cardinal's is large and short. Furthermore, this bird is usually not very timid.

'Elepaio (*Chasiempis sandwichensis*)
This bird apparently earned its name because of its song. Once considered sacred by canoe builders, the *'elepaio* is a tiny white and brownish-beige flycatcher. It feeds on insects caught in midflight or found on leaves and tree trunks. Less colourful than others, it is less noticed.

Hawaii Creeper
(*Oreomystis*)
Five subspecies of this bird inhabit the five largest islands: the *'alauahio* (O'ahu and Maui), the *kakawahie* (Moloka'i), the *'akikiki* (Kaua'i) and the *oreomystis mana* (Hawaii). Rather small (approximately 4in or 10cm), they have a shorter and straighter bill than other Hawaiian forest birds. Their plumage ranges from olive green to yellow. The O'ahu creeper is the rarest, while the Hawaii creeper is the most common. It lives on higher windswept slopes and prefers *koa* forests.

'Iiwi (*Vestiaria coccinea*)
The most renowned of the Hawaiian forest birds is also the most beautiful. Entirely cloaked in a blood-red shade, except for its black wings and tail, it has a long, curved orange beak used to extract nectar from flowers. Its feathers were once used to make ceremonial clothes for the *ali'i*, a custom which explains the origin of this bird's scientific name. Despite this practice, it is one of the more common endemic bird species and can be seen on all the islands (except Lana'i) especially the Big Island, Kaua'i and Maui.

Palila (*Loxioides bailleui*)
Related to the hawfinch, the *palila* is a small bird with grey and white feathers and a yellow head, throat and wings. Becoming scarce, it lives in the dry forests on the higher slopes of the Mauna Kea on the Big Island, where it feeds on the green seeds of the *mamane*.

Hawaii Thrush
(*Myadestes*)
All of the several subspecies of Hawaiian thrushes are fairly rare. However, it is still possible to see the *kama'o* and the *puaiohi* on Kaua'i, the *oloma'o* on Moloka'i and the *'oma'o* on the Big Island. Rather large for a forest bird, the thrush is more noticeable for its melodious song than for its

green, grey and brown plumage, which is rather dull.

Japanese White-Eye
(*Zosterops japonicus*)
Don't confuse this lovely little bird with an olive-coloured head and grey body with other endemic species. The Japanese white-eye is very common all over the archipelago and is easily recognizable by its white-circled eye, hence its name. It came from Japan in the years between the two world wars.

Birds of Prey

'Io or **Hawaiian Falcon**
(*Buteo solitarius*)
The Hawaiian falcon very nearly disappeared because of the massive destruction of its habitat. But thanks to protection programs, it made a strong comeback on the Big Island as well as on Kaua'i and Maui. Fairly small in size (about 14in or 35cm), it can easily be spotted flying as it scans the ground looking for its prey. The *'io* comes in two colours: entirely brown or with a brown back and yellowish-brown breast streaked with dark lines. Symbol of Hawaiian royalty, the *'io* represents for some Hawaiians the kind spirits of their ancestors (*'aumakua*).

Pueo or **Hawaiian Short-Eared Owl** (*Asio flammeus sandwichensis*)
Still relatively common except perhaps on

O'ahu, the *pueo* plays an important role in Hawaiian mythology. Sacred in the eyes of the elders, it also belonged to the *'aumakua*. It is a subspecies of the North American short-eared owl. Males and females look alike: brown and black bodies, black mask, yellow eyes and round head. They are often seen on cloudy days, flying at high altitudes to better spot their prey.

Water Birds

Ae'o or **Hawaiian Stilt**
(*Himantopus mexicanus knudseni*)
Similar in appearance to its North American congener, the Hawaiian stilt is also perched above long pink-coloured legs. The male is black on top and white underneath whereas the female is brownish. Stilts use their long black beak (2.4-2.8in or 6-7cm) to search for small fish, shellfish, worms and insects in the mud. Populating humid zones across the archipelago, except on Lana'i, they frequently fly from one island to the next (from 1,000 to 1,200 birds).

Koloa or **Hawaiian Duck**
(*Anas wyvilliana*)
Most of the population of Hawaiian ducks lives on Kaua'i as well as on O'ahu and the Big Island: approximately 2,000 frequent the last preserved swamplands. The *koloa* is a small brown bird with white

stripes. The mating parade provides the occasion for some spectacular aerial acrobatics: with the male close behind, the female does a vertical climb of about 98ft (30m) before starting a series of circles. The favoured male then plunges in a vertical dive to chase away his adversaries. Flying obviously does not frighten the *koloa*: a female was once spotted carrying her little ones between her legs in mid-air.

Nene or **Hawaiian Goose**
(*Branta sandwichensis*)
Virtually a national symbol, the *nene* goose was saved from extinction at the very last moment. Designated state bird in 1957, a time when the flock had dwindled down to about 40 birds, its population now numbers approximately 750. They live on the superior slopes of the Mauna Loa and the Kilauea on the Big Island, of the Hale'a'kala on Maui and on Kaua'i. This spectacular outcome is the result of considerable research and breeding in captivity programs. Over the years, this distant cousin of the Canadian barnacle goose, thought to have adapted itself to life in the isles of vegetation (*kipuka*) covering ancient lava flows, has also populated the lower humid zones. Two theories attempt to explain the disappear-

ance of its palms over time: some say that this is attributable to lava while others claim that it is because the *nene* perches itself in trees during the mating season. The *nene* feeds on plants, seeds and berries of the *o'helo* and the *pukiawe* and can live for over 35 years. Nesting occurs during the winter: it is then fairly common for mongooses to attack the eggs, if not the goose itself who never abandons its brood. The danger is even higher during moulting, when for a few days, the *nene* can no longer fly.

Sea and Migratory Birds

In addition to the species presented below, the list could include gannets (*'a*), either brown or with red feet, brown and black noddies (*noio*) and myriad terns that inhabit the archipelago.

Laysan Albatross

(*Diomedea immutabilis*)
So beautifully evoked by poet Charles Baudelaire, the king of seabirds spends several months a year without ever setting foot on ground as it glides on aerial currents. The Laysan albatross is the smallest of all the various species: it weighs between 6.6 and 8.8lbs (3-4kg), and its wingspan reaches "only" 5ft (1.6m) (half of the royal albatross's). It feeds on cuttlefish, fish, shellfish and seawater which is

filtered by its nasal glands. The Laysan albatross faithfully joins its mate every year for the nuptial parade and mating. The birds gather to form a colony of 800,000 (71% of the world population) on Midway Island starting in November. The symbolic nuptial parade includes strange postures such as the *sky moo*: both the male and the female take turns throwing their head back by extending their neck to the sky and making a mooing kind of sound. A single egg is laid, weighing a quarter of the female's weight. Both parents take turns sitting on the egg, starting with the male. It takes almost six months for the young albatross to take flight, and it remains at sea from three to seven years before returning to the island to mate. The albatross can live for 40 or more years.

Black-Footed Albatross

(*Diomedea nigripes*)
Although not as many black-footed albatrosses nest on Midway as the Laysan albatross, they nonetheless form a very respectable colony of 43,000 individuals. This timid bird has a magnificent, lustrous dark-brown plumage which is lighter on the breast and head. Occupying the northwestern islands, from Midway to Ni'ihau, it sometimes crossbreeds with the Laysan albatross.

'Iwa or **Frigate Bird**
(*Fregata minor palmerstoni*)
Often seen flying high above the main islands, the frigate bird only nests in the northwestern islands. With a wingspan of nearly 6.6ft (2m), this impressive bird is all black except for its chest, which is white. During mating season, the male attracts females by puffing out the red membranous pocket under its neck. In Hawaiian, the frigate bird is known as *'iwa*, meaning "thief," because it has the annoying habit of stealing prey from other birds.

Koa'e kea or **White-Tailed Tropicbird** (*Phaeton lepturus*)
Regularly seen throughout the archipelago, this graceful bird glides in and out of the clouds, followed by its train of long feathers. Although it is a fish-eating seabird, the white-tailed tropicbird nests in the mountains, where it is most commonly seen, such as in the Hawaii Volcanoes National Park, for instance, or in the Waimea Canyon on Kaua'i. There also exists a subspecies called the red-tailed tropicbird, or *koa'e 'ula* (*Phaeton rubricauda*), which prefers the northwestern islands and Midway but can also be seen near the Kilauea lighthouse on Kaua'i.

Kolea or Pacific Plover
(*Pluvialis fulva*)
Every autumn, as the first snow falls in Alaska, the Pacific plover begins its long journey: 3,100mi (5,000km), at an average speed of 62mph (100kmph), that brings it all the way to Hawaii to spend the winter, one of the longest known-of sea migrations.. Maybe it is its sense of orientation or its great oceanic travels that persuaded Hawaiians to make it one of their fetish birds. The *kolea* embodies the spirit of Kumukahi, a revered war god. Quite attractive and not very shy, this bird has long black legs and a colourful plumage with brown, white and golden specks.

'Ua'u or Hawaiian Dark-Rumped Petrel
(*Pterodroma phaeopygia sandwichensis*)
The Hawaiian dark-rumped petrel, similar to the Galapagós species, is one of the most rare in this large family. Seabird par excellence, similar to the albatross but smaller (3.3ft or 1m wingspan), it spends a great part of its life at sea. Mostly black, except for the lower part of its head and belly which are white, it is very agile in the air. The Hawaiian dark-rumped petrel now only counts about 900 couples, most of which have sought refuge between 8,200 and 9,840ft (2,500 to 3,000m) in the Hale'a'kala National Park. A large number nest in the crater itself where they dig burrows that can exceed 6.6ft (2m). Other kinds of petrels also frequent the islands; they can be observed at Kilauea Point NWR on Kaua'i.

Marine Life

In general, the farther away from the continental masses, the poorer the underwater kingdom. As such, Hawaii is certainly not as well endowed as other South Pacific archipelagos, especially those closest to Asia. Thus, there are five times less coral species in the waters around Hawaii than in Micronesia. Scuba-diving enthusiasts from colder countries, however, will not be disappointed. In addition to cetaceans (nearly 20 species) and dolphins (eight species), the coasts are home to a wealth of small reef fish while the open sea features great pelagic species greatly valued by fishermen, such as marlin, tuna and *mahi-mahi*.

Humpback Whale
(*Megaptera novaeanglie*)
Many kinds of whales swim in Hawaiian waters in addition to the occasional sperm whale, but one species in particular has captured our imagination: the humpback whale. Found in all oceans of the planet, they number over 15,000, one tenth of the population that existed before they were hunted, a practice that only stopped in 1966. Measuring over 49ft (15m) and weighing 40 tonnes, these giants propel themselves using very large pectoral fins (up to 16ft or 5m). Various populations of humpback whales live in the various oceans of the world. Whales in the North Pacific (estimated between 4,000 and 6,000) spend the summer in the cold waters of Alaska and Oriental Siberia, gorging themselves on one tonne of krill and small fish a day. Every autumn, they set off for the warmer waters of the tropics. Two thirds swim towards Hawaii, a three-month journey of 3,472mi (5,600km), at a speed of 3 to 6mph (5 to 10kmph). Others travel along the American littoral to lower

Mahi-mahi

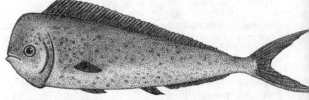

California or to the Sea of Japan. Scientific studies have shown that certain animals migrate one year to one destination and to another the following year. Cetaceans winter by living off their reserves of fat. Some arrive in late September but most gather at the end of November in the straight separating Maui and its neighbouring islands.

Although no direct observation of this phenomenon has taken place, it is probably here, or soon before arriving, that mothers give birth. Winter is also mating season, and confrontations between males give rise to some spectacular leaps. It is also the time when males sing their variety of songs, perhaps as a way to expand their seduction methods. It seems that it is mostly single females who reproduce. Gestation lasts close to 12 months, so they give birth the following year in the same waters. A young whale calf, weighing about 1.5 tonnes at birth and measuring 10 to 16ft (3 to 5m), can gain up to 110 lb (50kg) per day in the first weeks of its life thanks to fatty maternal milk (50%). In one year, it will double in size.

Hawaiian Monk Seal
(*Monachus schauinslandi*)
Sometimes seen on beaches of the main islands (Kaua'i in particular), the monk seal lives mostly in the far-off northwestern islands and is often seen on Midway. Aptly named *ilio holo kai*, which in Hawaiian means "dog that runs in the sea," this graceful animal is smaller than other kinds of seals.

Green Sea Turtle

Measuring up to 8ft (2.4m), it nonetheless can weigh 595lbs (270kg) and live 20 to 30 years. The population is estimated at 1,200 individuals.

Victims of overfishing, tiger sharks and drifting nets, seal monks have modified their behaviour in light of their declining numbers. Facing a cut-throat competition, males are increasing the mortality rate by fighting more and more violently, even attacking their own mates who are larger than them, to obtain favours willingly or by force (mobbing).

Honu or **Green Sea Turtle**
(*Chelonia mydas*)
Having been an endangered species for a long time, the Hawaiian green sea turtle is now a protected species that has made a remarkable comeback in the last decade. Named not for the colour of its shell but for the colour of its fat, it can live up to 50 years and reach 3.9ft (1.2m) and 551lbs (250kg). However, very few of the tiny babies hatched on the deserted beaches will reach this age and weight since they are easy prey for birds, crabs, sharks, fishing nets and pieces of plastic floating on the water which they mistake for jellyfish, part of their diet along with marine plants. The green turtle lays its eggs in May, at night. About the size of golf balls, it drops them (as many as 200 at a time) in a hole dug in the sand of a softly sloped beach, at the very spot where it was born several years before. The eggs hatch two months later.

Flora

Frangipani trees and their fragrant flowers, birds of paradise, flamboyant trees, hibiscus (the state emblem), bougainvillea, anthuriums as well as papaya trees, mango trees, guava trees, avocado trees and *lilikoi* (passion fruit)... Hawaii is covered in millions of exotic flowers and fruit trees. As close to paradise as it might seem, this teeming garden is not as natural as it appears. In fact, it is the result of two centuries of contact between the archipelago and the rest of the world. There are six major biological regions in Hawaii: coastal, dry forests, rainforests, epiphytic vegetation, marshlands and alpine zones. The main vegetation species are presented below.

Coastal and Transitional Regions

The coastal regions are the habitat of grasses and bushes able to withstand drought and salt, such as the soft green *naupaka* that often covers dunes. Very frequent along the littoral, the pandanus shrub (*hala*) is recognizable by its long pointed leaves. Imported by the Polynesians and very common at low altitudes, the *ti* exists in various species. Its large leaves are either dark green or a mixture of green and burgundy. The *ti* was used to wrap offerings in ancient temples. Just as common near the shores, the *kukui*, or candlenut tree, is an all-purpose tree from southeastern Asia, also brought here by the Polynesians. Endemic species such as the *lama*, the *naio* and the *mamane*, with pretty

yellow flowers resembling those of peas, grow higher up on the dry slopes of former lava flows. Lianas such as the delicate *maile* grow at even higher altitudes.

Forests

Forests here shelter a great diversity of species, in particular the *'ohia lehua* (*Metrosideros polymorpha*), a bush of the myrtle family whose red or yellow flowers provide pollen to a great number of endemic species of small birds. The *'ohi'a* blooms mainly between 984ft (300m) and 3,280ft (1,000m). No other plant has adapted as well to the harsh conditions of the neighbouring volcanoes: depending on the conditions, it can either exceed 16ft (5m) or remain a stunted shrub. If part of the trunk burns, new branches will sprout on the side that was saved, no matter how small it is. Of course, the *'ohi'a* does not always escape the furnace, as is shown by the ghost forests composed of fossilized tree trunks covered in lava. Dominated by bushes and ferns, thickets of *'ohi'a* often shelter other endemic species such as the *koa* (acacia). In former times, only the *kahuna* (priests) used to venture into the forests of *'ohi'a* to collect bird feathers or to cut the trunks that were necessary for construction.

Humid and High Altitude Zones

The undergrowth of humid zones is fertile ground for tree ferns such as the *hapu'u* (*Cibotium splendens*), which can grow up to 39ft (12m), and for most epiphytic plants (especially members of the Bromeliaceae family and orchids). Most marshlands in Hawaii are at high altitudes; the Alaka'i marshes on Kaua'i, for instance, feature plants which have evolved in complete autarky. Under such harsh conditions, many suffer from dwarfism. Finally, the alpine zone extends beyond 6,560ft (2,000m) and includes the great volcanoes on Maui and the Big Island. The most famous plant is surely the silversword (*'ahinahina*) which only grows in the cloud-shrouded crater of the Hale'a'kala. Having almost disappeared, the silversword is now the emblem of the state of Hawaii. The *naenae* and the *o'helo* bearing small red berries also flourish in altitude.

Plants Suitable for Cultivation

The Polynesians came to the islands with various kinds of bananas, sweet potato (*'uala*), sugar cane (*ko*), yam (*uhi*), breadfruit tree (*'ulu*) with its large and bumpy oval-shaped green fruits, and the

Sandalwood

Of the nearly 4,000 types in the world, three kinds of sandalwood grow in Hawaii, where it is known as *ili'ahi*. Reputed for its delicate fragrance, which can last up to 50 years, it was used by the ancient Hawaiians to scent the *kapa* and exported to China in great quantities, where it was used for furniture, fans and incense, among other items.

This trade was so important that the Chinese referred to Hawaii as the "Sandalwood Islands." However, in a desperate bid to abolish slavery in the 19th century, the Hawaiian population started to pull out all new shoots. Although it subsequently became quite rare, Hawaiian sandalwood managed to survive.

taro (*kalo*), a plant with tuberous roots that is prevalent throughout the Pacific and is similar to the North American potato. Grown with its roots in water, the taro is easily recognized by its large green leaves shaped like elongated hearts. Not greatly appreciated by Occidentals (it is said to taste like glue), it now only grows on Kaua'i and Maui. Coconut trees, also introduced by the Polynesians, have spread over the entire archipelago but are no longer picked. Rice-growing, which replaced taro in the 19th century, was later abandoned for the sugar cane, followed by the more profitable

pineapple and finally, by tourism.

History

The Polynesians

It is almost a miracle that Hawaii's solitary string of islands floating thousands of nautical miles from the closest land was ever colonized. The story begins at the end of the Würm glaciation age (around 40,000 BC), when the people of Borneo, taking advantage of the lowering sea level, crossed the straight to New Guinea and made their way to the Solomon Islands. Closer to the ocean, these people, known as Lapita,

became sailors and fishers.

Much later, around 1000-1200 BC, the development of marine construction techniques allowed them to travel east across the landless ocean. In only a few centuries, populations sailed to and colonized Vanuatu, Fiji, Tonga and the Samoa Islands. Laboratory of the Polynesian culture, these islands were the starting point of their extraordinary dispersion throughout the greater part of the immense Pacific, an ocean as big as a continent. No other people has colonized so much of the ocean.

From AD 200, perhaps because of a demographic explosion, wars or banishment, a group of Polynesians landed in the Marquesas Islands where they founded a very structured society. This archipelago defines the intangible borders of the "Polynesian Triangle" whose three angles are formed by New Zealand in the southwest (10th century), Easter Island in the southeast (9th century) and Hawaii in the north (5th to 7th century). With a common heritage, each group of islands developed its own distinct society with slightly different languages, customs and beliefs.

The Colonization of Hawaii

Over 1,300 or 1,500 years ago, the first Polynesians travelled from the Marquesas Islands to Hawaii. Perhaps even more impressive than the Vikings who made their way to North America, the Polynesians ended there a journey of nearly 2,480mi (4,000km) of open sea, without any guarantee of ever seeing land. Sailing aboard large double-hulled canoes (vaguely similar to modern-day catamarans), the Polynesians used nature to trace their route: they looked to the stars, the moon, the trajectory of the planets, the sun and the winds, as well as the smallest but unmistakable signs: seabirds, the greenish tinge of water or clouds announcing a nearby island, even seaweed drifting in the direction of the current. Pigs, chickens, dogs, breadfruit trees, sugar cane, coconuts, sweet potatoes and yams were crammed on board to provide food for several weeks at sea and once they arrived. Without any written records, many questions remain unanswered: How many intrepid men, women and families embarked on this long journey? How many survived and how many never got to the final destination and were lost in the immensity of the great Pacific?

The Tahitians

The islands were then forgotten as suddenly as they were discovered, and for several centuries, there seemed to be no communication with the Marquesas Islands. Then, around the year AD 1000, a second wave of migration arrived from Kahiki (Tahiti). Unaware of the presence of the first inhabitants, the Tahitians were more numerous and probably forced the Polynesians into slavery. Two centuries later, the great *kahuna* (priest) Pa'ao established a very strict religious and social system, regulating every second of daily life with a greater-than-ever number of *kapu* (taboos). Only fools would have dared disobey these rules, for they would be punished by death. The dominating class of *ali'i* (a type of nobility) distanced itself from the common people. New gods such as Pele, goddess of fire, were introduced, and human sacrifices were performed. Pa'ao welcomed the great chief Pili from Tahiti and together they established a dynasty that ruled Hawaii for over 600 years. Around the year 1400, relations between the two archipelagoes ceased, and Hawaii became completely self-sufficient.

As one would cut a cake, the land on every island was divided in equal parts (*ahupua'a*) between members of the *ali'i*, from the mountain summits to the shoreline. Based on a calendar of specific rituals, the *'ohana* (extended families) worked together on these slices of land in the spirit of *malama 'aina* ("caring for the land"). Soon, the god of agriculture Lono occupied an increasingly important place in the Hawaiian pantheon, rivalling Ku, the god of war. However, this did not prevent chiefs from engaging in frequent battles, originally innocuous, in bids to extend their land. In the 18th century, before the arrival of the Occidentals, the population included between 300,000 and 500,000 people.

The Westerners' Discovery of the Islands

As early as the 16th century, Spanish galleons wound their way across the North Pacific in their long journeys between the Mexican port of Acapulco and Asian trading posts. No official record mentions them ever stopping in Hawaii, despite it practically being on their route, yet some historians suspect otherwise. One story in particular tells of one or two ships, part of an expedition of three ships

Kapu

The English word "taboo" is a deviation of *tapu* which, in southern Polynesian, referred to any of the many religious prohibitions that have evolved in the Polynesian Triangle since time began. The people of the Marquesas Islands fostered a great number of *tapu*, which they brought with them to Hawaii. Revived by the religious inquisition led by the high priest Pa'ao, they served as divine law for several centuries during the great Hawaiian dynasties. Also used to exert social control, the *kapu* forbade common people from approaching members of the *ali'i*, the superior caste; to even cross their shadow meant death. Another infamous *kapu* forbade men and women from eating together. The men had to grow and prepare their own food because their wives were declared impure for life because of menstruation. There did, however, exist many useful *kapu* that oversaw the management of natural resources, for instance. Access to forbidden areas was simply prevented by two *pulo'ulo'u*, crossed sticks bearing a piece of white *kapa*.

To break a *kapu* was an insult to the divine order and was always punished by strangulation. By sentencing an individual in this manner, the community protected itself from the wrath of the gods: eruptions, cyclones... anything could happen as a reprisal. After their abolition in 1819, when King Kamehameha II and Queen Ka'ahumanu shared a meal together, the *kapu* progressively disappeared from Hawaii. Nevertheless, the *kapu* remain firmly established in other groups of islands in the Pacific.

sent by Cortès to the Moluccan Islands, that ran aground on the Hawaiian shores in 1527. Both the ship's captain and his sister were among the survivors and both married an *ali'i* to found a line of chiefs. Spanish portolans and maps of the period, some dating back to the 18th century, mention a group of islands baptised Los Monges, situated between 20° and 22° latitude, which might very well be Hawaii. Others maintain that the archipelago was discovered in 1542, perhaps 1555, by a certain Spaniard by the name of Gaetano. The discovery on O'ahu of a white-stone bust of unknown origin but with features evoking a Spanish nobleman lends weight to the theory that at least one Spanish ship called into port.

Captain Cook

Heading north from Tahiti on board the *Resolution* and the *Discovery*, Cook and his men, like the first Polynesians, happened upon Hawaii by accident. The English sailors, in search of a septentrional passage between the Pacific and the Atlantic (the infamous "Northwest Passage"), joyfully welcomed this unexpected port. Because it was so isolated, the archipelago was the last great territory of the Pacific to be discovered by the

Portrait

occidental world. Cook christened the archipelago the "Sandwich Islands" in honour of his protector in the court of England, John Montagu, First Lord of Admiralty and Fourth Count of Sandwich. The English navigator landed in the Bay of Waimea on Kaua'i on January 19, 1778. The Hawaiians were quite hospitable and ready to satisfy trading customs. Cook, knowing too well the danger of venereal diseases, attempted to forbid his men from being intimate with the lovely islanders, but to no avail. After three days on Kaua'i and a forced stopover on Ni'ihau because of strong headwinds, the two fully stocked ships departed on a one-year journey in search of the Northwest Passage without any project of returning. Captain Cook and his crew navigated to Alaska and passed the Strait of Bering but were soon blocked by ice flows. They decided to turn around and spend the winter in the Sandwich Islands.

One year day for day after seeing O'ahu for the first time, the English returned to the Bay of Kealakekua. The ship's log overflowed with enthusiastic descriptions of the thousand of dugouts that came to welcome them. Luck was on Cook's side: the bay was the

most sacred area of Hawaii and his ships came into sight in a clockwise direction as they came around the island, which corresponded to legends on the return of Lono to earth. His arrival also coincided with the Makahiki festival, dedicated to the god and protector of harvests. Cook himself was taken for the god. Greeted

HMS Endeavour,
Replica of Captain
Cook's ships

with great pomp and ceremony, the crew enjoyed Hawaiian hospitality. After two weeks of festivities the two ships set sail again, to the great relief of the Hawaiians whose supplies were running low. But no sooner had they left the coast that a violent storm ripped the sails and broke a mast on the *Resolution*, forcing the ships to return to Kealakekua for repairs. But the Makahiki celebrations were finished and the

area was deserted. This time, Cook was not greeted as warmly. The season dedicated to Ku, the god of war, had just begun. What's more, not only did the English arrive in a counterclockwise direction but their ship was damaged. The signs that had made them divinities were now reducing them to mere mortals, and on board, objects started to disappear, including one lifeboat. Inflexible by nature, Cook blockaded the bay. Accompanied by 11 men, he went ashore to capture the grand chief Kalani'opu'u and hold him hostage until the lifeboat was returned. In the ensuing scuffle, Cook was bludgeoned, stabbed and beaten to death by the very men who, not so long ago, had worshipped him as a god.

Back in England, the remaining crew told the world of the explorer's death and the existence of the islands. However, for six years, no ship set sail on the horizon: Cook's death had frightened the Europeans. Then, suddenly, the excitement was back. The location of the archipelago, in the middle of the Pacific Ocean, soon made it a favourite port of call for merchants.

The Unification of the Archipelago

When Cook discovered Hawaii, the islands were at the hands of enemy chiefs vying for power. On the Big Island, one man's domination soon became legendary: Kamehameha. For 10 years, from 1782 to 1791, he battled his two cousins, Kiwala'o and Keoua, sons of Kalani'opu'u and official heirs to the island's throne. The young *ali'i* then fought numerous other battles that led, for the first time in the history of the archipelago, to its unification.

Kamehameha quickly defeated Kiwala'o and took control of the Kohala Peninsula. Then a stroke of luck was interpreted by the belligerents as a foreboding sign from the gods: part of Keoua's army was killed by an explosion on the slopes of the Kilauea in 1790. The following year, Keoua himself was killed by Kamehameha's father-in-law during the inauguration of the temple of Pu'ukohola. This allowed Kamehameha to rule the Big Island, and from that moment on, events escalated. More and more foreign ships entered Hawaiian waters, and rival chiefs armed themselves with cannons and muskets.

Between 1792 and 1794, Captain George Vancouver, who had been part of Cook's expedition, visited the islands on three separate occasions. He befriended Kamehameha and negotiated peace between him and the Kahekili clan of Maui before recognizing him as the undisputed chief of the archipelago. The English captain refused to hand over military equipment to the king but, promising to send him a war ship, left him with two sailors to teach him European battle techniques. Aware of the military superiority of the British, Kamehameha asked Vancouver for England's official protection. Although a document was signed it was never ratified by the British Parliament.

In 1795, the "Napoleon of the Pacific," as Kamehameha was sometimes called, conquered the islands one by one: Maui, Moloka'i, Lana'i and O'ahu, where he landed with 1,200 canoes and over 10,000 men. The last resistance crumbled on the cliffs of Nu'uanu, where hundreds of soldiers preferred to jump to their death rather than surrender. Several attacks were launched on Kaua'i and Ni'ihau but failed. Finally, in 1810, under the pressure of European merchants, the king of Kaua'i, Kaumuali'i, accepted a deal: upon his death, which would occur in 1824, the two islands would be incorporated to the kingdom.

The Golden Age of the Adventurers

Kamehameha's reign was marked by the rapid transition from an ancient world dominated by gods to a society influenced by the Occident and the greatest of its precepts: commerce. Barely six years after Cook's visit, the first fur trader, an Englishman by the name of James Hanna, arrived in the islands en route to Asia. In his ship's hold were otter skins destined for the Chinese market. Long before the end of the 18th century, dozens of merchant ships sailed into Hawaii to stock up on fresh supplies, and many islanders joined the English and American crews. Some even moved to the northwestern United States, where some two centuries later, a city in Oregon is still called Aloha. After the otter population sharply declined, trappers turned to beavers, seals and even bears. But all the animals in the world were not enough to satisfy their great ambitions.

Other adventurers of various origins landed in the archipelago: English, German, American, Spanish and Russian. In 1804, under the reign of Alexander the First, the first Russian ship called into port in

Kamehameha

The life, and especially the birth of the first great king of the islands, Kamehameha, "the lonely one," is shrouded in a mystery cleverly maintained by centuries of legends. One story describes how, during her pregnancy, his mother Kekuiapoiwa had a strong urge to eat the eye of a chief. The *kahuna* interpreted this sign as the announcement of a rebel child, and frightened by the predictions of his priests, her father-in-law, King Alapainui, decided to do away with the child. But on the stormy autumn night of the baby's birth, the young mother arranged to have her newborn hidden in a basket. Relying on oral traditions which tell that on the eve of his birth a celestial object flew through the sky (probably Halley's comet), histo-

rians have estimated his date of birth to 1758. Some claim that the king came into this world earlier – in 1753, according to some, in 1736, according to others. Hiding from the chief's men who were sent on a manhunt, Kamehameha grew up in the secret valley of Waipi'o. He eventually returned to the world of the *ali'i* and learned to become a leader. Before reaching adulthood, Kamehameha, whose stature and physical condition were not simply the stuff of legends, succeeded in moving the enormous stone of Naha, which weighed close to 3.5 tonnes. This feat was considered as an announcement of the one who would one day preside over the archipelago's destiny.

When Cook came to the Big Island, Kamehameha already held uncontested power. It is said that the future monarch partook in the lynching of the explorer, and may have even kept his scalp as a symbol of prestige. Married numerous times (some say he had as many as 21 wives), the king truly loved his favorite wife, Ka'ahumanu, who became queen regent upon his death on May 8, 1819. Having ensured a fairly smooth transition between the Hawaiian past and the modern world – neither denying the first nor surrendering to the second, – islanders consider Kamehameha their greatest king, hero and conqueror but also a man who attended to the desires of his people.

Hawaii. A limited commercial agreement was signed with the kingdom. In 1815, the Russian brig *Rurik* anchored in the archipelago, and its commander, Captain Otto Von Kotzebue, became Kamehameha's minister of foreign affairs. The same year, Dr. George Schaeffer, working for the Russian-American Company of Alaska (which was still Russian territory), built a fort on Kaua'i. Supported by the grand chief Kaumuali'i, who had reluctantly accepted the suzerainty of Kamehameha, Schaeffer tried to overtake the archipelago but was soon ousted by Kamehameha.

During their calls to port, the captains started to notice the great abundance of sandalwood growing on the islands. Thus began a lucrative commercial triangle: the precious wood, obtained from the kingdom in exchange for weapons and consumer goods, was sold in Canton, China, and ships were then loaded with silk and porcelain to sell in the United States. The enormous profits attracted a growing number of shipowners. The more there were, the more Kamehameha's control over the destiny of the islands grew uncertain. The king became suspicious and refused to hand over his lands; he instituted a *kapu* on

sandalwood in hopes of better controlling its commerce. In 1816, he imposed harbour dues, but to no avail. After his death in 1819, his son Liholiho was persuaded to abandon the royal monopoly to the greater profit of the *ali'i*. The situation worsened: the Hawaiian chiefs, wanting to acquire more consumer goods and weapons, virtually forced their subjects into slavery. Forced to fell and transport the wood, the Hawaiians, already victims of unknown diseases brought by foreigners, no longer had time to tend to their fields. The islands were sporadically touched by famine and by 1829, the sandalwood forests were depleted.

The End of the Idols

Before Kamehameha's death, Tahitian Protestant missionaries, converted by the very enterprising London Missionary Society, landed in Hawaii. Their found an attentive ear in Ka'ahumanu, the king's preferred wife and de facto regent of the kingdom upon his death. Under her influence, her son-in-law Lihiliho, crowned Kamehameha II at the age of 23, accepted, during a meal that would be engraved in the history books of the islands, to defy the *kapu* forbidding men

and women from eating together. Seeing as the gods did not manifest themselves any more than they did to help the Hawaiians in their fight against the abuse of foreigners, the royal couple encountered very little resistance when they ordered the destruction of the idols and the *heiau* (temples). Only on the Big Island was there a revolt that was quickly subdued. In a matter of months, a religious system that was over 1,000 years old came to an end.

It was during this period that the first North American missionaries arrived from New England: on April 19, 1820, 23 members of the Congregationalist church headed by Pastor Hiram Bingham were on board the *Thaddeus*. Their six-month voyage led them from Boston to Hawaii by way of Cape Horn. Ensconced in their moral superiority and role as civilizers, the missionaries reacted to Hawaiian customs with suspicion, even horror. After founding their first mission in Honolulu, they invented a Hawaiian alphabet to translate the Bible, created schools to diffuse their teachings and built churches covered with palm roofs. They forbade all types of activities such as drinking, gambling and adultery but also surfing, *hula* dancing, singing, wearing *lei* (necklace made of flowers) or "indecent" clothes and interracial marriages. It took the full weight of the example given by Ka'ahumanu, one of the first to convert, to convince the Hawaiians to submit themselves to such inclement ways. It is hard to know whether the queen did this for political reasons or in gratitude towards the missionaries who cared for her during a severe illness.

Whale-Hunting

The arrival of the missionaries coincided with the coming of new players in September 1819: the whalers. Starting as early as 1789 in the Pacific Ocean, whale-hunting took on a new dimension from 1825 to 1860 with the creation of large fleets. At the time, oil was needed to supply all the lamps in North America, and the market seemed inexhaustible. Numerous whalers from New England, especially Nantucket, set sail for Hawaii. Despite the continual presence of cetaceans in the archipelago, they mostly came in the spring and autumn since it was halfway between the whaling zones of the Arctic and the Sea of Japan. Their principal port of call became Lahaina, the capital of Maui since 1802. The industry reached its zenith in the 1840s when a new boat sailed into port

every day. Between 1851 and 1860, the "harvest" was estimated at 6.5 million tonnes of whalebones and 116 million pints (66 million litres) of whale oil. Kamehameha IV even created his own fleet in 1854, composed of 19 ships displaying the Hawaiian colours. Meanwhile, many settlers established themselves as breeders and farmers in the islands to supply both the seafarers and the gold rush in California. Ships hired sailors from the islands (called *sailumoku*), New England (Native Americans from Massachusetts and Black Americans) and others from as far away as the Azores. The Hawaiians were the most appreciated for their loyalty... and because they were the only ones who could swim! Captains paid the royal Hawaiian government about $200 for each man, with the condition of bringing him safely home within three years. In the towns, conflicts brewed between sailors and missionaries whose interests were obviously in opposition. In 1825, an uprising took place after female visitors were banned from ships, a decree voted by the Hawaiian leaders under the influence of the religious powers. Two years later, an English second officer ordered the bombardment of a pastor's residence after his captain was detained on land for having performed a

trade for young girls to come aboard despite the restriction. In 1852, virtually all the whalersailors in town (approximately 4,000) started a riot after one of them was imprisoned.

As the years passed, the catches became more and more difficult, and the competition grew tougher and tougher. In 1860, the Civil War and the decrease in whale-oil prices, now competing against petroleum, was a hard blow to the industry. The last whaler captains finally gave up when faced with the quasi-disappearance of their prey and a tragic accident of 1871 when an early winter in the Arctic destroyed an entire whaler fleet.

The English Episode

In 1822, the ship promised to Kamehameha some 30 years earlier by George Vancouver finally arrived in Hawaii. Kamehameha II, who used the English protection as a security against the Russians and the Americans, decided to thank George IV in person. The Hawaiian monarch arrived in London in May 1824, accompanied by his favourite wife, Kamamalu, and the royal entourage. But Liholiho never had the chance to meet the king: they all contracted the measles and fell very ill soon after arriving. The queen died, followed by Liholiho a few days later. Their bodies were repatriated to Hawaii by Lord Byron, brother of the famous poet.

The rest of the decade, like the previous one, reflected the increasing role of England and the missionaries in Hawaii. More and more settlers came to the islands to work on the farms, such as the famous Mexican *paniolos*. In 1834, the Hudson Bay Company established itself in Honolulu. Richard Charlton, a British consular agent and businessman, tried at the end of the 1830s to instigate the return of the islands to Great Britain, a project that clearly went against American interests. He succeeded in 1843 but the kingdom was restored a few months later by the English troops themselves.

Land Issues

When Kamehameha II died in 1824, his brother Kauikeaouli ascended to the throne as Kamehameha III. At the time he was only 12 years old and was placed under the regency of the unshakeable Ka'ahumanu until her death in 1832. Educated by the missionaries, the young king was constantly torn between the interests of his people and

the teachings of his professors. The increasing number of foreign settlers only made matters worse, and the combined influence of rich merchants, white members of his cabinet and foreign governments forced him into making disastrous decisions. In 1840, the first Hawaiian constitution established a parliament and religious freedom, and guaranteed the right of vote to all male residents, including settlers.

But it was the 1848 decree in particular, known as the Mahele (division), that marked a turning point in the history of the islands. It revolutionized the Hawaiian concept of nonproperty by dividing the lands in the archipelago between the Crown (25%), the government (37.5%) and individuals – chiefs and general population combined (37.5%). Two years later, the right to property was granted to everyone without regards to nationality. The Hawaiians, for whom the principle itself was absurd, paid no heed to this provision. The settlers, on the other hand, who had been exerting pressure for years, hurried to endorse it. Many children of missionaries, or the missionaries themselves, as well as people of mixed parentage acquired considerably large pieces of land, soon depriving the Hawaiians of all

land suitable for cultivation. The numbers speak for themselves: even though there were no more than 2,000 foreigners in all the archipelago, only 0.9% of Hawaiians received land. These vast estates were at the root of the economic and political power to come for the *haole* (Whites).

The Sugar Era

Upon the death of Kamehameha III in 1854, the Kingdom of Hawaii was little more than a ghost of what it used to be. Alexander Lihiliho, adopted son and successor of Kamehameha III, ascended to the throne under the name of Kamehameha IV and witnessed the systematic dismemberment of the islands and the increasing financial power of the settlers thanks to an existing industry: sugar. Many of the first sugar-cane plantations were created in the 1820s and 1830s by Chinese immigrants and resold around 1835-1840 to occidental companies equipped with steam machines. With the progressive decline of the whaling industry, sugar took on new dimensions. Immense estates managed by English, German and American planters were created thanks to the Mahele. This act also opened the doors to immigration: because the Hawaiians had

A Brief History of Hawaii

400-700   The first Polynesians come to Hawaii, no doubt from the Marquesas Islands.

1000   A second migratory wave arrives from Tahiti; the first settlers are probably forced into slavery.

1200   The great Tahitian priest Pa'ao makes his way to the islands and founds the dynasty that rules the archipelago until the 19th century. A very strict system of religious interdictions is established.

1580   Although there is no record to prove it, one or more Spanish ships land in the Hawaiian isles at the end of the 16th century.

1778   En route from Tahiti to a hypothetical "northwest passage," Captain Cook officially discovers O'ahu, Kaua'i and Ni'ihau. He names them the Sandwich Islands.

1779   Upon his return to Hawaii the following year, Cook is mistaken for the god Lono and given a divine welcome on the Big Island. Days later, he is killed during a skirmish with the native people.

1795   Following many bloody battles, Kamehameha, a chief from the Big Island, rules the entire archipelago except Kaua'i and Ni'ihau. For the first time, Hawaii forms a unified kingdom. Western ships begin calling to port en route between America and China.

1810   King Kaumuali'i of Kaua'i finally agrees to have his island join the kingdom – on condition that this takes places after his death (in 1824).

1819   Kamehameha's death. The first whaling ships land in Hawaii.

1820   The first Protestant missionaries arrive. Despite difficult beginnings, the Christian religion spreads in the islands, partially thanks to Queen Ka'ahumanu. Many traditional activities are forbidden or condemned on moral grounds.

1848 Bowing to the pressure of the ever-increasing number of foreign businessmen in the archipelago, Kamehamaha III decrees the Great Mahele, opening the way to private property (1850). The missionaries and their children, as well as numerous entrepreneurs, acquire lands for sugar-cane plantations. Overnight, many Hawaiians are left without land.

1860 A great influx of foreigners, Chinese, Japanese and Portuguese, among others, goes to work in the plantations.

1876 The Reciprocity Treaty (customs duty traded for the disposition of Pearl Harbor Bay) opens the doors of the United States to Hawaiian sugar.

1893 Queen Lili'uokalani is overthrown by a group of western business people who demand the return of the islands to the United States. A provisory government is set up and quickly replaced by the "Republic of Hawaii".

1898 In due time, the United States, now expanding its activities across the Pacific, decides to make Hawaii a U.S. territory.

1910 A new wave of immigrants comes to the islands, particularly from the Philippines, to work on the flourishing pineapple plantations.

1927 Tourism surfaces in Hawaii with the inauguration of the San Francisco-Honolulu ocean liners.

1936 The first flight makes the journey between San Francisco and O'ahu in over 21hrs.

1941 On December 7, the Japanese launch a surprise attack on Pearl Harbor. As a result, the United States enters the Second World War.

1959 The U.S. Congress makes Hawaii the 50th state of the Union, a decision approved by 90% of the residents of the archipelago.

massively succumbed to illnesses, the planters had to turn towards a new workforce. The Chinese arrived as early as 1852 but very few remained since working conditions were hard and the pay poor. From 1868 on, the Japanese and Okinawans followed, more numerous and desirous to settle down. Between 1885 and 1924, about 180,000 made Honolulu their home. The total number of sugar-cane workers in the archipelago between 1850 and the Second World War is estimated to be about 350,000.

In an attempt to counter the ever-increasing influence of the Americans, King Kamehameha IV developed diplomatic ties with a number of other countries. However, he died suddenly in 1862 at the age of 29, perhaps poisoned. His older brother Lot became Kamehameha V and succeeded in introducing a new constitution that reinforced royal powers but also those of foreigners. He died in 1872 without an heir. His successor Lunalilo was named king in 1873 by a college of dignitaries. He held the throne for little more than a year before succumbing to consumption, at which time the white members of his cabinet lobbied for the annexation of the archipelago to the United States. Meanwhile, immigra-

tion doubled, with the massive arrival of Portuguese from the Azores and Madeira.

Kalakaua

Kalakaua was "elected" king in 1874 to succeed Lunalilo. His ambiguous reign was marred by a rift between the Hawaiian traditions he tried to infuse new life into, his taste for the splendours of the royal courts and his dependence on the financial power held by foreign industrialists. Unable to breach the gap between these three entities, he was widely criticized and denounced for his thoughtlessness, numerous trips abroad and dissolute lifestyle. As soon as he was nominated by the Cabinet, he was victim of a revolt orchestrated by the followers of Queen Emma, widow of Kamehameha IV.

No sooner had he come to power that the king travelled to Washington to negotiate a reciprocity treaty with President Grant: in exchange for the surrender of Pearl Harbor Bay, the American government would import

Hawaiian sugar duty-free on its territory – a substantial victory for Hawaiian planters. The sugar industry and the economy of the islands had an unprecedented boom brought forth by the influx of mostly American capital. Important industrialists began investing, such as the German Claus Spreckles, known as "the king of Hawaiian sugar." In 1877, he bought half the annual harvest before its value

Kalakaua

skyrocketed. He then acquired over 39,536 acres (16,000ha) of land on Maui. Kalakaua soon became one of his friends and debtors since the king had the unfortunate habit of losing substantial amounts of money at poker, which made it quite difficult for him to refuse to allow the suspicious sale of lands. Thousands of new immigrants arrived, including unskilled workers from Asia and Southern Europe as well as foremen and engineers from North America. Irrigation canals were dug to increase the surface suitable for cultivation. In 1881, Kalakaua's sister, Princess Lili'uokalani, inaugurated the first railway on Kaua'i.

In 1887, increasingly criticized for his superfluous spending, Kalakaua tried to strengthen his power. Several hundreds of landowners joined the Hawaiian League and forced the king, decidedly too dependent on finances, to adopt the Bayonet constitution. Kalakaua lost many of his prerogatives. All white landowners were allowed to vote with the notable exception of Asian immigrants and Hawaiians, of course. Facing this unbearable situation, a group of islanders led by Robert Wilcox tried to overthrow the government in the summer of 1889 and obtain the cancellation of the constitution. But the revolt was subdued. Kalakaua died in 1891 during a trip to San Francisco.

Lili'uokalani

Having acted as regent during the repeated absences of her brother, Lili'uokalani became his successor. Determined to restore the royal power, she formed a new cabinet that was less likely to be influenced by entrepreneurs and settlers. In January 1893, supported by the population and the Hawaiian members of her cabinet, she tried to instate a new constitution that would not be as favourable to the *haole*. But this project was immediately opposed by a public security comity, which included certain American ministers. Troops from the American warship *Boston* disembarked under pretext of ensuring peace in Honolulu. On Tuesday, January 17, some 500 armed members of the public safety comity marched on the royal palace. To avoid bloodshed, the queen ordered her

troops to not intervene. Lili'uokalani was overthrown, the monarchy was abolished, government buildings were taken over and a provisory government of four influential American settlers was put in place. Its president, Sanford Dole, was the son of a missionary and heir to the Dole dynasty, now famous for its fruit and vegetable packaging business. With the exception of England, all western powers recognized the new government. The very next day after the queen was overthrown, a commission was sent to Washington to demand the annexation of the archipelago to the United States. Martial law was decreed. For the American press of the day, the military intervention was the obvious result of Lili'uokalani's autocratic government. For the Hawaiians, however, it was the result of shameless industrialists and power-hungry landowners.

The Downfall of the Hawaiians

Heiress to the throne, Princess Kaiulani went to Washington to demand the restoration of her aunt, the queen. After listening to her request, President Cleveland refused the annexation. In 1894, the Republic of Hawaii was born, with Sanford Dole as president. Land belonging to the Crown

The Kings of Hawaii

Kamehameha I (1795-1819)
Kamehameha II, Liholiho (1819-1824)
Kamehameha III, Kauikeaouli (1824-1854)
Kamehameha IV, Alexander Liholiho (1854-1863)
Kamehameha V, Lot (1863-1872)
Lunalilo (William Charles, 1873-1874)
Kalakaua (David, 1874-1891)
Lili'uokalani (Lydia, 1891-1893)

was resold to influential wheelers and dealers, and new laws were passed, prohibiting the Hawaiian language as well as certain customs. In 1895, Lili'uokalani's followers led again by Robert Wilcox rebelled, but had no more success than the first time and most were sentenced to death. Hidden weapons were found in Lili'uokalani's garden. The queen was arrested and sentenced to five years of hard labour, which she commuted under house arrest. In 1898, in full expansionism, the United States finally annexed the archipelago; during the same year, at the end of the Hispano-American war, it also took over Puerto Rico, the Philippines and Guam. The accession to the status of American territory in 1900 changed very little with regards to the social structure in Hawaii. President McKinley named as first governor no other than... Sanford Dole. A new wave of immigration hit the islands: Spanish and Puerto Rican workers, thousands of Japanese and, starting in the 1910s, Filipinos. Pineapple became the second most exported product after sugar.

The Early 20th Century

Soon after annexation, the American army began building the Pearl Harbor base,

destined to become the most critical army base in the world in the decades to come. The First World War, which the United States only joined in 1917, came and went relatively unnoticed in Hawaii if only for the capture of the first German navy ship which was in the islands at the moment war was declared. German immigrants were the most afflicted since they were distrusted by other communities and the government in particular. In 1920, the Hawaiian Home Lands were created to give back to the Hawaiians some of the land they had lost on account of the Mahele. But this program, implemented by major landowners, served their own benefits and not those of the Hawaiian people. The inter-war years were also marred by the Great Depression and Prohibition but Hawaii, now the refuge of American millionaires attracted by its budding tourism industry, suffered little during this time.

The Second World War

If the first world conflict barely skimmed the archipelago, the second hit it head-on. At 6am on December 7, 1941, 183 Japanese airplanes, followed an hour later by another 167, attacked the Wheeler, Hickam and Bellows air bases as

well as Battleship Row in Pearl Harbor, where numerous warships belonging to the Pacific fleet were docked. Before anti-aircraft defences could react, 19 ships were sunk or damaged, 164 planes were destroyed, 2,346 men were killed – almost half were aboard the USS Arizona alone – and 1,143 others wounded. 58 civilians were also killed by American anti-aircraft missiles which had not exploded in mid-air but rather once they fell to the ground. The Japanese lost 29 planes, five mini-submarines and 64 men.

The defeat was all the more devastating because of the element of surprise: the United States and Japan had not yet officially declared war. Of course, there were hints of the attack. Relations between the two countries had severely deteriorated over the past 10 years, especially since the occupation of Manchuria in 1931 and the invasion of China in 1937 by Japan. Furthermore, Pearl Harbor was reported to be the safest port in the Pacific and allowed control of the great ocean. Army services had decoded a message announcing a large-scale attack on an unknown site, but strategists leaned more towards the Philippines, refusing to believe it could be Hawaii. To save fuel, the army had decided to limit its naval and submarine patrols, and to avoid sabotage, American fighter planes were disarmed at night and parked close together, providing the perfect target for the Nipponese planes. Supreme confusion, 30min before the attack, radars picked up planes coming from the west but mistakenly thought they were American.

Following the greatest tragedy ever provoked on American soil by a foreign country, the United States entered the Second World War. Despite the great damages it caused, the December 7 attack eventually played against the Japanese. Not only were most of the sunk ships raised but American public opinion, which had been divided until then, became pro-war.

An iron curtain fell on Honolulu: martial law was decreed, civil courts were laid off and vast parcels of land were handed over to the army. Barbed wire appeared on all shores. Thanks to their great numbers, residents of Japanese origin avoided the internment camps that held their compatriots on the continent captive. But Japanese schools were closed, community representatives were imprisoned and interrogated, and soldiers and government employees of Japanese descent were released from duty.

Towards the end of the war, the army did however authorize the creation of two battalions reserved for Japanese-American citizens.

Hawaii Today

The post-war period provided the stage for the first social conflicts in the islands. In 1949, a strike by longshoremen paralyzed commercial activities for nearly six months. Following this, repeated movements against major landowners led to a notable improvement of the working conditions of farm workers. But the cold war was raging, and Hawaii, like the rest of the United States, was soon plunged into the anti-communist paranoia of McCarthyism. For several years, debate raged in Congress as to whether or not Hawaii should become a full-fledged state. The strategic importance of the area, shown by the Second World War, tipped the scale in favour of integration. But the political turmoil and unique multi-ethnic composition of the islands worried those in power. Finally, in 1959, Hawaii became the 50th member of the United States, and the results of a referendum reserved for American citizens having resided for at least one year in the islands confirmed this new status by 90%.

Politics

The State is divided into four administrative counties: O'ahu, Maui (including Moloka'i and Lana'i), Hawaii and Kaua'i. Like the rest of the nation, representatives are elected to the Senate and the House of Representatives. A governor is elected every four years; the most recent, Ben Cayetano, is of Filipino descent. Since joining the United States, Hawaii has undergone a virtually unexpected turn of events. In the midst of the intellectual and political effervescence of the 1960s, between the fight for the equality of rights and desegregation in the southern United States, a Hawaiian political conscience was born and manifested itself through, among other ways, a strong cultural revival. Today it has brought the subject of sovereignty to the table.

The Department of Hawaiian Home Lands (DHHL)

In 1920, to remedy the great poverty of land-deprived Hawaiians, Prince Kuhio, territorial delegate in Congress, created the homestead lands. These former Crown lands seized by the state were to be rented out to the Hawaiian population for a token amount. If the

Portrait

Hawaiian Flag

Until the end of his reign, Kamehameha kept the British Union Jack as the state emblem. But in 1816, Hawaii adopted its own flag. While the English banner still adorned the upper left corner, eight blue, white and red stripes were introduced, representing the eight main islands of the archipelago. The Hawaiian flag is occasionally seen hanging upside down, the rallying sign of sovereignty movements.

idea seemed generous at first, its practical implementation was much less so: resulting from a compromise made for the sole benefit of major landowners (about 50 controlled half the territory), barely 309 sq mi (800km²) of the most infertile and inaccessible lands in the archipelago, especially on the Big Island, were handed over. Consequently, very few Hawaiians benefited from the homestead lands, and the few lucky ones, confronted with their barrenness, contented themselves most often with building homes.

Even though Hawaii was given the status of state in 1959, partially removing the major landowning families from power, it did not change the abusive policy of the local and federal governments. To replenish state coffers, the Department of Hawaiian Home Lands (DHHL) rented more and more land to private investors, such as the immense Parker ranch on the Big Island. Collusions were brought to light a posteriori, demonstrating the converging interests of DHHL representatives and certain important landowners. But the latter were not the only ones to benefit: at least 40 decrees authorized the concession of lands belonging to the Hawaiian Home Lands to the army. Many were cancelled in 1984 by Governor Ariyoshi. But rather than shooing away the "illegal" occupants, the government opted for a financial settlement. Hence, DHHL managers accepted $10 million worth of damages and interests. In 1997, only 6,400 people were granted leases by the DHHL, representing barely 20% of the total surface area of the Hawaiian Home Lands. Meanwhile, the waiting list includes nearly 30,000 requests that have not been processed, even some that were filled out in the 1950s! Such corrupt practices are presently being denounced by

sovereignty groups, who demand the right to manage the lands granted to them by law.

The Office of Hawaiian Affairs (OHA)

In 1978, the state recognized the failure of its Hawaiian politics frequently corrupted by breaches of trust. In accordance with federal texts, island residents of all origins voted to add an amendment to the Hawaiian constitution that would oversee the creation of a fund to improve the living conditions of Hawaiians by birth. This was to be financed by 20% of the revenues generated by the "ceded lands," former Crown lands taken over in 1894 by the young Republic of Hawaii and now rented by the state of Hawaii to individuals and companies. Managed by the Office of Hawaiian Affairs (OHA), this fund was aimed at those whose Hawaiian heritage was at least 50%.

The OHA was mainly a consultative political body, but also held decisional power in local matters. In 1998, over 100,000 people were able to voice their opinion on all kinds of subjects such as immersion schools, health and Hawaiian culture. It also held elections on a regular basis to name its board of directors. However, this specificity did not please everyone. In 1996, a certain Mr. Rice, a *haole* breeder living on the Big Island, lodged a complaint against the state on the basis of discrimination. Twice dismissed, he brought his case all the way to the Supreme Court of the United States who, against all odds, decided in his favour at the end of February 2000. This decision forced the OHA, whose mission was to defend the interests of Hawaiians, to open the elections of its board of directors to all. Because Hawaiians had long been a minority, this basically consisted of dissolving the only representative body they could count on. To counter this decision, the state of Hawaii is considering transferring some of the OHA's powers to the Department of Hawaiian Home Lands. Until the next lawsuit launched by the next Mr. Rice. To be continued...

The Army

A main player in Hawaii, the army occupies nearly as much land as the Hawaiian Home Lands. What's worse, it occupies some parcels of land that officially should go to Hawaiians in accordance with the program. At least one quarter of the island of O'ahu is under its absolute control. The general headquarters of the Pacific American Armed Forces, composed of the marines, submarines, shipyards, airforce and ground army, forms the largest military base in the world. With 50,000 people stationed in the islands (115,000 including their families), the army is the second most important economic sector in Hawaii. But for a growing number of residents, this financial godsend does not justify the presence of such a force, which makes Hawaii the most militarized state of the country. The occupation of such large surfaces, the use of the sacred island of Kaho'olawe as a shooting target and the training using real bullets in certain sectors have raised discontent. Despite the return of Kaho'olawe to the public sector and the initiation of clean-up programs, the Hawaiian population remains, for the most part, hostile towards the army.

Towards Sovereignty?

A survey sponsored by the OHA in 1999 revealed growing support for sovereignty: over one third of the 4,000 members questioned said they were in favour of this option. Three years earlier, only 12% had voiced this opinion. This new piece of information in the Hawaiian political scene is the result of several factors. A major factor is undoubtedly the 1993 centennial celebration of the overthrow of Queen Lili'uokalani and the official pardons presented by the government at this occasion. Since then, the question of sovereignty, previously considered radical and discussed behind closed doors, is now openly tackled, including by the press.

What sovereignty means to individuals remains to be seen. Some 300 Hawaiian interest groups are scattered throughout the archipelago, most appearing to lean towards the transfer of some 3,088 sq mi (8,000km^2) of land (combining the former "ceded lands" and the Hawaiian Home Lands) to Hawaiians by birth and the creation of a political body inspired by Native American nations in the southwestern United States and Alaska, which are independent for local matters but under the federal government for matters such as justice and foreign affairs. Some wish to restore the monarchy while the more radical "Independent Nation of Hawai'i" demands the creation of a 100% independent state. Even though this movement continues to grow in size, it is very hard at the present time to imagine the United States relinquishing their rights to the archipelago. However, the judicial aspect of the matter leans in favour of sovereignists: legally, the Kingdom of Hawaii, once recognized by occidental countries, has never ceased to exist.

Economy

Extremely dynamic in the 1980s, the Hawaiian economy was profoundly shaken in the 1990s because of the end of the great farms and the decrease in tourism. Furthermore, the extremely high cost of living prevented businesses from being competitive, and an increasing number of them were forced to relocate. In 1997, Hawaii had the lowest growth rate in the country: 1.7% as opposed to the national average of 4.5%. Island residents are obviously the first to pay the price of such changes. The lack of land coupled with the multiplication by 10 of the population within the last century, the considerable buying power of Japanese investors in the 1970s and of retired Americans today, the importation of 80% of all consumer goods, the isolation... all of these factors contribute to making Hawaii a state where the price of land and homes as well as the cost of living greatly surpass the means of most residents.

Agriculture

Since the 19th century, two crops have had their glory days in Hawaii: first, the sugar cane was the motor behind the economic boom of the 1870s but also the reason why Hawaiians lost their lands, and second, the pineapple market skyrocketed at the turn of the 20th century thanks to James Dole's invention of the fruit-packaging machine. He even went as far as buying the entire island of Lana'i and turning it into the largest pineapple plantation in the world. The sugar industry had its maximal growth in the 1930s and a record production of over 1.2 million tonnes in 1966. It gradually disappeared due to the collapse of world markets as, one by one, sugar mills closed. As for the pineapple industry, it could not compete with the cheap labour in poorer countries and only survived as a "folkloric" enterprise. However, other specialized cultures have been more fruitful, such as coffee, macadamia nuts, flowers and tropical fruit. Today, agriculture represents less than 2% of Hawaii's GNP.

The Big Five

Originating from the colonization and growth at the end of the 19th century, five major groups, Alexander & Baldwin, Amfac, Brewer, Castle & Cook, and Dole and Davies, nicknamed The Big Five, made their fortune in the agricultural sector. Despite antitrust laws implemented when Hawaii became a state in 1959, their immense estates (60% of all private land) made them giants in a wide variety of sectors: they escaped the farming slump and invested into tourism, real estate (converted farm lands) and finances in Hawaii as well as in the rest of the continent and the world. They remained major economic forces in the archipelago, controlling, among others, the transportation of all merchandise. For a time, the jobs lost in farming were absorbed by tourism but with this industry slowing down as well, concern is mounting.

Tourism

Tourism in the islands began in the 1920s, especially on O'ahu. Initially reserved for well-lined purses, travelling became more accessible over the decades. In the 1960s, for the first time, tourism brought in the most revenue, even surpassing agriculture. The 1980s saw a spectacular increase, accompanied by unbridled property speculation. Then, suddenly, at the beginning of the 1990s, the sector began to decrease due to the Gulf

War, federal budget cuts (the second source of revenue in the archipelago), hurricane Iniki in 1992 and the Asian crisis. It hit rock bottom in 1993: 6.1 million tourists visited the islands that year as opposed to 7 million in 1990 (today 6.8 million for $10 billion); 60% came from America and 35% from Asia. The sector was overdeveloped and suffered from the ageing of the destination. Subsequently, it is trying to renew itself by focusing on ecotourism and upper-scale travellers. Numerous real-estate projects were stopped, seemingly indicating a new priority given to natural resources and cultural projects. Best to wish the islanders a smooth transition since tourism represents nearly one in three jobs.

Population

When Cook discovered Hawaii, its population was estimated between 300,000 and 500,000 people. Quickly though, contact with Occidentals turned fatal for the islanders. Much more than the skirmishes, small pox, mumps, whooping cough, influenza and venereal diseases transmitted by sailors in 20 years caused the first demographic fall of 10%. Sadly, this was only the beginning. A century after the first contact, the population, which was still more

than three-quarters Hawaiian, decreased to 57,000 individuals. Several factors were added to the epidemics: high infant mortality, poor hygienic conditions, insufficient medical care and malnutrition, among others.

The strong immigration that accompanied the sugar boom saw the arrival of a substantial foreign workforce at the end of the 19th century: Portuguese, German and Japanese. Given that they accounted for 76% of the population in 1878, Hawaiians represented a little over 50% six years later and, at the turn of the 20th century, merely one in five inhabitants of the archipelago. In the 20th century, the population grew by 10, sustained this time by a strong Asian and South Europe immigration: Filipino, Chinese, Korean, Spanish and Puerto Rican. The island population reached one million inhabitants in the 1980s and, based on the last census, in 1996 it reached 1,186,815 inhabitants, including 50,000 American military personnel. With 70% of the entire population (approximately 885,000 inhab.), O'ahu is 1.5 times more densely populated than Belgium, a country reputed for the density of its population. The Big Island counts about 137,000; Maui 100,000; Kaua'i 56,000.; Moloka'i

Menehune

In Hawaiian folklore, the *menehune* elves are famous for their construction projects. Numerous *heiau*, fishponds, ancient roads and irrigation canals throughout the archipelago have been attributed to them. Said to live deep in the forests far from prying eyes, industrious brigades of *menehune* work at night to avoid being seen. They disappear into the wilderness at sunrise or as soon as they are disturbed. Still today, when something strange or inexplicable happens, many half-jokingly attribute it to the *menehune*.

6,700; Lanai 2,800; and Ni'ihau less than 200.

Ethnic Origins

Based on the kind of poll that is conducted, the Hawaiian portion of the island population varies between 13% (people who consider themselves Hawaiian) and 19% (people who have Hawaiian blood but whose domi-nant ethnic group is other). The first number is more accurate and was used by the American Census Bureau in its research. The most recent results indicate: Caucasians 33% (this rate is constantly on the rise with the arrival of American retirees); Japanese 22%; Filipinos 15%; Hawaiians 13%; Chinese 6%; others 11% (many from the Pacific islands).

Hawaiians

Upon seeing these numbers, one conclusion becomes quite clear: Hawaiians have long been a minority on their own territory. In the 1960 census, they were even classified under the category "Others." A study conducted by the OHA revealed that of all those who declared themselves of Hawaiian descent, more than half had in fact less than 50% of Hawaiian blood. One in three (that is, 48,000 people) had between 50% and 99%, and only one in 25 was a direct descendant of Hawaiian ancestors, without any outside blood: in other words, about 8,000 people or less than 1% of all the inhabitants of the islands. Hardly more even know the language of their ancestors. The statistics speak for themselves: Hawaiians are the least educated, the least well paid, the least cared for and the most often sentenced to imprisonment. A tough case to win. Moreover, many Hawaiians now live on the continent: nearly 35,000 live in California and about 17,000 have sought exile in the western United States to flee the high cost of living in Hawaii.

Caucasians

The British were the first Europeans to settle in the islands: adventurers, sailors desperate to set foot on land and all sorts of merchants arrived as early as the 18th century. England, not the United States, was the first to leave its mark on the archipelago, which is still today shown by the Hawaiian flag that dedicates a large place to the Union Jack. The first Protestant missionaries arrived from New England as long ago as 1820 and are the ancestors of many of the prominent landowning dynasties still in the islands today. The Portuguese (named *Pokiki*), who came from Madeira and the Azores in the 1870s, formed the largest European community to have immigrated to Hawaii after the Anglo-Saxons.

Hokule'a

Originally farm workers, they quickly became landowners. If their language essentially disappeared in the 1960s in the great Hawaiian melting pot, some traditions have withstood the test of time, such as the annual Pentecost celebration.

Asians

The Chinese were the first Asians to find work on the plantations in the 1850s. Many left but those who remained despite the racism opened shops. A second wave of Chinese immigration in the 1870s-1880s was accompanied by the arrival of many Japanese workers, who now constitute the largest ethnic group of Asian descent. Forming the second largest community, the Filipinos arrived in the islands between 1910 and 1930 and replaced the Japanese and Chinese on the plantations whose social status had improved. Despite the insults and suspicion resulting from the Second World War (during which many remained loyal to the United States), the Japanese community managed to establish itself. Many of their offspring climbed the social ladder through commerce, tourism or administration. The Chinese, for their part, play a major role in real estate, restaurants and tourism,

Religion

In Hawaiian society each element used to be represented by a divinity, and ceremonies were centered around four main gods. Ku and Hina (the Moon) formed the sacred couple, guardians of paradise and Earth, rulers of the Hawaiian pantheon – he of male deities, she of goddesses. Embodied in various forms, Ku was also Ku'ula, god of fishing, or Ku'kailimoku, the all-powerful god of war. Introduced by Tahitian settlers, Lono represented the elements (rain), fertility, harvests as well as peace; he was the soul of the Earth (*mana 'aina*), and Kane was the forefather of the man he created. The fourth great god, sombre-faced Kanaloa, ruled over the dead and spirits. In addition, about 40 other minor deities presided over natural phenomena and human activities: Pele, volcanoes and fire; her sister Na Maka, the sea; another sister, Laka, the *hula*; Poli'ahu, snow; Kane kekili, thunder; Laieikawai, rainbows; Kamoho-ali'i, sharks, guardians of the nourishing waters, etc.

and have maintained many of their customs, such as the Chinese New Year.

Doorway to the Pacific

Other smaller groups came later: Koreans, Puerto Ricans, as well as many inhabitants of the Pacific Islands (Samoans, Tongans, Micronesians and many more) today form about one tenth of the archipelago's population. Their cultural influence on the revival of Hawaiian culture is far from negligible. The very traditional island of Tonga, still governed by a king, provides a model of continuity and wisdom to followers of Hawaiian monarchy, which some would like to draw inspiration from. Many Hawaiians look to their cousins in Tonga to rediscover the art of the *tapa*, or to the Samoa Islands to rediscover ancient forms of tattooing.

Marriage

In this true cultural melting pot, a sense of ethnic belonging is often hard to determine. It is not rare for one person to have Hawaiian, English, German, Chinese or Japanese origins. Mixed marriages are the most common in Hawaii today; nearly one in two unions is mixed. Fact is, to their great misfortune, Hawaiians, along with the Chinese, are the most exogamous residents of the archipelago.

Culture and Traditions

Hawaiian traditions very nearly disappeared when Protestant missionaries condemned their "futile" (surfing) or "lewd" (*hula*) nature and forbade most of them. A first cultural revival movement was instigated by King David Kalakaua at the end of the 19th century and contributed several years later to the growing popularity of surfing by Duke Kahanamoku, an Olympic gold-medal swimmer. In the 1970s, when a double-hulled canoe (the *Hokule'a*) made the first great trans-oceanic voyage between Tahiti and Hawaii, the islands again rediscovered their traditions. The lasting movement has since constantly grown thanks to the ancient language, *hula* dance, music, tattooing and the art of *tapa*.

Language

The official language in the islands along with English, Hawaiian is a direct descendant of the Polynesian tongue spoken by the first settlers. Over the centuries, numerous local specificities and transformations have turned it into a full-fledged language, as close to Polynesian as French is to Italian. The vocabulary for cultural and natural elements is very extensive. For example, there are 64 different ways of describing rain! Although the popularity of the Hawaiian language is once again on the rise thanks to the cultural revival that has been sweeping over the islands for the past 20 years, it is rare to hear it on a day-to-day basis (except on the private island of Ni'ihau where everyone speaks it fluently). It is more frequently heard in songs and during *hula* dances. Bits of Hawaiian are sprinkled into the everyday language along with Pidgin (Creole) which originated from contacts

between the settlers and their workers. In 1980, Hawaiian organizations obtained the creation of Hawaiian immersion schools such as those reserved for Native American communities in the western United States and French-speaking Cajuns in Louisiana. Going one step further, the parents of children enrolled in these classes must also take classes to reappropriate the language of their ancestors. In the spring of 1998, the first class reached the university level.

Hula

"Hula is the language of the heart and therefore the heartbeat of the Hawaiian people," wrote King David Kalakaua. True expression of the Hawaiian soul, the *hula* is undoubtedly one of the most graceful and meaningful dances. Over and above its obvious beauty, the sometimes slow and fluid, other times jerky and war-like movements of the body, feet, arms and eyes evoke using a precise code

Hula Dancer

the entire universe of Hawaiians: the moon, sun, sea, anger of the gods, the wonders of nature... Its themes are drawn from the history of the islands, their heroes and their legends. Some relate happy events, others sadness and death. Accompanied by music or repetitive *mele* (songs) chanted by men, the stories often evoke Pele, goddess of fire, soul of volcanoes and guardian of *hula* dancers. According to legend, Pele herself composed the oldest and most beautiful forms of *hula* at the foot of the Kilauea at the end of her long journey through the archipelago. Thus, it was originally to honour the gods, by praying to the elements that frightened them, that Hawaiians danced. Moreover, the *hula* was a means of transmitting legends and cultural beliefs without requiring any writing. Like the rest of society, the *hula* schools (*halau*) created in the temples also had to respect numerous strict *kapus*. Originally, the *hula* was only performed by men.

Hula Today

Ever since the 1970s and the rebirth of the Hawaiian culture, *hula*

Ukulele

Contrary to popular belief, although it is often associated with Hawaiian music, the ukulele was not invented in the archipelago. It owes its origins to the *braguinha*, a small four-stringed guitar introduced by the first Portuguese immigrants. King David Kalakaua liked the sound of this instrument and contributed to its popularity with Hawaiian musicians. The term ukulele, which means "jumping flea," alludes to the rapid movement of fingers along the neck and appeared soon after three immigrants from Madeira started a factory in Honolulu. The continent caught on a few years later, in 1915, thanks to the Panama Pacific Exhibit in San Francisco. Today, although most instruments are made in Asia, a few family businesses such as Kamaka Ukulele in Honolulu, established in 1916, continue to make the instruments.

('umeke), conch and maracas might have been heard. Each instrument had a specific role: the *pahu* signalled ceremonies taking place in the temple and the conch announced arrivals by land or sea. The missionaries introduced many instruments used in liturgy and initiated the Hawaiians to their sounds. Songs composed by queens are still hummed today such as Lili'uokalani's "Aloha Oe." With immigration came the ukulele ("jumping flea"), derived from the Portuguese *braguinha* and the Hawaiian guitar with its pronounced vibrato. During the inter-war years, these two instruments became indissociable with the Hawaiian sound popularized in the 1930s by the radio show *Hawai'i Calls* broadcast from Waikiki. Singer Don Ho crooned the sensual, slightly melancholic songs of this period which evoked the timeless sweetness of life.

has been taught throughout the archipelago, and the number of students never stops growing. The Hawaiians, whose cultural pride suffered greatly under the oppression of the missionaries in the 19th century, have used the *hula* to retrace their steps back to the past. Although numerous *hula* shows are given in the archipelago, it is during the Merry Monarch Festival in April on the Big Island that one finds the true essence of the Hawaiian heart. This celebration was named after King David Kalakaua ("the merry king"). The *hula kahiko* (ancient) is distinguished by a cappella chants and floral or fern *lei*, whose colours are chosen based on the theme of the dances. Very popular in all tourist shows, the *hula 'auana* (modern), more dressed, evokes the present-day diversity of the islands to rhythmic music.

Music

Traditionally, musical instruments were rarely used to accompany Hawaiian songs. On rare occasions, the *pahu*, calabash

Umeke Player

Contemporary Rhythms

Over time, the islands have became the stage for all kinds of music: from the *paniolo*-style country of Ernie Cruz Senior to *jawaiian*, a combination of Hawaiian sounds and reggae, performed by the likes of Bruddah Walta, Marty Dread and the Manao Company. Record stores sell rock music by groups like Kalapana or The Krush, recipients of numerous Hanohano Awards (Hawaiian music), alongside folk songs by Chris Rego and Jerry Santos. Despite the death in 1997 of its figurehead, Israel Kamakawiwo'ole (IZ), the music of Hawaiian-speaking singers surely has the strongest wind in its sails. Popular singers include the Cazimero Brothers, Makaha Sons (from Ni'ihau), Keali'i Reichel, the Hapa duo and newcomer Kekuhi Kanahele who draws her inspiration from the *mele* chants that accompany the *hula*. For concert listings, consult the Honolulu Weekly Magazine.

Tattooing

In Tahiti, where Cook first observed this art form, they called it *tatau* (*kakau* in Hawaii). In the islands of the Polynesian Triangle, tattooing was originally created to scare away enemies and had a very specific social function.

Kahuna

Once upon a time, Hawaii had over 20 kinds of priests, or kahunas, who practised various activities. The kahuna nui (grand priest), who was the grand chief's alter ego, counselled the tribe leader on religious matters, advising him at the most opportune moment on important decisions, especially on those related to war. Religious activities were shared between several priests, each having their own specific prerogatives.

Medical kahunas, who outnumbered the others priests, included herbalists, masseurs, and mind and body specialists. Ancestral Hawaiians believed that illness resulted primarily from negative thoughts. Each consultation was thus preceded by a ho'oponopono session, in which people close to the patient accompanied him or her to discuss their relationship problems. Once the problems were resolved, all joined the practitioner to pray for the patient's recovery.

It was used to mark the passage of young men into adulthood; it was also used to manifest relations to gods and spirits, the pain caused by death, the shame of infamy or the pride of a heroic act. The drawings, essentially geometric and often very elaborate, alternated with sections that were completely black. Following precise codes, they sometimes included the variations, reflections and tastes of the epoch. Individuals were tattooed to mark significant events in their lives, transcribing their personal journey into their very skin. Tattoos were done using shark teeth and sharpened bones dipped in ink made by burning the nuts of the candlenut tree (*kukui*) and applied using a small mallet. Ceremonies surrounding tattooing sessions generally lasted several days, which this is still done today in the Samoa Islands. The tattooers, *kahuna* who passed their skills on from generation to generation, occupied a high social rank. Instruments have been found that dated back nearly a millennium BC.

Designs

Tattoos differed according to sex. Originally tattooed between the waist and the knees, men developed little by little more complex designs that covered the entire body. Hawaiian tattoos drew much of their inspiration from those in the Marquesas Islands. Warrior tattoos were particularly impressive: one side of the body was left intact whereas the other side was completely covered in black. Women generally had less tattoos, which were limited to certain body parts. In 1819, French traveller Jacques Arago, author of many engravings, described the "very elegantly tattooed" legs, left-hand palm and tongue of Queen Ka'ahumanu – the last tattoo having been applied following the death of her mother-in-law. Symbols of prestige or sadness, tattoos could also evoke the unworthiness of a slave or prisoner (eyelids were tattooed on the inside). Even more surprising, it was discovered that lepers living on the Kalaupapa Peninsula on Moloka'i had created their own tattoo motifs.

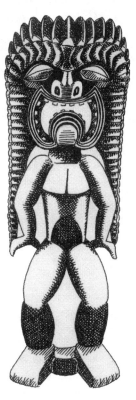

A Return to Roots

Originally condemned by the missionaries as superstition and devil's practice, tattooing virtually disappeared from the Hawaiian population due to the introduction of occidental clothing. Irony of fate, some of the sailors in Captain Cook's expedition were tattooed and proudly showed off their Hawaiian mementoes back home. The fashion then spread like wildfire in ports across Europe. Once again popular across Polynesia, tattooing, once used to challenge colonial governments, is now first and foremost a way of reinforcing a sense of belonging to a culture.

Practical Information

This chapter will
help travellers better plan their trip to Hawaii.

Hawaii's area code is 808.

Entrance Formalities

To enter the United States, Canadian citizens do not need a visa.

Most Western Europeans need only a valid passport to enter the United States and no visa is required for stays of up to three months; a return or continuation plane ticket is sufficient. If Honolulu is not your first port of entry to the United States, which is most likely unless you are coming from Asia or the Pacific, you will clear customs at your first port of entry.

There are very strict rules in Hawaii regarding the importation of plants and organic matter in order to protect the fragile Hawaiian ecosystem from aggressive foreign species. These rules equally apply to exportation: only plants and flowers approved by customs are allowed to leave the archipelago.

Embassies and Consulates

Consulates in Hawaii

Canada, Great Britain, Spain and the Netherlands do not have consulates in Hawaii.

BELGIUM
745 Fort St. Mall, 18th floor
Honolulu, HI 96813
☎533-6900

ITALY
735 Bishop St., Suite 201
Honolulu, HI 96813
☎531-2277

SWITZERLAND
4231 Papu Circle
Honolulu, HI 96816
☎737-5297

U.S. Embassies and Consulates Abroad

AUSTRALIA
Moonah Place, Canberra
ACT 2600
☎(6) 214-5600

BELGIUM
27 Boulevard du Régent
B-1000 Brussels
☎(02) 512-2210
⇒(02) 511-9652

CANADA
2 Wellington Street
Ottawa, Ontario K1P 5T1
☎(613) 238-5335
⇒(613) 238-5720

Consulate
Place Félix-Martin
1155 Rue Saint-Alexandre
Montréal, Québec H2Z 1Z2
☎*(514) 398-9695*
⇋*(514) 398-9748*

Consulate
360 University Avenue
Toronto, Ontario M5G 1S4
☎*(416) 595-1700*
⇋*(416) 595-0051*

Consulate
1095 West Pender
Vancouver
British Columbia V6E 2M6
☎*(604) 685-4311*

DENMARK
Dag Hammarskjölds Allé 24
2100 Copenhagen Ø
☎*(35) 55 31 44*
⇋*(35) 43 02 23*

FINLAND
Itaïnen Puistotie 14B
FIN-00140, Helsinki, Finland
☎*358-9-171-931*

GERMANY
Clayallee 170, 14195 Berlin
☎*(30) 832-2933*
⇋*(30) 8305-1215*

GREAT BRITAIN
24 Grosvenor Square
London W1A 1AE
☎*(171) 499-9000*
⇋*(171) 491-2485*

ITALY
Via Veneto 119-a
00187 Roma
☎*(06) 467-41*
⇋*(06) 467-42217*

PORTUGAL
Av. Das Forças Armadas
1600 Lisboa
Apartado 4258
1507 Lisboa Codex
☎*(351) (1) 727-3300*
⇋*(351) (1) 727-2354*

Aloha

Hello, goodbye, welcome, love – aloha conveys in a single word the warmth of the Polynesian people. Each of its five letters stands for a quality: akahai (gentleness), lokahi (harmony), 'olu'olu (kindness), ha'aha'a (humility) and ahonui (patience).

NORWAY
Drammensveien 18
0244 Oslo
☎*22448550*

NETHERLANDS
Lange Voorhout 102
2514 EJ, Den Haag
☎*(70) 310-9209*
⇋*(70) 361-4688*

SPAIN
C. Serrano 75
Madrid 28006
☎*(1) 577-4000*
⇋*(1) 564-1652*

SWEDEN
Strandvägen 101
11589 Stockholm
☎*(08) 783 53 00*
⇋*(08) 661 19 64*

SWITZERLAND
93 Jubilam Strasse
3005 Berne
☎*31-43-70-11*
⇋*31-357-73-98*

Tourist Information

Outside Hawaii

Hawaii Visitors and Convention Bureau
c/o Comprehensive Travel Industry Services
1260 Hornby St., Suite 104
Vancouver, BC
V6Z 1W2 Canada
☎*(604) 669-6691*
⇋*(604) 669-6075*

Hawaii Visitors and Convention Bureau
180 Montgomery St., Suite 2360
San Francisco, CA 94104
☎*(415) 248-3800*
⇋*(415) 248-3808*

Hawaii Visitors and Convention Bureau
P.O. Box 208
Sudbury on Thames
Middlesex, TW16 5RJ
Great Britain
☎*(44) 181-941-4009*
⇋*(44) 181-941-4011*

In Hawaii

Hawaii Visitors and Convention Bureau
2270 Kalakaua Ave., Suite 801
Honolulu, HI 96815
☎*923-1811*
☎*800-GO-HAWAII*
⇋*924-0290*
www.gohawaii.com
The Hawaii Visitors and Convention Bureau is the only source of information on the archipelago, but don't expect a miracle here; service is neither quick nor efficient. You may be better off contacting the bureaus of each island you will be

staying at, which may be fastidious if you plan on visiting several, but also more reliable. The coordinates of each bureau are listed in each chapter. Most bureaus can send you information by mail.

The Visitors Bureau has set up red and gold signs with the image of Kamehameha throughout the archipelago to indicate tourist attractions, lookouts and various points of interest. Not everything is marked though, and some attractions, such as libraries, are of little or no interest to visitors. The red and gold markers will nevertheless help you find your way around.

Most visitors consult the free magazines featuring each of the four main islands – O'ahu, the Big Island, Maui and Kaua'i – such as *Spotlight's Gold*, *101 Things to Do* and *This Week*. Although these magazines are heavy on advertising, they are nonetheless useful sources of information.

Internet

As hard as it may be to believe, Hawaii still isn't on-line. Cybercafés are few and far between outside of Waikiki. Before your trip, you might want to visit these interesting sites in addition to those of the tourism bureaus:

www.enewshawaii.com
A new, informative Web site on Hawaii, designed like a daily newspaper.

honolulu.about.com
All kinds of information on the archipelago, with the opportunity to read newspaper and other articles.

www.hawaii-nation.org
One of the main Hawaii independence movements.

www.kahoolawe.org
The Protect Kaho'olawe 'Ohana Web site, which is responsible for occupations of the island and supports its return to the fold of the State of Hawaii.

www.moolelo.com
Web site of Uncle Charlie (Charles Kauluwehi Maxwell Sr.), Hawaiian cultural consultant, storyteller and husband of the *kumu hula* of Maui's main *halau* (*hula* school).

Getting to Hawaii

By Plane

Hawaii has four main airports, one on each of the largest islands. Although 90% of planes still land in Honolulu, you can now fly directly from the mainland to Kona (the Big Island), Kahului (Maui) and Lihu'e (Kaua'i). Hilo Airport on the Big Island receives many inter-island flights.

Several airports or aerodromes strictly serve small airplanes and chartered flights: Kapalua (West Maui), Hana (Maui), Kalaupapa (Moloka'i) and Kamuela-Waimea (the Big Island). A description of each of these airports is provided in their respective chapter.

International Flights

Hawaii's central location has made the island a major hub of air traffic in the Asia-Pacific region: no less than 24 carriers currently fly to Honolulu from the mainland. Nearly all North American carriers take part in this profitable market and most adjust their fares. There are no direct flights from Europe, but Honolulu is a popular stop for round-the-world trips. If you wish to continue your trip after Hawaii, you will find good deals on fares. The best thing to do is to consult the "Travel" section of the *Honolulu Advertiser* on Sundays.

The two main Hawaiian-based airlines also fly to several continental and international destinations.

Founded in 1929, **Hawaiian Airlines** (☎800-367-5320 on the continent or 800-882-8811 in Hawaii, except O'ahu ☎838-1555, www.hawaiianair.com) flies to Los Angeles (three flights per day), San Francisco (one flight per day), Las Vegas (one flight per day via Los Angeles), Seattle (one to two flight(s) per day) and Portland (one flight per day) from Honolulu, and offers direct Maui - Los Angeles and Kona - Los Angeles flights. The carrier soon plans to offer flights east of the Rocky Mountains. Hawaiian Airlines also flies to Anchorage (Alaska) in summer, Papeete (Tahiti) and Pago Pago (Samoa).

Aloha Airlines (*☎800-367-5250 on the continent or 800-432-7117 in Hawaii, except O'ahu ☎484-1111, www.alohaair.com)* has been expanding its international network for several years now. Since February 2000, the carrier offers two daily flights to Oakland, near San Francisco, one departing from Honolulu and the other from Kahului. The airline also flies to several Pacific islands: Midway (*☎888-477-7010)*, Christmas Island *(a dependent atoll of the State of Kirbati; ☎839-6680 or 888-800-8144)*, as well as Majuro and Kwajalein of the Marshall Islands.

Among the less expensive travel agencies offering no-frills flights, you can contact **Cheap Tickets** (*☎800-377-1000, www.cheaptickets.com)*, which has a dozen offices in Hawaii, on the U.S. West Coast and in New York. You can make airplane, car and

hotel reservations by Internet or by telephone and have tickets and travel coupons mailed to you anywhere in North America.

For **domestic flights**, refer to the "Transportation" section (see p 58).

Health

No vaccinations are required for Hawaii. The basic hygiene rules and advice that follow should steer you clear of most health problems.

Sun

As pleasant as the sun's warm rays may be, they can also be quite harmful. In order to have as much fun on the beach as possible and in complete safety, always opt for sunscreen with a high SPF number. And don't forget to apply it regularly! Ideally, you should put sunscreen on 20 to 30min before going out into the sun. Even with proper protection, though, extended sun exposure on the first few days may cause sunstroke, causing symptoms such as dizziness, vomiting and fever. A parasol, a hat, sunglasses and perhaps even a T-shirt will help protect you from the sun's harmful rays as you enjoy the beach.

Swimming

Be extremely cautious of currents that violently sweep Hawaii's coasts and make swimming dangerous. Just because there are surfers in the water doesn't mean conditions are safe: they are generally used to the rough waters and know how to deal with them. As a general rule, the islands' northern coasts are most dangerous in winter and the southern coasts in summer. Be careful though, as this is not an absolute rule. If you have any doubts before going into the water, ask a lifeguard on the beach if it is safe. If there is no lifeguard around, do as the Hawaiians do: if nobody is in the water, swimming is out! Indeed, you should never swim alone. If you get carried away by a current, swim parallel to the shore until the current becomes weaker.

Also, watch out for rising tides if you are swimming in the natural basin of a torrent. The best way to avoid this risk is to avoid swimming on rainy days. In some places, the water level may rise by a metre or more in a few minutes, pushing swimmers downstream where they inevitably hurt themselves on the rocks or even drown. Swimming in torrents or ponds is not recommended due to the risk of contracting leptospirosis, an condition spread by infected water, which may result in fever, aches and pains, and even meningitis.

Marine Environment

Do not touch the coral reefs when snorkelling. Not only will you kill them, but you risk injuring yourself as well: cuts and scratches from coral scar boldly. Also be careful of the many sea urchins. In case you do hurt yourself, it is imperative that you make sure the stinger is entirely removed. Among the more dangerous sea creatures are medusas, the largest of which (Portugese men-of-war) can inflict severe burns, even after having been washed up on the beach.

Sharks, which preoccupy the thoughts of many tourists, are a minor risk. Surfers regularly encounter small ones and rarely have problems. The only shark that poses a threat is the tiger shark that sometimes swims near the coast, though few fatal accidents have been reported in the last 20 years. If you see albatrosses on the island of Midway, however, be careful: tiger sharks often swim in the lagoon looking for a snack.

Don't pick anything up off the ocean floor

when diving in Molokini off the coast of Maui. Though it is now a marine reserve, the island once served for U.S. Army target practice and not all unexploded munitions were removed in the clean-up that followed.

Altitude

You may experience altitude-related malaises at the top of Hale'a'kala (10,020ft or 3,055m) on Maui, Mauna Kea's summit (13,792ft or 4,205m) and at the top of Mauna Loa (13,674ft or 4,169m) on the Big Island. The first two are both accessible by car and pose the biggest risk due to the quick rise in altitude. It can be extremely dangerous to climb so high or fly if you have gone diving in the last 24hrs. If you feel sick – nausea, headache, shortness of breath – it is best to cllimb down as soon as possible. Watch for signs of hypothermia when hiking: it can get rather cold high up there at night.

Climate

Hawaii is known the world over for its trade winds, sunshine and blue skies, but depending on the time of year, the island, slopes, altitude and conditions can vary drastically. Hawaii has two main seasons: winter, which is cooler (77°F or 25°C

on average) with frequent and extensive rain; and summer, which is warmer (86°F or 30°C) and sunnier, cooled by the trade winds blowing from the northeast. In winter, the trade winds are replaced by *kona* winds from the southeast, which bring hot temperatures and bad weather.

The islands' orientation and relative location have significant consequences. Subject to dominant trade winds that bring rain, the north and east littorals are more humid. The west and south coasts, however, are "under the wind" and drier, which explains why all seaside resorts are located here. In fact, because of this phenomenon, five times as much rain can fall just a few kilometres away.

Each island has its own weather service that can be consulted any time, especially if you plan to go for a hike or out to sea. There is in addition a general number, ☎*973-4380* (24hrs).

Safety

Like any other tourist destination, Hawaii has its share of theft. It is advisable that you leave nothing in your car, especially if it is parked near a beach, tourist attraction or in a shopping centre parking lot. Islanders almost always leave their own

Practical Information

cars unlocked. This is not a bad idea, especially in O'ahu, as it may keep you from having to pay for a damaged door or broken window. The smaller the island, the more peaceful it is.

Public drunkenness, though much improved, is another problem; avoid downtown Honolulu late at night and anywhere else you might encounter intoxicated individuals. As a general rule, and unless otherwise noted in the text, respect private-property signs, not only because Hawaiians are often annoyed to see tourists in their garden, but also because *pakololo*, or marijuana, is grown illegally in certain areas. Police interventions have greatly reduced this activity in recent years.

Transportation

By Plane

Hawaiians talk of *holoholo* while North Americans refer to island hopping. Visiting one's family or friends on other islands is one of the favourite activities of archipelago residents. Several carriers, both big and small, are in great competition intensely for this extremely profitable market.

Hawaiian Airlines
☎800-367-5320 *(continent)*
☎800-882-8811 *(Hawaii)*
☎838-1555 *(O'ahu)*

Island Air
☎800-323-3345 *(continent)*
☎800-652-6541 *(Hawaii)*
☎484-2222 *(O'ahu)*

Aloha Airlines
☎800-367-5250 *(continent)*
☎800-432-7117 *(Hawaii)*
☎484-1111 *(O'ahu)*

Pacific Wings
☎873-0877 *(Maui)*
☎888-575-4546

Moloka'i Air Shuttle
☎567-6847 *(Moloka'i)*
☎545-4988 *(Honolulu)*

Flight Coupons

Inter-island flight coupons issued by Aloha and Hawaiian Airlines can be purchased at any local travel agency at a good price. The downside to these coupons is that they can only be bought in Hawaii, but reservations can be made in advance.

Packages

Aloha and Hawaiian Airlines both offer packages for an unlimited number of flights within a given period. Both airlines also offer additional promotions regularly: don't hesitate to inquire.

Maritime Service

The archipelago's maritime service is extremely limited.

There is currently only one shuttle operating between Lahaina (Maui) and the port of Manele Bay (Lana'i), with five daily round trips. A weekly boat excursion to Moloka'i, also departing from Lahaina, is also available.

American Hawaii Cruises
☎800-513-5022
www.cruisehawaii.com
This cruise company offers a one-week cruise in the archipelago.

By Car

Unless you don't mind riding in a minibus or spending your entire vacation in Waikiki and taking advantage of the O'ahu bus network, a car is practically indispensable on the outer islands. Rentals are relatively affordable and offer more freedom.

Overall, the road network is good. The only highways in the archipelago are on O'ahu and circle Honolulu. Elsewhere, roads run more or less along the coast, the central mountains having caused problems for the Bridges and Roads Department. On several islands, Maui and the Big Island (Saddle Road) in particular, you will find many unpaved roads. Note that it is forbidden to drive rental vehicles on these. Lana'i is a particular case, as most of its road network consists of dirt roads. If you really want to explore the entire island, we can't stress enough that you might consider renting a four-wheel-drive vehicle despite the high price. One last point: do not be fooled by the word "highway," a term which is sometimes given to winding roads that take you nowhere fast.

Hawaii may be an island paradise, but you will unfortunately find mainland problems here too: monster traffic jams, not only in the region of Honolulu but on Maui as well; there is slightly less traffic on the eastern coast of Kaua'i and around Kona on the Big Island. Traffic has considerably increased these last few years and since no improvements have been made to the road network, there is little else to do but to sit patiently and wait in your car.

Highway Code

Road regulations in Hawaii are, on the whole, similar to those of the United States. The legal alcohol limit is one of the lowest in the country, with a maximum of 0.08% for people over 21 and only 0.02% for people under 21 – one beer is enough to reach this limit. Speed limits rarely reach 55mi/hr (90km/hr); the limit on wider roads is usually 45mi/hr (70km/hr) and often only 25mi/hr (40km/hr) on smaller roads.

Those over 18 years of age who rent a scooter are not required to wear a helmet, but goggles are a must.

Addresses are rarely used on the island and directions are usually given by referring to mile markers. For this reason, all directions in this guide will refer to mile markers.

Parking

The lack of space in Hawaii is a constant nightmare, particularly on O'ahu, but also in certain resorts where there is a charge for parking. Rates range between $3 per day and $10 per day in Waikiki (see p 86).

Car Rentals

All of the big international agencies are found in Hawaii, at least on the islands that are most popular with tourists. It is advisable to make a reservation in advance, not only to benefit from better rates but also because some agencies on the outer islands do not have enough cars to supply demand.

The Hawaiian government imposes a road surtax of $3 per day.

Most large agencies require that drivers be at least 25 years of age, sometimes only 21 with a daily surcharge. Some local agencies on more popular islands, however, rent cars to 18 to 21 year-olds, sometimes even without a credit card (though a cash deposit is required). Upon signing of the contract, you will be asked for your local address (hotel, friends). If you tell the agency you plan on camping, they might refuse to rent you a vehicle.

Alamo
☎*800-327-9633*

Avis
☎*800-321-3712*
☎*800-331-1212*

Budget
☎*800-527-0700*

Dollar
☎*800-342-7398*
(Hawaii)
☎*800-367-7006*
(continent)

Harper
Big Island
☎*800-852-9993*

Hertz
☎*800-654-3011*

National
☎*800-CAR-RENT*

Thrifty
☎*800-367-5238*

Scooters

You can rent scooters at most resorts in Waikiki, Lahaina, Kihei and Kona. Sports enthusiasts can also rent bicycles.

Practical Information

Exchange Rate

$1 CAN	= $0.68 US	$1 US	= $1.46 CAN
1 EURO	= $1.09 US	$1 US	= 0.92 EURO
1 FF	= $0.16 US	$1 US	= 6.03 FF
1 SF	= $0.65 US	$1 US	= 1.54 SF
10 BF	= $0.28 US	$1 US	= 36.15 BF
100 PTA	= $0.54 US	$1 US	= 185.19 PTA
1000 ITL	= $0.59 US	$1 US	= 1706.74 ITL

Public Transportation

Hawaii's public transportation system is not extensive. The only exception to the rule is O'ahu, where The Bus provides efficient service at a good price *($1)*. Most lines service the region around the Ala Moana Center. Kaua'i and the Big Island have smaller bus fleets offering limited service.

Money and Banking

Currency

Hawaii's currency is the U.S. dollar ($), which is divided into 100 cents. Bills come in one-, five-, 10-, 20-, 50- and 100-dollar denominations, as well as one- (penny), five- (nickel), 10- (dime) and 25-cent (quarter) coins. Two-dollar bills exist, as do dollar and fifty-cent coins, but are rarely used. The Central American Bank is currently trying to replace older bank notes, as there are two types of $20, $50 and $100 bills.

Banks and Exchange

There are banks on every island except Midway and they are generally open Monday to Friday from 8am or 9am to 3pm. Not all banks have an ATM though, which is the easiest and most efficient way to withdraw cash with a credit or debit card. Money (especially the Canadian dollar and the yen) can be exchanged in most large banks and at Honolulu Airport.

Traveller's Cheques

Traveller's cheques can be changed at banks upon presentation of a piece of identification (and commission) and are accepted by most merchants as cash.

Credit Cards

In addition to allowing you to withdraw cash from an ATM, credit cards are accepted just about everywhere. It is essential to have a credit card to rent a car; if you do not have one, you will be asked to make a cash deposit or the agency might simply refuse to rent you a vehicle. The most readily accepted cards, in ascending order, are Visa, MasterCard, Diners Club and American Express.

Telecommunications

Post Office

With the exception of small islands, which have their own service, post offices are only found in larger cities. Most post offices are open between 8am or 8:30am and 4pm or 4:30pm, Monday to Friday, and sometimes Saturday morning. Stamps can also be purchased in stores selling postcards.

Telephone and Fax

Despite higher rates, Hawaii is linked to the North American telephone network and thus functions the same way. To make a call on the island you're on: $0.30 from a phone booth, free from home without a time limit, dial only the seven-digit number. If you are calling another island, you must dial 1, then the area code (808) and the seven-digit number you wish to reach. Rates are quite high, especially from a phone booth (*starting at $3 for only 3min*). All numbers preceded by 800, 888 or 877 are toll-free, some accessible from Hawaii, most of the United States and often Canada as well. These numbers do not work from Europe, but if you have an alternative number, you can nevertheless call (there is a fee) by replacing 800 with 880, 888 with 881, and 877 with 882.

For long-distance service from a telephone booth, you can either have a supply of quarters ($0.25), which is somewhat inconve-

nient, or purchase pre-paid calling cards that are readily found in stores. Some phones allow callers to pay by credit card, but rates are even higher in these cases. To make life easier, you can simply call from your hotel room, but be aware that rates are most often hiked by 20% to...50%!

A fax machine is available in nearly all hotels. Sending a fax costs a few dollars and certain hotels charge for receiving faxes, as well.

Calling Home

To call Canada, all you need to do is to dial 1, followed by the area code and the number you wish to reach.

To call other places in North America from Hawaii, dial 1 then the area code and the seven-digit number you are trying to reach.

To call other countries, dial 011, then the country code, the regional or city code, and the number you are trying to reach.

Country Codes

Australia	61
Belgium	32
Germany	49
Great Britain	44
Holland	31
Italy	39
New Zealand	64
Spain	34
Switzerland	41

It is sometimes cheaper to call long-distance by using the direct access numbers below to contact an operator in your home country:

Canada Direct
☎*800-555-1111*

United States
AT&T
☎*800-CALL ATT*
MCI
☎*800-888-8000*

British Telecom Direct
☎*800-408-6420*
☎*800-363-4144*

Australia Telstra Direct
☎*800-663-0683*

New Zealand Telecom Direct
☎*800-663-0684*

Accommodations

Hotel, resort, apartment, cottage rental, bed and breakfast, youth hostel, campground... in Hawaii there are accommodations to suit all budgets. The comfort level and prices are generally quite high, althought it should be said that some of the hotels are a bit old. Rates listed in this guide do not include taxes. To calculate the full price, add 11.416%, which is not refundable to non-residents. Note that significant discounts are sometimes offered to seniors, sometimes even those as young as 50. Savings are also often offered if you spend a few nights at the same place.

Practical Information

Pidgin

Like other simplified languages born in most recently discovered places, Hawaii Creole English developed through the contact between Western colonizers, island natives and immigrants who came to work on plantations. Hawaiian Creole features a strong glide in pronunciation and broken English grammar, and is enriched with words borrowed from all languages such as Japanese, Chinese and Portuguese, and especially Hawaiian.

Spoken daily by all long-time residents, Hawaiian Creole suffers from its low of status. Recognized as a language all on its own in the West Indies or in the Indian Ocean, the language awkwardly sits between English (the official language) and everyday reality in the islands. The problem is heightened by young people's loss of basic English grammar, and there is currently widespread debate on whether Hawaiian Creole should either be completely eradicated or recognized.

Here are a few Hawaiian Creole words and expressions, but using them will not be appreciated by islanders.

Pidgin	English
Babooze	Dummy
Brah, braddah	Brother
Broke da mouth	Delicious
Choke	Lots, plenty
Choke waves!	Lots of waves!
Howzit?	How is it?
Kaukau	Eat, food
Shaka	Great, perfect
Try	Please
Utu utu	Sex
Wassup	What's up?

The high season is roughly the third week of December (beginning of Christmas holidays) to late March. If you plan on visiting Hawaii during this period, it is recommended that you make reservations well in advance. Reservations that are made in establishments that offer the best quality/price ratio should be made in summer for a winter trip, and sometimes up to a year in advance.

Rates are 10% to 30% lower the rest of the year, especially from May to June and October to early December. Also, be aware that no matter the type of accommodation, rooms with an ocean view almost always cost 30% to 50% more. In large and sometimes small resorts, rooms on higher floors, which offer a great view, are more expensive than rooms on lower floors. Another factor affecting cost is beach proximity; simply having to cross the street might save you 20% to 30%.

If you are travelling on a tight budget, remember that the four main islands have youth hostels.

Condominiums (apartment rental)

Condominiums refer to both a furnished group of apartments sharing certain facilities such as pool, whirlpool and barbecue area, and the apartments themselves. They may consist of studios or units of one, two, three and even four bedrooms. Each is always equipped with a kitchen or kitchenette, and often a living room. Many also include a washing machine and dryer. The main advantage to renting a condominium is that it allows you to save money, you prepare your own meals, and also provides more space than a hotel room. Larger condominiums often have as many bathrooms as bedrooms, which make them ideal for sharing.

Most condominiums are found on the outer islands. Some are rented through classified ads, but most are either partly or fully managed by a hotel chain or real-estate

agency. It is therefore not unusual for a condo to be represented by three or four real-estate agencies, each having one or more apartments or a renting mandate from the owners. You therefore cannot show up at the last minute. Certain places do not even have a reception desk.

Bed and Breakfasts

There are hundreds of types of bed and breakfasts throughout the archipelago, catering to different budgets.

Most of Hawaii's bed and breakfasts are poorly or not advertised at all, due to strange local by-laws forbidding signs in residential districts. Be aware that most, if not all, require a reservation.

Here is a selection of reservation services. Most require a minimum three-night stay:

All Islands Bed & Breakfast
463 Iliwahi Loop, Kailua
HI 96734-1837
☎*263-2342 or 800-542-0344*
⌨*263-0308*
www.home.hawaii.rr.com/ allislands/
This service offers bed and breakfasts, studios and cottages for prices ranging between $65 and $300.

Bed & Breakfast Hawaii
P.O. Box 449, Kapa'a, HI 96746
☎*822-7771 or 800-733-1632*
⌨*822-2723*
www.bandb-hawaii.com
There are more than 200 bed and breakfasts, studios and cottages on all islands, except Lana'i. Rates vary between $65 and $325.

Bed & Breakfast Honolulu (Hawaii)
3242 Kaohinani Dr., Honolulu
HI 96817
☎*595-7533 or 800-288-4666*
⌨*595-2030*
www.aloha-bnb.com
Hawaii's largest reservation service offers more than 800 units, including bed and breakfasts, studios, cottages and houses. Each reservation costs $10. You can also reserve a car and purchase inter-island flight coupons.

Hawaii's Best Bed & Breakfasts
P.O. Box 563, Kamuela
HI 96743
☎*885-4550 or 800-262-9912*
⌨*885-0559*
www.bestbnb.com
A choice of the best (and most expensive) bed and breakfasts in the archipelago, all with private bath. The most affordable range between $70 and $80, but most cost between $90 and $100.

Camping

All Hawaiian islands have at least one campground. They are often managed either by the National Parks Department (free), the Hawaiian government (free) or the four counties of the archipelago *($3 per person)*. While some are pleasant, others are not very attractive. Several campgrounds, especially those on O'ahu where rent is extremely high, have become a permanent residence for homeless families who are regularly expelled by park officials. With no other option but the street, these homeless families move to another campground, whence they will be driven out once again after a few weeks, months or sometimes even years.

Some state parks also offer wooden bungalows, which are rather rustic but equipped with basic necessities: kitchen, bathroom and bedrooms. Simpler bungalows do not have electricity. You are advised to reserve as early as possible.

Restaurants

Through their mixed descent, Hawaiians have created a popular cuisine influenced by the four corners of the world, with Japan, the United States, Portugal, China, the Philippines and Korea each making a contribution. More discrete, but essential to understanding the islands, Hawaiian cuisine has its own specialties. Add to this all of the recent ethnic restaurants such as Italian and Mexican

Hawaii's Fishponds

Hawaiians developed Polynesia's most complex and efficient aquaculture system, which features two types of fishponds: those located around coastal springs (*lokowai*) and those that stretch along shallow coasts (*loko* Kuapu), formed in lava stone so that they are always above high tide. They were designed to allow young fish to swim through the stake fences (*makaha*), which then hold them in once they have fattened up.

(very popular), Thai, Filipino, French, Greek and even German.

As is generally the case in North America, and even more so here, dinner is always more expensive than lunch.

Prices listed in this guide are for dinner for one person, unless otherwise indicated. Drinks and tip (approximately 15%) are not included.

Daily Cuisine

The meal generally begins with *pupus*, Hawaiian-style hors d'oeuvres, as you have a beer or wait for dinner to be served.

The **plate lunch**, a favourite dish of all Hawaiians, is served at roadside canteens or in small local restaurants and consists of two scoops of rice, macaroni salad and one or more specialties such as beef or chicken teriyaki, *kalua* pork, ground beef, breaded *mahi-mahi*, the catch of the day, *kal-bi* and various stews, all of which covered with gravy or not. This may not be a gourmet meal, but it will satisfy your appetite! The plate lunch is a variation of the basket lunches women once prepared for plantation workers. The *loco moco*, another variation, features a mountain of rice covered with ground or corned beef, a fried egg and lots of gravy. Incidentally, corned beef is something Hawaiians love to indulge in: Hawaii consumes 3.5 times more corned beef than any other U.S. state.

The *bento*, which is just as popular, is the Japanese equivalent of the plate lunch and includes a variety of sushi, marinated vegetables and fish or grilled chicken.

Saimin, meaning "food of the poor," is a delicious noodle soup made with chicken or shrimp broth, green onions, strips of pork, *char sui* (marinated meat), *kamaboko* (fish cake) or simply *surimi*.

Hawaiian Specialties

In olden days, when thanking the gods, it was customary to celebrate important events such as the triumph over a rival tribe, the birth of a child and harvesting with a feast called *'aha'aina*. During this feast, men sat on one side and women on the other, as a *kapu* forbade women to eat at the same time as their husbands, to prepare food for them and even to taste several dishes such as bananas, coconuts and certain fish. On this occasion, a pig was stuffed with hot stones and braised in a pit oven (*imu*) for an entire day. It is much later that the term *lu'au*, referring to the taro leaves used to wrap the food, appeared.

Inseparable from Hawaiian culture, the *lu'au* is enjoyed by both local families and tourists. In both cases, the centrepiece is *kalua* pork, with side dishes of chicken, fish, *poi*, bananas, *laulau*, *lomilomi* salmon, *poke*

and *haupia* for desert (see below). Commercial *lu'aus* are more of a show than a cultural experience. The event begins with the sounding of a conch, announcing the arrival of an imaginary king and his court in costume. The *imu* is then opened, and the meal begins with an all-you-can-eat buffet served on a huge table covered with food. A *hula* show, consisting of Polynesian dances and "fire knives," usually follows.

- *Kalua* pork: pork braised in an *imu*.

- *Poi*: a purée made from taro tubers, which is a little pasty and rather flavourless. *Poi* is best eaten as a side dish with *kalua* pork or *lomilomi* salmon.

- *Laulau*: fish or pork steamed in taro leaves, covered with *ti* leaves.

- *Lomilomi* salmon: diced, marinated with tomatoes and onions.

- *Poke*, a favourite of islanders: fresh fish, octopus or squid cut into small pieces and marinated in soya sauce with onions and *limu* (green seaweed), sometimes with peppers.

- *Haupia*: pineapple and coconut milk pudding. Never found in restaurants but always at *lu'aus*.

Hawaiian Regional Cuisine

Originating from "Pacific Rim" cuisine, popular north of the U.S. West Coast, and incorporating the culinary influences of Asian minorities and fresh local products, Hawaiian regional cuisine (HRC) offers even greater variety. Immigrants spread out in the Hawaiian melting pot and exchanged recipes, which gave rise to new local specialties. Developed at the discretion of chefs, these specialties served as a base for the emergence of an original cuisine, a bouquet of a thousand flavours featuring blends of sweet and salty, Asian sauces and spices, soy, sushi, tempura, *bentos* (Japanese), citronella (Vietnamese), *won* ton and *dim sum* (Chinese), ginger, and much more. Add to this European know-how, Japanese presentation, vegetables (usually organic), island fish and exotic ingredients such as *o'helo* berries, fern growths and Macadamia nuts. This regional cuisine bridges classic and modern cooking, Eastern and Western flavours and can be considered nothing less than a

Practical Information

perfect mélange of cultures.

Fish

Hawaii's location in the middle of the Northern Pacific makes it a fish-lover's paradise. Often eaten raw or marinated Polynesian- or Japanese-style, the fish is equally delicious seared, grilled or cooked in sauce. Here is a list of the main fish served in restaurants of the archipelago:

- **'Ahi**: this red-fleshed albacore tuna is the most popular fish served, often as sashimi (raw) or seared. Available nearly year-round. The *aku*, another type of tuna, has a stronger taste than the *ahi*. Often eaten in *poke* or dried.

- **Mahi-mahi**: very popular, this is a type of sea bream with pinkish flesh. Served in a thousand ways, fresh *mahi-mahi* is found especially in fall and spring. The rest of the year, it is often substituted with frozen fish or *ono*.

- **Ono**: meaning "good" in Hawaiian. The royal mackerel (*wahoo*) is a firm fish, delicious sautéed. Increasingly popular and especially fresh in spring and fall.

- **Opah**: pretty rare, this sunfish has a light, flavourful flesh and is extremely tender.

- **Snapper**: there are several kinds. The pinkish *onaga* is tender and melts in your mouth; the *opakapaka* is firmer and deeper in flavour, and is often fried or prepared with pepper; the *uku* has an even stronger flavour, which explains why it is rarely served.

Shopping

Opening Hours

Store hours vary greatly. As a general rule, stores open between 9am and 10am in shopping centres and close at around 8pm or 9pm, sometimes later. In Waikiki, stores often close at 11pm or later. Grocery-store hours are even longer, opening at 7am (sometimes earlier) and closing between 5pm and 8pm. Some supermarkets are open 24hrs.

Souvenirs

Natural items top the list of potential purchases. Hawaii produces many kinds of jams because of its large variety of tropical fruit; the Kukui brand is excellent.

You will find **Macadamia nuts** everywhere, grilled, salted, less often plain, as well as covered with chocolate, caramel or coffee. Cookies and oil made of Macadamia nuts are also available, with the latter apparently being good for your health, too! The nuts are sometimes also sold in their pretty shells, which are tough to crack.

Add Kona coffee to your list. We suggest you taste it before you buy it, though; despite what locals claim, it is not necessarily the "world's best." *Kiawe*, eucalyptus or macadamia **honey**, exotic teas (such as *noni*-flavoured), taro chips, smoked marlin and Asian products that cannot be found in North America and Europe make great gifts and souvenirs.

Noni

Fresh **flowers** can be brought back if they are purchased from a florist or horticulturist recognized by the Sanitary Control Department. Some will even offer to have the flowers shipped directly to their North American destination. The short-lived, sweet-smelling

Lei

Throughout the Polynesian islands, *lei* are given as a symbol of affection and fondness. These beautiful flower necklaces are traditionally hung around the neck of guests to welcome them or bid them farewell. Though always decorative, the necklaces also symbolize rites of passage such as graduations, weddings and anniversaries.

While jasmine (related to matters of the heart), orchids and especially the sweet-smelling frangipani are today used to make *lei*, residents of the Forbidden Isle of Ni'ihau continue to thread and braid thousands of tiny seashells. Making these necklaces takes such a long time that they are sold for a high price. If you are in the islands on May 1 (Lei Day), join the party and wear a *lei*.

flowers used to make *lei* would unfortunately not last the trip.

Some of Hawaii's most beautiful crafts are made with the archipelago's natural resources. *Lauhala*, pandanus fibers, are braided into mats, bags, hats and other accessories. *Leis* (necklaces) are made with seeds and feathers, but also with seashells. Those from Ni'ihau, well known throughout the Pacific, are exquisitely beautiful, but are quite expensive. Bracelets are more affordable.

Wood sculpting is a very popular traditional craft. Co-operatives produce superb objects made from *koa*, but also from *kou* and *milo* wood. Bowls and culinary utensils are magnificent, but again, are extremely pricy. Be careful: you can find bargain-priced items, but they are not made with the same wood and are often imported from the Philippines.

The elitist **scrimshaw** is a modern version of the ancient form of carving on whale teeth. Today Lahaina craftspeople carve fossil teeth or walrus tusks. The cost of the raw materials and the time it takes to produce these carvings justify their extremely high price tag, which unfortunately makes them affordable only to collectors.

Lahaina also has numerous **art galleries**, as do other cities in the archipelago. Many specialize in paintings,

others in Hawaiian crafts or even imported antiques.

Some shops specialize in **quilts**, most often featuring plant designs. It takes weeks to create a quilt. One of the loveliest designs is the green *ulu*.

Flowery Hawaiian shirts, or **aloha shirts**, are ready to wear, as are *mu'umu'us* (large Hawaiian dresses), pareos and T-shirts, sold by the truckload. Red Dirt Shirt, found throughout the island, dyes T-shirts with laterite.

Miscellaneous

Time Difference

Hawaii does not move its clocks forward in summer. The islands are 5hrs behind the U.S. East Coast from November to March and 6hrs in summer. Midway is an extra hour behind the rest of the archipelago.

Electricity

As is the case throughout North America, voltage in Hawaii is 110 volts (60 cycles). Electrical plugs are two-pinned and flat. Europeans wishing to use their electrical appliances will need an adapter and a transformer.

Practical Information

Kapa / Tapa

Kapa (*tapa* cloth) was at one time the only material known to Polynesians and was used to make men's *malos* (loincloths) and women's *pans* (skirts). Women beared the heavy burden of making these clothes, not by weaving, but by pounding the bark of certain young trees. They would strip the branches by removing the hard outer bark to uncover the inner bark, which was soaked in salt water for several days. The softened pieces of bark were then laid on a flat stone and pounded for hours with a cylindrical pylon (*hohoa*) to form large bark "pancakes." After being soaked a second time, they were laid out on a stack of extremely hard *kawaw* wood where they were pounded again with a four-sided pylon, each of its sides engraved with a different design. This delicate step required great skill so not to pierce the bark. By the end of the process, the bark had stretched to several times its original size.

Hawaii is the only archipelago in the Pacific where pink, blue and green dyes were known and used. The dyes were extracted from plants, soil, charcoal, bark and even sea urchins. After being soaked in candlenut (*kukui*) or coconut oil to be softened, the *tapa* cloth was finally ready to be used.

Smokers

It is forbidden to smoke in public places and smoking has fallen out of fashion here, as in the rest of the United States. Many restaurants have smoking and non-smoking sections.

Holidays

Hawaii has three extra holidays than the rest of the United States:

January

New Year's Day
January 1

Martin Luther King Day
third Monday

February

President's Day
third Monday

March and April

Prince Kuhio Day
March 26

Easter Monday
variable

May

Lei Day
May 1

Memorial Day
last Monday of May

June

Kamehameha Day
June 11

July

Independence Day (U.S.)
July 4

August

Admission Day
third Friday

September

Labor Day
first Monday

October

Columbus Day
second Monday

November

Veteran's Day
November 11

Thanksgiving
last Thursday

December

Christmas
December 25

All offices are closed on those days, but stores are usually open. For festivities specific to each island, please refer to the appropriate chapter.

Taxes

The state tax, one of the lowest in the United States, is set at 4.167%. Taxes on hotel services are higher (11.416%).

Tipping

Tipping applies to all table service, i.e. in restaurants or other places where you are served at your table (fast-food service is therefore not included in this category). It is also compulsory in bars and nightclubs.

You should calculate around 15% of the bill before tax, depending, of course, on the quality of service received. Unlike in Europe, the tip is not added to the bill; customers must calculate it themselves and give it to the server. Service and tip go hand in hand in North America.

It is also standard practice, though not compulsory, to tip tour guides, taxi drivers, hairdressers, hotel porters and chambermaids.

Gay and Lesbian Life

For a long time, the main bastions of Hawaii's gay community were located on Kuhio Avenue in Waikiki, but they had to move when faced with expanding real estate speculation. The archipelago's only gay hotel (Hotel Honolulu) and two long-standing bars (Angles and Fusion) remain in the area, with all of the other points of interest being spread out. On the outer islands, only a few bed and breakfasts cater to a gay clientele.

For information on Hawaii's gay community and services, visit *www.gayhawaii.com*. The editors are also the managers of **Pacific Ocean Holidays** (☎923-2400 or 800-735-6600 *from the United States only*, ⇔923-2499, or by E-mail: *reservations@ gayhawaii.com*), whose Web site lists a large number of gay or gay-friendly establishments. Their rather commercial list, however, is not exhaustive. Pacific Ocean Holidays also publishes the *Pocket Guide to Hawai'i*, which is revised three times a year and lists the main gay and related businesses. You can order the guide on the Internet or by mail *(P.O. Box 88245, Dept. PGO, Honolulu, HI 96830-8245)* for $5 each or $12/year. For specific information on Waikiki and on bars and nightclubs, consult *Odyssey* magazine *(1750 Kalakaua Avenue, ☎955-5959, www.hawaiiscene.com/ odyssey).*

Practical Information

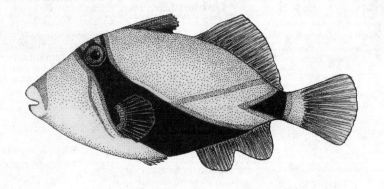

Outdoors

A lthough they appear as little more than specks dotting the immensity of the ocean, the Hawaiian Islands actually form an endless playground.

All kinds of national and local parks, both in the interior and along beaches covered in white or black sand, provide myriad opportunities for hiking and swimming. Of course, water sports top the list, especially wave-riding activities such as surfing, boogie boarding and kitesurfing. During the winter, colossal waves crash on the eastern coasts of the islands, much to the delight of surfing fanatics.

Out at sea, the ocean floor offers a vast territory for scuba divers and snorkellers to explore. Coral reefs abound with schools of brightly coloured fish, and rocky shores reveal unexpected underwater lava formations.

If you prefer the comforts of a boat, you can enjoy such wonders with dry feet or in a thousand other ways: the options are virtually endless and include touring the islands in a submarine, taking a sunset dinner cruise or embarking on a whale or dolphin photo-safari.

This chapter contains general information on the most popular types of outdoor activities. For more information on each activity, consult the pertinent section in each chapter. Keep in mind that wholesalers such as

Activity Mart obtain rate reductions on many activities and excursions, especially when booked at the last minute. Just make sure you know what you're getting for the price. The special prices offered by some agencies end up being the same as the regular prices offered by others, if not slightly higher. As always, the best thing to do is to shop around and compare prices and services.

Parks

National Parks

As is frequently the case in the United States, national parks have been adapted to the human race and can easily be reached and visited by car. There are two national parks on the archipelago: the **Volcanoes National Park** on the Big Island and the **Hale'a'kala National Park** on Maui. Entrance is $10 per vehicle and is valid for one week, and the Golden Eagle pass *($65)* is accepted. The latter also provides entry to several historical and nature parks operated by the U.S. National Park Service, such as Puuhonua o Honaunau on the Big Island and the Kilauea peninsula on Kaua'i. The main campgrounds in the national parks are free and do not require reservations or special permits. The only restriction is the length of stay (five days). Wilderness camping, usually accessible by hiking trails, requires a permit that which is free of charge.

State Parks

Hawaii has 55 State parks which encompass 40 sq mi (105km²) on five of the main islands. They are divided into State Natural Parks, State Recreation Areas, State Monuments, State Historical Parks, State Underwater Parks and State Wayside Parks (small parks located along roads). Most allow various sports activities such as swimming, snorkelling, surfing, boogie boarding, fishing and hiking. About a dozen have campgrounds, while others provide wooden bungalows, which are generally fairly rustic but very popular with locals and vacationers – as much for their attractive price as for their natural setting.

A permit is required to camp and can be obtained free of charge at the State Park district offices in each county: O'ahu, the Big Island, Maui (including Moloka'i) and Kaua'i. For addresses, see their respective chapter in this guide. If your tour has already been planned out, you can ask for permits in advance except if you plan to camp on O'ahu or on the Na Pali coast in the summertime – because of the high demand, permits are only handed out in person at the designated offices. Another exception are the cabins in Malaekahana (O'ahu) and Koke'e (Kaua'i) which are available for a fee and reserved through companies mandated by the government.

Permits are emitted a year ahead of time except for those on O'ahu (30 days) and the Na Pali coast in the summer (four weeks). When demand exceeds available space, priority is given to permits requested first in person, then by mail and lastly, by phone. Park headquarters are usually open Mon to Fri from 8am to 4pm, except on holidays. For weekends it is best to plan ahead. Parks are open every day, except on O'ahu. For more information and a description of each park in the state of Hawaii, you can obtain the Hawaii State Parks brochure at one of the park offices or by writing to:

Department of Land & Natural Resources Division of State Parks
P.O. Box 621
Honolulu, HI 96809

County Parks

Numerous county parks are scattered across the archipelago, especially along the coasts. Some are little more than paved surfaces by the sea while others are vast, untamed expanses of sand. Each of the four counties manages its own parks, yet all parks seem to share one point: their mediocre condition.

A few allow camping but, again, the infrastructures are not always particularly inviting. Only the better sites are described in this guide. While camping is free on O'ahu (but impossible for two days of the week), the three other counties charge $3 to $5 per person per day. In all cases, it is obligatory to obtain a permit from the authorized services, indicated in each chapter. As a general rule, park offices are open from 7:45am to 4pm from Mon to Fri, except on holidays.

Depending on the island, the maximum stay permitted on a site ranges from three days (Maui) to two weeks (the Big Island during the winter months). In certain instances, it is forbidden to camp twice on the same site in the same month. Permits can be obtained ahead of time in most cases, but usually must be requested in person.

Nature Conservancy

Created in 1951, the Nature Conservancy is an international agency involved in the protection of ecosystems and biodiversity. It has played a major role in Hawaii since 1980 where it manages 10 preserves. These preserves account for over 90 sq mi (237km²) of land spread across the archipelago that were bought from or leased by major landowners concerned about preserving the hydro-

graphic basin uphill from their farmlands, in order to guarantee constant water supply.

Access to preserves is restricted and sometimes forbidden. However, volunteers usually organize monthly walks lasting a few hours. It is recommended to reserve in advance since the waiting list is often quite long. It usually costs $10 for Nature Conservancy members and $25 for non-members. Membership is available for $25 per year; this includes a subscription to the bimonthly *Nature Conservancy* magazine which describes the accessible preserves on each island.

The Nature Conservancy of Hawaii
1116 Smith St., Suite 201
Honolulu, HI 96817
☎*537-4508*
⇌*545-2019*
www.tnc.org/hawaii

Outdoor Activities

Swimming

Good news! All beaches in Hawaii, without exception, are open to the public, and many have facilities such as toilets and showers. At first glance, you'll think you're in a

swimmer's paradise: islands, coconut trees, miles of pale sand and quiet beaches far from the hordes of tourists... What more could you ask for?

However, a closer look reveals that the strong currents and powerful waves famous in these parts jeopardize your chances of swimming. Furthermore, just because a beach is supervised, it is not necessarily any less dangerous, since lifeguards are often called upon to help surfers and Boogie-Board amateurs in need. If you don't see anybody swimming in the water, the simplest thing to do is to ask the lifeguards. If there aren't any, it is best to continue on your way. Generally speaking, it is preferable to stay close to the shoreline on many beaches. That said, rest assured: favourable areas abound and water temperatures fluctuate between 72°F and 77°F (22°C and 25°C). Watch out for coral reefs which are fragile and sharp, as well as giant jellyfish that approach the shores (especially in the north) when a westerly wind blows or in the days following a storm.

Cruises

Although not a sport in the strict sense of the

word, cruises are so popular in Hawaii that it is impossible not to mention them. You can hop aboard a sailboat, catamaran, raft or even a canoe to discover the shores or the seabed. By far the most sought-after, catamarans allow passengers to jump right into the water to seek coral fish and turtles, or to simply enjoy the setting sun out at sea. Glass-bottomed boats are also well liked but this activity is marginal when compared to the whale-watching excursions that take place every year from December to April. A great many depart from the Lahaina port on Maui but it is also possible to board one from Moloka'i, Lana'i, the Big Island and other islands. In the off-season, excursions seek out friendly dolphins.

You can also hire a sailboat and skipper or rent your own boat, but keep in mind that strong currents make for challenging navigation. If you can do without the sea spray but have always dreamed of shipwrecks and the open sea, you can descend into one of the tiny submarines that cruise through the islands. Finally, to top off your day, you can indulge in a dinner-cruise, complete with Hawaiian show.

Scuba Diving

Because the archipelago is so isolated, the underwater kingdom of Hawaii is not as bountiful as other seascapes. Yet amateur divers will not be disappointed. From the shores, reefs reveal myriad rainbow-coloured species of tropical fish, surgeonfish, butterfly fish, parrot fish, lionfish and other members of the Balistidae family, in addition to sea urchins, octopuses and moray eels. Erosion caused lava to break up into grottos, arches, tunnels and other underwater sea caves, favorite exploratory grounds for divers. Here, they can see Hawaiian green turtles, rays and small reef sharks. The visibility is excellent most of the time, especially in summer when the sea is calmer.

Certified divers can either dive from boats or the shore (less expensive). On average, it costs between $85 and $100 for two oxygen tanks, sometimes more for remote destinations (Molokini or Ni'ihau for example). Novices can register for diving lessons at any of the numerous diving centres. Competition is fierce, so quality is assured. Most of the professionals who provide diving excursions and lessons oper-

ate modern boats, often with showers and toilets. If you are near-sighted or astigmatic, you will be provided with a mask that suits your eyesight. The majority also rent underwater cameras.

Invented in the late 1980s, "snuba" is a cross between scuba diving and snorkelling: a long pipe connects the diver's regulator to an air tank floating on the surface. The main advantage of snuba is that no certification is required – only a brief 20min introductory class. Its disadvantage is that it is still very expensive.

Snorkelling

Snorkelling requires the bare minimum in equipment: mask, snorkel and fins. Bring your own or, even simpler, rent it wherever you go in the islands. Prices depend on the competition. You might pay $10 to $15 to rent equipment for a week in Waikiki, while other less frequented places might charge just as much for a single day. For a slightly higher fee, many rental agencies provide masks that are adapted to an individual's eyesight. In addition to offering good prices, Snorkel Bob will allow you to rent the equipment on one island and return it on another island. Snorkel Bob shops can be found on the four main islands.

Protected from the strong ocean currents, coves and bays, such as the magnificent Hanauma Bay on O'ahu, are the best places to snorkel. The inconvenience, however, is the sport's great popularity, which often results in cloudy water and makes the experience a little too "common" for the tastes of some. For this reason, you might want to join an ocean excursion and snorkel from the boat. This solution promises quieter sites like the Kealakekua Bay on the Big Island or the islet of Molokini.

Surfing

Long practiced by Polynesian men and women, surfing (*he'e nalu*) probably came to Hawaii with the second wave of immigration from Tahiti, where Captain Cook saw it for the first time. In Hawaii, strict codes regulated its practice. Even the way a tree was cut down and carved into a board demanded the observation of precise rituals, as was its first launched into the water. People prayed to

the gods for good waves.

Everyone surfed: men, women, the *ali'i* and the general population; on nice days, villages and fields were deserted. But again, a number of rules had to be respected. Only the *ali'i* had access to the best places and were allowed to use long boards (*olo*) in *nawiliwili*, measuring up to 23ft (7m). Commonly 4in (10cm) thick, these boards often weighed over 150lb (70kg). The other half had to content itself with less prestigious boards of about 6.5ft (2m) long. Very often, the Hawaiians competed among themselves and bet ferociously: a piece of *tapa*, a fishing net, a canoe,

sometimes their own freedom...

Almost disappearing under the yoke of the missionaries who condemned its futility, surfing became popular again thanks to King David Kalakaua – who was a surfer himself – and the Outrigger Canoe Club in 1908. It was during this period that a certain Duke Kahanamoku appeared, future gold-medal swimmer in the Stockholm Olympic Games and big promoter of the sport. He subsequently introduced surfing to Australia and from there, it conquered the rest of the world. The first continental surfers landed in Hawaii in the winter of 1954. Living in makeshift huts on the beach, they started a lifestyle which, nearly a half century later, has come to symbolize the entire archipelago.

Today, two worlds coexist without ever meeting: the high-flying surfers and the tourists. The first, who often have made a career out of surfing, attack the world's greatest rollers on the eastern coasts of the islands during the winter. Neophytes, on the other hand, are quite content with riding reasonable waves. Were they to venture onto the same sites as the professionals, say on O'ahu's North Shore, Honolua Bay on

Maui or along the Hilo coast on the Big Island, they would probably drown in less than five minutes.

Surf schools, generally operated by former professionals, are located on the four main islands, particularly in Waikiki, in Lahaina and Ka'anapali on Maui and in Po'ipu (Kaua'i). You can learn to surf on a standard board or on a longboard. Both are used in Hawaii and each has its aficionados and favorite spots. Measuring 10ft (3m), the longboard allows beginners to get their balance a little easier. Boards can be rented throughout the archipelago; rates range from $10 to $25 per day.

Boogie Boarding

In the beginning, bodysurfers put fins on their feet and rode the waves using their body as a board, with their arms glued to their torso (open sea) or pointing ahead to control their trajectory (near the shore). In the 1980s, this exercise was facilitated by the invention of the bodyboard. Today commonly known as a Boogie Board, this board measures between 3 and 4ft (1-1.2m) and supports the upper body only. Much easier than surfing, the Boogie Board doesn't provide the same intense sensations as surfing but is none-

Surf 'n' Turf

Not only did the Polynesians invent surfing, but they also concocted another, far more surprising sport – land surfing! Known as *holua*, this sport was practised on downhill runs made of stone paths covered in mud and slippery rushes measuring up to 6.6ft (2m). Spectators were said to wager heavily on this bizarre sport. At least once in history, the winner of one such competition, Umi, became Chief of the Big Island by defeating his elder rival.

theless a lot of fun, especially when you tumble head first into a wave. Accessible to all, this sport particularly targets younger people. It is practiced all throughout the archipelago, near the shore at the point where the waves break. Boards can be rented virtually anywhere for $4 to $10 per day.

Wakeboarding

Obsessed with riding the waves, Hawaiians continually invent new water sports. A good example of this is wakeboarding, a hybrid of surfing and water

skiing and its advantage is that it is easy. The objective is to surf on the wake created by the boat pulling you. Like waterskiing, all kinds of styles are possible.

Kitesurfing

Having recently appeared on Hawaiian coasts, kitesurfing is winning over more and more fans. With feet secured on a rather small board (like air surfing), the surfer is pulled by a 26 to 30ft- (8 to 9m) wide sail, similar to those used for paragliding, which serves as a huge kite. With the help of a good wave or a strong wind, the surfer can fly up to 30ft (10m) high before hitting the water, gently or not. Kitesurfing requires strength to work the sail so that it constantly catches the wind. But when Aeolus blows, the pleasure of taking off is intense! Kailua Bay on O'ahu and the central northern coast of Maui are two favourite spots.

Windsurfing

Like surfing, the world of windsurfers is divided into two separate entities: the professionals who every year gather on the rollers of the northern coast of Maui or O'ahu and the visitors who enjoy the constant winds at their own rhythm, far from the breakers that carry their idols. The most impressive is wave jumping (with looping, circumstances permitting) but competitions also include slalom and speed events. Windsurfing equipment can be rented at any of the main seaside resorts and near favourite sites such as Kailua Bay on O'ahu as well as the central coast between Kanaha and Ho'okipa on Maui. Remember that the first surfer to reach a wave has priority. And if two surfers approach a wave at the same time, priority is given to the one who is farthest out to sea with the wind astern.

Personal Watercraft (Jet-Skiing)

Very popular with tourists, personal watercraft are used around all the main islands, especially near seaside resorts. They are forbidden around Maui from December 15 to May 15, when whales return to the waters. It generally costs between $30 and $40 for 10 to 15min, and learning how to jet ski is fast and easy. The sensation of speed is exhilarating, but steer clear of beaches. Accidents frequently happen between personal watercraft and swimmers or divers seen at the last moment.

Deep-Sea Fishing

For years now, Hawaii has been established as a sport-fishing paradise. Numerous world records have been set here, especially along the Kona coastline, in the waters off the Big Island where the World Billfish Tournament is held every year, and near Midway. But fishing is good everywhere in the archipelago. Many captains rent out their boats for half, three-quarter or full days. As prices are relatively high *(from $200 to $600)*, another option is to share a boat. In many cases, rates are reduced for non-fishing passengers.

The king of all fish is the Pacific blue marlin, a monster that can weigh over 1,764 lb (800kg)! Prize catches also include the *ahi* (tuna), *ono* (wahoo), *mahi-mahi* and swordfish. For the past few years, an increasing number of catches, especially marlins, have been thrown back to the sea in an effort to save these precious natural resources. A program launched by the Pacific Ocean Research Foundation involves tagging young marlins to better understand their development. When the fish are kept however, only the fillets are given to fishers, which, in many instances, they can have prepared at their hotel. Record catches are displayed as trophies. To find out what to expect before setting out to sea, ask the captain.

Kayaking

Sea kayaking is very popular in Hawaii. You can either rent a boat *($20 to $25 per day)* or join an organized excursion. This means of gliding on water will allow you to visit otherwise unreachable coasts, like Kealakekua Bay on the Big Island or Na Pali on Kaua'i, and to navigate to islets sitting out in the open sea (Kailua Bay on O'ahu). Kaua'i is surely the best place for sea kayaking because of its numerous navigable waterways. Kayaking in a simple boat or a two-seater is a wonderful way to discover nature and fauna in Olympian calm. Most rental outlets also provide a

Outdoors

waterproof bag (to store camera equipment, for example) and a cooler.

Hiking

The great variety and natural beauty of its landscapes, its mountains furrowed by deep valleys, its untamed shores... all this and more makes Hawaii ideal for hiking. Virtually anything is possible: you can enjoy a simple walk out in the wilderness or embark on an expedition of several days to scale the highest volcanoes. Trails meandering through superb tropical forests high above Honolulu or paths leading through Volcanoes National Park on the Big Island are accessible to all. On the other hand, hiking in Koke'e Park or along the Na Pali coast on Kaua'i (the Kalalau Trail), in the crater of the Hale'a'kala on Maui, in the central mountains and northern valleys of Moloka'i or to the summits of the Mauna Kea and Mauna Loa are incontestably reserved for more experienced hikers who are willing to hike for several days by the sweat of their brow.

Before setting off on an excursion, reserve the wilderness campsite or shelter where you plan on spending the night in advance where necessary (for example, in national and state parks). Demand is high, so it's best to plan ahead of time as much as possible. You can also buy a detailed map in national parks' shops or specialized stores. While hiking, watch out for dehydration, which is aggravated by altitude and heat, altitude sickness caused by scaling the highest peaks too quickly, as well as short days (the sun sets before 7pm).

I'iwi

In addition to this guide, you can obtain detailed information on hiking trails in Hawaii by contacting agencies such as the Hawaii State Department of Land and Natural Resources (State Parks) which distributes free maps and brochures. If you prefer organized expeditions, guided walks are offered by several Hawaiian agencies such as Hawaii Forest & Trail, which will introduce you to the fauna, especially endemic bird species, flora and preserved ecosystems (including those on private land).

Cycling

Both tour and mountain biking are practised in Hawaii. With regards to the first, although you can ride your bike virtually anywhere in the islands, heavy traffic can sometimes make cycling quite unpleasant. And don't forget that some of the volcanoes are quite high! To circumvent such difficulties, numerous companies on Maui and Kaua'i propose downhill biking – from the summits of the Hale'a'kala and the Koke'e Park along the Waimea Canyon. This activity might not have much to do with the sport itself but is nevertheless very popular with tourists.

True fans of wild trails can surrender themselves body and soul to mountain biking along trails and forest paths on any of the islands. Although only a limited number of trails allow mountain bikes, they nonetheless provide a great variety of rides, ranging from a few miles to a complete day. If you're feeling particularly brave, you can even cycle to the top of the Mauna Kea on the Big Island – provided you stop to catch your breath once in a while.

Rentals generally cost about $20 to $25 per day. A touring bike can be rented for as little as $10, whereas competition mountain bikes often exceed $30. Because of these high prices, some visitors prefer to buy their own bike when they arrive in Hawaii and transport it from island to island by plane. This feasible solution doesn't cost too much but is not worthwhile unless you plan on staying in the islands for a long period of time. Depending on the airports and airlines, it is possible to ship a bicycle without taking it apart (at the very least, pedals and handlebars).

Horseback Riding

The more rural the island and the more open spaces it features, the better it is for horseback riding. The Big Island and Maui, well-endowed in such respects, provide a wide selection of short rides for beginners and day outings for more accomplished riders. Lana'i and Moloka'i are also good grounds for saddling up, as are, albeit to a lesser degree, O'ahu and Kaua'i. Prices start at $40 to $50 for a 1hr ride and can exceed $200. If you can, join an excursion to one of the many ranches which will give you the chance to meet

some Hawaiian cowboys, called *paniolos*.

The four main islands also feature polo fields. Most visitors are satisfied just to watch.

Golf

The archipelago has over 80 golf courses, for the most part 18-hole fairways. Landscaped by such noteworthy designers as Robert Trent Jones Jr., Ted Robinson and Greg Norman, they count among some of the country's most beautiful. O'ahu is by far the best-endowed, embracing nearly half of all the greens in the archipelago, including the very difficult Ko'olau Golf Course. However, many of the loveliest courses can be found on other islands: on Kaua'i in particular (Prince Course and Po'ipu Bay Resort Golf Course), Lana'i (Experience at Ko'ele and Challenge at Manele), Maui (Kapalua and Wailea Golf Courses) and the Big Island where the largest clubs are gathered along the Kohala coastline.

Althought it is expensive to tee off on these grounds, many hotels offer package deals including accommodations and golfing. Otherwise, expect to pay anywhere between $150 and $200 for the

top-notch courses (*$100 if you are staying at the hotel that owns the golf course*). Municipal golf courses are more affordable (*$10 to $40*) but are in high demand. In the high season on O'ahu, it is sometimes necessary to reserve weeks in advance. During the warmest hours of the day, many private courses offer attractive "twilight" rates, sometimes starting as early as noon or 1pm, but usually from 2pm or 3pm until closing time. Whatever the type, the price almost always includes a cart. On the main islands, Stand-by Golf (*every day 7am to 9pm, ☎322-2665 or 888-645-BOOK on all islands*) offers discount prices on same-day playing fees (or the next day at the very latest).

Tennis

With the exception of Waikiki where space is limited, most upscale and intermediate hotels feature tennis courts that are often lit up at night. Otherwise, you can practice your backhand in public courts, which are free or fairly inexpensive (*$5 per hr*). Playing time, however, is usually limited to give everyone a chance to play.

Flying and Aerial Sports

A bevy of helicopter and small-plane companies offer low-altitude flights over O'ahu, the Big Island, Kaua'i and Maui (with or without Lana'i and Moloka'i). If you are visiting several islands but only wish to fly once, opt for an aerial view of the Big Island if the volcanic activity is high, or of Kaua'i for its stupendous Na Pali cliffs and Waymea Canyon. Helicopter excursions are more expensive than small planes but the views are certainly more commanding.

Aerial-sports enthusiasts can take to the skies in gliders (O'ahu) or ultralights (O'ahu, Kaua'i) or by parachuting (O'ahu), hang-gliding (O'ahu) or paragliding (Maui).

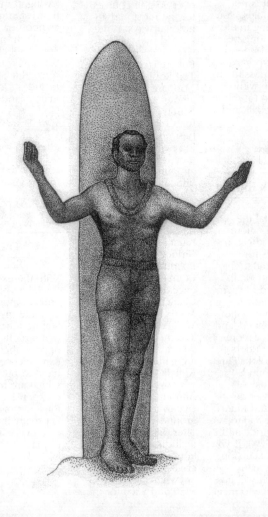

O'ahu

The third largest

island of the archipelago, O'ahu is actually the most important one in many respects.

Representing only 10% of Hawaii's land, the island is home to some 885,000 people – nearly 75% of the state's population. Discovered by sailors en route to China at the beginning of the 19th century, the island owes its rapid development to its thriving port. Seat of the government since Kamehameha III moved the capital here in 1850, economic powerhouse, university and artistic centre – not to mention the main destination of tourists who flock to Waikiki – the island has appropriately long been known as "The Gathering Place."

The island of O'ahu was formed three to three-and-a-half million years ago after the eruption of two shield volcanoes. About 500,000 years ago, a second series of eruptions rocked O'ahu along the Ko'olau fault

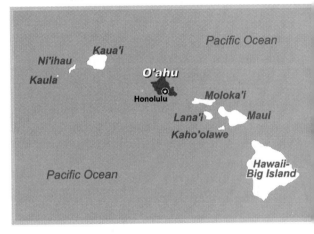

and led to the formation of the famous Diamond Head crater. Today, the only vestiges that remain are the Wai'anae and Ko'olau mountain ranges. The Wai'anae Range, located on the western side, is the oldest of the two ranges. It conceals an arid and rarely visited region facing the plateau near Pearl Harbor and features the last pineapple plantations. Honolulu and Waikiki are to the southeast, while the towering Ko'olau barrier lies to the northeast. Facing the northeasterly trade winds, the Ko'olau Range acts as an umbrella, pushing precipitation up north to the lush, rainy coast. Until modern roads were built, only one path linked the south to the north.

O'ahu's diverse geology and history have created an island of two faces. Honolulu and Waikiki, on one side, are extensively developed cosmopolitan tourist areas. The backcountry, on the other side, with its papaya and coconut trees, carved cliffs and pristine beaches, has a timeless charm. In winter, violent storms that form in the north Pacific unleash their wrath here, and in some places waves swell up as high as small buildings – a surfer's paradise. The island only measures 113mi (70km) at its widest point, so technically it is possible to see it all in one day. However, we recommend you take your time to leisurely explore the island, region by region, beginning first with its capital.

Finding Your Way Around

Honolulu International Airport

Location

Situated less than 13mi (8km) west of downtown, Honolulu International Airport was built between Pearl Harbor and the Hawaiian capital. The trip via the H1 Freeway takes only about 12min

(20min to Waikiki) when there aren't any traffic jams. During rush hour, however, the trip to Waikiki can take up to 1hr. You can also get to Honolulu via the Nimitz Highway, which turns into Ala Moana Boulevard near the downtown area and then heads to Waikiki.

Terminals

The airport has three different terminals. The largest, with more than 20 million passengers annually, handles international and U.S. flights. Since there are no services offered here, it's best not to arrive too soon before entering the gates. Don't forget that if you're returning to the continent, your bags have to pass through health inspection. In stark contrast to its drab exterior, the interior of the airport offers an impressive selection of boutiques, concession stands and bars. The terminal even has a mini-hotel (see p 151) and an Aeronautical Museum (*every day 9am to 6pm*) with many interactive exhibits. There are also many electronic storage lockers.

The second terminal, which is an extension of the first, handles flights of the Aloha and Hawaiian (Inter-island Terminal) carriers. The third terminal, located farther away, only serves the smaller commuter airlines (Commu-

ter Airlines Terminal). Flights to Lana'i and Moloka'i with Aloha Islandair and to Hana and Kalaupapa with Pacific Wings depart from this terminal.

The three terminals are connected by the Wiki Wiki shuttle service, which runs from Waikiki every 20min. The service only operates between 6am and 10:30pm. Surf boards and pets are forbidden.

Information

Tourist information booths are located in both the international and the inter-island terminals. To contact the airport, dial ☎*836-6411*.

Bus

The City Bus stops in front of the inter-island terminal as well as at lobby 4 and 7 for departures at the international terminal (top floor). Nos. 19 and 20 Eastbound follow the same path via the Nimitz Highway to downtown Honolulu and via Ala Moana Boulevard to Waikiki. The Westbound no. 19 goes to the Hickham Air Force Base and no. 20 heads to Pearl Harbor (Arizona Memorial), Aiea and Pearlridge. Buses come by about every 30min between 5am and 11:45pm (*5:30am and 11:25pm Sat, Sun and holidays*). The fare is $1. Note that large pieces of luggage is forbidden.

Shuttle Buses

Waikiki Express (☎*566-7333 8am to 5pm,* ☎*845-8707 after hours)* offers a 24hr shuttle service to Waikiki, with departures approximately every 30min. The one-way trip, which costs $8, doesn't make sense for two people since you can grab a taxi for about the same cost and get there a lot faster. The round trip by shuttle bus costs $13 and departures are at the arrival level of the international terminal. Round trips can be booked upon arrival. There are also a number of companies that offer transportation from Waikiki to the airport at a lower cost *($4 to $6)*.

Taxis and Limousines

The trip by taxi between the airport and Waikiki is a flat rate of $12. Some limousines occasionally match this price when business is slow, but they usually charge between $25 and $30.

Car Rentals

The main car rental agencies have outlets at the airport. Their shuttles continually circle from one terminal to another, and they can drive you to the depot. Note that Alamo is situated 1.2mi (2km) out-

side of the airport. Every company should automatically provide you with the O'ahu Drive Guide. If they don't, just ask for it since it can be very helpful.

To and From Honolulu

Honolulu is situated at the heart of a network of roads that serve the entire island. The H1 Freeway, which heads west along the south coast, leads to the airport (5mi or 8km), **Pearl Harbor** (10mi or 16km), the outskirts of **Pearl City** (15mi or 24km) and **Waipahu** (18mi or 29km). The H1 Freeway ends near the **Wai'anae coast**, which is bordered by the Farrington Highway. The H1 Freeway is flanked by three two-lane service roads (which have many traffic lights): the Nimitz Highway (leading to the airport), the Kamehameha Highway and the Farrington Highway. Shortly after Pearl City, a fork in the road, The H2 Freeway, leads to **Wahiawa** in the north on the North Shore Road. The Kamehameha Highway follows the same path and completes the tour of the island via the windward coast back to **Kane'ohe**.

The H1 Freeway veers east towards **Waikiki** and soon ends near the residential area of Kahala. At **Kahala**, it

becomes the Kalaniana'ole Highway, which circles the eastern tip of the island and then heads back to Kane'ohe on the windward coast. Ala Moana Boulevard, which runs along the sea front, connects Honolulu and Waikiki, and turns into the Nimitz Highway near the downtown area.

From the H1 Freeway, three main roads allow you to make your way to the north coast through the **Ko'olau Range**, thanks to several tunnels. The Paili Highway (61), the most popular road for tourists, begins in downtown Honolulu at Nu'uanu Avenue. The Likelike Highway (63) begins farther north and runs parallel to the Pali Highway. The recently built the H3 Freeway connects Pearl Harbor and Kane'ohe.

Wherever you're headed, expect traffic jams during rush hour *(from 6am to 9am and 3:30pm to 6pm)*.

Downtown

Downtown is divided into three different districts. The business district, whose main street is Bishop Street, is dominated by skyscrapers, while Chinatown to the west is more unpretentious and lively. The second district, located just to the east between Vineyard Boulevard to the

O'ahu

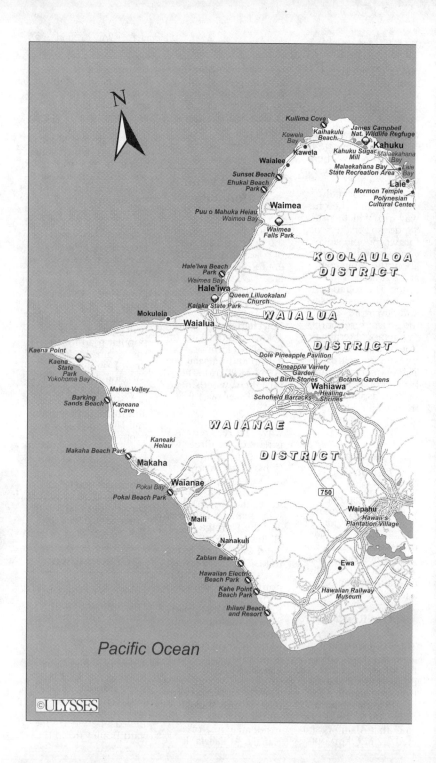

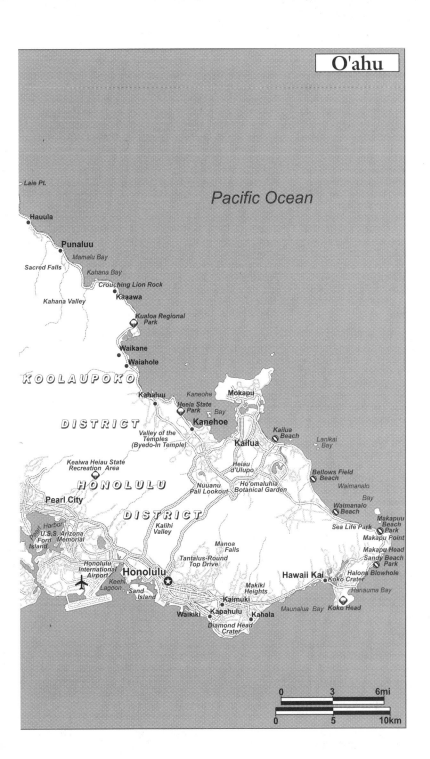

north and Queen Street to the south, is the historic area where Honolulu emerged as capital in the 19th century. In addition to the Ioloani Palace and the mission houses, this is where the main government buildings are located: City Hall, the Capitol and the Supreme Court. To the south, Bishop Street leads to the sea front where the famous Aloha Tower stands. Buses nos. 2 and 13 (also nos. 19 and 20) go to most of the sites in downtown Honolulu.

The town is also divided into many other areas. The most important ones are Kalihi, to the west, where the Bishop Museum is located (on the way to the airport); Moiliili to the east, on the road from Waikiki; and, farther along, Kahala. There are also the districts of upper Honolulu, including the two main areas of Makiki and the Manoa Valley, which overlooks the University.

If you're asking for directions and someone tells you to head towards Diamond Head or 'Ewa, this means east or west, respectively. Two other frequently used terms are *mauka*, which means towards the mountains, and *makai*, towards the sea.

Parking

Parking is always a problem in downtown

Honolulu. If you want to avoid the rather expensive underground parking, you can try to find a spot on Queen Emma Street facing the Kamamalu playing field (just north of Vineyard towards Punchbowl), where you can park for an unlimited amount of time. Otherwise, the simplest solution is to leave your car in the parking area at the intersection of Smith and North Beretania. Parking here costs $1 per hr with a limit of 3hrs – elsewhere, the time limit is either 1 or 2hrs.

Parking is even more expensive in Waikiki, and most hotels charge for parking. In the cheaper hotels, parking costs $5 to $6 per day, while in the more luxurious establishments, expect to pay between $9 and $10 per day. A few rare hotels do offer free parking, while some leave it up to their guests to find their own. If this is the case, you'll have to pay for a spot in another establishment – or simply look around for a spot. If you're staying in the northeastern part of Waikiki, things are a little rosier, as most of the streets that have free parking are between Kuhio Avenue in the south and Ala Wai Boulevard in the north, mainly on Ohua, Paoakalani, Kaneloa, Pualani and Wainani. However, pay attention to the No Parking signs, to sidewalks marked

with a red line and to yellow fire hydrants. You can also leave your car for the night on the borders of Paki'olani Park, but note that you have to pay for these spots between 10am and 6pm. Another option is to park along the Ala Wai Canal. However, except for weekends and holidays (when it is even more difficult to find parking), parking is forbidden here between 6:30am and 8:30am and between 3:30pm and 5:30pm, which means you won't be able to leave your car there – unless you plan to wake up before the crack of dawn.

Transportation

Car Rental Agencies

Alamo
☎800-327-9633
airport
☎327-9633
There are outlets at the **Royal Islander Hotel** (*2164 Kalia R.,* ☎923-3337) and at the **Ilikai Hotel** (*1777 Ala Moana Blvd.,* ☎947-6112).

Avis
☎800-321-3712
airport
☎834-5536
There are outlets at the **Hilton Hawaiian Village** (*2005 Kalia R.,* ☎973-2624), at the **Outrigger East Hotel** (*148 Ka'iulani Ave.,* ☎971-3700) at the **Sheraton Waikiki** (*2255 Kalakaua Ave.,* ☎922-4422).

Budget
☎*800-527-0700*
airport
☎*838-1111*
There are outlets at the
Outrigger Reef
(2169 Kalia Rd.), at the
Outrigger East Hotel
(2379 Kuhio Ave.) and at
the **Hyatt Regency**
(2424 Kalakaua Ave.).

Dollar
☎*800-800-4000*
airport
☎*831-2003*
There are outlets at the
Coral Seas Hotel
(250 Lewers St., ☎*952-4264)*, at the **Discovery
Bay Center** *(1765 Ala
Moana Blvd.,* ☎*952-4242)*, at the **Hale Koa
Hotel** *(2055 Kalia Dr.,*
☎*952-4264)* and at the
Hawaiian Regent Hotel
(2552 Kalakaua Ave.,
☎*952-4264)*.

Hertz
☎*800-654-3011*
airport
☎*831-3500*
There are outlets at
Alana Waikiki Hotel
(1956 Ala Moana Blvd.,
☎*941-7275)*, at the
Hilton Hawaiian Village
(2005 Kalia Rd., ☎*973-3637)* and at the **Hyatt
Regency** *(2424 Kalakaua
Ave.,* ☎*971-3535)*.

National
☎*800-CAR-RENT*
airport
☎*831-3800*
There are outlets at the
Discovery Bay Center
(1778 Ala Moana Blvd.,
☎*922-3331)*, at the
Hilton Hawaiian Village
(2005 Kalia Rd., ☎*941-4891)* and at **Kahala
Mandarin Oriental**
(5000 Kahala Ave.,
☎*737-4681)*.

Thrifty
☎*800-FOR-CARS*
airport
☎*831-2277*
325 Seaside Ave., Waikiki
☎*971-2660*

Some local companies,
following the example
of **Paradise Isle Rentals**
(151 Uluniu Ave., Waikiki,
☎*926-7777)* will rent
vehicles to people un-
der the age of 21.

Taxi

Here are a few of the
main companies:

Charley's
☎*531-1333*

City Taxi
☎*524-2121*

Sida Taxi
☎*836-0011*

TheCab
☎*536-1707*

Bus

TheBus *(*☎*848-5555,
every day 5:30am to
10pm)* offers the most
extensive bus service of
the archipelago, cover-
ing most of the island.
Whatever the distance,
the fare is $1. You can
obtain a bus schedule
for each bus line at the
main office *(811 Middle
St.)* or you can buy a
complete guide at one
of the many ABC Dis-
count Stores. All the
buses marked "Hono-
lulu" are based at the
Ala Moana Center,
which is where you'll
have to transfer if
you're coming from
Waikiki. Don't forget to
ask the driver for a free

transfer when you
board. It only takes
4hrs to circle the island
(2hrs to Turtle Bay).
Buses are equipped
with bike racks so that
you can combine both
activities.

Trolleybus

The **Waikiki Trolley**
(☎*596-2199 or 800-824-8804, www.enoa.com)*
serves the main tourist
sites of O'ahu every
day, with three lines
and 37 stops: red for
Honolulu up to the
Bishop Museum *(every
20min from 8:30am to
6:45pm)*, yellow for
Waikiki to Ward Center
only *(every 10 to 20min
from 8:50am to 11:35pm)*
and blue for the eastern
part of the island to Sea
Life Park *(every hour
from 8:30am to 7:15pm)*.
Narration is provided
along the way and pas-
sengers can get on and
off at their leisure.
You can choose a one-
day pass *($18)*, which
is good for two lines
(yellow and blue or
yellow and red), or a
four-day pass for $30
(two lines) or $42
(three lines). It's expensive, but you can often
find two-for-one cou-
pons. Get a free copy
of the *Trolley Map Guide*,
which is essential to
find your way around.
Note that the trolley
only stops for a few
minutes in Hanauma
Bay. For couples or
groups who plan to
leave Waikiki or Hono-
lulu, a rental car will
not cost much more
and will give you much
more freedom.

O'ahu

Motorcyle and Moped Rentals

This is another transportation option for Waikiki and the surrounding area. There are over a dozen rental agencies, and prices are about the same everywhere (*$15 to $20 per day not including insurance*).

Practical Information

Tourist Offices

Hawai'i Visitors and Convention Bureau
Mon to Fri 8am to 4:30pm
2270 Kalakaua Ave.
Waikiki Business Plaza
☎923-1811

Hawai'i Visitors Information Center
☎528-1566
Since tourist offices can only provide limited help, most visitors consult the many free brochures and guides distributed in all tourist sites (such as *This Week O'ahu, O'ahu Gold, 101 Things to Do on O'ahu*). Although the information is purely commercial, you can take advantage of the enclosed coupons.

Foreign Exchange Offices

Thomas Cook Currency Services
☎949-2813

National Parks Service

Department of Land and Natural Resources Division of State Parks
Mon to Fri 8am to 3:30pm
P.O. Box 621
1151 Punchbowl St.
Honolulu HI 96809
☎587-0399
Located in the Kalanimoku Building (*suite 131*) just north of Honolulu Hale, the State Parks office issues free camping permits and offers information on all parks on O'ahu as well as the other islands. For more information, refer to the section on camping in the introductory chapter (see p 63). Suite 130 (☎587-0300) sells the helpful *O'ahu Recreation Map ($4)*, which has a list of 22 hiking trails on the island.

County Park Services City & County Parks
Mon to Fri 7:45am to 4pm
Municipal Building
650 South King St., main floor
☎523-4525
The county of Honolulu authorizes free camping in 13 of its parks for a maximum of five days. All campgrounds are closed from 8am Wed to 8am Fri. You have to obtain a permit in advance at City Hall Services at the address above, or at one of the many satellite offices. The Ala Moana center is the most convenient office, but you can also obtain one at Fort Street, Pearlridge, Kane'ohe, Kailua, Wahiawa, Wai'anae, Waipahu, as well as at a dozen "mobile" stations, usually located in shopping centres. You can get a complete list by calling ☎527-6695. The permits, which must be obtained in person, can be issued up to two weeks in advance, up to the same day.

Emergencies

Emergencies
☎911

SOS Doctors
971-6000

Hospitals

Castle Medical Center
☎263-5164

Kaiser Permanente
☎800-966-5955

Queen's Medical Center
☎538-9011

Schriner's Children Hospital
☎941-4466

Safety and Security

O'ahu's reputation for safety is not very good, but has nevertheless gotten better in the last few years. Avoid

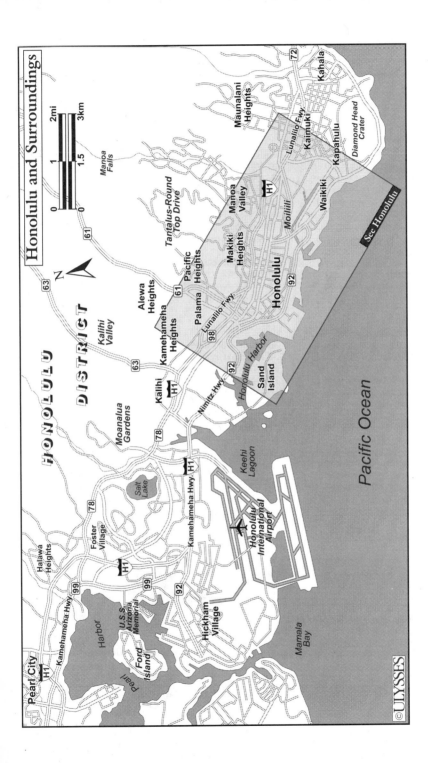

downtown Honolulu at night and watch out for car theft, which is quite frequent near the most popular beaches (especially on the north coast). Many people prefer to leave their vehicle empty and the doors open – that way, the thieves won't break the windows to see what's inside.

Post Offices

Waikiki
Mon, Tue, Thu and Fri 8am to 4:30pm, Wed 8am to 6pm, Sat 9am to noon
330 Saratoga Road

Ala Moana Center
Mon to Fri 8:30am to 5pm, Sat 8:30am to 4:30pm
street level, below Longs Drugs

There is also a small post office in the Hilton Hawaiian Village complex by the ABC store on the main floor *(Mon to Sat 8am to noon and 1pm to 4pm)*.

Internet

All of the Internet cafés are located in Waikiki (and Honolulu).

Cappucinos Cafe
$6/hr with a minimum of $3 and one drink
every day 10am to midnight
Waikiki Joy Hotel
320 Lewers St, Waikiki
☎921-3534

Coco's Internet Cafe
$1/10min
Mon to Fri 6am to 1am, Sat to Sun 9am to midnight
2310 Kuhio Ave., Waikiki

Coffee Cove
$1.50/15min
Mon-Fri 7am to midnight, Sat and Sun from 10am
2600 South King St., Honolulu (corner of University)
☎955-2683
www.coffeecove.com

Fishbowl Internet Cafe
$1/10min
every day 8am to 1am
Kuhio Village, Waikiki
2463 Kuhio Ave.
☎922-7562

Web Side Story Cafe
$6/hr, with a minimum of $3; $1.50 for each additional period of 15min
every day 9am to 11pm (bar 3pm to 11pm)
Ewa Hotel
2555 Cartwright Rd., Waikiki
☎922-1677

Laundromats

The Hotel Outrigger East's laundromat, situated at the corner of Kuhio Ave. and Kaiulani St., is open to everyone from 6:30am to 11pm *(last load at 10:30pm)*. It is on Kuhio across from the hotel's parking lot. You can get change at the liquor store next door.

Macadamia Nuts

Exploring

Honolulu and Waikiki

In Hawaiian, Honolulu means, "sheltered bay," a more recent term for what the first Hawaiians used to call Ke awa Kou ("prosperous harbour" or "the harbour of Kou," a rare wood). The only natural harbour of the archipelago, it was created by the Nu'uanu Stream whose mouth carried fresh water to this area and prevented coral from forming at this spot. The islanders, however, didn't need to use the harbour since their large canoes had very shallow draughts. Since the *ali'i* (noble Hawaiians) preferred Waikiki with its waves and greenery, the Honolulu harbour area was very sparsely populated and merely had a temple dedicated to Lono.

In November 1793, Captain William Brown, a British fur trader, was the first Westerner to dock his ship, the *Jackal*, in what is now called Honolulu Harbour. Two years later, after conquering O'hau, Kamehameha built a palace known as Halehui on the seashore of Honolulu (it has today disappeared). By the turn of the century, merchant ships en route to Asia began to flock to Honolulu and a shipyard was eventually built in 1825, complete with hotels, bars and brothels.

A quarter of a century later, Kamehameha III, realizing that Honolulu was booming, left Lahaina and moved the capital to Honolulu. Under his reign (as well as his successors'), the city became a thriving port. After the land was divided in 1848 and sugar-cane plantations were established, corporations that were owned by powerful business people – mostly heirs of the original missionary families – built offices in the centre of town. Chinese buildings and shops also sprung up, marking the beginning of what was later to become the financial centre and Chinatown. After the 'Iolani Palace was built in 1874, King David Kalakaua firmly established Honolulu as the political centre of the islands, a role it still maintains today.

In just two centuries, Honolulu went from being a deserted land to becoming a metropolis. Huts were replaced with skyscrapers and Hawaiians were superseded by an international population consisting of immigrants from all over the Americas, Asia and Europe. Today, Honolulu and surroundings has a population of 400,000 and stretches 64mi (40km) from west to east.

In Waikiki, Honolulu's alter ego, hotels sprung up on the beaches only a few kilometres to the east. In the 19th century, noble Hawaiians had already built homes on its beautiful shore, where they surfed when the mundane troubles of this world became too boring.

★★
The Historic Centre of Honolulu

The area where the Hawaiian capital was born is situated just east of Honolulu's skyscrapers. It was here that the first missionaries came in 1820, where the first permanent church in town was located, and where the 'Iolani Palace, now a symbol of the dethroned Hawaiian monarchy, was built.

"The Only Royal Palace in the U.S.," **'Iolani Palace ★★★** *($15; guided tours every 15min Tue to Sat 9am to 2:15pm; bags, cameras, video cameras and children under five years not allowed, ☎522-0832 for reservations or ☎538-1471 for information)* stands in the middle of a spacious park with large trees,

O'ahu

'Iolani Palace

between the state capitol to the north and the Supreme Court (Ali'iolani Hale) to the south. Built between 1879 and 1881 for King Kalakaua who lived here until his death in 1891, this "bird of paradise" palace then became the royal palace for his sister, venerable Queen Lili'uokalani, the last Hawaiian monarch. After her overthrow in 1893 and until 1968 the palace became the capitol – first for the republic, then for the territory and later for the state of Hawaii. If it hadn't been for the intervention of a citizens' organization, the place would have been demolished and turned into a parking lot. Its

restoration took nine years. Today, the site is impeccably well maintained; visitors must even wear slippers to protect the hardwood floors.

The guided tour, which is headed by a volunteer and lasts about 45min, leads visitors through the 10 rooms of the palace. Since the main entrance has been boarded up, you must enter by the back entrance via the grand central hall. The walls on both sides of the magnificent central *koa*-wood (Hawaiian acacia) staircase are covered with portraits of Hawaiian monarchs. The first room you visit is the Blue Room, dec-

orated with paintings of Kalakaua and of his sister, as well as a portrait of... King Louis-Philippe of France, which shows how important international relations were to the Hawaiian monarchy. A sliding door opens onto the dining room where the royal couple had breakfast every morning – a seven- or eight-course meal! Flamboyant personalities, poker players, captains and even seamen dined at the table of King Kalakaua, who was known to be fond of colourful characters.

The decoration and objects reflect the king's fondness for European luxuries:

● ATTRACTIONS	
1. Honolulu Academy of Arts	7. University of Hawaii
2. Royal Mausoleum	8. John Young Museum of Art
3. Sand Island	9. East-West Center
4. Ala Moana Beach	10. Pu'u 'Ualaka State Park
5. Aina Moana	11. Contemporary Museum
6. Bishop Museum	12. Punchbowl Cemetary

◯ ACCOMMODATIONS	
1. Central YMCA	5. Pagoda Hotel (R)
2. Fernhurst YMCA	
3. Hostelling International	(R) Property with restaurant (see description)
4. Manoa Valley Inn	

● RESTAURANTS	
1. Ala Moana Center	13. Maple Garden
- Hanako Restaurant	14. Ono Hawaiian Foods
- Honolulu Coffee Company	15. Rumours
- Makai Market	16. Sam Choy's Nimitz
- Pearl's Seafood Chinese Restaurant	17. Sam Choy's Kapahulu
2. Alan Wong's	18. The Pyramid
3. Anna Bannana's	19. Wa'ioli Tea Room
4. Auntie Pasto's	20. Ward Warehouse
5. Bubbies	- A Pacific Cafe
6. Camellia Yakiniku	- Brew Moon
7. Chef Mavro	- Compadres
8. Coffee Cove	21. Ward Center
9. Coffeeline	- Kincaid's Fish, Chop & Steak House
10 Down to Earth Natural Foods	- Stuart Anderson Cattle Company
11. Leonard's Bakery	- The Old Spaghetti Factory
12. Liquid	

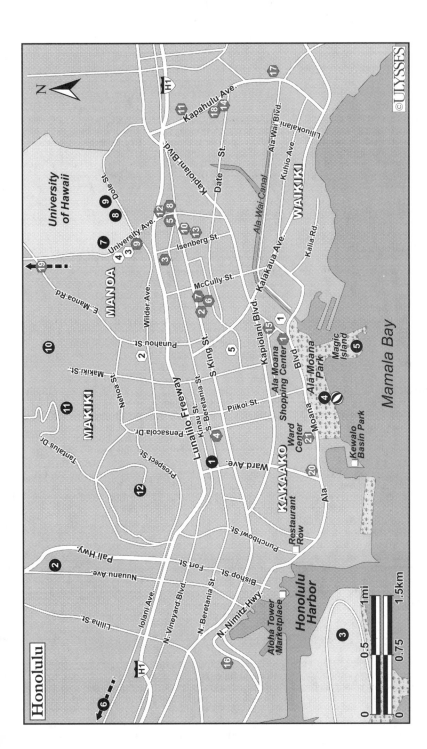

Honolulu

MANOA

MAKIKI

WAKIKI

KAKAAKO

University of Hawaii

E. Manoa Rd.

Tantalus Dr.

Wilder Ave.

University Ave.

Dole St.

Isenberg St.

McCully St.

Kapiolani Blvd.

Date St.

Kapahulu Ave.

Ala Wai Canal

Ala Wai Blvd.

Kuhio Ave.

Kalakaua Ave.

Liliuokalani

Kalia Rd.

Punahou St.

Makiki St.

Nehoa St.

Piikoi St.

S. Beretania St.

S. King St.

Kinau St.

Pensacola Dr.

Prospect St.

Lunalilo Freeway

Ward Ave.

Ala Moana Blvd.

Ala Moana Shopping Center

Ward Center

Moana Blvd.

Ala Moana Park

Magic Island

Kewalo Basin Park

Ala Moana

Ala

Restaurant Row

Punchbowl St.

Bishop St.

Fort St.

Iolani Ave.

Nuuanu Ave.

Pali Hwy.

Liliha St.

N. Vineyard Blvd.

N. Beretania St.

N. Nimitz Hwy.

Aloha Tower Marketplace

Honolulu Harbor

Mamala Bay

N

H1

© ULYSSES

0   0.5   1mi

0   0.75   1.5km

French porcelain, English silverware and Bohemian crystal. The east wing of the main floor consists entirely of the thrown room, decorated in crimson and gold, conjuring up images of fantastical fairy tales. The crown and sceptre, which Kalakau instituted in Hawaii, are displayed. On some evenings, this room was transformed into a ballroom where a dance card was presented to each woman with the name of the dancers. It is also here that, in 1893, Queen Lili'uokalani was tried and convicted of "treason".

The bedrooms are found upstairs. The west wing was reserved for the king; the east wing for the queen. In Kalakaua's Victorian-style bedroom, a photograph shows that it used to be filled with 14 tables, eight chairs, a bed, and numerous paintings and works of art that he picked up during his trips abroad. After the monarchy was overthrown, the furniture was sold and dispersed throughout the world, thanks to the various ports of call of many ships.

Unfortunately, none of the original period furniture is left. The next place you visit is the king's office. Kalakaua was a technology fanatic; he installed one in the first telephones of the Pacific and even had electricity before the White House in Washington. In addition to the study and the music room is Lili'uokalani's room, where the deposed queen spent eight-and-a-half months under house arrest. To pass the time, she read, wrote songs and worked on a large quilt, which is on display.

Several annexes surround the palace, such as the **Queen's Barracks**, which now houses the museum's ticket office. This is where the Royal Household Guards lived. Today it also features the museum's boutique and a room where you can watch a 15min film on the palace's history *(every 30min)*. The **Coronation Pavilion** ('Iolani Bandstand) was built for the coronation of Kalakaua and Kapi'olani on February 12, 1883. Every Friday from 12:15pm to 1:15pm the Royal Hawaiian Band performs concerts here.

It was Kamehameha V who launched a project to construct a building that would house the Parliament, the cabinet and the courthouses. The king envisioned a European-style capitol, but he died soon after the first stone was laid. His successor, Kalakaua, inaugurated **Ali'iolani Hale** ★ *(free admission; Mon to Fri 7:45am to 4:30pm)*, "The House of the Heavenly King," in honour of Kamehameha V, during the legislative session of 1874. In this building in 1893, a "revolutionary committee," consisting of business people and influential people from the U.S., illegally overthrew the monarchy and created a provisory government. Since then, Ali'iolani Hale only houses the Supreme Court.

Standing in front of Ali'iolani Hale is the majestic **Statue of Kamehameha** ★, who is depicted wearing a golden cloak and helmet (*mahiole*). The commissioned work of British sculptor Thomas Gould, molten in France and sent by ship, the statue sank near the Falkland Islands. It was eventually recovered, but in the meantime, a second version of it had already been placed by Kalakaua in 1883. The original statue now stands in Kapa'au, on the Big Island, the birthplace of the great king.

In addition to the courtrooms, which are still in use, Ali'iolani Hale also houses the **Judiciary History Center** ★ *(Mon to Fri 10am to 3pm)*, a museum that traces the history of Hawaiian law. Although the theme sounds rather dull, don't let that discourage you – this really is a fascinating exhibit. The tour begins with an introduction to the system of *kapu* (taboo) of the ancient Hawaiians and then turns to the surprising provisions of the penal code introduced in 1827 by Ka'ahumanu, the widow of Kamehameha, under the influence of the missionaries. Those found guilty of gambling or adultery were put in chains, while those convicted of prostitution or selling alcohol merely received a fine! On the way out, you can see a courtroom set up like those found in 1913, and two short videos dealing with controversial topics (such as the sharing of land and water resources).

Just east of Ali'iolani Hale stands the **Kawaiaha'o Church ★ ★** *(free admission; 8am to 4pm; 957 Punchbowl St., ☎522-1333)*, "the Hawaiian Westminster Abbey," which is the oldest stone church on O'ahu. There used to be a spring here where Chiefess Ha'o used to bathe, giving her name to it: Ka Wai a Ha'o ("the water of Ha'o"). It was at this site that the missionaries, soon after their arrival, chose to build

their first church. It took four palm-leaf thatch churches for Kamehameha III, under the influence of Ka'ahimanu (Kamehameha's favourite wife, who was baptized here in 1825), to finally authorize the construction of a permanent structure here. It was begun in 1838 and finished during the summer of 1842 – an incredible feat considering that it's made of 14,000 slabs of coral hacked from the reef, each with an average weight of half a tonne and depth of between 10ft (3m) and 20ft (6m)!

Upon entering, you will notice the seats at the back of the church marked by the *kahili* emblem of yellow and red feathers, which are reserved for the descendants of royalty. Upstairs are portraits depicting the 21 most important Hawaiian *ali'i*. It is here that Kamehameha V was crowned in 1854 and where he married Emma

two years later. Volunteer tour guides are usually available from 9am to 3:30pm from Monday to Saturday. Sunday is reserved for mass in Hawaiian at 10:30am.

Just in front of the entrance stands the **tomb of King Lunalilo**, who was elected by the cabinet as the brief successor to Kamehameha V. To assure popular support, the new king resorted to a plebiscite. He only ruled for a little more than a year before his death on February 3, 1874, at the age of 39.

Walk around the church past the fountain, which replaced the former spring, to the peaceful little cemetery, the oldest Christian burial place in Hawaii. Some of the founding missionaries and their children, many of whom died very young, rest here under the frangipani. From Waikiki, where many *ali'i* lived, the entrance to the church used to be via the arch that today opens onto Kawaiaha'o Street and the Mission Houses Museum.

The spot now occupied by the **Mission Houses Museum ★ ★** *(Tue to Sat 9am to 4pm; guided tours $8, last tour at 2:30pm; 553 South King St., ☎531-0481)* marks where the first missionary families of O'ahu built their houses in 1819. These fervent Protestants who

O'ahu

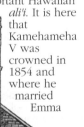

Kawaiaha'o Church

arrived from Boston had committed themselves to a religious revival movement in the northeastern and southern U.S., the American Board of Commissioners for Foreign Missions (ABCFM). Many of them had never left their home before, and, after the gruelling six-month trip via Cape Horn, the cultural shock was mind-boggling. But disciplined in spite of everything, they immediately began building houses, churches and schools. They received the unexpected support of the ambitious Queen Ka'ahumanu, who regarded them as staunch allies – and rightly so. She was baptized and soon thousands of *kanaka* ("men" in Hawaiian) became churchgoers. From 1821-1865, the Honolulu mission was the centre of all missionary organizations in Hawai'i.

Three New England-style homes, the birthplace of the missionaries, have been meticulously restored. The oldest western-style home in Hawaii, the Frame House was shipped from New England in pieces and put back together in Hawaii in 1821. Four missionary families were once crammed into this house. Built in 1831, the Chamberlain House was made from 3,000 coral blocks and was the home of Levi Chamberlain, the mis-

sion's liaison officer. The Printing House (1841), which is an extension of the Frame House, holds a replica of the printing press – a powerful new tool for the missionaries – that was used to print the Bible in the Hawaiian language in 1822. The building is only accessible by guided tour, which lasts 45min, but there is no admission fee so you can walk around and take a peek through the windows. The exhibit traces the history of these devoutly religious people from the arrival of the first "company" in Hawaii on October 23, 1819, to the 12th and last mission in 1848. There is also a scale model of the early mission. Every Wednesday and second Saturday of each month are "Living History" days, in which costumed guides re-enact the bygone era with cooking and printing demonstrations.

On the other side of King Street stands City Hall, also known as **Honolulu Hale**, which has an ornate Spanish Mission-style design. The interior of the building is not that interesting, but there are occasionally temporary exhibits, especially in the hall, but also in the Lane Gallery or on the second floor *(Mon to Fri 8am to 5pm)*, with a variety of local themes. To the west lies the **Hawai'i State Library** *(Mon and Fri and Sat 9am to 5pm, Tue and*

Thu 9am to 8pm, Wed 10am to 5pm; 478 South King St., ☎586-3500), open to the public since 1913.

A pedestrian path leads to the **Capitol ★**, a large building that took over the function of its neighbour, the 'Iolani Palace, in 1969. Its open-court design represents a volcano around a crater, while the entire structure is encircled by a large pool, symbolizing the ocean. A statue of Queen Lili'uokalani stands in front of the southern entrance, and in front of the northern entrance is a modern statue of Father Damien. You can see the House of Representatives through the windows and look down on the downtown area from the veranda located on top of the building.

Located north of the Capitol on the other side of Beretania Street (meaning "Great Britain" in Hawaiian), the **War Memorial**, dedicated to the Hawaiian men and women who fought in the American Armed Forces, stands at the end of two rows of stately palm trees. Just next door, **Washington Place** (no visitors allowed) is a more successful architectural experiment. This two-storey colonial-style wooden mansion has a porch decorated with white columns on the western side. By the entrance is a commemorative plaque that features the lyrics of the song "Aloha 'Oe," composed by Queen Lili'uokalani who lived here until her death in 1917. Today, it is the governor's official residence.

Just west of Washington Place towers the great Neo-Gothic-style **St. Andrews Cathedral ★★**. King Kamehameha V and his wife, Queen Emma, who was a devout member of the Episcopal Church, decided to have this church built in 1867. The large stained-glass windows framing the entrance are magnificent. The royal couple is depicted on the right, as well as several other local personalities who played an important role on the islands and the taro plantations.

A few minutes' drive by car along South Beretania Street brings you from downtown to the **Honolulu Academy of Arts ★★** *($7, free admission on the first Wed of the month; Tue to Sat 10am to 4:30pm and Sun 1pm to 5pm; 900 South Beretania St.: ☎532-8701, www.honoluluacademy.org, bus no. 2).* The main art museum in the Hawaiian capital, it was founded in 1927 by Anna Rice Cooke. The Academy has a superb, eclectic collection, including a few exquisite pieces. The mix of different cultures and time periods makes it easy to lose your bearings.

There's the Garden Cafe *(Mon to Fri 11:30am to 2pm)*, a video room and a bookstore.
The museum is renowned for its permanent European collection (first room), including works by Matisse, Bonnard, Vlaminck, Monet, Modigliani, Cézanne, Gauguin, Van Gogh, Fernand Léger, Braque and Picasso – nearly all the masters are represented here. Although small, the collection is very impressive, especially considering that it's in the middle of the Pacific. The Academy also holds some fascinating depictions of Hawaii by visiting artists, such as Jacques Arago, who came to the islands at the end of the 18th century during a French scientific expedition. The periods and styles follow one another in a rather haphazard order: religious Medieval Italian paintings, European works from the 17th and 18th centuries, as well as Asian and American Art-Deco works. The Mediterranean Court displays a wonderful mosaic of Roman animals, which was discovered at Antioch (Syria), as well as a few Cycladic statuettes. This is followed by some rich collections of Eastern art. China (furniture, calligraphy, porcelain, ancient bronzes) and Japan (lacquers, Samurai armour, swords, *ukiyo-e* etchings) are best rep-

resented, but there are also sections devoted to Cambodia, Vietnam, India and Indonesia. At the end of the exhibit is a hodgepodge of African, Central American, Oceanic (such as the beautiful crocodile totem from Sepik) and American Indian artwork.

★★
The Financial Centre and Chinatown

(half-day to full day)

It was here that Honolulu's first buildings were built, between Bishop and King Street, during the 19th century. Although most of the ancient buildings have now been replaced by glass and steel, there are still a few old facades left. Most streets in the financial district also feature modern sculptures.

On Fort Street between King and Beretania, an old Russian blockhouse made out of coral once stood here during the 19th century. Transformed into a fort in 1816 by Kamehameha, it protected the port entrance, served as a prison and welcomed ships full of drunken sailors. The building was destroyed in 1857 and its stones were used to create the small peninsula on which the Aloha Tower stands today. The street was renamed **Fort Street Mall**

O'ahu

and is now home to a lively pedestrian shopping mall, which is frequented by students from Hawaii Pacific University (whose campus is situated at the north end of the mall). A few of the buildings huddle around the **Cathedral of Our Lady of Peace** *(every day 6:30am to 5:30pm; 1184 Bishop St.)*, the oldest Catholic cathedral in the U.S. (1843). There are also some fast-food restaurants in the mall.

Pauahi Street leads to the nearby **Hawai'i Theater** ★ *(1130 Bethel St.; ☎528-0506)*, the former "Carnegie Hall of the Pacific." The theatre, which is decorated with gold, mural paintings and Corinthian columns, was recently restored and now hosts all kinds of events. Guided tours *($5)* are organized on the first and third Tuesday of each month.

A stone's throw from the theatre near the intersection of Hotel Street and Nu'uanu Avenue, the bronze lions of the **Chinatown Gateway Park** mark the entrance into Chinatown. They were donated by the town of Kaohsiung (Taiwan) to commemorate the first Chinese emigration to the island at the end of the 18th century.

After the first Chinese workers on the plantations finished their contracts in the 1860s, a lot of them decided to make the island their new home. By the end of the decade, more than 70 of them had opened shops in Honolulu. Eventually, the oldest **Chinatown** ★★ in the U.S. became well established, overflowing with successive immigration from Asia. Although the area was practically abandoned for a long time, it is now slowly but surely undergoing a renaissance of sorts.

This lively area adds character to the grid of streets and skyscrapers of the adjacent downtown area. All day, its shops bustle with

● **ATTRACTIONS**

1. 'Iolani Palace	11. Notre-Dame de la Paix Cathedral
2. Ali'iolani Hale	12. Hawai'i Theater
3. Statue of Kamehameha I	13. Chinatown Gateway Park
4. Kawaiaha'o Church	14. Downtown Market
5. Mission Houses Museum	15. Maunakea Marketplace
6. Honolulu Hale	16. Izumo Taisha Shrine
7. Hawai'i State Library	17. Kuan Yin Temple
8. Capitol	18. Foster Botanical Garden
9. Washington Place	19. Aloha Tower
10. St. Andrews Cathedral	20. Hawai'i Maritime Center

◐ **ACCOMMODATIONS**

1. Executive Centre Hotel	2. Nu'uanu YMCA

⬣ **RESTAURANTS**

1. A Little bit of Saigon	10. Mabuhay Cafe and Restaurant
2. Aloha Tower Marketplace	11. Maunakea Marketplace
- Chai's Island Bistro	12. Maxime
- Don Ho's Island Grill	13. Murphy's Bar & Grill
- Gordon Biersch Brewery & Restaurant	14. O'Toole's Pub
- The Pier Bar	15. Restaurant Row
3. Cafe Peninsula	- Ocean Club
4. Duc's Bistro	- Payao
5. Havana Cabana	- Ruth's Chris Steak House
6. Indigo	- Sunset Grill
7. Krung Thai	16. Shung Chong Yuein
8. Legend Seafood Restaurant	17. Tô-Châu
9. Legend Vegetarian Restaurant	

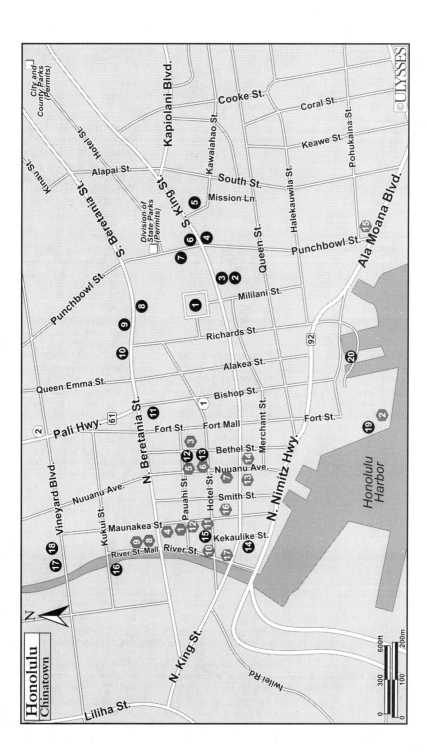

activity and locals shopping at the noodle factories and rotisseries that display Peking ducks in their windows. Here there are acupuncture specialists, herbalists, tattoo artists, kung-fu schools, Vietnamese, Chinese and Filipino restaurants – a walk through Chinatown is like taking a trip to Asia. Saturday mornings are especially lively. Chinatown is bordered to the north by Vineyard Boulevard, to the west by River Street, to the south by the waterfront and to the east by Nu'uanu Avenue.

Two blocks past Nu'uanau Avenue, Hotel Street crosses Maunakea Street, where all the *lei* **shops** are located. If you have the irresistible urge to wear a flower garland around your neck, then head to Sweethart's Lei Stand *(Mon to Fri 6:30am to 8:30pm, Sat 7am to 8:30pm, Sun 7am to 6:30pm; 69 A North Beretania, ☎537-3011)*, which is the islanders' favourite shop. At the southwest corner of the square stands the Wo Fat restaurant, a Chinatown landmark featuring neo-Chinese roofing. Originally founded in 1882, the restaurant was unfortunately recently closed.

Head makai *(towards the sea) down Maunakea Street to North King Street. Go west on North King Street.*

At the intersection of North King and Kekaulike is the **Downtown Market ★**; the meat market is on one side and the fish market is on the other. Many island cooks come here to buy their ingredients. From here to River Street, the thoroughfare is lined with strings of shops that sell fruits, vegetables and other provisions. Everything the Asian cook needs is on display: durians, nashis, star fruits, longans, persimmons, Chinese cabbage, okra and ginger – not to mention a few items that are usually a bit too "exotic" for most Westerners.

Just before Hotel Street crosses the Nu'uanu Stream, follow the stream along River Street. River Street passes several small restaurants and leads to the **Maunakea Marketplace** *(1120 Maunakea St.)*, the main shopping centre in Chinatown. Although there's an excellent selection of fast-food restaurants (see p 166) and Asian boutiques here, the place lacks a certain charm.

A statue of Sun Yat-Sen, the Hawaiian-raised Chinese revolutionary leader, stands at the entrance to the **River Street Mall**. Right next to it is the Lum Hai So Tong Taoist temple. Founded in 1899, it is located in an unusual setting, right above a second-hand

store. Visits are rare since the street-level door is usually locked.

Across the river on Kukui Street, the magnificent **Izumo Taisha Temple ★★** is marked by a large Torii, a symbolic door in the shape of pi. There are more than 400 similar temples in Japan, where this dissident branch of Shintoism originated, then came to Hawaii in 1905. Its pantheon is dominated by the universal *kami* (god) of love (*Okuninushi-no-Okami*), happiness, farming and marriage. Don't miss the temple's wooden portico which is adorned with a magnificent wicker ornament. Just right of the entrance is a small pool where followers wash their hands to purify themselves before entering the prayer room where you will see a beautiful *kodo* (ceremonial drum).

Continue along River Street to Vineyard Boulevard.

On the other side of the artery is the **Kuan Yin Temple ★** *(every day 8:30am to 2pm)*, named after the Chinese goddess of mercy, located near the entrance to the Foster Botanical Garden. The oldest Asian temple in Honolulu, it's quite a peaceful place in spite of its location near the road. It has impressive carved altars covered with offerings, statues of Buddha and the goddess, as well as two prayer ovens, whose smoke rises to the sky by the liberating fire.

Behind the temple is the entrance to the **Foster Botanical Garden ★** *($5; every day 9am to 4pm; 50 North Vineyard Blvd.,* ☎*522-7066; Bus no. 4)*, which is a great place for a stroll. The garden took root when William Hillebrand, a German botanist and Queen Kalama's head doctor, planted rare Hawaiian and tropical trees here in 1850. The Foster family bought the property in 1867 and continued planting the grounds until it was bequeathed to the city of Honolulu in 1930. It has some extremely rare trees, a large collection of palms (including 20 species indigenous to Hawaii), but very few flowers, except for the section devoted to orchids. Guided tours are organized from Mon to Fri at 1pm. Unfortunately, the garden is located near the freeway, which takes away from the serenity of the site. At the entrance, which faces the ticket office, is a small exhibit that displays a variety of the unusually shaped seeds of species featured in the garden.

To finish the tour, you can head up Nu'uanu Avenue by car to the Royal Mausoleum.

Located in a park trimmed with royal

John Young

Born in Liverpool, John Young was the boatswain on the *Eleanora* when, in 1790, the ship, which was filled with furs bought in Alaska, docked in Kealakekua Bay. The young man came on shore to get some provisions, but was captured by Kamehameha, who was in a war with his cousins for control of the island. Young soon became fond of his abductor, calling him Olohana and made him a Hawaiian chief. With the help of Isaac Davis, the only survivor on board the *Fair American,* they helped develop Kamehameha's military strategy by introducing western techniques to Hawaii. In particular, he taught the troops of the future king to use muskets and cannons, which insured their success in the attempt to unify the islands. Always at Kamehameha's side, John Young was then put in charge of building the fort of Honolulu and was named governor of the Big Island.

palms trees, the **Royal Mausoleum ★** *(free admission; Mon to Fri 8am to 4:30pm; 2261 Nu'uanu Ave.; Bus no. 4)* contains the remains of nearly all of the Hawaiian monarchs – except for Kamehameha, who was secretly buried on the Big Island. Originally placed inside the mausoleum, coffins were later placed into three crypts: one for descendants of Kamehameha, another for Kalahaua and a third for the Wyllie family (a former governor). There are also monuments dedicated to Kamehameha II, III, IV and V, near the one to Charles Reed Bishop, husband of Princess Bernice Pauahi and founder of the Bishop Museum. At the back of the chapel is the crypt of John Young, who died in 1835 at the age of 93 years.

Just across the Royal Mausoleum is a lovely wooden **Japanese house** *(2236 Nu'uana Ave)*, which has a two-tiered roof covered with lacquered tiles. Unfortunately, the building is not open to the public.

From the old Honolulu cemetery on the other

O'ahu

Hokule'a

Hokule'a was an important star to the ancient Hawaiian navigators. Meaning "Star of Gladness," this star reaches its zenith above Hawaii, and indicating that they had arrived at destination. Founded in 1973 to showcase the art of Polynesian navigation without way-finding instruments, the Polynesian Voyaging Society built its first vessel in 1976 and named it *Hokule'a*. Though constructed with modern materials, its design was based on the traditional double-hulled canoe. The *Hokule'a* embarked on its maiden voyage to Tahiti in 1976 and reached the island in only 30 days.

Since its maiden voyage, the *Hokule'a* has completed five other expeditions, sailing more than 62,000mi (100,000km) across the Pacific guided only by the night sky. One person in particular has become famous in this historic and spiritual quest: Nainoa Thompson, who eventually became chief navigator of the *Hokule'a*. In October 1999, he announced his decision to retire so that younger people could take his place. From the summer of 1999 to the beginning of 2000, the *Hokule'a* completed its final voyage, sailing from Hawaii to Easter Island via the Marquesas Islands. In 1995, the *Hawai'iloa*, built using traditional materials (of *koa* wood), completed its maiden voyage.

side of the street, you can see the peak of a large **Japanese pagoda**. To get a closer look, drive south down Craigside Place, a small side street that passes through a large field of Japanese gravestones. The pagoda is closed to the public since the site is poorly maintained. There is a temple beside the pagoda (also closed), which is surrounded by a pretty garden and a pool filled with swimming goldfish. The tranquility of the place almost makes you forget the noisy Pali Highway.

The Waterfront

(half-day to full day)

Discovered in the early 19th century by American and European commercial vessels en route to Asia, Honolulu Harbor quickly became an important port of call. Well aware of its influencial economic potential, Kamehameha III decided to make it his capital in 1850. By the end of the 19th century, nautical clubs sprung up in the port and regattas were often organized here. In 1911, Olympic surfing champion Duke Kahananmoku achieved his first world record off the shores of Honolulu Harbor. During the early 20th century, great ocean liners began making regular trips to Asia: Hawaii's tourism industry was born. Today, cruise ships still dock here, and the port has become the heart of Hawaii's economic powerhouse. Over 80% of goods consumed here still pass through Honolulu Harbor.

The **Aloha Tower** ★ *(free admission; Apr to Sep*

*every day 9am to 7:30pm,
Oct to Mar to 7pm; guided
tours at 11am and 1pm
departing from the infor-
mation booth; bus no. 19
or no. 20)* was built in
1926 so the harbour
captain could control
the port's traffic, the
arrival of passengers, as
well as the loading and
unloading of goods.
The great steamships
used to dock here – an
event that attracted a
large crowd. The Royal
Hawaiian Band greeted
new arrivals with mu-
sic, and *hula* dancers
put welcoming *leis*
around their necks.
Before leaving, visitors
took part in an unusual
ritual: they threw a
snake to a bystander on
the pier, who had to
hold it as long as possi-
ble. The Aloha Tower
is Hawaii's largest
tower and one of the
most important towers
in U.S. history. Ships
used to syncronize their
clocks with the tower,
when, at exactly noon
every day, a 4ft (1.2m)-
diametre sphere (called
a "time ball") was
dropped by an infalli-
ble mechanism. The
tower clock even ran
during the war years, at
which time it was cam-
ouflaged with army
colours. An elevator
goes up to the 10th
floor for a panoramic
view of downtown Ho-
nolulu and its skyscrap-
ers, Sand Island, the
harbour and the nearby
marine centre with its
old rigs. That's basically
the tower's only draw.

After the Second World
War, cruise ships were
again welcomed in the
same way, and every-
one rejoiced in the
festivities. The *S.S. Independence* leaves every
Sat at 9pm *(Pier 10)*. For
other departures, call
☎*566-2337*.

Beneath the tower is
the **Aloha Tower Market-
place**, a large shopping
centre built in 1994
with about 80 stores
(see p 189).

Located nearby at Pier
7 is the fascinating
**Hawaii Maritime
Center** ★ ★ ★ *($7.50
with audio-guide; every
day 8:30pm to 5pm;
☎536-6373; bus no. 19 or
no. 20)*, which has been
run by the Bishop Mu-
seum since 1994. It
traces Hawaii's seafar-
ing past from the colo-
nization by the Polyne-
sians to its rediscovery
by Captain Cook to the
modern era. The first
section displays objects
brought by the great
British explorer, the
story of his death on
the Big Island, the fur
trade (especially otter-
skins from Alaska) and
sandalwood.
Kamehameha's unifica-
tion of the islands is
presented in the histori-
cal context of the diplo-
matic manoeuvring
between England, Rus-
sia, France and the U.S.
The whaling industry is
also covered, with ex-
hibits displaying im-
pressive iron try-pots in
which fat was boiled,
and beautiful pieces of
scrimshaw (chiselled
and carved whale
teeth). The skeleton of
a humpback whale
hangs on the first floor,
above other sections
that are devoted to the
golden years of ocean
liners, with an entire
collection of trans-Pa-
cific line mementoes, as
well as an exhibit on
modern navigation and
flying boats. There's
also a film on *Hokule'a*'s
voyages, the first canoe
to travel from Tahiti to
Hawaii without the aid
of modern navigation
instruments.

The visit continues on
the main floor with a
beautiful collection of
traditional Hawaiian
objects, such as fishing
implements and tools,
on display in windows
shaped like huge
double-hulled canoes.
Don't miss the surfing
section where you'll
learn that the ancient
Hawaiians also surfed
on land! Right beside
the surfing exhibit is a
display devoted to
Hokule'a and the Poly-
nesian Voyaging Soci-
ety.

After going through the
museum, you can climb
the observation tower
which looks out onto
the *Falls of Clyde*, the
last four-mast ship to
sail the Hawaiian wa-
ters. Built in Glasgow
in 1878, it measures
266ft (81m) and trans-
ported all sorts of
goods, such as tea,
spices and sugar, be-
fore being converted
into an oil tanker in
1907. Just before it was
scheduled for sinking
in 1963, a group of
Hawaiians raised funds
to rescue and restore

O'ahu

the ship. Visitors can stroll the deck.

Usually moored at the pier but inaccessible to the public are the *Hokule'a* and the *Hawai'iloa*, both double-hulled Polynesian canoes, built using traditional materials and methods.

Sand Island faces Honolulu Harbor, only a few fathoms from the coast. During the First World War, an internment camp here "welcomed" several hundred Japanese-Hawaiians – a drop in the bucket compared to the 115,000 Japanese-Americans interned in a dozen or so camps across the U.S. Entirely artificial, the island is used as a base for the Coast Guard as well as a recreational park *(free admission; every day 7am to 6:45pm; washrooms, camping)*, which is frequented by Hawaiian families on weekends. The beach is nothing to write home about and few tourists come here, although Hawaiians find in it some of the tranquillity lost on other beaches of O'ahu. The eastern point of the island has a panoramic view of the downtown skyscrapers, with the Aloha Tower and the Maritime Center buildings in the foreground. The only way to get here is via a circuitous route – and it's not really worth the effort. But if you insist on doing so, follow Nimitz Highway to the

western exit of Honolulu, and then take Sand Island Access Road (no. 64) to the end.

East of the port, Ala Moana Boulevard passes the complex of stores and restaurants known as Restaurant Row (see p 165), and then the Ward Centers, consisting of five shopping centres (see p 189). Facing the Ward Centres is the Kewalo Harbor, which was the tuna-industry base in the early 1900s. An auction takes place here at 5am every morning. Shortly before Waikiki, the boulevard leads to the huge Ala Moana Center, the largest shopping centre in Hawaii (see p 189).

Ala Moana Center is located opposite a large 74 acre (30ha) public park, which is bordered by **Ala Moana Beach** ★★ (washrooms, outdoor showers, volleyball court, tennis courts). Ala Moana is a recent expression that means "path to the sea." The beautiful strand of artificial beach runs along the lawn and juts out along the peninsula of **Aina Moana** ★★ *(washrooms, picnic tables, water fountains)*, also known as Magic Island. The park is located across from the Waikiki Yachting Harbour at the mouth of the Ala Wai Canal. Closed to traffic, the park is a vast recreation area with inviting picnic tables on a grassy lawn. A cy-

cling path runs alongside a walking path all the way to the point. There's another beach at the point, almost entirely closed by a pier, which makes swimming there not as interesting. Most people prefer the lovely cove formed at the base of the peninsula; the water here is calm and shallow.

★★★

Bishop Museum

(half-day to full day)

From the H1 Freeway west of Honolulu, take Kalihi Street *mauka* (away from the sea), then turn right at MM1 onto Bernice Street.

The **Bishop Museum** *($15, $12 children from four to 12, family packages $40 for one or two adults and unlimited number of children under 17; every day 9am to 5pm; guided tours every 20min from 10am to 3pm; 1525 Bernice St., ☎847-3511, www.bishopmuseum.org, bus no. 2)* is a must-see. Dedicated to the history of Hawaii and the Pacific, it was founded in 1889 by Charles Reed Bishop in memory of his wife, Princess Bernice Pauahi Bishop, the last direct descendant of Kamehameha the Great. Visited by more than a million people every year, it was originally devoted to the Hawaiian islands only, but it soon began to focus on the rest of the great ocean,

Feathers

In ancient times, feathers symbolized the spiritual power and the social status of the person who wore them. The red, yellow and black *mahiole* (helmets) and *'ahu'ula* (cloaks) made from feathers collected from forest birds were worn by the most important chiefs. Women, on the other hand, wore feather *lei* around their necks and heads. To catch the birds, the Hawaiians used the natural tar from the seeds of a bougainvillea species or a mix of *kukui* nuts and resin from the bread tree. They coated the branches of a tree with it and waited until an *'i'iwi*, an *'apapane* or a *mamo* landed. After plucking part of its feathers, they would clean the bird and then release it alive.

eventually amassing the world's finest collection of Pacific artwork with more than one million artifacts and 21 million animals specimens (insects and shells mostly). Wildlife educational programs were set up from the get-go. Today, the museum continues to educate

and protect the Hawaiian biotope.

The museum also houses Hawaii's only planetarium. Its Hawaiian Hall is dedicated to the history and natural sciences of Hawaii, while the Polynesian Hall, next door, is devoted to all the cultures of the Pacific – which are all housed in the same building made of volcanic rock. The Castle Memorial Building and several annexes (such as the Paki Hall, which features Hawaii's Sports Hall of Fame and a shell collection) all have excellent temporary exhibits. Unfortunately, the buildings are in a state of disrepair.

Just right of the entrance, the **Planetarium** ★ has a small exhibit on traditional Polynesian navigation techniques and the origins of the islands' population. Films are shown three times a day *(11:30am, 1:3pm and 3pm)* on the same theme. The exhibit also illustrates how the Polynesians used the movement of the stars to determine their distance from the horizon, their position in relation to the horizon and their latitude. Nainoa Thomson, the most famous of the new Hawaiian navigators, spent many days here in his quest to rediscover the trail of his ancestors. It's a pity that the show ends with a section devoted

to U.S. space exploration. Although this is an appropriate topic for a planetarium, it doesn't have much to do with the rest of the exhibit. A new planetarium as well as an IMAX theatre are planned to open in the future.

The Polynesian Hall faces the entrance in the main building. The room on the right is dedicated to traditional Hawaiian activities: bone and stone carving, *lauhala* (the leaf of the hala tree) weaving, quilting, flower and seed *lei* (garland) making and other traditional crafts. The activities change, but there's at least one per day *(9am to 2pm)*.

The museum was recently in the process of relocating some of its objects to other rooms. Last time we were there, we noticed a wicker representation of the war god Kuka'ilimoku just before entering the next room. He's depicted with a gnarly dog-like smile and is covered in feathers.

The **Hawaiian Hall** ★★★ has three
floors covering the cultural history of Hawaii. It is also the home of a giant sperm-whale skeleton. The main floor definitely has the most beautiful collection of Hawaiian artifacts in the world, a few of which deserve particular mention. The large sculpture depict-

O'ahu

ing Ku (the god of war) made of 'ohi'a wood (end of the 18th century) probably stood on a *luakini heiau*, a temple where human sacrifices took place. There are two lithographs by Jacques Arago entitled "Killing a Criminal" and "Strangling a Criminal," a collection of *kapa* (the bark-cloth also known as *tapa*), as well as some wood dishes (including a waste bowl made out of driftwood and inlaid with human teeth – quite the insult to the donor!). On a magnificent carved *koa* platter stands the representation of a defeated chief and his wife, whose open mouths served as condiment containers. This is followed by a display of musical instruments, and a beautiful collection of feather *leis*. But the most impressive display has to be the *'ahu'ula* and the *mahiole*. The *'ahu'ula* is a cloak consisting of thousands of red and black feathers from three endemic birds, the *'i'iai*, the *'o'o* and the *mamo*. The *mahiole* is a feather helmet. Before going upstairs, take a look at another section dedicated to the three Hawaiian rulers and Queen Lili'uokalani, the last monarch of Hawaii. A *hula* show is presented in this room every day between 11am and 2pm.

On the first floor are collections of objects, not all of them Hawai-

ian. Like the rest of the museum, the displays here lack unity, and the quality of the objects doesn't make up for the rather trite cultural and historical presentations.

The second floor is entirely devoted to the contributions of immigrants who made Hawaii their home: Germans, Portuguese, Spanish, Puerto Ricans, Filipinos, Koreans, Okinawans, Chinese and Japanese (this large section has samurai armour and beautiful kimonos). The collections include objects used by the immigrants on a daily basis, as well some ancient historic pieces, which seem a bit out of place in this context.

In the same building, the **Polynesian Hall** ★★★ is dedicated to the arts of the Pacific rim cultures, including Melanesia, Micronesia and especially Polynesia. This section – one of the most fascinating parts of the museum – is filled with priceless treasures. Among the centrepieces of the collection, don't miss the magnificent Tahitian mourning costume, worn by the great priest or relative after the death of a chief, the stunning wooden statuettes from Easter Island, the Melanesian ceremonial masks, the superb Papua New Guinean dagger with an obsidian blade and the large, red feather money roll from the Solomon Is-

lands (which was, until recently, used for marriages and purchasing pigs). The second floor contains objects from Fiji, Tonga, the Samoas and New Zealand (with two beautiful stone puzzles). A small window has an interesting display of different types of traditional currency used in the Pacific: shells in Micronesia and the Solomon Islands, tortoise shells from Palau and stones from Yap. There's also a natural-history section connected to the second floor of the Hawaiian Hall. Before leaving the building, take a peek in the room situated to the left of the main entrance. This exhibit is devoted to royal insignia, with Lili'uokalani's horse-drawn carriage and a collection of *kahili* (feather sceptres that symbolize the *ali'i*).

If you have any energy left, head to the **Castle Memorial Building** ★★, which showcases temporary exhibitions. The most recent and very interesting displays, entitled "Backyard Aliens," were dedicated to invasive plants that threaten the Hawaiian ecosystem and to the history of Waikiki. Some of the past exhibitions covered the Japanese and Filipino heritage of Hawaii. To educate the young and captivate their interest, museum organizers have often used interactive displays. Hawaii's Music Hall of

Fame is upstairs. Along the same lines, Hawaii's Sports Hall of Fame is housed in Paki Hall, which is situated behind the main building. Unless you're really an avid sports and music buff, you might as well bypass this section.

★
The University Area and Honolulu Heights

(one day)

To escape the hustle and bustle of the coast and to breathe in some fresh, cool air, do as the Hawaiians do: head for the hills. Lush wilderness and panoramic views await.

On the Manoa Valley Road, you can stop by the large campus of the **University of Hawai'i**, which has about 20,000 students and more than 90 fields of study. It is home to a museum and several exposition halls. At one of the checkpoints, you can purchase a $3 card that allows you to park for free and explains how to get to the different attractions, which are free on Sunday. However, this doesn't guarantee that you'll find parking since many of the spaces are reserved for students and staff during the day. If you can't find any spots, head to the parking lot on the southern campus on Dole Street. Bus no. 4 goes from Waikiki to the university.

Situated in Krauss Hall, the **John Young Museum of Art** *(Tue 10am to 1pm, Fri noon to 3pm and Sun from 1pm to 4pm; 2500 Dole St.,* ☎*956-5666, www.outreach.hawaii.edu/JYMuseum)* is the first campus museum and was opened in 1999. Contrary to what one might think, the museum doesn't get its name from Kamehameha's famous English advisor; rather, it was named in honour of the Chinese-Hawaiian painter who passed away in 1997 and bequeathed a portion of his personal collection. There you will see many ancient Chinese and Korean artifacts as well as a few works from Japan and southeastern Asia. The Pacific region is also represented by some beautiful Papau New Guinean, Maori and Melanesian pieces.

Located in the arts department, the **University of Hawaii Art Gallery** *(free admission; late Aug to mid-May Mon to Fri 10:30am to 4pm, Sun noon to 4pm;* ☎*956-6888, www.hawaii.edu/artgallery)* houses some decent temporary exhibits. The subject matter varies from history to contemporary art (Asian costumes, icons and the like).

The **East-West Center** *(free admission; open during exhibits Mon to Fri 8am to 5pm, Sun noon to 4pm; 1601 East-West Road* ☎*944-7111)* was established to promote mutual understanding among the East and the West. It organizes temporary drawing, painting and ceramic exhibits with one specific country featured. The exhibitions take place in the John A. Burns Hall on East-West Road east of the campus. It's best to call in advance to inquire about the program.

The university is not far from the **Manoa Valley** ★★, nicknamed the "Rainbow Valley." Rainbows are a frequent occurrence here, resulting from the extreme difference in precipitation between the coast in Honolulu and the heart of this vast amphitheatre of lush, hilly terrain. The beautiful Princess Kahalaopuna (a creation of ancient Hawaiian poets), the daughter of the wind and rain gods, was said to have been assassinated here by a jealous lover. She was then brought back to life by the Pueo owl, *'aumakua* ("protective spirit"). Kings sought refuge here, and later on, a flux of immigration brought a large population of Japanese who planted fields of taro, which they used to made *poi* (taro paste). At the turn of the 20th century, the first settlers had already left, and Manoa eventually became a well-to-do residential neighbourhood of Honolulu. Today, there are many homes in the valley;

O'ahu

only the Upper Manoa Valley remains relatively untouched.

First head up University mauka. *When the street name changes to O'ahu, continue straight ahead, and then turn right onto Manoa Road.*

A trail runs along the Manoa Stream amid a lush, damp tropical forest before ending at the lovely **Manoa Falls ★★**. Although rocky in some places, the trail is relatively easy to follow, especially since it was covered with gravel so that hikers wouldn't slide on the mud after the daily rainfall. After about a 20min gradual climb, you arrive at the waterfall which gently flows along a cliff and then spills into a shallow pool at its base. Many hikers cool off in the pool here despite the temperature of the water. If you come here in the springtime, the ground will be covered with pink stamen from the trees surrounding the end of the path, which has the peculiar common name "Red-capped gum" (indigenous to the Indian Ocean). Be sure not to leave any valuables in your car at the foot of the trail.

Just before the road ends, it makes a sharp turn towards the **Harold L. Lyon Arboretum ★** *(suggested donation $1; Mon to Sat 9am to 5pm, 3860 Manoa Rd., ☎988-0456, bus no. 5 then a 0.6mi or 1km walk)*, which belongs to the University of Hawaii and is renowned for its hybridization experiments. The park is the result of a reforestation project that began in 1918 in the area that had been stripped clean by livestock. This is exactly how one usually imagines Hawaii's forests, with their intertwined, sprawling fruit-bearing trees and an abundance of flowering plants. However, nothing here is untouched. The arboretum is an excellent example of the dispersion of plant species around the world (by human intervention) and their propagation in the fragile Hawaiian ecosystem.

Over a 30-year period, some 2,000 plants have been introduced here. Amid the tangle of vegetation, related species are clustered together: herbs, the Demonstration Garden with ferns and bromeliads, the palm garden, the Hawaiian section and the fruit-bearing tree section. The trails that run through these last two sections are muddy, but they lead up to a breathtaking lookout called Inspiration Point. You'll probably catch a glimpse of (or hear) cockatoos, which escaped from an animal park and then made the valley their home. Visitors are asked to sign in at the reception centre, where you can obtain a map of the trails that crisscross the park.

Before leaving the Manoa Valley, enjoy a snack or a cup of tea at the **Wai'oli Tea Room ★**, *(see p 178, bus no. 5)*, a tea room that dates from 1922. Next door is a charming **chapel** with modern stained-glass windows depicting Biblical scenes *à la* Hawaiian.

*In front of Panahou High School, turn from Manoa Road onto Nehoa Street, which quickly crosses Makiki Street. Head up Nehoa Street mauka; at the top of the hill is Round Top Drive, which makes a large loop through Honolulu Heights and offers spectacular **views** of the coast.*

The entrance to **Pu'u 'Ualaka State Park** *(every day 7am to 6:45pm)* is 2.5mi (4km) up Round Top Drive; keep to the left when the road forks. Drive past the first parking lot and continue to the end of the road, from where you can enjoy an incredible panoramic view of Honolulu. The airport and Punchbowl are on the right; Waikiki and Diamond Head are on the left. Down below, the Manoa Valley, which is dotted with houses on its lower slopes, disappears into the Ko'olau mountains.

The main road continues the climb up to dense forests at the **Maikiki Tantalus**

Reserve ★, whose slopes are usually cloud-covered and rainy while Waikiki basks in sunshine. At around Mile 5 or 6, Round Top Drive becomes Tantalus Drive, where the road begins to descend. The entire area is crisscrossed with wonderful hiking trails. The only problem is that you'll be walking through mud most of the time. On the return trip, philodendrons, bamboo, mango and giant *kukui* (candlenut) trees, eucalyptus, passifloras and elephant-ear taro are easily identified midst the dense tropical growth. Farther down below, you'll catch a glimpse of some houses.

Ohia-lehua

After driving 9.3mi (15km) on Tantalus Drive, turn left onto Makiki Heights Drive.

The **Contemporary Museum** ★ *($5; Tue to Sat 10am to 4pm, Sun noon to 4pm; guided tours every day at 1:30pm; 2411 Makiki Heights Dr., ☎526-1322, www.tcmhi.org; bus no. 15)* is 450yds (500m) farther, on the left-hand side. Housed in the former residence of Anna Cooke, who bequeathed the home

to the town after her death, the museum holds a small collection of modern art from the 1940s up to today, including a portrait by David Hockney inspired by Maurice Ravel's composition entitled *L'Enfant et les Sortilèges* (The Child and the Magic Spell). There are also some temporary exhibits that display some of the museum's inventory. However, most of the works announced in the brochures were not all on display at the time due to a lack of space. The most impressive exhibit has to be the great tropical garden, which is adorned with sculptures. The embankment offers a magnificent view of Honolulu and Waikiki. You can have breakfast here in this peaceful setting at the Contemporary Cafe *(Tue to Sat 11m to 2pm, Sun noon to 2pm)*.

If you have the time, you can end your visit to the Honolulu Heights with a tour of Punchbowl. To get here, head down Tantalus Drive above the fork that leads to the Modern Art Museum. Turn left at the fifth street down Puowaiana Drive.

Perched above downtown Honolulu, the **Punchbowl National Me-**

morial Cemetery of the Pacific ★ *(free admission; Oct to Feb every day 8am to 5:30pm, Mar to Sep until 6:30pm; 2177 Puowaina Dr., ☎566-1430, bus no. 15)* stands in the former Puowaian crater, which the early Hawaiians called "the hill of sacrifices." In ancient times, this is where the *ali'i* were buried and the *kapu* breakers were strangled. The tombs of 33,143 men and women who died during the Pacific and Korean wars are simply marked with crosses, and stand in rows at the foot of a memorial that bears the names of more than 26,000 service personnel listed as missing in action. At the entrance is a small orientation centre, which houses a small Second World War photo exhibit and a biography of Ernest Pyle, the distinguished war correspondent who was killed during the final days of the war. Some also come here to pay their respects to astronaut Ellison Onizuka, the Big Island native who perished in the 1986 Challenger disaster, while others come here simply to enjoy the beautiful view of Honolulu, the coast and Diamond Head, which stands out in the east. To get to Punchbowl from downtown, head north down Queen Emma Street. Just past the bridge above the freeway, turn left on Lusitana Street. Puowaina Drive, which is on your right, leads to the turnoff for the monument.

★★★
Waikiki

(one day)

The "most famous beach of the Pacific" is only a stone's throw from Honolulu. Bordered by Diamond Head to the east and Ala Wai Yacht Harbor to the west, the entire area, which is covered with buildings and palm trees, only measures 0.6 sq mi (1.8km²)! More than five million tourists cram into this small space every year, and its hundreds of hotels, restaurants and stores employ more than 39,000 people – with annual revenues of more than $5 billion US.

Waikiki has long since lost its meaning, "gushing waters," in reference to the springs that once flowed behind its narrow beachfront and vast swamps where Hawaiians planted taro patches, and later, in the 19th century, rice paddies. Well before the 20th century, Waikiki Beach was the early Hawaiians' preferred spot. The most important figures of the state, including Queen Ka'ahumanu, Kamehameha's favourite wife, could be seen here. For this reason, many *ali'i* built homes here. The most famous estate was called Kalehuawele, "take off the *lehua*," in reference to the legendary hero who took off his flower *lei* and gave it to the wife of a chief with whom he was surfing. More and more homes were built over the

● ATTRACTIONS

1. Kahanamoku Beach	8. Kapahulu Groin
2. Fort de Russy Beach	9. Queen's Surf Beach
3. U.S. Army Museum of Hawai'i	10. Honolulu Zoo
4. Halekulani Beach	11. Kapi'olani Park
5. Central Waikiki Beach	12. Waikiki Aquarium
6. Kuhio Beach	13. Sans Souci Beach
7. Damien Museum	

○ ACCOMMODATIONS

1. Aston Waikiki Circle Hotel	21. Queen Kapi'olani Hotel
2. Banana Bungalow	22. Royal Grove
3. Coconut Plaza Hotel	23. Royal Hawaiian
4. Ewa Hotel	24. Seaside Hostel
5. Halekulani (R)	25. Sheraton Moana Surfrider (R)
6. Hawaiiana Hotel	26. Sheraton Waikiki Hotel
7. Hawaii Polo Inn	27. The Breakers
8. Hawaiian Waikiki Beach Hotel	28. Waikiki Beach Tower
9. Hilton Hawaiian Village (R)	29. Waikiki Beachside Hostel & Hotel
10. Holiday Inn Waikiki	30. Waikiki Beachside Hotel
11. Hostelling International	31. Waikiki Grand Hotel
12. Hotel Hale Pua Nui	32. Waikiki Joy Hotel
13. Hotel Honolulu	33. Waikiki Hana Hotel
14. Hyatt Regency Waikiki (R)	34. Waikiki Parc Hotel (R)
15. Ilima Hotel	35. Waikiki Prince Hotel
16. Imperial of Waikiki	36. Waikiki Sand Villa Hotel
17. Island Hostel & Hotel	37. Waikiki Surf Ohana
18. Ohana Coral Seas	38. Waikiki Village Ohana
19. Outrigger Islander Waikiki	39. Winston's Waikiki Condos
20. Polynesian Hostel Beach Club	
	(R) Property with restaurant (see description)

● RESTAURANTS

1. Acqua	11. Nick's Fishmarket
2. Arancino	12. Oceanarium
3. Cha Cha Cha	13. Padovani's Bistro & Wine Bar
4. Cheeseburger in Paradise	14. Perry's Smorgy
5. Duke's Canoe Club	15. Shore Bird Beach Broiler
6. Eggs'n Things	16. Singha Thai Restaurant
7. Fatty's Chinese Kitchen	17. Sushi Koh
8. International Marketplace	18. Tanaka of Tokyo
9. Keo's	19. Top of Waikiki
10. Moose McGillycuddy's	20. Trattoria Restaurant

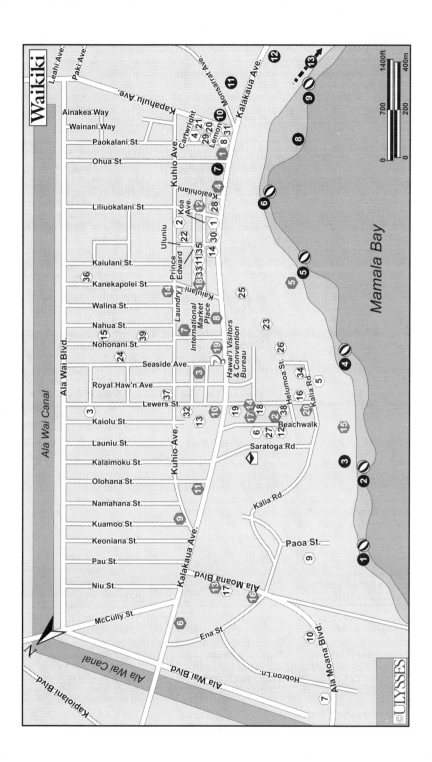

Waïkïkï

Leahi Ave.
Paki Ave.
Kapahulu Ave.
Ainakea Way
Wainani Way
Paokalani St.
Ohua St.
Liliuokalani St.
Kaiulani St.
Kanekapolei St.
Walina St.
Nahua St.
Nohonani St.
Kaiolu St.
Launiu St.
Kalaimoku St.
Olohana St.
Namahana St.
Kuamoo St.
Keoniana St.
Pau St.
Niu St.
McCully St.

Monsarrat Ave.
Cartwright
Lemon
Koa Ave.
Kealohilani
Uluniu
Prince Edward
Kaiulani
Ala Wai Blvd.
Seaside Ave.
Royal Haw'n Ave.
Lewers St.
Kuhio Ave.
Kalakaua Ave.
Ala Moana Blvd.
Ena St.
Hobron Ln.

Ala Wai Canal
Kapiolani Blvd.
Ala Wai Blvd.
Ala Wai Canal

Kalakaua Ave.
Kuhio Ave.
Kalakaua Ave.

International Market Place
Laundry
Hawai'i Visitors & Convention Bureau
Helumoa St.
Kalia Rd.
Beachwalk
Saratoga Rd.
Kalia Rd.
Paoa St.

Mamala Bay

0   700   1400ft
0   200   400m

© ULYSSES

N

years, and, during the second half of the 19th century, the first tourists, who were Victorian to the bone, arrived. A few small hotels sprung up on the beaches, including the Sans Souci Hotel, where Robert Louis Stevenson spent five weeks in 1893. Others like him came here to paint the perfect picture of paradise, which the entire continent would soon dream about. In 1904, a tramline was constructed to connect Waikiki to downtown Honolulu, where cruise ships were already docked. The Moana Hotel opened its doors, and meanwhile, Hawaiian music was taking the world by storm with its languorous rhythms evoking the gentle trade winds and palm trees.

Modern Waikiki took root in 1922 when the Ala Wai Canal was dug to divert the streams, which flowed into Waikiki, and the water was drained out of the swamps. Six years later, Waikiki became an artificial island. Over the course of several years of successive construction, a concrete watershed was eventually built. Recent construction has modified the coastal point to divert the spring from the huge waves, which used to surge here. In the past, the waves used to reach more than 33ft (10m) high; today, however, they rarely surpass 6.5ft (2m). Novice surfers won't complain, and even the more experienced ones still enjoy its wide waves, which can be over 330ft (100m) long. The world surfing record was achieved here by the eminent Duke Kahanamoku, Hawaii's patron son and multiple Olympic medal winner, who surfed on a 33ft (10m) wave here for more than 3mi (2km)!

The watershed has started to show its age, so in 1999, a series of private and public development projects were launched.

Give credit when credit is due: **Kahanamoku Beach ★★**, where the famous Duke learned to surf, is a wonderful place for surfing – something you have to try at least once in your lifetime. The Duke's maternal grandfather, descendant of an *al'i* family, obtained the land from Kamehameha III during the Great Mahele ("Division of Lands"). Today, the impressive Hilton Hawaiian Village stands here. The beach, which is watched over by a strip of coconut trees, seems timeless – the only thing that matters is the present, that magical moment when the visitor discovers white sand and warm sea.

A walking path runs along the length of the beach and ends in the west at the Ala Wai Yacht Harbor. The Aina Moana Peninsula (Magic Island) and Ala Moana Beach (see p 145) are on the other side of the Ala Wai Yacht Harbor. Head in the opposite direction towards Diamond Head. The border between Kahanamoku Beach and **Fort De Russy Beach ★★**, which is a good place for swimming, is not that obvious. The beach borders a pleasant little park that offers shade beneath trees, picnic tables, beach volleyball courts and games for children. And behind the park is the Fort De Russey Military Reservation, which houses the **U.S. Army Museum of Hawaii ★** *(free admission, Tue to Sun 10am to 4:30pm, audio guides $3 from 10am to 2pm)*. The museum traces the military history of Hawaii from the time of its unification to today. Although the theme is based on war and the slant is obviously American, you can nevertheless learn some interesting things here. It showcases some ancient weapons and a superb puzzle made from shark teeth. There's also an exhibit about Hawaii's annexation by the U.S. and its expansion into the Pacific, the beginnings of aviation and the tensions leading up to the Second World War. This last section, which covers the attack on

Pearl Harbor and Hawaii's passage through a period of martial law, is explored in great detail. The entire island, Waikiki included, was surrounded with barbed wire to prevent a Japanese invasion by land. The sensational military treatment of some exhibits, such as the M2A1 flame-thrower, glamorize war. This is infinitely regretful. The tour then ends with a section on the Vietnam War.

East of the Fort De Russy beach, the pedestrian walkway disappears into the sand. The coast narrows into a thin strip of beach known as Gray's Beach, or **Halekulani Beach** – the name of the deluxe hotel that borders it. This is not the best place for swimming, but a few old *hau* trees, with low, intertwined branches, offer sun worshippers a shady reprieve. Near the Waikiki Sheraton, the beach is so narrow that it virtually disappears at high tide.

Farther east, the beach widens again and the most beautiful beach of

the seaside resort appears, simply known as **Central Waikiki Beach ★★**. The beach stretches out in front of the two luxury resorts, the pink Royal Hawaiian and the Sheraton Moana Surfrider. This is an ideal spot for swimming, boogie boarding, surfing, sailing and even canoeing.

At the point where Kalakua Avenue veers toward the coast, the hotels stand farther back from the beach. **Kuhio Beach ★★**, one of the most pleasant beaches to swim at in Waikiki, begins here. The place is named after Prince Jonah Kuhio Kalaniana'ole Pi'ikoi, the Territory of Hawaii's delegate to the U.S. Congress from 1902 until his death in 1922. He is known for

initiating the Hawaiian Home Lands project. He lived here in a home called Pualeilani, "flower from the wreath of Heaven." After his death in 1922, the property was bequeathed to the city. Today, it is the only stretch of beach not

flanked by a concrete wall.

In the morning, the new arrivals have blissful smiles on their faces as they discover under the coconut trees the bronze **statue of Duke Kahanamoku ★**. There are usually one or several fine *lei* around his neck or out stretched arms. Four sacred stones, installed on a *paepae* (platform) and protected by a barrier, stand near his feet. Called Na pohaku ola Kapaemahu a Kapuni by the Hawaiians, these sacred **Wizard Stones** commemorate the visit of four great *kahuna ho'oli* (healers), Kapaemahu, Kapuni, Kinohi and Kahaloa, who came from Tahiti around the 15th century. After spending several years on the islands, they gave the Hawaiians a gift: four stones to which, during a ceremony when a young *ali'i* girl had to be sacrificed, they gave their *mana* (spiritual power). Legend has it that the stones were brought here from Kaimuki in one night, a town situated 5mi (3km) away, and that the largest one weighed nearly 7.5 tonnes. Every afternoon, just a few steps away on the concrete tables, people play chess and cards here.

With its spire towering above Kalahaua Avenue, St. Augustine's Catholic Church marks the **Damien Museum** (*free*

Statue of Duke Kahanamoku

admission; Mon to Fri 9am to 3pm; 130 Ohua Ave., ☎923-2690), devoted to Father Damien, the Belgian priest who is famed for his work at the leprosy colony at Kalaupapa on Moloka'i. This small museum displays liturgical objects, tools, old photos, the colony's register of baptisms and marriages, a few of Father Damien's personal possessions, as well as a wooden chest made from *koa*, in which one of his relics was brought from Belgium to Hawaii. There is also a 20min video presentation.

Kapahalu Groin, the pier that demarcates the second basin of Kuhio Beach, is the favourite spot of boogie boarders in Waikiki. Although the beach on its eastern border is called **Queen's Surf ★**, boogie boarders call it Graveyards because of the pier they have to avoid crashing into. One of the widest beaches in Waikiki, it is bordered by a walkway and Kapi'olani Beach Park, which has a pleasant picnic area.

If you feel like it, cross Kalahaua Avenue at Kapahalu Groin and head to the **Honolulu Zoo** *($6, $1 children from six to 12; every day 9am to 5:30pm, doors close at 4:30; 151 Kapahulu Ave., ☎971-7195)*, which was inaugurated in 1916 with the arrival of a young and gentle elephant named Daisy.

The fauna, which includes African animals, tigers, alligators, tropical Hawaiian birds, *nene* (the national goose) as well as a recent addition of Komodo dragons, is varied and well looked after. This 42 acre (17ha) zoo has been designed to re-create the natural habitat of the animals (especially the African Kabuni Reserve). A few days per month, you can visit the zoo under the moonlight *($9, 6:30pm to 8:30pm)* and even camp there *($35)*.

The vast **Kapi'olani Park** stretches out in front of the zoo, bordered by Waikiki's hotels to the west and Diamond Head's ridges to the east. King Kalakaua opened it in 1877 and dedicated it to his wife, Queen Kapi'olani. There used to be a racetrack for horses and some ornamental gardens here. The same day the U.S. annexed the Hawaiian islands (August 12, 1898), American troops settled here and established Camp McKinley, but abandoned it in 1907. Although there were only 75 cars on the island at the time, the former horese racetrack became a racetrack for cars, and shortly thereafter, it became home to one of the first aerodromes in Hawaii. Sports complexes and a large spectator area have since replaced the aerodrome.

In the years following the Second World War, the Waikiki Shell, an outdoor amphitheatre, was opened in the park. Since 1969, tourists have poured into the building to watch the festive **Kodak Hula Show ★★** *(free admission; Tue to Thu 10am, ☎537-2927)*. Having begun in 1937 as a promotional venture on Sans Souci Beach, this fairly stereotypical – but true all the same – *hula* show presents the different styles of Polynesian dances. The show lasts about one 1hr and the last 10 minutes are devoted to photo shoots with the dancers. Be sure to arrive on time as latecomers must wait until the end of the first scene before entering.

Along the waterfront walkway is the **Waikiki Aquarium ★** *($7, free for children under 12; every day 9am to 5pm; 2777 Kalakauna Ave., ☎923-9741)*, which was founded in 1904 and is renowned for its marine-study programs. Its "farm" can grow some 75 varieties of coral from branches gathered in nature (the most prolific species can grow up to 17in or 8cm per year). The aquarium also breeds nautiluses, an extremely rare mollusc that has a unique spiral-chambered shell, lives at great depths and has been traced back to prehistoric times. There are two research areas here as well as some more traditional aquariums presenting dozens of fish species from the Pacific. The fish are divided according to the type of coral reef they are found in, and classified according to their diet. The exhibit also touches on the biology of coral and sharks, as well as the problems of pollution and the destruction of their habitat. Outside you'll find two monk seals splashing about in a pool.

The walkway ends in front of a decaying building, the **Natatorium**, a saltwater swimming pool that opened in 1921 for a competition between Duke Kahanamoku, Johnny Weissmuler and his successor in the role of Tarzan, Buster Crabbe. It is now in a state of disrepair after many years of neglect. The government planned to level the facility, but an organization intervened. The first stage of restoration has already been finished, and the four eagles of the monument arch have been given a new lease on life. For the time being, however, the pool remains closed and its future is uncertain.

Just east of the Natatorium, the **Sans Souci Beach** ★★ is an escape

from the main tourist scene of Waikiki beach. Robert Louis Stevenson, the renowned author of *Treasure Island*, stayed here for several weeks during his stop on the island at the end of the 19th century.

The last part of the tour is by car and can very well make up a separate trip. Between the zoo and Kapi'olani Park, take Montsarrat Avenue, which soon becomes Diamond Head Road. Just after the Kapi'olani Community College, take the turnoff on the right through the tunnel to Diamond Head.

Situated southeast of Waikiki, **Diamond Head** ★★★ *(every day 6am to 6pm, bus no. 58)* is undeniably Hawaii's most famous landmark. The crater, which has a diameter of 0.6mi (1km), was formed by a violent residual explosion about 300,000 years ago, a relatively recent geological event considering that O'ahu was formed three million years ago. It mostly consists of tuffs, which are volcanic ashes and particles fused together by the rain and wind. Thousands of years of erosion have already claimed 100ft (30m) of the crater. Diamond

Silversword

Head gets its name from the British sailors who found calcite crystals here in the early 19th century and mistakenly thought they were diamonds. The Hawaiians called the volcano Le'ahi, which can either be translated by "wreath of fire" (in reference to beacons lit on the summit to guide their canoes as they approached the coast), or by "brow of the 'ahi fish"(tuna), in reference to the way it looks from Waikiki.

Once with a lake and fields, today Diamond Head is a dried basin overgrown with shrubs. The U.S. Army occupied the crater in 1906 and quickly drained the basin to build Fort Ruger, which was protected by the walls of the crater. They built artillery on the rim and inside of the crater, as well as an observation post at the summit, which still stands today. But it's been a silent sentinel whose guns have never fired – even during the Second World War. Nevertheless, the crater remained off-limits until 1976, when one section was opened to the public. Today, more than one million visitors come every year to admire the panoramic view of Waikiki from Diamond Head.

There are washrooms, a telephone and drinking water at the foot of the 0.6mi (1km) trail (20-25min), which

O'ahu

climbs up to 558ft (170m). Built by the military in 1908 to service their observation stations, the first part of the trail is paved, and then less so as you climb higher up. Halfway up is a series of 72 steps leading to a long, dark tunnel whose curves hide the exit. When you come back out into daylight, you will see an abandoned artillery. A spiral staircase continues into an unlit bunker and then leads to the upper platform. A flashlight will come in handy here. Your journey comes to an end after the 52 final steps that lead to the summit at 761ft (232m), where there's a fantastic view of the crater and the mountains in one direction, whose lower slopes are dotted with homes, and Waikiki, Kap'olani Park and the Diamond Head lighthouse in the other direction. A *heiau* (an ancient place of worship) dedicated to the god of wind once stood at this site to pray to him that the beacons used to guide the canoes would not go out. To avoid the oppressive heat and crowds, the best time to make the climb is at sunrise or at the end of the day.

As you finish the Diamond Head tour by the north, you reach the coast along Fort Ruger Park. On your left, Kahala Road leads to the chic residential area of the same name,

while on your right, Diamond Head Road heads back to Waikiki. Along the way are breathtaking views of the sea and the coral reefs near the coast. During good weather, the sea is an intense turquoise colour. The road soon reaches the **Diamond Head lighthouse**, which was put in operation in 1899 and is now automated. Ships as far as 17mi (27km) away from the island can spot its light. Just east of the lighthouse, a path goes down to the beach, a haven for surfers and windsurfers.

Pearl Harbor

(Half-day)

Exit Honolulu via the H1 Freeway, then take the turnoff for Highway 78 West (Aiea/Pearlridge).

On the road to Pearl Harbor, you can stop for a few minutes or enjoy a picnic at the **Moanalua Gardens** *(free admission; Exit no. 3 Puuloa Road/Tripler Hospital from Highway 78 West)*. The gardens are in fact a large public park whose serenity is somewhat disturbed by the nearby highway. On the left side of the basin is a well-maintained taro plantation, which is nestled at the foot of Kamehameha V's former residence.

You can also take another route to get to the Honolulu forest at **Keaiwa Heiau State Park**

(washrooms, picnic tables and barbecue pits, camping -- see p 164; every day 7am to 6:45pm in winter, 7:45pm in summer). The *ho'ola heiau*, planted with *ti*, situated just left of the park entrance, is not that impressive but used to be renowned for the power of its healing *kahuna*. It was probably built around the 16th century. Most visitors come here to enjoy a family picnic on the weekend or to go hiking under the canopy of large trees. The Aiea Loop Trail (4.8mi or 7.7km) departs from the summit (past the campground) and is a popular spot for a day hike. To get to the park, exit Highway 78 West at the Stadium Area exit. The junction is called Moanalua Road. Aiea Heights Road, the third road on your right, climbs 2.5mi (4km) to the park.

To get to Pearl Harbor, take the same exit as for the Keaiwa Heiau State Park (Stadium Area) from Highway 78 West. However, instead of continuing straight, take the road to the south on Highway 99 East to the park. Another option is to come directly via the H1 Freeway, take the 15A exit to Highway 99 West towards the Arizona Memorial and not Pearl Harbor. Go straight ahead for a little less than 0.9mi (1.5km) until you see the sign for the parking-lot entrance on your left. Bus nos. 20 or 47 go to the visitor centre. You can also take the Memorial Shuttle Bus directly from Waikiki ($3), but there are only five return trips (☎839-0911).

Named for its pearl-bearing oysters, **Pearl Harbor** ★★ is Hawaii's most famous bay. Hawaii was still a kingdom when, in 1887, the United States gained free entry to the bay in return for granting Hawaiian sugar duty-free access to U.S. markets. No other port in the entire Pacific offered better shelter. In 1906, after Hawaii's annexation, the U.S. Marines began building what was to become the largest military base in the world, the U.S. Pacific headquarters.

At 6am on December 7, 1941, a first wave of Japanese bombers took off 217mi (350km) northwest of O'ahu. The fleet of six aircraft carriers and 26 escort vessels left Japan on November 26, commanded by Admiral Yamamoto, who was opposed to war with the U.S. but was convinced that it was a tactical necessity to get rid of the U.S. Pacific fleet. Yamamoto chose a northerly course, near the icy waters of the Arctic, to avoid being detected. The strategy was a resounding success: even as the Japanese fleet approached the coast of the island, nobody had a clue about the imminent attack to come. Thirty minutes later, a second

squadron, this time mostly made up of torpedo planes, took off. Meanwhile, the Americans had spotted and sank a Japanese mini-submarine approaching the harbour, but no one seemed to make a big deal of it. There were actually five Japanese subs positioned right in the middle of Pearl Harbor in order to inflict the greatest amount of damage during the aerial attack. No bombs had fallen yet, but just before 7am, a radar station on the north coast of O'ahu detected the approach of several aircraft. It reported the news to the headquarters, who confidently declared that, although its position was quite unusual, it was a squadron of B-17s arriving from California. Less than 1hr later at 7:55am, Commander Mitsuo Fuchida sent the code "*Tora! Tora! Tora!*" (Tiger! Tiger! Tiger!), and the Battleship Row and seven other warships that were moored in the harbour went up in flames. The shock was immense. Only 14 U.S. planes managed to take off; all the others were destroyed on the ground. Then, 45min later, a second assault pummelled Pearl Harbor. When the last Japanese planes retreated at 10am, 21 U.S. vessels had been sunk or damaged, 164 planes were destroyed, approximately 2,400 were dead

and 1,200 were wounded.

Widely commented and analyzed, more than half a century later the Japanese attack on Pearl Harbor is still present in the memory of natives and visitors, American and Japanese alike. It is surprising to see how the National Park Service actually offers a balanced viewpoint, completely devoid of patriotism. Every year on December 7, a remembrance ceremony brings together the former archenemies, and every day, thousands of tourists flock to this site. Situated on the eastern side of Ford Island, the memorial above the *USS Arizona* wreck is Hawaii's most visited attraction.

The visitor centre and the memorial (☎422-5905 or 422-5664) are jointly run by the Marines and the National Park Service. The National Park Service gives away free tickets on a first-come first-served basis (*every day 7:30am to 3pm*). Unfortunately, waiting lines usually begin to form between 8am and 9am, especially in summer. Reservations are not accepted and you can't send someone to pick up tickets for groups; everyone must show up in person at the counter.

The tour lasts about 75min. The first one takes place at 8am and

O'ahu

the last at 3pm, with departures every 15min. The tour begins with a video presentation, followed by a boat ride to the memorial. Each ticket has a number; go to the theatre when your number is called. While waiting, you can visit the small museum, the bookstore or buy something at the snack bar. If have a couple of hóurs to kill before your tour begins, you might want to stroll past the parking lot and head to the *USS Bowfin* Submarine Museum.

In addition to the many scale models of boats and the old photos, the **museum ★** houses different objects that belonged to the two enemy armies and some of their troops. In front of the museum, on the seaward side, is a semicircle memorial that lists the names of the soldiers, classified according to rank, who died in the Pearl Harbor attack. Civilians who perished in the attack are also remembered.

The excellent 25min **film ★★** presented at the beginning of the visit traces the historical circumstances that led up to the attack on Pearl Harbor. It includes scenes filmed by the two armies during the attack and the rest of the war. Except for

the *Arizona*, the *Utah* and the *Oklahoma*, all U.S. ships that were sunk or damaged were re-floated and sent back into battle. After the film, small boats ferry visitors across the port to the **memorial ★★**, a large white monument sculpted in the shape of a ship. Surprisingly, the existence of this memorial is largely due to the efforts of Elvis Presley. Realizing that organizers were having difficulties funding the project, the singer gave all the proceeds of one concert to Honolulu, a gesture that persuaded the authorities to free up the missing sum needed for the monument. Finally conceived in 1962 and opened to the public in 1980, the memorial was placed on pylons anchored on both ends of the battleship, and not

Arizona Memorial

on top of it. The *USS Arizona* rests in about 40ft (12m) of water and 20ft (6m) of its hull is buried beneath the silt of the bay. Only the tip of a turret rises to the surface; it's difficult to make out the engulfed ship in windy or cloudy weather. Even today, 60 years after it went

down, it continues to ooze oil, which forms iridescent spots on the surface. At the bottom of the memorial, a wall is inscribed with the names of the 1,177 men who perished on board. Most of their bodies remain entombed in the wreckage and the ashes of 14 veteran survivors have since joined them. You might find the 15 to 20min wait after the visit here a bit long.

On the other side of the Arizona Memorial parking lot, another museum, the **Submarine Museum & Park ★** *($8 museum and submarine, $4 museum only; every day 8am to 5pm;* ☎*423-1341, free shuttle from Waikiki every 45min from 9:30am to 4:15pm, bus no. 20 and no. 47 from Waikiki, nos. 49, 52 and 62 from the Ala Moana Center)*, examines another page of naval history. The entrance to the "park" (which is in fact a lawn decorated with torpedoes and other missiles), is free. There's a memorial dedicated to the 3,500 submarines and 52 American vessels lost during the Second World War. The museum, although military in nature, is quite fascinating. It traces the development of submarines, beginning with the first American trial conducted on September 16, 1776, in the port of New York by Sargent Ezra Lee. Sargent Lee unsuccessfully attempted to attach an explosive from his mini-submersible, named *Turtle*, to the ship of British Admiral Lord Richard Howe. There are uniforms, old photos, posters encouraging people to join the army, scale models and a letter carried by U.S. pilots in the Pacific, with translations in French, Vietnamese, Thai, Chinese, Korean, Lao and even Japanese: "I am an American pilot. My plane is destroyed. I cannot speak your language. I am the enemy of the Japanese. Please be so kind as to protect me, take care of me and direct me to the nearest ally military office. The government of my country will reward you." Take a look at the diving suits worn in the 1960s: the equipment weighed 300 lbs (135 kg)!

After the visit to the museum, head to the *USS Bowfin* ★, a submarine that was commissioned exactly one year after the attack on Pearl Harbour. This 312ft-long (95m) and 16ft-wide (5m) tube weighs 18,000 tonnes and has eight compartments sealed off by watertight doors. There is a free self-guided audio tour narrated by the former captain of the ship, explaining the functioning of the vessel, the daily routines, as well

as the details of Operation Barney, conducted in Japanese waters in May of 1945. The first thing you'll notice is the lack of space, making it hard to believe that a crew of 83 men slept in its two torpedo rooms. Some bunks were even jammed between the bombs, each of which contained nearly 660 lbs (300kg) of explosives. Several watertight doors separated the crew and officer quarters and the control room. Crew members who were off duty played cards in the mess, which had 36 bunks – those who were taking the watch replaced those who were ending it. As for the washroom, only the cooks were allowed to take a fresh-water shower – and only once a week! The tour ends in the engine room where the temperature often went over 100°F (40°C).

As soon as you exit the submarine, take a look at the large, black Japanese torpedoes called *kaiten* (near the tables of the refreshment stand). Invented in 1944, these were operated by pilots condemned to suicide missions.

In addition to the submarine museum, it is also possible to board the *USS Missouri* (*$10, every day 9am to 5pm, ticket sales end at 4pm; departures about every 20min, ☎877-MIGHTY-*

MO), also known as *Mighty Mo*. It was on this bridge that General MacArthur received the surrender of the Japanese army on September 2, 1945. Having begun its career only a few months earlier, the ship was decommissioned in 1991. While it was in operation, 2,500 men lived on board. Those interested in historic blood baths will appreciate "The True Story about WWII, the Korean War and Desert Storm" (*$4*). There are also packages that include the *USS Bowfin* tour (*$14*).

Around the Island

★★
The Eastern Point

(one day)

The following itinerary covers the eastern point of the island and explores several swimming spots, rugged coastlines, a crater, as well as an attraction park. You can turn the famous Hanauma Bay into a separate trip from Waikiki if you want to spend more time on its magnificent beaches and beautiful waters.

East of Honolulu, the H1 Freeway ends near the affluent Kahala neighbourhood and becomes Kalaniana'ole Highway (72). From Waikiki, you can easily get to the highway 2mi (3km) before it ends by taking Kipahul Avenue, or by going around Diamond Head on the coastal road (Diamond Head Road, which becomes Kahala Avénue).

The **Koko Head** volcanic ridge towers along the coast, flanked to the east by Maunalua Bay, while the cone of the **Koko Crater**, whose slopes have been ravaged by erosion, stands out on the left. On Koko Head's west side is a residential neighbourhood; access to the coast is forbidden here. The road that begins around Hanauma Bay and leads to the summit of the cape is also closed off to the general public. Once a month, between January and April, the Nature Conservancy *(1116 Smith St., Suite 201, Honolulu HI 96817,* ☎*537-4508)* organizes tours to the **'Ihi'ihilauakea Reserve**, which protects a rare species of fern *(marsilea villosa)*. The only entrance to the Koko Crater is situated on the northern side, which is gorged by the crater (see p 121).

One of the most visited sites in O'ahu, **Hanauma Bay ★★★** *($3, parking $1, Wed to Mon 6am to 6pm in winter, until 7pm in summer; bus no. 22 or no. 58)* forms a deep indentation in the eastern coast, created when an old volcano collapsed. The bay is blessed with superb beaches, bordered by

beautiful coral reefs. Since 1967, Hanauma Bay has been a Marine Life Conservation District – the first in Hawaii. There are thousands of tame tropical fish here, including the unpronounceable *humuhumunukunukuapua'a*. You can also occasionally see some rare green Hawaiian turtles. Tourists could not overlook such a place for long;

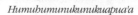

Humuhumunukunukuapua'a

hundreds of people now flock here every day to swim and admire the fauna in the bay. As a result of this throng of tourists, an entrance tax has been imposed and feeding fish is now strictly forbidden, since this not only disturbs their diet, but also because many people have complained about bites.

There is a small display devoted to coral and marine life near the entrance (above the beach and the bay). Most people, however, rush down the 1,000ft (300m) steep slope to get to the water. A trolley *($0.50 to go down, $1 to go back up, 8am to 5pm)* makes a non-stop

return trip. To avoid the swarm of tourists, it's best to come very early in the day, when the water's visibility hasn't yet been spoiled by hundreds of feet stirring up the sand. On the beach *(washrooms, showers)* is a snack bar with a predictable selection of hot dogs, sandwiches, pizza and ice cream, as well as a stand that rents snorkel gear. Two sites, which are not visible from the park entrance, regularly attract experienced divers: Witch's Brew, a tiny cove formed by a short rocky point that juts out into the western coast of the bay at the foot of the protective Koko Head ridge, and Toilet Bowl, a small, remote inlet dug into the opposite side of the bay. The entrance to the bay, which is swept by violent currents, is reserved to experienced scuba divers.

In the spring of 2000, there was a controversy surrounding the planned construction of a new visitor centre.

Shortly past Hanauma Bay, the road emerges at the foot of Koko Crater, then runs along the stratified cliffs of the coast, carved out by the continually breaking waves. The Ka Iwi Channel, known as one of the most dangerous in the world, and Moloka'i Island can be seen in the distance. At

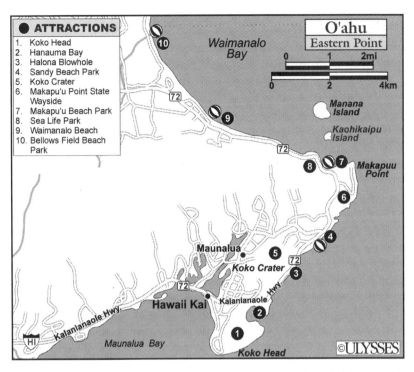

ATTRACTIONS
1. Koko Head
2. Hanauma Bay
3. Halona Blowhole
4. Sandy Beach Park
5. Koko Crater
6. Makapu'u Point State Wayside
7. Makapu'u Beach Park
8. Sea Life Park
9. Waimanalo Beach
10. Bellows Field Beach Park

O'ahu
Eastern Point

Waimanalo Bay

Manana Island

Kaohikaipu Island

Makapuu Point

Maunalua

Koko Crater

Hawaii Kai

Kalanianaole

Kalanianaole Hwy

Maunalua Bay

Koko Head

©ULYSSES

Mile 11.1, just before the parking lot, is a small altar put up by Japanese fishers. From the parking lot, you can easily go down to the small and usually peaceful **Cove Beach**, but this is not a good place for swimming since the waves crash against the rocks around the cove. Cross the paved parking lot for a lovely view of Sandy Beach to the north and the **Halona Blowhole ★**. The waves have carved out an opening in the volcanic rock, and as each breaker rushes in, the water spouts out of the hole reaches up to 50ft (15m).

At Mile 10.7, the **Sandy Beach Park ★** (*wash-*

rooms, showers, telephone) includes a grassy field popular with kite-flyers and a large beach with golden sand, a favourite place for boogie boarders. Swimming is not recommended here. At low tide, you can spot some petroglyphs in the lava by the coast.

At Mile 10.1, north of Sandy Beach, Kealahou Street allows you to visit the inside the **Koko Crater**. After 0.6mi (1km), turn left towards the Koko Crater Stables. From the entrance, a trail leads around the crater's exterior and interior, where the **Botanical Garden ★** (*free admission; every day 9am to 4pm,*

☎522-7060, bus no. 58), which belongs to the Honolulu Botanical Gardens, is located. In the mailbox is a map that indicates the location of the different sections: past the frangipani are the American cacti and Hawaiian plants, followed by the Madagascar and African sections. All the species here are xerophiles, which means that they are adapted to the dry microclimate of the Koko Crater. A large part of the land is still occupied by some *kiawe*, thorny plants that were introduced to Hawaii in the 19th century. The best place to admire the crater and its eroded face, which is shaped like a large

O'ahu

pothole, is the African section (left at the fork in the road). The entire 2.5mi (4km) hike takes 40 to 60min.

The rocky Makapu'u Point, the eastern point of the island, forces the road to veer from the coast into the Kalama Valley, where the Hawaii Kai golf course is situated. At Mile 8.8, as the road climbs the last stretch of the Ko'olau mountain range, a sign marks **Makapu'u Point State Wayside ★**. The entrance road is closed to traffic, but you can park your car along the road and hike the 2mi (3.2km) to Makapu'u Point. Along the way are some stunning views, but be careful – the jaunt is steep and exposed to the sun. The point is particularly popular with hang-gliders.

Less than 450yds (500m) away, a large parking lot offers a panoramic view of the north coast, Makapu'u Beach, and the islets of Kaohikaipu (the closest) and Manana (the largest), also known as Rabbit Island. These two islets are home to a large population of marine birds. Towards the north, beyond Waimanalo Bay, is Makapu Point, which is almost entirely taken up by a Marine military base and easily mistaken for an island. Head down to **Makapu'u**

Beach Park ★ *(washrooms, telephone)*, whose lovely beach, made famous by the risqué scene from *From Here to Eternity*, today attracts many boogie boarders. Even if you're dying to go swimming in the winter, don't try it here, as the waves and currents are known to be very dangerous.

Immediately opposite the beach stands the entrance to **Sea Life Park** *($24, children $12; every day 9:30am to 5pm, 41-202 Kalaniana'ole Hwy., ☎259-7933; bus nos. 57 or 58 or the trolley)*. A cross between a marine park and a theme park (but closer to the latter), this undeniably popular tourist attraction is beginning to show its age. The spiral ramp around the large aquarium is particularly well conceived (you can even swim in

Dolphin

it for an extra $75!), but the predictable dolphin and sea lion shows hold much greater appeal for children than adults. Kids are given lettuce to feed the green turtles, which live in groups of 20 in crammed tanks, and for $2 you can buy a piece of fish to feed the ravenous sea lions. As for the Whaling Museum

advertized on the orientation sign, don't look for it: a souvenir shop has replaced it. The only way to truly get your money's worth is to spend the entire day here, going from one attraction to the next. However, there's only one activity every 30min. While you're here, say hello to the park's mascot, Kekaimalu, the world's first cross between a killer whale and a "tursiops" dolphin, aptly called a "wholphin." Shuttle buses make the trip from Waikiki ($5 return).

Continuing along the coast, you reach Mile 7.8, opposite Rabbit Island, where **Kaupo Beach Park** *(no services)* is located. You can snorkel here, but the undertow is more popular with surfers.

The first city on the north coast, **Waimanalo** is nestled at the foot of the Ko'olau mountain range, with sheer slopes and rocky ridges. The majority of the town's population is Hawaiian. There's a life-size statue – and what a size – of the town's hero, Chad "Akebono" Rowan, the first non-Japanese person to be crowned Sumo wrestling world champion. The long stretch of attractive beach, which has beautiful white sand, is trimmed by fir trees, which conceal a nearby residential district. The water here is excellent for swimming. Coming from the east, you first pass Mile 5.7, **Waimanalo Beach Park ★** *(washrooms, showers, picnic tables, telephone).* During calm weather, this is a great place for surface diving. Technically, Camping is allowed, but the site, which has become the home of several homeless families, is not well adapted. The best place to camp is the **Waimanalo Bay State Recreation Area ★** *(Mile 4.4, every day 7am to 6:45pm),* where you can pitch your tent underneath the pines behind the beach (see p 161). The park, whose entrance is opposite the polo field, is popular with swimmers and boogie boarders.

At Mile 4.1 is the marked entrance of Bellows AFS (Air Force Station). **Bellows Field Beach Park ★** *(washrooms, showers, picnic tables)* is open to civilian beach-goers on weekends only, and many residents from the north coast come here with their boogie boards under their arms. The beach is in fact the northern end of Waimanalo beach. You can also camp amidst the pine trees on weekends (see p 161).

Four miles (6.5km) further, past the residential neighbourhood surrounding the large

Kaelepulu pond, the Kalaniana'ole Highway hooks up with the Pali Highway (61), which leads straight to Honolulu through the central mountains.

★★
The Windward Coast

(one day)

This tour first covers the few sites scattered along the Pali Highway, which crosses the island, and then heads to the central north coast. The Pali Highway cuts through the Ko'olau Range (whose name means "windward coast") and ends up at the vast basin where the town of Kane'ohe is located, near the large, shallow Kane'ohe Bay. To the east is the town of Kailua, the mecca of windsurfers. Although the two sprawling towns do not hold much interest, this area, which used to be the political and religious centre of the island, does contain a few relics from Hawaii's past, such as *heiau* (ancient places of worship) and fishponds. Heavy rainfall from the northeast beats down on the Ko'olau foothills, and the region is therefore blessed with many thriving gardens. Buses nos. 56 and 57 serve the Kane'ohe region.

Just before Mile 2 along the Pali Highway, time seems to stand still at

the summer palace of Queen Emma, granddaughter of Charles Bishop and wife of Kamehameha IV. Built in the lower part of the Nu'uanu Valley, the tiny **Queen Emma Summer Palace ★★** *($5; every day 9am to 4pm; 2913 Pali Hwy., ☎595-6291; bus no. 4),* which only has six rooms, stands on the site where Kamehameha deliberated in 1795 before beginning his final attack to conquer and unify the island. Built in 1848, the house, which was sent from New England in pieces, was bought two years later by the son of John Young, the great king's British adviser. Emma, his niece, inherited it in 1857. Since 1913, the palace and gardens have been run by an organization called the Daughters of Hawaii that has brought impressive restorations to the building. Many items that once belonged to the royal couple were re-bought and are now on display. The rooms evoke the original Victorianera style. There are also some magnificent royal insignia: *kahili* and feather *leis, 'ahu'ula* (feather cape), dishes made from *koa* wood and porcelain. A stereoscope (an optical instrument for viewing pictures in relief), given to Emma by Napoleon III during her visit to Paris in 1865, sits imposingly in the hallway.

Oʻahu

Rather than continuing along the busy Pali Highway, take Nu'uanu Pali Drive on your right just past the palace. The road almost immediately plunges into a natural tunnel created by large 100-year-old banyan trees. After about 0.9mi (1.5km), the **Judd Trail**, which quickly leads to a torrent forming a series of small basins, begins near a bridge. Swimming is possible if you don't mind chilly – very chilly – water. If you cross the stream, the trail continues creating a loop among the bamboo, banyan and other large trees.

Nu'uanu Pali Drive hooks up with the main road 0.6mi (1km) farther, just before the turnoff (Mile 5.3) to **Pali Lookout ★★** *(every day 8am to 4pm)*, which is a part of the Nuuanu Pali State Park. At this place is an opening in the Ko'olau Mountains, which form the backbone of O'ahu. The lookout, which is very popular with organized tours, is quite windy but offers breathtaking views of Kane'ohe Bay and the jagged cliffs. At this very spot, the last act of O'ahu's conquest was played out in 1795. Thanks to his cannons, Kamehameha led Kalanikupule's army up the Nu'uanu Valley and surrounded it above this fearsome cliff. Kalanikupule's men had nowhere to go. The ensuing battle, known as

Kaleleka'anae, "'anae's jump" (a kind of fish), ended with about 400 soldiers jumping to their death.

An ancient trail that seems to have been there forever runs through the mountainous barrier. The only other way to get to the windward coast is via a circuitous trip by canoe around the island's point. Paved in 1845 for horses, the path was widened a half-century later using dynamite and finally became a surfaced road in the 1950s. Travellers now get from one side of the mountain to the other via a tunnel. The trip to Kane'ohe offers many hidden lookouts onto the central north coast.

Just past the turnoff from Kamehameha Highway (83), Anoi Road and Luluku Road lead to the **Ho'omaluhia Botanical Garden ★** *(free admission; every day 9am to 4pm; 45-680 Luluku Rd., ☎233-7323)*. This huge 400 acre (160ha) garden stretches out at the very foot of the Ko'olau cliffs. If it's been raining, you'll see lacy waterfalls streaming down the cliffs. The cloud-covered Konahuanui summit, at 3,100ft (946m), towers above this picturesque setting. The region, which was first covered with fields of taro, rice and then pineapple, only became a park in 1982 after some severe floods, and it was then

that Waimaluhia Lake, an artificial reservoir, was dug. The park has several sections which are all connected by a road and a network of trails. You can go for a walk by yourself or take part in one of the free guided tours that take place at 10am on Saturday and at 1pm on Sunday. The visitor centre offers information on those tours as well as camping possibilities. Here, there is also a small exhibit on the various plants that were once used by Hawaiians.

Continue on the two-lane road (61), which follows the same course as Kalaniana'ole Road (72). Two miles farther, Kalaniana'ole Road branches off to the east towards Waimanalo and the eastern point of the island. At this point, continue driving straight on Kailua Road (61).

Taro

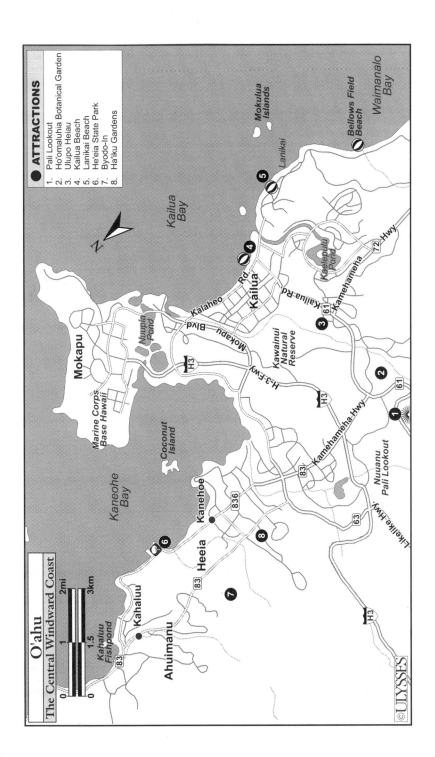

O'ahu
The Central Windward Coast

0   1   1.5   2mi
0   1.5   3km

● ATTRACTIONS
1. Pali Lookout
2. Ho'omaluhia Botanical Garden
3. Ulupo Heiau
4. Kailua Beach
5. Lanikai Beach
6. He'eia State Park
7. Byodo-In
8. Ha'iku Gardens

Kaneohe Bay

Mokapu

Marine Corps Base Hawaii

Nuupia Pond

Coconut Island

Kailua Bay

Mokulua Islands

Lanikai

N

Kahaluu Fishpond

Ahuimanu

Kahaluu

Heeia

Kanehoe

Kaelepulu Pond

Kailua

Kalaheo Blvd

Kalaheo Rd

Mokapu Blvd

Kailua Rd

Kawainui Natural Reserve

Kamehameha Hwy

H-3 Hwy

Kamehameha Hwy

Nuuanu Pali Lookout

Likelike Hwy

Bellows Field Beach

Waimanalo Bay

83

836

83

63

61

61

72 Hwy

H3

H3

H3

© ULYSSES

The first small street on the left, past the turnoff opposite the Aloha service station, is called Uluoa Street. Turn onto this street, turn right on Manu Aloha Street and then right again on Manu'o'o. You can park at the Windward YMCA and then walk on foot to the **Ulupo** *heiau* ★. This ancient temple towers over Hawaii's largest swamp, the Kawainui Swamp, which is the habitat for a variety of birds. Legends say that it was built by the Menehune, a legendary tribe of small men known for their building skills. The only part left is the top platform, which is 138ft (42m) long and 30ft (9m) wide. It is said that Ulupo was placed under the protection of Hauwahine, *mo'o*, the swamp's guardian spirit, which could take the form of a giant lizard or a beautiful woman, and insured that riverside residents would have plenty of fish.

About 1,000 years ago, at a time when Kailua was no doubt an important religious and political centre, the central north coast was quite different. There were clusters of villages around the edges of a lagoon, which was at that point still connected to the sea. Progressively, though, the channel was filled with sand and the lagoon became a swamp. Much later, after fresh-water replaced the

Hawai'i State Seabird Sanctuary

All of the islets and islands off O'ahu's windward coast are protected by the Hawai'i State Seabird Sanctuary. These eroded rocks are vestiges of cliffs that were once part of the coast, remnants of ancient eruptions or pieces of coral from the reef. The islands form a mini-archipelago that is home to threatened endemic plant species as well as a large population of marine birds.

brackish water, the swamp took the name Kawainui, "the great fresh water." The town of Kailua now stands on the fringes of the former lagoon.

It is this distinctive geographic feature that created the gorgeous, wide beach that borders Kailua Bay, which is 5mi (8km) long. Gently lulled by the trade winds and voted "best beach in the U.S.," **Kailua Beach** ★★★ *(washrooms, showers, picnic tables, bus no. 70 from Kailua)* offers the best conditions on the island for the windsurfers who flock here every weekend. Some have recently taken up kitesurfing. Carried up by the force of the wind driving the kite they're towing, they can fly through the air for up to 10 seconds. Those who are not really into sports can enjoy a pleasant swim.

Farther east, **Lanikai Beach** ★ is bordered by a residential area. In some places, the thin strip of sand turns into rocks. Only a few access roads allow you to get from the road to the beach, but unless you're planning to stay in the area, it's almost impossible to park on the lower side. Beyond Wailea Point is Waimanalo Beach (see p 145), but you can only get there by a circuitous route around Kailua and the Bellows Air Force Station.

Kala'heo Avenue passes through Kailua and then heads towards Mokapu Peninsula, which used to be separated from the rest of the island by former brackish waters that were transformed into fishponds by the Hawaiians. Unfortunately, the area is off-limits to the public since the army occupies most of the peninsula. When

Kala'heo Avenue crosses Mokapu Boulevard, instead of taking the two-lane road, continue straight ahead towards Kane'ohe.

The main town on the north coast, **Kane'ohe** is basically a charmless dormitory town with sprawling suburbs and shopping centres. Although the shallow bay is sheltered, there is no beach here. What's more, the bay is flanked by coral reefs that make navigation perilous. In ancient times these distinctive features made the bay an important fish-farming centre.

The Kamehameha Highway crosses through the middle of Kane'ohe and then heads north up the coast and connects to the Kahekili Highway (83), which completes the tour of the island.

Along the way (at Mile 1.5) is the **He'eia State Park ★** *(Friends of He'eia, ☎247-3156)*, built on a finger of land known as Pealohi Point. The visitor centre looks out onto the bay and reefs, sparkling under the sun with

beautiful shades of green. In the foreground, at the base of the peninsula, you can clearly see a large fishpond, partly covered by vegetation, which legends say was protected by Mehau, a supernatural being that could transform itself into a woman, frog, lizard or eel. Used until the 1950s, its walls are more than 10ft (3m) thick. In the background lies Moku O Lo'e Island, a small island also known as Coconut Island, where the Hawai'i Institute of Marine Biology has a research station. The 15 acre (6ha) park is home to a small collection of indigenous and imported plants used by the ancient Hawaiians.

Past the park, the road quickly leads to **He'eia Kea Boat Harbor**, where glass-bottomed boat trips allow you to discover the rich underwater world of the bay. The paved road veers to the left along the coast, offering lovely views of the turquoise waters as well as the Ko'olau Mountains, which have dense forests in the north. Just before reaching High-

way 83, you'll notice the **Kahaluu Fishpond** on your right.

Take the Kahekili Highway (83) to the south, and at Mile 37.6, turn mauka onto Hui'iwa Street. Past the ticket booth, cross the cemetery until the end of the road.

At the foot of the mountains, whose cloud-covered peeks are overgrown with lush vegetation, stands one of the most beautiful monuments in Hawaii, the **Byodo-In ★ ★ ★** *($2; 8am to 4:30pm, 47-200 Kahekili Hwy., ☎239-8811, bus no. 65).* This replica of Uji, a 900-year-old Japanese temple near Kyoto, was built in 1968 to celebrate the 100-year anniversary of Japanese immigration to Hawaii. The shape of this beautiful red building with lacquered tile roof evokes the mythical Phoenix, and is reflected in the serene pond where thousands of *koi* (carp), symbol of perseverance, frolic about. Refreshing gardens surround the babbling pond, while a magnificently chiselled, three-tonne gong that was

O'ahu

Byodo-In

molten in Japan is sounded. The temple houses a 10ft (3m) statue of Buddha Amida (the Buddha of the western paradise). He's seated on lotus flowers behind an altar from which incense rises. Sometimes a few peacocks roam the gardens and strut up the steps.

About 1mi (1.5km) before the turnoff from the H3 Freeway, Ha'iku Road (Mile 29) heads to **Ha'iku Gardens** *(46-336 Ha'iku Rd., ☎247-6671)*, a small tropical garden surrounding a pond. Filled with lotuses, the garden is nestled below the terrace of the Chart House restaurant. The tropical scene is meant to lure customers, but you are free to take a pleasant stroll by the calm waters.

Pali Highway (61), which leads to Honolulu and Waikiki), is only 4mi (6.5km) farther.

★★★
The North Coast

(two to three days)

This tour leaves Honolulu on the Pali Highway and completes the trip around the island via the north. You'll discover a more peaceful side of O'ahu in the north, with sugar-cane fields, papaya orchards, scenic landscapes and idyllic beaches along the way. The north coast beaches are pounded by powerful waves in the winter,

and, consequently they have become a popular destination for international professional surfers. When a storm is brewing, waves can reach up to 50ft (15m).

This area of the island is served by bus no. 52 and no. 55 Circle Island (make sure it says "Circle Island" since other buses don't do the entire tour).

The tour up the northwest coast begins past Waiahole, north of Kane'ohe, where lush, tropical vegetation thrives here in the high humidity. Orchid and banana plantations lie on both sides of the road between patches of dense forest and the green foothills of the jagged Ko'olau mountain chain. Fruit vendors have set up stands along the way.

Shortly after intersecting with the Kamehameha Highway, Pulama Road (Mile 24.8) veers to the left and heads to **Senator Fong's Plantation** *($10, $6 children; every day 10am to 4pm, last tour at 3pm; 47-285 Pulama Rd., ☎239-6775)*. Senator Fong, the first Asian-American to be elected to the U.S. Senate, created with his family a large 740 acres (300ha) tropical garden on land that formerly belonged to King Lunalilo. Each of its five sections bares the names of presidents under which the senator served. Unfortunately, the only way to

visit the garden is by tramway with groups of Japanese tourists *(10:30am, 11:30am, 1pm, 2pm and 3pm)*. The vegetation is extremely varied, including tropical fruit-bearing trees, Hawaiian flowers, coniferous forests in the hills, rainforest, all sorts of palm trees, as well as the last Hawaiian sandalwood groves. There's a snack bar, a souvenir shop and a fruit stand on the premises.

The mountains soon draw near the coast. Pu'u Ohulehule at 2,264ft (690m), whose majestic face is covered with vegetation, plays a game of hide-and-seek with the clouds. Down below, the forest is dotted with green pastures where black and white cows graze. **Kualoa Regional Park ★** *(every day 7am to 8pm, washrooms, picnic tables)* faces Molili'i Island, also known as Chinaman's Hat because of its conical shape. The park, whose lawn is meticulously trimmed, is very peaceful during the week. On weekends, however, it resonates with the laughter of families who flock here to picnic or camp (see p 162). The beach is not very wide, but the water is quite shallow. Protected by a reef, it is a safe place to swim. At low tide, you can even wade out to Chinaman's Hat. Behind the campground is the Moli'i Fishpond, the

'Elepaio

'Akiapola'au

'Apapane

'Amakihi

'Akohekohe

Cardinal

Ti

White hibiscus
Koki'o ke'oke'o

Frangipani

Mamane

Ohelo

Silversword
Ahinahira

'Ohi'a lehua

Hawaiian stilt
Ae'o

Hawaiian dark-rumped petrel
'Ua'u

White-tailed tropicbird
Koa'e'ula

Pacific plover
Kolea

Laysan albatross

Frigate bird
'Iwa

Japanese white-eye

'Akepa

I'iwi

Hawaiian falcon
'Io

Hawaiian goose
Nene

Hawaiian short-eared owl
Pueo

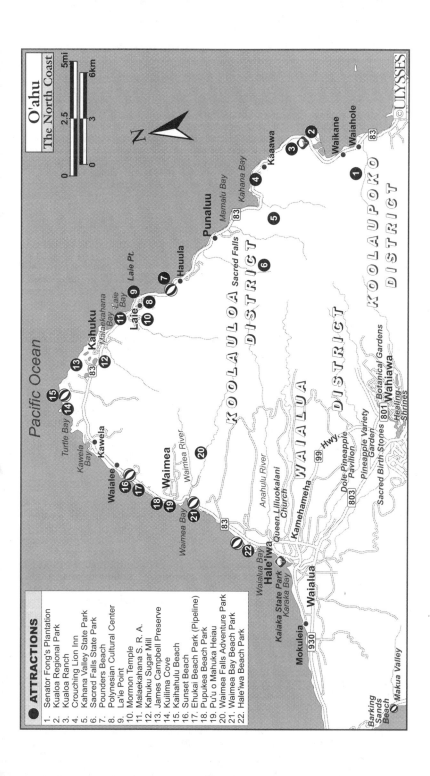

O'ahu
The North Coast

Pacific Ocean

© ULYSSES

0   2.5   5mi
0   3   6km

ATTRACTIONS

1. Senator Fong's Plantation
2. Kualoa Regional Park
3. Kualoa Ranch
4. Crouching Lion Inn
5. Kahana Valley State Park
6. Sacred Falls State Park
7. Pounders Beach
8. Polynesian Cultural Center
9. La'ie Point
10. Mormon Temple
11. Malaekahana S. R. A.
12. Kahuku Sugar Mill
13. James Campbell Preserve
14. Kulima Cove
15. Kaihahulu Beach
16. Sunset Beach
17. Ehukai Beach Park (Pipeline)
18. Pupukea Beach Park
19. Pu'u o Mahuka Heiau
20. Waimea Falls Adventure Park
21. Waimea Bay Beach Park
22. Hale'iwa Beach Park

KOOLAULOA DISTRICT

KOOLAUPOKO DISTRICT

WAIALUA DISTRICT

Waikane
Waiahole
Kaaawa
Kahana Bay
Mamalu Bay
Punaluu
Sacred Falls
Hauula
Laie Pt.
Laie Bay
Kahuku
Malaekahana Bay
Laie
Turtle Bay
Kawela Bay
Kawela
Waialee
Waimea
Waimea River
Waimea Bay
Hale'iwa
Waialua Bay
Kaiaka Bay
Kaiaka State Park
Queen Liliuokalani Church
Kamehameha Hwy.
Anahulu River
Waialua
Mokuleia
Barking Sands Beach
Makua Valley
Dole Pineapple Pavilion
Pineapple Variety Garden
Sacred Birth Stones
Botanical Gardens
Wahiawa
Healing Shrines

only fishpond still in operation in O'ahu.

Just north of Kualoa Park lies the **Kualoa Ranch** *(Mon to Fri 7am to 5:30pm; 49-560 Kamehameha Hwy., ☎237-7321 or 800-231-7321, www.kualoa.com)* that stretches across land bought from Kamehameha III in 1850 and kept to this day by the Judd family. In ancient times, the group of *ahupua'a*, including the valley, were considered as a *puuhonua* (refuge for *kapu* breakers). Since animal rearing was not as lucrative as tourism, the *paniolos* (Hawaiian cowboys) opted for the horseback-riding business in the Ka'a'awa Valley, where the ranch is located. You can also go for the bus or the quad, as well as a range of activities enjoyed by Asian tourists: clay-pigeon shooting, diving, helicopter rides, four-wheel-drive vehicles and mountain biking. The half-day trip to Secret Island is one of the most popular tours. Prices range between $28 and $45 (except for helicopter rides) and a package that includes three activities costs $99.

The road follows the coastline past the ranch. There are numerous beaches along the way that are quite narrow at high tide: **Kanenelu Beach**, with golden sand, situated at the mouth of a wide valley; **Kalae'io Beach**

Park, with a few tables under the pine and bancoulier trees; and **Ka'a'a Beach Park**, which is an extension of Kalae'io Beach Park. All three beaches are protected by a reef, but swimming isn't recommended here.

Around Mile 27, a rock formation known as Crouching Lion is outlined on the left-hand side of the road. But you'll probably have trouble seeing the stretched-out lion for which it is named; in Hawaiian folklore, the rock is said to be a demigod who was chained to the cliff. Featuring a restaurant (see p 181), the site remains one of the most popular stops for tours around the island.

The Kamehameha Highway runs along Kahana Bay and passes through the mouth of the Kahana Valley. From the road, you can see the Huilua Fishpond, which has recently undergone restoration.

The bottom of the bay is trimmed with a beach where camping is possible. At this precise spot (Mile 25.8), a turn-off leads to the orientation centre of **Kahana Valley State Park ★** *(☎237-7766)*. The centre is often closed, but you can obtain a trail map showing two possible hikes.

The Kahana Valley, one of the least developed

valleys on O'ahu, stretches from the Pu'u Pauao summit to the sea. It is the only publicly owned *ahupua'a* (land division) on the island. At the beginning of the 20th century, taro fields were replaced by sugar cane, and then by soldiers who came to learn jungle survival techniques. But the course of history now seems to be reversed: the State Parks department recently implemented a new plan with the creation of a "living park," and the 31 families residing in Kahana have been encouraged to stay and grow their crops in the traditional Hawaiian way.

Although the ancient sites are invisible or inaccessible, you can still explore the valley along the **Nakoa Trail**. This 2.5mi (4km) loop trail passes through rainforest and twice crosses the Kahana Stream, where brave souls can take a swim. Hiking is not particularly difficult here, except for the mud, a consequence of the continuous year-round rain. The 4mi (6.6km) trail begins about 0.8mi (1.3km) from the parking lot (just before a railing).

A second trail begins at the orientation centre and follows the coastline of the bay from a distance. It first follows the tracks of the former Ko'olau Railway line, and after about 0.5mi (1km), reaches a former Hawaiian fishing altar (Kapa'ele'ele Ko'a) and a lookout point.

At about Mile 24, **Punaluu Beach Park** *(washrooms, showers, picnic tables, telephone, and other conveniences)* is unfortunately situated a little too close to the road, but has a pretty crescent-shaped beach that is protected by the offshore reef. Just before the beach is **Sacred Falls State Park** *(Mile 22.6)*, which has been closed to the public since a deadly landslide in May 1999. If the park opens again in the future, you'll be able to hike a 2mi (3.2km) trail (one-way) leading to some lovely 80ft-high (24m) waterfalls. The last stretch of the trail passes through a narrow canyon, home of Kamapua'a, the boar demigod. Be careful: although the falls are accessible, watch out for storms that can make the water level rise quickly.

Just past the Sacred Falls parking lot, on the left-hand side of the road, stands the **Kamalamalama o Keao Church**, a pretty little church made of green wood. (It is usually closed to visitors). The Hauula Beach Park at Mile 21 has a few unattractive buildings and a nondescript campground. If you're planning to pitch your tent, it's best to head to **Kokololio Beach Park** (see p 162), which has a peaceful beach situated off the road. Just north lies **Pounders Beach ★**, another pretty beach that is devoid of buildings and is lined with pine and pandanus trees. As its name suggests, this beach is pounded by strong surf, which makes swimming out of the question here, and the tides unfortunately leave garbage on the shore. Only diehard boogie boarders dare venture out in the water here.

You can't miss the thatched roofs of the **Polynesian Cultural Center ★** *($27, $47 with buffet, $64 with* lu'au*; children 5 to 11, $16/$30/$43; Mon to Sat 12:30pm to 9:30pm; 55-370 Kamehameha Hwy., ☎293-3333 or 800-367-7060, www.polynesia. com; bus no. 55 Circle Island)* at the entrance to **La'ie** (Mile 19.1). Run by the Mormon Church, this cultural theme park has seven "villages" consisting of a few pandanus or palm *hale* (thatched buildings) representing seven Polynesian islands: Samoa, Aetearoa (New Zealand), Fiji, Hawaii, Tahiti, the Marquesas and Tonga. Many of the dancers, artists and souvenir vendors working in the villages are originally from these islands, and most of them work for low wages and are students from nearby Brigham Young University. The students do, however, receive credits towards their economics classes. The small amount of authenticity is basically provided by the workers; the rest consists of a large dose of kitsch and American-style show business. If that's what you have in mind, you won't be disappointed. The shows are well organized, with performances by top-notch professionals.

The shows take place between 12:30pm and 7pm, but most are presented between 2pm and 5:30pm. The two most popular shows are "Ancient Legends of Polynesia" (2:30pm), a costumed dance presentation that takes place in canoes, and "Horizons" (7:30pm), a show with more than 100 singers, dancers and musicians. For the price of admission, you'll even be able to see a simulated volcanic eruption. There's also an IMAX theatre *(12:30pm, 1:30pm, 3pm, 4pm, 5pm and 6pm)*, which presents films on a variety of topics, some of them unrelated to the park's Polynesian theme.

About 730yds (800m) farther, **Brigham Young University** *(55-220 Kulanui St., ☎392-3660, www.byuh.edu)* is a little removed from the coastal road (via Naniloa St.). "Founded by prophets," it bears the name of the first president of the Mormon Church, the father of Salt Lake City and

O'ahu

husband of more than 30 women. Renowned for its liberal-arts program, it welcomes about 2,000 students every year, most of whom come from the islands of the Pacific. While the church assists them with their college expenses, in return they must work at the Polynesian Cultural Centre. Classes are therefore designed to allow students to dance and sing for 19 hours every week.

You can take a detour off the main road to **La'ie Point** (*via Anemoku and Naupaka Sts.*), which boldly juts out into the sea's raging waves. Fishers appreciate the solitude this place has to offer – only the occasional tourist drops by to enjoy the lovely view of the Mokualai islet, of a sea ark and of the windward coast.

Just 700yds (800m) farther is the imposing **Mormon Temple**, which looks more like a government building than a church. Built between 1914 and 1919, this stately temple stands at the end of a wide promenade lined with royal palm trees. As in Salt Lake City and other Mormon communities around the world, the church is only used for special occasions (marriages, baptisms, and the like); non-Mormons are not allowed to visit the temple.

Even Mormons themselves wait several years before feeling worthy of entering. The Visitor's Center (*every day 9am to 8pm; 55-645 Naniloa Loop; ☎293-9297*), which is more of an information centre on the Mormon Church than a tourist attraction, has a few photographs of the temple's interior, a scale model of the Salomon Temple, as well as two short films (*5min and 15min*) on the credo of The Church of Jesus Christ of Latter-day Saints (its official name), "which restored on earth true faith in God." Even if you don't share the same beliefs, the presentation provides insight into a different way of thinking about the world. A free shuttle service is offered between the Polynesian Cultural Center and the temple (*every 20min*).

Petrel

Situated along a large remote beach past La'ie, the vast **Malaekahana Park ★** (*6am to 6:45pm, washrooms, showers, picnic tables, campground – see p 163*) is a great spot for a picnic, facing the islet of Mokuauia. Unfortunately, the waves wash up a lot of debris onto the beach, but the campground is nevertheless one of the nicest ones on the island.

North of Malaekahana Bay, **Kahuku** surrounds a former sugar factory that is at the centre of the touristic rebirth of the town. Built in 1900 with a capacity to produce 650 tonnes of sugar every day, the steam-powered **Kahuku Sugar Mill ★★** (*free admission; Mon to Sat 9am to 5pm, 56-565 Kamehameha Hwy., ☎293-8747*) went out of business in 1971, a victim of the drop in the "white gold" market price. The town has been meticulously restored by committed citizens and now offers visitors an opportunity to see how cane is transformed into sugar. In order to follow the production process, machine parts have been colour-coded according to their former function, just like a toy construction set with giant gearwheels – it looks like something out of *Modern Times*. The complete list of machine parts is posted above the steps. The oldest steam engine dates back to the time of the American Civil War!

At the exit from Kahuku, the road runs alongside aquafarm pools where shrimp are raised and served on the tables of the few restaurants on the north coast. At this spot are two ponds that are part of the **James Campbell Nature Reserve**. The Punanmano pond was formed naturally by a spring; the Kii pond was built during the plantation era. You can see several species of indigenous and migratory birds by contacting the administration of the reserve *(66-590 Kamehameha Hwy., Room 2-C, P.O. Box 340, Hale'iwa HI 96712-0340, ☎637-6330)*.

The Kamehameha Highway veers away from the northern tip of the island and heads west towards Turtle Bay, where a massive Hilton hotel stands on the remote coast. At the foot of the hotel lies the sandy **Kuilima Cove** ★, one of the few spots on the north coast that are suitable for swimming all year. Towards the east, a path leads to **Kaihahulu Beach**, which is lined with pine trees and pounded by waves. However, its rocky bottom makes the beach a poor place for swimming. To get to one or the other beach without having to pay the Hilton's entrance fee, you can park at a small parking lot on the right-hand side, just before the tollbooth. There are only about 15 parking spaces, so you might end up parking at the hotel *($1.50 for the first 30min, then $0.50 for every extra 30min)*. An old sign with a red arrow indicates the Kaihahulu dirt road.

A few miles (5km) farther, you will arrive at the most famous beach on the North Shore, **Sunset Beach** ★★★, which marks the northern limit of the "7 Mile miracle," a group of the best surfing spots on the planet. With its colossal waves, this pretty stretch of golden beach draws the best surfers in the world every winter. If you come in December or January, you'll get the chance to attend one of the competitions counting for the prestigious Triple Crown. Hundreds of spectators come here, and Sunset is transformed into bedlam, with loudspeakers announcing competitors and sponsors. The rest of the year, you'll have the beach to yourself. Swimming is not possible here in winter, but there's nothing to stop you from enjoying the soft sand for an afternoon nap or a picnic. On the other side of the road are a few snack bars where you can get a bite to eat.

A little farther (Mile 7.8), **Ehukai Beach Park** ★★★ *(washrooms, showers)* draws everyone who's not at Sunset. This beach is also renowned for its winter waves, especially the Pipeline and the Banzai, situated on the left side of the park, whose names allude to their strength

The Triple Crown

From mid-November to mid-December, the best surfers in the world come to O'ahu for the most important competition of the year: the Triple Crown. Within one month, there are three consecutive high-calibre competitions: the Hawaiian Pro at Hale'iwa Beach Park, the World Cup of Surfing at Sunset Beach, and by the Pipe Masters at Banzai Pipeline. Although the points allocated in the Triple Crown are part of the world championship, a separate title is also at stake – not to mention a large purse. The oldest competition, which dates back to 1971, is at Banzai Pipeline. It is also the best place to watch surfers in action on the colossal waves that form near the coast. The waves have been particularly high over the past few years thanks to El Niño.

and character. In this spot, waves are so straight that they form nearly perfect surfing conditions. The cur-

O'ahu

The Makahiki at Waimea Falls

Each year for four months, the ancient Hawaiians celebrated the Makahiki, a traditional harvest festival dedicated to Lono, the god of agriculture. During this period, wars were forbidden, games were held and the *kapu* (taboos) were relaxed. The start of the festival was marked by the first sighting of the constellation Pleiades, usually around the end of October or beginning of November. For a two-month period on each island, the great chiefs would bring *tiki* from their personal temples and travel across the land they owned to collect part of the harvests as an offering. The two subsequent months were devoted to purification rituals. The *tiki* were finally replaced in the temples, the *kapu* were re-instated and Lono symbolically left for Kahiki (Tahiti), returning the pre-eminence to Ku, the totem of chiefs.

In Waimea Falls, the *makahiki* is celebrated during the first weekend in October on the Hale O Lono *heiau* – a tradition that dates back to the 15th century when the temple was built on this site. You can attend a *hula* competition with music as well as the Hawaiian games, just like the ones hundreds of years ago.

rents are violent, as they are everywhere along the north coast, and are therefore reserved for experienced surfers. When water conditions are calmer, in the summer, swimmers and boogie boarders join in. The park has several picnic tables, but the action is in the water, not on the grass – you can't see anything from there.

Only 2.4mi (1.5km) farther lies **Pupukea Beach ★** *(washrooms, showers)*, whose waters are part of a waterpark. The currents here are also too violent for water sports in winter, but during summer, you'll probably see snorkellers and scuba divers. The Old Quarry, opposite the parking lot, is too shallow, but there are two famous sites on both its sides: on the left, the formation of Three Tables, which is pounded by strong waves even in summertime, and on the right, the calmer Shark's Cove, whose rocky coast is riddled with caves. The most beautiful lava caverns are located outside the cove, which, incidentally, does not have any more sharks than the rest of the archipelago.

Near the Foodland supermarket (Mile 6.5), turn *mauka* on Pulukea Road. After about 730yds (800m), a turn-off leads to the **Pu'u O Mahuka Heiau State Monument ★**, perched on a rocky bluff overlooking Waimea Bay from the north. The largest temple in O'ahu, it was probably built around 1600 and was later expanded and transformed into a *luakini heiau*, where human sacrifices took place during wartime. A *lele* was reconstructed, and it's usually covered with offerings.

Carved out by the stream flowing from the cloud-covered peaks of the Ko'olau chain, the Waimea Valley was once one of the most important *ahupua'a* of the north coast. The main political and religious centre of the region, the territory, with its many taro fields, was home to several thousand inhabitants. During the first half of the 19th century, most of the valley's occupants left under the pressure of sandalwood merchants, who still needed more workers. The valley was completely abandoned after a devastating flood in 1860, followed by an equally catastrophic drought. Traces of the settlement, graves and *heiau* still remain.

The valley is today occupied by the **Waimea Falls Adventure Park ★★** *($24, $12 for children under 12, $10 after 4:15pm, parking $3; every day 10am to 5:30pm; 59-864 Kamehameha Hwy., ☎638-8511, two shuttles/day from Waikiki $5 or bus no. 52)*, which is a botanical garden, cultural preserve and tourist park wrapped into one, with a dash of American-style showmanship – guaranteeing renewed success with organized tours.

The park offers three main attractions in three different locations. The first is a rather successful historical presentation of a restored village on its original site. The guide tells about the early Hawaiian's daily life, and introductory craft-making workshops are offered. At the Nature Center, you can attend demonstrations of (ancient) *kahiko hula* dances and traditional Hawaiian games. The highlight attraction of the park, the third option, consists of a series of high-flying dives off the rocks dominating the large natural pool into which the Waimea Falls plunge – a fall of 46ft (14m). Activities begin at 11:15am and take place every 15 to 45min. There is also a host of other attractions, including butterfly greenhouses and the Hale O Lono *heiau*, located near the park entrance. A shuttle runs about every 20min along the sloping path through the valley to the waterfalls. You can also sign up for an entire range of activities, including tours in fou-wheel-drive vehicles, mountain biking and kayaking on the Waimea River. Each activity costs $35. If you're hungry, you'll find a snack bar at the entrance and another one near the waterfalls.

Frangipani

For a more nature-related visit, some come here to appreciate the 6,000 or so tropical and subtropical species in the botanical garden, which is not run by the park but by a nonprofit organization. The $10 reduced price after 4:15pm (the time of the last shows) caters to these visitors. There are 36 gardens along the trails (you will have to share with a few peacocks): Hawaiian, Micronesian, Australian and Asian plants, bromeliads, ferns, bamboo, canna, palms, hibiscus... the list goes on. Of these species, some 400 are rare or very rare.

Almost across the park entrance (Mile 5.6) is a short road leading to the **Waimea Bay Beach Park ★** *(washrooms, showers, picnic tables)*. Its wide sandy beach lines the bay at the mouth of the Waimea Stream. This is a prized site for expert surfers who defy the waves at the northern point. In the winter, the waves outside the sandbar can reach phenomenal heights. Boogie boarders prefer the relative safety of the nearby beach, the only one accessible to them on the North Shore. In summer, the waves dissipate and swimming and snorkelling become possible.

Further south, you can watch surfers in action on Chun's Reef break from the parking lots

O'ahu

(Miles 3 and 3.5). On the eastern side of Waialua Bay, **Hale'iwa Beach Park ★** *(Mile 1.5, 62-449 Kamehameha Hwy.)* draws mostly fishers and, in the evening, members of a local canoe club. The beach is protected by a reef and Puaena Point, which makes it one of the few beaches on the north coast where you can safely swim. Right before the bridge that crosses the Anahulu River, don't miss the legendary "Surfer X-ing" sign in front of the Surf & Sea store *(every day 9am to 7pm;* ☎*637-9887)*, a wooden building dating from the 1920s. Inside, a collection of old surfboards hangs from the ceiling.

In ancient times, the *ali'i* sought refuge at **Hale'iwa ★★** (the frigate house) in the summer to enjoy the refreshing breezes of the trade winds. Queen Lili'uokalani herself had a home here. At the end of the 19th century, the village experienced rapid development during the height of the sugar era and the arrival of the train in 1898. The Hale'iwa Hotel, a vacation resort, was soon built, making it a popular refuge for Honolulu residents. When the sugar era ended, the town took on a new look, preserving some of the old facades of wooden buildings but abandoning the white smoke of the sugar mills for the sand and suntan lotion of the surfers and beachboys. This new role of surfing capital has transformed Hale'iwa into a town where shops are overflowing with surf boards and T-shirts, and streets are lined with friendly cafés, organic-food stores, yoga schools and art galleries.

After crossing the bridge, you have two options: continuing straight ahead to the centre of Hale'iwa, where there are restaurants and shops, or turning west along the coast. If you decide to head towards town, you'll soon see **Lili'uokalani Church**, a Protestant church founded in 1832 whose actual building is from a later date. As a gift, the queen attended mass here during her retreats to Hale'iwa. She gave the congregation a stunning clock that displays the letters of her name in lieu of numbers. The interior of the church is quite modern. Situated slightly back from the road, on the other side, **Matsumoto's** is the most popular place for "shaved ice" (crushed ice sweetened with syrup) in Hawaii (see p 180). If you choose to follow the coast via Hale'iwa Road instead, you'll soon reach **Hale'iwa Ali'i Beach Park** *(every day 6am to 10pm, washrooms, showers, telephone, picnic tables)*, located at the centre of Waialua Bay. The park is popular with intermediate-level surfers, but swimming is not recommended here. Farther west, an access road leads to **Kaiaka Bay Beach Park** *(washrooms, showers, telephone, picnic tables, campgrounds – see p 163)*, forming a large grassy stretch on the point enclosing Kaiaka Bay to the west. The park is mostly deserted, except for a few locals who come jogging here.

At the traffic circle located at the southern exit from Hale'iwa,

Baywatch in Hawaii

After 12 years of *Hawai'i Five-O* and eight years of *Magnum P.I.*, a new television series just made its home in Hawaii. Given the worldwide popularity of *Baywatch*, a show about lifeguards on the Californian coasts, the producers decided to move the series to Hawaii. The first episode aired in the fall of 1999.

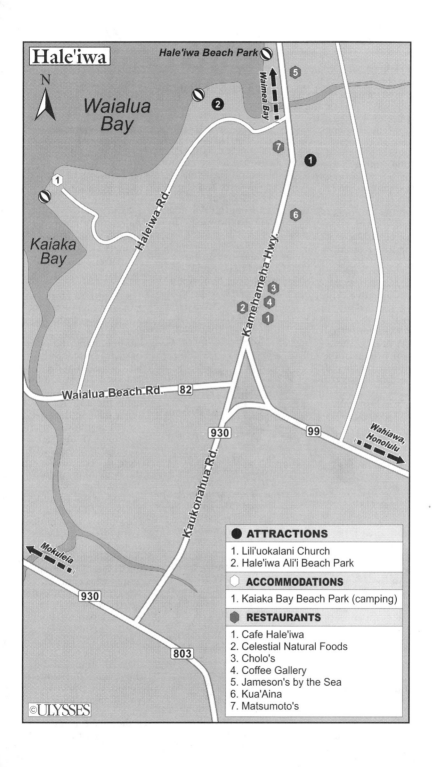

Hale'iwa

N

Waialua Bay

Hale'iwa Beach Park

Waimea Bay

Kaiaka Bay

Haleiwa Rd.

Kamehameha Hwy.

Waialua Beach Rd. 82

930

99

Wahiawa, Honolulu

Kaukonahua Rd.

Mokuleia

930

803

● **ATTRACTIONS**

1. Lili'uokalani Church
2. Hale'iwa Ali'i Beach Park

◇ **ACCOMMODATIONS**

1. Kaiaka Bay Beach Park (camping)

⬡ **RESTAURANTS**

1. Cafe Hale'iwa
2. Celestial Natural Foods
3. Cholo's
4. Coffee Gallery
5. Jameson's by the Sea
6. Kua'Aina
7. Matsumoto's

©ULYSSES

Waialua Beach Road (82) leads to Waialua, a former plantation town, still dominated by the chimney of its sugar mill. The buildings have now been transformed into the **Waialua Coffee Mill** ★ and information centre *(every day 9am to 5pm, ☎637-2411)*, which explains the ins and outs of coffee production. The coffee fields, south of the town, are now on their way to replacing the sugar cane and pineapple, which are less lucrative. You can see them along the road on the way back to Honolulu (Highway 803 or 99). The coffee beans ripen in the fall, but the plants only yield beans after five years. To get to the factory, turn left on Goodale Avenue from the 82, and then right on Kealoha nui Street.

Coffee-tree Branch

To the west, the Farrington Highway passes by **Mokule'ia Beach**, which is popular with local families, and then heads to the **Dillingham** airfield. Several companies offer rides on glider planes, biplanes and motorized ultra-light planes, as well as parachute jumping. The road soon ends near **Ka'ena Point**, the westernmost point of the island, which can only be reached on foot along a sunny trail.

★
The Central Plateau

(one day)

This day trip leads from the edge of Pearl Harbor's bay to the central plateau of Leilehua, which separates the Ko'olau chain to the east from the Wai'anae chain to the west. The last 11,450 acres (4,650ha) of pineapple plantations can be found here. Some of the places on this itinerary can also be visited on the way to the leeward coast, while others can be visited on the way to the North Shore.

Leave Honolulu via the H1 Freeway to the west. At Mile 7.2, take Exit 8B to Waipahu, then Route 7101 to the town centre. From here, signs indicate Hawaii's Plantation Village. Follow the signs on Waipahu Depot Street, then turn left at the light.

Situated northwest of the bay of Pearl Harbor, the Waipahu suburb offers an unusual setting to one of the most interesting museums on the island, **Hawaii's Plantation Village ★★** *($7; Mon to Fri 9am to 3pm, Sat 10am to 3pm; 94-695 Waipahu St.; ☎677-0110)*. Within sight of a large sugar mill, which was still functioning not too long ago, an early

20th-century-style plantation village has been reconstructed. You can discover its secrets on the 90min guided tour *(departures every hour)*. In addition to the dormitories and the employees' homes, which were furnished according to their ethnic origin, you will discover a secret Chinese organization, a tofu manufacturer, a Shinto temple from 1914, a plantation store and even a Sumo ring!

The Visitor Center's museum completes the tour with an insightful look at the sugar plantation era and the people who brought it to life. The sign at the entrance displaying the Hawaiian Islands highlights the importance of sugar mills in the past and their gradual disappearance: of the 130 or so sugar refineries that were in operation at the beginning of the 20th century, only seven are still running today. With the help of old photos, quotations and personal possessions, the museum clearly illustrates the harsh life of the immigrants who came to work in the sugar-cane fields: Chinese, Portuguese, Japanese, Puerto Ricans, Okinawans, Koreans and Filipinos were awakened at 5am every morning, and if they weren't up within 30min, the police would take them from their beds. "Deserters," if they were caught, were either thrown in prison, fined or worse, subjected to double the working hours for every day they missed. Take a look at the *bangos*, identification badges that were introduced in 1905. Workers had to present their badge to receive their pay and to buy things on credit at the plantation store.

From the centre of Waipahu, Farrington Highway heads west to the junction of Fort Weaver Road (76).

Those who are fascinated by old trains can make a side trip to the **Hawaiian Railway Museum** (☎681-5461). To get here, take Highway 76 South, turn right at Renton Road, and then drive 4mi (2.5km) to the end. The road crosses **Ewa**, a former plantation village that is now mostly residential areas. A revitalization project is currently under way to rejuvenate the old centre, which still features a few wooden homes. If you're coming from the highway, take Exit 5 (Mile 5) towards Ewa to reach Fort Weaver Road.

More than just a museum, you'll discover a large warehouse packed with a jumble of locomotives and freight cars from another era. "Ewa 1," a little red locomotive standing near the entrance, was the first locomotive to be put in service on the Ewa plantation in 1890 – and the only one left. Every Sunday, volunteers from the Hawaiian Railway Society organize 90min excursions *($8, 12:30pm and 2:30pm)* aboard old open-air (but covered) freight cars. Every second Sunday of the month, the luxurious Dillingham Parlor Car, built in 1900 especially for the founder of the O'ahu Railway Company, is hitched up to the train *($15)*. The train heads 6.5mi (10.5km) to the Wai'nae coast, one of the last surviving stretches of the line that once ran from Honolulu to the northwest coast. The section of railway from Pearl Harbor is still in good condition and it may be restored in the future. Ewa Beach, at the end of Highway 76 South, has a bit of a view of the distant buildings in Honolulu, but is not really worth the trip.

North of its intersection with the Farrington Highway, Fort Weaver Road becomes **Kunia Road** ★ *(exit at Mile 5.7 on the H1 Freeway West).* This road to the North Shore is a quieter alternative than the H2 Freeway. After a few miles, you will see the first Del Monte pineapple fields, whose production centre is situated just north of the town of Kunia. The carpet of fields sprawl below the foothills of the Wai'anae mountain chain, and they are among the last ones in Hawai'i, in addition to the ones on the central plain of Maui. The international market has made Hawaiian pineapple too costly, so other crops, such as the more lucrative coffee plantations, have gradually replaced pineapple plantations. Since pineapple production is year-round, you'll be able to see every stage of the fruit's development.

Twice a month, the **Nature Conservancy** *(1116 Smith St., Suite 201, Honolulu, HI 96817, ☎537-4508)* organizes guided hikes in the **Honouliuli Preserve**, one of the last corners of unspoiled wilderness in O'ahu, nestled in the southern slopes of the Wai'anae chain. The park has 45 species of rare plants and animals, some of which are endemic. Brightly coloured snails share this space with forest birds such as the *'elepaio*, *'i'iwi*, *'papane*, *'amakihi*, as well as the *pueo* (owl). Of the two trails, the Palikea Trail, which goes through mountain crests, offers the most beautiful viewpoints of the coast and Pearl Harbor.

After 7mi (11km), the rural scenery on Kunia Road changes to wire netting and barbed-wire fences in the area of the Schofield Barracks, headquarters of the 25th battalion, an

O'ahu

infantry of 11,000 soldiers. Take Highway 99 South, then turn left on Highway 80 North to the centre of **Wahi'awa**. This charmless GI town, which is filled with uniformed soldiers and lined with fast-food restaurants, is the gateway to several gardens and ancient sites of varying interest.

From Highway 80, drive 1mi (1.5km) along California Avenue to the **Wahi'awa Botanical Garden** ★ *(free admission; every day 9am to 4pm, 1936 California Ave., ☎621-7321, bus no. 52 or no. 62)*. This pleasant tropical park, a lovely green space in the middle of town, is the result of a business experiment initiated in the 1920s. To determine what species of trees would be suitable to reforest Hawaii, dozens of different trees from around the world were planted here. A few short trails crisscross the side of the ravine where the park lies. Here you will walk among bamboo, chicle, fig, choketree, Mindanao eucalyptus (protected) with its rainbow-coloured bark, jacaranda, camphor, as well as other tree ferns. Part of the park is laid out with markers; at the visitor centre, you can obtain a map to show you where the different species are located. The park does make for a pleasant stroll, but no need to go out of your way to see it.

On the other side of Highway 80, California Avenue leads this time near the three **Healing Stones**, which are usually adorned with *lei* that for a long time were thought to have healing powers. The stones are housed inside a small shelter, covered with rather ugly white marble. Again, not worth the detour.

North of Wahi'awa, just past Mile 1 near Whitmore Avenue, a short dirt road on your left leads to the **Kukaniloko Birthstones** ★, which are shaded by a cluster of eucalyptus and coconut trees. Legend says that the children of chiefs born here were promised a great future. The event was marked by a ritual involving not less than 48 *ali'i*, who were in charge of watching the newborn or of playing sacred drums announcing the birth to the people. Fruit offerings and stones wrapped in *ti* leaves are still regularly laid on the rocks – and occasionally even an entire piglet! Some stones bear vague traces of petroglyphs, but they are hard to make out.

About 275yds north (300m), at the intersection of Highways 80 and 99, the Del Monte company created the **Variety Garden** ★, an astonishing garden with several dozen species of pineapples – from the minuscule Brazilian *ananas ananassoides*, which is just a few centimetres long, to the red-coloured Indo-Chinese *Saigon Red*. You can also see the different stages of development of the Smooth Cayenne, the commercial variety grown in both Hawaii and the Ivory Coast. As the signs explain, this type of pineapple yields only one fruit 11 to 13 months after shoots are planted, and only reaches maturity seven months later.

The Dole company, Del Monte's first competitor, built the **Dole Plantation Pavilion** *(free admission; every day 9am to 6pm; 64-1550 Kamehameha Hwy., ☎621-8408; bus no. 52 or no. 55)* only 0.8mi (1.3km) from there on Route 99. A frequent stop on organized tours, it basically consists of a large souvenir shop offering a selection of T-shirts, mugs and cuddly pineapple-shaped toys. The free juice-fountain is

Pineapple

gone, but you can still buy delicious pineapple whips sold in the snack bar alongside the chocolate pineapples and pineapple cheese cakes. Behind the boutique lies a pineapple garden similar to Del Monte's, but accompanied with a short historical portrait of the fruit and the Dole family business. Recognized in the *Guiness Book of Records* as the largest in the world, the nearby maze *($4.50, every day 9am to 5:30pm)* is shaped in the form of a pineapple. Created in 1997, it is made of tropical plants only.

From here, you can reach the north coast at Hale'iwa in about 10min or head back to Honolulu via the 99 and then the freeway (about 45min).

★
The Leeward Coast

(one day)

Nestled at the foot of the Wai'anae peaks, the **Wai'anae Coast** is the least touristic side of the island. It has always lived in relative isolation, due in part to the rocky mountainous barrier, and was one of the last areas to be converted to Christianity. With its rural, laid-back feeling, it's definitely more authentic than the rest of O'ahu. The leeward coast offers a string of pretty, white-sand beaches lapped by waves that become more powerful as you head north,

making it a popular spot with local surfers. Ka'ena Point is the westernmost point of the island. Nothing here is really geared for tourists and you will have to settle for the conveniences found in a few towns. The coast is served by bus no. 51.

The southwestern tip of the island, around Barbers Point (named after the German captain who ran aground here in 1796), has recently seen the development of Kapolei, a new residential area that the government wanted to turn into a dormitory suburb of Honolulu. A new hydroplane service (still in trial period) began in the fall of 1999.

Via Exit 1 (past Kapolei), shortly before the end of the freeway, you'll reach the Hawaiian Waters Adventure Park.

O'ahu has often been criticized for not having any amusement parks, and this has been partially remedied by the **Hawaiian Waters Adventure Park** *($30, $20 from 4 to 11; every day 10:30am to 6pm; 400 Farrington Hwy., ☎945-3928, www.HawaiianWaters.com)*, whose many slides, waves pools and artificial rivers delight Hawaiian children and families every weekend. Obviously, the best time to come here is on weekdays to avoid the long lineups.

Along the coast stretches the Ko'Olina tourist complex, with golf course, marina, and the large Ihilani Hotel. Between the two lie the four coconut-studded, sandy indentations of **Ihilani Beach ★★** *(washrooms, showers, telephones, water fountains)*, which were built right into the rocky coastline. These wide, shallow artificial lagoons look like coves and are large enough to become fun swimming spots (year-round) for both children and adults. What's more, thanks to its distance from Waikiki, Ko'Olino only receives a small amount of visitors. A paved path follows the coast to the marina. Tell the parking-lot attendant that you are going to the public parking lot.

The H1 Freeway ends 3mi (5km) from the southwest coast, just past the exit for the Ko'Olina Resort. Farrington Avenue, which runs along the coastline, is a busy two-lane road. Coming from the south, make sure you put on your turning signal to cross it – which doesn't necessarily guarantee success! The best thing to do might be to head to the end and make a few stops on your return trip.

Just after reaching the coast, the **Kahe Point Park** *(washrooms, telephone, picnic tables)* appears just before a

O'ahu

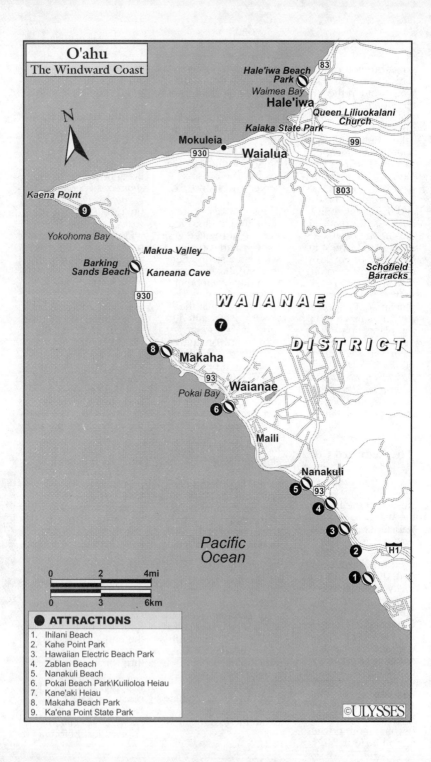

large power station. The park is popular with fishers and divers – who dive in front of the point – but holds little interest for others. North of the power plant, the lovely **Hawaiian Electric Beach Park** (which surfers have nicknamed "Tracks" because of the former railroad line it borders) is shared by boogie boarders on its southern edge and by longboarders on its northern tip, who are drawn by the waves even in the middle of summer. Swimmers will enjoy the sandy, shallow water, but not the noise of the power plant's generators and the cars on the highway.

The village of Nanakuli, along Farrington Highway, is situated on land belonging to the Hawaiian Home Lands settlement and is home to a large Samoan community. There's a supermarket, several fast-food eateries and two beaches. The southern-most beach, **Zablan Beach** ★ (*washrooms, showers, picnic tables*), is a good spot for swimming and usually has lifeguards. Since surfing and boogie boarding are not possible here, it's often deserted. The actual **Nanakuli Beach** (*washrooms, exterior showers, picnic tables*) is situated further north (Mile 5.7). Narrower and covered with rocks, it is clearly not the best place for swimming.

Farther north, between Miles 8 and 9, stretches **Ulehawa Beach Park** (*washrooms, showers, picnic tables*). This long white-sand beach, which has a view of the eroded Wai'anae chain, is fringed with a few coconut trees. On weekends, Hawaiian families come here to picnic. Just past it lies **Ma'ili Beach Park** (*washrooms, showers, picnic tables and barbecue pits*). Camping is officially allowed here, but the park lacks shade and the noise of cars constantly zooming by disturbs the tranquility. Surfers flock to the northern part of the beach near the pier.

Just past Mile 10 is **Wai'anae**, the main town on the west coast. It has several supermarkets and a selection of fast-food chains. At the entrance (Mile 10.2), turn left onto Polai Bay Street. Drive past Lualualei Beach Park and continue to the Kaneilio Peninsula where the **Polai Beach Park** ★ (*washrooms, showers, picnic tables, beach volleyball*) is nestled. Kaneilio Point is the site of **Kuilioloa Heiau**, a three-tiered structure that offers a gorgeous view of the coast, dominated by the eroded Wai'anae mountain chain. The bay, whose entrance is partly protected by a long pier and is a favourite spot for fishers, is where you will find one the few calm

beaches on the west coast.

*At the northern exit from Wai'anae (Mile 12.6), Makaha Valley Road, as its name suggests, heads through the rocky amphi-theatre of the **Makaha Valley**.*

Drive past the Country Club, turn right before the Golf Club, then turn right again onto Mauna'olu Street, which leads to the Mauna Olu Estates guard post. With permission from the security guards at the gate, you can visit the **Kane'aki Heiau** ★ ★ (*Tue to Sun 10am to 2pm, ☎695-8174*), one of the most interesting *heiaus* in Hawaii. Sometimes there's no security guard here when the site opens – but he eventually shows up. After passing through security, follow the signs to the site.

Founded between the mid 15th and the 17th century, the temple seems to have first been devoted to agricultural deities – Lono was first – before being transformed into a *luakini heiau* and dedicated to Ku, the god of war. At the end of the 18th century, the great Kamehameha himself sought refuge here. The central part of the *heiau*, its most sacred area, shaded by great *kukui* (candlenut trees), was authentically reconstructed based on the Hawaiian temples described by the first explorers. There are

O'ahu

two thatched huts (Hale Mana and Hale Pahu, the house of spirits and the house of drums), an altar where offerings were laid (*lele*), situated between the two houses, as well as two *anu'u* (ceremonial ovens) and a *ki'i* (*tiki*) representing Ku. It is no longer possible to go inside the temple since the walls could crumble at any moment; you'll have to settle for a walk around the structure.

Back on the road, at Mile 14.3 you will reach **Mahaha Beach Park** ★★ (*washrooms, showers*), a mecca for surfers and especially longboarders on the Wai'anae coast. The first international surfing competition was held here in 1952 – it's still the only contest on the west coast. If water conditions are too rough for swimming, you can always watch the surfing action from the carpet of soft sand. Some boogie boards also hit the waves near the beach. There's usually a van selling drinks and snacks on the weekends.

At Mile 17.3, a parking lot on the opposite side of the road leads to **Kaneana Cave**, a rather uninteresting cavern whose entrance is covered in graffiti. Near Mile 18.7 lies the unmarked **Barking Sands Beach**, situated on Yokohama Bay in the vast Makua Valley (occupied by the army). The green cliffs and ridges here form a vast amphitheatre.

The Farrington Highway ends at the entrance to **Ka'ena Point State Park** where a road leads to a U.S. Air Force station that specializes in satellite tracking. The beach (*washrooms*), which is bordered with rocks, is swept by strong currents and pounded by waves. Only experienced surfers and boogie boarders dare to go in the water – but sometimes a few swimmers venture out in summer after consulting with the lifeguard on duty.

A trail, reserved exclusively for mountain bikes, runs along the coast. A walk to **Ka'ena Point** (2.7 mi) will take about 60min, where you will find an automated lighthouse. The landscape is arid and shade virtually inexistant (after all, the word Kaena does mean "heat"). You'll pass the nesting site of gannets and, with a little luck, in the morning you'll be able to see some dolphins.

Outdoor Activities

Swimming

With 100mi (160km) of white sand, there's no shortage of beaches on O'ahu. However, always keep in mind that the currents, like everywhere in Hawaii, can be dangerous. Waikiki and the south coast have the calmest water conditions, especially during winter, when the waves pound to the north. This is the only spot where you can safely swim all year, although there are sometimes strong currents offshore. Be careful not to step on the coral reefs; not only does this kill the reef, but you can also cut yourself. Lastly, watch out for jellyfish, which appear in cycles.

Stretching from Kahanamoku Beach in the west to Sans Souci Beach in the east, **Waikiki**'s beaches form a long string of sandy shoreline, separated in places only by a pier or a low concrete wall. Most beaches offer good swimming conditions. Heading west to east, you'll discover **Kahanamoku Beach** and **Fort de Russy Beach**, which have the same boardwalk; narrow

Halekulani Beach; and Central Waikiki Beach, the widest beach, shaded by the first large hotels of the resort.

Its neighbour, **Kuhio Beach**, is protected by a seawall, creating two basins that are excellent spots for swimming – but the only time you'll be here by yourself is perhaps at the crack of dawn. The most popular spot is in front of the Moana Surfrider Hotel where the two beaches join up, forming a crescent-shaped cove. The first surfing lessons are given at 9am, and all day long, cruisers and sun worshippers mix with fashion fanatics and happy sandcastle builders. Farther east, the Kapahulu Groin pier marks the border of **Queen's Surf Beach**, one of the widest in Waikiki. It's a popular spot for locals as well as the gay community. Swimming is a bit more invigorating here compared to elsewhere in Waikiki.

Just beyond Queen's Surf Beach is one of the loveliest beaches in Waikiki, **Sans Souci Beach**, which is shaded by a row of slender palm trees.

One other beach lies west of Waikiki, **Ala Moana Beach**, across from the shopping centre of the same name between Kewalo Harbor, frequented by fishers, and Ala Wai Harbor, where yachts are

Duke Paoa Kahanamoku

This strange name is in fact a title. Duke Kahanamoku was given the same name as his father, born on July 21, 1869, the day the Duke of Edinburgh visited Honolulu. At a very early age, Duke learned to swim and surf the waves of Waikiki. His surfboard, which has been preserved, measured 16ft (5m) long and weighed nearly 110lbs (50kg)! He quickly acquired a certain reputation. After his first world record for the 50m freestyle achieved in Honolulu Harbour in 1911, he represented the United States at the 1912 Olympics in Stockholm, where he won two gold medals and established a new world record. His unique swimming style soon got the name "the Hawaiian crawl." Deprived of medals during the war, he turned to surfing and introduced the sport in Australia in 1915. In 1917, he achieved a world surfing record when he glided on a 33ft (10m) wave for nearly 1mi (2km). After the war, he cleaned up at the 1920 Olympics in Anvers where he won another gold medal. Now internationally famous, he appeared on the silver screen with John Wayne, and in 1925, he was catapulted to heroic status when, on his board, he saved eight people on a fishing boat that ran aground off Newport Beach in California. He participated in three more Olympic Games. Duke Kahanamoku died in January of 1968 at the age of 77.

moored. To the east, in the cove formed by the base of the Aina Moana Peninsula, the sand is finer and the beach is particularly enjoyable for a dip.

As you travel around the island, you'll discover a number of other beaches that are ideal for swimming. Most of them are found along the windward coast: **Waimanalo**, stretching 3.7mi (6km) and ending in the north at **Bellows Beach** (a great beach for children); and **Kailua Beach**, voted O'ahu's best beach for

O'ahu

swimming, windsurfing, kayaking and other water sports. Protected by a coral reef, it has a sandy bottom and is quite peaceful on weekdays. Farther north, the beach at the **Kualoa Regional Park**, although narrow, is suitable for swimming since the water is quite shallow. **Hanauma Bay**, although not very peaceful, has two advantages: calm waters and a coral reef teeming with thousands of fish.

On the north coast, the only beach that is safe year-round is at the **Hale'iwa Beach Park**. The popular winter surfing beaches, especially those of **Waimea Bay**, are much calmer in summer, but always ask the lifeguard about the current water conditions. As for the Wai'anae Coast, except for **Pokai Beach Park**, the water is never very calm.

Surfing and Boogie Boarding

Every morning at the crack of dawn, surfers and boogie boarders religiously head for the waves, boards under their arms. Although the waves at **Waikiki** aren't what they used to be, hundreds of boarders – especially Japanese – flock here to try the legendary sport of the gods. The day usually begins with a balancing and positioning lesson on land at Kuhio or Waikiki Beach itself – and then it's off to the waves! Most schools guarantee that you'll be able to stand up on the board within 24hrs and that you'll be able to surf more or less correctly within a week. A word of advice: it is (logically) much easier to learn on a longboard – it's in fact the board of choice for surfers who swarm to the south coast to test its waters in summer when the North Shore waves peter out. Their favourite waves are off the **Fort De Russy** and **Kahanamoky Beaches**, as well as **Diamond Head Beach**, east of Waikiki. Some of the famous breaks here include Old Mans, Tonggs and Suicide. **Canoes** and **Queens**, opposite Moana, may not be the most spectacular, but the setting is lovely. Lastly, Bowls (or Kaiser Bowl), on **Ala Moana Beach**, delights both longboarders and boogie boarders alike. The north coast is a surfer's paradise: **Sunset** (4 to 6m in winter), **Pipeline** and **Banzai**, which have absolutely perfect waves, **Waimea Bay** (10 to 13ft or 3 to 4m) inside the reef, much higher outside), **Chun's Reef** and **Hale'iwa**. All of these have become legendary in the surfing world, and are all unquestionably reserved for specialists. The waves begin to pound the north coast in September and then gradually subside between March and April. The same holds true for the Wai'anae Coast, where **Makaha Beach Park** is one of the most popular gathering spots for longboarding enthusiasts.

In Waikiki, boogie-board enthusiasts swear by **Kapahulu Groin**. Another option is **Point Panic**, facing Kewalo Harbor. At the eastern point of the island, **Sandy Beach** is also an all-time favourite. Although the water looks very shallow, it quickly descends to over 10ft (3m), creating violent waves, some of which break close to the beach. In summer, watch out for the strong current. A bit further north, **Makapu'u Beach** is also popular with boogie boarders. The waves break a long ways from the shore and can reach up to 13ft (4m) in winter. **Waimanalo, Bellows** and **Kailua** are calmer beaches that are very safe for both children and beginners. On the north coast, try **Waimea Bay**.

Many inns in Waikiki and a few bed and breakfasts lend boogie boards and sometimes surfboards to guests at no charge or for a few dollars. A more expensive alternative is to rent a board at one of the beaches or at one of the specialty shops. You'll have to pay about $8 for a boogie board and anywhere between $18 to $25 for a surfboard (longboards are even more expensive).

For water conditions, call Surf Report: ☎*596-7873 or 593-2170* ☎*538-1961*

Windsurfing

Although you might be able to find places it rent sailboards in Waikiki, that is not the best spot for windsurfing since the winds that blow offshore can quickly carry you away. Savvy windsurfers instead choose **Diamond Head** (especially in the spring and summer) and **Kailua Beach**, in the slipstream of the trade winds that are constantly blowing. Kailua Beach is perfect for beginners (there are no waves inside the reef) and even experts (thrill-seekers head outside the reef to Jump City). You'll find many specialty stores right along the beach. Naish Windsurfing Hawaii *(155 Hamakua Dr.,* ☎*262-6068),* founded by Robby Naish, a world-renowned windsurfing specialist, rents equipment and offers lessons for all levels. The windward coast and the north coast provide a few other surfing opportunities at **Secret Island** (all levels) with Kualoa Rand;

"Backyards," off **Sunset Point** (experts), which has gigantic waves, **Hale'iwa Beach Park** (several shops including Surf & Sea) and **Mokule'ia**, which has the most reliable winds on the north coast. Regulars come here mostly in the spring and fall; beginners prefer the summer when the waves take a bit of a vacation.

Scuba Diving and Snorkelling

Although the Hawaiian underwater world perhaps doesn't offer the most interesting marine life in the Pacific, scuba diving and snorkelling are nevertheless popular here. In Waikiki, there are two sites worth mentioning: **Sans Souci Beach** and the renowned **Rainbow Reef**, opposite Ala Moana Park, where the fish are used to being fed. But this is nothing compared to the wonderful **Hanauma Bay**, whose reefs are teeming with thousands of colourful fish that swim about in its turquoise blue waters. You can rent a mask and flippers on the site *($6, $8 for a mask with a magnified lens, $5 deposit, no credit cards; every day 8am to 4:30pm).*

Among the other popular locations on the island are **Secret Island**

(Kualoa Ranch), **La'ie Beach**, **Malaekahana Beach Park** on the windward coast, and **Hale'iwa Beach Park** on the north coast. In summer, the waves dissipate and divers have free reign. **Shark's Cove**, at Pupukea Beach Park, is popular for its cave and lava formations, while the nearby **Three Tables**, just beyond Shark's Cove, are famous for their three sections of coral that emerge at low tide and for their reef fish. Surf & Sea, at Hale'iwa, rents equipment and organizes transportation for its customers to various dive sites. They also offer lessons. There are also several dive sites off the **Wai'anae Coast**: Electric Beach, an ideal spot for beginner divers – fish and turtles are drawn by the warm water coming out of the nearby power station; Nanakuli Beach Park at Ma'ili Point, which features the Mahi shipwreck, a renowned dive site frequented by manta rays; and the lava caves of Makaha.

Snorkelling equipment is readily available on some beaches, but it's cheaper to rent the gear at specialty shops. It costs about $5 a day to rent a mask and fins *(between $10 and $15 per week).* One of the least expensive is Snorkel Bob's *(702 Kapahulu Ave.,* ☎*735-7944),* a shop that allows you to take the equipment to other islands (for example, you can borrow the equipment in Waikiki and return it in Maui). For one dive, expect to pay at least $80 to $90 per person.

Snuba of O'ahu (☎396-6163) offers non-certified dives using a long breathing tube attached to an air tank on an inflatable raft. Ideal for first-timers, the diver can descend to 16-20ft (5-6m). But the downside is the price: $85 for only 30min (divers must be over eight years old). Diving is possible in Maunalua Bay and Hanauma Bay, as well as at Ko'Olina.

Water Sports

Waikiki offers a great variety of water sports, including parascending ($30 to $40), which allows you to fly above the beach, motor-boating ($30 to $40), water-skiing, wakeboarding and canoe surfing. All the Koko marina outfitters at Maunalua Bay (on the road to Hanauma Bay) offer the same type of activities at similar prices.

Sea kayaking (with one- or two-seat boats) is quite popular. Boats can be rented on Kuhio Beach and Fort de Russy Beach in Waikiki, but the best place for sea kayaking has to be Kailua Bay. The most enjoyable excursions ($50 to $70), on bright

turquoise waters, head to the Molukua Islands where there's a bird sanctuary across from **Lanikai Beach**. For information, contact **Kailua Sailboard and Kayak** (130 Kailua Rd., ☎262-2555) or **Twogood Kayaks** (345 Hahani St., ☎262-5656). Waimea Falls Park also offers guided (or unaccompanied) 60min tours ($35) between the park and Waimea Bay.

Deep-Sea Fishing

The **Hawai'i Charter Skippers Association** (☎594-9100) can give you a list of companies offering one-day, half-day and three-quarter-day fishing trips to catch the tuna or swordfish of your dreams. Daily departures are at **Kewalo Harbor** and **Kailua Harbor**. Most companies have a policy of releasing catches, some allow fishers to keep them, while others sell the catch of the day! Ask before signing up. An economical alternative is sharing a boat with several people.

Cruises

This category covers a great range of activities, including catamaran rides along the Diamond Head coastline,

excursions to Pearl Harbor (without possibility of getting off at the *Arizona* Memorial), snorkelling excursions off Waikiki and sea rafting, not to mention tours on offshore vessels and even bumper-boat rides! For the best deals, consult the free brochures.

Several travel agencies also offer **dinner-theatre** sunset cruises. Prices vary significantly ($20 to $70) depending on the tour operator or vendor, and you can often find some great deals. Among the most reputed excursions are the *Star of Honolulu*, a magnificent ship with four decks (☎983-STAR, 800-334-6191, www.paradisecruises. com), the *Navatek I* and the catamaran *Ali'i Lai* (☎539-9400). All of them feature a Polynesian-style show after dinner. Later in the evening, the dining room transforms into a dance floor.

If you have always dreamed of stepping aboard a **submarine**, **Atlantis Adventures** (☎973-9811 or 800-548-6262, www.atlantisadventures. com) will take you down to depths of 100ft (30m) to see an artificial reef that was created around an old tanker. Through the portholes you can see fish and shipwrecks. Visitors are whisked to the sub aboard a catamaran. The tours last about 2hrs and cost between $50 and $90. Other companies offer similar trips: **Voyager** *($90 for 45min)* and **Nautilus Subsea Adventures** *(☎591-9199)*, which has a boat that is a cross between a submarine and a glass-bottomed boat *($30-$60)*.

There is an infinite number of activities around the island, including **dolphin-watching** with **Dolphin Excursions** *(☎239-5579)* along the Ka'ena coast, home to some 300 dolphins, and a harmless hunt for **humpback whales** from January to April (Maui, however, is the best place for this kind of trip). There are also **glass-bottomed boat rides** from the Koko Marina and Kane'ohe Marina, and **yacht rides** in Kailua Bay.

Cycling

Although it is possible to rent road bikes and mountain bikes *(Blue Sky Rentals, 1920 Ala Moana Blvd., ☎947-0101)*, it's practically impossible to cycle around the island because there's so much traffic. However, the Department of Land and Natural Resources Division of Forestry and Wildlife *(DOFAW, ☎973-9782)* maintains a 60mi (100km) network of trails, three quarters of which are open to mountain bikes. The length of the trails

varies between one and 9mi (two and 15km). One of the most popular trails (5mi or 8km return) leads to Ka'ena Point, at the tip of the Wa'anae coast. Waimea Falls Park and the Kualoa Ranch also organize bike trips.

Golf

O'ahu is home to nearly half the golf courses in all of Hawaii. There are 36 in total, mostly located in the south. Not all of them, however, are easily accessible. Six municipal courses *(Ala Wai, Pali, Ewa Village, Ted Makalena, West Loch and Kahuku)* are so popular that it's nearly impossible to get to play on them, although you'll have a better chance on weekdays. The rest of the golf courses are either private or semi-private, or owned by hotels. If you're staying at one these hotels, you're in luck. Another option is to brave the afternoon heat between 1pm and 3pm, when there are often reduced rates. In general, green fees range between $80 and $120, golf cart included. At $75, the **Hawaii Country Club** is one of the least expensive golf courses on the island. It often offers specials as low as $50. If you're looking for a challenge, opt for the golf course at the Turtle

Bay Hilton (**Links at Kuilima**), where the last three holes are right beside the sea. If that's not challenging enough, try the golf course at the **Ko'olau Golf Club** beyond Kane'ohe. It has a majestic mountain setting, with no less than 81 bunkers and an equal amount of lakes! At every hole, you have to be careful not to sink your ball. Other popular courses are the following: Hawaii Prince and 'Ewa Beach International Country Club, both near 'Ewa; Hawaii Kai, designed by golfing expert Robert Trent Jones; Bayview and Makaha on the Wai'anae coast, which mostly attracts local players.

Tennis

Given the high price of land, no hotels in Waikiki offer tennis courts. However, you can play on the free courts at Kapi'olani Park and Ala Moana Park.

Hiking

The **Moanalua Gardens Foundation** *(☎839-5334)*, the **Hawaii Nature Center** *(☎955-0100)*, the **Sierra Club** *(☎538-6616)* and the **Hawaiian Trail & Mountain Club** *(☎674-1459 or 377-5442)* offer

O'ahu

organized hiking excursions, usually on weekends.

In addition to **Diamond Head** (see p 115), there are numerous hiking possibilities in the Honolulu area. The most popular trails climb the southern slopes of the Ko'olau mountain chain and offer both a refreshing forest setting and magnificent views of the coast. Some of the most popular trails are **Manoa Falls Trail** (1.6mi or 2.6km return, see p 108), **Aiea Heights Trail** (a 4.8mi or 7.7km loop trail, see p 116) and the paths that crisscross the Tantatus forest (Makiki Heights), including **Manoa Cliffs Trail** (3.4mi or 5.5km in each direction). Note that all of these trails are often muddy.

There are also numerous options around the island: **Makapu'u Lighthouse Trail** (2mi or 3.2km return, see p 122) offers fine views of the coast; **Nakoa Trail** (5mi or 8km return, see p 130) explores the Kahana Valley, and swimming in its stream; the **Sacred Falls** trail (if it has reopened) leads to lovely waterfalls (3.1mi or 5km one way, see p 131). In addition, there's a guided hiking tour with the Nature Conservancy at the **Honouliuli Preserve** (see p 139) and an easy 2.5mi (4km) trail to **Ka'ena Point** (see p 144) along the remote coast.

Horseback Riding

Horseback riders, expert and novice, are not forgotten here. **Kualoa Ranch** (☎237-8515) trails rides for both beginner and experienced riders in the Ka'a'awa Valley. Farther north, the **Turtle Bay Hilton** (☎293-8811) has its own stable. It offers rides on the beach during the day as well as sunset rides on the weekends. Other options include **Happy Trails** (☎638-7433), situated in the **Waimea Valley**, and **Correa Trail Hawai'i** (☎259-9005), which offers rides at the foot of the Ko'olau mountains above **Waimanalo Bay**. You can also attend polo matches that take place in town every Sunday from May to October. Most of the excursions cost between $40 and $50 per hr.

Flying and Aerial Sports

Several **helicopter** companies offer flights around the island – you'll notice ads posted everywhere. It is difficult to recommend one company over another since they all offer similar trips (*from 10 to 60min*) at about the same prices (*from $50 to $150*). If you're looking for something out of the ordinary, opt for a **hydroplane ride** with **Island Seaplane Service** (☎836-7273).

From Dillingham Airfield west of Hale'iwa, the sky truly is the limit: you can ride on a **biplane**, **glider plane** (*$60*) or a motorized **ultra-light plane**. In addition, there is **parachuting** and **hang-gliding**, and if you're certified, you can fly alone. Tandem flights with a "driver" (no experience required) are also possible at Makapu'u Point, where the world record was beaten – 34hrs in the air!

Accommodations

Downtown Honolulu

Nu'uanu YMCA
$25/person, $143/week
sb, ≈, laundry, ⊘
1441 Pali Hwy., corner of Vineyard Blvd.
☎526-3556
The Nu'uanu YMCA has the same small, worn-out rooms (with shared bathrooms) as the Central YMCA. When it's hot, you can borrow a fan at the front desk – while supplies last, and they run out quite rapidly. Many Vietnam veterans seem to have taken up permanent

residence here. The only redeeming quality of this place is its excellent sports equipment.

Executive Centre Hotel
$170-$245 bkfst incl.
≈, ≡, △, laundry, ☉, ctv, ◉
1088 Bishop St.
☎ *539-3000 or 800-92-ASTON*
⇥ *922-8785*
www.aston-hotels.com
The only large hotel in downtown Honolulu, this Aston hotel caters almost exclusively to business travellers who will enjoy its range of services. The hotel offers sumptuous suites whose price varies according to the direction they're facing.

Near the Airport

Honolulu Airport Mini Hotel
$20 for 2hrs, $26 for 3hrs, $31 for 4hrs, $35 for 8hrs
open 24hrs
Honolulu Airport, International Terminal
☎ *836-3044*
⇥ *834-8985*
Not just near the airport, but actually right inside it, the Mini Hotel offers tiny rooms with single beds so that travellers can unwind for a few hours. This is a practical option if you have to wait until the next morning for a connecting flight to the outlying island after arriving late at night. During the day, it offers 2 to 4hr rates, and at night, you can rent a room for 8hrs at a flat rate of $35, which includes the use of a shower. If you wish, you can take only the shower for $8.50 (towel included). All prices are per person since the rooms are too small to accommodate couples. Reservations are recommended.

Nimitz Shower Tree
$18/person, $110/week
sb, laundry
3085 North Nimitz Hwy.
☎ *833-1411*
Located near the H1 Freeway, but reasonably quiet, the Shower Tree offers cubicle-style rooms like those found in some boarding schools or in budget hotels in Singapore. Each "compartment" is separated from the next one by a partition that doesn't quite go to the ceiling, which can be a little annoying if your neighbour starts snoring. That said, the rates are half those at the Honolulu Airport Mini Hotel. Many of its guests are Asian airline employees with small budgets, which explains why it's dark in the rooms all day long. The price includes a shower *(shower only $7.50)*. The hotel is open 24hrs and the reception is quite friendly. Reservations recommended.

Pacific Marina Inn
$90-$110
≈, ℜ, laundry, ≡, tv, ℝ
2628 Waiwai Loop
☎ *836-1131 or 800-367-5004*
☎ *800-272-5275 from Hawaii*
⇥ *833-0851*
Situated a little farther away from the highway than the other airport hotels, next to Keehi Lagoon Park, the Pacific Marina Inn offers lovely rooms with showers. Renovated in 1997 and a member of the Cast Resorts & Hotels chain, it offers a free shuttle service to the airport 24hrs a day.

Best Western
$110-$295
≈, laundry, ≡, ctv
3253 North Nimitz Hwy.
☎ *836-3636 or 800-800-4683*
☎ *800-327-4570 from Hawaii*
⇥ *834-7406*
gbdc@lava.net
Half of the rooms face the eight-lane the H1 Freeway, which passes halfway up the hotel. You should ask for a room on the lower floors – or bring your earplugs! The hotel offers three room categories, the difference mostly being the size. A shuttle service runs to the airport 24hrs a day.

Honolulu Airport Hotel
$112-$260
≈, laundry, ≡, ctv
3401 North Nimitz Hwy.
☎ *836-0661 or 800-800-3477*
☎ *800-327-5301 from Hawaii*
⇥ *833-1738*
www.honoluluairporthotel.com
Located only slightly away from the highway, this hotel is very similar to the previous one – it's location, size, rates and comfort are all comparable. For an additional $10, you can have an Executive room, which has an office and includes breakfast. A shuttle drives guests to the

airport 24hrs a day, every 30min during the day.

University Area

Hostelling International
members $12.50
Non-members $15.50
K, laundry, tv
2323 Seaview St.
☎*946-0591*
≈*946-5904*
Located a stone's throw from the main entrance to the University of Hawaii, this small youth hostel is very peaceful. It offers 43 beds divided in three dormitories, and two private rooms. To get here from the airport, take bus no. 19 or 20 to Ala Moana Center, then take the no. 6 Woodlaw or no. 18. Both drop you off at the corner of University and Metcalf. After getting off the bus, walk up to Seaview, the next street. Be careful: the hostel isn't located in the first house but rather the one at the end. If you're coming by car, you can park in one of the four spaces available in the evening. The front desk is only open from 8am to noon and from 4pm until midnight. Reservations are recommended if you're coming in summer or winter.

Manoa Valley Inn
$99-$190 bkfst incl.
2001 Vancouver Dr.
☎*947-6019*
manoavalleyinn@aloha.net
Located above the university at the base of

the Manoa Valley, this beautiful 1915 Victorian home houses one of the best bed and breakfasts in O'ahu. The veranda, where breakfast is served, towers over downtown Honolulu through the trees. The seven old-fashioned rooms are comfortable despite their age; the atmosphere is reminescent of the Hawaii of yesteryear. Each door is inscribed with the name of an important Hawaiian figure and decorated with objects that are associated with that person. Four rooms (including a suite) have their own bathrooms, while the three rooms on the second floor share one bathroom. You can also rent the separate cottage, which has an old-fashioned bathtub with feet. There has been a change of owners recently, and unfortunately, the new management is not very accommodating or welcoming.

Waikiki – Kalakaua Avenue (seaside)

Aston Waikiki Circle Hotel
$120-$180
≡, ◙, *ctv*, ☼
2464 Kalakaua Ave.
☎*923-1571*
☎*800-92-ASTON*
≈*926-8024*
www.aston-hotels.com
This hotel, which is a member of the Aston chain, is located across Kuhio beach, separated only by Kalahaua Avenue. Designed in the shape of a cylindrical

13-storey tower, each room, whose last renovations have not completely erased signs of ageing, is identical. The only difference with the higher-priced rooms is the view.

Hawaiian Waikiki Beach Hotel
$130-$230
≈, ℜ, K, ◙, ⋃, ℝ, *ctv*, ☼
2570 Kalakaua Ave.
☎*922-2511 or 800-877-7666*
≈*923-3656*
www.hawaiianwaikikibeach
.com
This hotel has 713 nondescript rooms and comfortable suites, all of which have balconies and 80% have more of less direct ocean views. There are many promotional offers with substantially reduced rates, such as the "Valueline," which starts at $79 and includes breakfast as well as the fifth night for free.

🌴 **Kaimana Beach Hotel**
$125-$705
≈, ℜ, K, ◙, ℝ, *ctv*, ☼
2863 Kalakaua Ave.
☎*923-1555 or 800-35-OTANI*
≈*922-9404*
www.kaimana.com
Member of the New Otani chain, this relatively small hotel (compared to its neighbours to the west) stands on a lovely beach far from the hustle and bustle of Waikiki, but still only a 10min walk from downtown. This establishment is one of the best values on the coast. The cozy rooms are decorated in tropical pastel colours. For

an extra $25, you can rent a studio with kitchenette (but no view). You can also have a snack at the Hau Tree Lanai, whose terrace offers a magnificent view of the area (see p 176).

Waikiki Beachside Hotel
$180-$325 bkfst incl.
≈, ≡, ◙ ℝ, *ctv, vcr*
2452 Kalakaua Ave.
☎*931-2100*
☎*800-92-ASTON*
⇸*931-2129*
www.aston-hotels.com
Don't confuse this hotel, one of the most luxurious members of the Aston chain in Waikiki, with the establishment of the same name located on Lemon Street, which is actually a youth hostel (see p 156). The Waikiki Beachside Hotel is a medium-sized facility located right near the beach, which lies on the other side of Kalakaua Avenue. It offers comfortable rooms and an attractive decor, accented with pleasant touches, such as the kimonos that are offered to guests. Breakfast is served on the patio, where you can also enjoy afternoon tea.

Halekulani
$310-$520
ℜ, ≈, ⊘, ℝ, ◙ *ctv*
2199 Kalia Rd.
☎*923-2311 or 800-367-2343*
⇸*926-8004*
www.halekulani.com
Originally built in 1917, the Halekulani has expanded quite a bit. Member of the Leading Hotels of the World

chain, it now has 456 luxurious rooms and suites which are pleasantly subdued rather than posh. About 90% of the rooms have ocean views. Often rated as one of the best hotels in the country, especially for its personalized service, the Halekulani caters to a wealthy clientele. From the pool, which is decorated with a hibiscus mosaic, to the king-size bathtubs in the rooms to the impeccable service of La Mer restaurant (see p 177), this establishment exudes elegance – elegance that reflects its name, which is translated as "house befitting heaven."

Hilton Hawaiian Village
$220-$445
≈, ℜ, ⊘, △, ≡, ◙, *ctv,* ⛱
2005 Kalia Rd.
☎*949-4321 or 800-221-2424*
⇸*947-7803*
Situated west of Waikiki away from busy Kalakaua Avenue, the Hilton and its four towers are situated between Kahanamoku Beach, one of the loveliest beaches in Waikiki, and the Hilton Lagoon, a small lake that was used as a fishpond by the Hawaiians in former times. The biggest hotel in Hawaii, it has over 2,500 rooms. It has excellent quality services, and a wing (Ali'i Tower) with its own reception desk, pool and exercise room. As one might expect, the rooms are very cozy and the ones in the Ali'i Tower even

have mini-televisions in the bathrooms! The hotel has two highly rated restaurants, the Bali by the Sea (see p 175) and the Golden Dragon (see p 176). Just across the main entrance stands a huge shopping centre, which has attractive Chinese-style architecture, and more than 100 boutiques. If you find yourself a little bored, take a stroll in the garden with its turtles, carp and pink flamingoes, or attend one of the free daily shows. This establishment lives up to its name: it is truly a village where you could (if you wanted to) stay for your entire trip.

Hyatt Regency Waikiki
$250-$465
≈, ℜ, ≡, ℝ, ◙, *ctv,* ⛱
2424 Kalakaua Ave.
☎*923-1234 or 800-233-1234*
⇸*923-7839*
www.hyatt.com
Although it's not situated directly on Kuhio Beach (it is actually across the street), the Hyatt boasts one of the best locations among the luxury establishments in Waikiki. Facing the statue of Duke Kahanamoku, this huge complex, which has two enormous towers engulfing an atrium with a waterfall, has 1,230 cozy rooms, five restaurants offering a variety of cuisine (see p 175), as well as more than 60 boutiques in its shopping centre. The Hyatt is a favourite for honeymooners.

O'ahu

Young couples stay in the rooms of the Regency Club, on the upper level, and enjoy little extras such as a bottle of champagne upon arrival, newspaper in the morning, breakfast served in a room reserved exclusively for club members, and so on.

🦐 Royal Hawaiian
$205-$590
ℜ, ≈, ≡, ℝ, K, ctv, ☂
2259 Kalakaua Ave.
☎ 923-7311 or 800-325-3589
⇆ 924-7098
www.royal-hawaiian.com
Founded in 1927, at the time of trans-Pacific liners, this birthday-cake-like building ("Pink Palace") with a touch of Art Deco represents Waikiki's architectural style. The building commands a great expanse of beach, overlooking the terrace gardens and surrounding a shopping centre with dozens of boutiques. A peaceful haven in the middle of the Waikiki bustle, this exclusive resort now boasts a modern high-rise wing with spacious rooms. The rooms in the original building, which are smaller and by definition older, have an atmosphere that would be a shame not to experience. Whatever section you choose, you will be greeted by a lovely *lei* and tasty banana bread will welcome you upon arrival. Children (up to 18) sharing a room with their parents stay for free. Every Saturday, between 9am and

10am, the Mai Tai Bar hosts the Eddie Sherman Radio Show, broadcast by more than 25 stations across the U.S.

🦐 Sheraton Moana Surfrider
$265-$495
ℜ, ≈, ≡, ℝ, ◙, ctv, ☂
2365 Kalakaua Ave.
☎ 922-3111 or 800-782-9488
⇆ 923-0308
www.sheraton-hawaii.com
When it opened its doors in 1901, the Moana Hotel shared its beach with only a few small buildings, which have since disappeared. It quickly became a popular spot for American jet-setters who arrived here on ocean liners. During the 1930s, the establishment broadcast the radio show *Hawaii Calls*, which popularized "Hawaiian" music – guitar and languorous rhythms with undulating tremolos, the very image of palm trees fluttering in the breeze by the seaside. Listeners could just imagine palm trees gently bending in the soft breeze. An enormous banyan tree, planted in 1904, now towers over the interior courtyard, with a pool facing the ocean. Every morning there's a harp player here, and every afternoon, British-style high tea is served. The rooms of the original building, which were completely renovated about 10 years ago, are cozy and filled with old-fashioned charm, with quilts on the beds

and drawings on the walls. For the same price as the two modern wings, these rooms have much more character; and for a touch of nostalgia, don't miss the two daily historic tours of Waikiki's "First Lady" *(11am and 5pm)*, in the neo-colonial-style reception area of the hotel.

Sheraton Waikiki Hotel
$250-$425
≈, ℜ, ≡, ◙, ctv, ☂
2255 Kalakaua Ave.
☎ 922-4422 or 800-9488
⇆ 923-8785
www.sheraton-waikiki.com
If you've made a reservation for this colossal tourist factory (1,700 rooms and 150 suites), don't forget to bring your compass, as you can easily get lost in the maze of passageways. The hotel may stand right on Waikiki Beach, but the beach is so narrow here that it practically disappears at high tide. What's more, the rooms are overpriced. However, there are a few redeeming features, including two pools, four restaurants, a nightclub, as well as free aerobic classes.

🦐 Honolulu Diamond Head Hotel
$295-350
≡, ℝ, ◙, ctv, vcr, ☂
2885 Kalakaua Ave.
☎ 924-3111 or 888-924SURF
⇆ 923-2249
www.colonysurf.com
Known until recently as the Colony Surf, this hotel is located east of Waikiki just behind Sans Souci Beach. Catering to a jet-set clien-

tele looking for peace and quiet, this luxurious hotel only has 44 rooms and four suites. All rooms have marble bathrooms and are tastefully decorated with a Balinese touch, featuring rattan furniture and green plants. The establishment has personalized service and boasts dozens of little extras at no charge. An excellent choice in this category.

Waikiki Beach Tower
$430-$1,000
≈, K, △, ◙, ctv, ⚲
2470 Kalakaua Ave.
☎926-6400
☎800-92-ASTON
☎800-321-2558 from Hawaii
⇄926-7380
www.aston-hotels.com

Located in a 40-storey tower facing Kuhio Beach, Aston's premier hotel is an all-suite luxury establishment. It has apartments with one or two rooms, including kitchen, living room, bathroom, large *lanai*, as well as a washer and dryer. The paper is even delivered to your door every morning.

Waikiki – Beyond the Coast

Banana Bungalow
Dormitories $16
Private room $60-$105
sb/pb, laundry, K, ≡, ℝ, ◙, ctv
2463 Kuhio Ave.
☎924-5074 or 888-2-HOSTEL
⇄924-4119
Hlres@bananabungalow.com

The most recent addition to the Banana

Bungalows family, a budget-accommodation franchise for students, that already has locations in London, Miami Beach and Hollywood, has established itself in an old hotel that was no longer popular. The reception desk is located in Kuhio Village, from where you are taken to the elevator and guided to your room or dorm. The dorms, which sleep up to six people, are either co-ed or for women only. The rooms, on the other hand, are very small, but clean and fully equipped. The $90 suites can easily accommodate four or possibly six people. Guests can take advantage of the many daily activities offered, gettogethers, free services (such as lockers and mats), but some may not like its impersonal, tourist-factory atmosphere. On the main floor is the Fishbowl Internet Cafe (see p 90), a grocery store, and a bar-grill (Spinner's). You can also rent a car, scooter or bike *($25 per day)* right next door.

🛏 Hostelling International – Waikiki
Dormitories $16/members, $19/non-members
Private room $40-$46
sb, laundry, ⊗
2417 Prince Edward St.
☎926-8313
⇄922-3798

The best-located youth hostel in Waikiki (only 180yds or 200m from the beach) is also the only one that belongs

to an international network. Relatively small, it only has three dorms with four beds and four private bedrooms, all of which share two bathrooms. Guests have access to a kitchen, television, living room, washing machines, Internet *($0.10/min)* and a few parking spaces *($5/day)*. From the airport, take bus no. 19 or no. 20 and get off at the corner of Kaiulani Street and Kuhio Avenue. The former manager of the hostel, a geologist, organizes trips to the tropical forest that are a little pricey *($25)*, but nevertheless very interesting.

Island Hostel & Hotel
Dormitories $16.75
Private room $40-$60
sb/pb, K, ≡/⊗, ctv
1946 Ala Moana Blvd.
☎942-8748

Not quite in the thick of things, this youth hostel is the only one in Waikiki that doesn't ask to see a return plane ticket before you rent a bed in one of its dorms. Amenities include kitchenette, washroom and television shared between a maximum of four people. The private rooms are exactly the same as the dorms, except they have two beds and air-conditioning, and are rather drab. There are two types of rooms: the old ones and the recently renovated ones. The facility offers rebates on all types of accommodation if you reserve in advance or if

O'ahu

you call from the airport.

Polynesian Hostel Beach Club
Dormitories $16.75
Private room or studio $38-$50
sb/pb, laundry, K, ⊗, ctv
2584 Lemon St.
☎*922-1340*
☎*877-50-HAWAII*
⇌*923-4146*
www.hostelhawaii.com
Located just behind the Queen Kapi'olani Hotel, this youth hostel offers a range of accommodations, from single beds in dorms that sleep four people, to studio and semi-private rooms that are in fact apartments bathrooms and kitchens shared with another couple. Guests can borrow Boogie Boards or surfboards, or snorkel sets at no charge. In the lounge, you'll meet travellers from around the world. The hostel organizes many activities: Spaghetti Night, weekly barbecues *($5)*, inexpensive trips to different places on the island, boogie boarding at Sandy Beach *($7)*, hiking on the north coast *($15)*, and more. They'll even pick you up at the airport for free between 10pm and 6am if you're arriving on an international flight. There is a small discount on the first night if you reserve in advance. Internet access available.

Seaside Hostel
Dormitories $14.25-$16.75, $85.50-$99/week
Private room $37.50, $225/week
sb, K, laundry, ⊗
419 Seaside Ave.
☎*924-3306 or 800-492-7238*
www.hawaiianseaside.com
Situated in a quiet alley on the right side of Seaside Avenue as you head up Kuhio Avenue to the Ala Wai Canal, this pleasant youth hostel offers six dormitories that can accommodate up to six people, as well as seven private rooms. All bathrooms are shared, as are the two kitchens. Activities are organized every day (island tours, barbecues on the north coast, and the like) at very reasonable prices *($8 to $10)*. Guests can borrow Boogie Booards, surfboards or snorkels sets. If you stay at least three days, you receive a discount on the first night. They'll also bring you back to the airport for free. Internet access available at $3 for 30min.

Waikiki Beachside Hostel & Hotel
Dormitories $15-$16.50
Semi-private or private rooms $35-$115
sb/pb, laundry, K, ≡, ▣, ⊗, ctv
2556 Lemon St.
☎*923-9566*
⇌*923-7525*
www.bokondo.com
Although it's not far from Kuhio Beach (about 275yds or 300m), this other youth hostel isn't as "beachside" as its name

suggests. It offers a wide selection of accommodations: dorms, private and semi-private rooms and superior-category rooms with ocean view in the Waikiki Grand Hotel. The first three options have identical rooms, including washrooms, kitchenettes and cable television; the layout is different. Dorms have bunk beds and can sleep up to four people. Internet access is available at $5/hr.

Hotel Hale Pua Nui
$57, $349/week
K, ≡, tv
228 Beach Walk
☎*923-9693*
⇌*923-9678*
This unpretentious little hotel offers basic but decent rooms with kitchenettes. Friendly welcome from the manager.

Royal Grove
$42.50-$85, $255-$350/week
≈, K, ≡, tv, ♨
151 Uluniu Ave.
☎*923-7691*
⇌*922-7508*
www.royalgrovehotel.com
Don't be put off by the dilapidated facade – most of the rooms in this budget facility have been renovated and offer good value for your money. The less expensive rooms, which have no air-conditioning, are located in the oldest wing. The prices are the same all year long, but no weekly rate is offered between December and March.

Waikiki Prince Hotel
$40-$55
laundry, K, tv
2431 Prince Edward St.
☎*922-1544*
⇄*924-3712*
Situated only 90yds (100m) from Kuhio Beach (behind the Hyatt Hotel), this small hotel is one of the best deals in Waikiki. The rooms have just recently been renovated and are more than adequate. However, note that the least expensive ones are very small. The seventh night is free except at Christmas. Note that the front desk is only open from 9am to 6pm; it's therefore a good idea to call in advance if you're arriving later.

Coconut Plaza Hotel
$70-$120 bkfst incl.
≈, laundry, K, ℝ, ≡, ctv
450 Lewers St.
☎*923-8828 or 800-882-9696*
⇄*923-3473*
www.coconutplaza.com
A new member of the Aston chain, the Coconut Plaza offers quality accommodation at reasonable prices. Cheaper than its sister hotels because of its location, the beach nevertheless is only a short walk (450yds or 500m) away. The small standard rooms have mini-refrigerators and microwave ovens; the larger superior category and deluxe rooms offer kitchenettes, as do the suites, and can accommodate up to five people.

Ewa Hotel
$77-$100
K, ≡, ctv
2555 Cartwright Rd.
☎*922-1677 or 800-359-8639*
⇄*923-8538*
www.ewahotel.com
Situated 370yds (400m) from the beach and half that distance from the Honolulu zoo east of Waikiki, this small hotel has 74 basic but decent rooms that have been recently renovated. It's a popular spot for Japanese tourists, and offers excellent rates. Its packages for longer stays are quite interesting. The Ewa is one of the few hotels in Waikiki with public Internet access (see p 90).

Hotel Honolulu
$65-$119
laundry, K, ⊗
376 Kai'olu St.
☎*922-2824 or 877-922-3824*
⇄*922-5514*
hulagirl@hula.net
A relic of Waikiki's gay district, formerly found along Kuhio Avenue, the Hotel Honolulu caters to gay couples, but straights are also welcome. Located away from the bustle of town, this small hotel offers a selection of studios and different sizes of suites, a bit worn-out but still comfortable, with private bathrooms and tiny kitchenettes.

Waikiki Hana Hotel
$69-$99
≡, ctv, ℝ
2424 Koa Ave.
☎*926-8841 or 800-367-5004*
☎*800-272-5275 from Hawaii*
⇄*924-3770*
Although a little noisy because of the traffic and rather small for the price, rooms here are nevertheless more than adequate. The prices vary according to the size of the room. The least expensive ones are located on the lower floors and only have one bed; the superior rooms are larger and most have two beds.

Waikiki Sand Villa Hotel
$74-$148
≈, K, ≡, ◙, ℝ, ctv
2375 Ala Wai Blvd.
☎*922-4744 or 800-247-1903*
⇄*923-2541*
www.waikiki-hotel.com
The rooms of this midrange facility, situated north of Waikiki along the Ala Wai Canal, are divided between a tower and a low building (10 studios). The excellent soundproofing blocks out most of the noise from the traffic on the boulevard, and the distance from the beach is compensated by the good deals you can get here. The studios, which have kitchenettes, are comfortable but a bit drab. The standard rooms, however, are the best value for your money, provided that you ask for one that has been recently renovated.

O'ahu

Winston's Waikiki Condos
$75-$125
≈, K, tv, ☂
417 Nohonani St.
☎/⇌ *922-3894 or 924-3332*
☎ *800-545-1948*
winstonswaikikicondos.com

Patrick Winston, manager of the Hawaiian King Hotel, owns 17 out of the 64 units, and they are the best-kept ones, designated as Winston's Waikiki Condos. Although rather small, each apartment has a living room, kitchen, bedroom, bathroom with shower and a peaceful balcony. Some of them are decorated with specific themes (for example, Hawaii of the 1950s, Mount Fuji, and the like). Patrick, who is an excellent host, will tell you about the three months he spent on the vineyards of the Rhone Valley, as well as the best places to dine and visit. He offers a 10% discount to travellers who have the Ulysses guide, which should pay for the $25 cleaning fee charged per unit. Patrick doesn't take reservations for stays of less than four days, but he may have some space available if you're passing by.

Hawaii Polo Inn
$98-$159
laundry, ≡, ℝ, ctv, ☂
1696 Ala Moana Blvd.
☎ *949-0061 or 800-669-7719*
⇌ *949-4906*
www.waikiki.com/
hawaiipolo

Member of the Aston chain, this small, unpretentious hotel offers 68 classic rooms a stone's throw from the Ala Moana Center and the beach of the same name. Although the official rates start at $98, you can often get a much better rate with their promotional offers. Note that the rooms near Ala Moana Boulevard are quite noisy.

Hawaiiana Hotel
$85-$190
≈, *laundry*, K, ≡, ◙, ctv, ☂
260 Beach Walk
☎ *923-3811 or 800-367-5122*
⇌ *926-5728*

The entrance to this small hotel is marked with two large wooden *tiki*, showing how this hotel is suffused with Hawaiian culture. All staff members are also Hawaiian. Although the rooms are a bit antiquated and only have a shower, they're more than adequate. The ones that face the main pool cost $10 more (*$95*). The studios with *lanai* are lovely, but rather expensive. Avoid renting a room at the end facing Saratoga Road; they're quite noisy due to car traffic.

Ilima Hotel
$95-$295
≈, △, ☺, K, ≡, ctv, ☂
445 Nohonani St.
☎ *800-367-5172*
⇌ *888-TO-ILIMA*

Recently renovated, this condominium offers a wide selection of comfortable units, from a simple studio (which is in fact a large hotel room with kitchenette), to the large three-room apartments. The sixth night is free and there are discounts (up to 20%) for guests over 55. The facility has a few free parking spaces.

Imperial of Waikiki
$89-$189
≈, K, ≡, ◙
205 Lewers St.
☎ *923-1827 or 800-347-2582*
⇌ *923-7848*
www.imperialofwaikiki.com

This time-share apartment complex rents out unfilled rooms on a space-available basis for one or several days at a time. The studios, which have sofa beds, regular beds, kitchenette and bathrooms, are really good values. The two-bedroom units have two bathrooms, a kitchen and two *lanai*. All units have recently been renovated.

Ohana Coral Seas
$90-$130
K, ≡, ctv, ◙
250 Lewers St.
☎ *923-3881 or 800-462-6262*
www.ohanahotels.com

In December 1999, Outrigger created a new subdivision of budget hotels: the Ohana hotels. The Coral Seas is one of them. Some of its rooms have been renovated; others await necessary renovations. The higher prices are only justified by the fact that guests have a kitchenette at their disposal. The standard rooms are therefore the best value.

The Breakers
$91-$97
≈, *K*, ≡, ◙, *ctv*
250 Beach Walk
☎*923-3181 or 800-426-0494*
⇌*923-7174*
www.breakers-hawaiian.com
The rooms in this small family hotel surround a central pool and all are equipped with a kitchenette. Although they're nothing special, most provide minimum comfort. There are seven free parking spaces available to guests on a first-come, first-served basis. In the winter, the hotel fills up quickly, so make reservations well in advance.

Holiday Inn Waikiki
$117-$130
≈, ℜ, ◔, ≡, ℝ, ◙, *ctv*
1830 Ala Moana Blvd.
☎*955-1111*
☎*888-9-WAIKIKI*
⇌*947-1799*
www.holiday-inn.com
Situated west of Waikiki near Ala Wai Harbor, this mid-range hotel has rooms that are a bit on the small side, but are nevertheless good value. The main drawback is that it's quite a ways from central Waikiki. Unless you're willing to walk 20min to the beach, or if you plan on going to the nearby Ala Moana Center often, its location is not that great.

Outrigger Islander Waikiki
$159-$189
≈, *laundry*, ≡, ℝ, ◙, *ctv*
270 Lewers St.
☎*923-7711*
☎*800-OUTRIGGER*
⇌*924-5755*
www.outrigger.com
Located at the corner of Kalakaua Avenue, this latest addition to the Outrigger chain offers 287 rooms that have just been renovated. They're reasonably comfortable, but quite noisy and a bit expensive. What's more, you have to pay extra for everything – from the safety deposit box to coffee. There's a Starbuck's café on the main floor.

Queen Kapi'olani Hotel
$107-$180
≈, ℜ, *K*, ≡, ◙, *ctv*, ⚘
150 Kapahulu Ave.
☎*922-1941 or 800-367-5004*
☎*800-272-5275 from Hawaii*
⇌*922-2694*
A member of the Castle Resorts & Hotels chain, the Queen Kapi'olani is a decent mid-range hotel that is very popular with Mexican tour groups. The standard rooms are quite adequate, but some might find them a little dark. The prices climb according to categories, up to the studio category that offers a kitchenette and ocean view. Promotional offers are always available: you get the fifth night for free or free car rental (not including taxes and insurance).

Waikiki Grand Hotel
$119-$149
≈, *K*, *laundry*, ≡, ◙, ℝ, *ctv*
134 Kapahulu Ave.
☎*922-9700 or 800-535-0085*
⇌*922-2421*
Situated a short distance from the coast opposite the Honolulu zoo, this establishment belongs to the Marc Resorts chain. It draws both a working-class and gay clientele, which is not necessarily a contradiction. The rooms are quite small and a bit worn out. The studios with kitchenette are the best value, but the prices are a bit steep compared to similar options in the area.

Waikiki Joy Hotel
$155-$280 bkfst incl.
≈, △, *K*, ≡, ℝ
320 Lewers St.
☎*923-2300 or 800-922-7866*
☎*800-321-2558 from Hawaii*
⇌*922-8785*
www.aston-hotels.com
Member of the Aston chain, this small, chic hotel just north of Kalakaua Avenue offers cozy rooms and suites with or without a kitchen, and all rooms include a whirlpool and a stereo system. Breakfast is served on the veranda. Since the hotel has a strong Asian clientele, a room has been especially set up for karaoke – with individual boxes so you won't make a fool of yourself in public! The establishment also attracts a gay clientele and has an Internet café (see p 90).

O'ahu

Waikiki Parc Hotel
$175-$270
℟, ≈, ≡, ◙, ℝ, *ctv*, ♒
2233 Helumoa Rd.
☎*921-7272 or 800-422-0450*
⇌*923-1336*
www.waikikiparc.com
Set slightly back from the beach opposite the Halekulani Hotel (which belongs to the same company), the Waikiki Parc Hotel is a decent facility offering 300 identical, comfortable rooms, decorated with tropical themes. The ocean-view rooms have a *lanai*, while the rooms on the other side do not. The hotel offers various promotional offers including breakfast and free parking. Three-day packages are a particularly good value.

Waikiki Surf Ohana
$139-$179
≈, *laundry*, *K*, ≡, ℝ, ◙, *ctv*
2200 Kuhio Ave.
☎*923-7671 or 800-462-6262*
⇌*921-4959*
www.ohanahotels.com
A member of the Ohana chain, the Waikiki Surf offers four different categories of rooms. Standard rooms are quite small; the ones with kitchenettes are much larger and more pleasant; suites can accommodate up to four people; and two-bedroom apartments sleep up to six. For the small extra cost, the rooms with kitchenettes are definitely the best value. A few of them even have a view (albeit distant) of the ocean. Note that, no matter what category

you choose, all rooms have showers only.

Waikiki Village Ohana
$139-$179
K, ≡, ◙, ℝ, *ctv*
240 Lewers St.
☎*923-3881 or 800-462-6262*
⇌*922-2330*
www.ohanahotels.com
Also affiliated with the Ohana chain, the Waikiki Village occupies a charmless 20-storey tower. The rooms, which have recently been remodelled, are quite cozy, but only have a shower. During low season, rates are really attractive.

Around Town

Central YMCA
$29-$51.50
sh/pb
401 Atkinson Dr.
☎*941-3344*
⇌*941-8821*
Situated opposite the Ala Moana Center, a fairly noisy location because of the traffic, the Central YMCA welcomes both men and women. Men are offered tiny rooms that consist of narrow beds and shared bathrooms with no air conditioning or other amenities; the women's rooms are not much better, but they include private washrooms. For the same price, you can get something better almost anywhere else.

Fernhurst YWCA
$25-$30 bkfst incl.
1566 Wilder Ave.
☎*941-2231*
⇌*949-0266*
As expected, the Honolulu YWCA offers spartan rooms with two beds and a shared bathroom. There's no air-conditioning or television – just the bare essentials – but the price includes breakfast and dinner (except on Sat, Sun and holidays). On each floor is a small room with a shared fridge, hot plates and an ironing board. Only women are admitted; men are not allowed to go past the front desk.

Pagoda Hotel
$90-$145
≈, ℟, *laundry*, *K*, ≡, ◙, ℝ, *ctv*
1525 Rycroft St.
☎*941-6611 or 800-472-4632*
⇌*955-5067*
www.pagodahotel.com
Situated on a small street halfway between the H1 Freeway and the Ala Moana Center, the Pagoda Hotel is a little out of place. The rooms, although quite old, are well maintained and more than adequate. In addition to the main building, the adjacent Pagoda Terrace has studios with kitchenettes and two-bedroom apartments that can accommodate four people. Here you fill find the Floating Pagoda restaurant (see p 168).

The Eastern Point

Waimanalo Bay State Recreation Area
Free
Access every day 7am to 6:45pm in winter, 7:45pm in summer
Washrooms, outdoor showers, picnic tables
Situated amidst pine trees and north of the long Waimanalo Beach, this campground is quite pleasant, even though it's a bit noisy on weekends when many island families and friends camp here. The equipment is in average condition.

Bellows Field Beach Park
Free
41-043 Kalaniana'ole Hwy.
Washrooms, outdoor showers, picnic tables, telephone
Situated at the northern tip of Waimanalo Beach on the grounds of a military base, the park is open every weekend. You can camp here from Friday to Sunday as long as you quickly clear out Monday morning. The 50 campsites, of which only a few are usually taken, are nestled beneath pine trees near the beach, where you can go swimming, surfing or boogie boarding. Visitors must obtain a free camping permit with the county services.

Kahala Mandarin Oriental
$295-$665
≈, ℜ, ☉, ≡, ◉, ⊌, ctv, ☂
5000 Kahala Ave.
☎739-8888
East of Waikiki past Diamond Head, the coastal road leads to Kahala, a well-to-do residential neighbourhood. At the end of Kahala Road, the Mandarin Oriental stands alone, far from the bustle of town, on a pretty white-sand beach. This spacious establishment faces a pool, framed with palm trees, and a tank where three dolphins frolic. It attracts a jet-set clientele looking for an exceptional vacation. The cozy rooms are equipped with canopy beds and tastefully decorated with tropical wood tones. An architectural anomaly, half of the rooms don't have balconies (but at least the price is lower). The bar located in the entrance features piano and guitar concerts (jazz and classical).

The Winward Coast

Ho'olaluhia Botanical Garden
$5/person
Bathrooms, showers
45-680 Luluku Rd.
☎233-7323
The garden allows camping from 9am Friday to 4pm Monday, and you must obtain a permit at the Visitor Center (Mon to Sat) to camp. You can also make reservations in advance. Note that the entrance gate is closed to the public at 4pm and you should therefore arrive beforehand to register. You can still leave the park between 5:30pm and 6:30pm. Although humid and swarming with mosquitoes, the setting is peaceful and pleasant.

Schrader's Windward Marine Resort
$50-$350 bkfst incl.
≈, laundry, K, ctv
47-039 Lihikai Dr., Kane'ohe
☎239-5711 or 800-735-5711
≂239-6658
Don't be fooled by the name – Schrader's Windward Marine Resort isn't a luxury establishment but rather a sort of motel. Situated in a residential area on the tiny peninsula north of Kane'ohe Bay, the facility has 20 units, from studios to four-bedroom apartments. All of them have kitchens or kitchenettes, and most have a living room. Half of them have been renovated and the others need to be since they're rather dreary. The price includes a boat ride on the bay (Wednesday and Saturday). The listed price is for a room without a view. From Kamehameha Highway, turn onto Lihikai Drive 450yds (500m) from the Route 83 junction.

O'ahu

Ali'i Bluffs B&B
$60-$70
pb, ≈, ⊗
46-251 Ikiiki St., Kane'ohe
☎*235-1124 or 800-235-1151*
(U.S. only)
⇄*236-4877*
www.hawaiiscene.com/
aliibluffs
Situated in a residential
neighbourhood at the
western exit from
Kane'ohe, this house
has two rooms, each
with a private bath-
room. The rooms,
which are rather small,
are decorated (as is the
rest of the house) with
many paintings and
posters. One room has
a circus theme, and
another has a Victorian-
style decor. Donald is a
Scottish real estate
agent, and his partner
is a painter, as evi-
denced by the male
nudes displayed in the
living room. Breakfast
is served on the terrace
by the pool, which
faces Kane'ohe Bay.
Credit cards are not
accepted and the mini-
mum stay is three
nights. To get here
from downtown, drive
0.7mi (1km) from Lib-
erty House to 'Ipuka
Street. Ikiiki is the first
street on your left and
the house is at the cor-
ner.

Kailua Beachside Cottages
$80-$150
K, ⊗, ctv
324-328 South Kalaheo Ave.
Kailua
☎*262-1653 or 262-4128*
⇄*261-0893*
www.10kvacationrentals.co
m/pats
These four wooden
cottages of various
sizes house six apart-

ments, from studios to
three-bedroom units.
Situated behind the
main section of Kailua
Beach, they're sepa-
rated from it by a fence
that has a gateway. The
two apartments situated
near the road are a bit
noisy. Popular with
families and
windsurfers, the accom-
modations are quite
old, but are neverthe-
less more than ade-
quate.

Lanikai B&B
$90-$125 bkfst incl.
K, ⊗, tv, vcr
1277 Mokulua Dr., Kailua
☎*261-7895 or 800-258-7895*
⇄*262-2181*
www.lanikaibb.com
Rick and Nin Maxey,
who have lived in
Lanikai for more than
15 years, rent out a
one-bedroom apart-
ment and a studio (with
terrace) in their home
situated a short dis-
tance from the beach.
Both units provide sim-
ple but quite comfort-
able accommodation,
and each has a kitchen-
ette, bathroom and
private entrance. Al-
though the house is
situated on the "wrong"
side of the road,
Lanikai Beach is easily
accessible by a path
across the house.
Kalaheo Avenue be-
comes Kawailoa Road
east of Kailua Beach.
Turn left towards
Lanikai just past the
beach. There are two
roads – one in each
direction. Take the one
on your right,
A'alapapa Drive, for
seven blocks, then take
A'ala to Mokulua Drive,

which leads to the
Maxey's home.

The North Coast

If you're looking for
accommodation in
Hale'iwa, you'll see
several signs above the
entrance to Celestial
Natural Foods and the
Coffee Gallery (North
Shore Marketplace)
advertizing inexpensive
apartment or room
time-shares.

Kualoa Regional Park
Free
*Access every day 7am to
8pm*
49-479 Kamehameha Hwy.
*Washrooms, showers,
tables, telephone*
Situated right at the end
of the park, a camp-
ground lies between
Kualoa Point and Moli'i
Hawaiian fishponds.
The 30 pleasant camp-
sites are shaded by
pine and bancoulier
trees. Just a few hun-
dred metres away, the
park beach is a good
spot for swimming,
snorkelling and wind-
surfing. A permit is
issued by the county
park services.

Kokololio Beach Park
Free
*Access every day 7am to
8pm*
55-017 Kamehameha Hwy.
(Mile 20.3)
*Bathrooms, outdoor
showers, picnic tables*
One of the most pleas-
ant campgrounds on
the north coast,
Kokololio Beach Park
has five campsites
sheltered by pine and
bancoulier trees and is

situated far enough back from the road to allow you to enjoy peace and quiet. During the weekdays, you probably won't be disturbed by neighbours. Make sure you securely anchor your tent since winds are quite strong around here. Campers must obtain a permit with the county park services.

Malaekahana S.R.A.
$5/pers.
Access every day 6am to 6:45pm in winter, until 7:45 in summer
Kamehameha Hwy. (Mile 17.1)
Bathrooms, showers, picnic tables
The Maleakahan S.R.A. is definitely the most pleasant campground on the north coast. The beach and the campground are separated by a row of trees, which forms a screen that shelters the site in the wintertime. Shaded by pine and *kukui* trees, the campsites are extremely quiet. It's too bad the washrooms aren't in better shape. The permit, which you have to pay for, is available at Friends of Maleakahana *(Mon to Fri 10am to 3pm; 56-335 Kamehameha Hwy., Kahuku HI 96731; ☎293-1736).*

Kaiaka Bay Beach Park
Free
66-449 Hale'iwa Rd.
Bathrooms, showers, picnic tables, telephone
Surfers looking for accommodations in the Hale'iwa area sometimes pitch their tents here for a few days, but

most of the time, there's still plenty of space. A canopy of pine trees shelters the seven campsites. While not unpleasant, the campground lacks charm. A permit, available at the county park services, is required.

Backpacker's
Dormitories $15
Semi-private room $45-$55
Studio $80-$95
sb/pb, K, laundry, ⊗, ctv
59-788 Kamehameha Hwy.
Waimea (Mile 6.3)
☎638-7838 or 888-628-8882 *(from Hawaii)*
⇆638-7515
www.backpackers-hawaii.com
Backpacker's has two locations: the Vacation Inn and the Plantation Village. The Vacation Inn has dorms and semi-private rooms; the Plantation Village boasts nine bungalows with kitchens and bathrooms. In the green building opposite Vacation Inn facing the sea are eight expensive studios, which can sleep up to four people. The rooms are quite similar to hotel rooms with kitchenettes. Guests can borrow snorkel gear and Boogie Boards, and there's a shuttle to Waikiki airport once a day. Internet access is available at $7/hr. Reservations accepted. Bus no. 52 will drop you off in the vicinity.

Best Inn – Hukilau Resort
$79-$94 bkfst incl.
≈, ≡, ℝ, *ctv*, ☼
55-109 Laniloa St., La'ie
☎293-8115
www.nwhotels.com
Formerly the Rodeway Inn, the Best Inn is located only 180yds (200m) from the entrance to the Polynesian Cultural Center. It offers pleasant motel rooms better maintained and equipped than you might think upon seeing the appearance of the five buildings surrounding the pool. Each room has a coffee machine and some have microwave ovens.

Thomsen's B&B
$85 bkfst incl.
pb, K, ctv
59-420 Kamehameha Hwy.
☎638-7170 *(ask for Pete)*
Situated just back from the road near Ehukai Beach (Mile 7.6), this simple home is so popular with surfers in winter that you'll have to reserve months in advance. There's only one apartment (situated on the main floor), which has a bathroom (with shower) and private entrance. Three-night minimum stay. Note that the new owners plan to change the name of the establishment.

Turtle Bay Condos
$80-$175
≈, K, ⊗, ☼
☎293-2800
⇆293-2169
www.turtlebaycondos.com
Located on both sides of the access road from the Turtle Bay Hilton,

O'ahu

the apartments of the Kuilima Estates belong to a large condominium development. The unoccupied units, which range from studios to four-bedroom apartments, can be rented on a daily basis (minimum two days), by the week or by the month. It's not a good idea, however, to only stay a few days since there is a $50 cleaning fee. In addition to the pool, you can take advantage of the tennis courts, the nearby Kuilima Beach and the Hilton stable. To get the key, you have to go to the agency in Kahuku (next to the Sugar Mill Museum).

Hilton Turtle Bay Resort
$165-$295
≈, ℜ, ≡, ℝ, *ctv*
57-091 Kamehameha Hwy.
(Mile 12.6)
☎*293-8811 or 800-HILTONS*
⇌*293-9147*
www.turtlebayresort.hilton.com
Standing on a strip of land flanked by two bays at the northern tip of the island and pounded by the waves, the Turtle Bay Hilton seems a bit stranded, far from the main tourist attractions on the island. Consequently, this operation has not been very profitable; the buildings are ageing, and its main restaurant had to close down. Its rooms, though rather plain looking, are nevertheless comfortable. The hotel has two pools, 10 tennis courts and a 27-hole golf course. The nearby Kuilima Cove,

which is protected from the elements, is a good spot to go swimming.

Ke 'Iki Hale
$85-$195
laundry, ⊗
59-179 Ke 'Iki Road
☎/⇌*638-8229*
Situated just north of Pupukea Beach Park, this complex, which has one- and two-bedroom apartments, looks out onto the beach. Although the owner is very kind (the only asset in this place) the ageing units are rather expensive for the comfort they provide. The four rooms that face the road cost $85; the other units start at $145 – and a $65 cleaning fee is added on top of that.

The Central Plains

Keaiwa Heiau State Park
Free
Access every day 7am to 6:45pm in winter, until 7:45pm in summer
Bathrooms, tables, barbecues
You can pitch your tent here in the peaceful Honolulu Heights in a clearing surrounded by large trees. It's a pleasant site in a rural setting, but expect occasional downpours, strong winds and cooler temperatures in the wintertime. A permit is required.

The Leeward Coast

🌴 **Ihilani Resort & Spa**
$295-$440
≈, ☉, ≡, ◙, *mb, ctv,* ☂
92-1001 Olani St.
Ko'Olina Resort, Kapolei
☎*679-0079 or 800-626-4446*
⇌*679-0080*
www.ibilani.com
Member of the exclusive "Leading Hotels of the World" club, the Ihilani Resort & Spa is the only large vacation centre on O'ahu – and quite similar to those found on the Big Island. Far from the Waikiki bustle, its 14-storey building towers over a magnificent Mediterranean-like artificial cove whose sandy beaches are ideal for swimming. The rooms are very spacious and offer all the comforts you would expect to find at a luxury hotel, including a marble bathroom. Most rooms have ocean views. Opposite the hotel, a separate building houses a thalasso-therapy centre as well as a pool, tennis courts and an exercise club where you can also enjoy a massage. A shuttle whisks golfers to the Ko'Olina golf course, and there is a variety of other activities. Various package deals are available, including a discount on a car rental.

Restaurants

Downtown Honolulu

Cafe Peninsula
less than $10
1147 Bethel St.
☎531-5398
This local cafe on the edge of Chinatown has cozy sofas, good music, and a dark-blue, intimate decor, making it a popular hangout for students from the nearby university. You can have tea, a bagel, ice cream, a sandwich or a hot dish for just a few dollars. And for a European touch, smoking is allowed here.

Gordon Biersch Brewery & Restaurant
$10-$20
every day 10:30am to 2pm and 5:00pm to 11pm
Aloha Tower Marketplace
☎599-4877
Facing Honolulu Harbor, this restaurant-brewery offers a selection of pizza, salads, pasta and hamburgers, as well as a few refined dishes and fresh fish. Try the unique Tahitian *fafa* with coconut milk served on taro leaves. The distillation vats of four homemade beers are visible just behind the bar, which becomes lively especially after nightfall. Music on Wednesday and Saturday evenings.

Payao
$10-$25
Mon to Sat 11am to 2:30pm and every day 5pm to 10pm
500 Ala Moana Blvd.
Restaurant Row
☎521-3511
"The home of sticky rice" (steamed in a bamboo basket), Restaurant Row actually offers much more. Its 51 dishes, cooked up by chef Art Srivongsana, have earned it a fine reputation with Honolulu residents. Half the dishes are vegetarian and most are spicy, such as payao's evil shrimps, evil chicken and evil beef. But don't worry – you can ask for different levels of "spiciness"! A few tables outside face the Restaurant Row terrace. The lunch and dinner menus are both the same.

Don Ho's Island Grill
$15-$20
Aloha Tower Marketplace
With its mildly kitsch wooden decor, imitation palm trees, surf boards and canoes hanging everywhere, Don Ho's Island Grill clearly shows its pride in Hawaiian culture and has earned itself a popular following – just like its famous owner, Don Ho, former Hawaiian football star and singer of *Tiny Bubbles*. Hawaiian cuisine is definitely the specialty here, which, over the generations, has come to represent the world of the *kama'aina* (islanders) – the beach, the sun, the surfing, the

mixed origins and... taking the time to live. The hamburgers are served up with caramelized onions and taro, and the deserts feature sweet-potato and macadamia-nut pies. The pizza, which is to be commended for its originality, is served on a mini surf board. There's music on Friday nights.

Sunset Grill
$15-$30
Mon to Fri 11am to 10pm, Sat and Sun 5:30pm to 10pm
500 Ala Moana Blvd.
Restaurant Row
☎521-4409
Modern, convivial and slightly posh, the Sunset Grill has a new chef, Todd Wells, who worked for seven years on the island of Lana'i in the two highly rated restaurants of the tourist complex. Belonging to the new school of creative Hawaiian cuisine, his dishes have Italian influences (pasta, risotto) and his wine cellar is famous in the area. Introductory wine-tasting sessions are held regularly.

Sam Choy's
$20-$40
every day 6:30am to 4pm and 5pm to 10pm Brewery every day 10:30am to midnight
580 North Nimitz Hwy.
☎545-7979
The first of Sam Choy's restaurants, named after one of the top chefs in regional Hawaiian cuisine, made its home west of Chinatown at the edge of the indus-

O'ahu

trial area. The on-site brewery, open kitchen, the fishing boat prominently displayed in the middle of the room (where some tables are set up) – all of these add a touch of originality to the building, which used to be a hangar. More accessible than other big names in gourmet cuisine on the island, Sam Choy's offers generous portions – no doubt the source of his famous big belly! Here there is a prominence of fish and seafood dishes, with "new and improved" popular Hawaiian and Asian classics, as well as timeless ribs, sometimes served with paella. Or you can simply come to sample one of the five homemade beers, such as the unsual honey *kiawe*. Hawaiian groups perform here every Wednesday from 9pm until midnight.

Ruth's Chris Steak House
$25-$35
every day 5pm to 10pm
500 Ala Moana Blvd.
Restaurant Row
☎599-3860
Established in New Orleans during the 1980s, Ruth Fertel's original steakhouse immediately won over meat-lovers with its quality steaks and high-society ambiance. The Honolulu location is no exception. Although the prices are rather exorbitant, the portions are generous.

Chai's Island Bistro
$30-$40
every day 11am to 10pm
Aloha Tower Marketplace
☎585-0011
Eclectic is definitely the best word to describe Chai's cuisine. Hawaiian ingredients, a Thai chef, grilled meat as well as vegetarian fare – the cuisine is truly a mix of everything. The setting is charming and you can dine inside or outside. The restaurant is as famous for its varied menu as for its entertainment (Tue to Sat). Famous Hawaiian singers sometimes perform here, such as Hapa and the Cazimero brothers.

Chinatown

🛶 A Little Bit of Saigon
less than $10
every day 10am to 9pm
1160 Maunakea St.
☎528-3669
Voted Best Vietnamese Restaurant in Honolulu, this 100% authentic restaurant provides its guests with a detailed menu outlining the composition of each dish. The house speciality is obviously *pho*, a traditional Vietnamese noodle soup flavoured with lemongrass that can be accompanied with beef, chicken or seafood. But the menu doesn't stop there. You'll also find an excellent selection of spring and summer rolls, kebabs, sautéed vegetables with tofu, shrimp or meat, and more.

Krung Thai
less than $10
Mon to Fri 10:30am to 2:30pm
1028 Nu'uana Ave.
☎599-4803
This small, unpretentious Thai restaurant offers a plate lunch priced according to the number of courses you order (between one and four). All dishes are accompanied with rice or noodles, which vegetarians can choose as their main course (and which are ridiculously inexpensive).

Mabuhay Cafe and Restaurant
less than $10
Every day 10am to 10pm
River St.
Established in 1963, this small Filipino restaurant is one of best places in Chinatown. It has a mostly local clientele, obviously not necessarily all Filipino. If you wish to sample a traditional dish (and something a bit unusual), try a *balut* – but read the following before doing so... It's a soft-boiled duck egg that is about to hatch! The beak is a bit hard to chew. For a less adventurous choice, try the *halo halo* (advertized in the window), a kind of fruit sorbet covered with condensed milk.

Maunakea Marketplace
less than $10
every day 6:30am to 6pm
1120 Maunakea St. (between Pauahi, Smith and Hotel Streets)
Inside the shopping centre is a fast-food court with about a

dozen stands offering mostly Asian cuisine (Filipino, Korean and Vietnamese), as well as Italian and Mexican cuisine. This is a rather dark place, however. A better idea is to head to one of the affordable restaurants in the area for breakfast or lunch.

Maxime
less than $10
Thu to Tue 10am to 9pm
1134 Maunakea St.
☎*545-4188*
Another Vietnamese restaurant offers traditional quality cuisine at great prices. Here, there is a large selection of dishes such as *pho*, curry, Vietnamese crepes and noodles with or without tofu, lemongrass chicken, etc. Try one of the house specialties such as the *cuc quay*, marinated and fried quail served in pairs with rice, tomato and lettuce.

Shung Chong Yuein
less than $10
1027 Maunakea St.
This Chinese pastry shop offers a variety of traditional delicacies such as bean-filled cakes, as well as dried fruit: lotus roots, carrots, papayas, mangoes, water chestnuts, and the like. If you like caramel sesame snaps, you'll also find some of these treats with peanuts and macadamia nuts as well.

Tô-Châu
less than $10
every day 8am to 2:30pm
River St., near King St.
As evidenced by the long line-ups in front of its door, this local Vietnamese restaurant is really popular – especially since nothing is over $6. The speciality here is definitely *pho*, and the menu offers a dozen different variations of this dish. You can also order spring rolls or pork dishes. This is not a place for vegetarians since nearly everything has meat.

Legend Seafood Restaurant
$10-$25
Mon to Fri 10:30am to 2pm and 5:30pm to 10pm, Sat and Sun from 8am
Chinatown Cultural Plaza
100 North Beretania St., corner River St.
☎*532-1868*
The most highly reputed seafood restaurant in Chinatown, Legend Seafood Restaurant offers a great selection of oysters, crab, lobster, fish, as well as abalone, sea cucumber, shark-fin soup, and braised fins prepared according to traditional Chinese recipes. Those who are not fond of seafood can choose a beef, pork or

vegetarian dish. Although its interior decor is quite attractive, its exterior is downright ugly.

Legend Vegetarian Restaurant
$10-$20
Mon to Fri 10:30am to 2pm and 5:30pm to 10pm, Sat and Sun from 8am
100 North Beretania St.
☎*532-8218*
Situated right across from the Legend Seafood Restaurant, this establishment belongs to the same owner. As one might expect, it offers only vegetarian dishes, mostly consisting of vegetables and tofu, prepared many different ways – diced fried, steamed or braised. Those whose beliefs – and not their taste buds – dictate the diet should try the vegetarian "ham" or "pork."

Duc's Bistro
$10-$20
1188 Maunakea St.
☎*531-6325*
Duc Nguyen offers quality cuisine served in a refined decor. Its menu will please those looking for a selection of Asian and European dishes – a good choice for groups with different tastes. In addition to its Vietnamese influences, the cuisine is inspired from many different cuisines, especially French, with its rich sauces.

O'ahu

Indigo
$20-$25
Tue to Fri 11:30 to 2pm,
every day 6pm to 9:30pm
1121 Nu'uanu Ave.
☎521-2900

In a spacious and tropical setting, chef Glenn Chu offers excellent Eurasian cuisine, an eclectic blend of fresh Hawaiian items with Chinese, Vietnamese, Japanese and French influences. The duck confit coated with a pineapple and lemongrass sauce is recommended. The copious deserts will delight those who like chocolate, coconut and *crème brûlée*. The lovely terrace, located behind the restaurant, is the perfect place for a romantic dinner (see also p 183).

King Street

Auntie Pasto's
$10-$15
Mon to Thu 11am to 10:30pm, Fri 11am to 11pm, Sun and holidays 4pm to 10:30pm
1099 South Beretania St.
☎523-8855

This tiny Italian-American restaurant draws a lunch crowd from the offices next door. The service is efficient, the portions are generous and the prices are reasonable. That said, don't expect exceptional cuisine here – after all, Honolulu isn't Rome. The menu is posted on the wall and they'll bring you the wine list if you ask. The dishes are prepared in ancient ovens.

Camellia Yakiniku
$10-$16
930 McCully St.
☎951-0511 or 951-0611

This typical Korean restaurant only offers all-you-can-eat buffets, with a selection of spicy hors-d'oeuvres and sliced meat that you can grill yourself on a hot plate on the table. Rice and soup complete the menu. Don't expect any miracles here; both the cuisine and the decor are nothing to getting excited about. But it still is a good choice for famished carnivores.

Floating Pagoda
$11-$20
Mon to Sat 6:30am to 10:30pm, Sun 6:30am to 9:30pm; Mon to Sat 11am to 2pm and every day 4:30pm to 9:30pm; Sun brunch 10:30am to 2pm
1525 Rycroft St.
☎941-6611

The Pagoda Hotel's (see p 160) restaurant is not located right on King Street but just south of it, a few minutes from the Ala Moana Center. The two-storey rotunda, surrounded with bay windows, faces a pretty little Asian park with an artificial waterfall, a carp fishpond and a pavilion for private parties. Popular with Hawaiian families who come here for special occasions, the Pagoda only offers a buffet with many of Hawaii's cuisines represented – from Japanese to Chinese to North American.

Alan Wong's
$20-$50
every day 5pm to 10pm
1857 South King St.
☎949-2526

Voted Best Restaurant in 1996, 1997 and 1999, Alan Wong – with his personal touches – is the embodiment of regional Hawaiian cuisine. The vast cultural influences of this giant melting pot are represented in his cuisine, which uses high-quality ingredients. Of Chinese origin, Wong has kept a tradition alive in his chic establishment, which has become all the rage on the island during the past few years: the open kitchen that allows you to watch the chefs and their assistants at work. There are several different menus to choose from and the desserts are truly worth the trip.

Chef Mavro
Menus at $39, $57 and $77
Tue to Sun 6pm to 9:30pm
1969 South King St.
☎944-4714

Of Greek origin, George Mavrothalassitis grew up in southern France and was trained according to the region's tradition. From his diverse background and the Hawaiian cornucopia, an incredibly elegant menu was created, mixing classicism with exoticism, traditional techniques with tropical imagination. The result is shown in dishes such as caviar and tuna tartar with taro, goat cheese and eggplant terrine with cardamon and curried lobster risotto. A specific wine is recommended with each dish, but the customer is king here; guests are welcome to make their own choice.

University Area

Bubbies
less than $10
Mon to Fri noon to midnight, until 1am Sat and 11:30pm Sun
1010 University Ave., corner South King St.
☎949-8984
Located behind the shopping centre between King St. and Cayne St., this ice cream and pastry shop is so popular that it expanded to King's Village in Waikiki, Kahala Mall and all the way to Singapore! Needless to say, its products are excellent. If you come here, try the macadamia-nut ice cream, the "banana royal" (with strawberries), or, for something more adventurous, sample the green-tea ice cream. There's also a bewildering selection of sundaes with highly unusual names.

Coffeeline
less than $10
every day 7:30am to 4pm
1820 University Ave.
☎947-1615
Situated across from the main entrance to the University of Hawaii at Manoe, the campus

coffee shop is in fact a simple, pleasant place where students hang out to chat over a coffee. But the crowds don't come here for the coffee; they come to socialize. The entrance is situated near the corner of Seaview St. (where the youth hostel is located).

Down to Earth Natural Foods
less than $10
2525 South King St.
☎947-7678
This restaurant's slogan is "Love animals, don't eat them!" The largest supermarket for natural products in Hawaii, it also has a deli section offering an excellent variety of pastries, hot dishes and organic salads, all at reasonable prices.

Maple Garden
$10-$15
every day 11am to 2pm and 5:30pm to 10pm
909 Isenberg St.
☎941-6641
Located on a small street west of the large Down to Earth store, this Chinese restaurant has served up Szechwan specialties for more than 20 years. The selection is bewildering, and vegetarians are not forgotten. The lunch-time menu has an assortment of inexpensive dishes.

Ward Centers

The Old Spaghetti Factory
$10-$15
Mon to Fri 11:30am to 2pm; Mon to Thu 5pm to 10pm, Fri until 10:30pm; Sat 11:30am to 10:30pm and Sun 4pm to 9:30pm
1050 Ala Moana Blvd.
Ward Warehouse, second floor
☎591-2513
The menu, which is vaguely inspired by Italian cuisine, features a large selection of spaghetti and other pasta dishes. Many of its customers come here for the great prices and Victorian-style decor, with its wooden panelling and velvet-covered chairs.

Compadres
$15-$20
every day from 11am
1200 Ala Moana Blvd.
Ward Center, second floor
☎591-8307
Recognized as one of the best Mexican restaurants in O'ahu, Compadres offers a California-style menu; not authentic, but still good. The setting is actually quite refined, with a south-of-the-border theme. The crowds that flock here don't just come here to eat – they come to party. On weekends, there's live music, which you can enjoy while sipping a tequila or margarita. On Tuesday, you can sign up for a taco-eating contest, where the winner is announced at 2am!

O'ahu

**Kincaid's Fish, Chop &
Steak House**
$25-$30
*Sun to Thu 11am to
10pm, Fri and Sat until
10:30pm*
1050 Ala Moana Blvd.
Ward Warehouse, second floor
☎591-2005
Decorated with a nautical theme, the large dining room of this restaurant overlooks the Kewalo Yacht Harbor, located on the other side of Ala Moana Avenue. Kincaid's is popular with Honolulu residents who flock here for its fish and seafood dishes, prepared *à la* American, Asian or Cajun. Meatlovers aren't forgotten either: the rock salt-roasted ribs of beef are one of its specialties. Every Thursday *(from 6:30pm to 9:30pm)*, Friday and Saturday evening *(9:30pm to 12:30am)*, local groups perform here.

**Stuart Anderson's Cattle
Company**
$20-$30
*Mon to Thu 11am to
10pm, Fri and Sat until
10:30pm; Sun noon to
9:30pm*
1050 Ala Moana Blvd.
Ward Warehouse
☎591-9292
Stuart Anderson's Cattle Company is a meat-lover's delight, with succulent steaks, ribs and hamburgers. Beef is truly king here. The menu also offers a few salads and fish dishes. The restaurant also has a bar, which opens later.

A Pacific Cafe – O 'ahu
$30-$40
*Sun to Thu 5:30pm to
9pm, Fri and Sat until
10pm*
1200 Ala Moana Blvd.
Ward Center, first floor
☎593-0035
One of five restaurants owned by French chef Jean-Marie Josselin, A Pacific Cafe has become a figurehead of regional Hawaiian cuisine in just a few years. The restaurant's cuisine is an amalgamation of classical and exotic cooking styles, using simple ingredients and sophisticated recipes borrowed from Hawaii's many cultures. If you want to learn more about "Hawaiian nouvelle cuisine" and this restaurant's chef, you can watch his television program, "A Taste of Hawaii," broadcast every Saturday at 5:30pm on KGMB. Or better yet, come here for dinner and judge for yourself. Most Americans adore his cuisine, but many Europeans (of Latin origin, especially) are a bit confused by the eclectic mix of flavours, and are somewhat disturbed by the fact that the chef is not always in the kitchen. Several menus are offered.

Ala Moana Center

Makai Market
less than $10
*Mon to Sat 9am to 9pm,
Sun 9:30am to 7pm*
1450 Ala Moana Blvd.
Basement of Ala Moana Center
☎955-9517
At last count, this huge fast food area had no less than 27 restaurant signs set up around a vast field of 1,500 tables. Don't expect anything fancy, but there's something for everyone here, from predictable hamburgers and fried chicken to pastries and ice cream, as well as all sorts of ethnic specialties – Hawaiian (Poi Bowl), Chinese, Korean, Italian, Thai, Japanese and even Cajun. Yokozuna, near the main entrance facing Ala Moana Boulevard, offers a wonderful selection of sushi.

Hanaka Restaurant
less than $10
1450 Ala Moana Blvd.
Basement of Ala Moana Center
right of the main entrance
☎942-0132
The large number of dishes offered by this major Japanese fast-food restaurant (*bentos*, miso soup, noodles, sushi, etc.) are displayed in the window to help you choose.

Honolulu Coffee Company
less than $10
1450 Ala Moana Blvd.
second floor Ala Moana Center
If you're here in the morning, instead of descending into the depths of the

"neonified" shopping centre (where the food court is located), stop by this coffee-roasting café, where you can enjoy a good cappuccino and a pastry with jazz music in the background.

Pearl's Seafood Chinese Restaurant
$10-$30
every day 10am to 10pm
1450 Ala Moana Blvd.
Basement of Ala Moana Center, right of the main entrance
As its name suggests, this Chinese restaurant's specialty is seafood. It offers an excellent selection of dishes, from sea cucumbers and jelly-fish appetizers to the exotic bird's nest soup – a delicacy prepared using saliva concretions from salanganes (sea swallows from southeast Asia that live in caves).

Waikiki

Diamond Head Deli-Cafe
Less than $10 to $15
Mon to Fri 11am to 8pm, Sat 9am to 8pm and Sun 9am to 3pm
3046 Montsarrat Ave.
Its name says it all: situated on the road to Diamond Head, this small establishment is both a café and a deli. What it doesn't say is that the restaurant uses organic ingredients and that its tropical decor is quite pleasant. You can order sandwiches, vegetable salads, pasta, pastries, as well as fresh juice. The coffees and teas are also organic. For something a

little unusual, try the *kawa* tea (made from the root of the pepper plant) or the *noni* (a fruit used in certain anti-cancer treatments). Breakfast is only served on the weekends.

Eggs'n Things
less than $10
every day 11pm to 2pm
1911-B Kalakaua Ave.
☎949-0820
This plain-looking local restaurant is situated on Kalakaua Avenue just past the Ala Moana Boulevard junction. Why would you go this far for breakfast? The large crowd that gathers here every morning in front of the doors knows why. Omelets, pancakes, waffles – the concept is simple, the prices reasonable and the food scrumptious. The hours of operation here are not what you'd expect: closed in the afternoon, it is open all night long. It offers breakfast specials with three pancakes and two eggs at surprisingly low prices. Note that credit cards aren't accepted.

Fatty's Chinese Kitchen
less than $10
every day 10:30am to 9:30pm
2345 Kuhio Ave.
☎922-9600
For small and large appetites, this tiny Chinese restaurant nestled on a shopping lane behind the International Marketplace *(at the corner of Kuhio Ave. and Nahua St.)* draws many employees from the surrounding area.

Seated at the bar, you'll be able to have a free cooking lesson as you watch the simmering noodles and glowing flames.

International Marketplace
less than $10
2330 Kalakaua Ave.
☎923-9871
In the middle of thousands of souvenir shops, the International Marketplace restaurant complex houses about 15 stands around a covered space where you can have a seat. Pastries, pizza, hamburgers, Filipino, Japanese, Vietnamese and even Greek dishes – there are all sorts of variations on the fast-food theme. To finish your meal on a sweet note, sample a delicious pineapple ice cream.

Perry's Smorgy Restaurants
less than $10
every day 7am to 11am, 11:30am to 2:30pm and 5pm to 9pm
Sunday brunch 11:30am to 2:30pm
250 Lewers Street (Ohana Coral Seas Hotel)
☎922-8814
2380 Kuhio Ave.
☎926-0184
The two locations of Perry's Smorgy in Waikiki have been popular with budget travellers for more than 40 years. They both offer an all-you-can-eat buffet to satiate your appetite without breaking the bank. At this price, it's obviously not gourmet dining, but the drinks are included. The loca-

O'ahu

tion on Kuhio Avenue is the more attractive and more spacious of the two, which is good to know when you see the long queues.

Banyan Veranda
$10-$20
2365 Kalakaua Ave.
Sheraton Moana Surfrider
☎922-3111
Facing the ocean between Waikiki Beach and the Moana Hotel pool, the Banyan Veranda transports you to a bygone era. During the 1930s, the radio show *Hawaii Calls*, which popularized Hawaiian music, was broadcast from this establishment. It offers light fare and drinks, which you can enjoy under the famous 100-year-old banyan tree. Or you can come for British-style high tea *(every day)*, with a selection of high-quality teas, pastries and various snacks. After tea, Hawaiian musicians perform some heavenly Hawaiian tunes.

Cha Cha Cha
$10-$15
342 Seaview Ave.
☎923-7797
True to its name, Cha Cha Cha welcomes its guests with frenzied Latino rhythms. Start your evening off with a tequila, and then choose among the decent – although Americanized – Mexican dishes, as well as a few Caribbean offerings on the menu, such as vegetables with coconut milk. There's also a

house special every evening.

Hard Rock Cafe
$10-$20
every day 11:30am to 11pm (bar until midnight, except Fri until 1:30am)
1837 Kapi'olani Blvd.
☎955-7383
Situated west of Waikiki, this was one of the very first locations of the famous Hard Rock Cafe chain. In addition to the usual music, there are souvenirs of the great surfing legends. An old green Cadillac, filled with surfboards, hangs over the bar. The food, since we have to mention it, is neither better nor worse than other restaurants in Waikiki.

Moose McGillycuddy's
$10-$15
every day 7:30am to 10pm
310 Lewers St.
☎923-0751
If you meet a moose-headed human handing out flyers near Kalakaua Avenue and you happen to be looking for a good place to have breakfast, follow his directions. When you arrive at Moose McGillycuddy's, another creature with sunglasses greets you – this one propped up on the wall. Enjoy a Bill Clinton omelet (the menu tells you not to inhale it) or a Homer Simpson omelet (which fortunately does not contain radioactive peanuts and stale popcorn in a beer sauce, like the menu says).

Another option, for those who love spicy food, is the Speedy Gonzales omelet. There are about 21 different choices in total. The rest of the menu lists hamburgers and sandwiches. For small budgets, there's an earlybird breakfast special and an inexpensive "Quickie" lunch that includes half a sandwich, soup and salad. Many people come to McGillycuddy's for a drink or two (see p 184xx).

Sushi Koh
$10-$20
every day 11:30am to 2:30pm and 5pm to 10pm
255 Beach Walk
☎923-5526
This tiny, unpretentious Japanese restaurant, which mostly caters to Japanese tourists, looks like its right out of Tokyo or Sapporo. The inexpensive lunch menu offers miso soup, a main dish (sushi, tempura, chicken teriyaki or ginger pork), rice and a small salad. Try the "rock'n'roll sushi" with flying fish eggs.

Arancino
$15-$25
every day 11:30am to 2:30pm and 5pm to 10pm
255 Beach Walk
☎923-5557
Everything here evokes Italy: old photographs, tables covered with red tablecloths, green wrought-iron chairs, bottles of Chianti lined up on the wall, mu-

sic...everything except the waiters, who are mostly Japanese to cater to the touristic clientele. The menu is also completely devoted to The Boot. The pizza is delicious, as is the lobster linguini, served with a tomato sauce. But be careful not to order too much because the portions are generous. To accompany your meal, you can order wine by the glass or an Italian beer. This is an excellent, unpretentious restaurant, far from the bustle of the large hotels, and an incredibly good value at lunchtime.

Cheeseburger in Paradise
$15-$20
every day from 8am to 11pm
2500 Kalakaua Ave.
☎923-3731
The Cheeseburger in Paradise is a good example of typical tourist traps whose main draw isn't the food. Situated just across from Waikiki Beach, it has a slightly kitsch decor, with imitation palm trees and relics dating back to the 1930s. It has an American Beach Boy-style atmosphere, with waitresses in mini-shorts who serve up fries and hamburgers galore. It isn't cheap, and what's more, the service isn't that hot either. Groups and singers perform here from Wednesday to Sunday.

Duke's Canoe Club
$15-$20
every day 7am to 10:30pm, 11am to 2:30pm and 5pm to 10pm, bar until midnight
2335 Kalakaua Ave.
Outrigger Waikiki Hotel
☎922-2268
Bordering Waikiki Beach, Duke's is one of the most popular restaurants on the island. The tropical decor, including many black and white photos on the walls, pays homage to the accomplishments of Duke Kahanamoku, with Hawaiian music in the background. At lunch, the inexpensive menu offers an hors-d'oeuvre buffet, grilled *mahi-mahi*, teriyaki chicken and *kalua* pork (see also p 184).

Furusato
$15-$40
Sushi every day 11:30am to 1pm and 5:30pm to midnight
Restaurant every day 6:30am to 10:30am, 11am to 2:30pm and 5:30pm to 10:30pm
2424 Kalakaua Ave.
☎922-4991
Located in the basement of the Hyatt Hotel, Furusato is one of the best Japanese restaurants in all of Hawaii. It concocts impeccable quality cuisine, but the prices are a bit expensive. However, you can take advantage of the early-bird specials. Otherwise head to the sushi bar located on the street level; it has an excellent selection of high-quality offerings, and the prices, all things considered, are reasonable enough. The sushi is rolled before your very eyes by Japanese masters, exclusively men since, according to Japanese tradition, women's hands are too warm for this sort of activity. You can have a seat at the bar or at a table and order sushi à la carte, by the roll, or a combination plate that includes miso soup and tea. The *unagi* (river eel), though expensive, is simply divine. Risk-takers might want to try the "Russian roulette" special, which is not for anyone under 18 since it is incredibly spicy.

House Without a Key
$15-$20
every day 7am to 9pm
2199 Kalia Rd.
Halekulani Hotel (see p 153)
☎923-2311
The Halekulani Hotel's most affordable and laid-back restaurant lies between the pool and the ocean beneath the shade of a large *kiawe* tree. It gets its name from the first novel by local author Earl Derr Biggers. It tells of the adventures of a character named Charlie Chan, apparently based on the real life of a Chinese detective in Honolulu from the 1930s. House Without a Key is a wonderful place to stop for dessert, which feature the exotic flavours of Hawaiian fruit. The lychee sorbet is worth the trip alone. Every evening between 9pm and 10:30pm, guests are

O'ahu

treated to Hawaiian musical concerts and a *hula* show. A great place to sip a cocktail as the sun sets.

Keo's
$15-$25
every day 7am to 10am, 11am to 2pm, evening from 5pm
2028 Kuhio Ave.
☎951-9355
Closer to central Waiki-ki, Keo's compete with the Singha (see below) for the title of Best Thai Restaurant on the island. Although the cuisine is slightly Ameri-canized (there's even ribs on the menu), the setting is lovely, with straw chairs, a terrace that opens onto the street and a flowery decor featuring some beautiful pieces of Thai artwork, such as the two bronze winged dancers at the entrance. You'll also notice an incredible photo collec-tion showing Keo Sananikore, the owner, with many celebrities.

Parc Cafe
$15-$25
Mon to Sat 6:30am to 10am (Sun to 9am), 11:30am to 2pm (Sun 11m to 2pm), every eve-ning from 5:30pm
2233 Helumoa Rd.
Waikiki Parc Hotel
☎921-7272
Although you can order a few sandwiches and salads à la carte here, most people come to the Parc Cafe for its award-winning buffets. Breakfast is followed by a lunch featuring Asian cuisine on Mon-days, Tuesdays, Thurs-days and Saturdays, and Hawaiian cuisine on Wednesdays and Fridays. On Sundays is a pricey sushi brunch. Dinner buffets feature ribs from Monday to Thursday and fish and seafood from Friday to Sunday.

Shore Bird Broiler
$15-$20
every day 7am to 11pm (buffet) and 4:30pm to 10pm
2169 Kalia Rd.
Outrigger Reef Hotel
☎922-2887
According to its ad, the Shore Bird Beach Broiler claims to have "the best ribs on the island." That's perhaps a slight exaggeration, but those who enjoy grilled meat will defi-nitely find large enough helpings here to satisfy their appetite. You can grill the meat yourself, if you so desire. Each order includes one trip to the hors-d'oeuvre buffet. (See also p 184).

Acqua
$20-$30
every day from 5:30pm
Hawaiian Regent Hotel, second floor of the Kalakaua Tower
2552 Kalakaua Ave.
☎924-0123 or 924-0531
With its tropical theme, the menu is obviously influenced by Hawaiian nouvelle cuisine. Meat and seafood make up a large part of the menu, prepared with Asian and French touches. Among the recom-mended dishes are guava barbecue prawns, sautéed rock shrimp risotto with asparagus and wild mushrooms, and the coconut-crusted island *'ahi*, (seared tuna with coconut and Szechwan sauce). The dining room, which towers above Kalakaua Ave-nue, has a lovely view facing the sea.

Oceanarium
$20-$30
Mon to Fri 6am to 2pm; Sat 6am to 9:30am and 11am to 2:30pm; Sun 6am to 8:30am and 10am to 2:30pm; every day 5pm to 10pm
Pacific Beach Hotel
2490 Kalakaua Ave.
☎922-1233
Oceanarium is not as famous for its food as it is for its 26ft (8m) high aquarium, which con-tains more than 260,000 gallons (1,000,000 litres) of water. To the guests' delight, more than 60 species of fish swim about the tank. Several times a day, divers hand-feed them. As for the food, buffets are a regular feature, especially for breakfast and lunch on week-ends. Seafood, of course, makes up a large part of the menu, but there's meat as well. You can also come here simply to admire the aquarium on the first floor.

Singha Thai Restaurant
$20-$30
Mon to Fri 11am to 4pm, every day 4pm to 11pm
1910 Ala Moana Blvd.
☎941-2898
You can't miss the rep-lica of a Thai temple west of Waikiki at the intersection of Ala

Moana Boulevard and Ena Road. Recognized as one of the best – if not *the* best – Thai restaurant in Hawaii, Singha only uses organic Hawaii-grown products. The presentations are eye-catching and the service is impeccable. To top it all off, every evening there's a show featuring costumed Thai dancers *(6:45pm to 9pm)*.

Top of Waikiki
$20-$30
every day 11m to 2pm and 5pm to 9pm
Waikiki Business Plaza
☎*923-3877*
Perched on the 21st floor of an office building, the only revolving restaurant in Hawaii transports guests back to the 1970s. Don't be fooled by its appearance: while the cuisine can hardly be called gourmet, it offers good value for your money, especially at lunchtime. Here you can enjoy a *mahi-mahi* hamburger or a Louis crab salad. The dinner menu is more expensive and the menu offers a sophisticated selection of fish and steak. From 5pm to 7pm are early-bird specials, such as the lobster with mushrooms on a bed of *farfales*.

Trattoria Restaurant
$20-$30
every day 5:30pm to 10pm
2168 Kalia Rd.
Edgewater Hotel
☎*923-8415*
For nearly 30 years, customers at this Italian restaurant have enjoyed its cuisine, which features specialties from northern Italy such as Milanese escalopes and cannelloni. Dinner includes minestrone soup or salad and coffee.

Bali by the Sea
$25-$50
Mon to Sat 6pm to 10pm
2005 Kalia Rd.
Hilton Hawaiian Village
(see p 153)
First floor of the Rainbow Tower
☎*949-4321 ext. 43*
Facing the ocean, the Hilton's premier restaurant was voted Best Restaurant in Hawaii. Run by Jean-Luc Voegele, a French chef, it offers a menu that combines fresh Hawaiian-grown products, traditional savoir-faire and Hawaiian nouvelle cuisine influences. The chef's specialty is cuisine *à la Provençale*, featuring dishes like bouillabaisse, shrimp and *coquille Saint-Jacques*, as well as leg of lamb with julienne vegetables and macadamia nuts!

Ciao Mein
$25-$40
2424 Kalakaua Ave.
Hyatt Regency Waikiki
(see p 153)
second floor Ewa Tower
☎*923-1234*
This restaurant's name lets you know what to expect: Chinese and Italian cuisine – and you won't be disappointed. Rather than mix the two cuisines, Ciao Mein instead offers a selection of both. It also offers a few extravagant fusion dishes, such as Chinese duck roasted with cannelloni – after all, both Chinese and Italian cuisines have pasta in common! The Marco Polo menu traces the culinary adventures of the Venetian explorer: carpaccio and minestrone for starters, followed by shrimp with nuts and honey, and a Mongolian casserole. The voyage back to Italy concludes with a good cappuccino. The decor, which has mostly Asian accents, is refined.

Padovani's Bistro & Wine Bar
$25-$85
Bistro every day 6am to 10pm, Mon to Fri 11:30am to 2pm and every day 5:30pm to 10pm
Wine bar every day 6am to 9pm and 4pm to midnight, Sat and Sun 11:30am to 2pm
1956 Ala Moana Blvd.
Doubletree Alana Waikiki Hotel
☎*946-3456*
Under the management of Philippe Padovani, Mediterranean influences and Hawaiian-grown products combine to create a flavourful menu that would impress even royalty. Try the salmon confit with olive oil and leeks, pasta and beluga caviar. Or for something a bit more extravagant, try the lobster stuffed with a mango salad, accompanied by a vegetable *brunoise* and vinaigrette. The dessert tray is really something else. The wine bar up-

O'ahu

stairs, which has a modern decor, has a cellar with more than 9,000 bottles – a sizeable number for Hawaii. You can also come here for coffee and pastries in the morning.

Tanaka of Tokyo
$25-$30
Mon to Fri from 11:30am, every day from 5:30pm
131 Kaiulani Ave.
King's Village
☎922-4233
Tanaka of Tokyo West
Ilikai Hotel Nikko
1777 Ala Moana Blvd.
☎945-3443
Tanaka of Tokyo Central
Waikiki Shopping Plaza
2250 Kalakaua Ave.
☎922-4702
Tanaka has been voted Best Japanese Restaurant in the U.S. Now a well-known concept, guests sit around a large cooking plate on which the chef, armed with long, sharp knives, cooks up beef, chicken, salmon and seafood, doing a juggling act with salt and pepper shakers. All sorts of combination dinners are offered. The portions are smaller at lunch, but the prices are much lower. All dinners include miso soup, rice, vegetables, salad and green tea. Excellent service.

David Paul's Diamond Head Grill
$30-$40
every day 7am to 10:30pm, Mon to Fri 11:30am to 2:30pm, every day 6pm to 10pm
Bistro Thu to Sat 10am to 11:30pm
2885 Kalakaua Ave.
West Honolulu Diamond Head Hotel, first floor (see p 154)
☎922-3734
A renowned chef in the Hawaiian culinary scene, David Paul has two restaurants, the Diamond Head Grill and another one in Lahaina on Mauai (see p 363). In a chic, modern bistro, the chef, who's a nouvelle-cuisine fan, offers a menu that brings together an eclectic assortment of dishes: there's pasta and fresh fish, Hawaiian-inspired dishes (such as the caramalized *kalua* pork sandwich with pineapple mustard and marinated mangoes), Japanese-inspired creations (a napoleon of *hamachi*, lobster and river eel). You can order wine by the glass, as well as a variety of portos and Madeira wines. From Tuesday to Saturday, there's jazz music in the background.

Golden Dragon
$30-$50
Tue to Sun 6pm to 9:30pm
2005 Kalia Rd.
Hilton Hawaiian Village (see p 153)
☎949-4321 ext. 42
Perched above the lake at the foot of the Rainbow Tower, the

Golden Dragon serves up high-quality Chinese cuisine in an elegant Asian decor. Known for its Szechwan and Cantonese specialities, the presentation of the fish and seafood dishes is particularly impressive. The Golden Dragon offers several menus, including its Healthy Chinese Menu – it's hard to believe that these dishes have less than 500 calories. For dessert, the lychee ice cream is a must.

Hau Tree Lanai
$30-$40
every day from 7am
2863 Kalakaua Ave.
New Otani Kaimana Beach Hotel (see p 152)
☎921-7066
Facing Sans Souci Beach on a terrace sheltered by two old *hau* (hibiscus) trees with split branches, 20 wrought-iron tables look out onto the sea. Robert Louis Stevenson relaxed on the beach at this very spot more than 100 years ago. The extensive menu has something for everyone, including tossed salads, seafood galore and a selection of sandwiches with Asian touches. If you're travelling on a tight budget and would like to enjoy the enchanting setting of the Hau Tree Lanai, come here for lunch when the prices are about half. From Friday to Sunday, there's live guitar music. The service unfortunately is very slow.

Michel's
$30-$40
every day 5:50 to 9pm
2885 Kalakaua Ave.
W. Honolulu Diamond Head
Hotel (see p 154)
☎*923-6552*
The dining room, which directly faces the small beach in front of the hotel, creates a harmonious and refined atmosphere for serving its French-style cuisine, which features warm goat-cheese salad, lobster bisque, snails, Chateaubriand and the like. You can order one of its fine portos or cognacs with dessert.

Bird of paradise

Nick's Fishmarket
$30-$40
every day 5:30pm to 2am
2070 Kalakaua Ave.
☎*955-6333*
This popular but expensive seafood restaurant features a large sampling of local products from Hawaiian waters (such as *'ahi*, *mahi-mahi* and *opakapaka*) or the result of migratory movements that have populated the archipelago (shiitake mushrooms, *shoyu* sauce, and even a few Italian touches (all a result of immigration to the islands). Those not fond of seafood will also find a selection of meats. Nick's turns into a nightclub on some evenings after dinner.

Orchids
$30-$40
Mon to Sat 7:30am to 11am, 11:30am to 2pm and every day 6pm to 10pm
Sunday brunch 9:30am to 2:30pm
2199 Kalia Rd.
Halekulani (see p 153)
☎*923-2311*
Located right by the ocean, the Helekulani Hotel's second restaurant blends the charm of the tropics, with an orchid at each table, and the elegance of this deluxe hotel. It offers a selection of fish and seafood served with vegetables and fresh Hawaiian fruit. The paella is highly recommended.

La Mer
Menus from $75
every day 6pm to 10pm
2199 Kalia Rd.
Halekulani (see p 153)
☎*923-2311*
Under the direction of chef Yves Garnier, the menu features dishes seasoned with the flavours of Provence and southern France. Using local products, he concocts dishes such as red and white tuna tartar and salmon with three caviars and three sauces. The decor is extremely refined, the cheese plate is the best within a 1,900mi (3,000km) radius and the view of Diamond Head and the coconut trees is absolutely breathtaking. As if that weren't enough, the wine list has more than 300 wines, including a few rare vintages, such as Château d'Yquem, Petrus and Mouton-Rothschild. The service is impeccable. There's only one drawback: it's a little strait-laced (men must wear a jacket).

Kapahulu Avenue

Running from Waikiki to the University area, Kapahulu Avenue, with its many sports shops, drive-inns and inexpensive restaurants, is a favourite spot for local residents.

Leonard's Bakery
less than $10
every day 6am to 9pm, Fri and Sat until 10pm
933 Kapahulu Ave.
☎*737-5591*
Established in 1952, Leonard's Bakery is *the* place for *malassadas*, a delicious fritter whose recipe was brought by Portuguese immigrants. "Malassada" means "poorly made," and legend has it that the first *malassadas* were a result of a botched bread dough, which was then fried and covered with sugar. For two generations, the Leonard family has crisscrossed the island on their red and white van, now aided by a few extra helping hands.

O'ahu

Ono Hawaiian Foods
less than $10
Mon to Sat 11m to 7:30pm
726 Kapahulu Ave.
☎737-2275
In Hawaiian, *ono* means "good," which is à propos for this restaurant. For more than 35 years, this family business has had a popular following of local residents and throngs of adventurous tourists. Ono is one of the rare restaurants on O'ahu that offers a selection of traditional Hawaiian dishes. Some of the most popular dishes include the *kalua* pork dinner, served with salmon *lomilomi* as an appetizer, chicken with rice, *poi*, as well as many other scrumptious dishes. The *poke* is excellent, and if you're not intimidated by the regional cuisine, try the *na'au* (pork intestines). Credit cards are not accepted.

The Pyramid
$10-$20
Mon to Sat 11am to 2pm and 5:30pm to 10pm; Sun noon to 3pm and 5pm to 9pm
758 Kapahulu Ave.
☎737-2900
For something a little out of the ordinary, try this fine Egyptian restaurant, the favourite place of Honolulu's Arabic community, which is always growing. Its specialties include eastern Mediterranean dishes like tabouli, falafel, as well as stuffed grape leaves, Greek salad with feta cheese or pita,

moussaka, baklava and Turkish coffee. There's an all-you-can-eat buffet at noon. In the evening, you can watch belly-dancers for no additional charge. The owners run the Mediterranean grocery store next door, the only place in Hawaii where you'll find couscous and *dolmas* (a vine leaf stuffed with a filling of meat and rice).

Sam Choy's
$25-$35
Mon to Thu 5:30pm to 9:30pm, Fri to Sun 5pm to 10pm
Sunday brunch 9:30am to 2pm
449 Kapahulu Ave.
Hee Hing Plaza, first floor
☎732-8645
Somewhere between the past and the present, Sam Choy and his chefs feature classic recipes from yesteryear adapted to today's tastes. Although often considered as representative of Hawaiian cuisine, Sam has a style unto his own. His approach is more traditional than his accomplices, and he's also much closer to his customers. For a Hawaiian note, enjoy the appetizer of *poke* or *laulau* seafood and fish (with a *béarnaise* sauce), steamed in a *ti* leaf. If you're looking for something original, try the grilled duck with soy sauce, honey and macadamia nuts, or the lobster stuffed with shrimp and served with a miso soya sauce and white truffles.

Around Town

Wai'oli Tea Room
Less than $10 to $16
every day 8am to 4pm
2950 Manoa Rd.
☎988-5800
Established in 1922, this institution has become a historic monument over the years. The Salvation Army orphanage next door originally created the Tea Room to educate young girls about "cooking, baking and the arts of gracious living." Throughout the years, socialites have replaced the orphans. Today, you can have a quick breakfast or lunch (sandwiches, salads and pastries), but most people come here for the tea. At 2:30pm on Sundays, English-style high tea, a tradition from a bygone era, is served, with an extensive selection of canapés, pastries and chocolates. It's a bit pricey, but a unique experience nevertheless. Reservations required.

The Eastern Tip

Roys
$20-$40
6600 Kalaniana'ole Hwy.
Hawaii Kai Corporate Plaza corner Keahole St.
☎396-7697
The modern, refined decor here tries to make you forget where you are – in a sterile shopping centre by the roadside. The Oahu restaurant of Roy Yamaguchi, host of a famous television cook-

ing program and one of the founding fathers of Hawaiian nouvelle cuisine, offers classic dishes featuring the culinary traditions of all of Hawaii's peoples. Many celebrities have come here, as evidenced by the pictures of Roy with the Clintons and the menu dedicated by Paul Bocuse.

The Windward Coast

In each of Kane'ohe's shopping centres and in the surrounding area, you'll find a selection of nondescript fast-food restaurants. Here are the ones in Kailua:

Bar-B-Q n'Things
less than $10
Mon to Sat 10:30am to 9pm, Sun 4:30pm to 9pm
201 Hamakua Dr., Kailua
☎261-7223
This small, unpretentious family restaurant offers both a Korean and Japanese menu, which makes sense since the former borrows a lot from the latter. Here you can order Korean-style grilled meat, tempura, noodles or Japanese-style seafood. A different fish special is offered every day.

Jaron's
$10-$20
201 Hamakua Dr., Kailua
☎261-4600
This restaurant has vinyl booths and offers an extensive menu featuring Thai-style or Moroccan-style chicken

salad (with tabouli), fish of the day, hamburgers and steak, Cajun-spiced salmon, vegetarian plates...the restaurant's policy is clear: something for everyone. It's not gourmet cuisine, but you can enjoy one or two hours of music by a local group every Thursday, Friday and Saturday evening after dinner is served *(around 10:30pm).*

Los Garcia's
$10-$15
every day 11am to 9pm, Fri and Sat until 10pm
14 Oneawa St., Kailya
☎231-0306
This tiny, authentic (therefore spicy!) Mexican restaurant is very popular with Kailua residents, who flock here on weekends. The owner is from Jalisco and the dishes reflect his origins. Dinner is accompanied by enjoyable Latino music, with mariachi duets every Tuesday and Wednesday from 5pm to 8pm.

Zia's
$10-$20
every day 11am to 9pm
201 Hamakua Dr., Kailua
☎262-7168
The bottles of olive oil and balsamic vinegar on the tables will make you think you're in Italy. But don't get carried away: when the tomato salad with mozzarella cheese arrives at your table, you'll notice something's missing – the tomatoes and the mozzarella! That said, the pasta is no worse than elsewhere, the

portions are generous and the service is attentive. If you're watching your weight, you can ask for a half-order and replace the second half with a salad.

Casablanca
$15-$25
Mon to Thu 6pm to 9pm. Fri and Sat until 9:30pm
19 Hoolai St., Kailua
☎262-8196
For a completely different experience, try this authentic Moroccan restaurant, an unexpected find in this part of the world. Those who crave couscous or something exotic – or both – will be enchanted by this place. The decor, between whitewashed archways and rugs, conjures up the famous town in a refined manner.

The North Coast

There are very few restaurants on the northwest coast between Kane'ohe and La'ie. For example, it is impossible to find a place to have breakfast here. There are a few fast-food restaurants in La'ie, including a McDonald's in the shape of a Polynesian building, two Chinese restaurants and a large supermarket. Keep your eye out for the red and white van owned by Leonard's, the *malassada* specialist (see p 177). Beyond La'ie, the selection is a little better thanks to a number of stands and snack bars along the

O'ahu

road. But you have to head west to Hale'iwa for a larger selection, mostly consisting of simple coffee shops and fast-food joints.

Cafe Hale'iwa

$

Mon to Sat 7am to 2pm
66-460 Kamehameha Hwy.
Hale'iwa
☎637-5511
Situated at the southern entrance to Hale'iwa (Mile 0.3) across from McDonald's, this café has become a hangout for international surfers. It's a great place to eat your fill before heading out to surf the breaks at Sunset or Waimea. There's an excellent selection of American and Mexican breakfasts at very reasonable prices, the warm banana bread is delicious, and the hamburgers and sandwiches served at lunch are not bad either. What more could you ask for?

Celestial Natural Foods

$

Store: Mon to Sat 9am to 6:30pm
Café: Mon to Sat 9am to 5pm, Sun 10am to 5pm
66-443 Kamehameha Hwy.
Hale'iwa
☎637-6729
In the style of Russian dolls, this well-stocked natural-foods store is home to a real find: Cafe Paradise Found, which offers a variety of soups, salads, chili, sandwiches, hummus and fresh fruit juices (such as celery-ginger and beet-parsley) for only a few dollars. Have a seat on one of

the three red vinyl booths, where you can nibble on your vegetarian plate, accompanied with rice, salad and sautéed tofu.

Coffee Gallery

$

Every day 7am to 8pm
66-250 Kamehameha Hwy.
North Shore Marketplace
Hale'iwa
☎637-5355
This small roasting house gives a taste of what's to come with its ceiling covered with bags of coffee from Kona. To accompany your espresso, latte or cappuccino, you can order a few pastries or a bowl of vegetarian chili for lunch.

Hukilau Cafe

$

Mon to Sat 7am to 2pm
55-662 Wahinepe St., La'ie
☎293-8616
A favourite with La'ie residents, many white-collar workers grab a quick bite here for lunch. Hukilau Cafe serves simple, family-style cuisine, without an ounce of sophistication. There's a large breakfast menu, from fruit pancakes to the Hungry Hawaiian, a copious serving of the classic American breakfast. The lunch-time portions, with four or five specials every day, are also gargantuan – and all at very reasonable prices. Credit cards are not accepted.

Kua'aina

$

every day 11am to 8pm
66-214 Kamehameha Hwy.
Hale'iwa
☎637-6067
This hole in the wall has a few tables inside and on the street. It offers a great selection of sandwiches as well as "the best hamburgers in the world." It's true, they are good, made to order with or without grilled onions, and the meat cooked the way you like it. The recipe is so good that Kua'aina has expanded to Honolulu – and even all the way to Tokyo!

Matsumoto's

$

66-087 Kamehameha Hwy.
Hale'iwa
☎637-4827
The father of Hawaiian "shaved ice" (crushed ice saturated with sweet syrup) is located opposite Lili'uokalani Church. The former grocery store from the early 1900s has been replaced by a souvenir shop, but thanks to the success of the homemade recipe, you can still order giant, multicoloured ice cream cones in a variety of flavours.

The Spaghetti Shack

$

Mon to Sat 11am to 8pm, Sun 2pm to 8pm
56-565 Kamehameha Hwy.
Kahuku
☎923-5959
Built beside the Kahuku Sugar Mill, this Italian-American restaurant has an enclosed terrace and offers a

good selection of pasta (spaghetti and penne) as well as a few specialties such as lasagna and eggplant parmigiana. You can also order a simple sandwich.

'Ahi's
$10-$15
Mon to Sat 11m to 9pm
53-147 Kamehameha Hwy.
Punaluu (Mile 24.7)
☎*923-5650*
At the southern entrance to Punaluu, an old van from the 1930s displays a giant, worn-out sign marking 'Ahi's, an old greenwood building. The house specialty is shrimp, served grilled, sautéed with garlic butter, steamed, fried and even tempura style. You don't have to worry about freshness: they come from the shrimp farm located past Kahuku a few kilometres to the north. Add to this all sorts of combination dinners with steak, fish and chicken, as well as a few sandwiches and salads, not to mention *poi*, which is not for everybody. Local groups perform here on Friday and Saturday nights starting at 6pm. Credit cards not accepted.

Cholo's
$10-$15
every day 8am to 9pm
66-250 Kamehameha Hwy.
North Shore Marketplace
Hale'iwa
☎*637-3059*
This small Mexican restaurant, with walls covered its masks,

paintings, rugs and other souvenirs, prepares standard Mexican fare such as burritos, quesadillas, tacos, fajitas and other *antojitos.* The menu is the same all day; the only things that change are the portions and the prices. The house specialties are chili relleno, peppers stuffed with melted cheese, and fish tacos.

Giovanni's
$10-$15
Kahuku
☎*923-1839*
The old white van, covered with graffiti, is parked on the side of the road at the northern exit from Kahuku. For many years, locals lined up for its excellent fresh shrimp, served in a lemon butter sauce, with African spices or with garlic and white wine. But at those prices, tourists are pretty much the only people who still stop at Giovanni's.

Crouching Lion Inn
$15-$25
every day 11am to 3pm and 5pm to 9pm
51-666 Kamehameha Hwy.
Ka'a'awa
☎*237-8511*
A favourite spot for vacationers on the north coast road, the Crouching Lion, which has been around for more than 40 years, offers an extensive menu with something for everyone: hamburgers, fish of the day, shrimp, chicken, salads, steak, *kalua* pork and even a vegetarian plate.

You can also opt for the hors-d'oeuvre buffet. For dessert, try the mud pie, one of the house specialties.

Jameson's By the Sea
$15-$25
Mon to Fri 11m to 9pm, Sat and Sun from 9am
62-540 Kamehameha Hwy.
Hale'iwa
☎*637-4336*
A little bit more upscale compared to most establishments in Hale'iwa, this restaurant chain, which is always located by the sea, serves sandwiches, salads, steak and hamburgers on the main floor during the day, and fresh fish upstairs in the evening. The catch of the day varies between *'ahi, ono, ulua* and *'opakapaka.*

Hilton Turtle Bay Resort
$10-$40
57-091 Kamehameha Hwy.
(Mile 12.6)
☎*293-8811*
Since The Cove, the hotel's premier restaurant, closed, there are still three options to get something to eat. The Palm Terrace Cafe *(every day 7am to 10pm, Fri and Sat until 11pm)* has an unimaginative menu, mostly buffets, which can be quite expensive in the evening. The Sea Tide Room, the large octagonal dining room at the tip of the peninsula, faces the sea on all sides. There's a Sunday brunch *($27, 10am to 2pm)* with ribs, seafood and sushi. The Bay View Lounge, located near the reception

O'ahu

desk, is a bar with pool tables serving mostly cocktails but also a few hot dishes.

The Leeward Coast

The selection of restaurants in this region is very limited. If you don't want to spend a small fortune at the Ihilani Resort, then you'll have to settle for a quick bite or a picnic, which is probably your best option in any case.

Makaha Valley Country Club Restaurant
less than $10
every day 7am to 5pm
Makaha Valley Country Club
(Mile 12.6)
84-627 Makaha Valley Rd.
☎*695-7111*
If you're expecting a strait-laced establishment, don't worry – this Country Club, which is popular with local golfers, is one of the most laid-back clubs around. On Sundays and Mondays, the club transforms into a sports bar. In addition to sandwiches and hamburgers, there are a few Japanese noodle dishes.

Tsunami's
less than $10
Sat and Sun 7am to 10:30am, every day noon to 8:30pm (Fri and Sat until 10pm)
87-064 Farrington Hwy.
(Mile 9.5)
☎*696-3975*
Looking at the outside of the restaurant, you might expect something a little more posh inside, but here

you'll have to settle for hamburgers, sandwiches, salads and other greasy lunch plates. But it's only fitting – after all, it's a sports bar. Crowds gather here every Sunday and Monday to watch football games.

Ihilani Resort & Spa
$30-$90
92-1001 Olani St.
Ko'Olina Resort, Kapolei
☎*679-0079*
The restaurants at the Ihilani Resort, although good quality, are very expensive. **Azul** *(Mon, Wed, Fri and Sat 6pm to 9pm)* offers Hawaiian-Mediterranean-style cuisine with eclectic influences, serving dishes such as ravioli, couscous and osso buco. Seafood is mostly offered as an appetizer. **Ushio-Tei** *(Tue, Thu, Sat and Sun from 6pm to 9pm alternating with Azul)* is a quality Japanese restaurant whose menu is rather limited (sushi bar). And finally, **Naupaka Terrace** *(Mon to Sat 6am to 2pm, every day 5:30pm to 10pm; Sun brunch 10am to 1:30pm)* is the simplest and most affordable of the hotel's restaurants. Pleasantly facing the pool, its Sunday brunch, which offers American, European and Asian dishes, is very popular. The price includes an assortment of sushi as well.

Entertainment

Bars and Nightclubs

Most of the nightlife is concentrated in Waikiki, where nearly all of the bars and nightclubs are still located. During the past few years, however, downtown Honolulu has undergone a progressive revival. But don't expect a frenzied scene – after all, Honolulu isn't Los Angeles or San Francisco. You'll often find mediocre local productions and DJs from the mainland putting on evenings of groove, R&B, house and hip-hop music – including some catering to an under-21 crowd.

Downtown Honolulu

Havana Cabana
1131 Nu'uanu Ave.
☎*524-4277*
Ever since the latest cigar rage swept across the United States, Honolulu has had its own cigar-smoking club. You don't have to be a member to enjoy the posh ambiance and sample a Montecristo made in the Dominican Republic (there are no Cuban cigars because of the U.S. embargo). Every room plays funky

music *(Wed to Sat)* from the 1970s, with slightly jazzy rhythms, occasionally even hip-hop. You can also have a decent lunch or dinner on the premises.

Indigo
1121 Nu'uana Ave.
☎*521-2900*
Every Thursday and Friday evening, the Indigo restaurant turns into a dance club beside the recently opened Green Room. It's quite a classy place, with mostly jazz and groove music, and it's now becoming one of the most popular spots in town with a 20-30 year-old crowd.

Murphy's Bar & Grill
2 Merchant St.
At the intersection of Merchant Street and Nu'uanu Avenue stands Honolulu's "Irish Corner." And it's a pretty rowdy place on weekends when students swarm to Murphy's, one of the most popular bars in downtown Honolulu. Your draft is served up by a barman dressed like the ones you find in Europe or occasionally on the east coast of the United States – a rarity in Hawaii.

Ocean Club
500 Ala Moana Blvd.
Restaurant Row
☎*526-9888*
The latest yuppie hangout in Honolulu, the Ocean Club is opened to all (minimum 23 years old), but asks that its patrons wear "appropriate attire." Regu-

lars from the business district come here to shoot the breeze over a beer and watch the night come to life. Over the past few months, it has become one of the hippest bars in Honolulu, with rock and dance music *(Tue to Sat)*.

O'Toole's Pub
902 Nu'uanu Ave.
Just across from Murphy's, O'Toole's is an Irish pub with an intimate atmosphere and a touch of class. This truly is a bar "where everybody knows your name." Excellent musicians perform here regularly.

The Pier Bar
Aloha-Tower Marketplace
☎*536-2166*
Situated right at the foot of the Aloha Tower opposite the harbour, the Pier Bar, which is quiet during the day, becomes a wildly popular watering hole in the evening. Local groups perform every day between 8pm and 9:30pm. There's something for everyone: modern and classical Hawaiian music every second day, swing music on Wednesdays, reggae on Thursdays, and so on. Sunday is improv night.

Around Honolulu

Anna Bannana's
2440 South Beretania, Honolulu
☎*946-5190*
The two "n"s in its name are supposed to make it sound more Mexican. Anna

Bannana's offers typical Mexican fare, but most people come here to watch the American football games upstairs or to down a beer at the pub on the main floor in a sombre and rather shabby decor featuring antiquated surf boards, license plates and photos plastered all over the walls and ceiling. On Thursday, Friday and Saturday evenings (and occasionally other days as well), local groups perform here and students arrive in droves. Groove, blues, hip-hop and rock – you can dance to all kinds of music.

Brew Moon (Restaurant & Microbrewery)
1200 Ala Moana Blvd.
Ward Center, second floor
☎*593-0088*
This microbrewery, a local branch of the eastern U.S. chain, makes five home-made beers that you can sample at the bar or the restaurant. If you want to sample all of them, ask for a "lunar sampler." The rather dull atmosphere is livened up on Wednesdays and Thursdays with local music groups. On Sundays, the DJ plays techno and hip-hop.

Liquid
No cover charge
1035 University Ave.
☎942-7873
This beer bar, frequented by a large number of students from the University of Hawaii, transforms into

O'ahu

a nightclub later in the evening.

Waikiki

Duke's Canoe Club
2335 Kalakaua Ave.
Outrigger Waikiki Hotel
☎922-2268
In addition to its restaurant, Duke's is famous for its bar, where you can arrive bare-foot from the beach and not have to worry about being turned away. The entertainment livens up as the afternoon wears on, with the first set of Hawaiian music between 4pm to 6pm, culminating from 10pm to midnight with a second installment of modern Hawaiian music.

Eurasia
No cover charge at the night club after 10pm
On the second floor of the Kalakaua Tower, Hawaiian Regent Hotel
2552 Kalakaua Ave.
Eurasia is one of the most popular hot spots in Waikiki. This sports bar, with two giant screens and 15 televisions, pool tables and electronic dart boards, obviously caters to American football-lovers. The nightclub, which has theme nights, is frequented by many young Honoluluans. The Utopia Bar, situated inside the nightclub, is popular with karaoke fanatics. There's rock, country, modern Hawaiian music and even Japanese, Chinese and Korean songs!

Hard Rock Cafe
every day 11:30am to midnight, Fri until 1:30am
1837 Kapi'olani Blvd.
☎955-7383
Just another of the famous chain, the Hard Rock is still overflowing with people every evening. When the last diners have left, the musicians arrive and people kick up their heels. Every Friday from 11pm to about 1am, there are live bands.

Moose McGillycuddy's
310 Lewers St.
☎923-0751
In addition to its famous breakfasts, Moose draws a large number of barflies and partygoers who come to down a few beers or to have a ball on the dance floor after 9pm. A local group performs here every evening. On Sunday, there's a bikini contest.

Rumours
410 Atkinson Dr., Ala Moana Hotel
☎955-4811
This stylish bar-nightclub offers different entertainment every day: afternoon American football on Mondays at 2:30pm; Latino night on Tuesdays from 7pm to 3am, with free dancing lesson between 9pm and 10pm; karaoke and dancing Wednesdays from 9pm to 4am, and so forth. There's no cover charge, but there's a two-drink minimum.

Scruples
2310 Kuhio Ave.
Waikiki Marketplace
☎923-9530
Surfboards on the wall, waitresses in bikinis and mini-pareos – the atmosphere here is totally laid-back and a bit flashy. The "international discotheque" advertized on the brochure is hopping every evening to the latest pop hits played by a tireless DJ.

Shore Bird Oceanside Bar & Grill
2169 Kalia Rd.
Outrigger Reef Hotel
☎922-2887
Next to the Shore Bird Beach Broiler, the atmosphere at this bar and grill is very relaxed. People come here to wolf down a sandwich or down a drink as the sun beats down on the beachside tables. You can hear local groups perform here every evening from 4pm to 8pm, and if you're a karaoke fan, you can sing your heart out from 9pm till 1am.

Wave Waikiki
No cover charge
1877 Kalakaua Ave.
☎941-0424, ext. 12
Situated at the corner of Kalakua Avenue and Ala Wai Boulevard, Wave is one of Honolulu's hottest dance clubs, frequented by both a young local and tourist clientele. Every night features a particular style of music: R&B, hip hop, house, jungle, groove, hard rock on Wednesdays and rock on Fridays. The upstairs

bar, which is framed with windows, overlooks the dance floor. On Thursday, there's no cover charge until 1:30am.

Gay Bars

Angles Waikiki
2256 Kuhio Ave. (third floor) Waikiki
☎923-1130
More rowdy than Hula's, this gay dance club, which has been around for many years, has drag shows, pool tournaments, variety shows and dancing on Fridays and Saturdays. The establishment organizes catamaran cruises on Sundays ($10) – but the cruise is simply a pretext to "cruise" (☎221-0069).

Fusion Waikiki
No cover Thu to Sat
2260 Kuhio Ave. (third floor) Waikiki
☎924-2422
Take the red and black staircase on the left-hand side of the entrance to Paradise Barbecue. Fusion Waikiki is upstairs. This long-established gay pub is situated right across from Angles, so you can easily bar-hop from one club to another. Although Monday nights are devoted to karaoke until 2am, the rest of the night and the other nights are dedicated to dancing, with different DJs every evening. On Friday and Saturday nights, the house organizes variety shows (at 9:30pm and 11:30pm).

Hula's Bar & Lei Stand
134 Kapahulu Ave., Waikiki
☎923-0669
Honolulu's most popular gay club has moved to the third floor of the Waikiki Grand Hotel after 25 years on Kuhio Avenue. From now on, you'll be able to sip your drinks on the terrace and enjoy a lovely view of Diamond Head, or play pool while waiting for the place to get hopping. There are different themes every night: dance music on Mondays, disco on Wednesdays, rumba on Thursdays, and so on. On Tuesdays and Thursdays, Hula's broadcasts the British sitcom *Queer as Folk*, which has yet to make its American television debut.

Festivals and Cultural Events

January

Ala Wai Canoe Challenge
☎967-7676

Narcissus Festival
☎533-3181

February

Hawai'i Mardi Gras
☎538-1441

Chinese New Year
(with parades and lion dances)

March

Kite Festival
at Kapi'olani Park
☎922-5483

Big Board Surfing Classic
in Makaha Beach
☎696-3878

Saint Patrick's Day Parade
at Waikiki on Kalakaua Avenue
Mar 17
☎946-1010

Prince Kuhio Day
(with a parade)
☎546-7573

Cherry Blossom Festival
between Feb and Apr
☎949-2255
(the most important Japanese event of the year)

April

Buddha Day Celebration
☎536-7044
(festival of flowers)

Carole Kai Bed Race
on Kalakauu Avenue
☎735-6092
(race on beds with wheels)

May

Lei Day
May 1
mostly in Kapi'olani Park
☎521-9815

June

King Kamehameha Celebration
lei ceremony near the statue of the king opposite Ali'iolani Hale

Kamehameha Day Parade
☎586-0333

O'ahu

July

Independence Day
July 4
mostly at Ala Moana Beach Park

Prince Lot Hula Festival
Moanalua Gardens
☎839-5334

Ukulele Festival
end Jul
☎487-6010

August

Na Hula o Hawaii Festival
at Kapi'olani Bandstand
☎521-9815

Queen Lili'uokalani Keiki Hula Competition
☎527-5400

Duke Kahanamoku Canoe Races
between Aina Moana Peninsula and Kailua Beach Park on the north shore

September

Aloha Festival
☎944-8857
(with canoe races, parades, Hawaiian music, *ho'olaule'a* – an arts and crafts exhibition)

Na Wahine o Ke Kai
between Moloka'i and O'ahu. Finish line at Fort de Russy Beach
☎525-5413
(women's canoe races)

October

Moloka'i Hoe
between Moloka'i and O'ahu. Finish line at Fort de Russy Beach
☎923-9871
(canoe race)

Orchid Show
☎527-5400

Makahiki Festival
at Waimea Falls Park
☎923-8448
(with Hawaiian games, *hula*, music, and more)

Bishop Museum Festival
☎847-3511
(music, *hula*, arts and crafts)

November

International Film Festival
☎944-7007

December

Pro-Surfing Championship
☎926-0611

Bodhi Day
Buddhist temples
☎536-7044

Honolulu Marathon
☎734-7200

First Night
December 31
downtown Honolulu
(stands, activities, arts and the like)

Theatre and Shows

City Hall has an up-to-date list of free activities planned in Honolulu. The calendar is available on Internet (*www.co.honolulu.hi.us/moca/calender*) or by calling ☎527-5666. For a more complete list of events, you can obtain one of the brochures called *O'ahu Gold* or *This Week O'ahu* (week-

lies) or a buy the Sunday edition of the *Honolulu Advertiser*. You can purchase tickets for the shows at the theatres and concert halls themselves, or by calling **TicketPlus** at ☎526-4400.

Free Shows

To begin with, there's the popular **Kodak Hula Show** (☎627-3300), which has delighted Waikiki tourists with Polynesian dancers for more than 60 years. The show takes place every Tuesday, Wednesday and Thursday at 10am at the Waikiki Shell (see p 114).

Molehu I Waikiki ("Dusk in Waikiki") is a night show in Waikiki featuring a light show, Hawaiian music and *hula*. It takes place every Saturday and Sunday at 6pm next to the Waikiki Aquarium (☎843-8002).

A *hula* show takes place every evening at 6:30pm at the **Hilton Hawaiian Village**. Every Friday, the hotel also hosts King Kalakaua's Jubilee, with fireworks.

The **Royal Hawaiian Band** (☎922-5331), established in 1836 under King Kamehameha III as the "King's Band," performs public concerts every Friday at the 'Iolani Palace at 12:15pm and every Sunday at Kapi'olani Park Bandstand at 2pm. The Royal Hawaiian Band plays everything

The Royal Hawaiian Band

Established in 1836 by Kamehameha III and under the baton of German conductor Heinrich Berger, the Royal Hawaiian Band is the last surviving institution dating from the time of the monar- chy. Financed by the city of Honolulu, it offers a program of free concerts all week long, featuring 40 musicians who per- form Hawaiian, classi- cal, jazz and pop tunes.

from classical music to pop tunes.

A concert called **Mayor's Aloha Friday** takes place every Friday from noon to 1pm at the corner of Bishop Street and South King Street in Tamarind Park. There is tradi- tional Hawaiian music, modern music, jazz, mariachis, and the like.

Many hotel and shop- ping centres organize *hula* shows, arts and craft demonstrations, such as *lei* making, and even free ukulele les- sons. The **Royal Hawaiian Shopping Center** hosts dancers from the Poly- nesian Cultural Center every day (*Mon, Tue and Fri 6pm to 8pm; Tue, Thu and Sat 10am to 11:30am*). Every Friday from 8pm to 10pm, dancers from the Na Mea Hula o Kahikiuaokalani *hula* school ("**Strolling Hula**") perform along Kalakaua Avenue, stop- ping at the Royal Ha- waiian Shopping Center

and at the King Kalakaua Plaza. Not to be outdone by the **Ala Moana Center**, which has more than 500 shows annually (*hula*, singers, dancers, choirs, and more).

Neal S. Blaisdell Center (*corner King St. and Ward Ave.,* ☎527-5400) hosts Broadway musi- cals, such as *Miss Sai- gon*. There's a concert hall, as well as the **Ha- waii Opera Theatre** (*987 Waimanu St.,* ☎596- 7372 or 800-836-7372, *www.hawaiiopera.org*). Within a short six-week season, the opera puts on three shows.

Opened in 1922 and completely restored in 1996, the **Hawaii Theater** (*1130 Bethel St.,* ☎528-0506, *www.hawaiitheatre.com*) welcomes up to 1,400 spectators for a variety of shows, including touring theatre compa- nies, classical concerts, local and national musi- cians, cultural events,

and so forth. The open- ing and closing film of the Hawaii Interna- tional Film Festival is presented here, as is the Jazz Festival.

Established in 1915 under the name "The Footlights," the **Diamond Head Theater** (*$10-$40, Thu to Sat 8pm and Sun 4pm, 520 Makapu'u Ave.,* ☎734-0274, *www.starrtech.com/diam ondhead/*) has become the main venue for Honolulu actors. A once unknown actress named Bette Midler made here debut here. Six local theatre pro- ductions are put on every season, as well as musicals and other popular road tours.

Founded more than a decade ago, the **Hono- lulu Symphony Orchestra** (*$12-$50,* ☎538-8863, *www.honolulusymphony. com*) is proud to be "the oldest symphony orchestra west of the Rockies." Concerts take place in the Neal S. Balisdell Center as well as at the Waikiki Shell in Kapi'olani Park.

Lu'aus

The only *lu'au* in Wai- kiki is the **Royal Lu'au**, which takes place on the lawn of the Royal Hawaiian Hotel (*2259 Kalakaua Ave.,* ☎923- 7311) every Monday. The celebration fea- tures dancing and sing- ing – not to mention a mountain of food, which can be a good opportunity to sample a few Hawaiian special-

O'ahu

ties. The show concludes with a fire dance.

Situated by the sea north of the Ko'Olina Resort, about 40min from Waikiki, **Paradise Cove Lu'au** *(92-1089 Ali'i Nui Drive in Kapolei,* ☎*842-5911 or 800-775-2683)* organizes one of the most popular *lu'aus* on the island – and it's quite an extravagant affair. There's a pig *imu* roast, a royal march as well as *hula* and Polynesian dance shows. You can even give a helping hand to the pretend fishers of a mock village and assist them with their nets. A free shuttle service from Waikiki is available to guests. Depending on where you buy your ticket, price ranges between $40 and $60.

Just south, near Barber's Point, **Germaine's Lu'au** *(*☎*949-6626 or 941-3338)* is more of a family event. The show is essentially the same, however, with a Hawaiian troop arriving by canoe, a typical pig roast in the imu and a dance show. The all-you-can-eat buffet is half-Hawaiian and half-American. You'll find coupons for 20% off by reserving directly.

Packages including the **Ali'i Lu'au**, the Polynesian Cultural Center *(*☎*293-3333)* and a park visit are available. The show and the meal are from 5pm to 6:40pm, followed by a show

called "Horizons" (see p 131).

Other Shows

Perhaps the most famous show in Hawaii, the **Don Ho Show** *($22, Waikiki Beachcomber Hotel, 2300 Kalakaua Ave.;* ☎*923-3981)* has been an institution for nearly 30 years. The famous singer performs Hawaiian classics, from *Tiny Bubbles,* his hit tune, to *Aloha Oe,* composed by Queen Lili'uokalani. Several other artists join Don. The dinner-theatre show takes place daily *(except Fri and Sat)* at 5:15.

Also at the Waikiki Beachcomber is "**Magic of Polynesia**" *(*☎*971-4321)*, a large-scale production mixing Polynesian songs and dances with magic tricks. The show is presented twice every evening under the direction of John Hirokawa, the renowned Hawaiian illusionist.

"**Creation – A Polynesian Odyssey**" *(Sheraton Princes Ka'iulani, 120 Ka'iulani Ave.,* ☎*931-4660)*, which features dazzling special effects, transports visitors back to the time of the early Polynesians. Legends tell the story of how the islands were created, the birth of the first couple and the battles between rival warriors. Two shows take place daily, with or without diner.

Shopping

In Waikiki, shops take up every square inch of land that is not occupied by hotels and restaurants. There are clothing stores, large chain outlets, hardware shops, mini-markets, and more. For basic necessities, many visitors turn to the popular ABC Stores, which offer a selection of souvenirs and foods.

There are shops and stands galore at the **International Marketplace** *(2330 Kalakaua Ave.)*, which surrounds a 100-year-old banyan tree. You'll find tasteful clothing, jewellery and souvenirs here. The **Waikiki Town Center** *(2301 Kuhio Ave.;* ☎*922-2724)*, an extension of the shopping centre, houses a slew of other stores.

If that's not enough, the **Royal Hawaiian Shopping Center** *(every day 9am to 11pm; 2201 Kalakaua Ave.,* ☎*922-2724)*, across from the International Marketplace, has four floors have with more than 150 chic stores, including Chanel, Versace and Prada.

Just west of the Royal Hawaiian Shopping Center, the recently built **King Kalakaua Plaza** *(every day 9am to 11pm, 2080 Kalakaua Ave.:* ☎*955-2878)* stands out with its gigantic Nike Town store.

With more than 50 acres (20ha) of shops, restaurants and snack bars, the **Ala Moana Center** *(Mon to Sat 9:30am to 9pm, Sun 10am to 7pm; 1450 Ala Moana Blvd.; ☎955-9517; www.alamoana.com)* was in 1959 the largest shopping centre in the world. Tourists and islanders alike enjoy shopping here, and the largely Japanese and American clientele tends to influence the stock in the stores. In winter, therefore, you'll find sweaters and jackets in addition to T-shirts and *mu'umu'us*. All sorts of activities are organized here, from fashion shows to concerts to *hula* shows, and much more. A bus service heads to the shopping centre from Waikiki every 15min *($1, Mon to Sat 9:30am to 9:30pm, Sun 10am to 7:30pm)*. You can also come by car to take advantage of one of the few free parking lots in Honolulu!

Halfway between downtown Honolulu and Waikiki, the five shopping centres of **Ward Centers** *(☎591-8411, www.victoriaward.com; Bus no. 8 Ward, nos. 19 or 20)* stand along Ala Moana Boulevard north of Auahi Street, which runs parallel. The two main buildings, **Ward Center** *(1200 Ala Moana Blvd.; Mon to Sat 10am to 9pm, Sun 10am to 5pm;*

☎591-8411*)* and **Ward Warehouse** *(1050 Ala Moana Blvd., every day 10am to 9pm; ☎591-8411)* are separated by Kamakee Street. There is no passageway between the two buildings, so you have to cross the street. This long maze of shops is definitely not as pleasant as the boutiques at Ala Moana Center, but there are numerous restaurants. Each shopping centre has its own free parking lot.

There are several shopping centres downtown, all competing for your dollars. **Restaurant Row** *(500 Ala Moana Blvd.; ☎538-1441)*, as its name indicates, features many restaurants, but it also has a few boutiques. At the foot of the famous tower, the **Aloha Tower Marketplace** *(every day 9am to 9pm, Fri and Sat until 10pm; ☎566-2337 or 528-5700; bus no. 19, 20 or 47)* has over 80 stores and restaurants.

Farther west, **Dole Cannery** *(Mon to Sat 9am to 6pm, Sun 9am to 4pm; 650 Iwilei Rd.; ☎528-2236, bus no. 19)* housed a Dole canning factory up until 1992. After closing its doors, it later reopened as a shopping centre with boutiques, restaurants and movie theatre. From 9:30am to 3:30pm, you can watch a film about the history of the Dole company and pineapples. The landmark water tower shaped in the form of a

pineapple, which was in operation from 1928 to 1993, will soon be reinstalled. Opposite the Dole Cannery is the largest store of the **Hilo Hattie** chain *(every day 7am to 6pm, ☎537-2926)*. Japanese tourists and retired Americans arrive here en masse, leaving with armfuls of clothes, macadamia nuts and kitsch souvenirs decorated with palm trees and *hula* dancers (made in Taiwan). It has some of the best prices around.

Daiei (Usa) *(Mon to Sat 9am to 9:30pm, Sun 9:30am to 8pm; Kaheka St., ☎973-4800)*, situated behind Ala Moana Center, is the largest discount shopping mall in Hawaii. You'll find everything from beach gear to macadamia nuts to Asian products, at much lower prices than anywhere else.

The island has many other shopping centres, which are in stiff competition with each other. In the Waikiki area, shopping fanatics can head to the **Kahala Mall** and to the **Hawaii Kai Towne Center** *(on the road from Hanauma Bay)*, which has wholesale outlets. In addition, the largest shopping centres are those of Maunalua Bay (**Koko Marina Shopping Center**, ☎395-4737), with a few stores specializing in travel and beach gear, and the Kane'ohe **Windward Mall** *(Mon to Sat 9:30am to 9pm; Sun 10am to 5pm; 46-056*

Kamehameha Hwy.; ☎253-1143), which has more than 80 restaurants, gift shops and clothing stores.

Arts & Crafts

Museum boutiques often offer beautiful crafts. The **Bishop Museum** *(every day 9am to 5pm)* is the best one, with books, CDs, and more.

There are also many stores in Honolulu and Waikiki that specialize in arts and crafts. The two boutiques of **Native Books & Beautiful Things** *(Ward Warehouse, ☎596-8885 and 222 Merchant St., ☎599-5511)* have been set up by a group of about 20 artists. Here you'll find a large selection of quilts, jewellery, *hulas,* hats, *lauhala* bags, jams and dried fruit.

Established by Leone Kamana Okamura, a Hawaiian "living treasure," **Quilt Hawaii** *(Mon to Sat 9am to 5:30pm; 2338 South Kin St.)* also offers an excellent selection of crafts, but specializes in quilts of all shapes and sizes.

If you like antiques, don't miss **Garakuta-Do** *(☎955-2099),* which

sells Japanese arts and crafts. In the Furumono-ya tradition, this Ali Baba's cave – whose name means "second-hand shop" – has lacquers, bronze lamps, pottery and ceramics, wooden dishes, and the like.

Opposite Kapi'olani Park, the outside gate of the zoo facing Montsarrat Avenue is the site of an art market every weekend *(10am to 4pm)* called **Art at the Park** *(☎923-4354),* where local artists sell their creations.

Eventually you'll come across one of the many **Wyland** galleries *(Aloha Tower marketplace, Hyatt Regency Waikiki, Kalakaua Center and also in Hale'iwa),* which specialize in slightly tacky seascapes, with whimsical scenes of whales and thousands of fish frolicking under the moonlight. A surfer named Wyland started the trend in the early 1970s, and his canvases now fetch ridiculously high prices.

On the north coast, you can take a peek at the beautiful items at **Hale Ku'ai** *(Tue to Sat 10am to 6pm; 54-040 Kamehameha Hwy., next to the Hauula Church;*

☎293-4477), an Hawaiian arts and crafts cooperative that sells jewellery, *lauhala* headgear, musical instruments, all sorts of gourmet foods, clothing, T-shirts, and much more.

Markets

Every Sunday, the **Aloha Stadium Swap Meet & Flea Market** *(flea market entrance $0.50; Wed, Sat and Sun 6am to 3pm; ☎486-1529)* draws nearly 300 stands and thousands of onlookers. Stalls are spread out on the parking lot of the huge Aloha Stadium, and here you'll find everything from junk to uninspired artwork to "new age" items to fruit.

Every Saturday on Maunakea Street downtown is the **Chinatown Night Market** *(between 6pm and 2am),* where you'll find a slew of arts and crafts, food items, and more.

During your island tour, make sure to visit a **Farmer's Market** if you see one. Local farmer come here to sell their fruit (often organic) and flowers. There are often craft and clothing stands as well.

Hawaii – Big Island

I ts very name
embodies the entire archipelago: Hawaii.

Cradle of Hawaiian culture, this island was once the setting of the most important events in Hawaii's history. It is here that the first Polynesian explorers are thought to have landed around AD 500; Kamehameha the Great, who unified the Hawaiian Islands, was born here; and Captain Cook, the once deified British explorer, died here. This royal capital maintains a sacred link to its past through remnants of numerous *heiau* (temples), fields of petroglyphs and its beliefs in Pele, the fire goddess.

According to legends, it is she, the incarnation of the all-powerful geology, the feared and respected goddess, who gave birth to the island and its five volcanoes: the Kohala to the north-west, which has been dormant for a long time; tiny Hualalai, towering over Kailau-Kona and whose last

eruption dates back to 1801; the dormant Mauna Kea and the active Mauna Loa, the highest mountains in the world when measured from their foot at the bottom of the ocean and virtually forming the entire island; and finally, the constantly erupting Kilauea, whose fires are still expanding Pele's territory. Nowhere else in the world does a volcano allow you to walk right up to it like this, mezmerizing visitors with its glowing red lava and many secrets.

Only 800,000 years old, Hawaii is not only the youngest island of the archipelago, but also one of the youngest islands in the world. Commonly called the Big Island, a logical reference to its size, it is actually larger than all the other islands combined but only has 15% of the total population of the archipelago (137,000 inhabitants). With a touch of humour, its inhabitants call the North American continent "the Big, Big Island." Its size, altitude and the power of spiritual forces have made Hawaii an island of contrasts. As proof of this, scientists point out the Big Island's climatic diversity: it has no less than 11 of the 13 known climatic zones in the world!

While the lava spewing out everywhere has created, layer by layer, a lunar landscape blackened by fire, the rainfall pattern has dictated the land's future. To the west near the Kona Coast, which has almost constant sunshine – a paradise for tourists – the land is infertile, but about 1,000ft (300m) higher is the famous "coffee belt" where most of Hawaii's plantations are found. To the north on the Hamakua Coast, facing the trade winds, a lush tropical forest replaces desolate lava flows. This was once the site of sugar-cane plantations, and macadamia and papaya trees still grow here. The landscape in Hilo, the capital, located on the humid eastern coast, is similar. Hawaii's official nickname, "The Orchid Island," is highly appropriate. As for the rest of the island, the land-

scape ranges between two extremes: lush pastures in Waimea, capital of the *paniolos* (Hawaiian cowboys), with one of the largest ranches in the United States; and forests of arborescent ferns bathing in the mist near the Kilauea crater.

Finding Your Way Around

By Plane

Kona Airport

Keahole's airport, built on Hualalai's last lava flow (dating back to 1801), is located about 10min north of Kailua-Kona. It receives mostly inter-island flights (Honolulu, Maui, Lana'i and Hilo), but also a few long hulls from the mainland (Los Angeles and San Francisco on United) and even from Vancouver and Japan. At the arrival area, you will find a small information booth (with mostly brochures), a snack bar, and car rental agencies across from the terminal. Vehicles are parked on the premises, but the line-up can be long when major flights arrive. To get your car faster, it is a good idea to have one person wait by the luggage conveyor belt

while another person takes care of the rental. Guests of large tourist centres are welcomed by their hotel's shuttle bus. For other travellers, there is no public transportation – only taxis. To obtain flight information, call ☎329-2484.

Hilo Airport

The airport is situated approximately 2mi (3km) east of downtown. Despite its name, Hilo International Airport does not receive any flights from the mainland or from Japan – only from Honolulu and Maui, as well as a daily flight from Kona. There is an information booth at the arrival area. Car rental outlets are also just in front of the terminal. A shuttle bus will take you to the company's depot nearby. To obtain information on flights, call ☎934-5801.

Airlines

Aloha
☎800-367-5250 or 935-5771

Hawaiian
☎800-367-5320 or 326-5615

United
☎800-241-6522

By Car

Car Rental Agencies

Alamo
☎800-327-9633
☎329-8896 or 961-3343

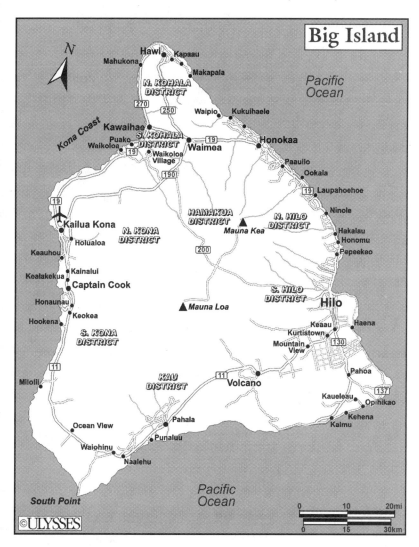

Avis
☎*800-321-3712*
☎*327-3000*
☎*935-1290 or 885-2821*

Budget
☎*800-527-0700 or 329-1229*

Dollar
☎*800-800-4000*
☎*329-2744 or 961-6059*

Hertz
☎*800-654-3011*
☎*329-3566 or 935-2896*

National
☎*800-227-7368*
☎*329-1674 or 935-0891*

Very few companies allow customers to drive through Saddle Road. **Harper Car & Truck**

Rental (*456 Kalaniana'ole Ave. in Hilo,* ☎*969-1478 or 800-852-9993, Kona* ☎*329-6688,* ⇢*961-0423, www.harpershawaii.com*) is the only agency that allows its four-wheel-drive vehicles to go up to the Mauna Kea summit. These vehicles are priced at $100 per day in addition to insurance for $600 per week. There is unlimited mileage and the minimum age is 25.

Kailua-Kona

The former capital is not reached by the Hawaii Belt Road, but rather the Palani Road that exits Highway 11 at Mile 100 – the most logical route to take if you're arriving from the airport. Ali'i Drive runs along the seafront and continues south to Keauhou, where you can head back to Highway 11 via Kamehameha Road.

Hilo

The city of Hilo sprawls across the wide, sheltered Hilo Bay. Kamehameha Avenue runs along the bay, leading to the old town centre and then heading towards the Hamakua Coast via Highway 19. Just east of the bay, Banyan Drive runs along the Wai'akea Peninsula where most of the hotels are found. Further along, Kalaniana'ole Avenue follows the coast, which features several coastal parks, and then ends at Richardson Beach Park. Perpendicular to the coast, the two-lane Kanoelehua Avenue (Hwy. 11) runs to the airport and then heads to the interior towards the Hawaii Volcanoes National Park.

Parking

Finding a parking spot is not really a problem on the Big Island except in the centre of Kailua-Kona. Since you cannot park on Ali'i Drive, you can use the large parking area located between Luana Lane and Kuakini Highway. Unfortunately, it's usually full on weekends. Another option is the $1 or $2/day parking lots along Sarona Road further east. Every shopping centre offers parking to its customers.

Bicycle and Moped Rentals

Expect to pay $25 to $30 per day for a moped and $45 to $50 for a two-person scooter. The cost for a one-week rental is four or five times the daily rate.

By Taxi

Here are a few taxi companies:

Ace One Taxi
Hilo
☎935-8303

Aloha Taxi
Kona
☎325-5448

Hilo Harry's Taxi
Hilo
☎935-7091

Kona Airport Taxi
☎329-7779

Paradise Taxi
Kona
☎329-1234

Public Transportation

A limited bus service (*Hele On*, ☎961-8744) links the main towns on the Big Island. Since they make frequent stops, you'll have to be patient or only travel short distances. Most buses only run on weekdays, but a few offer service on Saturdays (Kona-Hilo). The service is limited; for example, only two buses make the daily Kona-Hilo trip, but the fare is inexpensive ($5.25, 3hr trip via Waikoloa, Waimea and the Hamakua Coast). Other lines serve Honoka'a from Hilo (three per day) and Ka'u from Hilo via Volcano and all the villages in between (two per day). There is also service to Kona's south coast between Kailua-Kona and Honaunau (four per day).

The **Kona Coast Express** (☎331-1582) shuttle serves the entire Kona Coast with three lines (every 80min on average). The **Waikoloa Resort Express** runs between the tourist centres along the south coast of Kohaha from 6am to 9pm, and the **Kona Town Express** departs from King's Shops and heads to the centre of Kona (*7am, last return bus at 8:20pm*).

There is also a **trolley** service that goes to the hotels and condominiums between the King Kamehameha Hotel in Kona and the Kona Surf Hotel in Keauhou. The latter operates from 7:40am to 8:20pm. The fare for each of the three lines is $5 per day, $15 for the entire network.

Another company, **Ali'i Shuttle** *(☎775-7121)* serves the row of hotels and condominiums lined up between Kona and Keauhou with a bus every 90min from 8:30am to 10pm *($2 one way, $5 per day, $20 per week).*

Practical Information

Tourist Information Offices

Hawai'i Visitors Bureau
Mon to Fri 8am to 4:30pm
250 Waikoloa Beach Dr.
King's Shops, Suite B-15
☎886-1655
⇋886-1651
The Visitors Bureau on the west coast moved in the fall of 1999 from the centre of Kona to the King's Shops in Waikoloa. Located upstairs in building B, it offers mostly brochures and maps that can also be found everywhere else.

Hawai'i Visitors Bureau
Mon to Fri 8am to 4:30pm
250 Keawe St., Hilo
☎961-5797 *or 800-648-2441*
⇋961-2126

You'll also find mostly brochures here.

You can also check out the Big Island's web site: *www.bigisland.org*

State Park Services

Department of Land and Natural Resources Division of State Parks
Mon to Fri 8am to 4pm (permits issued only until noon)
State Office Building (no. 204)
75 Aupuni St.
P.O. Box 936, Hilo HI 96720
☎974-6200

County Park Services

Department of Parks and Recreation
Mon to Fri 7:45am to 4:30pm
25 Aupuni St., Hilo
☎961-8311
This is the main office on the island.

Department of Parks and Recreation
Mon to Fri 7:45am to 4pm
Kona Aquatics Center
Kuakini Hwy.
0.6mi (1km) west of downtown (past Kiawi St.)
The ticket office is located at the pool entrance.

You must obtain **permit** *($5 per day per person)* to camp at one of the County Park's 11 camp-

grounds. In addition to the offices in Hilo and Kailua-Kona, you can also head to Captain Cook *(Yano Hall, Mon to Fri from noon to 2pm)* or Waimea-Kamuela *(Waimea Community Center, Mon to Fri 8:30am to 10:30am).* Reservations are accepted and stays are limited to one week during summer, two weeks during the rest of the year.

Accommodations

The Big Island has its own bed-and-breakfast association. The **Hawai'i Island B&B Association** *(P.O. Box 1890, Honoka'a HI 96727, www.stayhawaii.com)* brings together more than 50 homeowners around the island, from budget to luxury accommodations.

There are also more than 10 home and apartment rental agencies, most of which are located in the same condominiums. Here's a list of a few popular agencies:

Action Team Realty
75-6082 Ali'i Dr.
(second floor)
☎329-6020 *or 888-311-6020*
www.konacondo.com
This agency manages apartments in more than 20 condominiums and also offers home rentals.

Knutson & Associates
75-6082 Ali'i Dr.
☎ *329-6311 or 800-800-6202*
⇄ *326-2178*
planet-hawaii.com/knutson
A selection of popular condominiums and a few rental homes, with a minimum stay of three nights. The prices range between $75 ($65 in summer) and $180 ($165) for the condos.

Kona Hawaii Vacation Rentals
75-5776 Kuakini Hwy.
at the upper reception desk of the Islander Inn
☎ *329-9393 or 800-622-5342*
⇄ *326-4136*
www.konahawaii.com
A small-scale condominium park with low prices.

West Hawaii Property Services
78-6831 Ali'i Dr., suite 237
☎ *322-6696*
☎ *800-799-KONA*
⇄ *324-0609*
www.konarentals.com
This company offers a 10% discount on reservations made on the Internet for stays of at least one week (condominiums, homes and cars).

Internet Access

The Big Island is not really well equipped when it comes to the Internet.

Island Lava Java
$10/hr with purchase
$12 without
75-5799 Ali'i Dr., Kona
Ali'i Sunset Plaza
☎ *327-2161*

Bytes and Bites
$2.50 for 15min and $8 per hour
every day 10am to 10pm
223 Kilauea Ave.,
corner Ponahawai St., Hilo
☎ *935-3520*

Lava Rock Cafe
$1 for 10min
Mon 7:30am to 5pm, Tue 6:30pm, Wed to Sat 9pm and Sun 4pm
Old Volcano Rd.
☎ *967-8526*

Laundromats

Kona

The Hele Mai Laundromat
every day 6am to 10pm, last machine at 8:45pm
75-5629 Kuakini Hwy., North Kona Shopping Center
☎ *329-3494*
The Hele Mai Laundromat has many machines and dryers in good condition.

Hilo

Tyke's Laundromat
6am to 10pm, last machine at 8:30pm
1472 Kilauea Ave.
☎ *935-1093*

Volcanoes National Park

Don't forget that the Volcanoes National Park is quite remote; don't expect to find a bank here, and as for gas, fill up in Volcano – there is no other gas station beyond this town. Most of the village and the park is found at high altitudes; there are frequent

drizzles and the nights are chilly, so plan accordingly, especially if you are camping.

The **Volcano Village Square**, at the intersection of Old Volcano Road and Haunani Street, has a grocery store (Volcano Store, every day 5am to 7pm), a gas station, Surf's restaurant and the Steam Vent Cafe. A stone's throw away is the **Kilauea General Store** *(Mon to Sat 7am to 7:30pm, Sun until 7pm)*, which actually dares post its prices; there's also a gas station.

To obtain information about ongoing eruptions, in addition to the Visitor Center, you can also tune in to the radio at 530 AM. Most bed and breakfasts offer their guests a copy of the Hawaii Volcanoes National Park guide, an 80-page guide that covers all aspects of the park. You can also pick it up at other places for $2.

If you're planing a difficult hike, you can call the weather service at
☎ *961-5582*.

Organized Tours

The Kona Historical Society *(☎ 323-2005)* organizes 90min guided walking tours in Kailua-Kona *($10, Tue to Fri at 9:30am and Fri at 1:30pm)*. The organization also runs tours *($15, Tue and Thu at 9am)* at the D. Uchida

Volcanic Eruption

The ongoing volcanic eruption began in January 1983 when lava flowed from an isolated area on the eastern side of Kilauea. The lava gradually fortified Pu'u 'O'o's cone, where the eruption originally occurred, although its precise location is always moving. An eruption at the end of the 1980s buried 10km (6mi) of the Chain of Craters Road and Kalapana's magnificent black-sand beach, and destroyed 181 homes. Volcanic activity intensified at the beginning of the 1990s, and at the end of January 1997, Pu'u 'O'o's cone collapsed after its lava lake flowed into the crater. Activity then ceased for 23 days, the longest recorded period since 1983. The eruption, however, regained its strength the following month, and 100ft-long (30m) lava flows entombed the sacred Waha'ula *heiau*. The lava lake is now building up and could very well collapse again.

According to the latest news, the lava is flowing towards the coast via a network of tunnels. Pu'u 'O'o' produces about 4,409,200lbs (2,000 tonnes) of sulphur dioxide and discharges 387,130 cu yd (296,000m³) of lava every day. Since the start of the eruption, it has spewed 2.09 billion cu yd (1.6 billion m³) of lava – enough to pave a road around the earth 50 times! The Big Island is now 571 acres (231ha) larger.

Farm (Kona Coffee Living History Farm), a coffee and macadamia-nut farm established in 1900 by a Japanese family – one of hundreds of typical farms that were scattered in the region up until the Second World War. Costumed guides demonstrate the farming techniques used in the 1930s. Past the fields you can see the farm, with the *kuriba* (roasting centre), the drying platforms (*hoshidara*) and the annexes. The tour lasts about 3hrs and starts at the Greenwell Store (Kona Historical Society Museum), while the farm itself is located at the beginning of Napo'opo'o Road. Reservations are a must for both tours.

In Hilo, the **Lyman Museum** (☎935-5021) offers a guided tour of the town one Saturday a month with a variety of themes.

Excursions

The two largest agencies, **Roberts** (☎329-1688) and **Polynesian Adventure Tours** (☎329-8008), offer day tours of the island ($45-$65) for those who don't have a lot of time.

Safety

The Big Island isn't Honolulu and incidents are rare here. However, don't tempt fate by leaving valuables in your car, especially near the tourist beaches.

The biggest safety hazard is nature: falls in crevasses, the collapse of the lava bed near the sea, burns, and the like. If you walk near the active lava flow, follow the advice of the guard on duty.

Hawaii – Big Island

Exploring

The Kona Coast

★★
Kailua-Kona

(one to two days)

In the beginning, there was nothing, or rather, just "two streams" (Kailua) along the "wind-swept" coast (Kona) – not to mention the fearsome Hualalai mass, one of five volcanoes that created the island, born on the northwest slopes of Mauna Loa. A former surfing region, the coast began to drastically change when Kamehameha, after having unified the islands, retreated here in 1812, only 11 years after the Hualalai lava flows had dried up. Up until the king's death seven years later, Kailua, which wasn't even a village yet, was Hawaii's centre of political power. With the development of trade during the second half of the 19th century, Kailua became a commercial port. At the time, most of the population lived on the high-altitude plantation villages on the hillside, and today, this region is still covered with fields of coffee trees.

It may be hard to believe, but until the 1970s, Kailua only had a few hundred inhabitants; today, it has a population of 35,000. In spite of extensive tourist development and real-estate speculation over the past few years, the tourist capital of the Big Island, bathed in an often dazzling sunshine, has not lost its small-town feel. Just take a stroll along the seafront, from the oldest church in Hawaii to the Hulihe'e Palace, and you'll agree.

It's at **Kamakahonu** ("eye of the turtle"), north of the seafront, where the hotel bearing his name stands today, that Kamehameha spent his last days. His makeshift "home" which was called Hale Nana Mahina'ai, "the home to watch over the farms," was a simple hut built on a *paepae*. There's a replica of it on the beach. The hut beside it was where the guard stayed. All around it were buildings, fishponds and farmland, and it is here that the king is thought to have died. His remains were prepared for burial in a secret place. Later, Governor Kuakini, Kamehameha's brother-in-law, built a fort armed with canons, of which today only one face of a wall remains.

Occupying a basalt *paepae* nearly enclosing Kamakahonu Beach, the **Ahu'ena heiau** ★★ was rebuilt between 1812-1813 by Kamehameha and re-dedicated to Lono. The Hale Mana, where prayers were conducted and state affairs of the state were

Ahu'ena Heiau

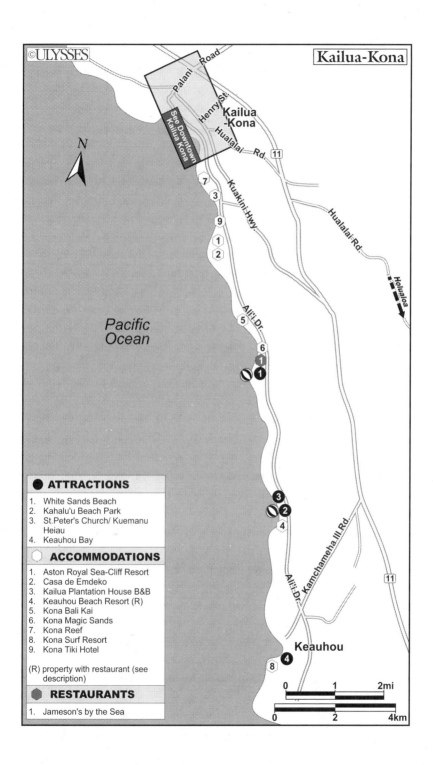

Kailua-Kona

©ULYSSES

Pacific
Ocean

ATTRACTIONS

1. White Sands Beach
2. Kahalu'u Beach Park
3. St.Peter's Church/ Kuemanu Heiau
4. Keauhou Bay

ACCOMMODATIONS

1. Aston Royal Sea-Cliff Resort
2. Casa de Emdeko
3. Kailua Plantation House B&B
4. Keauhou Beach Resort (R)
5. Kona Bali Kai
6. Kona Magic Sands
7. Kona Reef
8. Kona Surf Resort
9. Kona Tiki Hotel

(R) property with restaurant (see description)

RESTAURANTS

1. Jameson's by the Sea

discussed, also served as a classroom for the king's son, Liholiho, the future Kamehameha II. The building had an interior chimney used to cook bananas. The Hale Pahu, with its pandanus roof, housed ceremonial drums. You can also see the *lele*, where the offerings were laid, and the *anu'u*, the "oracle tower," which gets its name from the great *kahuna* who expressed the gods' answers to his questions. The *ki'i akua* (*tikis*) symbolized the help from the ancestral deities. The largest, in the form of a bird (*kolea*, or plover), is the incarnation of Koleamoku, a healing god.

Bordered by sand, the small **Kamakahonu Lagoon** ★★ is ideal for children since the water is both calm and shallow. You can rent kayaks, pedal-boats and snorkelling gear, but the prices are quite high. In the background is the **King Kamehameha Beach Hotel**, which deserves a visit for several reasons. First, you can watch the pig be put in the *imu* (oven) in the morning on *lu'au* days, and you can also sign up for historical tours (1:30pm during the week), which are free even if you're not a guest. Take a stroll through the lobby to see the displays of Hawaiian musical instruments, games, *kahili*, feather clothing as well as fish-

ing trophies. At the front desk, you can ask for an interesting brochure called "Aloha Mai," which traces the history of the site and describes the displayed objects.

A stone's throw from the hotel, the **Kailua Pier** is the departure point for most sea excursions (except for deep-sea fishing). It is here, near the tiny Kaiakeakua Beach, that the Ironman, the most famous triathlon in the world, begins and ends every year.

Further along the seafront, **Hukihe's Palace** ★★★ (*$5; unaccompanied or guided tours, Mon to Fri 9am to 4pm, Sat and Sun 10am to 4pm; 75-5718 Ali'i Dr., ☎329-1877*) was built in 1838 by foreign sailors for Kuakini, one of the first chefs to adopt western customs. Built from wood, coral and lava, the two-storey palace only had six rooms. It then became the home of Princess Ruth, Kuakini's successor as governor of the Big Island, but she never really lived here because she weighed 330lbs (150kg) and had trouble climbing up to her bedroom. Kalakaua redecorated the palace in 1884 when he made it his summer residence, then the building was passed on to Prince Kuhio. After it was restored, it was transformed into a museum in 1927 under the aegis of "Daughters of

Hawai'i" and housed an extraordinary collection of ancient furniture and Hawaiian art.

On the main floor, don't miss the old photographs of the royal family, Kalakaua's guitar, incrusted with mother-of-pearl and made in Paris in 1886, jewellery, puzzles incrusted with shark teeth, the "toboggan," used for *papa holua* (land surfing), the gorgeous *pahu* (drum), whose size indicated that is was crafted for an *ali'i*, as well as the superb *koa*- and *kou*-*wood* dishes. There's an anecdote about these dishes: since Kamehameha did not like the taste of food in *koa* dishes, he only used dishes made from *kou*, of which the museum has an example (with "ears" for condiments).

The upper level is surrounded by a balcony that looks out towards the sea, and has two rooms and a living room, all of which are attractively furnished. In the room on the left, you'll see an astonishing collection of hats. One of them stands out: Queen Kapi'olani's, with its peacock feathers. Even if you haven't paid to see the museum, you can still go for a stroll in the small park, which offers a pretty view of the seafront. A *hula* class is held here twice a week in the afternoon. Take a look

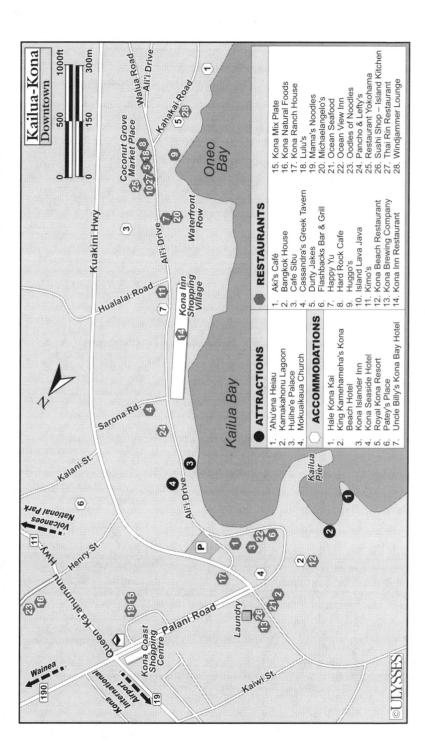

Kailua-Kona
Downtown

| | 0 | 500 | 1000ft |
| | 0 | 150 | 300m |

● ATTRACTIONS

1. 'Ahu'ena Heiau
2. Kamakahonu Lagoon
3. Hulihe'e Palace
4. Mokuaikaua Church

☐ ACCOMMODATIONS

1. Hale Kona Kai
2. King Kamehameha's Kona Beach Hotel
3. Kona Islander Inn
4. Kona Seaside Hotel
5. Royal Kona Resort
6. Patey's Place
7. Uncle Billy's Kona Bay Hotel

⬡ RESTAURANTS

1. Aki's Café
2. Bangkok House
3. Cafe Sibu
4. Cassandra's Greek Tavern
5. Durty Jakes
6. Flashbacks Bar & Grill
7. Happy Yu
8. Hard Rock Cafe
9. Hugo's
10. Island Lava Java
11. Kimo's
12. Kona Beach Restaurant
13. Kona Brewing Company
14. Kona Inn Restaurant
15. Kona Mix Plate
16. Kona Natural Foods
17. Kona Ranch House
18. Lulu's
19. Mama's Noodles
20. Michaelangelo's
21. Ocean Seafood
22. Ocean View Inn
23. Oodles of Noodles
24. Pancho & Lefty's
25. Restaurant Yokohama
26. Sushi Shop – Island Kitchen
27. Thai Rin Restaurant
28. Windjammer Lounge

© ULYSSES

at the fishpond located behind the boutique.

Opposite the palace stands **Mokuaikaua Church** ★★ *(free admission)*, a large lava stone church decked with a white wooden steeple – the oldest one in Hawaii. Built with permanent materials in 1837, it replaced two former temporary structures that had palm roofs. This majestic building is both sober and spacious, with wooden *'ohi'a* pillars, and the choir loft is framed by the royal red and yellow *kahili*. At the back is a small exhibit tracing the history of the mission, with a delightful scale model of the 10ft (3m) brig *Thaddeus*. The first missionaries arrived aboard this ship in 1820. They left Boston on April 4, took the Cape Horn route and reached Hawaii 164 days later. When the arrived, they learned that Kamehameha had died and that the *kapu* system had been abolished – a blessing that must have involved some kind of divine intervention. After being greeted in Kailua by Liholiho, the new king, and his regent, Queen Ka'ahumanu, the group then left for O'ahu where they had gotten the authorization to establish a mission for one year. Four people stayed behind and founded the first church in Hawaii. The scale-model boat was made in 1934 by a group of Navy soldiers based in Pearl Harbor. The small exhibit also shows a portrait of the first Hawaiian converted to Christianity by Tahitian missionaries, even before the *Thaddeus*.

As you leave the Kailua seafront, continue along Ali'i Drive towards Keauhou.

Towards Keauhou, the coast is for the most part covered with tourist resorts and condominiums. Past the Hale Halawai o Holualoa church (1855), the road reaches the appropriately named **White Sand Beach** ★★ *(Mile 3.8; washrooms, outdoor showers)*, with its magnificent blanket of white sand. It is also known as Magic Sands and Disappearing Sands, as a large part of the sand is carried away in winter, only to miraculously reappear in the spring. Very popular with local families and tourists, the cove is nestled under a few coconut trees. There is a beach volleyball court and many experienced boogie boarders.

At Mile 4.7 is **Kahalu'u Beach Park** ★★ *(every day 7am to 11pm; washrooms; showers, picnic tables, telephones)*, which was established on land that used to belong to Princess Bernice Pauahi Bishop. Stretching across the sheltered Kahalu'u Bay, the black- and white-sand beach (from basalt and coral) is very popular despite its small size. The rocks that border the beach form small, shallow sandy basins, ideal for young children. But it's snorkelling that has put Kaha'lu'u on the map since this is one of the best spots on the island to practice the sport. You can also have a picnic under the coconut trees behind the coast. In winter, some surfers come here to take advantage of the waves that form at the bay's entrance.

Beside the park stands the small **Saint Peter's Church** ★★, an adorable white and turquoise wooden Catholic chapel. Nestled between the palm trees and bougainvillea, it is a popular place to get married. A few photos on the walls show the aftermath of Hurricane Iniki in 1992. The cross on the tiny altar is often adorned with one or two *lei* with heady fragrances.

In the spirit of continuity, the church stands beside the **Ku'emanu Heiau**, marked by a *paepae* replica. On the platform, a *lele* bears a few offerings: coconuts, dried flower or shell garlands and small sculpted wooden *tikis*. This temple is said to have been used to ask the gods for good surfing conditions!

The point enclosing Kahalu'u Bay by the south is occupied by the large **Aston Keauhou Beach Resort ★**. In ancient times, this site was reserved for *ali'i* and today still has a number of relics from this era. One of the most striking vestiges from the Hawaiian past is the reconstructed small home of Kalakaua. Although it is closed, if you take a peek in the window you'll be able to see a room on one side and a reception room on the other, with a portrait of the king in uniform. The king used to bathe in the natural pool, which was fed by a spring and designed as a fishpond. Legend has it that whoever fished here would have bad luck or bring misfortune to their family.

Beside the pool at the end of the point are the **Ka-Pua-Noni Heiau** ruins, marked by an old *tiki*. Further south, still facing the sea, you can see the meagre remnants of another temple located on the other side of a small bridge. Cycling enthusiasts will enjoy riding along the rocky coast, whose water holes reveal traces of petroglyphs at low tide as well as tiny creatures such as the red sea urchin.

Further south, the road heads around Keauhou Bay.

Small but deep and protected, **Keauhou**

Bay ★ still has a few anchored sailboats. In the park *(washrooms, showers)* located on the shore, a few quiet tables make a pleasant spot for a picnic. More adventurous travellers can rent a kayak and paddle along the rocky coast for a few hours.

Coffee-tree Branch

You can get to the bay in two ways: via Kamehameha III Road from Ali'i Drive, or via Kaleiopapa Street, which begins a ways back on Ali'i Drive. On this side, you'll notice a plaque at the end of the road commemorating the birth of Kamehameha III on March 17, 1814, the second child of Kamehameha the Great and Keopuolani. For a panoramic view of the bay, head to Kona Surf Resort (see p 257), the site of the battle of Kuamo'o, in which Hawaiian Christians fought against partisans of the old religion. In the evening, floodlights attract manta rays (see p 256).

★★★
The South Coast of Kona

(one day)

About 2mi (3km) inland from the Kona Coast on the slopes of the Kualalai and Mauna Loa volcanoes stand rows of plantation villages: Holualoa, Honalo, Kainaliu, Kealakekua, Captain Cook, Honaunau – all nestled in dense vegetation among tropical fruit and coffee plantations. The "coffee belt," which is home to all the farms on the island, sprawls across 20mi (30km) of land, rising between 820ft (250m) and 1,640ft (500m). The ancient Hawaiians had long ago made this land their garden.

From Highway 11, passing by Kona, Hualalai Road heads 3mi (4km) to the town of Holualoa.

Tucked into the lower Hualalai slopes far from the bustle of Kona, the small town of **Holualoa ★★** cultivates both its plantation-village character and its coffee groves. The cool, rainy climate at this altitude nurtures the lush vegetation. In the centre of town, many houses still have wooden displays in their windows, often with art galleries inside. The old Kona Hotel, established in 1926, hasn't changed a bit. Holualoa doesn't really

Hawaii – Big Island

have any attractions, but it would be a pity not to come here and breathe in some of the nostalgia hanging in the air – and to visit the *lauhala* boutique Kimura (see p 290).

From Holualoa, head south via Mamalahoa Highway (180), which snakes through the hillside. There are coffee plantations and flower gardens all the way up to the junction with Highway 11, to the entrance of the town of Honalo 9mi (14km) south of Kailua-Kona.

Honalo *(Mile 113.9)*, another plantation village, has a Daifukuji *(soto)* Buddhist temple, a large red wooden building with a pagoda-like roof. A few old photographs inside are mementoes of the Japanese community, with a gallery of portraits of young soldiers who enlisted in the American army during the Second World War. In addition to two simple altars are several *kodos* (ceremonial drums).

Here, it's one plantation village after the other, making it hard to know where one town ends and the other begins. Just past Honalo is **Kainaliu** *(Mile 113.3)*, whose old Aloha Theater houses both a restored cinema and a restaurant (see p 277). Soon after, you'll reach **Kealakekua** *(Mile 112)*, which is famous for the bay where Captain

Cook died. The village, like its neighbours, is nestled in the slopes between coffee groves and orchards, and you have to continue along the road to reach the bay (see p 206).

At the exit from Kealakekua *(Mile 111.7)*, the small **Kona Historical Society Museum ★** *($2; every day 9am to 3pm; 81-6551 Mamalahoa Hwy.; ☎323-3222)* is found in the old Greenwell Store, founded in 1873 by Henry Nicholas Greenwell, a British settler. Greenwell had arrived here more than 20 years earlier and established a prosperous farm based on trade, livestock and coffee, which he exported to Europe. The museum is devoted to his farms and traces his life with old photos and 19th-century tools. It also has the archives of the Kona Historical Society as well as a number of books on the history of Hawaii.

Just before the museum lie **Greenwell Farms ★** *(free guided tour Mon to Sat 8am to 4pm, ☎323-2862)*. The first trees were planted here in 1903. A 15min tour allows visitors to go through the steps of coffee processing. First, the coffee is bought at the nearby farm and husked using a special machine made in Costa Rica. The beans are then fermented for 24hrs and dried in the

sun for two days. So that they don't "cook," they are regularly turned with a rake, and if it rains, a roof is quickly placed over the beans. The next step consists of leaving the coffee under shelter for four or five days until its inner shell is gone. The beans are then sorted by size before being roasted. The thickest beans are considered the best ones. At the end of the tour, you're invited to taste the homemade coffee…and stock up.

Other coffee producers (17 at last count) offer tours of their farms from one end of the "coffee belt" to the other. None of them charge admission, but most have a store filled with a variety of products and souvenirs. Such is the case for the **Captain Cook Coffee Company** *(every day noon to 5pm, Mile 113.1)*; **Royal Kona Museum & Coffee Mill** *(every day 8am to 5pm, Mile 106.4)*, which is more of a souvenir shop than a museum; the **Coffee Roasting Factory**, on Middle Ke'ei Road *(towards Napo'opo'o, Mon to Sat 9am to 5pm, Sun 10am to 5pm)*, with a beautiful photo exhibit illustrating coffee production, from germination to the final product; and the **Bay View Farm** *(every day 9am to 5pm, close to Painted Church)*. Located on Middle Ke'ei Road just below the junction of High-

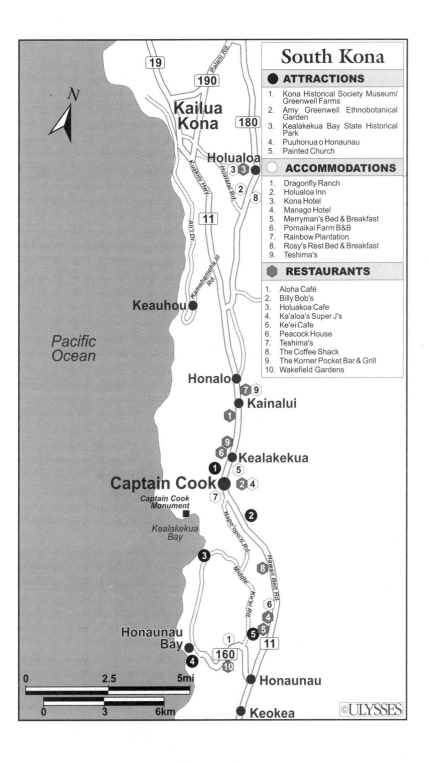

South Kona

● ATTRACTIONS

1. Kona Historical Society Museum/ Greenwell Farms
2. Amy Greenwell Ethnobotanical Garden
3. Kealakekua Bay State Historical Park
4. Puuhonua o Honaunau
5. Painted Church

⬡ ACCOMMODATIONS

1. Dragonfly Ranch
2. Holualoa Inn
3. Kona Hotel
4. Manago Hotel
5. Merryman's Bed & Breakfast
6. Pomaikai Farm B&B
7. Rainbow Plantation
8. Rosy's Rest Bed & Breakfast
9. Teshima's

⬢ RESTAURANTS

1. Aloha Café
2. Billy Bob's
3. Holuakoa Cafe
4. Ka'aloa's Super J's
5. Ke'ei Cafe
6. Peacock House
7. Teshima's
8. The Coffee Shack
9. The Korner Pocket Bar & Grill
10. Wakefield Gardens

N

19
190
180

Kailua Kona

Palani Rd.

Holualoa

Hualalai Rd.

Kaiminii Hwy.

11

Kamehameha III Rd.

Ali'i Dr.

Pacific Ocean

Keauhou

Honalo

⬡7 ⬡9

Kainalui

⬢1

⬡9
⬢6
Kealakekua

●1 ⬢5

Captain Cook

⬢2 ⬢4

Captain Cook Monument

⬡7

●2

Napo'opo'o Rd.

Kealakekua Bay

●3

Middle Ke'ei Rd.

Hawaii Belt Rd.

⬢8

⬢6
⬢4
⬢5
Honaunau Bay

⬡1
160
●4
⬢10

11

●4

Honaunau

Keokea

0   2.5   5mi
0   3   6km

©ULYSSES

Macadamia

Macadamia nuts are Hawaii's third most important agricultural product after pineapples and sugar cane. Macadamia trees produce nuts all year long, which means that you can see flowers, inflorescences, green fruit as well as ripe fruit all on the same tree. As soon as the nuts ripen, they fall to the ground, which explains why the ground is always swept clean on plantations. One tree yields between 8lbs (3.5kg) and 20lbs (9kg) of nuts every year by the time it is six years old, and by the age of 20, its production peaks with an average annual yield of between 88lbs (40kg) and 143lbs (65kg).

way 11 *(Mile 105.9)*, the **Macadamia Nut Factory** is along the same lines, featuring of course the macadamia nut.

At Mile 110.4, the short Napo'opo'o Road heads down towards Kealakekua Bay.

Take a short 1,650ft (600m) detour on the main road to the **Amy Greenwell Ethnobotanical Garden** ★ *(suggested donation $4; sunrise to sunset;* ☎ *323-3318)*. This botanical garden, created by the descendant of the man who founded the Greenwell Store, was bequeathed to the Bishop Museum after his death. The garden has an area displaying a Hawaiian garden as it would have looked like before the Europeans arrived.

It contains both endemic plants and plants that were introduced by the Polynesians: celebasses, bread trees, 'uala (sweet potato) and ko (sugar cane). You can still see remnants of the walls the Hawaiians built to section off the lots of farmland. They were long and narrow, heading towards the slope. Here, there are interesting descriptions about the farming organization system.

About 825ft (300m) past the turn-off on Napo'opo'o Road begins the trail leading to

Kealakekua Bay ★★, the famous spot where Captain Cook died. It was the attempted capture of the great chief Kalani'opu'u by the crew (who stole a canoe the night before) that triggered the argument that led to the death of the famous navigator and four of his men. Only a few weeks earlier, Cook had been welcomed here with all the honours of a distinguished host. Kealakekua means "pathway of the god," in reference to Lono who, according to legends, used the Manuahi cliff overhanging the bay as a slide to reach the sea. It was also from here that he left for far away, promising to return one day – seemingly in the person of Captain Cook, whose boat evoked the raft described in tales related to Lono.

You can park on the other side of the road.

Don't take the right turn-off just past the beginning of the trail; instead, continue straight ahead through the high grasses that tend to swallow up hikers. The path gradually clears up. After about 30min, you will reach an old lava flow and the first view of the

Macadamia Nuts

sea – but not yet the bay. The trail climbs down a gentle slope at first, but gradually becomes steeper as it passes through the basalt field. The stony trail is a bit difficult on the way back in the midday heat. The trail reaches the coast 20min later, and shortly thereafter is a **monument** erected in memory of James Cook, "who discovered these islands on the 18th of January A.D. 1778 and fell near this spot on the 14th of February, A.D. 1779."

The first monument was inaugurated in 1825 by Lord Byron. Erected in November of 1874 "by some of his fellow countrymen," the white obelisk that can still be seen today is held by anchor chains, standing to the north of the vast Kealakekua Bay on a narrow piece of land at the foot of Pali o Manuahi, whose lava is lapped up by the ocean. The nearby plot of land was given to the British and the monument was maintained by the crews of passing Anglo-Saxon ships. Just across is a small pier where passing ships have mounted plaques bearing their coat of arms. Unfortunately, souvenir hunters have pulled out many of them. In the surrounding area, you'll notice the ruins of many dwellings and several *heiau*, but the only thing left is the foundations, which are

overrun by vegetation and torn apart by tree roots.

The bay, a marine reserve where fishing is forbidden, is famous for its crystal-clear waters that make it ideal for snorkelling. Every day, groups come here to do just that. The pier is the best place to take a dip. Parakeet and butterfly fish, *awa*, Moorish idols and other reef fish swim around the coral. About 138ft (50m) north of the monument, a plaque embedded in a rock and covered by water marks the precise spot where Captain Cook died. Some people prefer to come here by kayak (see p 250) from Napo'opo'o rather than on organized tours. It takes 20 to 30min to cross the bay, and you can sometimes see dolphins along the way if you stay close to the coast.

The lower part of the trail makes for a peaceful walk along the coast in the opposite direction of the monument. The sea here has carved many natural pools in the ancient *pahoehoe* lava flow. You will soon reach **Cook Point**, which is pounded by unpredictable waves at the bay's entrance. Further along stands a signal station.

Napo'opo'o Road winds all the way down the southern coast of Kealakekua Bay.

The **Kealakekua Bay State Historical Park ★**, at the end of the road, has the restored *heiau* from Hikiau and a plaque commemorating the funeral oration of William Whatman, a sailor on Cook's expedition who died of a heart attack here on January 28, 1779. It was the first Christian service in Hawaii's history and the first time Hawaiians witnessed the mortal character of the British. Those who want to kayak to the Cook monument, situated on the other side of the bay, can launch their boat along the small pier located across from the end of Middle Ke'ei Road.

From the park, a narrow coastal road heads to Pb'uhonoua o Honaunau, situated a few kilometres away.

To relive the glorious past of the Big Island, be sure to visit the historical park of **Pu'uhonua o Honaunau ★ ★** *($2; every day 7:30am to 5:30pm, guided tours between 10am and 3:30pm;* ☎*328-2288 or 328-2326, www.nps.gov/pubo).* Cutting along the rocky coast, the tiny beach at Honaunau (Keone'ele) Bay was once reserved for the *ali'i* residence on the Kona Coast. As if to warn the lower castes to stay away, fearsome *ki'i* (carved wooden statues) watched over the canoes and nearby reserved waters – just like the fishponds further inland. No *maka'ainana* ("commoners") dared set foot here for fear of losing their lives. When they weren't busy waging war, the *ali'i* retreated here to enjoy the sea and *holua* (land surfing). Several buildings have been reconstructed, as well as a model of a temple.

To the south is a lava stone wall (10ft high and 17ft wide, or 3m by 5m) that marks the boundary of one of the island's rare *pu'uhonua* (place of refuge), a sanctuary where defeated warriors and *kapu* breakers were given a second chance. If they managed to make it all the way here, often forced to swim, their lives would be spared and a ceremony of absolution would ensue. The enclave owes its sacred character to the presence of Hale o Keawe, located by the sea, where the bones of 23 great *ali'i* were placed – including those of the great chief Keawe'ikekahiali'i o Kamoku, Kamehameha's great-grandfather. The reconstructed sanctuary, surrounded by images of gods, stands here at the foot of a flowering coconut grove.

Each year, the park organizes a Hawaiian cultural festival on the weekend closest to the first day of July. During the rest of the year, you

can often attend craft demonstrations.

Past the parking lot, a trail has been created right from the lava and follows the edge of the park, leading to picnic tables and barbecue pits beneath coconut trees. Near the washrooms are several natural, nearly enclosed shallow pools that the ocean has carved into the rocky coast – an ideal spot for a pleasant sea bath. A path, off-limits to vehicles, leads to Ho'okena (see below).

Located north of the historical park, the cove of **Honaunau Bay** ★ *(required parking $2, picnic tables, washrooms)* is a popular place to snorkel, especially beside the rocks that protect its entrance. The water is crystal clear, but avoid swimming when the sea is rough. The lava rocks, warmed up by the sun, often attract avid sun worshippers. The canoes of the Keoua Honaunau Canoe Club are lined up on the shore.

Heading up Pu'uhonua o Honaunau towards Highway 11, be sure to make the slight detour to **Painted Church** ★★, located on Painted Church Road *(turn-off near Mile 1)*. The interior of this small, whitewood Catholic church is entirely painted with naive biblical scenes reflecting local influences – the work of Father Velghe

between 1899 and 1904, a priest from Belgium who wanted to illustrate the Bible for his illiterate congregation. Columns erupt into palm leaves on the vaulted ceiling of a tropical sky, and the choir loft, painted with a trompe l'oeil, evokes the massive pillars and overhead domes of a cathedral. A lovely piece of *kapa* (cloth made from pounded bark) covers the altar, and in front of the entrance stands a bust of another Belgian priest, Father Damien de Veuster (1840-1889), who became well known when a film came out in 1999, retelling his life on the Kalaupapa Peninsula of Moloka'i.

As Highway 11 descends south, it becomes less and less sinuous and gradually leaves the tropical ambiance of Kona's central coast. The sun often becomes hazy, and the forest replaces the flowers and coffee groves.

At Mile 101.2, a road on the right leads to **Ho'okena State Park** ★ *(washrooms, showers, picnic tables, camping – see p 258)*, where a few isolated homes are scattered. During the 19th century, there was a lively port (now abandoned) where steamships docked. The grey-sand beach fronts a small cliff; the remains of lower-ranking *ali'i* were once placed in caves here. The sea is not usually calm here, but when it is, it's an interesting spot to snorkel. Failing that, you can take a dip in the water holes left by the tide.

Past Mile 93, the lava begins to appear, alternating with sections of forest that have covered the oldest lava flows. At Mile 88.9, a short, windy road, which first crosses macadamia plantations and then undergrowth, leads to **Miloli'i ★**, known for being the most traditional town in Hawaii. Miloli'i is not a tourist destination; there's nothing to see or do here. The first homes were built right on the desolate surface of the lava – quite the example of the quality of land distributed under the Hawaiian Home Lands program! Other homes are scattered along the coast in a rather austere setting, slightly cheered up by a few clusters of palm and pine trees. In theory, camping is allowed in Beach County Park (which actually doesn't have a beach, just a mix of lava or coral), but the site is not well equipped and the Miloli'i inhabitants choose to live here mostly to keep their peaceful way of life.

At Mile 86, Highway 11 crosses the vast macadamia plantations of Mac Farms of Hawai'i, spread out over more than 3,700 acres (1,500ha), towards Ka'u and Ka Lae, the southern tip of the island. You can either head in this direction (see p 246) on the way to Volcanoes National Park, or you can turn back to Kona.

★
The North Coast of Kona

(half-day)

Shortly after leaving Kailua-Kona, the lava again carpets the ground with its blackish mantle. Once a hostile region, the coast's landscape now reveals a few treasures: deserted beaches that are sometimes difficult to reach, with blankets of white sand lapped by crystal-clear waters and fringed by clusters of coconut trees. Halfway between idyllic and chaotic, the first great tourist resorts made this region their home. The first port of call past Kona, the **Honokohau** marina is the departure point for many tour boats and deep-sea fishing excursions. You can also watch the boats return just before noon or between 3pm and 4pm when they come to weigh their catches. Only the prize catches are kept; all the others are thrown back into the sea. A good place to swim is in the tiny cove south of the port.

Most sun worshippers, however, prefer the long, peaceful beach on the north side, at the southern edge of **Koloko-Honoko-Hau ★** (☎329-6881), a large national historical park. Extending towards the airport, the park houses several fishponds that are frequented by migratory birds, ancient Hawaiian sites, as well as a natural pool known as Queen's Bath. The remains of Kamehameha the Great are supposedly buried here near the Koloko fishpond.

The main entrance to the park is presently being renovated near Mile 97 on Highway 19; in the meantime, only the southern entrance is accessible. To get here, take the first turn-off on the right before arriving at the Honokohau Harbor. You'll pass in front of the marina buildings and then cross the dry docks. Park near the pontoons and then walk to the gate at the park's border.

At Mile 94.1, a road leads to Keahole Point where the Hawai'i Ocean Science & Technology Park (OTEC) and the Natural Energy Laboratory of Hawai'i are located. The two institutions work on research programs exploring new energy sources, aquaculture and marine sciences. Guided tours take place on Thursdays between 10am and noon (reservations ☎329-7341). Before the research

Marine Research

The Hawai'i Ocean Science & Technology Park (OTEC) and the Natural Energy Laboratory of Hawai'i have together developed a variety of revolutionary techniques based on using seawater. Algae, salmon, flounder, lobster, oysters, sea cucumbers, sea urchins, shrimp and even tilapia are raised here thanks to an ingenious cooling system. At a depth of 2,198ft (670m), where the water is rich in organic matter and very pure, cold water at 43°F (6°C) is pumped up and mixed with warm water at 49ft (15m). With this technique, which involves rather large displacements of water to one or the other, a constant temperature can be maintained in each tank – colder water for non-tropical species and warmer water for endemic species. Scientists have even developed an energy-production system that harnesses the temperature difference between cold and warm water.

buildings is the **Wawaloli Beach Park** *(6am to 8pm)* at the spot where the road reaches the coast. The entire length of beach here is bordered by a lava barrier protecting a natural basin *(about 330ft or 100m left of the washrooms)* with a sandy bottom where you can wade out at high tide. The water is quite warm since the sun heats it. You can also enjoy a picnic in the park.

Back on Highway 19, you'll soon cross the road that leads to the Kona airport *(Mile 93)*. Those who are interested in space exploration can visit the **Astronaut Ellison S. Onizuka Space Center** *($3; every day 8:30am to 4:30pm; ☎329-3441)*, dedicated to the memory of the astronaut who was born in Kona and died in the Challenger space shuttle explosion of 1986. The museum covers great achievements in space exploration, from the first walk on the moon to the Pathfinder mission on Mars. It also illustrates the role Hawaii has played in this great movement, from the importance of telescopes on Mauna Kea to the return to Earth (or rather, the return to Hawaiian waters) of the Apollo mission to the training of astronauts on the desolate slopes of Mauna Kea. Onizuka and his colleagues have not been forgotten.

At Mile 90.9, just before the "Speed Limit 55 mph" sign, a large lava tube (on the right-hand side of the road) opens up in the rock. However, it's not as impressive as the one in the National Volcanoes Park.

A few hundred kilometres further, a chaotic trail branches off towards the left to **Kona Coast State Park** *(Thu to Tue 9am to 7pm)*. It crosses a former *pahoehoe* lava flow for 1.6mi (2.5km) before arriving at two consecutive parking lots – the first one in the middle of the lava fields, and the second one on the edge of a large sandy beach, trimmed by rocks next to a brackish pond. During the day, you can have a bite to eat under the coconut trees at the snack bar. Suntanning is more popular here than swimming, but if you're looking for peace and quiet, head to

Mahai'ula or Makalawena.

These two beaches are located towards the north. **Mahai'ula ★★** is not far from the first parking lot. One of the most beautiful beaches on the island, it lies next to a thin canopy of vegetation, which conceals the flow, an abandoned house, as well as a few picnic tables. The large trees here offer welcome shade when it gets hot. At each end of the cove are clusters of palm trees. This would be an idyllic setting if it weren't for the huge waves that pound the coast – although surfers don't complain in winter.

Further on, the coastal trail, an integral part of the former King's Trail, crosses another wide, sun-beaten lava flow on the way to **Makalawena Beach ★★** – often considered the most attractive beach on the island. The trail continues to Kua Bay (4.5mi or 7.2km), passing Pu'u Ku'ili at midpoint, a small volcanic cone whose summit offers a lovely panoramic view.

You can also reach Kua Bay, which is a part of the Kona Coast State Park, by a path (off-limits to rental vehicles) branching off Highway 19 at Mile 87.9.

At Mile 86.9, Ka'upuleha Road leads to the Kona Village Resort (see p 260). Ever since the Four Seasons

Resort opened, the lovely white sand of Ka'upulehu Beach (swimming forbidden) has been accessible. Since it used to be off-limits, it is still rarely frequented.

Between Miles 85 and 87, don't miss the "Donkey Crossing" signs along the road. These little donkeys were once used to transport coffee harvests; they now run wild. You can usually see them in the evening or at dusk, rarely during the daytime.

The views of **Kiholo Bay** at Mile 82.1 reveal clusters of coconut trees – surprisingly, in the middle of a lava desert. A trail *(every day 8:30am to 3:30pm)*, which starts about 1,100ft (400m) before the lookout, allows you to get closer to the bay.

Kohala

The Tourist Coast

(one day)

Black and desolate, volcanic and sterile – this is the south coast of Kohala. But in some spots, it is fringed by fine white sand, a gold mine in which enlightened developers saw a promising future as early as the mid-1960s. Add to this a climate that is almost always sunny, and a few hundred palm trees and millions of dollars later, you have the Gold

Coast's mega-resorts, Waikoloa, Mauna Lani and Mauna Kea, which welcome the majority of tourists to the Big Island every year. These small "islands" far from civilization are virtually self-sufficient communities. Tennis, golf, exercise rooms, beaches, water sports – everything is easily accessible to guests. In fact, they don't even have to leave the resort since these also feature ancient Hawaiian ruins, petroglyphs and fishponds.

At Mile 76, Waikoloa Beach Drive heads down to **Waikoloa ★★**, the main tourist centre on the coast. Don't confuse the Waikoloa Resort on the coast, where the tourist complexes are located, with the Waikoloa Village (the turn-off at Mile 77), a modern town built in the hills in the middle of the lava desert to accommodate workers – there are also condominiums here that are a lot less expensive than on the coast. In addition to its hotel complexes and two golf courses, the Waikoloa Resort has the only shopping centre on the coast (King's Shops), as well as a number of vestiges from Hawaii's past. Whatever you do, be sure to visit the Hilton Waikoloa Village (see p 261), which is served by a canal and a monorail! If you stay here, you'll be able to participate in all sorts

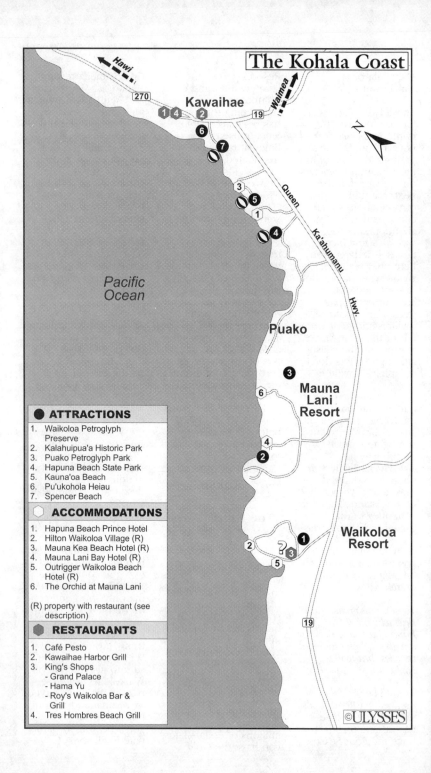

The Kohala Coast

ATTRACTIONS
1. Waikoloa Petroglyph Preserve
2. Kalahuipua'a Historic Park
3. Puako Petroglyph Park
4. Hapuna Beach State Park
5. Kauna'oa Beach
6. Pu'ukohola Heiau
7. Spencer Beach

ACCOMMODATIONS
1. Hapuna Beach Prince Hotel
2. Hilton Waikoloa Village (R)
3. Mauna Kea Beach Hotel (R)
4. Mauna Lani Bay Hotel (R)
5. Outrigger Waikoloa Beach Hotel (R)
6. The Orchid at Mauna Lani

(R) property with restaurant (see description)

RESTAURANTS
1. Café Pesto
2. Kawaihae Harbor Grill
3. King's Shops
   - Grand Palace
   - Hama Yu
   - Roy's Waikoloa Bar & Grill
4. Tres Hombres Beach Grill

©ULYSSES

of activities and water sports.

It appears that the Waikoloa site was inhabited by the first guardians of Anaeho'omalu, the royal fishpond, around the year AD 900. Several fishing villages were home to a few families, especially on the outskirts of Nawahine Rock, on the Wailua Bay (opposite the Hilton), where you can still see traces of the past. For some unknown reason, all of these villages were abandoned near the end of the 18th century, perhaps because of a tsunami, or perhaps due to the arrival of the first Western ships.

Petroglyphs

From the entrance to King's Shops, a 1,350ft (500m) trail along the golf course leads to **Waikoloa Petroglyph Preserve** ★, which contains nearly 9,000 drawings engraved by the ancient Hawaiians on basaltic rock. A map on the site points out the most important petroglyph, probably in memory of a passage by 'Anaeho'omalu, or in honour of a birth, to insure that the child has a long life. The Puako petroglyphs to the north are easier to make out.

Across from the King's Shops, a road leads straight south to the superb **'Anaeho'omalu Bay** ★★ *(every day 6am to 8pm; washrooms, showers, sail-board and beach-gear rentals, drinks)*, the recreation area of the hotel complexes. Featuring a long, curved beach with tall coconut trees, it is popular with swimmers, sun worshippers, divers, sail boarders and boating enthusiasts. After one last dip in the water, this site, where sailboats are usually anchored, is an ideal spot to watch the sunset.

Behind the beach is the **Ku'ualali'i** fishpond, extended to the north by the **Kahapapa** fishpond. Interconnected fishponds were once created in this spot, as evidenced by the reappearance of an underground river that met up with seawater. The name of this place, 'Anaeho'omalu, suggests that the fish (*'anae*), which were fed here, were reserved (*ho'omalu*) for travelling *ali'i*.

Behind the bay, the **King's Trail** crosses a place known to have been used as a rock quarry, where the ancient Hawaiian used stones to polish wood for canoes and to make fishhooks. It seems that these products were exported throughout the entire island.

At Mile 73.4, Mauna Lani Drive leads to the two luxury hotels of the Mauna Lani Resort: Mauna Lani Bay Hotel and Orchid at Mauna Lani.

Just before reaching the Mauna Lani Bay Hotel, Pauoa Street veers left to **Kalahuipua'a Historic Park** ★★ *(every day 6:30am to 6:30pm)*. From the parking lot, a paved trail crosses open lava, passing near two lava tunnels. The second tunnel, which was inhabited between 1500 and 1700, is in better condition. The cool interior is in stark contrast with the sun-beaten exterior. After about 1,350ft (500m), the path crosses a road and reaches the Kalahuipu'a ponds, bordered by the villas of the Mauna Lani Resort. Fed by springs, the ponds create an oasis of greenery, with many coconut and bread trees. The ancient Hawaiians, realizing that the ponds became filled with salt water at high tide, converted them into fishponds, where they raised mullet, barracudas, eels and shrimp. This is one of the few fishponds on the island that are still in operation. The walk between the ponds continues right up to Shoreline Trail along the coast.

Hawaii – Big Island

Just before the entrance to the Orchid at Mauna Lani, a road veers right to Holoholokai Beach and **Puako Petroglyph Park ★★**, which has the largest collection of rock carvings on the Big Island. Park in the first parking lot, which is the departure point of the Malama Trail. You'll soon see some reproductions of the most beautiful petroglyphs on the sides: mostly characters on the right, and turtles and other animals on the left. The trail continues for about 0.6mi (1km) right up to the actual petroglyphs. Though not difficult, the trail crosses rocky terrain, remnants of an ancient lava flow now overgrown with shrubs. The trail is sheltered from the sun nearly until the end, where you'll discover from a platform a patch of *pahoehoe* (flat, smooth lava) engraved with about 3,000 stylized human forms. Most of them are found near the mountains. Archaeologists, who want to find out their meaning, wonder what drove the ancient Hawaiians to engrave these images here during a time when lava flows were still active in the area.

Just 270ft (100m) from the beginning of the

trail, **Holoholokai Beach Park** *(every day 6:30am to 7pm; washrooms, barbecues, picnic tables),* along the rocky coast, has a striking black and white (basalt and coral) pebble beach. There's no swimming here, only net fishing, enjoyed by a few Hawaiians.

Back on Highway 19, at Mile 70.3, you'll cross a road leading to Puako. This is not another way to get to the petroglyphs but rather a mostly residential village. It sprawls along the rocky coast that has many basins formed by the tide. The access roads are mostly private. Along the way, you will see the small Hokuloa church, which is only open on Sundays for services.

At Mile 68.2, another turn-off leads to the Mauna Kea Resort.

The third and last tourist resort in southern Kohala was also the first. In 1965, a man named Rockefeller invested money to build the Mauna Kea Beach Hotel; in 1994, that hotel was joined

by the Hapuna Beach Prince Hotel. The two neighbouring establishments both have their own stretch of superb beach, Hapuna Beach to the south and Kauna'oa Beach to the north. According to Hawaiian law, all beaches are public, so you can enjoy them even if you're not staying at the hotels.

To get here, at Mile 69.3, take the road from **Hapuna Beach State Park ★★★** *(every day 7am to 8pm; ☎882-7995).* The white-sand beach – the loveliest on the island – is quite wide and bathed by turquoise waters. The park lies to the south, while the Hapuana Beach Prince Hotel stands on the promontory enclosing the cove to the north. Swimming is generally possible when the sea is calm, although you should stay close to the shore. Bodysurfing is popular when the waves are high (watch out for the currents). There's a snack bar on the premises that also serves as a grocery store and offers fin, mask and boogie-board rentals. In addition to picnicking, you can camp just behind the beach (see p 260).

The nearby *(Mile 68.1)* **Kauna'oa Beach ★★**

makes a lovely 825ft (300m) crescent at the foot of the Mauna Kea Resort. You'll have to share the beach with the hotel guests, but that is usually not a problem. The beach is the ideal spot to tan, swim and snorkel.

Past the tourist resort, at Mile 67, Highway 19 branches off to the east and heads towards Waimea. The coastal road (Hwy. 270), also called Akoni Pule Road, runs along the coast of the Kohala Peninsula.

Just past the junction *(Mile 2.4)*, the **Pu'ukohola Heiau ★★** *(free admission; every day 7:30am to 4pm; ☎882-7218)*, the temple of the "whale's hill," stands at the top of a hill that has become a historical park. It is the most important *heiau* on the island, Kamehameha's most ambitious project and the last major temple built in Hawaii. This is how the story goes: When the great chief Kalani'opu'u died, his two sons initially shared the island. Three quarters of the island went to Keoua, the eldest son, and one quarter was given to Kiwala'o, the youngest. Their cousin Kamehameha, who was guardian of the totem of Kuka'ilimoku, the war god, was entrusted with the Waipi'o valley. But Kamehameha's ambitions extended well beyond sharing control of the island – and his conviction was

supported by prophecies. He soon defeated the youngest brother, and when he was killed in 1782 at the battle of Moku'ohai, Kamehameha became ruler of Kohala. After Kamehameha failed to conquer Keoua when he invaded Maui, Lana'i and Moloka'i, he decided to turn to his aunt, who consulted the prophet Kapoukahi. The prophet told the young chief that if he wanted to conquer the entire archipelago, he should built a large-scale temple to honour his war god, Kuka'ilimoku. Kamehameha did so, taking meticulous care in its construction. Apparently, the stones of the *heiau*, with massive 20ft-high (6m) walls, were brought from the Pololu valley, located more than 19mi (30km) north, by a continuous chain of men. Not even the combined attacks of all the other island's chiefs managed to slow down construction. The temple was completed in 1791 and the future king invited Keoua to the inauguration. Keoua reluctantly accepted the invitation – after all, many of his soldiers had been killed the previous year by a volcanic gas explosion as they passed beneath the slopes of the Kilauea Crater. This is the only known volcanic explosion in Hawaiian history, and was interpreted as divine intervention. Before coming to the island,

Keoua apparently cut off the tip of his penis as a precaution so that Kamehameha would not be able to give his body as an offering, now incomplete and impure. But it was all in vain: Keoua was immediately sacrificed to Ku, speared by Ke'eaumoku, a relative of Kamehameha and father of Ka'ahumanu, as soon as he reached the shores. The debate continues: was it an isolated act or was it premeditated?

The temple has three narrow terraces facing the sea that are unfortunately off-limits to the public, except during the cultural festivities that take place in August. The rest of the year, you'll have to settle for a walk underneath. However, you'll be able to see the ruins of a second *heiau* close up. This one, which is a slightly smaller, is dedicated to Lono (Mailekini Heiau). During Kamehameha's reign, John Young transformed it into a fort. Hale o Kapuni, an altar in honour of the shark god that is no longer visible, once stood in the hollow of the cove. A short distance to the north, Young had his lavastone house built here, and it was there that Queen Emma was born. A trail just past a small bridge on Highway 270 leads to this place, but there's not much left to see.

Just south of the historical park lies **Spencer Beach ★★**, with its blanket of golden sand at the foot of large trees. The beach forms a wonderful cove that is a pleasant place to swim. You can also camp here in this tranquil setting (see p 261).

Just past the beach and park (Mile 3.5) is Kawaihae Harbor, where the Parker Ranch cattle once roamed (see p 222).

★★

The Kohala Peninsula

(one to two days)

Arid, windy, pounded by powerful waves and violent currents and dominated by the old Kohala volcano, which has been silent for 60,000 years, the western coast of the peninsula is hardly an inviting landscape. Yet some people, mostly fishers, have made it their home. Kamehameha the Great was born here, facing the island of Maui. To the north, the trade-wind-swept coast suddenly plunges into dreamy tropics. From the 1860s onwards, sugar-cane plantations, sugarhouses and small towns sprung up here, and by the early 1900s, 11 different nationalities made up two thirds of the population. Hundreds of these people joined forces and dug an incredible mountain of irrigation canals, crossing ravines, ditches and entire valleys. A century later, the villages, having abandoned the sugar industry and now buried under vegetation, are slowly coming back to life thanks to tourism.

Near Mile 14, **Lapakahi State Historical Park ★** *(free admission; every day 8am to 4pm; ☎882-7995)*, is home to the partially restored ruins of a 15th-century Hawaiian fishing village. Lapakahi was one of the rare sites where canoes could approach this rather hostile coast – not on a beach, but on a white bed of coral pebbles, starkly contrasting with the basaltic rock. Along a 1mi (1.5km) loop trail (30 to 40min) you'll discover ancient games such as *konane* (similar to checkers), a *hale* where boats were once stored, as well as some partially hollowed stones that were filled with sea water to obtain salt. A visitor centre is currently under construction.

At Mile 14.8, a turn-off descends to **Mahukona Beach County Park** where a port was once used by sugar companies. Opposite the former railroad house (1930), the road splits in two: the road on the right leads to a former wharf, a great place to snorkel during calm weather; the road to the left leads to a small campground *(washrooms, showers, no drinking water)*, which is guarded by a family of grey cats.

Just before reaching Hawi, take the road to the Upolu airport at Mile 20, then take the path to the left just before the entrance. Although the road is accessible during dry and even bad weather, the only way to get here after heavy rainfall is with a four-wheel-drive vehicle. After about 1.7mi (2.8km), you'll see a sign on the left indicating the heiau. *Leave your car here and hike the last 825ft (300m) on foot.*

The **Mo'okini Heiau ★** stands at the northwestern tip of the island on a remote site that is difficult to reach. Associated with Kamehameha the Great, this *heiau*, which is one of the oldest in Hawaii, was built by the first settlers from the Marquesas Islands in the year 480 (according to the oral tradition). It is maintained by a direct descendant of the great priests who once presided here. At first hidden by the hill, the *heiau* suddenly appears just past a turn. With its massive walls, reaching 16ft (5m) in certain places, it evokes the incredible power of the great king and of Hawaiian legends, and this feeling of power is reinforced by the constant winds, frequent mist and relative absence of visitors. The

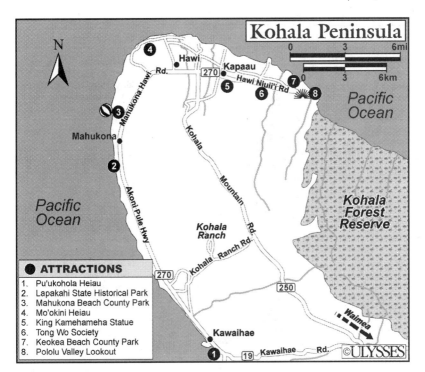

ATTRACTIONS

1. Pu'ukohola Heiau
2. Lapakahi State Historical Park
3. Mahukona Beach County Park
4. Mo'okini Heiau
5. King Kamehameha Statue
6. Tong Wo Society
7. Keokea Beach County Park
8. Pololu Valley Lookout

temple forms an enclosed rectangular-shaped enclosure that is almost the length of a football field, in which human sacrifices were performed. Outside the enclosure, a hut has been reconstructed and, all around, like wooded islets in the cattle country, you'll discover other forgotten structures.

Back on the main track, head 2,190ft (800m) further to the double enclosure that marks the supposed birthplace of Kamehameha in 1758. On the inside wall, offerings are still made in honour of the old king and gods: a few coins, a pendant

bearing words of peace and love, a pebble wrapped in *ti* (a sacred plant) leaves, pine cones and shells.

At Mile 21, Highway 270 reaches the town of Hawi and just beyond, the town of Kapa'au.

The village of **Kapa'au** (*Mile 23*) was populated between 1905 and 1920 by a wave of immigrants who came to work in the sugar-cane fields. Most of them came from Japan and Puerto Rico, but also from Korea, Portugal and the Philippines. The sugar refinery shut down in 1975, and until tourism was developed, Kapa'au went through a difficult period.

Downtown, a polychrome statue of **Kamehameha the Great ★★** stands next to the Kohala Civic Center, towering above the road on the centre divider strip. The king, wearing a feather cloak and helmet, is holding out his right hand while holding a spear in his left hand. This statue has an eventful story behind it. It was placed in Ainakea (Kohala) in 1883, then was moved to its present location in 1912. Commissioned from Boston sculptor Thomas Gould for the sum of $10,000, it was originally supposed to stand in front of Ali'iolani Hale in Honolulu. The sculptor completed the mould in

Florence and then had the statue cast in Paris. But the ship delivering it sank near the Falkland Islands, so another copy was ordered with the insurance money. However, before the replacement was completed, the original sculpture miraculously reappeared in Honolulu: a captain passing through the Falkland Islands had bought it after it was taken out of the icy waters! The copy was placed in O'ahu and the original was sent to the Big Island. Volunteers are almost always on duty at the Civic Center; they are retired sugar-factory workers who have many interesting stories to tell.

At Mile 23.9, a short road, which crosses a macadamia plantation, heads right to **Kalahikiola Church** (1855). Usually closed, this massive Episcopal church is made of stone and has a wooden steeple. On a curve just past a small bridge at Mile 25.7 is a large rock known as

Kamehameha Rock. A Visitors Bureau sign points out its location. The future king is said to have demonstrated his legendary strength by lifting this rock above his head.

At the next curve (Mile 25.8), don't miss the pretty red and green wooden building of the **Tong Wo Society ★**, located a little farther from the road. During plantation years, there was a Chinese school here during the day and a fraternity during the evening where local employees socialized. The building is closed to the public. At its foot, on the edge of the road, the old Wo On Store, a former plantation store, was transformed into an art gallery a few years ago.

Around Mile 26, the road winds through small valleys, crossing several one-lane bridges along the way.

Soon after *(at Mile 27)*, the road crosses the hamlet of **Makapala**, with its few wooden

Statue of Kamehameha the Great

houses nestled in front of a small church. The name of the village means "slanting eyes," a reference to an old Hawaiian legend that says that the Chinese were here even before the Europeans. Just opposite the "All Saints Church" sign is a small fruit stand. As the sign says, don't hesitate to ring the doorbell of the house out back. Gene, a former Alaskan gold digger and inveterate pipe smoker, will take you on a tour of his garden with its macadamia-nut trees and will also offer you a game of miniature golf for a few dollars.

At Mile 27.3, a small road leads to **Keokea Beach County Park**, which, despite its name, doesn't really have a beach, just a kind of shallow pool, formed after a large lava-stone dike was built. Camping is possible here (see p 262).

The road ends at Mile 28 where a magnificent panoramic viewpoint overlooks the great **Pololu Valley ★★** and the phenomenal cliffs of the Hamakua Coast sink into the sea. The cliffs are flanked with almost imperceptible valleys: Waimanu, the refuge of wild-pig hunters, up to Waipi'o, which is not visible from this spot (see p 228). Despite frequent tsunamis, the valley was inhabited for a long time, but it was gradually deserted after the Kohala Ditch began operating at the beginning of the 20th century. The irrigation canal that was built in the middle of the mountain diverted a large portion of the water resources – to the benefit of the sugar-cane fields in the large plantations, but to the detriment of Pololu's taro plantations.

Only accessible by foot, the valley is not as difficult to reach as it may seem. Past the first 825ft (300m) stretch (the steepest part), the trail, although muddy during rainy weather and stony in places, is not long or difficult. Depending on the shape you're in, you'll reach the bottom in 15 to 20min; the return trip barely takes longer. Make sure to bring a hat if it's sunny since part of the path is exposed.

The trail ends by the sea on the left bank of the Pololu Stream. Wide and peaceful, the valley is crisscrossed by the stream, which, at its mouth, looks like a river. When the water level is low, it forms a volume of water like a dam behind the coast and no longer reaches the ocean – a blessing for hikers. On the other hand, after rainfall, the stream can swell up into a violent flow within a few hours, at which time it is dangerous to cross. Although the fields in the interior are for the most part no

longer planted, all are private property and therefore inaccessible to the public, as the signs throughout this region indicate.

The beach lying next to a blanket of large pebbles and a vast pine grove is covered with fine grey sand and dotted with driftwood and rocks, which have been piled into mounds and are incredibly stable considering their height. Sometimes the tide also leaves behind garbage that was thrown into the sea. Swimming is out of the question, but you can hike down the trail to the next valley if you so desire. The trail, which becomes more difficult and muddy as you go along, is mostly used by hunters and experienced hikers.

If you prefer the (relative) comfort of a saddle rather than hiking, mule rides are organized daily (see p 254).

From Hawaii, Highway 250, which runs by the foot of the old Kohala volcano (4,708ft or 1,435m), links up with Waimea-Kamuela after 20mi (32km). This picturesque road passes through a region of high pastures and ranches between patches of forest. The surrounding area is known as Ahualoa, which means "long heap" (of volcanic matter) in Hawaiian.

The North of the Island

Waimea-Kamuela

(half-day)

If there's one town on the Big Island that displays an original personality, it's got to be Waimea-Kamuela, the headquarters of Parker Ranch. Located at an altitude of nearly 2,300ft (700m) on the plateau separating Kohala from Mauna Kea, Waimea is focused around one activity: cattle rearing. With the often rainy and windy climate, vast stretches of pastures, white fences and the last real *paniolos* (cowboys) dressed in cowboy boots, you'll think you're in Montana or Wyoming.

Officially called Waimea ("red waters"), the town is known by its inhabitants as "Kamuela" to avoid confusion with other Waimeas on Kaua'i and O'ahu. Kamuela is simply a Hawaiian corruption of "Samuel," the son of John Palmer Parker, who took over the ranch in 1868. Although the days when everything belonged to the family are gone, the ranch still covers more than 225,000 acres (91,000ha) of land, with more than 50,000 head of cattle and 300 horses. Wherever you look, you'll see signs advertizing it. In town, you'll find the Parker

John Parker

John Palmer Parker, a 19-year-old U.S. marine originally from New England, jumped ship in Kealakekua Bay in 1809. At the time, the Big Island was overrun by wild cattle, the offspring of the first five cows Captain Vancouver had given Kamehameha in 1793. The British captain suggested to the king that a *kapu* be placed on the cattle to allow the population to grow – it was such a success that they ended up having to destroy the herds.

In 1815, Parker, who had learned to speak Hawaiian, convinced Kamehameha to give him permission to hunt the hordes of wild cattle. Once slaughtered and salted, it was then sold to islanders and visiting ships. The scene was a little like the Hispaniola buccaneers – except that Parker had the blessing of the authorities. Business was brisk. The following year, Parker married Kipikane, one of Kamehameha's granddaughters, and on that occasion he landed himself his first plot of land – less than 2.5 acres (1ha). Thirty years later, during the Great Mahele, Kipikane, because of her royal blood, received 665 acres (269ha) of land. Today, this land has become the foundation of the largest private ranch in Hawaii and the United States, with an area of more than 328 sq mi (850km²) – twice the size of Lana'i!

Ranch Center, the Parker Ranch Grill, Parker Square, Parker Realty, and, if you're here during Independence Day celebrations (Fourth of July), you'll be able to attend the Parker Ranch Rodeo. Since the death of Richard Palmer Smart in 1992, Parker's last heir, the ranch (which was then worth $450 million) has been run by an association whose profits are invested in hospitals and charities.

At the entrance to Waimea on Highway 19 *(just past the turn-off from Hwy. 250)*, don't miss the **Kamuela**

Museum ★★ *($5; every day 8am to 5pm; 66-1655 Kaweheonalani Rd., ☎885-4724).* Visitors are greeted by a statue that you wouldn't expect to encounter in this part of the world: a bust of Kaiser Wilhelm I, brought to the islands in 1840 and taken down during the First World War. Albert and Harriet Salomon, whose combined age adds up to 181 years, give a hearty welcome to visitors. Albert is the grandson of an Arabic-Jewish immigrant and a great *kahuna* who predicted in 1913 that he would open a museum, while Harriet is one of John Palmer Parker's great-great-granddaughters.

The prediction came true and the Salomons passionately care for their "priceless collection of over 50 years." More than a museum, this vast and eclectic collection recalls the days when, in the 16th and 17th centuries, wealthy and important people collected all sorts of rare and unusual objects from the four corners of the world. Everything is classified by category (from "old" to "rare" to "quite rare") and the descriptions are handwritten on cardboard. Because of their advanced age, they are thinking about selling their collection. So, unfortunately, the collection may no longer be there when you come.

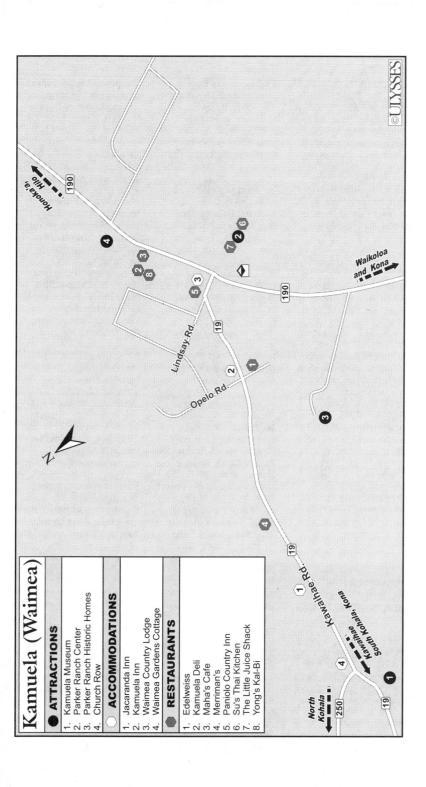

Kamuela (Waimea)

● ATTRACTIONS

1. Kamuela Museum
2. Parker Ranch Center
3. Parker Ranch Historic Homes
4. Church Row

○ ACCOMMODATIONS

1. Jacaranda Inn
2. Kamuela Inn
3. Waimea Country Lodge
4. Waimea Gardens Cottage

● RESTAURANTS

1. Edelweiss
2. Kamuela Deli
3. Maha's Cafe
4. Merriman's
5. Paniolo Country Inn
6. Su's Thai Kitchen
7. The Little Juice Shack
8. Yong's Kal-Bi

© ULYSSES

Honoka'e, Hilo

Waikoloa and Kona

Lindsay Rd.

Opelo Rd.

Kawaihae Rd.

Kawaihae, Kona

South Kohala, Kona

North Kohala

Located in the heart of town, the **Parker Ranch Center** ★ *($5; every day 9am to 5pm, no admission after 4pm;* ☎*885-7655)* houses a visitor centre and a small museum devoted to the history of the village and its main developer, John Palmer Parker, founder of the Parker Ranch. There is a re-creation of a saddle workshop, the dresses of the Parker daughters dating from the 1880s, a gallery of portraits of Parker descendants and important figures of the 19th century, a gorgeous quilt with Hawaiian colours, as well as a few beautiful Hawaiian artifacts: taro pounders, *koa*-wood *poi* bowls, lava bowls and *tiki* replicas. Don't miss the reproduction of Captain Vancouver's uniform. Vancouver brought the first five cattle to Kawaihae in 1793, which was the (indirect) source of the Parker fortune. The following year, long-horned Mexican cattle and sheep were also introduced.

In a separate room, you can watch a short 20min **film** that traces the epic tale of this ranch and presents the life of *paniolos* today: horses, lassoes, winter births, calf-counting and branding in spring (at the rate of 400 per hour!). It's just like the Wild West, except that orders are shouted in Hawaiian and there are sounds of ukulele, adding an exotic touch.

Life here has barely changed in 100 years. The only thing that is different is that the cattle are no longer attached by the horns to the small boats that used to transport them to the ships anchored in deep waters. A biography is devoted to Richard Palmer Smart, the last heir to the ranch, who "saw the lights of Broadway."

If you don't want to take one of the carriage rides that give a rather superficial look of the ranch (every hour, maximum 20 people), you can head to the boutique and buy a beautiful hat or a pair of cowboy boots.

At the entrance to Waimea-Kamuela on Highway 190, a short road flanked by eucalyptus trees leads to the **Parker Ranch Historic Homes** ★★ *($7.50, $10 combined with the Parker Ranch Center Museum; every day 10am to 5pm;* ☎*885-5433)*. You can see two homes here that were once owned by the Parker family: Mana Hale and Pu'uopelu. Pu'uopelu, which has been a family dwelling since 1862, has been expanded over the years. Its style is more reminiscent of a French manor than an American ranch. Today, it houses the museum. It features period furnishings, Chinese art objects (Tang and Ming horses and camels), 16th-century engravings (including several by

Dürer and Rembrandt) and a few paintings by Richard Palmer Smart, the last family heir. A small room traces his career as a Broadway musical star.

The more modest Mana Hale was the home of the patriarch, John Palmer Parker. This magnificent *koa*-wood home is essentially of saltbox construction, a popular design in Parker's native Massachusetts. Originally built more than 16mi (10km) from here, it was later brought here for the museum.

Near the entrance to the Parker Ranch Historic Homes, Camp Tarawa Memorial is dedicated to the 55,000 soldiers who trained here between 1943 and 1945 before being sent to various combat zones in the Pacific.

East of the town centre, Waimea's churches are lined up side by side in an area called **Church Row** ★. There's a Buddhist temple (*hongwanji*), as well as a dark-green church known as Ke Ola Mau Lao Church ("church of eternal life"), which is decked with a silver steeple. Next to it stands the beige-coloured Imiola Congregational Church, originally a grass hut built in 1832. It was replaced in 1837 by a wooden structure, and then a stone building was erected between 1855 and 1856 under the supervision of Reverend Lorenzo Lyons of Massachusetts, as attested by his grave located to the left of the entrance. The interior is covered with *koa*-wood panels.

★
Saddle Road

(half-day to full day)

Leaving Mamalahoa Highway 16mi (10km) south of Waimea, Saddle Road (Route 20) crosses the Big Island from one end to the other. The pastures, where large cacti seem to be a bit out of place, quickly give way to an increasingly solitary land covered with lava fields and bushes quavering in the mountain wind. At 6,560ft (2,000m), the pass creeps between the base of Mauna Kea to the north and the base of Mauna Loa to the south before heading down to Hilo. Many car rental agencies forbid their clients to drive on Saddle Road – although this rule isn't justified by the condition of the road, which is quite good. If you are keen on making this trip, enquire in advance, or contact Harper's Car Rentals (see p 193), which allows its four-wheel-drive vehicles to be driven up to the Mauna Kea summit. Saddle Road is supposed to be improved soon and then it will finally be accessible to everyone.

After passing through 20mi (30km) of endless desolate desert landscape, shortly after passing the Pohakuloa military camp, Saddle Road reaches **Mauna Kea State Recreation Area** *(Mile 35.1)*. At an altitude of nearly 6,560ft (2,000m), the park is mostly frequented by hunters, but anyone can spend the night here (see p 264).

At Mile 28, John Burns Way climbs towards Mauna Kea.

For 5,000 years, **Mauna Kea ★★** hasn't budged. Specialists, however, say that the highest point of the archipelago, at 13,796ft (4,205m), is probably only dormant. The accumulated lava of this classic shield volcano alone makes up more than a good third of the island. From its ocean base, at a height of 32,680ft (9,961m), it is in fact the highest peak in the world!

Mauna Kea, whose name means "white mountain," was the legendary territory of the mysterious Poli'ahu, goddess of snow and enemy of Pele, reputed for her beauty and her conquests of men. The mountain boasts a crown of snow every winter, to the delight of skiers. It's not the Alps, make no mistake, but the runs, including Poi Bowl, Pele's Parlor, Prince Kuhio, King Kamehameha, are all the rage – what could

be more original than skiing in the tropics?

More than its sporting capacities, Mauna Kea is famous for its astronomy facilities: at its summit, there are no less than nine telescopes operating around the clock, run by research institutes from a dozen countries who take advantage of clear nights and dark skies to scan the heavens. With 40% of the earth's atmosphere at its feet and 98% of the water vapour eliminated, the site is ideal. It was here, at the W.M. Keck Observatory and at the VLBA (Very Long Baseline Array), the largest telescope in the world, that the most important recent discoveries have been made – including the discovery that the configuration of planets orbiting around extremely distant suns is similar to that of the earth. To avoid interfering with these observations, all streetlights on the island have been equipped with orange bulbs, which are not as bright. Despite opposition from Hawaiian organizations, for whom the site is sacred (a rock quarry used to make axes and adzes was once found here), a new telescope is under construction.

At an altitude of 9,186ft (2,800m), the **Onizuka Center of International Astronomy Visitor Information Station** (VIS) *(Thu 5:30pm to 10pm, Fri 9am* *to 12pm, 1pm to 4:30pm and 6pm to 10pm, Sat and Sun 9am to 10pm;* ☎*961-2180 for VIS,* ☎*969-3218 for the weather service, www.ifa.hawaii.edu/info/vis/)* marks the end of the paved road. It's important to stop here (at least 1hr) to get used to the high altitude – and avoid the nausea and headaches often associated with altitude sickness, which can strike anyone.

In the centre, you'll discover a small museum where you can watch a film that traces the history of astronomy at the summit of Mauna Kea since the installation of the first telescope in 1964, and explains the current state of research. Most visitors, however, come on weekends (Thu to Sun 6pm to 10pm) at dusk to attend a free stargazing show. The weather is an important factor, and it is preferable to go on moonless nights, but the elevation of the observatory guarantees a clear view 80% of the time. That is also usually the time to put on your anorak. Be well prepared, as it can really be very cold. On a regular basis, the telescope operates during the day with a filter in order to see the sun.

The track leading from the observatory centre to the summit of Mauna Kea is only accessible to four-wheel-drive vehicles. The steep, windy road rises 7mi

(11km) up to the sky and takes about 30min in good weather. At the top, the land, which is bald in the summer, is red and bare. Walking enthusiasts or those who don't have a four-wheel-drive vehicle may prefer the **Mauna Kea Trail**, which passes through lunar landscapes *(allow 6 to 8hrs for the return trip)*. It is important to register at the Visitor Station, which organizes a summit tour on Saturdays and Sundays from 1pm to 5pm, with a visit to one or two telescopes open to the public during the day. This trip is only possible if you have your own vehicle.

Failing that, **Mauna Kea Summit Adventures** *(*☎*322-2366)* organizes 7hr tours to the summit ($135) departing from the tourist complexes on the Kona Coast (or the Waimea Coast) to observe the stars with the help of a telescope. The tour to the summit on a four-wheel-drive vehicle is longer and less expensive with **Hawaiian Eyes** *($99 for 9hrs;* ☎*937-5230)*, whose guides are geologists and naturalists. Other options are **Eco Tours Hawai'i** *($125 for 6hrs;* ☎*968-6856)* and **Waipi'o Valley Shuttle** *($80 for 6hrs;* ☎*775-7121)*. **Arnotts Lodge**, from Hilo, organizes its own tour on Tuesdays at the lowest prices *($70;* ☎*969-7097)*. It's not advisable to go to the summit if you suffer from obesity, cardiac or

respiratory problems, if you are pregnant or if you have been diving within the past 24hrs.

If you have your own vehicle, be careful about two things. First, with the high altitude and lack of oxygen, all vehicles use much more gas. Make sure to fill up your tank before coming (there's no gas station on the premises). Second, when driving down, be very careful: entire stretches of the track face the sun when it's setting, making it difficult to see oncoming vehicles.

Established between 1978 and 1987 by the successive acquisition of five plots of land by the Fish & Wildlife Service and the Nature Conservancy group, the **Hakalau National Wildlife Refuge** *(*☎*933-6915)* today remains the largest reserve on the archipelago. It sprawls for 51 sq mi (133km²) from the eastern slope of Mauna Kea, at an altitude between 2,625ft (800m) and 6,562ft (2,000m), and covers a significant part of the largest *koa* and *ohi'a* forest on the island. Hakalau is the first reserve of the country created to protect forest birds. Amateur ornithologists will discover seven rare endemic species here: *'akiapola'au, 'akepa,* scansorial birds, Hawaiian falcons, *o'u, 'elepaio* and *'oma'o*. There are also *amakihi, i'iwi, apapane* and *kolea*, as well as the small

The Mighty Tsunami

Underwater earthquakes can sometimes cause gigantic waves known in the Pacific as *tsunami* (from the Japanese word *tsu*, meaning "port," and *nami*, meaning "wave"). The tidal wave is barely noticeable at sea, but it swells up near the coasts. There can be up to a dozen successive waves over a period of a few minutes or an hour. They usually reach up to 33ft (10m) high, but it's not their height that makes them so destructive – it's their speed, which can reach up to 500mph (800km/hr).

On average, Hawaii is touched by one of these sea monsters once or twice every 10 years. Since 1819, more than 40 such waves have been recorded and two tsunami during the last 50 years have devastated the islands and remain in the collective memory. The first one, caused by movements in the Aleutian Islands trench, happened on April 1, 1946. It took only 5hrs for it to reach the Hawaiian Islands, travelling at an estimated speed of 453mph (730km/hr)! It hit Hilo and Hamakua head-on and killed 159 people. Less than 15 years later, on May 23, 1960, the same region was ravaged by another major tsunami, which was caused by an underwater earthquake measuring 8.5 on the Richter scale, whose epicentre was situated off the coast of Chile.

Since 1948, there has been a monitoring and warning system based on a real-time information network between all the seismological stations in the Pacific Rim. If you hear a siren or feel a tremor, immediately leave the coast and head for shelter on higher ground.

Hawaiian bat, which is on the verge of extinction. The reserve is only open on the weekend, and you must call the number above to obtain the code to the gate's padlock. After 2mi (3km) on the road from Mauna Kea, take Keanakolu Road on your right for 14mi (22km).

During your descent to Hilo, 5mi (8km) before arriving in town, you can stop at **Kaumana Caves**, which faces a vast lava tunnel created by the eruption of Mauna Loa in 1881 and is now overgrown with ferns.

★★

The Hamakua Coast

(one day)

Facing the trade winds, the Hamakua Coast has the most amount of rainfall and is covered with lush vegetation that makes you forget about the lava flows everywhere on the rest of the island. And yet just above lie the slopes of Mauna Kea, notched with streams flowing down successive valleys and overrun by profuse, thick vegetation. Taking advantage of this godsend, sugar-cane plantations began to spring up here at the end of the 19th century. Gradually abandoned after the decline of the sugar industry, deserted for

Hawaii – Big Island

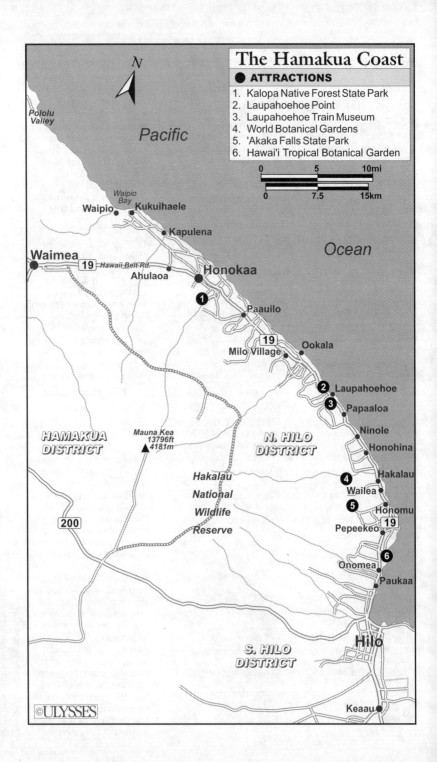

The Hamakua Coast

● ATTRACTIONS
1. Kalopa Native Forest State Park
2. Laupahoehoe Point
3. Laupahoehoe Train Museum
4. World Botanical Gardens
5. 'Akaka Falls State Park
6. Hawai'i Tropical Botanical Garden

| 0 | 5 | 10mi |

| 0 | 7.5 | 15km |

N

Pololu Valley

Pacific

Ocean

Waipio Bay

Waipio ● Kukuihaele

● Kapulena

Waimea ● [19] *Hawaii Belt Rd.*

Ahulaoa ● **Honokaa**

①

● Paauilo

[19]

Milo Village ● Ookala

② Laupahoehoe

③ Papaaloa

Ninole ●

HAMAKUA DISTRICT

Mauna Kea 13796ft ▲4181m

N. HILO DISTRICT

Honohina ●

Hakalau

National

Wildlife

Reserve

④ Hakalau

Wailea ●

⑤ Honomu

[200]

Pepeekeo ● [19]

⑥

Onomea ●

Paukaa ●

S. HILO DISTRICT

Hilo

©ULYSSES

Keaau ●

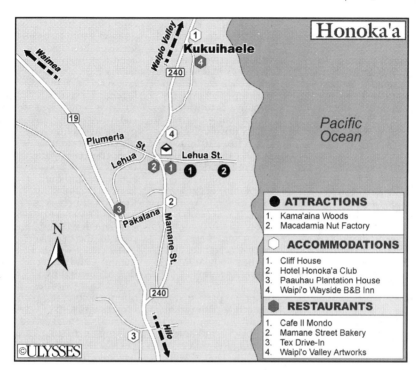

Honoka'a

Kukuihaele

Waimea

Waipio Valley

Plumeria St.

Lehua

Lehua St.

Pakalana

Mamane St.

Hilo

N

©ULYSSES

Pacific
Ocean

● **ATTRACTIONS**
1. Kama'aina Woods
2. Macadamia Nut Factory

○ **ACCOMMODATIONS**
1. Cliff House
2. Hotel Honoka'a Club
3. Paauhau Plantation House
4. Waipi'o Wayside B&B Inn

⬢ **RESTAURANTS**
1. Cafe Il Mondo
2. Mamane Street Bakery
3. Tex Drive-In
4. Waipi'o Valley Artworks

employment in town, Hamakua's villages have slowly begun to come back to life thanks to tourism. The Mamalahoa Highway (19) runs more or less continuously near the coast from Honoka'a to Hilo.

At Mile 52.1, at the Waimea exit, is the Old Mamalahoa turn-off on the right, which is a pleasant alternative to Highway 19. The paved road snakes in between pastures, patches of forest and hamlets, leading to Highway 19 just beyond Honoka'a – past the first road leading to the village centre. If you decide to take the main road, the turn-off for Honoka'a is at Mile 42 (a second is

found at Mile 43.5 if you're coming from the east).

A stopover on the road from the Waipi'o Valley, the plantation village of **Honoka'a**, founded in 1873, was once the third town of the archipelago. Although isolated, for a long time it had a reputation for being quite lively. Here too, sugar was its strength and destiny. Once forgotten after the gradual desertion of the sugar refineries, the town has regained its former vitality. In the town centre, the wooden buildings, which are now looking radiantly youthful, have been restored and are now home to restau-

rants and shops. The old People's Theater (1930) has also been renovated and films are shown here on weekends. You can also have a good time in Honoka'a at its annual rodeo.

On Lehua Street, about 2,200ft (800m) from downtown towards the sea, the **Macadamia Nut Factory** *(every day 9am to 5pm; ☎775-0020)* is rather a boutique offering products made with macadamia nuts and other souvenirs bearing the effigy of Keoki, the small mascot donkey of the house. Sometimes you can see employees behind the windows in the process of roasting coffee or nuts. You'll also have an opportunity to look at the macadamia trees surrounding the parking lot. Along the way, don't hesitate to stop at **Kama'aina Woods**, a Hawaiian co-operative that makes beautiful quality wooden objects (see p 290).

From Honoka'a, a dead-end road runs along the coast for long way towards the Waipi'o valley. Just before reaching the end (Mile 8.1) an access road on the right passes through the hamlet of Kukuihaele, where you can stop at Waipi'o Valley Artwork (see p 283 and p 290).

From the end of the paved road, where there is a large parking lot, the view plunges down to one of the most sacred spots in Hawaii, **Waipi'o Valley ★★**. In ancient times, the royal residence and "capital" of the island were located here. It is said that Kamehameha grew up and learned to surf here. Once one of the most populated valleys, Waipi'o still has houses and taro fields owned by several families. Evenings in Kukuihaele are becoming a little more lively, but the lifestyle has essentially not changed that much: fishing, agriculture, and wild-pig hunting in the recesses of the valley, overgrown by the jungle.

Unless you have a four-wheel-drive vehicle, it's

impossible to head down by car. The road that leads through the valley is paved but so steep (25%) that a regular vehicle can't climb back up. The only alternative is to walk or take a tour – by four-wheel-drive vehicle ($135 from 10am to 3pm), carriage ($40 for 90min, four departures a day), minibus ($35 for 90min) or by horse ($75, descent by minibus). If you're on foot, allow 15 to 20min to go down and almost double to come back up. It's best to take this trip when it's sunny.

When you arrive at the bottom, a path (often muddy) leads right to the black-sand **beach** fringing the valley (10min). Dotted with rocks and pounded by waves, it is split in the middle by the mouth of the Waipi'o River. The western end of the beach is the best place for swimming if you don't venture too far from the coast, but to reach it, you have to go around the valley. Since tours aren't allowed to go to the beach, you won't see it if you choose this option. There's free camping under the pine trees (see p 264).

If you keep your left below the access road rather than your right, you'll enter the heart of the valley and will soon discover a dramatic view of two waterfalls: **Hakalao'a**, on the left, and **Ki'ilawe**, the largest,

on the right, which has gouged a tributary valley over the course of centuries. Both waterfalls occupy an important place in Hawaiian legends – especially Ki'ilawe, which is associated with Lono, the god of agriculture. A plateau that dominates Waipi'o is cut by the bed of two rivers, the Hakalao'a and the Lalakea, channelling the rainfall between Mauna Kea and Kohala. On the edge of the plateau, the two rivers come closer – without joining – and plunge down, creating two spectacular cascades. Shortly before, the path crosses a first river (10min), then a second, making an arc of a circle to reach the beach to the west (30min).

From here, a wild trail that first climbs steadily and then runs along the sides of cliffs from valley to valley allows you to get to the **Waimanu Valley ★★** in one day. One of the most remote trails in Hawaii, with slopes streaked with seven or eight waterfalls, it is mostly frequented by hunters and die-hard hikers. You can camp here behind the beach before returning the next day, or you can head on to Pololu. This stretch of the journey is even more arduous and is reserved for experienced hikers who are not afraid of mud.

Back on Highway 19, continue driving towards Hilo. At Mile 39.5, Kalpa Road, and then Kalaniai Road, two small tourist roads, head 3mi (5km) to Kalopa Park.

Kalopa Native Forest State Park ★,

as its name indicates, is home to a rare section of mostly endemic forest covering the lower slopes of Mauna Kea. A short loop trail (0.6 mi or 1km) offers a good view. All along the trail grow 'ohi'a, kolea, with its young rose petals, and akala, the delicate Hawaiian raspberry that has lost most of its thorns with evolution. You'll also see an endemic hibiscus garden and an arboretum, founded in 1978, which has many Hawaiian plants as well as introduced plants from Polynesia. What's more, those who have a four-wheel-drive vehicle can drive on the trails climbing to the pastures overlooking the forest. You can camp at a pleasant site or rent a bungalow (see p 264).

Along Mamalahoa Highway, you will find one old plantation village after another, and for the most part, all of them preserve the memories of ancient times with their old wooden buildings and their family grocery stores. Near Mile 36, you'll pass Pa'auilo and about 8mi (15km) further, Laupahoehoe, followed by Papa'aloa, Honomu, etc.

Halfway between Honoka'a and Hilo (Mile 27.2), a short road quickly descends to **Laupahoehoe Point**, a rocky point enclosing the Laupahoehoe Bay from the west. Its name reflects its shape and its history: lau, "leaf," and pahoehoe, "lava," discharged from an eruption of Mauna Kea. From the park (washrooms, tables), situated next to a tiny port that is pounded by the swell of the sea, emerges a lovely viewpoint of the cliffs that are covered with vegetation on the Hamakua Coast. Less poetic, a monument stands in memory of 24 victims of the tsunami on April 1, 1946, children and teachers of the town school. At the point, with its sharp lava rocks, thickets of pine trees make an ideal setting to have a picnic or to camp (see p 264).

In "town" (Mile 25.2), the **Laupahoehoe Train Museum** (suggested donation $2; every day 9am to 4:30pm; 36-2377 Hwy. 19, ☎962-6300) will be of interest to old-locomotive buffs. Occupying the former residence of the Laupahoehoe stationmaster, it is devoted to the brief railroad history of the Hamakua Coast and the Big Island – brief because the lines were damaged and abandoned after the tsunami in 1946.

Just past the Pohakupuka church, a short road heads mauka towards the **World Botanical Gardens of Umauma** ($5; Mon to Sat 9am to 5:30pm; Mile 16; ☎963-5427), recently opened to the public. You'll be able to see a lovely series of three small waterfalls flowing from basin to basin (Umauma Falls), as well as a wall of orchids, and stroll along the flower-covered path dominating the Hamakua Coast.

At Mile 13.4, Highway 220 climbs to Honomu, a small farming town situated in the heart of the sugar-cane plantations, which saw better days at the beginning of the 20th century. The old Honomu Theater (1931) and a few other wooden buildings from this prosperous era are still standing. A little less than 3mi (5km) further is the **Akaka Falls' State Park ★★**, which has the highest waterfall in Hawaii. A loop trail, about 2,200ft (800m) long, first leads (to the right) to the Kahuna waterfall, which plunges 443ft (135m) in a white torrent in the middle of the jungle. Along the path, bamboo thickets, lush vegetation typical of the tropical rainforest and flowering plants create a life-size botanical garden. Via a series of steps, you will reach the great Akaka Falls, the most frequently depicted waterfall on postcards, which some legends say is the territory of the god Akaka. Particularly large after winter rainfalls (the spectacle can be a bit disappointing in summer), over the course of time, it has gorged a vast "pot" surrounded by mossy cliffs.

Instead of heading to Hilo via Highway 19, at Mile 10.9, take the **Pepe'ekeo Scenic Drive** ★ ★ on your left. For 4mi (6km), the road gently winds through the heart of the tropical vegetation, mingled with banana, palm and tulip trees. Crossing several small valleys on single-lane bridges, it offers lovely viewpoints of the rocky coast, which is lined with vegetation and pounded by the waves.

Occupied right until the beginning of the 19th century by Kahali'i, a Hawaiian fishing village, the Onomea valley then became the home of a rudimentary port that served the sugar mill it overlooked. In 1978, the founder of the **Hawai'i Tropical Botanical Garden** ★ ★ (*$15, $5 children 6 to 16, family package $35; every day 9am to 5pm; ☎964-5233, www.htbg.com*) bought it back. Returned to its original state, it then served as a dump and, before they were able to begin building the gardens, 35 car wrecks and 25 truckloads of garbage had to be removed. Twenty-five years later, filled with 2,000 species of plants,

the botanical garden, where the tropical forest meets unrestrained vegetation, is without a doubt the most beautiful in all of Hawaii. On the shores of the Onomea Stream, tumbling like small waterfalls above a forest of palm trees, heliconias, slender orchids, hibiscus sprinkling the ground, passion fruits with their heady scent, majestic banyan and bread trees abound. The trail, which is steep at first but well designed, leads right up to the seaside near the four graves of the last inhabitants of the valley. The luxuriant vegetation is the result of continuous year-long rainfall. You can borrow an umbrella at the entrance and even get sprayed with insect repellent if you so desire. After the visit (60 to 90min), you can take a look at the small museum in the visitor centre, which has all sorts of objects discovered in the valley as well as a small collection of Oriental art.

Pepe'ekeo Scenic Drive meets up with Highway 19 at Mile 7.3, shortly before reaching Hilo.

The East Coast

Hilo

(half-day to full day)

During his visit to the island in 1825, Lord Byron, through a cer-

tain lack of modesty, named the port Byron's Bay. But the inhabitants took revenge by quickly discarding this name in favour of the Hawaiian word Hilo. At the confluence of the Hamakua Coast and the region of Puna, on the way to the Volcanoes National Park, Hilo is strategically placed at the bottom of the large bay that cuts across the northeastern coast of the island. This position allowed it to shelter its main port, which was frequented by whalers, and later by merchant ships. After the two tsunamis of 1946 and 1960, it lost its role as a commercial centre to the benefit of the west coast. Nevertheless, it is still the capital of the county of Hawaii and stands in the heart of a large horticultural region – a sign of its relative humidity, which is, if not constant, quite high. Less touristic than the Kona Coast because of its climate, the town is more of a port of call than a vacation centre. This explains why it seems to have retained a certain authenticity, reaching its peak during the annual Merrie Monarch *hula* competition.

Facing the bay on several blocks of houses, the old town centre – bordered by Kamehameha Avenue on the seaward side, Keawe to the south, Haili Street to the west and Mamo to the east – which was spared by

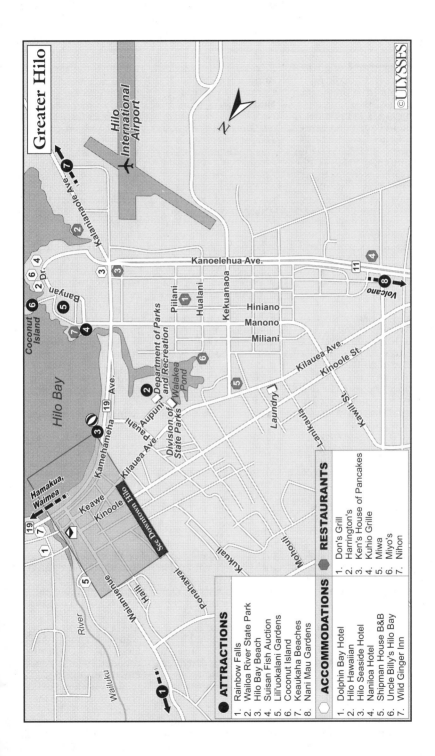

Greater Hilo

Hilo International Airport

Kanoelehua Ave.

Kanoelehua Ave.

Coconut Island

Banyan Dr.

Hilo Bay

Department of Parks and Recreation

Walakea Pond

Division of State Parks

Piilani

Hualani

Hiniano

Manono

Miliani

Kekuanaoa

Kilauea Ave.

Kinoole St.

Volcano

Kamehameha Ave.

Aupuni

Kilauea Ave.

Pauahi

Laundry

Lanikaula

Keawe

Kinoole

See Downtown Hilo

Hamakua, Waimea

Ponahawai

Kukuau

Manono

Kawili St.

Kawili St.

Waianuenue

Hall

River

Wailuku

©ULYSSES

N

● ATTRACTIONS

1. Rainbow Falls
2. Wailoa River State Park
3. Hilo Bay Beach
4. Suisan Fish Auction
5. Lili'uokalani Gardens
6. Coconut Island
7. Keaukaha Beaches
8. Nani Mau Gardens

◇ ACCOMMODATIONS

1. Dolphin Bay Hotel
2. Hilo Hawaiian
3. Hilo Seaside Hotel
4. Naniloa Hotel
5. Shipman House B&B
6. Uncle Billy's Hilo Bay
7. Wild Ginger Inn

● RESTAURANTS

1. Don's Grill
2. Harrington's
3. Ken's House of Pancakes
4. Kuhio Grille
5. Miwa
6. Miyo's
7. Nihon

the tsunamis, still has some old buildings dating from the beginning of the 20th century. A good number of them have been carefully restored by businesses that have set up shop here. They're not as interesting as the tourist office would have you believe, but a stroll through the heart of town is nevertheless pleasant. The surrounding area is particularly lively on Wednesdays and Saturdays when the market is held (see p 291).

At 130 Kamehameha Avenue, at the corner of Kalakaua Street, the old building of the First Hawaiian Bank (1930) has been occupied since the summer of 1998 by the **Pacific Tsunami Museum** ★ *(suggested donation $5; Wed to Sat 10am to 4pm; ☎935-0926, www.planet-hawaii.com/tsunami/).* The museum is devoted to natural disasters, eruptions and devastating tidal waves that have struck Hilo twice in the last half-century. You can see some old photos, a film with original footage, as well as the testimony of survivors, which sheds light on the topic.

Haili Street, *mauka*, is nicknamed Church Row for its numerous churches: Saint Joseph's Church, a pink, Mexican-style Catholic church; and Haili Church, founded at the beginning of the 19th century by the first

Protestant missionaries. At the corner of Laimana, the **Lyman Museum** ★ *($7, family package $12.50; Mon to Sat 9am to 4:30pm; 276 Haili St., ☎935-5021)* was undergoing restoration, but it was still open nevertheless. You'll discover collections of tools and Hawaiian objects placed in context by explanations on the different aspects of daily life, sports, games, beliefs, etc. The museum also houses a small section of Chinese art and, like the Bishop Museum, an exhibit devoted to the different communities that settled on the islands. Notice the Portuguese *braginha*, the ancestor of the ukulele, the colourful Korean clothing, as well as the mortar – powered by feet – used by a Chinese herbalist who lived in Puna in 1873.

Next to the museum is **Lyman Mission House** ★ *(guided tours every hour from 9:30am to 11:30am and from 1pm to 4pm),* which immerses the visitor in the day-to-day life of this family of missionaries who came to Hilo in 1832. After living in a hut for a few years, they built this house in 1839. Less than a century later, it was restored and transformed into a museum by their own daughter, Emma, whose room you can see upstairs.

The Waluku River defines the western limit of the downtown area.

Although the surrounding area is not that interesting, some guides and documents mention **Maui's Canoe**, a rock of little interest except for its legend, and the **Kalakaua Park**, on Waianuenue Avenue, where you'll find an old pond filled with hyacinths, a seated statue of the "Merrie Monarch" and a plaque commemorating the solar eclipse of July 11, 1991. Messages have been buried under the flagstone, to be opened on May 3, 2106, the date of the next total eclipse in Hilo! A little further, before the bookstore, the **Historic Stones**, one lying, the other standing, will hardly leave you with enduring memories. The legend says that Kamehameha managed to move the larger of the two, called the Naha Stone, whose estimated weight is 7,716lbs (3.5 tonnes). A prophecy declared that anyone who managed to move the stone would find boundless fame.

You'll more likely find something more satisfying by heading up Waianuenue Avenue 1.5mi (2.4km) to **Rainbow Falls** ★★. This lovely 80ft-high (24m) waterfall plunges into a large, round basin surrounded by lush vegetation. Breathtaking rainbows often extend above, formed by the refraction of light on water particles – you can see them quite well

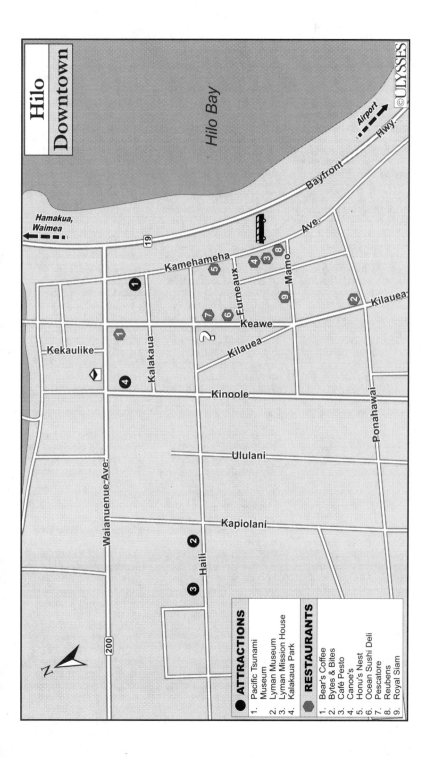

Hilo
Downtown

Hilo Bay

Hamakua,
Waimea

Bayfront Ave.

Airport
Hwy.

© ULYSSES

Kamehameha

Kekaulike

Keawe

Kalakaua

Kilauea

Kilauea

Kinoole

Ululani

Kapiolani

Haili

Furneaux

Mamo

Waianuenue Ave.

Ponahawai

N

ATTRACTIONS
1. Pacific Tsunami Museum
2. Lyman Museum
3. Lyman Mission House
4. Kalakaua Park

RESTAURANTS
1. Bear's Coffee
2. Bytes & Bites
3. Café Pesto
4. Canoe's
5. Honu's Nest
6. Ocean Sushi Deli
7. Pescatore
8. Reubens
9. Royal Siam

on sunny mornings. A legend says that the cave concealed at the base of the waterfall was once the home of Hina, the mother of Maui. The falls are part of the Wailuku River State Park, as is **Boiling Pots** ★, 1mi (1.6km) further. Via Waianuenue, crossing a residential area, then Peepee Falls Street, you will reach this area *(every day 7am to 6:30pm)*. Upstream, the Wailuku River forms a second waterfall at the cliffs, which are dotted with impatiens plants, then it flows through a series of "boiling" pools gauged in volcanic rock, whose basaltic structures you can see very clearly. Here, the name of the river makes sense: Wailuku means "destroying waters."

East of downtown, the **Wailoa River State Park** includes the Wai'akea Pond (an ancient fishpond) and a vast stretch of flat, grassy region between the flanks of the river and Kamehameha Avenue. Here, families and joggers pass by all day long, heading over the small bridges that cross the many lakes. The surrounding area, once known as Shinmachi, a neighbourhood of Japanese immigrants, suffered the most damage from the tsunami of 1946. Reached via Pi'opi'o Street, the **Wailoa Center** *(Mon to Fri and Thu to Fri 8am to 4:30pm, Wed noon to*

4:30pm and Sat 9am to 3pm) houses a centre of temporary exhibits and a gallery showing the aftermath of the 1946 and 1960 tsunamis. Just outside, a large lava-stone memorial pays homage to their victims. A little further north, on a mound, stands a black and gold statue of Kamehameha, a copy of the ones in Kapa'au and Honolulu.

Opposite the park, on the other side of the avenue, stretches **Hilo Bay Beach**, a long grey-sand beach where canoe clubs meet on Saturdays. Kamehameha launched his fleet of 800 canoes here in an unsuccessful attempt to conquer Kaua'i. Note that the water is quite murky.

Beyond the park and the mouth of the Wailoa River, the Wai'akea Peninsula defines the eastern limit of Hilo Bay. At the base of the peninsula, from Monday to Saturday, wholesalers and restaurant owners from the region come to bid for the catch of the day at the **Suisan Fish Auction** ★★. The event takes place early, but if you miss the auction, you can still buy a tuna filet at the store next door.

The peninsula is crossed from end to end by Banyan Drive, whose trees were planted by visiting celebrities of the time. A number of hotels are

clustered along the road, and at the centre of the peninsula lie the **Lili'uokalani Gardens**. This large public park commemorates the signing of a friendship treaty between Hilo and the Japanese island of O-shima with a marble monument, a Japanese garden around several lakes, and a teahouse. Unfortunately, everything is poorly maintained. More popular for a picnic or for a bit of *ulua*, tiny **Coconut Island** ★ *(washrooms, showers, picnic tables)*, called Mokulua by the ancient Hawaiians, is connected to dry land by a bridge opposite the Hilo Hawaiian Hotel. There are a few coconut trees and a lawn. In the past, there used to be a *pu'uhonua* as well as a "place of refuge." The ancient Hawaiians believed that the springs that flowed around the islet were beneficial for your health.

Continue driving east on Kalaniana'ole Avenue and you'll discover the row of **Keaukaha Beaches** ★, the playground for Hilo inhabitants on weekends. The surrounding area is occupied by one of the oldest Hawaiian Home Lands of the State and by no less than 14 former fishponds. First, there's Onekahakaha Beach Park *(washrooms, showers, picnic tables, barbecues)*, which is popular for its natural rocky basin designed for swimming; then James Kealoha Beach Park, the meeting place for fishers and surfers – and, in the evening, the place to enjoy a beer among friends. The Leleiwi Beach Park *(picnic tables, barbecues)* is just in front of the **Richardson Ocean Park** *(washrooms, showers)*, right at the end of the road, a popular place for snorkelling. Via a trail heading to the right along the coast, you reach a small peaceful beach, where you can swim, as long as you don't go too far from the shore.

On the Volcanoes National Park road, 3mi (5km) from Hilo, a large number of tour groups file through the **Nani Mau Gardens** *($10, $6 children 6 to 18; every day until 8am; 421 Makalika St., ☎959-3541)* all day long. It has a beautiful collection of orchids and typical fruit trees that are omnipresent on the islands, but the Japanese garden is tiny, and as for the rest, Nani Mau looks more like a public park than a botanical garden. Not only is the admission expensive, everything is extra.

From Highway 11 at Mile 4.1, Stainback Highway, then West Mamaki Street, lead to the **Panaewa Zoo** *(free admission; every day 9am to 4pm)*. If you have children, they will enjoy the rather small menagerie it is expand-

ing however, and take advantage of the natural tropical setting, with lemurs, white Bengal tigers, all kinds of frogs, pygmy hippopotamuses and even miniature horses!

Back on Highway 11, you'll soon cross Macadamia Road *(Mile 5.8)*, which leads 3mi (5km) through macadamia plantations to the processing factory of **Mauna Loa** *(free admission; every day 8am to 5pm; ☎966-8618)*. The Visitor Center is in fact a large souvenir shop and very popular with organized tours. Through the windows of the factory, you can see several stages of processing and packaging of nuts and chocolate macadamia nuts, but that's about it. Unless you have an irrepressible desire for nuts or for kitschy souvenirs, you might as well forego this visit.

★★
Puna

(one day)

Often ignored by visitors, Puna lies across the eastern bow of the island, just north of Volcanoes National Park. The region has suffered a lot from the fury of the volcanoes, right up to the wonderful black-sand beach of Kalapana and the town, which went up in smoke in 1990. The longer you stay, the more you'll discover one of the most au-

thentic coasts of the archipelago, with an oasis of vegetation hiding hot springs – a memorable place for a swim.

At Keaau, 7mi (11km) south of Hilo, Highway 130 veers towards Pahoa; 10mi (16km) further, don't miss the exit leading to town.

Founded in 1908 around a sawmill set up to supply crossbeams to the Santa Fe Railroad which was in the middle of construction, **Pahoa ★** sprung up in the heart of sugar-cane fields. Today surrounded by horticultural greenhouses and papaya plantations, the town retains a certain charm of bygone days. One thousand strong, the town has an old centre with wooden storefronts, connected with a long grating. The shops have been fixed up and have become restaurants, antique stores and galleries. The Akebono Theater (1910), which has also been restored, is the oldest cinema in Hawaii.

Shortly past Pahoa (Mile 11.3), Route 132, to the left, indicates Kapoho. Drive 2.5mi (4km) to Lava Tree State Park.

Crossed by a 0.6mi (1km) loop trail, the **Lava Tree State Park ★** *(washroom, picnic tables, barbecues)* protects a forest of fossilized *ohi'a* trunks that look like

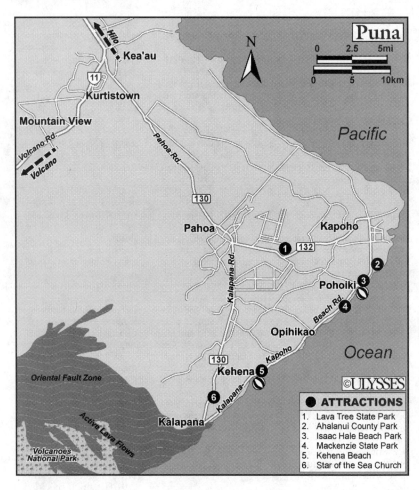

Puna

0   2.5   5mi

0   5   10km

Hilo

Kea'au

11

Kurtistown

Mountain View

Volcano Rd.

Volcano

Pahoa Rd.

Pacific

130

Pahoa

Kapoho

1   132

2

Pohoiki   3

Kalapana Rd.

Beach Rd.

4

Opihikao

Kapoho

Ocean

130

Kehena   5

Kalapana

6

Oriental Fault Zone

©ULYSSES

Kālapana

Active Lava Flows

Volcanoes National Park

● **ATTRACTIONS**

1. Lava Tree State Park
2. Ahalanui County Park
3. Isaac Hale Beach Park
4. Mackenzie State Park
5. Kehena Beach
6. Star of the Sea Church

strange, blackish termite mounds. These famous lava trees are the result of a smooth, quickly moving lava flow in 1790 that didn't have the time to instantly burn all the trunks – which explains the formation of these "mounds."

As you approach the coast, the road crosses vast lava fields, vestiges of the eruption of the Kapoho Cinder Cone in 1960. At Cape Kumukahi (reached by a track), marking the easternmost point on the Big Island and therefore the archipelago, the lava spared the lighthouse by surrounding it.

The sterility of the landscape quickly changes when you take Route 137 to the south. Near Mile 10.6, the **Ahalanui County Park** ★★★ *(7am to 7pm)*, a well-

kept secret in the middle of palm trees, has a large natural pool formed by hot springs. On weekends, many families come here to picnic between two relaxing pools that are connected to the sea.

A little further, **Isaac Hale Beach Park** ★★ is situated on the edge of the magnificent Pohoiki Bay, which is frequented by a large number of surfers, boogie-board enthusiasts and divers. From the parking area near the small port, a 550ft (200m) trail running along the coast to the south (behind the red house) leads to an incredible "bathtub" of fresh water. Hidden beneath trees slightly behind the seaside, it is ideal for a bath for two or on your own.

From the park, continue to follow the coast to the south via the sinuous and bumpy Route 137, which penetrates into magnificent dense vegetation.

After Mile 13, **Mackenzie State Park** is popular for family picnics on weekends. Camping is possible (see p 268).

At Mile 15 near the hamlet of **Opihikao**, with its pretty wooden homes beneath palm and other large trees, the Pahoa turn-off heads back to Route 130. Just past Mile 19, in the opposite direction, you'll notice a large parking area. About 270ft (100m) before, a trail (whose point of departure is indicated by a red sign marked "Government Property") quickly descends between the rocks to **Kehena Beach** ★★. This magnificent black-sand beach, next to a strip of coconut trees, is very popular.

In April 1990, the eruption of Pu'u 'O'o wiped most of **Kalapana** ★ off the face

of the earth, a town once famous for its superb black-sand beaches. The road stops here, cut across by an infinite field of lava, which goes beyond some charred remnants of the engulfed town. Access to the area is restricted due to cliffs that cross it. The *haole* (Caucasians) that live along the coast saved what they could; some homes were taken away on the back of trucks. The Catholic congregation moved its church, the tiny **Star of the Sea Church** (1929), called Painted Church because of its naive frescoes of the Nativity, which are visible on the side of Route 130 near Mile 20. The Protestants put their trust in God's will, from which a debate arose about the vanity of material possessions. For the Hawaiians, upsetting the course of events was out of the question, and according to the wishes of the population, the govern-

ment did not attempt to divert the lava flows, as it had done for Hilo in 1935. But let's face it: that didn't achieve great results.

Via Route 130, you return to Pahoa and Highway 11.

★★★
Volcanoes National Park

(two days)

In a landscape of sterile lava flows and small islands of vegetation, craters and forests of aborescent ferns, Volcanoes National Park encompasses two champions of volcanic activity: Mauna Loa, the largest volcano in the world, 13,681ft (4,170m) at its highest point, and Kilauea, which was born on its slopes as the island drifted west with the Pacific plate. Stretching more than 600 sq mi (1,550 km²), Kilauea is the most active volcano in the world. This unusual volcano does not form a cone but rather a vast caldera and a series of vent holes along a fault area extending 129mi (80km) out to sea.

The first European to witness its activity in 1823 was William Ellis, a missionary. From 1846, a temporary building welcomed the most intrepid visitors. The national park saw the light of day in 1916 and became a UNESCO

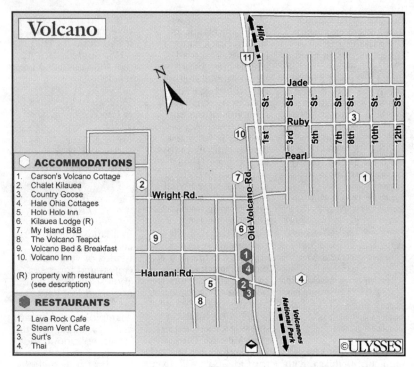

Volcano

N

Hilo

11

Jade

St.   St.   St.   St.   St.   St.   St.

Ruby

3

1st   3rd   5th   7th   8th   10th   12th

10

Pearl

ACCOMMODATIONS

1. Carson's Volcano Cottage
2. Chalet Kilauea
3. Country Goose
4. Hale Ohia Cottages
5. Holo Holo Inn
6. Kilauea Lodge (R)
7. My Island B&B
8. The Volcano Teapot
9. Volcano Bed & Breakfast
10. Volcano Inn

(R) property with restaurant
    (see descritption)

RESTAURANTS

1. Lava Rock Cafe
2. Steam Vent Cafe
3. Surt's
4. Thai

Wright Rd.

Old Volcano Rd.

Haunani Rd.

Volcanoes National Park

©ULYSSES

Biosphere Reserve in 1980. Hundreds of thousands of people now come every year to see Kilauea, which has been almost continuously erupting since 1983. No one can predict when it will stop but in the meantime, this is a unique opportunity to watch its activity from up close. Provided that you respect a few safety rules, you have nothing to fear: Kilauea is so harmless that it's the only drive-in volcano in the world!

From Hilo, Highway 11, which passes Kurtistown then Mountain View, gradually heads towards the park. Before reaching it, at Mile 27.5, a series of small, secluded roads lead on both sides of the highway to the residential neighbourhood of Volcano Village, where a number of bed and breakfasts are located. Born as a lumbering town at the beginning of the 20th century, Volcano gradually became a vacation resort, especially appreciated by artists. The park entrance lies 1mi (1.6km) further.

The checkpoint is open during the day only ($10, entrance valid for seven days; P.O. Box 52, Hawaii Volcanoes National Park HI 967180052, www.nps.gov/havo), but access is possible 24hrs a day. Before beginning the tour, allow yourself a stop at the **Visitor Cen-** **ter** *(every day 7:45am to 5pm, ☎985-6000)* located just past the checkpoint. You'll be able to obtain useful information about the hiking trails and the latest news about volcanic activity–to find out if it is possible to see the lava flow. A small exhibit presents the different types of lava found in the park and two short films are shown. You can also consult an interactive monitor that provides a variety of interesting information about the park.

The Visitor Center offers 45min guided walking tours twice a day by the edge of the Kilauea caldera, a good

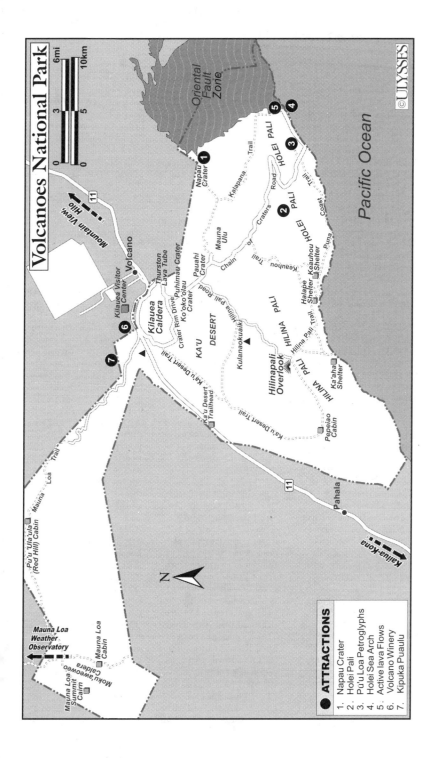

Volcanoes National Park

Mountain View, Hilo

Oriental Fault Zone

Pacific Ocean

Napaū Crater

Kalapana Trail

HOLEI PALI

HOLEI PALI

Chain of Craters Road

Mauna Ulu

Pauahi Crater

Keauhou Trail

Keauhou Shelter

Puna Coast Trail

Halape Shelter

Thurston Lava Tube

Puhimau Crater

Ko'oko'olau Crater

Crater Rim Drive

Kilauea Visitor Center

Volcano

Kilauea Caldera

Hilina Pali Road

KA'U DESERT

Kulanaokuaiki

HILINA PALI

Hilinapali Overlook

Hilina Pali Trail

HILINA PALI

Ka'aha Shelter

Ka'u Desert Trail

Ka'u Desert Trailhead

Pepeiao Cabin

Ka'u Desert Trail

Mauna Loa Trail

Pu'u 'Ula'ula (Red Hill) Cabin

Mauna Loa Cabin

Mauna Loa Summit Cairn

Moku'aweoweo Caldera

Mauna Loa Weather Observatory

Kailua-Kona

Pahala

N

© ULYSSES

0   3   6mi
0   5   10km

ATTRACTIONS

1. Napau Crater
2. Holei Pali
3. Pu'u Loa Petroglyphs
4. Holei Sea Arch
5. Active lava Flows
6. Volcano Winery
7. Kipuka Puaulu

opportunity to learn about the plants, animals and beliefs associated with this site. Departures take place at the Visitor Center. Longer guided hiking tours are also organized as well as very interesting films, once a week in the evening (in the auditorium), on a variety of themes – lava fountains, meteorology in the park, etc. For schedules, consult the program on the centre's notice board.

Not far away, the **Volcano Art Center** (every day 9am to 5pm; ☎967-7565), an arts and crafts gallery, occupies an old wooden building dating from 1877, the location of the first real hotel of the park. At the end of the 19th century, it cost $5 – a good price at the time – to stay in one of its six rooms and have dinner before being driven in the evening to the edge of the lava lake that was then in the Halema'uma'u crater. When there were too many people, the last ones to arrive slept in the entrance near the chimney or under the porch, which was a lot cooler…

From the Visitor Center starts Crater Rim Drive, one of the park's two roads, which make the tour of the Kilauea caldera. Crater Rim Trail runs parallel to Crater Rim Drive for its entire length (11.5 mi or 18.5km).

The first stop is usually at the **Sulphur Banks** ★, whose sulphurous vent holes create a tableau of yellow spots. A 1,350ft (500m) trail leads to the visitor centre and another (Iliahi Trail) heads in the opposite direction to the rim of the caldera (1,650ft or 600m). Near the departure, fumaroles leak out from the depths of the earth. They appear out of cracks created by landslides heading towards the crater. Rainwater seeps into the crevices and turns into vapour as soon as is it comes into contact with the deep rock that is still hot. Back on Crater Rim Drive, you'll discover other vent holes (Steam Vents) at a spot where a short trail allows you to reach the bank of the caldera. The hot temperature of the ground makes it difficult for trees to grow here.

Past the military camp, the chapel and the cinema, the road heads close to the rim of the immense **Kilauea caldera** ★★, which has a diameter of more than 2mi (3km). Lower down (400ft or 120m) is a desolate surface full of holes created by the unavoidable fumeroles. Ten thousand years ago, Kilauea most likely had a summit. An explosion probably contributed to the creation of a first caldera, formed by the collapse of the magma reservoir inside the mountain.

Then it gradually filled with lava after successive eruptions, followed by lulls that could last several centuries. The last period of intense activity began with an explosion in 1790 that formed the Halema'uma'u crater on the floor of the caldera – and killed some of the troops that were led by Keoua, cousin of Kamehameha, in the Ka'u desert.

You'll soon reach the **Hawaiian Volcano Observatory** (closed to the public; hvo.wr.usgs.gov), the worthy inheritor of the first observatory built in 1912 on the current site of Volcano House. The centre has volcanologists, seismologists and geochemists who all watch Kilauea's activity while trying to improve their understanding of volcanoes. A cable connecting the observatory to a seismograph set up on the floor of the caldera takes the earth's pulse.

Next to the observatory, the **Thomas A. Jaggar Museum** ★★ (free admission; every day 8:30am to 5pm; ☎985-6049) bears the name of one of the first volcanologists to have developed surveillance methods and volcanic activity prediction at the beginning of the 20th century. You can explore an interesting exhibit devoted to the geology of the island and park, with an introduction to the different

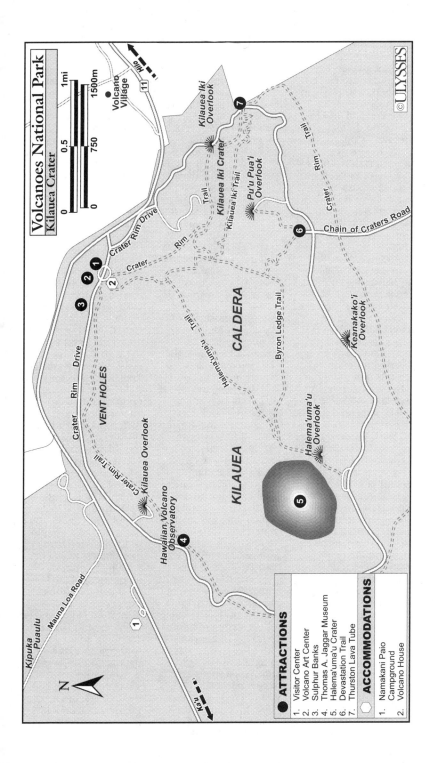

Volcanoes National Park
Kilauea Crater

ATTRACTIONS

1. Visitor Center
2. Volcano Art Center
3. Sulphur Banks
4. Thomas A. Jaggar Museum
5. Halema'uma'u Crater
6. Devastation Trail
7. Thurston Lava Tube

ACCOMMODATIONS

1. Namakani Paio Campground
2. Volcano House

N

© ULYSSES

types of lave and volcanic emissions. The last eruption, which began in January 1983, is quite detailed and information on its weekly progress is provided. You can also see a short film showing old footage of the volcano and watch in real time the work of seven seismographs measuring the activity of the different areas of the park.

From the esplanade, the view looks down on **Halema'uma'u Crater ★ ★**, Pele's legendary abode. The activity was concentrated here during a period of a little less than 200 years, causing a dozen eruptions in periods of a few hours to several months. A lava lake, with variable levels, appeared here in 1823 and was described by Mark Twain during his visit to the islands. Its sudden disappearance into the depths in 1924, following an explosion that doubled the size of the crater, put an end to the romantic custom of picnics on the banks wearing crinoline petticoats... Postcards, burnt at the edges by the volcanic beast for more authenticity, were all the rage at the time. For 50 years, the crater had a rapid succession of eruptions, whose paroxysm was embodied by over 30ft-high (10m) lava fountains, in 1952 (during 136 days) and again in 1967, during no less than eight months. The first of

these two episodes was enough to nearly fill the crater, which went from 1,280ft (390m) in depth to only 100ft (30m), its current state. In 1974, "embankments" created along the fault lines by a succession of small lava fountains appeared in the caldera. One last small eruption occurred in 1982, lasting only 19hrs, then the activity definitely confirmed its shifting on the eastern slopes of Kilauea, where it continues today without respite.

After the museum, the road, crossing the Kilauea fault zone, makes a loop around the Halema'uma'u crater. In the hollows of lava, remnants of the 1974 eruption, a few ferns are taking root, an imitation of the appearance of life on earth. From the large parking lot, a short trail (750ft or 300m), leading through the desolate surface of the lava, paralyzed with solfatara which emit the smell of rotten eggs, allows you to approach the bank. At the bottom of the vast basin, which is 2,625ft (800m) in diameter, you can make out fumaroles and sulphurous vent holes – some of the them are bright yellow. On the rim, offerings to Pele have often been laid: *lei*, cigarettes, shells and sometimes even piglets are offered to the divine appetite. In the crater, volcanologists have even found de-

formed but intact bottles of gin swallowed by the lava. Beyond the access trail, the 3mi (5km) Halema'uma'u Trail heads to Volcano House, crossing right through the caldera.

Bordering the southern limit of the gored crater, Crater Rim Drive goes beyond the small Keanakako'i crater, which was partially filled in 1877 and 1974. Hawaiians had made a rock quarry out of it to make their tools. The road soon meets the *ohi'a* forest and reaches a junction. Chain of Craters Road begins on your right and heads all the way down the coast, while **Devastation Trail ★** begins on your right. After 0.6mi (1km), the trail crosses an area devastated by the eruption of Kilauea Iki, a crater adjacent to the Kilauea caldera, where the activity was concentrated in 1959. Large lava fountains, which bubbled for 36 days, formed a 165ft-high (50m) cinder cone and covered a section of Crater Rim Drive. The highest reached 1,900ft (579m)! All along the trail are bleached tree trunks destroyed by a shower of pumice stones mixed with cinders. The surrounding area is home to the *nene*, Hawaii's national goose, which is now protected from extinction. At the end, the trail reaches Pu'upua'i Overlook, also accessible by the road, which dominates

Renewal of Life

There seems to be no sign of life on the desolate surface of the cooling lava. While the abundant ashes of the dangerous "explosive" volcanoes make for soil fertile, the type of volcanoes found in Hawaii, known as "effusive" volcanoes, turn the land into rock.

Yet life infiltrates everywhere as soon as it is able to. The first signs of life are found in the *pahoehoe* lava flows: condensation in the steamy vents creates small puddles of warm water where microscopic creatures begin to grow. Algae, carried by the wind, also make their home here. When the water evaporates, the spores are carried away by trade winds in search of new miniature worlds. In the same way, in the cracks of the magma, condensation of vapour when it comes into contact with cool air brings water, the essential ingredient for life. Some of the first plants to appear are tiny mosses, which are only about 1/100th of an inch (3mm) long. As they decompose, they become food for insects and molluscs. Then the birds arrive, and the life cycle begins anew.

the depths of the cool crater.

Passing through a beautiful forest of *ohi'a* and aborescent ferns, which are often surrounded in a nourishing mist, Crater Rim Drive reaches one of the most visited sites of the park, **Thurston Lava Tube** ★★ *(Nahuku)*. This former lava tunnel, created 350 to 500 years ago, formed when the eruption was losing its intensity and no longer allowed the lava to flow in contact with the cooling air. It is facing towards the north. More than 6.6ft (2m) of annual precipitation nourishes lush vegetation here, with magnificent *hapu'u*

ferns. The trail, which overflows with groups during the day, soon reaches the tunnel, whose main 16.4ft (5m) tube is lit for more than 330ft (100m). Rainwater seeps through the rock, dripping on visitors and allowing small ferns to grow on the ceiling. You can explore the longest and usually ignored part of the 2,000ft-long (300m) tunnel, provided that you come equipped with a flashlight. Simply push the door located at the main exit.

From the parking lot, on the other side of the road, begins the Kilauea Iki Trail, a 2.4mi (3.9km) loop trail that crosses the crater

before reaching Byron Ledge Trail. You can also reach Volcano House via the Crater Rim Trail, which passes by the place where the Crater Rim Trail was once located before it partially collapsed in the caldera in 1983. On the left-hand side, a lookout allows you to scope the hilly landscape you are about to descend.

The loop of Crater Rim Drive ends at the park entrance.

The second road that is open to the public, Chain of Craters Road, begins a bit further to the south. You can head in this direction after having visited the Thurston Lava

Hawaii – Big Island

Tube by retracing your path, or choose to come back here another day to spend more time.

The first part of the **Chain of Craters Road** ★★ passes the string of craters that gave it its name: Lua Manu, the impressive Puhimau and Ko'olo'olau, which is overgrown with vegetation.

After 2mi (3km), the short **Hilina Pali Road** veers right to the Kulanaokuaiki campground (5 mi or 8km), and then reaches Hilina Pali (9mi or 14km). From one spot to the other, hikers head to the remote coast from Ka'aha park (3.6 mi or 5.8km) or at Halape (7.9 mi or 12.8km), a coral beach dotted with palm trees at the foot of a rocky barrier. Hilina Pali Road is often closed during periods of reproduction or droughts.

Back on the main road, you'll pass more or less recent lava flows and other craters: Hi'iaka and Pauahi. From the parking lot of the latter begins the **Napau Trail** ★, which runs along Kilauea's eastern fault zone that stretches from the summit of the caldera to 50mi (80km) out to sea. Pu'u Huluhulu appeared on this fault line 400 years ago in the crater that was overgrown with ferns – a short trail (1.5mi or 2.4km) leads to its summit. The trail

then passes near Mauna Ulu, which means "mountain that grows" in Hawaiian. Its eruption, from 1969 to 1974, one of the most prolific of the 20th century, completely cut off the former Chain of Craters Road. Further on, you'll reach the immense double crater of Makaopuhi, which is very deep and 500 years old, then the Napau crater (7mi or 11.2km). The location of regular eruptions, Napau had a short episode of lava fountains in January 1997. From here you can see Pu'u 'O'o's smoking summit, the site of the current eruption. The area is very unstable and ridden with numerous faults.

Another trail, leaving before the Chain of Craters Road, reaches **Keauhou** (6.8mi or 10.8km) on the remote coast, where a few patches of black sand are nestled between the rocks by the seaside and beyond Halape (8.4 mi or 13.5km). Both have a shelter, a rainwater recovery system and rudimentary washrooms.

All along the descent to the sea, the road crosses an increasingly lunar landscape, with lava everywhere. Parking lots often reveal viewpoints of the coast, which now spreads below, each time detailing a few points of geological history of the park. Past two

Lava

There are two types of lava: *'a'a* and *pahoehoe*, two Hawaiian terms that are today used by volcanologists around the world. The first type, which appears sporadically, takes the form of metallic scoria. It is formed when rocks fuse with lava at the end of its journey, without or almost without gas; as the lava cools, it forms a rough, jagged surface. The second type of lava, *pahoehoe*, is typical of long eruptions. This type of lava flows in a more fluid way. Like a wave of caramel, it traps obstacles in its way, creating a smooth, shiny-looking surface forming waves in places. The chemical composition of the two types of lava is identical; in fact, it is common for *pahoehoe* to change to *'a'a*.

sharp turns, sea level is nearly reached. Past Mile 14, you'll notice the two kinds of lava seen most often in Hawaii, shiny *pahoehoe* and dull, black *'a'a* chaotically tumbling down the heights of the **Holei Pali** cliff in a cascade formed by the eruption of Mauna Ulu.

In the vicinity of Mile 16.5, a 0.6mi (1km) one-way trail leads across a former flow at the **Pu'u Loa Petroglyphs ★★**. Several thousand drawings have been carved here on the rock, of which only about 30 are actually legible. Most of them represent human forms, including an unexpected one of a surfer. At this spot, holes were dug in the lava where fathers would place a part of the umbilical cord of new-borns to guarantee a long life.

As soon as you reach the coast, the road climbs towards the north along the cliffs pounded by waves. On your way, take a look at the **Holei Sea Arch ★**, created by the insidious undermining process of the waves. A little further, everything suddenly stops. The asphalt road, which once ran to Hilo, is cut across by recent lava flows for more than 6mi (10km). Here, two huts have been built by the park services, with a guard on duty who provides explanations about the eruption – and lends his telescope, if necessary, to better see the **current flow ★★★**.

Since July 1997, the flow has been situated more than 3mi (5km) from the end of the road, too great a distance to really see anything, even from the lookout built 825ft (300m) from the guard station. Since September 1999, the lava no longer reached the sea, which deprived visitors of the spectacle of the gigantic coils of vapour laden with hydrochloric acid that formed on contact with the ocean. But when you visit, the scenario may be reversed.

Some don't hesitate to travel the distance on foot to get close to the molten lava. It's not impossible, but it is advisable to take certain precautions, outlined by a brochure distributed on site. You have to walk across a solidified flow, which is sometimes still hot beneath the hardened surface; good shoes are therefore a must. You'll also have to take along a flashlight, without which it is impossible to return after nightfall. While waiting for conditions to change, which will certainly happen, the best thing to do is still to come at night. That way you'll be able to see the orange-coloured aura of the flow from afar. If you're hoping to see large lava fountains, the view might be a bit disappointing. West of the park entrance, those who have the time can take (at Mile 30.1) Pi'i Mauna Drive, where you'll find the **Volcano Winery** *(every day 10am to 5:30pm;* ☎*967-7479)*, whose wines are mostly made without grapes – which would have difficulty growing at this altitude.

At Mile 30.8, just past the golf course, Launa Loa Road climbs the lower slopes of the volcano. Since 1832, it has begun erupting on 37 occasions, the last time being in 1984. On the way, the road passes the forest-bird reserve of **Kipuka Pualulu ★**, set up on a *kipuka*, a 100 acre (40ha) islet of vegetation spared by the former lava flow. A 1.2mi (1.9km) long trail crosses the forest where the songs of birds resonate. They are so tiny and fast that it's very difficult to spot them.

Mauna Loa Road climbs tight curves for 13.5mi (21.7km) up to the Mauna Loa Lookout, perched at 6,663ft (2,031m). The viewpoint, however, is not that impressive since the mass of the "long mountain" blocks the view. The end of the road marks the beginning of the **Mauna Loa Trail**, which allows you to reach the summit after 19.6mi (31.6km) – a three-day hike, two days to climb up and one day to climb down (see p 253).

★
Ka'u

(half-day to full day)

It is here, in an austere setting of lava and coasts swept by waves, that the first Hawaiians are thought to have arrived. To the south, a few fertile valleys disappear into the land, but the coast is for the most part sparsely populated and the centres of interest are few and far between. Ka'u means "warm wind," alluding to the *vog* laden with sulphur and hydrochloric acid that constantly blows from the volcano.

To the south of the Volcanoes National Park entrance, the road crosses a monotonous stretch dominated by the lava and the *'ohi'a*, with red flowers somewhat enlivening the landscape at the end of spring. The infertile land is explained by the fact that this windy region is constantly swept by the *vog*. At Mile 37.7 is the beginning of the **Ka'u Desert** trail, which reaches the coast in 16.6mi (26.7km) via the Hilina Pali Overlook. With the sun beating down on the lava, winds and sometimes violent downpours, the desolate landscape here is reserved for experienced hikers. Less than 2mi (3km) further, the road leaves the enclosure of the Volcanoes National Park.

As you head down towards the south, the lava, which is older here, has gradually become overgrown with vegetation. At Mile 51.2, a turn-off leads to the town of Pahala. At the stop sign, turn right onto Pikake Street then continue for 4.5mi (7km) across the macadamia plantations.

Shortly after entering the forest, stone markers indicate the entrance to **Wood Valley Temple ★★** (☎928-8539), from its Tibetan name **Nechung Dorje Drayang Ling** ("immutable island of melodious sound"). At the heart of a vast clearing

Green Sea Turtle

in a peaceful setting, this small, red saffron-wood temple has occupied the building of an old Japanese mission since 1973, which was founded by immigrants who came to work in the Wood Valley at the beginning of the 20th century. Established under the supervision of the oracle Nechung, it was consecrated by the Dalai Lama himself in 1980 (he came back here in 1994). The temple is both a centre for the spreading of Buddhist thought and a retreat (see p 271). At each end of the portico

surrounding the stairs, notice the heads of white elephants, symbols of purity.

Back on the main road, you'll cross vast stretches of pastures and other macadamia plantations growing on former lava flows. At Mile 55.8, don't miss taking the turn-off leading to **Punalu'u Black Sand Beach Park ★★**, which protects a long beach of jet-black volcanic sand beside a screen of coconut trees. This is one of the places in the archipelago where it is easier to see the rare green Hawaiian turtle, which comes to feed on algae growing in the shallow waters near the coast – a gushing spring at sea level stimulates their growth. Have a seat on the rocky promontory overlooking the beach from the south and wait until they come to breathe at the surface. Sometimes the creatures even climb up onto the land to sunbathe. In addition to green turtles, you can occasionally see hawksbill turtles that come to lay their eggs on the beach at night. Camping is possible *(showers, washrooms)*, but the site is windy and lacks privacy – the first groups arrive starting at 9 or 10am.

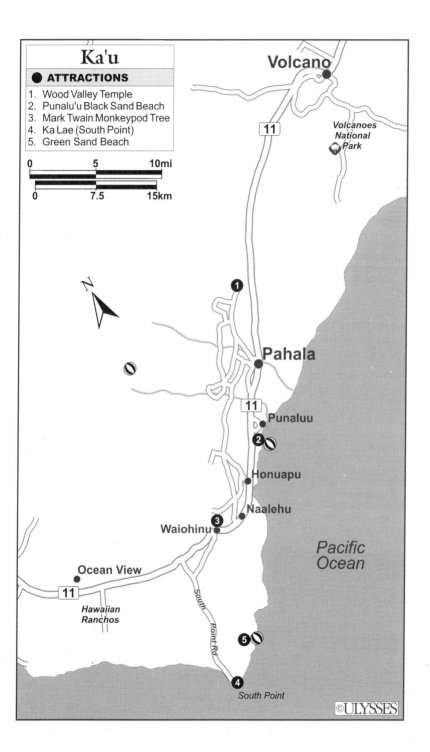

About 9mi (14km) further, Mamalahoa Highway reaches Na'alehu, then Wai'ohinu, two small towns nestled in a green valley that, compared to the lanscape you just left behind, will look like a true oasis.

Wai'ohinu has the distinction of being the southernmost town in the United States. At Mile 65.3, the Mark Twain Cafe (see p 287) is popular with tourists stopping along the road from Hilo to Kona. The hut stands next to a large *monkeypod* planted in 1866 by Mark Twain during his visit by horse. Uprooted by a storm in 1957, the tree survived by growing new roots. That is the site's only draw.

At Mile 69.5, a turn-off heads 10mi (16km) to **Ka Lae ★**, South Point, the most southerly point in the United States, remote and often overlooked, pounded by waves and winds. The first Polynesian settlers are said to have arrived here. Besides the logical aspect, considering the geographical location of Ka Lae, excavations have conclusively revealed human presence during the eighth century and probably as early as the third century. In more recent times, Ka Lae nearly became the unlikely base for launching space shuttles – made possible due to the fact that equatorial and polar orbits were

both attainable. A field of windmills stands at mid-point.

Shortly before arriving, there's a fork in the road past a sign marked "Kalae National Historic Landmark District."

On the right, you'll soon reach a parking lot and South Point Park, a stone's throw from Ka Lae itself. Near a wharf, with pulleys and ladders, 40ft (12m) below, many fishers sit on the rocks, which are splashed with sea spray. Standing out to the north are the black cliffs of Kulani and the slopes of Mauna Loa, whose summit often plays hide and seek. At the point, at the foot of a signal station, the Kalalea *heiau* faces the open sea. Shell offerings and *lei* have been placed on the small altar. Down below, a sign indicates the astonishing "buttonholes" dug into the rocks by the ancient Hawaiians to moor their canoes.

Further east are two burial sites. If you continue a bit further, you'll come across Lua o Palahemo, a large natural well in the shape of a sinkhole dug behind the coast. Its level changes with the tides. The area of South Point is infested with flies, which can make walking very unpleasant.

Via the fork on the left, you'll soon be within sight of a small infor-

mation centre, across from which visitors are allowed to park. The stand provides information on Mahana Beach, more commonly known as **Green Sand Beach ★★**, a stunning beach with greenish-grey sand mostly composed of olivine. It is located about 45min from here (1hr if you walk slowly).

Since the end of 1999, it is forbidden to come here by four-wheel-drive vehicle and a gate blocks the entrance of the track to make sure that no one disregards the ban. First head down via the road, then a large dirt path up to Kaulana Bay, 5min away, where an approach ramp for fishers is located. The trail leading to the beach begins east of the bay. The easy trail runs along the coast through a rather bleak landscape of coastline swept by waves and ancient lava flows. Only in winter is it enhanced by the presence of a few slender golden plovers. A rocky barrier gradually emerges in front of you: the summit of cliffs bordering Green Sand Bay. At times, several tracks crisscross each other, but all of them head in the same direction. To get there by the shortest way, it's usually best to stay near the coast. You'll finally reach the ridge dominating the cove, surrounded by crumbling volcanic rocks to the west and a tuff cliff (compressed ashes) to the east. The simplest way to head down to the beach is to follow the ridge to the centre and let yourself "slide" down the steep slope – being careful not to hurtle down too fast...

At Mile 81 on Highway 11, **Manuka State Park** *(washrooms, picnic tables)* has a former arboretum from the 1930s crisscrossed by a 2mi (3km) loop trail. On the way, between the forest and lava flows, you'll discover a crater hidden by a canopy of ferns.

Further on, the road reaches the south coast of Kona.

Outdoor Activities

Swimming

The young age of the island means that its coasts are not yet trimmed with endless beaches like those of the rest of the archipelago. Calmer and much sunnier, the **Kona Coast** from Honaunau to Kawaihae is unquestionably the best place for swimming.

In Kona itself, take advantage of the **Kamakahonu** beach

facing the Kamehameha hotel, ideal for children, and towards Keauhou, **Kahalu'u** beach, which is a popular place to snorkel. North of the town, the most pleasant area of the coast to enjoy a dip is at **Mahai'ula Beach** (in good weather), in the Kona Coast State Park.

However, the most beautiful beaches are located on the Kohala Coast, logically where the main tourist resorts have now opened: **Anaeho'omalu Beach**, at Waikoloa Resort, where you can watch the fish in total safety, and better yet, the superb **Hapuna Beach**, which has a sandy bottom (be careful in rough weather). Its neighbour at the foot of Mauna Kea Resort, **Kauna'oa Beach**, is ideal for swimming thanks to its protective reef. Just to the north, the same goes for Spencer Beach Park, whose waters are almost always calm.

Swimming on the east coast is mostly limited to places near Hilo: **Coconut Island**, where the water is quite shallow; and the sandy-bottomed basin of **Onekahakaha Beach County Park**, which is very popular (be careful during strong tides since the waves can go over the pier); **Richardson Ocean Park**, located next to the Beach County Park. Unique of its kind, don't miss Ahalanui Park in the

district of Puna, where you'll find an exceptional pool that was built around 95°F (35°C) hot springs and, nearby, the natural "bathtub" of **Isaac Hale Beach Park** (Pohoiki Bay).

Surfing and Boogie Boarding

The Big Island is not really the best place for surfing. As a general rule, the best conditions are found on the west and north coasts in winter, where **Kahalu'u Bay** and the site of **Pinetrees** (about 1 mi or 1.6km south of Natural Energy Lab), Lyman's and Banyan's are located. Boogie and surf boarders flock en masse to **White Sands Beach** or **Hapuna Beach** when the waves swell up (watch out for currents on both beaches). Hapuna Beach is ideal for beginners when the sea is calm – as is its neighbour **Kauna'oa Beach**, at the foot of the Mauna Kea Resort. In Kona, even though the conditions are not ideal, you'll find several schools, including: **Ocean Eco Tours** (☎*937-0494*) and **Hawaii Lifeguard Surf Instructors** (☎*324-0442*). To the east of the island, where the waves arrive in summer, the picture is even easier to paint. Surfers and bodyboarders come to

Honoli'i Beach Park, just north of Hilo at the mouth of the Honoli'i River.

Scuba Diving and Snorkelling

The Big Island has advantages over its sister islands, starting with the clarity of its water (less beaches mean less sand) and some of its sites are practically untouched and accessible only by boat. Here, like in the rest of the archipelago, the underwater rocky formations (arches, caves, tunnels, canyons, etc.) form an endless playground, frequented by a great variety of reef fish and often turtles, manta rays and dolphins. Diving (*$70*) and snorkelling (*$40*) with the manta rays at the foot of **Kona Surf Resort** is offered by many companies. You'll often encounter more than 10 of these giants who come to feed on moonless nights on the plankton mass attracted by the hotel's underwater floodlights.

The Kona Coast is still the best place for diving and snorkelling. From the north to the south, you will find good sites everywhere: Mahukona Beach Park (during calm weather, off the old wharf), Spencer Beach State Park (where there are

often turtles to the south), Kauna'oa Beach (at the end on the left), Hapuna Beach (the cove north of the beach), Anaeho'omalu Bay, Kona Coast State Park, Kona, opposite the King Kamehameha Hotel, White Sands, Kahalu'u, Kealakekua Bay and Honanunau (during calm weather). Of all these sites, the last three stand out: **Kahalu'u**, whose bay is protected in mild weather by the remnants of a former Hawaiian fishpond, is frequented by an array of Moorish idols, parrot fish, moray eels, butterfly fish, whistlers and turtles; and **Honaunau**, just next to Pu'uhonua o Honaunau, is also superb (but avoid it in rough seas). Trips to Kealakekua Bay and Pawai Bay are detailed in the paragraph devoted to sea tours (see p 251).

You can easily rent equipment for a small price. **Snorkel Bob's** (*Ali'i Dr., near Huggo's, every day 8am to 5pm;* ☎*329-0770*), the most well-known store, is also found here, with possible return trips on the neighbouring islands.

To the east, the beaches of **Keaukaha**, right next to Hilo, are the most suitable for diving – especially at Richardson's Ocean Park where you can sometimes see turtles and dolphins, and at Onekahakaha Beach Park, in the small cove

situated to the west, regularly frequented by locals. Further south is another unique site: **Punalu'u Black Sand Beach**, where there are a large number of green turtles. The water is cold due to the springs, which they are drawn to, and the currents are sometimes violent, especially south of the beach, but meeting turtles beneath the water is an extraordinary experience. Make sure you don't touch them or get too close.

Scuba diving generally costs $80 to $90.

Water Sports

Unlike O'ahu or Maui, **windsurfing** is not very common on the Big Island. Among one of the few suitable sites is Anaeho'omalu Bay, where you can take lessons or rent equipment.

One of the most popular **kayak** tours is the one that crosses Kealakekua Bay up to the monument of Captain Cook. **Kona Boy's Kayaks** (☎*328-1234*), at Mile 112.4 on Highway 11 rents boats at reasonable prices: $25 for 24hrs for a one-seat and $40 for a two-seat kayak. This includes a life jacket, a mask and fins, an icebox, and they'll even put the kayak on the roof of your car for you! The best thing to do is spend the night and then head out on the bay early the next day – that's when there are less people and more dolphins. You can also rent a kayak at **Kealakekua Bay Kayak** (☎323-3329), situated beside the McDonald's restaurants, or at **Ocean Safaris Kayaks** (☎326-4699), which is a bit more expensive. Organized tours are also becoming more and more popular.

Only one company in Kona (UFO, ☎325-5UFO) offers **parascending** outings. Depending on the company, they cost between $35 and $50, which is a bit expensive considering its duration (maximum 10min).

Deep-Sea Fishing

Since the launching of the Hawai'i International Billfish Tournament in 1959, **Kona** has become synonymous with deep-sea fishing. It is hands down the best place in the archipelago to enjoy this activity – and one of the excellent sites in the Pacific to catch one of the huge blue marlins that haunt the offshore waters. Except for record catches, most are released in order to protect reserves. The best season stretches from March until October and, apart from

marlin, aficionados focus on *mahi-mahi*, tuna and *ono*. **Honokohau** Harbor, next to Kailua-Kona, is becoming more and more popular for deep-sea fishing and there are numerous tour operators here.

Many only have one boat. The prices begin at less than $100 for a half-day on a shared boat and climb up to $600 per day for the most recent chartered models. With some companies, it is possible to combine fishing and snorkelling. **Charter Services Hawai'i** (☎334-1881) is a reservation service offering about 10 well-maintained boats.

Cruises and Whale-Watching

These very popular tours lead to two magnificent snorkelling sites: the bays of **Kealakekua** and **Pawai** (*between Kailua-Kona and Honokohau Harbor*), two marine reserves. Pawai is frequented by many reef fish and sometimes turtles and manta rays. Kealakekua is known for its rather tame dolphins. You can get there with **Fair Wind** (☎322-2788) and **Body Glove** (☎326-7122) on a large high-profile catamaran ($50 to $80 depending on the length of the tour), or with **Lanakila** (*$64,*

☎326-6000). The prices are only slightly cheaper for trips on inflatable dinghies (*$50-$65*) with **Captain Zodiac** (☎329-3199), **Sea Quest** (☎329-7238) or once again Fair Wind. You'll rarely save more than $5 by booking with agencies. To enjoy the depths of the ocean, you might prefer the comfort of a glass-bottomed boat (*$20,* **Kailua Bay Charter Company**, *☎324-1749, departures every hour from 10am to 2pm from Kona Pier*), a submarine of **Atlantis** (*$70 to $80, departure at 10m from Kona Pier, ☎800-548-6262*), or even the **Nautilus** (☎326-2003), which is a cross between a glass-bottomed boat and a submarine.

If you prefer to watch the waves and the coast, **Kamanu Charters** (☎329-2021) offers 3.5hr catamaran rides. A bit too simple? In winter, count on whales. One of the most highly recommended companies, **Whale Watch Learning Adventures** (*$50 for 3hrs;* ☎322-0028), has been created by a marine biology specialist (*departs from Honokohau Harbor*). Many of the boats have a hydrophone to broadcast the whale songs. During off-season, you can also head out to look for dolphins on small boats (*$42 to $70,* **In To Spirit**, ☎936-1470).

To end this long list of options, we should

mention dinner-cruises, which are also still popular. The prices range between $45 and $50. Among the most popular are **Captain Bean's Dinner Cruise** (☎329-5541) aboard a replica of a high-profile Polynesian canoe equipped with sails.

Cycling

The **Big Island Mountain Bike Association** (P.O. box 6819, Hilo HI 96720-8934, ☎961-4452, www.interpac.net/mtbike) publishes a brochure presenting the different possibilities of mountain-bike rides on the Big Island, from a simple ride of a few miles (3km) on a paved road to rides of more than 43mi (70km) through pastures, reserved for experienced cyclists (Mana Road, around the north of Mauna Kea). Mauna Kea Mountain Bikes (☎883-0130) in Waimea organizes bike trips, from the simple trip down to Hawi to "Mauna Kea Kamikaze," a wild trip down the summit of the "white mountain." Prices vary depending on the number of participants ($45 to $115). The company also rents bikes ($30 per day, $25 per day for two to four days, $20 per day for five to seven days, $130 per week).

Golf

With 19 courses (including two nine-holes), the island is the second best equipped after O'ahu. Most of them are found between Kona and Waimea, especially along the Kohala Coast where there is the largest concentration of high-calibre golf courses in the world. All of them have stunning, meticulously well-kept greens, which is in stark contrast with the obvious hostility of the lava flows on which they were built. If you have to choose one, make it the **Mauna Kea Beach Golf Club**. Green fees vary greatly according to the type of establishment. The golf courses of the tourist resorts are obviously the most expensive; they can be as high as $200 (usually –40% for hotel guests), except for the **Waikoloa Village Golf Club** ($80; ☎883-9621), which is not on the coast but, as its name indicates, in Waikoloa Village.

The best prices are offered by the most remote courses or those located in less sunny regions: **Waimea Country Club** ($65, $45 seniors; ☎885-8777), with lakes, eucalyptus trees and frequent drizzle; **Volcano Country Club** ($60; ☎967-7331), where it might not be very hot; **Sea**

Mountain Golf Courses, lost in Punalu'u ($40; ☎928-6222). With a few rare exceptions, green fees include the use of a golf cart. Most clubs offer attractive reduced fees (twilight) if you play during the warmer hours of the day.

Hiking

With its geographical diversity, no other island of the archipelago is more suitable for hiking than the Big Island. In ancient times, the Big Island was circled by the Ala Loa, a coastal trail that allowed you to make your way around the island. **King's Trail** was built on this base by the first settlers and still runs along part of the Kona Coast – at times, you can follow it in the Kona Coast State Park in particular (from Mahai'ula to Kua Bay). Still on the western coast, the most popular hike is no doubt the one that leads to **Kealakekua Bay** (less than 2hrs return). You can also walk along the coast between Pu'uhonua o Honaunau and Ho'okena.

Further north is the hike down to **Waipi'o**, but it cannot really be called a hike – rather, a challenging walk. Same thing to reach the **Pololu Valley**, although the trail is paved, at least. The trail connecting the two valleys by **Waimanu** (Muliwai Trail) is reserved for seasoned hikers – mud and steep climbs guaranteed.

The largest playground for hiking-lovers is unquestionably at the **Volcanoes National Park**. You'll find some 150mi (240km) of trails of varying difficulty, from the short walk from Devastation Trail (0.6mi or 1km) to the difficult three-day hike up to Mauna Loa (see below). Between the two extremes are all the paths running through the central craters – Kilauea Iki Trail, Halema'uma'u Trail, Crater Rim Trail – and the more remote trails – Napau Trail leading within sight of Pu'u 'O'o's active crater, Keauhou Trail heading to the remote Puna Coast, etc. When the trails cross wide lava flows, the direction is usually indicated by *abu* (cairns). Don't stray from the marked areas as the faults covering the ground can be very dangerous. The park publishes descriptives of the main trails for great hiking: Napau Backcountry guide, Mauna Loa Backcountry and Coastal and East Rift Backcountry.

It takes three days to hike up to the summit of Mauna Loa. The first day is spent on a journey from Mauna Loa Lookout, at the end of Mauna Loa Road, up to

Red Hill (7.5mi or 12.1km), at more than 9,840ft (3,000m). A refuge can accommodate eight people (allow 6 to 8hrs). The next day, there are 12.1mi (19.5km) to travel (8 to 10hrs) to arrive at the refuge perched on the eastern slope of the Moku'aweoweo caldera – which is 3mi (5km) long and reaches 590ft (180m) deep. The summit, at 13,678ft (4,169m) faces the caldera. You can reach the summit the next day by going around the crater (4.7mi or 7.6km). You can also get there faster (6.4mi or 10.33km) from the weather station (11,151ft or 3,399m) located on the north side of the volcano – a road climbs 19.3mi (31km) from Saddle Road. This path, however, is not recommended, as it is very steep and the risk of altitude sickness is much greater. Hikers are asked to report their return.

As in all U.S. parks, you must obtain a hiking and camping permit in the remote regions. It is issued free of charge at the Visitor Center (7:45am to 4:45pm), the night before the planned departure at the earliest, subject to availability (no reservations). You are not allowed to spend more than three days on the same site. You'll find three rudimentary shelters at Ka'aha, Halape and Keauhou on the

remote coast, and a hut with three beds at Pepeiao, located further west. All have rainwater collectors. It might be a good idea to bring a tent since the shelters are small. You can also camp on the two remote sites at Apua Point, on the Puna Coast Trail and beside the Napau crater (no water).

Other more remote options include: the climb to **Mauna Kea** summit from the Visitor Station (one full day) and the more peaceful walk to Green Sand Beach, located east of Ka Lae (South Point).

Bird-Watching

Bird-lovers sometimes come to the Big Island specifically to see certain rare bird species. The **Hakalau** (see p 224) and **Kipuka Puaulu** (see p 245) reserves inside Volcanoes National Park are the best places for bird-watching. But you can also participate in one of the tours organized by **Hawai'i Forest & Trail** (☎322-8881 or 800-464-1993), *www.hawaii-forest.com*), which are rather expensive but allow you to go on private land.

Horseback Riding

It was here, in the first years of the 19th century, that the first Hawaiian horses arrived – a sight that truly surprised the islanders. The *paniolos* have since become masters of the art of horseback riding, and the Big Island, with its vast pastures and hidden valleys, is one of the most suitable islands in the archipelago for this activity.

Two companies offer rides in **Waipi'o**, one in the valley (*Waipi'o on Horseback and taro farm,* ☎775-7291, *$75 for 2.5hrs*), the other on the fringes, up to the summit of Hi'ilawe Falls (*Waipi'o Ridge Stables* ☎775-1007, *same price and duration*). Na'alapa Stables offers a ride at the foot of the **Kohala Volcano** (*$55 for 90min, $75 for 2.5hrs;* ☎889-0022). In the same region, but on the back of mules this time, you can reach the **Pololu Valley** with Hawai'i Forest & Trail (*$95, at 8:30am and 12:30pm;* ☎331-8505 *or* 800-464-1993), whose stable is located just before the end of Route 270. Rides are in groups of six and last about 3hrs. Another region, another volcano, Hauoli Trails (☎985-7263) is the only one in the vicinity of **Volcanoes National Park**. Its rides are long and expensive (*$180 to*

$255). Rather original, King's Trail Rides (☎323-2388) offers rides down to **Kealakekua Bay** to the Captain Cook monument; it's best to have some experience since the descent is steep! Most tour operators offer discounts of 10% to 15% on these prices.

Skiing

Yes, skiing! Anything is possible in Hawaii, at least in winter, when **Mauna Kea**'s summit is capped with a crown of snow. Whatever your level, **Ski Guides Hawai'i** (*based in Waimea*) will take you to the "white mountain" for unforgettable downhill skiing – from November and usually until the beginning of summer.

Fluming

North of the Kohala Peninsula and on the Hamakua Coast, planters in the 19th century built a vast network of irrigation canals cutting through the mountains to bring rainwater to their sugar-cane fields. In some places, narrow tunnels had to be dug right into the rock. Generation after generation, children in the region got in the habit of sliding down these endless slides, floating on an old inner tube or a makeshift buoy. For the past few years,

people have been able to experience the joys of *fluming* in an inflatable kayak with **Kahala Mountain Kayak Cruise** (*55-519 Hawi Rd., at the intersection of Routes 270 and 250 in Hawi,* ☎889-6922, *www.kohalakayaks.com*). The outings, which cost $80, last about 3hrs and take place in the morning and afternoon.

Flying and Aerial Sports

If you want to go on a helicopter ride and don't know which island to do it on, the Big Island, with the appeal of its volcano, is a good candidate. You can often see active lava flows, but note that the lava often flows underground, so find out in advance. Unless you want to go on a complete tour of the island, (*2hrs., $260 to $300, $230 with operators*), departures from Hilo are preferable. Since the town is located near Volcanoes National Park, flights are shorter and therefore less expensive (*45 to 60min, $100 to $140*). Obviously, if you don't want to spend too much and you're staying on the Kona Coast, you can also choose a flight above the Kohala Peninsula and the Hamakua Coast, with a volcano and waterfalls (*$120 to $140*). Many companies are competing for your dollar. The largest ones serve both Hilo and Kona cone: **Sunshine Helicopters** (☎882-1223), **Blue Hawaiian** (☎961-5600), **Mauna Kea** (☎885-6400) and **Safari** (☎969-1259 or 800-326-3356). **Hawai'i Helicopters** (☎800-994-9099) is only based in Kona and **Tropical** (☎961-6810), which was recently offering the best price/time ratio flight, is based exclusively in Hilo.

The companies offering plane rides have more affordable prices, starting at $70 *(departing from Hilo)* and up to $190 for a round-island tour: **Big Island Air** (☎329-4868) from Kona; **Safari Aviation** from Hilo (☎969-1259), the least expensive; **Hawai'i island Hoppers** (☎969-2000) and **Mokulele Flight Service** (☎326-7070).

Accommodations

Kona – Keauhou

Patey's Place
dormitory $17.50
private room $41.50 to $46.50
sb, tv, ⊗
75-195 Ala Ona Ona St.
☎326-7018
⇔326-7640
www.hostels.com/patey's
Located in a residential district, the only youth hostel in Kona offers both dorm accommodations (four to six

beds) and private rooms, with or without TV. Whatever the case, bathrooms are shared. Guests have access to a communal kitchen and a common lounge, as well as the Internet (free for up to 30min). The establishment picks up guests at the airport and regularly offers excursions, including one to the beach and another that features snowboarding on the slopes of Mauna Koa in winter. Guests over the age of 21 can also rent an economy car, but only within a range limited to in and around Kona. To reach the hostel from Kuakini Highway, take Kalani Street, then the second street on the left (Alahou Street). Ala Ona Ona is the first street on the right.

Kona Islander Inn
$60-$79
≈, K, ≡, tv, ☼
75-5776 Kuakini Hwy.
☎329-3333 or 800-622-5348
⇔326-4137
www.konahawaii.com
Located right in the centre of town, the Islander Inn's very decent studios are scattered throughout several buildings, some of which surround a small central swimming pool nestled in a verdant setting. Individually furnished, they offer one of the best deals in Kona. Though many visitors show up at the last minute, reservations are strongly recommended – at least one week to 10 days in advance, especially in

winter. Minimum stay of three nights.

Kona Tiki Hotel
$62-$69
≈, K
75-5968 Ali'i Dr. (Mile 1.5)
☎329-1425
⇔327-9402
Though pleasant, airy and with a view of the ocean, the Kona Tiki Hotel's rooms have no TV, air conditioning or even telephone. The idea is that you come here to get away from it all – something the proximity of the road to Keauhou occasionally prevents during rush hour. As for the rest, the place is top-notch, offering truly good value for the price. Because there are only 15 rooms, would-be guests looking to stay here during peak season are advised to make reservations as much as a year in advance.

Hale Kona Kai
$95-$105
≈, laundry, K, ≡, tv, ☼
75-5870 Kahakai Rd.
☎/⇔329-2155
☎/⇔800-421-3696
Situated near the Royal Kona Resort (see p 257), this small, slightly "long-in-the-tooth" condominium is right on the ocean. Apartments have a small kitchen, bedroom, living room and balcony. For an extra $10, it is best to opt for a unit facing the surf. Discounts for extended stays are offered. The reception desk is closed on Sunday.

Kona Magic Sands
$85-$129
≈, *laundry, K*, ≡, *tv*
77-6452 Ali'i Dr. (Mile 3.7)
☎/⇌*326-1280*
www.coupledopinion.com
Standing at the northern edge of the beautiful White Sands Beach, this condominium offers two categories of studios: standard, which are older, smaller and have no air conditioning, and deluxe, which have been renovated and are air conditioned. Some of the latter are very appealing, with a thick wall-to-wall carpet and large picture windows looking out on the ocean. Three-night minimum stay. You can contact Dr. Milton (Suite 214) at the above coordinates, or the representative on the mainland, RM Fine Art *(600 Canyon Dr., Santa Fe, NM 87501, ☎505-983-9533, ⇌505-983-1454, morafine@aol.com)*.

Kona Seaside Hotel
$98-$115
≈, ≡, ℝ, *tv*, ♨
75-5646 Palani Rd.
☎*329-2455 or 800-367-7000*
from the U.S.
☎*800-654-7020*
from Canada
⇌*329-6157*
Owned by a Hawaiian family-run chain, this mid-range hotel takes up an entire block and is located right next to the Kamehameha Hotel. Though prices have risen considerably over the last few years, the hotel remains popular with senior citizens. The most expensive rooms are larger and

feature a bath, but are also noisier since they overlook the intersection of Ali'i Drive and the Kuakini Highway. The others, which come with a shower, are spread out over several buildings, some of which are built around a swimming pool.

Uncle Billy's Kona Bay Hotel
$92-$122
≈, ℜ, *laundry, K*, ≡, ℝ, *tv*, ♨
75-5744 Ali'i Dr.
☎*329-1393 or 800-367-5102*
⇌*935-7903*
www.unclebilly.com
Very popular with Hawaiians for its worthwhile *kama'aina* rates, Uncle Billy's has a hotel in Kona and another in Hilo. Granted, the hotel is conveniently located right in the centre of town, but prices are nevertheless a tad high. Offering standard comfort, the rooms are priced according to the age of furnishings. Those set up on the other side of Ali'i Drive, overlooking the ocean, have a kitchenette and a small balcony.

Casa de Emdecko
$100-$155
≈, *laundry, K*, ≡, ♨
75-6082 Ali'i Dr. (Mile 2.1)
☎*329-2160*
Located between Kona and Keauhou, this fairly pleasant condo development boasts some 100 one- to two-bedroom apartments distributed throughout two

Mediterranean-looking buildings that surround a swimming pool and a small garden. A third of them are rented out by absent owners, who can be contacted directly – or simpler yet, through one of the local estate agencies (Knutson has its office on the premises).

Keauhou Beach Resort
$115-$200
ℜ, ≈, ☺, ≡, *tv*, ◙, ♨
78-6740 Ali'i Dr. (Mile 5)
☎*322-3441*
☎*800-92-ASTON*
☎*800-321-2558*
from Hawaii
⇌*322-3117*
www.aston-hotels.com
Sprawled along the south shore of Kahalu'u Bay, fringed with one of the few beaches in Kona, the hotel occupies a place once reserved for the *ali'i* (royalty). It tastefully cultivates its link to the Hawaiian past, preserving a collection of old artifacts (including a *koa*-wood canoe) and offering all kinds of traditional activities (such as *hula* and *lauhala*-weaving lessons). Guests can also stroll the gardens and check out a replica of King Kalakaua's beach house and neighbouring natural cleansing pool, as well as the vestiges of two *heiaus*. The hotel's 311 newly

Red from laterite and dry except at its highest points, Lana'i is almost deserted and therefore ideal for cattle and plantations.
- *Claude Hervé-Bazin*

In Hawaii, the ocean is not the only thing making waves; indeed, lava also forms strange designs as fire and ash blend together.
- *Claude Hervé-Bazin*

At a height of 82ft (25m), the twin Wailua Falls majestically fall into a large basin that is surrounded by lush vegetation.
- *Claude Hervé-Bazin*

The old Waimea Foreign Church, featuring a truncated steeple covered in shingles, is one of many lovely stone churches on the island of Kaua'i.
- *Claude Hervé-Bazin*

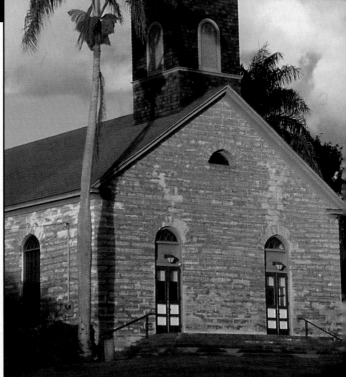

From the belvedere overlooking the great Pololu Valley, you can see the Homeric cliffs of the coast of Hamakua sinking into the sea.
- *Claude Hervé-Bazin*

Every year since 1963, after Easter, the streets of Hilo are the setting for the Merrie Monarch, the most important Hawaiian *hula* festival.
- *Claude Hervé-Bazin*

Adorned with a *lei* of flowers and seashells, this young Hawaiian girl will soon become a beautiful *wahine*.
- *Claude Hervé-Bazin*

No other plant is better adapted to the harsh volcanic environment than the *ohi'a lehua*, which continues to grow despite lava flows.- *Claude Hervé-Bazin*

renovated rooms are comfortable.

🏄 King Kamehameha's Kona Beach Hotel
$120-$195
ℜ, ≈, ☉, △, ≡, ℝ, *tv*, ◙, ☕
75-5660 Palani Rd.
☎*329-2911 or 800-367-6060*
⇌*922-8061 (reservations)*
www.konabeachhotel.com
Member of a chain with links throughout the archipelago, King Kamehameha's is one of the most venerable major hotels in Kona. Located right near the town centre, the oceanfront hotel boasts its own (small) beach on which stands one of the loveliest restored *heiaus* in Hawaii. It doesn't get much better than this. Though the rooms have seen better days, they are nonetheless comfortable, and guests have access to a whole range of services and activities, including tennis, water sports and shopping in the in-house mall. What's more, the common areas feature an exhibition of magnificent Hawaiian *objets d'art* (see p 200).

Kona Surf Resort
$129-$199
≈, ≡, *tv*, ℝ, ☕
78-128 Ehukai St. (Mile 6.6)
☎*322-3411 or 800-367-8011*
⇌*322-3245*
www.konasurfresort.com
Designed in a trident-like shape to provide most rooms with an ocean view, the Kona Surf Resort stands on the headland at the south end of Keauhou Bay. The location is spectacular, but the

hotel is a little too sprawling – so much so that it tends to lack clients. Just below the attractive oceanfront swimming pool, guests can observe manta rays, fed every night to lure them closer. A free Polynesian revue is offered to hotel guests every Tuesday and Friday. To get here, go past the Keauhou Shopping Center and the Country Club, then turn right on Kaleioipapa Street.

Royal Kona Resort
$140-$250
ℜ, ≈, *laundry*, ≡, *tv*, ℝ, ◙
75-5852 Ali'i Dr.
☎*329-3111*
☎*800-774-KONA*
⇌*329-7230*
www.royalkona.com
Set on the rocky promontory overlooking Kailua Bay, this large resort features 454 rooms distributed throughout three buildings. Though somewhat dated, the hotel offers rooms with all the modern conveniences. All are identical, their prices varying with the view. Various kinds of packages are available, reducing the official rates considerably. The resort features tennis courts, shops and a small artificial beach sheltered by a low wall. Stairs go down into a saltwater lagoon nestled between the rocks, making it a lovely place for a swim.

Aston Royal Sea-Cliff Resort
$190-$280
≈, △, *laundry*, K, ≡, ◙, *tv*, ☕
75-6040 Ali'i Dr. (Mile 2)
☎*329-8021*
☎*800-92-ASTON*
☎*800-321-2558*
from Hawaii
⇌*326-1887*
www.aston-hotels.com
Located between Kona and Keauhou, the oceanfront Royal Sea-Cliff Resort is a very comfortable establishment run by the Aston chain. One-, two- and three-bedroom condo apartments can be rented here. All are very well equipped and, as is often the case in this type of accommodation, decorated according to the owner's taste.

Kailua Plantation House B&B
$160-$235 bkfst incl.
≈, *tv*, ℝ, ☕
75-5948 Ali'i Dr. (Mile 1.4)
☎*329-3727*
⇌*326-7323*
www.tales.com/KPH
This luxury bed and breakfast, which mainly caters to honeymooners and couples celebrating their wedding anniversary, is nestled between the road and the ocean. Three of the five rooms overlook the water. Each individually decorated room has its own bathroom, and some have a whirlpool bath. Guests can take advantage of the very pleasant oceanfront lounge, the hot tub and the small, oddly shaped dipping pool set on the coast's rocks. Friendly reception, but children

under 12 are not welcome.

Kona Bali Kai
$169-$279
≈, *laundry, K, tv*, ≡, 🔲, ♻
76-6246 Ali'i Dr. (Mile 2.7)
☎329-9381 or 800-535-0085
⇒326-6056
www.marcresorts.com
Run by the Marc Resorts & Hotels chain, the Bali Kai condo resort (located between Kona and Keauhou) offers studios and one- to three-bedroom apartments. Services and room conditions largely depend on the owners. As a general rule, the units facing inland have air conditioning, while those facing the ocean do not, the ocean breeze ostensibly serving as a replacement. Conversely, only those overlooking the ocean have a washing machine. Reduced rates are offered both directly and through real-estate agents.

Kona Reef
$155-$330
≈, *laundry, K*, ≡/⊗, *tv*, ♻
75-5888 Ali'i Dr. (Mile 1.1)
☎329-2959 or 800-367-5004
☎800-272-5275
from Hawaii
⇒329-2762
www.castle-group.com
Owned by the Castle Resorts & Hotels chain, this condo resort offers one-, two- and three-bedroom apartments. The largest ones are those with an ocean view. The decor varies greatly from one unit to another according to the owner's tastes, ranging from amusing and very tropical to

utterly lacklustre. Rates include either the fifth night for free or a rental car.

The South
Coast of Kona

Ho'okena Beach Park
$5/pers. (see p 195)
washrooms, outdoor showers, picnic tables
At the southernmost end of the Kona Coast, in a rather lonely setting, the Ho'okena campground (see p 208) lies by a lovely grey-sand beach. Campers can pitch their tent at the south end, under the coconut trees – well, maybe not quite "under" the coconut trees...

Kona Hotel
$26-$30
sb
Mamalahoa Hwy.
Holualoa town centre
☎324-1155
Establishments of this kind, veritable plantation hotels, are a dying breed in Hawaii. Founded in 1926 by the Japanese-born parents of current owner Mr. Inaba, the Kona Hotel houses only 11 rooms, all of which are very simple, with neither television nor air conditioning, and with a shared bathroom. But history – still-living history – rather than comfort is the draw here.

Manago Hotel
$28-$46
ℜ, *sb/pb*, ⊗
Mamalahoa Hwy.
Captain Cook (Mile 109.8)
☎323-2642
⇒323-3451
Founded by Mr. Manago senior in 1913, this venerable all-wood plantation hotel offers two kinds of rooms. The less expensive, Spartan ones, with shared bathroom, are located in the main building and are a little noisy due to the traffic along Highway 11. The others, with private bathroom, occupy a new building set back from the road. Prices vary with the floor – but trees block any view there may be from the ground-floor rooms. You can even request the Japanese Room, complete with *furo* (bath) and tatami mats. Triple- and quadruple-occupancy rates are roughly the same as those for double occupancy, which can be very advantageous.

⚓ Teshima's
$35
ℜ, ⊗
Mamalahoa Hwy.
in the centre of Honalo
☎322-9140
Right behind their restaurant (see p 278), the Teshima family offers 10 rooms, five of which are rented out full time. Small but very decent and with a private bathroom, they are a great deal for budget travellers. Wonderful reception, too.

Pomaikai Farm B&B
$50-$60 bkfst incl.
sb/pb
83-5465 Hwy. 11 (Mile 106.7)
☎*328-2112*
☎*800-325-6427*
from the U.S.
≈*328-2255*
Simple and very friendly, American francophile Nita's bed and breakfast offers two rather standard rooms in the main house and three others that are considerably less so. Two of the latter are located in a "greenhouse," while the third occupies an old restored coffee barn. But in all three, some upper-wall sections have been replaced with mosquito-net panels, letting in the breeze wafting through the banana trees. The comfort is rustic, the shower is outdoors and the traffic along Highway 11 somewhat of a nuisance in the morning, but Pomaikai (or "lucky") Farm is charming for its congenial atmosphere. Many of its guests, mostly young and European, come here to leave their cares behind for a few days. A refrigerator and microwave oven are at guests's disposal.

Merryman's Bed & Breakfast
$75-$125 bkfst incl.
sb/pb, tv, ☂
Captain Cook
☎*323-2276 or 800-545-4390*
≈*323-3749*
www.konabedandbreakfast.com
From this large, modern wooden house's covered terrace, guests can get a glimpse of the ocean in the distance through leafy trees – a perfect setting for breakfast. Dominating Highway 11, the house offers four comfortable, flowery rooms, two of which come with a private bathroom. In the tropical gardens, guests can relax in the whirlpool or a hammock, or borrow a diving mask and flippers or beach gear for the day.

🏯 Rainbow Plantation
$75-$95 bkfst incl.
K, tv, ℝ
P.O. Box 122, Captain Cook
HI 96704
☎*323-2393 or 800-494-2829*
outside Hawaii
≈*323-9445*
www.aloha.net/konabnb/
A long country road, on the *makai* side, leads to this relaxing, peaceful refuge. The garden, filled with parrots, hens and peacocks in abundance, not to mention Petunia the house pig, is something of a cross between a jungle and a farmyard. The happy couple that owns this Noah's Ark are German, and after being knocked about a lot, they settled here in the heart of a 3ha coffee and macadamia-nut plantation. The establishment's four rooms and apartment, all with a private entrance, are in the main house, in a remodelled nut-sorting shop, and, for the utmost in originality, in a retired fishing boat – complete with built-in shower and washrooms – named the Jungle Queen.

Rosy's Rest Bed & Breakfast
$80 bkfst incl.
laundry, K, tv, ☂
76-1012 Mamalahoa Hwy.
Holualoa
☎*322-7378*
≈*322-7378*
www.stayhawaii.com/rosy.html
Rosy's offers two comfortable studios with all the essentials: one on the ground floor and the other upstairs. The latter, featuring a large balcony overlooking the ocean in the distance, is the most pleasant and comes with a kitchenette. Breakfast spotlights garden-fresh fruit and pastries.

Dragonfly Ranch
$85-$200 bkfst incl.
sb/pb, K, ℝ
Hwy. 160 (Mile 1.3)
Near Pu'uhonua o Honaunau
☎*328-2159 or 800-487-2159*
≈*328-9570*
www.dragonflyranch.com
At the very entrance, guests are greeted by a huge dragonfly in a meditation position. Housed in a large and ungainly wooden "expansion mansion" watched over by Oriental goddesses, the guestrooms are partly open on the hammock-festooned trees. The very New Age, over-40 clientele has been coming to this "healing arts retreat" for over 20 years, more in search of encounters than holidays. All meals are taken communally, which does not prevent

everyone's tastes from being taken into account. From the humble campsite to the Honeymoon Suite with view of the bay, guests are offered a very large choice of accommodations. Those who are truly hard up can even work for their room and board, provided they commit themselves to staying on for some time and become well integrated.

 **Holualoa Inn**
$150-$195 bkfst incl.
≈, ⊗
76-5932 Mamalahoa Hwy.
Holualoa
☎*324-1121 or 800-392-1812*
⇌*322-2472*
www.konaweb.com/HINN
This luxury bed and breakfast offers six rooms in a magnificent wooden house overlooking coffee plantations, pastureland, Kona and the ocean. Each has its own bathroom and a view of the coast and the ocean beyond. The estate also features a garden whirlpool, an oceanfront lounge with fireplace, a pool table and a telescope for stargazers. No children under 13.

The North Coast of Kona

Four Seasons Hualalai Resort
$450-$625
ℜ, ≈, *laundry,* ≡, ℝ, *tv*
100 Ka'upulehu Dr.
Mile 86.9 on Hwy. 19 via Ka'upulehu Rd.
☎*325-8000 or 800-332-3442 from the U.S.*
☎*800-268-6282 from Canada*
⇌*325-8100*
www.fourseasons.com
The newest addition to the west coast's holiday-resort scene, the Four Seasons Hualalai Resort shares the desolate lava-rock landscape with its neighbours. With the help of a great deal of watering, architects managed to create a pristine golf course (designed by Jack Nicklaus) and a rather successful establishment with many small units overlooking the links or the ocean. The rooms are essentially priced according to the view, except for the suites. Various kinds of packages, including one with a rental car or breakfast at a reduced rate, are available. Many activities are offered and guests can enjoy a game on one of eight tennis courts, a dip in one of three swimming pools or the oceanfront saltwater "lava pond."

Kona Village Resort
$450-$795
ℜ, ≈, ⊘, *laundry,* ℝ, ⊗
Mile 86.9 on Hwy. 19
via Ka'upulehu Rd.
☎*325-5555 or 800-367-5290*
⇌*325-5124*
www.konavillage.com
To play Robinson Crusoe while enjoying all the creature comforts (or almost), you can opt for one of the Kona Village Resort's 120 bungalows with traditional Polynesian-style thatched roofs. The bungalows are spread out over such extensive grounds that guests are driven to their *hale* in a golf cart – the first time, at any rate. On one side stretches an old stream of sun-scorched lava, while on the other lies Kahuwai Bay, lined with a well-sheltered but rather unexceptional grey-sand beach. Though comfortable, the bungalows have neither air conditioning, telephone, nor television – somewhat of a compulsory relegation back to nature. Prices, although very steep, include all meals and a wide variety of activities.

The Kohala Coast

Hapuna Beach State Park
$20 for a bungalow
(see p 214)
access from 7am to 8pm washrooms, outdoor showers, picnic tables
It's not every day that one sees a campground sharing a beach with a luxury hotel – especially when that beach

is one of the most beautiful on the island. And yet, the park, to the south, and the Hapuna Beach Prince Hotel (see below), to the north, live in harmony. It's hard to imagine a more idyllic camping spot. Permit-holders can simply pitch their tent on one of the campsites beneath the trees, just set back from the strand. Barbecue, picnic tables, drinking water: everything is within reach. There is even a grocery store/snack bar on site. It is best to set up camp at the end of the day, when the stream of sunburnt tourists heads back to the neighbouring hotels. You can also opt for one of the park's *A*-frame cabins, each of which provides rather rudimentary accommodations for up to four people (who sleep on wooden platforms).

Spencer Beach County Park
$5/pers. (see p 195)
access closed at 11pm washrooms, showers, telephones, barbecues, drinking water
Located right next to the Pu'ukohola Heiau National Historic Site, the Spencer Beach (see p 216) park will appeal to camping buffs who can set up their tent right by the beach's lovely mantle of golden sand, an enticing swimming spot. The scores of picnic tables are nestled between old trees with twisted trunks, which offer

welcome shade during the day.

Hapuna Beach Prince Hotel
$325-$520
ℜ, ☺, ≈, ≡, *tv*, ☂
62-100 Kauna'oa Dr.
☎*880-1111 or 800-882-6060*
⇄*880-3412*
www.hapunabeachprince hotel.com
Adjacent to the Mauna Kea Beach Hotel (see below), from which it is only separated by a rocky bluff, the Hapuna Beach Prince Hotel overlooks the north end of the beautiful beach of the same name (see p 214). Named after a long-known Artesian source (*hapuna* means "source of life"), it was built in 1994 in the same style as the Mauna Kea, it too open wide onto the ocean. Every one of its 350 rooms overlooks the water. The hotel is very popular with Asian tourists, justifying the opening of a prestigious Japanese restaurant, Hakone. In addition to the many activities offered, guests can enjoy an astronomy session four nights a week.

Hilton Waikoloa Village
$360-$430
ℜ, ≈, ☺, ≡, ▣, *tv*, ☂
425 Waikoloa Beach Dr.
☎*886-1234 or 800-HILTONS*
⇄*886-2900*
www.waikoloavillage.hilton. com
Huge, excessive and luxurious: the Hilton Waikoloa is all that and more. Just beyond the entrance, a monorail

takes you to your room, housed in one of three towers surrounding the huge central lagoon and the 4.5-acre-plus (1.5ha) gardens – unless you prefer taking the slower but more romantic shuttle boats travelling along the canal that runs parallel to the monorail. On the way, you may even get the chance to see one of the resident dolphins. Swimming sessions with the dolphins are organized; in fact, they are so popular that guests must now draw lots to enjoy this treat. Free and open to all is the magnificent collection of Asian and Melanesian art gracing the long corridors, a collection richer than that of many museums. It's almost enough to forget the beach, however magnificent, and all the activities available. In this riot of luxury, the rooms are predictably very comfortable, and offer Internet access.

Mauna Kea Beach Hotel
$325-$480
ℜ, ☺, ≈, ≡, ℝ, ☂, *tv on request*
62-100 Mauna Kea Beach Dr.
☎*882-7222 or 800-882-6060*
⇄*882-5700*
www.maunakeabeachhotel. com
The first holiday resort on the Kohala Coast, the Mauna Kea stands on a magnificent spot overlooking a small bay fringed with vegetation and the white-sand Kauna'oa Beach. The rather sober decor features a clearly Japanese

theme, enhanced with numerous plants. Most of the 310 comfortable rooms overlook the ocean, while some look out on the golf course. Many activities as well as tennis and golf packages are offered. The hotel also houses two renowned restaurants, Batik (see p 280) and the Pavilion (see p 280).

Mauna Lani Bay Hotel
$335-$465
ℜ, ⊘, △, ≈, ≡, ⊗, ☕
68-1400 Mauna Lani Dr.
☎*885-6622 or 800-367-2323*
⇌*885-1484*
www.maunalani.com
The Mauna Lani Bay Hotel is the only five-star hotel on the Big Island. The arrow-shaped hotel, within which is a vast atrium complete with coconut trees and a river, juts out to the edge of a lovely white-sand beach planted with palm trees. The very comfortable rooms all feature a *lanai* and most offer at least a partial view of the ocean. Bungalows and villas with one to three bedrooms and a private swimming pool are also available. The price even includes limo service from the airport and a full-time chef! Golf course (laid out right on an ancient lava flow), water sports, tennis: activities are plentiful and include a guided tour

through the Puako petroglyphs.

The Orchid at Mauna Lani
$385-$650
ℜ, ≈, ⊘, △, ≡, *tv*, ℝ
One North Kaniku Dr.
☎*885-2000 or 800-274-4884*
⇌*885-5778*
www.orchid-maunalani.com
The former Ritz-Carlton, taken over by the Sheraton chain, is located near a palm-lined beach. The rooms are most comfortable; unfortunately, only a few have an oceanfront view, the others looking out on the gardens with a swimming pool and an artificial river. But the many activities, massage centre, golf course, tennis courts, four restaurants, three bars and the staff's attentive service will soon banish this minor drawback from your mind. On the other hand, the $12 a day the Orchid automatically charges guests for services that are seldom used is reproachable.

Outrigger Waikoloa Beach
$210-$290
ℜ, ≈, ⊘, ≡, ◼, *tv*, ☕
69-275 Waikoloa Beach Dr.
☎*886-6789*
☎*800-OUTRIGGER*
⇌*886-7852*
www.outrigger.com
The former Royal Waikoloan has been given a new lease on life since it was bought by the Outrigger chain,

which is proceeding with its expansion. Though more modest than other hotel complexes on the Kohala Coast, its rates are more affordable. The rooms are decorated with a pleasant tropical note, and the Voyagers Club, offering a range of free services, also includes breakfast.

The Kohala Peninsula

Keokea Beach County Park
$5/pers. (see p 195)
washrooms, outdoor showers, picnic tables, barbecues
Here, campers can pitch their tent on the patch of grass at the base of the park's pavilion (see p 218) and be lulled to sleep by the rhythmic sound of the waves. It is best, however, to avoid weekends, when family gatherings can prove a little noisy *(lights out at 11pm)*. Beware also of pests of another kind: mosquitoes, which are rather plentiful.

Kohala Country Adventures Guest House
$55-$105 bkfst incl.
K, *tv*, ℝ
P.O. Box 703, Kapa'au, HI 96755
☎*889-5663*
www.kcadventures.com
This turquoise-coloured bed and breakfast houses three rooms. The largest one comes with a kitchenette and a large terrace, and all three have a private bathroom and entrance.

Kohala Guest House
$59-$125
K, tv
52-277 Keokea Beach Rd.
P.O. Box 172, Hawi
HI 96719
☎*889-5606*
⇌*889-5572*
home1.gte.net/svendsen
Located on the right side of the small road leading to the Keokea Beach County Park, the Kohala Guest House offers two brand-new, reasonably priced apartments: one studio and one three-room unit. Both have their own entrance and a tropical-themed decor.

Kohala Village Inn
$47-$79
ℜ, tv
55-514 Hawi Rd., Hawi
☎*889-0419*
This unpretentious establishment offers simple but very clean rooms for those in search of affordable, no-frills accommodations. The cheapest rooms are the smaller ones, with no television, and the highest-priced rooms have three to four beds. The hotel adjoins the Kohala Village Restaurant, which, though rather humdrum, hosts local musicians every Sunday and Monday night.

Waimea – Kamuela

Kamuela Inn
$59-$99 bkfst incl.
K, tv, ☂
65-1300 Kawaihae Rd.
☎*885-4243 or 800-555-8968*
⇌*885-8857*
www.hawaii-bnb.com/kamuela.html
Halfway between the hotel and motel, the Kamuela Inn has a good selection of rooms of various sizes. The cheapest ones are simple and fairly small but very decent, while those in the new (Mauna Kea) wing are more expensive but most pleasant. The decor is a bit Victorian, a bit kitsch, with different furnishings, carpets and gilded mirrors that give each room a personal touch. There is no air conditioning but there are blankets, which are much more useful.

Waimea Country Lodge
$84-$108
K, tv
65-1210 Lindsey Rd.
☎*885-4100 or 800-367-5004*
☎*800-272-5275*
from Hawaii
⇌*885-6711*
www.castle-group.com
A member of the Castle Resorts & Hotels chain, the Waimea Country Lodge offers decent, if slightly expensive, standard motel rooms.

Jacaranda Inn
$185-$425 bkfst incl.
65-1444 Kawaihae Rd.
(Hwy. 19)
☎*885-8813*
⇌*885-6096*
tji@ilbawaii.net
Kamuela's latest luxury bed and breakfast is housed in the former home of the Parker Ranch (1897) manager, a mauve-painted house matching the colours of the flowers of the jacaranda tree that stands at the foot of grass-covered volcanic mounds. On a decidedly purple, Victorian note, the eight very comfortable rooms (some with canopy beds), six of which are suites, are housed in adjacent cottages. The antique furnishings are made of *koa* wood and the communal areas include a Victorian lounge, a library-cum-billiard-room, a dining room and a patio. Minimum three-night stay.

Waimea Gardens Cottage
$135
K, tv
P.O. Box 563, Kamuela,
HI 96743
☎*800-262-9912*
⇌*885-0559*
bestbnb@aloha.net
Run by the owner of Hawai'i's Best Bed & Breakfasts (through which reservations are made), these two restored wooden cottages are only rented by reservation. The Waimea Wing has a kitchenette, a small living room with fireplace and a patio, while the Kohala Wing features a kitchen and a bathroom with

Japanese bath looking out on the garden. Both are furnished in the old-fashioned style. Credit cards are accepted, but with exorbitant fees for Europeans.

Saddle Road

Mauna Kea State Recreation Area
$45-$55 (see p 195)
Mile 35.1, west of Hilo
Located some 6,000ft (2,000m) above sea level, the Mauna Kea State Recreation Area bungalows can accommodate either up to six people or a whole group. What's more, the park offers hunters, walkers and cyclists a good base for exploring the surrounding area. Nights are cold, but there is heating.

The Hamakua Coast

Waipi'o Valley
no facilities
Campers can pitch their tent free of charge beneath the pine trees, east of the black-sand beach, with a view of a small waterfall that flows right into the ocean. There are no facilities on site, just a great deal of peace and quiet during the week. On weekends, a few families come here to spend the day fishing.

Laupahoehoe Beach Park
$5/pers. (see p 195xx)
washrooms, showers, barbecues, drinking water
The park (see p 229), spread out over the wave-swept rocky promontory, is one of the most popular camping sites on the island. Winds can be strong here (make sure your tent pegs are well anchored), but the setting, offering a view of the cliffs of the Hamakua Coast, is hard to beat. Peace and quiet assured.

Kalopa State Park
bungalow $55
showers, washrooms, barbecues and picnic tables
A vast clearing, watched over by eucalyptus trees and carpeted with soft grass, offers a very quiet spot where you can put up your tent. Nights are a little cool and often damp, but although the sun hardly shines here, you won't regret your choice. And, worse case scenario, you can move your tent under one of the three protective awnings. The park also has two large wooden cabins, right next to the hibiscus garden, each of which houses two units that can accommodate up to eight people. Each unit has a bathroom and a communal kitchen with fireplace is at guests's disposal in the neighbouring building.

Tom Araki's
$15
sh, K
Waipi'o Valley
☎ 775-0368
The Arakis offer seven bare-bones rooms in the building next to their faded-pastel-green home, located about 600ft (200m) past the first ford at the bottom of Waipi'o Valley. Time has done its work on the place, and the communal washrooms and showers are fairly rusty, but, for immersion in local culture, you won't find anything better in Hawaii. At 80, bon vivant Tom, renowned for his taste for sake, has partly handed the reigns over to his granddaughter after a bout of illness. Don't take the risk of showing up without calling first.

Hotel Honoka'a Club
dormitory $15
room $35-$65 bkfst incl.
sh/pb, tv
45-3480 Mamane St., Honoka'a
☎/⇆ 775-0678
☎ 800-808-0678
home1.gte.net/honokaac
Built in 1908, this wooden house was first home to the manager of the Honoka'a plantation. Having gotten into the habit of welcoming passing travellers who had nowhere else to stay in the area, it gradually turned into a hotel. After some hard times resulting from the plantation's demise, the hotel got a new lease on life under the management of Kathy Kenyon, who is as obliging as she is wel-

coming. The establishment features two dormitories (three to five beds) as well as tiny rooms with shared or private bathroom. The most appealing ones are upstairs, done up like new, sharing a view of the ocean in the distance and the neighbouring houses buried in vegetation. The corner rooms are very bright (no shutters).

'Akaka Falls Inn
$65 bkfst incl.
sb, tv
P.O. Box 190, Honomu
HI 96729
☎ *963-5468*
⇌ *963-6353*
www.akakafallsinn.com
The old Akita Building, a former Japanese grocery store built in 1923, has been renovated by Sonia Martinez and her son, who turned the ground floor into a deli and the upstairs into a two-room bed and breakfast. In pleasant shades of white and blue, the rooms share a large bathroom and comfortable living room; one has a large bed, while the other has two small ones. As Mrs. Martinez is a professional cook and her son Anthony has a degree in tropical agriculture, breakfasts are lavish and feature products fresh from the garden, where superb mangos, avocados, lychees and star fruit grow.

Akiko's Buddhist B&B
$55-$85 bkfst incl.
sb, ⊗
P.O. Box 272, Hakalau
HI 96710
☎ ⇌ *963-6422*
alternative-hawaii.com/akiko
Located in the heart of the village of Hakalau, this modest yellow wooden house was built in the early 20th century, during the plantation era. Its Japanese-born owner has turned it into a bed and breakfast coupled with a relaxation centre, with retreat and massage programs as well as dance and yoga classes – not to mention the chance to take part in Akiko's meditation session every morning at 5:30am! The mostly Spartan rooms are scattered throughout the main house (with futons), a neighbouring house (with beds) and a retreat studio for a minimum two-week stay.

Kamuela Inn's Guesthouse (Log Cabin)
$59-$99 bkfst incl.
sb/pb, K, tv
☎ *885-4243 or 800-555-8968*
www.hawaiibnb.com/kamuela.html
In a style halfway between a lodge and a cottage, the Log Cabin is located on the lower slopes of Mauna Kea, some 2,400ft (over 800m) in altitude. It belongs to the owner of the Waimea Kamuela Inn and comprises a large kitchen, a library, a whirlpool and five guestrooms – two with private bathroom, three

without. The living room features a cozy fireplace, which is very pleasant on cool evenings. The entire house can also be rented.

Paauhau Plantation House
$100-$140 bkfst incl.
K, tv, ⊗, ♨
1 Kalopa Rd., Honoka'a
☎ *775-7222 or 800-789-7614*
⇌ *775-7223*
www.bbhost.com/bbpaauhauplantation
Dominating Highway 19 and the ocean at a distance, at the east exit of Honoka'a is an old wooden plantation house (1921) set in the heart of a vast park. Transformed into a bed and breakfast, it houses two rooms, the loveliest of which boasts a fireplace. Two of the four cottages set up at the back have one bedroom, while the other two have two. Well ventilated, each of them has a kitchen and is decorated in a tropical style with rattan furniture, but the most appealing is unquestionably the blue-and-white Hilo Cottage. Guests have free use of a tennis court and basketball court as well as the pool table and fireplace in the main house. Minimum two-night stay.

Waipi'o Wayside B&B Inn
$95-$135 bkfst incl.
⊗
Hwy. 240, 2mi (3km) west of Honoka'a
☎ ⇌ *775-0275*
☎ *800-833-8849*
www.waipiowayside.com
Overlooking the ocean from a distance, this

wooden 1936 plantation house offers five comfortable rooms of varying sizes, each with its own bathroom. At the back is a large terrace where you can soak up the sun in a hammock. Owner Jackie Horne, in self-imposed exile from Silicon Valley, is a veritable mine of information on the region (restaurants and hikes in particular). That said, prices are very steep and the highway – fortunately hardly busy – runs a little close.

Cliff House
$150
K, laundry, tv, ⚕
Kukuihaele
☎775-0005 or 800-492-4746
This large house, ready for immediate occupation and rented by the day, towers above the ocean, slightly set back from the Waipi'o Valley Lookout. Newly built, it houses two bedrooms, a living room and a large balcony with a view of the surf. Would-be guests must go to Waipi'o Valley Artworks before 6pm. From there, the house is only about 600ft (200m) away, at the end of a dirt road, on the right side, just past the intersection of Highway 240 and the highway going back up from Kukuihaele. No security deposit is required when making reservations.

Hilo

Arnott's Lodge
camping $9
dormitory $17
semi-private and private
rooms $42-$105
sb/pb, laundry, K
98 Apapane Rd.
☎969-7097
≈961-9638
www.arnottslodge.com
From the simple patch of grass where you can pitch a tent to the shared (or not) private suite, Arnott's covers all low-budget niches. Each dormitory has a kitchen, and showers are plentiful. You can even get a free space in exchange for a morning's work. The establishment organizes all kinds of activities: barbecues, bicycle rentals, day excursions (not necessarily cheap) to such places as Volcanoes National Park and Mauna Kea. Internet access. Free shuttle pickup from the airport with a simple phone call; drop off at the airport three times daily.

Wild Ginger Inn
$45-$60 bkfst incl.
tv, ⊗
100 Puueo St.
☎935-5556 or 800-882-1887
www.wildgingerinn.com
Recently bought out, this old hotel sports a fresh coat of pink and turquoise paint. The rooms are being renovated, but will essentially remain very simple. The cheapest ones, without a television, are on the ground floor and darker. In the

future, the Wild Ginger Inn should once again offer dormitory accommodations as it did in the past.

🚗 Dolphin Bay Hotel
$66-$98
K, tv, ⊗
333 Iliahi St.
☎935-1466
≈935-1523
www.dolphinbayhilo.com
Located in a residential district west of the town centre, this small 18-room hotel is a favourite with both travellers and locals. You can opt for a standard room, two categories of studios, or apartments with one to two bedrooms, a living room and *lanai*. Couples are sure to appreciate the Superior Studios as they feature a tiled bath big enough for two. As evidenced by the photographs at the reception, the owner is a volcano fanatic and can provide all kinds of information on current eruptions. To reach the hotel, cross the bridge over the Wailuku River, in the continuation of Keawe Street, and turn left onto Iliahi Street; the hotel is about 300ft (100m) away.

Hilo Seaside Hotel
$70-$110
≈*, laundry,* ≡*, tv,* ℝ
126 Banyan Dr.
☎935-0821 or 800-367-7000
≈969-9195
Established on the four main islands, this Hawaiian chain has seen its prices climb considerably over the last few years. The rooms are past their prime but

very decent, and most feature a lovely turquoise (!) carpet. The difference between the "standard" and "luxury" categories does not warrant the price differential, so opt for the former, except for rooms 1 to 15, which are noisy since they are located in the wing overlooking Kalaniana'ole Avenue.

Hale Kai Bjornen
$90-$110 bkfst incl.
pb, ≈, tv
111 Honolii Place
☎*935-6330*
⇄*935-8439*
bjornen@interpac.net
Everything here looks out onto the ocean: the wooden house, set on a bluff over Hilo Bay, the swimming pool and hot tub, and the five guestrooms – from which a whale can sometimes be glimpsed in winter. Paul, the owner, even affirms having witnessed a birth right in front of the balcony. His spouse, Evonne, is of Norwegian descent and brings a Scandinavian touch to the decor of the house and the fairly large and airy rooms. The style (or perhaps the rather high prices) seem to suit a middle-aged, largely European clientele. Free Internet access for E-mail; beach gear and flashlights are also loaned.

Uncle Billy's Hilo Bay
$84-$114
≈, ℜ, K, ≡, tv, ℝ, ☂
87 Banyan Dr.
☎*935-0861 or 800-367-5102*
☎*800-442-5841*
from Hawaii
⇄*935-7903*
www.unclebilly.com
Of the two Uncle Billy's hotels on the Big Island (one in Hilo, the other in Kona), this one is the most pleasant, offering newly renovated rooms and studios with a kitchenette. Also available are all kinds of appealing packages, particularly for senior citizens. Featuring a very stage-like Polynesian decor, the hotel restaurant (☎*935-0861*) specializes in fish and offers nightly *hula* shows.

Hilo Hawaiian
$107-$137
≡, K, tv, ℝ, ☂
71 Banyan Dr.
☎*935-9361 or 800-367-5004*
☎*800-272-5275*
from Hawaii
⇄*961-9642*
www.castle-group.com
This mid-range hotel offers comfortable, if rather small, rooms, half of which face Banyan Drive while the rest look out on the ocean and Coconut Island. Most rooms have a balcony, so those who fancy one should make a point of requesting it at the reception.

Naniloa Hotel
$100-$160
≈, ℜ, ◷, ≡, tv, ◙
93 Banyan Dr.
☎*969-3333 or 800-367-5360*
⇄*969-6622*
planet-hawaii/sand/naniloa
Officially at the apex of Hilo's top-of-the-range hotels, the Naniloa, very popular with Japanese tour groups, offers rather unexceptional rooms for the price.

Shipman House B&B
$140-$150 bkfst incl.
ℝ
131 Ka'iulani St.
☎/⇄*934-8002*
☎*800-627-8447*
www.hilo-hawaii.com
Perched on a hillock west of the town centre, this Victorian mansion is home to the cattle-ranching descendants of a missionary family. Established in 1901, the house welcomed both Jack London and Lili'uokalani, who the family claims was a friend of the current owner's great-grandmother. The queen is even purported to have played regularly on the 1912 Steinway piano, preserved in the parlour alongside magnificent *koa*-wood furniture. The three rooms in the main house and the two in the self-contained cottage are all large, comfortable and furnished in the old style – the last two with a distinctly tropical touch. They are very pricey, however, and the strait-laced atmosphere may not be everyone's cup of tea. Credit cards are ac-

cepted, but not children under 12 years of age.

Puna

Mackenzie State Park
washrooms, no showers or water
In a secluded spot along the Puna Coast, the small, pine-shaded park (see p 237) offers a serene campground near the ocean – provided you can manage to plant your tent pegs in between the roots. During the week, the place is deserted.

Robert's Cabanas
$40
Kalapana, at the end of the road
☎265-8764
Robert Keli'iho'omalu's house miraculously survived the volcanic eruption of 1990, which destroyed a large part of the village of Kalapana. A fatalist, Robert was already prepared to see it go up in smoke, but Pele decided otherwise. The family has recently set up two small, rudimentary wooden shacks with corrugated-iron roofs (noisy when it rains) offering a direct view of the cooled lava flow. While hardly the epitome of luxury, the place is sure to leave you with lasting memories. Outdoor shower.

The Village Inn
$40-$60
sb/pb, tv, ⊗
P.O. Box 1987, Pahoa,
HI 96778
☎965-6444
This old 1910 plantation hotel offers five rooms with wooden floors that show their age but have a certain charm – that of a bygone era. All are named after famous people, such as Stevenson, Lili'uokalani and Mark Twain (the most appealing), but only two have a private bathroom. Another antique, Coco the parrot, perched at the top of the stairs, is approaching the ripe old age of 40. Note that the reception is only open from 10am to 3pm and 5pm to 7pm.

Kalani Honua Retreat Center
$110-$135
camping $15-$20
sb/pb, ≈, △, K, ⊗
RR2 Box 4500, Pahoa –
Beach Rd., HI 96778
(Mile 17.7)
☎965-7828 or 800-800-6886
www.kalani.com
This New Age-inspired centre has, within a few years, gone from a spiritual retreat to an expensive mini holiday resort. All that remains is its original Spartan aspect. The rooms are four to a large lodge with a communal kitchen and living room. Only the priciest have their own bathroom. The rates, at least, include the use of a large swimming pool,

two whirlpools and a sauna. *Hula, lauhala-*weaving and yoga lessons as well as traditional massage therapies and a variety of seminars are also offered.

Volcanoes National Park

Except for the park and Volcano House campgrounds, accommodations are only available in the village of Volcano. A complete list can be obtained at the park's Visitor Center and reservations can be made through Volcano Reservations *(P.O. Box 998, Volcano, HI 96785, ☎967-8216 or 800-736-7140, ≈800-577-1849, bchawaii@aol.com).*

Namakani Paio Campground
free camping
bungalow $40
washrooms, picnic tables, barbecues
Volcano House
☎967-7321
Located 3 mi (5km) south of the Visitor Center (Mile 31.4), in a glade bordering Highway 11, this campground is pleasantly shaded by large eucalyptus trees. No permit is required for the self-service campsites (first come, first served). The place would be perfect if it didn't rain so much and if nights weren't so cold. Another drawback is that the showers are reserved for guests of the 10 neighbouring wooden cabins. Rather sombre, basic and

unheated, the cabins can accommodate up to four people and feature an canopy with a picnic table and barbecue grill. Blankets, sheets and pillows are supplied at the Volcano House reception inside the park, as is the key. Reservations can be made in advance (recommended in summer).

Kulanaokuaiki Campground
free
washrooms, picnic tables, barbecues
This new campground, located on Hilina Pali Road, has replaced the Kipuna Nene Campground, closed due to its impact on the diet of *nenes*. Campsites are available on a first-come, first-served basis (no permit required). The campground is somewhat off the beaten path, so be prepared.

Holo Holo Inn
$17-$40
sb, laundry, △, K
19-4036 Kalani Honua Rd.
☎967-7950
≈967-8025
www.enable.org/holoholo/
A member of the Hostelling International network, Volcano's pleasant youth hostel is run by Satoshi Yabuki, a great Japanese traveller who settled here after 20 years of globetrotting. The hostel's isolation, and until recently its lack of heating, have long kept travellers away, but it would be a shame to let this deter you. You

can opt for one of two five-bed dormitories or one of two private rooms, with shared bathroom. Guests can also take advantage of the upstairs TV room, the large communal kitchen with unlimited tea and coffee and, an unusual perk in a youth hostel, a sauna. Reservations are mandatory because Satoshi, who did not open the hostel to grow rich but rather to meet people, must work during the day to subsidize his business. The office is open from 6:30am to 9am and 4:30pm to 9pm only.

Volcano Bed & Breakfast
$45-$65 bkfst incl.
sb, K
Keonelehua Ave.
☎967-7779 or 800-736-7140
≈800-577-1849
www.volcano-hawaii.com/VBB.htm
Run by the owners of the Chalet Kilauea (see p 271), this two-storey 1912 wooden house offers six affordable, rather simple rooms with shared bathroom. The communal areas include a living room with a stove and TV, as well as a kitchen and a small library.

🌋 Volcano Inn
$45-$95 bkfst incl.
pb, ℝ, tv
19-3820 Old Volcano Hwy.
(at the very end)
☎967-7293 or 800-997-2292
≈985-7349
www.volcanoinn.com
A cross between a hotel and a bed and breakfast, with a manager in charge, the Volcano Inn offers a very

good level of comfort for the price. All five rooms have their own bathroom, including the smallest (the Lava Room), at only $45. Some are decorated according to a particular theme, including the Honu (turtle) Bedroom, which is one of the most appealing. The establishment also has four cedar cottages, of which the two most luxurious have a kitchen and a gas stove. Breakfast is prepared daily by a resident cook.

Country Goose
$75 bkfst incl.
tv
at Ruby and Eighth Sts.
☎967-7759 or 800-238-7101
≈985-8673
www.hawaii-bnb.com/congses.html
Homeowner Joan Earley rents out two rooms with private bathroom and heating in winter, including a wood-panelled one on the ground floor, with a private entrance, and another in the basement, with a sliding door opening out on patch of garden. A lavish communal breakfast is served.

My Island B&B
$65-$175 bkfst incl.
sb/pb, laundry, K, ℝ, tv
19-3896 Old Volcano Rd.
☎967-7216
≈967-7719
www.myislandinnhawaii.com
Gordon and Joann Morse initially set up three guestrooms in their wooden house, the old Hale Ohu, the

first house in Volcano, built in 1886 amidst lush vegetation for the Lyman family who were Hilo missionaries. Set above the family living room, one room has its own bathroom while the other two share another. In view of their bed and breakfast's success, the couple had two very pleasant garden units built, each with a private entrance and bathroom, then five cottages – one on site, the other four scattered throughout Volcano. The welcome is friendly, and those travelling alone get a 20% to 30% discount on rooms in the main house.

Volcano House
$85-$185
opposite the Visitor Center, in the park
P.O. Box 53, Hawaii Volcanoes National Park, HI 96718
☎*967-7321*
⇔*967-8429*
Its location, on the edge of the Kilauea crater, and its lodge atmosphere makes this a somewhat exceptional and thus very popular hotel. This, however, is hardly reason enough to charge so much for the rooms, which, though comfortable and equipped with a private bathroom, offer few amenities. Only the most expensive ones, in the main building, offer a view – but only on fine days. The cheapest rooms,

smaller and more sombre but still quite decent, are set up in a separate cottage (Ohia Wing), with a common living room and fireplace, sofa and kitschy armchairs. Whatever the category, reservations must be made at least two to three months in advance, and up to one year for the winter season and school holidays.

Carson's Volcano Cottage
$105-$165 bkfst incl.
K, R, tv
Sixth St.
☎*967-7683*
☎*800-845-LAVA*
⇔*967-8094*
www.carsonscottage.com
Nestled in a lush rainforest, Carson's Volcano Cottage comprises a large house with six rooms and five cottages, only one of which is on site. The latter include family cottages and others (more upscale) catering to couples. Amenities differ from one unit to another, but all are comfortable, featuring a wood-burning stove or kitchenette, a fireplace (in the cottages) and more. Each has a private entrance and bathroom, a coffee maker and microwave oven. The hosts are charming and collect Japanese glass floats, as well as poodles! Guests can take advantage of the hot tub beneath a garden pavilion nestled in tree ferns.

Kilauea Lodge
$120-$150 bkfst incl.
R, tv
Old Volcano Rd.
☎*967-7366*
⇔*967-7367*
www.kilauealodge.com
Built in 1938 as a YMCA children's camp, this large cabin was turned into an inn in 1986, and within a few years became one of the most highly rated establishments in Volcano. The main building now houses a restaurant (see p 286), and the 11 rooms are set up in annexes. All are comfortable, with private bathrooms, heating and a kettle for tea or coffee. The four rooms in the Hale Maluna Building and the Honeymoon Deluxe Room also boast a fireplace, very pleasant though somewhat difficult to use because of security systems.

The Volcano Teapot
$105 bkfst incl.
K
19-4041 Kilauea Rd.
Bill & Antoinette Bullough
P.O. Box 511, Volcano
HI 96785
☎*967-7112 or 800-670-8345*
For a bit of Mary Poppins in the land of Pele, let yourself be tempted by this small, fully restored early-20th-century wooden cottage nestled beneath the trees. Though the place is not exactly in the form of a teapot, the forest setting and the *vog* (a combination of "volcano" and "fog") falling at dusk will encourage you to take advantage of the bone-

china collection at guests's disposal and enjoy a nice hot cup of tea. The cottage, rented as a whole, features two bedrooms, a bathroom and kitchen. Minimum two-night stay.

🏠 Hale Ohia Cottages
$95-$130 bkfst incl.
K, ℝ
11-3968 Hale Ohia Lane
☎*967-7986 or 800-455-3803*
⇔*967-8610*
www.baleobia.com
Built in the 1930s in an elegant Tudor-like style, the historic Dillingham family summer estate offers four suites, including a very large one in the main house, and three cottages. Among the most appealing, the Ihilani Cottage, much appreciated by honeymooners, stands out for its flower-laden patio and fireplace facing the bed. Most cottages have a kitchen. A magnificent landscaped garden surrounds the house.

Chalet Kilauea
$135-$395 bkfst incl.
tv
998 Wright Rd., at Laukapu Rd.
☎*967-7786 or 800-937-7786*
⇔*967-8660 or 800-577-1849*
www.volcano-bawaii.com
Both a bed and breakfast and lodge, Chalet Kilauea cultivates a slightly formal opulence, with its living room designed around a fireplace, as well as afternoon tea and a whirlpool perched beneath a pavilion. The six predictably comfortable rooms and suites all feature a marbled

bathroom, and some a hot tub. Each is decorated according to a different theme, including "Out of Africa," "Oriental Jade" and the Art Deco "Owner's Suite." An equally lavish breakfast is served by candlelight. Those only here for a short stay may be unable to reserve a specific room.

Ka'u

Whittington Beach Park
$5/pers. (see p 195)
access 7am to 11pm washrooms, outdoor showers, barbecues, picnic tables
Mamalahoa Hwy. (Mile 60.5)
Despite its name, there is nary a beach here, just a rocky coast with remnants of an old dock and some sort of small lagoon formed by the ocean. The facilities are rather time-worn, but the campground is a good pit stop between Kona and Hilo. Most campers opt to pitch their tent in the brush, on the north side of the lagoon, for greater peace and quiet.

Shirakawa Motel
$35-$42
K
P.O. Box 467, Na'alehu, HI 96772
☎*929-7462*
"The southernmost motel in the United States" is set back from the road, in the middle of Wa'iohinu, right near the Mark Twain Monkeypod Tree (see p 248). The motel has only 12 rooms, popular

on weekends with islanders who have relatives in the area for their good rates. Very simple, all the rooms have their own bathroom, and some a kitchenette, but none have a television or air conditioning. The owner's son is a fisher and can sometimes be seen packaging freshly caught tuna right behind the motel.

Wood Valley Temple
dormitory $25
room $50
sb, K
P.O. Box 250, Pahala HI 96777
☎*928-8539*
⇔*928-6271*
nechung@aloha.net
If you're in need of serenity and Tibetan Buddhism intrigues or fascinates you, don't miss the opportunity to spend a few days at this retreat centre, a secluded haven of peace in the forest. Weekends are often booked by groups, but you shouldn't have too much of a problem getting a space during the week. Keep in mind that this is a temple, so the level of comfort is not the same. All guests have access to a communal kitchen.

Bougainvillea B&B
$65 bkfst incl.
≈, tv
Ocean Estate (Mile 80)
☎/⇔*929-7089*
☎/⇔*800-688-1763*
bi-inns.com/bouga/
An odd place for a bed and breakfast... Mr and Mrs Nietsche left Maui

to settle here, in the middle of a 1,000-year-old lava flow on which a new town was slated for development. The town never completely materialized, but there are a few dozen houses in the shadow of the Mauna Loa fault zone, where an ancient Hawaiian trail once ran. The house holds four very classic, comfortable rooms, each with its own bathroom. A swimming pool, hot tub, barbecue and ping-pong table are at guests's disposal, and the Nietsches will even lend their car to cyclists staying overnight so that they may go to the nearest restaurant. Very friendly welcome.

Macadamia Meadows B&B
$75-$120 bkfst incl.
≈, tv, ℝ, ♨
P.O. Box 756, Naalehu
HI 96772
☎/≈929-8097
☎888-929-8118
www.stayhawaii.com/macmed/macmed.html
Located near the village of Wa'iohinu, in the heart of a macadamia plantation, the large, modern cedar house housing this bed and breakfast promises unexpected comfort after a long day of walking. Canadian-born Charlene is very spontaneous and offers guests a warm welcome; her husband Cortney, who attends to the harvest, is equally

thoughtful. Their eldest daughter studies vulcanology at Hilo University, so the couple is well up on Kilauea's volcanic activity. The two rooms and two suites, all of which have a private entrance and bathroom, are very comfortable; the honeymoon suite, whose antique clawfooted bathtub is set up right on the *lanai* under the stars, is particularly charming.

Sea Mountain Condominiums
$108-$174
≈, laundry, K, ⊗
95-789 Ninole Loop Rd., Punalu'u
☎929-8301 or 800-488-8301
≈928-8008
www.seamtnhawaii.com
Originally there were supposed to be two condominium resorts, but only Colony One materialized, in view of tourists' lack of receptiveness. Located right above the Punalu'u black-sand beach, the studios and apartments are scattered throughout small buildings with thatched roofs meant to evoke Polynesian long houses. They are starting to show their age and have no air conditioning, but are very decent nonetheless. Guests can take advantage of the tennis courts and adjacent golf course, which seems somewhat forlorn in

the middle of nowhere. Minimum two-night stay.

Restaurants

The cuisine of the Big Island stands out from the rest of the archipelago because, here more than elsewhere, restaurateurs have recourse to locally grown organic products, particularly on the northern part of the island and in Hilo.

Kona-Keauhou

Though restaurants abound in Kona, a great many facing the ocean and others set up in shopping centres, the choice is, surprisingly, rather unexceptional.

Kimo's
under $10
every day 7am to 10am and 5:30pm to 8:30pm
75-5739 Ali'i Dr.
☎329-1393
Located next to Uncle Billy's, Kimo's specializes in low-priced buffets. Selections such as prime rib, chicken with barbecue sauce and seafood pasta are rounded out by a grilled fish of the day. In short, all the classics of the kind, not too exciting, but there is Hawaiian music on Friday, Saturday and Sunday evenings.

Kona Mix Plate
under $10 to $15
Mon to Sat 10am to 8pm
Kopiko Plaza,
near Long's Drugs
☎*329-8104*
This no-frills neighbourhood eatery is a favourite haunt of area workers. Good local food is served alongside American and Asian fare, such as teriyaki, fish, tempura, *saiman*, Portuguese bean soup, steaks and sandwiches, not to mention the hallowed plate lunch. Friday is "prime-rib day."

Kona Natural Foods
under $10
Mon to Sat 9am to 9pm, Sun 9am to 7pm
75-1027 Henry St.
Kona Crossroads Center (Safeway Plaza)
☎*329-2296*
This large health-food store, located north of the town centre, houses a small deli offering sandwiches with or without meat and a selection of fresh juices, including carrot and fennel.

Mama's Noodles
under $10
Mon to Fri 10:30am to 9pm, Sat until 8pm
75-5595 Palani Dr.
at the entrance to the Sack'n'Save supermarket
☎*329-2888*
This tiny, very simple fast-food noodle shop is perfect for those with little time or money. *Saimin, udon,* fried rice, plate lunches as well as vegetarian dishes are served here at very reasonable prices.

Ocean Seafood
under $10 to $15
Mon to Fri 10:30am to 9pm, Sat and Sun as of 11am
75-5626 Kuakini Hwy.
King Kamehameha Shopping Center
☎*329-3055*
Located in a rather uninteresting shopping centre, this Chinese restaurant is a good choice for an inexpensive lunch or dinner. The menu offers no less than 152 selections, featuring all the specialties of southern China, with a good assortment of seafood and meats as well as vegetarian dishes, spicy dishes, noodle soups and more. Saturday features dim sum, Cantonese appetizers that can make up a meal in themselves.

Ocean View Inn
under $10
Tue to Sun 6:30am to 2:45pm and 5:15pm to 9pm
bar from 9am until closing
75-5683 Ali'i Dr.
☎*329-9998*
It's not so much the view, partly obstructed by mosquito nets, that draw patrons to the Ocean View Inn, but the good prices – which makes it a popular family restaurant with the locals. A wide selection of sandwiches, steaks and Chinese dishes as well as Hawaiian and vegetarian selections are offered, but the snail-paced service makes the place a bad bet for those in a hurry. No credit cards.

Aki's Café
$10-$15
as of 8am
75-5699 Ali'i Dr.
Kailua Bay Inn Plaza
☎*329-0090*
This small café's streetside terrace looks out on the Kona pier. You can order from the American menu (which includes fish & chips, sandwiches, burgers and pasta) or the Japanese menu (including *ramen,* sushi and *udon*). No credit cards.

Bangkok House
$10-$15
Mon to Fri 11am to 3pm, every day 5pm to 9pm
75-5626 Kuakini Hwy.
King Kamehameha Shopping Center
☎*329-7764*
This small Thai restaurant features a flowery setting and good authentic fare at very reasonable prices. The dinner menu offers a grand total of 104 dishes, from noodles and curries to seafood and vegetarian selections.

Durty Jakes
$10-$15
as of 7am
75-5819 Ali'i Dr.
Coconut Grove Marketplace
☎*329-7366*
This oceanfront eatery (located on the "wrong" side of Ali'i Drive) is open all day but is especially popular for its terrace breakfasts and daily soups. Monday is football night and Thursdays

feature belly dancers, Las Vegas-style.

Kona Ranch House
$10-$20
every day 6:30am to 2pm
75-5653 Olohi St.
☎ *329-7061*
Located a stone's throw from the Kona Seaside Hotel, set back from the seafront, the Ranch House offers a wide, reasonably priced selection at breakfast, which makes it a popular choice with winter visitors. Nothing very special on the menu, save for an unexpected ratatouille among the omelets, sandwiches and burgers. Quiet, fairly pleasant setting.

Lulu's
$10-$15
75-5819 Ali'i Dr.
Coconut Grove Marketplace
(above Durty Jakes)
☎ *331-2633*
The sign above the door reads "Bar – Restaurant – Zoo," an apt description with the place's walls and ceiling covered in tacky objects ranging from a stuffed sunfish to a portrait of Mona Lisa with a screw through her nose. Burgers, sandwiches, Mexican snacks and beer galore are served without respite to football fans who flock here during matches, while others take advantage of the seafront terrace overlooking Ali'i Drive or the nightly music.

Restaurant Yokohama
$10-$20
Tue to Fri and Sun 11am to 2pm, Tue to Sun 5:30pm to 9pm
Ali'i Sunset Plaza
75-5799 Ali'i Dr.
☎ *329-9661*
Attractively decorated, this small, unpretentious restaurant, located at the back of the shopping centre, essentially caters to a Japanese clientele. It even boasts a small Japanese bookshop, and offers a good choice of sushi, salads, *udon* and other selections at reasonable prices for Kona.

Sushi Shop – Island Kitchen
$10-$15
Mon to Sat 9am to 6pm
75-5629 Kuakini Hwy.
North Kona Shopping Center
(at the back)
☎ *987-8490*
Those with a sudden craving for sushi who prefer eating in their hotel room should drop by the Sushi Shop. The place offers a good selection of rolls and platters of various sizes.

Thai Rin Restaurant
$10-$15
Sun to Fri 11am to 2:30pm, every day 5pm to 9pm
Ali'i Sunset Plaza
75-5799 Ali'i Dr.
☎ *329-2929*
Nothing fancy here, just a pretty decor of orchids, good Thai food and a friendly welcome – which really isn't bad at all. Try the *tom kah gai*, a chicken-and-coconut-milk soup flavoured with lemon grass and ginger; the

pineapple fried rice with cucumber and cashews; or the *pad krao* (Bangkok Jungle), consisting of meat, shrimp or calamari with basil, vegetables and chilies. The level of "spiciness" can be adjusted on request.

Sibu Cafe
$15-$20
every day 11:30am to 3pm and 5pm to 9pm
Banyan Court
75-5695 Ali'i Dr.
☎ *329-1112*
The decor may be nondescript, but the Sibu Cafe's Indonesian fare brings a touch of warmth and colour to Kona's gastronomic scene. Though relatively spicy, Indonesian cuisine also features specialties that will please more delicate palates, such as Balinese tarragon chicken or satays. Many dishes come with peanut sauce and all with a choice of white, paddy or fried rice with raisins. Prices are the same at lunch and dinner. No credit cards.

Happy Yu
$15-$25
every day 11:30am to 1:30pm and 5:30pm to 9pm
75-5770 Ali'i Dr.
Waterfront Row
☎ *326-5653*
Happy Yu is part sushi bar, with a whole array of platter choices (including delicacies such as marlin, octopus and salmon roe), part steakhouse, where a chef sautées your vegetables, shrimp or filet

mignon on a grill before your eyes. All dishes come with salad, rice and vegetables.

Kona Beach Restaurant
$13-$22
Mon to Sat 5:30pm to 9pm
75-5660 Palani Rd.
King Kamehameha's Beach Hotel
☎*329-2911*
The King Kamehameha's Beach Hotel's restaurant specializes in buffets, whose prices vary with the theme: Hawaiian on Mondays and Tuesdays (with such treats as *laulau*, *kalua* pork, poi and *lomilomi* salmon); pasta on Wednesdays and Thursdays with appetizer buffet; and seafood on Fridays and Saturdays with fish, *poke*, Alaska snow crab, sashimi, oysters and mussels, as well as prime rib and poultry.

Oodles of Noodles
$15-$25
Mon to Thu 10am to 9pm, Fri 10am to 10pm, Sat noon to 10pm, Sun noon to 7pm
75-1027 Henry St.
Kona Crossroads Center (Safeway Plaza)
☎*329-9222*
Japanese, Italian, Vietnamese, Thai, Chinese, wheat and rice: noodles here come in every way imaginable – and are well prepared, too. Though most soups and salads also include noodles, recalcitrants are sure to find more conventional dishes.

Pancho & Lefty's
$15-$20
every day 8am to 8pm
75-5719 Ali'i Dr.
☎*326-2171*
Located opposite Hulihe'e Palace, this large Tex-Mex bar-restaurant features a long narrow terrace and a menu with all the classics of the genre. Don't overlook the choice of (large) margaritas, tequilas and mescals – but refrain from smoking afterwards, especially near the impressive collection of retro gas pumps set up at the back of the Art Deco room, including Mobilgas, Dixie and Pemex models. Friendly welcome and generous portions, too.

🌴 Cassandra's Greek Tavern
$20-$25
Mon to Fri 11:30am to 4:30pm and every day as of 4:30pm
75-5719 Ali'i Dr.
Kona Plaza Shopping Arcade at the entrance to the Sarona Lounge
☎*334-1066*
With Greece's blue and white national colours so omnipresent, there's no mistaking this restaurant's affiliation. For those with a sudden craving for Mediterranean food, Cassandra's offers a string of famous Greek appetizers, such as *dolmades*, tzatziki, *keftedes* (meatballs cooked with herbs and onions), octopus salad and calamari. And let's not forget the not-to-be-missed Greek salad with tomatoes, cucumber, feta cheese,

onions and olives liberally sprinkled with lemon juice and olive oil. And there's no need to fret about your waistline or saturated fats since Greek food is one of the healthiest on the planet. At night, prices go up and the menu is enriched with *moussaka* and lamb chops, grilled fish and steaks. What's more, patrons are treated to belly dancing every Friday and Saturday night.

Huggo's
$20-$30
Mon to Fri 11:30am to 2:30pm and every day 5:30pm to 10pm
bar Mon to Fri 11:30am to 12:30am, Sat and Sun as of 5pm
75-5828 Kahakai Rd.
☎*329-1493*
Located east of the seafront, Huggo's boasts a waterfront terrace, the main draw for the crowd that flocks here every night. The eclectic menu features salads, pizza, burgers and sandwiches at lunch, and vegetarian dishes, pizza, steak and seafood for dinner, all enhanced with a few Asian touches. After dinner, the restaurant turns into a dance "club" (see p 287). You can also have breakfast, a snack or a drink at Huggo's On the Rocks, right next door.

Kona Inn Restaurant
$20-$30
every day 11:30am to 10:30pm
75-5744 Ali'i Dr.
Kona Inn Shopping Village
☎*329-4455*
At the time of its opening on the seafront in 1928, the Kona Inn was the first hotel on the Big Island. It first welcomed all the passengers disembarking from the steamships sailing from Honolulu, then a growing number of big-game fishers. The most impressive catches of the last 15 years are on display in the lobby, including the biggest mako shark (about 1157 lb or 525kg) ever caught and a colossal blue marlin (weighing in at approximately 1058 lb or 480kg and measuring some 9ft or 3m).
The establishment offers a daily "café grill" menu, with a wide array of salads and sandwiches, and a more upscale dinner menu featuring good *ono, mahi-mahi*, ultra-fresh *'ahi* or *'opakapaka*. But it is the setting more than the cuisine that is admittedly its most attractive feature. Adorned with rattan chairs, the large shaded terrace offers a most soothing panoramic view of the ocean. You can also make do with the view from the bar.

Jameson's by the Sea
$25-$35
every day 11am to 3pm and 5pm to 9:30pm
77-6254 Ali'i Dr.
☎*329-3195*
The main asset of Jameson's, part of an archipelago-wide chain, is its location "by the sea." The romantic terrace looks right on the water and White Sands Beach, on the road to Keauhou. Though the lunch menu primarily sticks to burgers, sandwiches and salads, the dinner menu prominently features island-fresh fish and seafood – with several recipes for *'opakapaka* alone. Wine is sold by the glass, but prices are rather steep. From Wednesday to Sunday, patrons dine to live Hawaiian music. Good desserts.

Michaelangelo's
$25-$35
every day 11am to 10pm dance club until 2am
75-5770 Ali'i Dr.
Waterfront Row (see p 288)
☎*329-4436*
When Italy meets Hawaii under the leadership of a California chef, the result is Michaelangelo's. The most obvious point in common being the presence of the ocean, the establishment offers a wide range of fish and seafood, including fresh *'ahi, coquilles Saint-Jacques* with macadamia nuts, lobster and

San Francisco-style *cioppino*. Not be overlooked, however, are a few more "down-to-earth" specialties, such as the marsala chicken and steak Capri. You can dine inside, in a pleasant if somewhat kitsch setting with a mess of girders and fake purple columns, or on the large oceanfront terrace.

The South Coast of Kona

Billy Bob's
under $10
Mon to Sat 5pm to 9pm, Sun until 8pm
at the entrance to Captain Cook (Mile 110.7)
☎*323-3371*
Every barbecue afficionado within a 14mi (20km) radius flocks here. The Bodacious Meal features a cut of meat (beef or pork ribs, chicken or pork) and two accompaniments (including salad, rice or corn bread). Those with smaller appetites can go for a bowl of chili, a vegetarian enchilada or chicken salad. Live music on Saturday nights.

Holuakoa Cafe
under $10
Mon to Sat 6:30am to 3pm
76-5901 Mamalahoa Hwy.
☎*322-CAFE*
Located in an old wooden house that also serves as a souvenir shop – which carries locally grown vanilla –, this café has a few tables inside and three

others by a small flowery garden. You can sample local coffees along with a piece of macadamia-nut pie or a fresh bagel.

Ka'aloa's Super J's
under $10
Mon to Sat 10am until nightfall
83-5409 Mamalahoa Hwy., Honaunau (Mile 106.3)
☎*328-9566*
The owners of Super J's may be Mormons, but the food here provides unmistakable proof of their Hawaiian origins. All the classics are offered, including *lomilomi* salmon, *poi* and *poke*, ordered individually or as plate lunches. Most clients come here for take-out, but there are a few tables on the premises.

Peacock House
under $10
Mon to Fri 10am to 8:30pm, Sat as of 11am and Sun as of 5pm
81-6587 Mamalahoa Hwy.
Pualani Terrace,
Kealakekua (Mile 111.8)
☎*323-2366*
This neighbourhood Chinese restaurant draws a fair number of regulars, Kealakekua police officers having, as it were, made it their canteen. The extensive menu (144 dishes) is rounded out by a selection of plate lunches at unbeatable prices. What's more, portions are ample.

The Coffee Shack
under $10
Mon to Sat 7am to 5pm
Hwy. 11 (Mile 108.3)
at the south exit of
Captain Cook
☎*328-9555*
A very humble stop, the Coffee Shack has a terrace with a few tables overlooking fields of coffee trees, the coast and the ocean beyond. Besides breakfast and fresh bread, pizza and salads make up a quick lunch topped off with Kona coffee.

The Korner Pocket Bar & Grill
under $10 to $20
every day 11am to 2am
Central Kona Center 2,
Kealakehua (Mile 112)
via the road going down to
McDonald's
☎*322-2994*
Appreciated by regulars, this billiard-bar/restaurant offers a fairly appealing decor and a choice of varied dishes, from chicken and ribs to steak and pasta with clams and marinara sauce that will not disappoint. Less expensive alternatives are the daily salads and sandwiches. Live country music is featured on certain nights.

Wakefield Gardens
under $10
every day 10am to 4pm
on the road to Pu'uhonua o
Honaunau (Mile 1.1)
☎*328-7441*
There was once a botanical garden here – hence the establishment's name. A young couple bought it, the land was sold and the

verdant spot is now home to a sandwich shop. The place offers all kinds of sandwiches, including the amazing Papaya Boat, made of papaya, tuna and vegetables and served with fruit and cole slaw. The macadamia-nut, coconut and *lilikoi* (passion fruit) pies are also good.

Aloha Café
$10-$20
Sun to Thu 8am to 3pm,
Fri and Sat 8am to 9pm
Kainaliu (Mile 113.3)
☎*322-3383*
Now restored, the old 1932 Aloha Theater not only screens films again, but also houses a café-restaurant offering a range of nachos, burgers, soups and salads as well as a selection of seven dishes inspired by Hawaiian regional cuisine, including taro-crusted 'ahi and Cajun-Hawaiian chicken marinated in Cajun spices, served with mango sauce and topped with macadamia nuts. Everything is a little expensive, though.

Ke'ei Cafe
$10-$20
Tue to Sun as of 5:15pm
Mamalahoa Hwy.,
Honaunau (Mile 106)
☎*328-8451*
Though it isn't much to look at from the outside, this small café run by a Hawaiian man and Brazilian woman is so popular that reservations have almost become a must. The varied menu combines all the influences ever to

have reached the islands, including, of course, the proprietress's Brazilian touch. The meats are excellent. No credit cards.

⚓ Teshima's
$10-$15
every day 6:30am to 1:45pm and 5pm to 9pm
Honalo (Mile 113.9)
☎322-9140
Established in the 1940s, this veritable institution is typical of family-run restaurants that combine cultural tradition (Japanese, in this case) and local staples. At lunch, people come to treat themselves to the dish of the day with rice, miso soup, *tsukemono*, *sunomono* and green tea, or drop by to enjoy such offerings as *bento* with meat, fried fish or *kamaboku* (fish cake). Despite the humble setting, dinner is more scintillating and includes sushi appetizers. Excellent welcome and very reasonable prices. Hotel, see p 258.

The North Coast of Kona

Beach Tree Bar & Grill
$30-$45
every day 11:30am to 8:30pm
Four Seasons Hualalai Resort (see p 260)
Mile 86, on Hwy. 19
via Ka'upulehu Rd.
☎325-8000
The parasol-shaded terrace of the Four Seasons's most affordable restaurant is located next to the swimming pool and almost as close to the beach. It is best to come for the setting rather than the food, which, though not bad, sometimes holds unpleasant surprises (dirty lettuce, for instance). The lunch menu is limited to a few daily specials and grilled fish. Theme buffets are organized several nights a week: Asian on Monday, Italian on Wednesday and Hawaiian to music on Saturday.

Hale Moana
$70
every day 7:15am to 9:45am, 12:30pm to 2pm and 6pm to 8:45pm
Kona Village Resort (see p 260)
Mile 86.9 on Hwy. 19
via Ka'upulehu Rd.
☎325-5555
Housed in a Polynesian-style building, the main restaurant of the Kona Village Resort offers a view of the ocean through its large picture windows. Patrons enjoy lunch on the shaded terrace and dinner inside, at which time shorts, tank tops and jeans are forbidden – as are neckties! The buffet prominently features fish and seafood, generally prepared according to the new methods of Hawaiian regional cuisine. Dishes change nightly and are accompanied by tropical rhythms from 6pm to 9:30pm. What's more, a *luau* is organized on Fridays.

Pahui'a
$30-$50
every day 6am to 11:30am and 5:30pm to 10pm
Four Seasons Hualalai Resort (see p 260)
Mile 86.9 on Hwy. 19
via Ka'upulehu Rd.
☎325-8000
This highly renowned dining establishment, whose name means "aquarium," offers Hawaiian regional cuisine with a twist, such as leg of mutton paired with coffee and served with polenta, or Thai conserve of duck with rice noodles and *rouille* (spicy sauce of red peppers and garlic). The view of the ocean is soothing, but the choice is ultimately rather limited.

The Kohala Coast

King's Shops
under $10
250 Waikoloa Beach Dr.
The food court at the Waikoloa shopping centre, the only one on the south Kohala Coast, features a limited choice of fast-food counters whose offerings include Mexican food, a coffee and juice bar and a pizzeria-grill.

Grand Palace
$10-$25
every day 11am to 9:30pm
250 Waikoloa Beach Dr., King's Shops
☎886-6668
All of China in your plate: the menu features no less than 155 dishes, including desserts. Also available are

special combination plates for one to four people.

Tres Hombres Beach Grill
$15-$20
every day 11:30am to 9pm, Fri and Sat until 10pm
Kawaihae Shopping Center
☎*882-1031*
Located upstairs in the small shopping centre facing Kawaihae Harbor (on Highway 270, just past the junction to the port) and boasting a pleasant terrace, Tres Hombres cultivates a nostalgic image. On the walls hang a row of film posters and mementos from the golden years of surfing. The menu features all the great Americanized Mexican classics, from tacos to burritos to enchiladas, with a few big salads and sandwiches thrown in for good measure.

Café Pesto
$20-$25
every day 11am to 9pm, Fri and Sat until 10pm
Kawaihae Shopping Center
☎*882-1071*
Located on the lower level of the Kawaihae Shopping Center, Café Pesto has garnered a chorus of praise from local critics for its "Hawaiianized" Italian cuisine – or is it "Italianized" Hawaiian cuisine? The result: such treats as *luau* pizza with *kalua* pork and slightly spicy seafood risotto, as well as thoroughly local *poke*. At lunch, the choice is essentially limited to salads, sandwiches and

a few pasta dishes. Café Pesto has a counterpart in Hilo, which is more into regional cuisine (see p 285).

Kawaihae Harbor Grill
$20-$30
every day 5:30pm to 9:30pm
Kawaihae
☎*882-1368*
Located in an old green wooden building at the entrance to Kawaihae, the Harbor Grill is popular for its fresh fish and seafood specialties. The restaurant's orientation is as regional (*laulau* with fish, *co-quilles Saint-Jacques* and steamed crab in *ti* leaves) as it is international (New England clam chowder). Monday is lobster night and Thursday, prime-rib night.

Palm Terrace
$18-$24
every day 6am to 11am and 5pm to 9:30pm
425 Waikoloa Beach Dr.
Hilton Waikoloa Village (see p 261)
☎*886-1234, ext. 54*
Breakfast and dinner alike are summed up in one word here: buffet. But what buffets! Monday and Friday evenings have a barbecue theme, while Tuesdays and Saturdays are Polynesian, Thursdays are international and Sundays devoted to ribs (all you can eat). Children eat at half-price. If you're making a special trip here, take the monorail, as it's a fair walking distance from the reception – even if you enjoy Asian art.

Donatoni's
$25-$45
every day 6pm to 9:30pm
425 Waikoloa Beach Dr.
Hilton Waikoloa Village (see p 261)
☎*886-1234, ext. 54*
For diehard fans of Italy, here is Venice in kit form, with a terrace along the Hilton Waikolao canal, old-fashioned lampposts and romantic candlelit tables. This top-notch restaurant is run by a Milanese chef who concocts Tuscany-style minestrone, gnocchi with gorgonzola and nuts, marsala veal escalopes and other Livorno-style *cioppinos*. The value offered for the price makes this by far the best restaurant on the Kohala Coast.

Hama Yu
$25-$40
every day 11:30am to 3pm and 5:30pm to 9pm
250 Waikoloa Beach Dr.
King's Shops
☎*886-6333*
This "authentic" (as the sign proclaims) Japanese restaurant offers a wide array of sushi, sashimi, tempura, fish, chicken or beef teriyaki and tofu dishes, not to mention seaweed salads, in a sober yet polished setting.

Hawai'i Calls
$25-$40
every day 6:30am to 2pm and 5:30pm to 9:30pm
69-275 Waikoloa Beach Dr.
Outrigger Waikoloa Beach Hotel (see p 262)
☎*886-6789*
Looking out on the hotel swimming pool and lagoons, this

oceanfront restaurant draws its name from the famous 1930s radio show that popularized Hawaiian music. Its menu is predictably devoted to regional cuisine, with a focus on surf (*laulau*, Tahitian salmon, lobster) and turf (tournedos, lamb chops, roast chicken with mango sauce). A few vegetarian dishes are also available.

Roy's Waikoloa Bar & Grill
$30-$45
every day 11:30am to 2pm and 5:30pm to 9:30pm
250 Waikoloa Beach Dr.
King's Shops
☎885-4321
One of famous chef Roy Yamaguchi's four highly acclaimed Hawaiian restaurants, the Waikoloa Bar & Grill mixes and matches local products with international culinary trends. Every night, a crowd of tourists flocks to this prized eatery. To treat yourself without breaking the bank, take advantage of the lunch special, which includes a soup of the day and a small salad, sorbet and a beverage. Otherwise, the vegetarian dishes are top-notch.

The Pavilion
$30-$50
every day 6:30am to 10:30am and 6pm to 9:15pm
Mauna Kea Beach Hotel
(see p 261)
☎882-7222
A huge oceanfront terrace is what has earned the Pavilion its most loyal clients. Although

there's no need to book a table at lunch, it is a good idea to do so at dinner if you wish to get a decent table. The food is good, if unexceptional, consisting of international cuisine alongside dishes closer to the new Hawaiian culinary trend.

Canoe House
$35-$50
every day 6pm to 9pm
Mauna Lani Bay Hotel
(see p 262)
☎885-6622
So named because of the big *koa*-wood canoe hanging from the ceiling, the Mauna Lani Resort's signature restaurant offers a rich and varied menu featuring Pacific Rim cuisine, as well as some continental classics. Those who just want to take advantage of the setting without spending a small fortune can opt for a salad, with or without lobster. The wine list is true to type, but pricy.

The Terrace
$36
Mauna Kea Beach Hotel
(see p 261)
☎882-7222
Every Sunday, a brunch renowned throughout the island is served at The Terrace. The rest of the time, the place is a bar, a great place to have a drink by the ocean with Hawaiian music playing in the background.

Batik
$40-$60
every day except Wed and Sat from 6:30pm to 9pm
Mauna Kea Beach Hotel
☎882-7222
The Mauna Kea Beach Hotel's flagship poolside restaurant features a refined setting and a very heterogeneous menu showcasing Asian (Thai or Indonesian curries), European (escargots, garlic scampi on a bed of pasta, roast breast of pheasant with mushrooms and with artichokes and foie gras) and Hawaiian (*'ahi* tartare, macadamia-nut *ono* with lemon grass and coconut milk) cuisine. A different selection is offered every week.

Imari
$40-$60
every day 6pm to 10pm
425 Waikoloa Beach Dr.
Hilton Waikoloa Village
(see p 261)
☎886-1234, ext. 54
Rather than taking the first plane to Tokyo, treat yourself to a sumptuous dinner in this traditional Japanese oasis, nestled amidst the Hilton Waikoloa Village's splendours. A pavilion looking out on the water, the restaurant is surrounded by a miniature Zen garden and watched over by *koi*. Patrons can sample all the classics of Japanese cuisine, high-priced but warranted by the setting and quality. You can also make do with the sushi bar or, conversely, rent out

the traditional tatami room.

The Kohala Peninsula

Jen's Kohala Cafe
under $10
Mon to Sat 10am to 6pm, Sun 11am to 5pm
Kapa'au, in front of the King Kamehameha statue
☎*889-0099*
The only snack bar in Kapa'au offers a selection of sandwiches, burgers and wraps, herb-garlic flat bread stuffed with such ingredients as lettuce, tomato and meat. The Kamehameha wrap is made with *kalua* pork, Maui onion and cheese. Most of the organic vegetables are locally grown. Ice cream is also available.

Kohala Coffee Mill (Tropical Dreams)
under $10
Mon to Sat 6:30am to 6pm
Sat and Sun 7:30am to 5pm
Hawi, town centre
☎*889-5577*
Part café, part coffee-roasting (and souvenir) shop, the Kohala Coffee Mill is an appealing stop on the road to Pololu Valley. Coffee, fresh bagels, sandwiches and ice cream are enjoyed here throughout the day in a fairly cozy setting with a large, soft sofa and tables outside.

Bamboo Restaurant
$20-$25
Tue to Sat 11:30am to 2:30pm and 6pm to 8:30pm
Sunday brunch 11am to 2pm
Hawi, town centre
☎*889-5555*
True to its name, this restaurant is largely decorated with bamboo. Housed in a former hotel founded in the 1910s to welcome plantation workers upon their arrival, it is even rumoured to have been a brothel at one time. Bought out in 1926, the hotel became a grocery store, then a restaurant, but still retains its original Hawaiian-saloon-style decor. The menu features full-flavoured Hawaiian regional cuisine with an Asian twist. The establishment's pride and joy are its Chicken Sate Potstickers (steamed Chinese-style ravioli-like dumplings served with a chili-mint sauce). If you find a flower in your salad, don't hesitate to bite into it – it's an orange pepper-plant blossom from the restaurant's very own organic vegetable and aromatic-herb garden. On weekends, Hawaiian music wafts through the place, which is also home to a local arts-and-crafts gallery (see p 290) and a billiard bar.

Waimea-Kamuela

Kamuela Deli
under $10
Waimea Shopping Center
65-1158 Mamalahoa Hwy.
☎*885-4147*
This fast-food counter, whose counterpart is located in Kona, is a favoured local spot for a quick lunch. A selection of varied Asian dishes ranging from pig-knuckle soup to noodles in all their incarnations (including Indonesian, Thai, Chinese and Japanese) are offered. The Singapore Fried Rice Noodles are particularly recommended.

The Little Juice Shack
under $10
Mon to Fri 7am to 6pm, Sat 9am to 4pm
Parker Ranch Center
☎*885-1686*
The Little Juice Shack uses fruits and vegetables in every way imaginable: pear, papaya and pineapple as well as carrot, beet and celery, whether individually or mixed, are freshly squeezed before your very eyes. Healthy light fare (bagels, sandwiches, salads) is also available.

Young's Kal-Bi
under $10
Mon to Sat 10am to 9pm
65-1158 Mamalahoa Hwy.
Waimea Shopping Center
☎*885-8440*
Eating at this 100% authentic Korean eatery is a two-step process: you order your meal at the counter and the boss serves you at your

table once it's ready.
The Bi Bam Bap, a dish
of fried vegetables and
rice with chicken, beef
and tofu topped off
with a fried egg, is a
local favourite.

Maha's Cafe
$10-$15
*Wed to Mon 8am to
4:30pm*
65-1148 Mamalahoa Hwy.
Waimea Shopping Center
(at the entrance)
☎885-0693
This café shares the
historic Spencer House,
a wooden structure
dating from 1852, with
a real-estate agency
(through which cus-
tomers enter). A local
favourite, it is the brain-
child of a Hawaiian
chef whose menu
showcases local ingre-
dients, with such dishes
as fish of the day with
sweet potatoes and taro
and smoked 'ahi with
lilikoi sauce (served in a
cheese-covered tortilla).

Paniolo Country Inn
$10-$15
every day 7am to 8:45pm
65-1214 Lindsey Rd.
☎885-4377
It would be unthink-
able to visit Waimea
without sampling
Parker beef, and meat-
lovers are sure to find
something here to
please their carnivorous
proclivities, be it rare
steaks or burgers.
Though not as fitting,
paniolo pizza and Mexi-
can snacks as well as
salads or sandwiches
are also available. Won-
derful welcome and
much better value for
the money than at the

next-door Parker Ranch
Grill.

Su's Thai Kitchen
$10-$20
varying hours
Parker Ranch Center
☎885-8688
This simple, authentic
little Thai restaurant
offers a selection of
curries, rice and noodle
dishes, salads and
more. At lunch, you
can count on a cheap,
big or small, daily spe-
cial. House specialties
such as the Volcano
fish or chicken are
slightly more expen-
sive.

Edelweiss
$20-$30
*Wed to Sat 11:30am to
1:30pm and 5pm to
8:30pm*
Kawaihae Rd. (Hwy. 19)
right before Opelo Rd.
☎885-6800
A hint of Europe in the
heart of Hawaii!
Opened by a German
chef in 1983, Edelweiss
offers good traditional
Teutonic food, from
sauerkraut to wiener
schnitzel (escalopes),
not to mention the
chicken-liver omelets
and the leg of lamb –
substantial fare fit for
the chilly Waimea-
Kamuela climate. At
lunchtime, both the
menu and prices are
scaled down consider-
ably, with mostly sand-
wiches, bratwurst and
sauerkraut.

Merriman's
$20-$30
*every day 11:30am to
1:30pm and 5:30pm to
9pm*
Opelo Plaza
Kawaihae Rd. (Hwy. 19)
☎885-6822
Highly renowned on
the Big Island and be-
yond, chef Peter
Merriman offers good
Hawaiian regional cui-
sine, providing the best
fresh (and often or-
ganic) products the
island has to offer. At
lunch, the *Niçoise* salad
with grilled fish is a
good choice. The wok-
charred 'ahi and the
meats are the restau-
rant's signature dishes.
Delicate palates may
bemoan the tad-too-
frequent recourse to
hot spices, however.

The Hamakua
Coast

'Akaka Falls Inn
under $10
centre of Honomu
☎963-5468
Opened by a profes-
sional cook, this
deli/bed and breakfast
offers a variety of good
sandwiches (vegetarian
or not), tamales,
quesadillas and organic
salads. Also available
are fruit salads and
daily pastries, as well
as cooking lessons!

Mamane Street Bakery
under $10
Mamane St.,
opposite Cafe Il Mondo
☎775-9478
Renowned for its morn-
ing baked goods (in-
cluding muffins, crois-
sants and turnovers),

this pleasant, friendly bakery was founded by an Egyptian who has called the archipelago home since 1986.

Tex Drive-In
under $10
every day 6am to 8pm
45-690 Pakalana St.
Honoka'a
below Hwy. 19 (Mile 43)
☎775-0598
Both a drive-in and fast-food counter, this local favourite is a relic of the 1960s that was "Creolized" in a Hawaiian style. You can therefore enjoy a good *'ahi* burger or a Hawaiian plate (with *laulau*, *kalua* and *poi*), as well as burgers and sandwiches. But the real house specialty is *malassadas*, Portuguese holeless "donuts" with such fillings as papaya, pineapple or chocolate.

Waipi'o Valley Artworks
under $10
every day 8am to 6pm
Kukuihaele
☎775-0958
Located just before the Waipi'o Valley Lookout, this crafts shop (see p 290) is home to the Fire Woods Cafe, which offers varied snacks as well as a selection of coffees and excellent ice cream.

Cafe Il Mondo
$10-$15
Mon to Sat 10:30am to 8:30pm, Sun 4:30pm to 8:30pm
45-3626 Mamane St.
Honoka'a
☎775-7711
Located right in the heart of Honoka'a, this former bar, which first

saw the light of day in 1924, has been taken over by a small pizzeria with warm colours and a flowery decor. The pizza is more American than Italian but colossal and cooked in a wood-burning oven, and sold by the slice until 5pm. Also available are a few salads, a good choice of sandwiches and a whole range of coffees to sip while leafing through the many magazines at your disposal.

Hilo

Bear's Coffee
under $10
106 Keawe St.
☎935-0708
Regulars crowd to Bear's Coffee, where the java is from Kona, of course, and can be enjoyed with a morning waffle. Later in the day, bagels, sandwiches and burritos satisfy those who are feeling a little peckish. The establishment's business hours are somewhat misleading, however, as food is only served from 7am to 2:30pm.

Canoe's
under $10
308 Kamehameha Ave.
☎935-4070
A dozen tables huddled together in a small shopping centre, in the shadow of canoes and paddles suspended from the ceiling, make up this aptly named café. Food-wise, pastries are offered as of 8am, breakfast at 9am, and a profusion of salads, paninis and

sandwiches as well as *poke* the rest of the day.

Honu's Nest
under $10
Mon to Wed 10am to 7pm, Thu and Fri until 8pm, Sun until 4pm
270 Kamehameha Ave.
☎935-9321
Located at the corner of Furneaux Street, this "turtle's nest" offers a good selection of Japanese dishes (*domburi*, tempura and delicious sashimi), salads and sandwiches, as well as *katsu* chicken, sautéed vegetables, curries and other fine choices.

Ken's House of Pancakes
under $10
24hrs
1730 Kamehameha Ave.
at Kanoelehua Ave.
☎935-8711
A local favourite for its family breakfasts, Ken's offers round-the-clock food that, while not the epitome of fine cuisine, satisfies hearty appetites. Pancakes, waffles, burgers, ribs and eggs as well as a few desserts – everything you'd expect from a typical American fast-food restaurant.

Kuhio Grille
under $10
Mon to Thu 5am to 10pm, Fri 5am straight through Sun 10pm
Prince Kuhio Plaza, at the entrance to Hilo (on the road to Volcanoes National Park)
☎959-2336
A popular local spot for its good prices and copious dishes, the Kuhio Grille is nothing fancy, offering eggs for breakfast, sandwiches,

chili, *saimin*, spaghetti and, on a revisited Hawaiian note, corned-beef-hash taro. For dinner, give into the famous one-pound *laulau* – a one-of-kind dish combined with poi, *lomilomi* salmon and *haupia* – or *kanak atak* with *kalua* pork into the bargain.

Royal Siam
under $10
Mon to Sat 11am to 2pm and 5pm to 9pm
70 Mamo St.
☎*961-6100*
One of the best Thài eateries on the island, Royal Siam serves generous, authentic fare at reasonable prices. You can opt for a curry, a salad (including one with tofu or papaya), a whole range of soups, seafood and a wide array of vegetarian dishes. But the restaurant's benchmark dish remains the hot garlic shrimp with coconut milk.

Don's Grill
$10-$20
Tue to Thu 10:30am to 9pm, Fri until 10pm, Sat and Sun 10am to 9pm
485 Hinano St.
next to the stadium
☎*935-9099*
Very crowded on weekends, this family restaurant par excellence concocts simple, popular dishes such as braised beef, pork-stuffed eggplant, pig's knuckles and fish of the day. Expect a long wait on Friday and Saturday nights.

Miwa
$10-$30
Mon to Sat 11am to 2pm and every day 5pm to 10pm (Sun until 9pm)
1261 Kilauea Ave.
Hilo Shopping Center (Suite 230)
☎*961-4454*
Its name says it and regulars confirm it: Miwa could be translated as "first-rate cuisine." The Wafu Steak in sake sauce is especially noteworthy, but you can also opt for Japanese and American specialties such as tempura, salmon or beef teriyaki, meat, *'ahi* or stuffed shrimp. Sushi-lovers can get their fill at the sushi bar, and fans of karaoke can cut loose and belt out a few tunes after dinner.

Miyo's
$10-$15
Mon to Sat 11am to 2pm and 5:30pm to 8:30pm
400 Hualani St.
(Waiakea Villas Complex)
☎*935-2273*
Featuring a simple, all-wood decor reminiscent of a Japanese house, Miyo's looks out on Wailoa Pond. The restaurant's home-style Japanese cuisine offers excellent value for the price, dinner rates being almost identical to lunch. No sushi, but tempura, noodles (excellent *udon* with *wakame* and seaweed), teriyaki, *domburi* and sashimi. The combination plate includes rice, salad and miso soup.

Ocean Sushi Deli
$10-$20
Mon to Sat 10am to 3pm and 4:30pm to 9pm
239 Keawe St.
☎*961-6625*
Run by two young couples of Japanese ancestry, this humble little deli makes excellent sushi with a classic and downright innovative touch. You will undoubtedly need to a few minutes to choose among the 107 versions, unless you opt for a combo, which makes choosing a lot easier. A daily all-you-can-eat sushi buffet is offered for $20 at lunch and $25 at dinner – an unbelievable deal! What's more, individual prices are rarely equalled and the welcome is friendly.

Reubens
$10-$15
Mon to Fri 11am to 9pm, Sat noon to 9pm
336 Kamehameha Ave.
☎*961-2552*
Its later hours alone will make you feel like you're south of the American border. This unpretentious but good-quality little restaurant dishes up all the Mexican staples, including enchiladas, tamales and *carne asada* (grilled meats), as well as all types of eggs. The two house specialties come in liquid and solid form: the highly renowned margaritas, and the *gallina adobada* (marinated chicken), which comes with rice and salad.

Seaside Restaurant
$10-$25
Tue to Sun 5pm to 8:30pm
1790 Kalaniana'ole Rd.
☎*935-8825*
This aquacultural farm has its own restaurant – specializing in fish, of course. So fresh is the fish, you can choose your own "catch of the day" from the on-site former Lokowaka Hawaiian fishpond stocked with trout, silurid and mullet; the other fish are bought at the Suisan Fish Auction. But meat-lovers will also get their fill, as steaks, teriyaki chicken and ribs are prominently featured on the menu as well. All dishes come with salad, vegetables, apple pie and tea or coffee.

Nihon
$15-$30
Mon to Sat 11am to 1:30pm, dinner as of 5pm
123 Lihiwai St.
☎*969-1133*
The Japanese cultural centre's restaurant offers a predictably traditional menu. At lunch, the "Hatamoto" includes two of seven choices and comes with rice, sushi, potato salad, *konomono*, miso soup and a small salad. Also offered is a wide array of sushi, ordered à la carte or in combo platters of 16, 30 or 45 pieces. The tuna is ultra fresh as it is unloaded daily from the boats at the Suisan Fish Auction, located just 600ft (200m) away.

Café Pesto
$20-$30
every day 11am to 9pm (until 10pm Fri and Sat)
308 Kamehameha Ave.
☎*969-6640*
Hilo's Café Pesto has set up shop in the old 1912 Hata Building, right in the centre of town. Like its Kawaihae clone, on the Kona Coast, it offers Italian-influenced Hawaiian nouvelle cuisine. Romans-at-heart will undoubtedly be only moderately pleased with its gourmet pizza, but may be tempted by other house specialties, such as crab cakes with honey-miso dressing, sesame-ginger *poke* and slightly spicy seafood risotto. Prices are a little steep, though.

Harrington's
$20-$30
Mon to Fri 11am to 2pm, every day 5:30pm to 9:30pm (Sun 9pm)
135 Kalaniana'ole Ave.
☎*961-4966*
The restaurant is perched over Reed's Bay, but the tranquillity of its terrace is disrupted by the proximity of the road. Rather standard at lunch (salads, sandwiches), Harrington's adopts a new image in the evening, offering a good selection of fish and seafood, including kebabs, calamari *meunière* and lobster. Steaks, prime rib, marsala and teriyaki chicken are also available for those who prefer meat.

Pescatore
$20-$35
every day 11am to 2pm and 5:30pm to 9pm; bkfst Sat and Sun 7:30am to 11am
235 Keawe St.
☎*969-9090*
This establishment's name perfectly epitomizes its gastronomic inclination: Italy and its fish-filled waters. But the choice is not confined to *cioppino* and the delicious fish carpaccio, as the eatery also offers such selections as tomatoes with mozzarella, minestrone and pasta. At lunch time, pizza and paninis are served, while the dinner menu includes soup or salad, a main course, dessert and tea or coffee.

Puna

Luquin's
$10-$15
every day 7am to 9pm
Pahoa, town centre
☎*965-9990*
Located on the main floor of the Village Inn, the only hotel in Pahoa, Luquin's is, though its name is no indication, a Mexican restaurant – and a very popular one at that. Regulars gather here every Friday and Saturday over a margarita or a *chile relleno* (stuffed pepper) whose quality remains undisputed.

Paolo's
$10-$20
Tue to Sun 5:30pm to 9pm
333 Pahoa Rd., Pahoa
☎ 965-7033
Appreciated by couples, this rather intimate Italian bistro offers a fairly limited but good-quality menu.

Sawasdee
$10-$15
Wed to Mon noon to 8:30pm
15-2955 Pahoa Rd., Pahoa
☎ 965-8186
This rather standard Thai restaurant prides itself on using nothing but organic products from its own garden.

The Godmother
$10-$20
every day 8am to 3pm and as of 5:30pm
15-2969 Pahoa Rd., Pahoa
☎ 965-0055
Scampi, marsala, parmigiana: The Godmother cultivates her ties to the New World, Italian-style. The "New York" steak, the house specialty, is served with sautéed mushrooms and onions, tomato sauce and mozzarella. All dishes come with soup or salad.

Volcanoes National Park

🌴 **Lava Rock Cafe**
under $10 to $15
Mon 7:30am to 5pm, Tue until 6:30pm, Wed to Sat until 9pm, Sun until 4pm
Old Volcano Rd.
☎ 967-8526
From breakfast to dinner, the Lava Rock Cafe offers a warm and friendly setting as well as good value for the money. In the morning, you can opt for such offerings as the classic "2-egg eruption," pancakes or an omelet. At lunch, give in to the "seismic sandwiches" or the "lava tube plate lunches." Service is rather slow, but the proprietress does her best, running to and fro and making enquiries. The place is also one of the few establishments on the Big Island to offer Internet access (see p 196).

Steam Vent Cafe
under $10
every day 6:30am to 8:30pm
at Old Volcano Rd. and Haunani St.
☎ 985-8744
Located behind Surt's restaurant and the gas station, this small, self-service deli-café offers a selection of soups, good salads, sandwiches and fresh pastries, all of which can be snacked on throughout the day on the handful of covered tables set up outside.

Rainbow Moon Pizza
$10-$17
Wed to Sun 4pm to 9pm
☎ 967-8617
Highly renowned in Volcano, Rainbow Moon Pizza, opened by a German woman and her American spouse, delivers throughout the village as well as in the national park. It's not an optical illusion: the pizza is well and truly rectangular. But don't go looking for the pizzeria – there is none; just delivery (you can pay by credit card).

Thaï
$15-$20
Thu to Tue 5pm to 9pm
79-4084 Old Volcano Rd.
☎ 967-7969
As its name unequivocally indicates, this restaurant offers (good) Thai cuisine – and in a rather elegant setting, too. Curries, more or less spicy, are prominently featured and the daily specials are noteworthy. Unfortunately, rice is not systematically included. All in all, the choice is rather limited and prices a little steep.

🍴 **Kilauea Restaurant**
$20-$30
every day 5:30pm to 9pm
Old Volcano Rd.
Kilauea Lodge (see p 270)
☎ 967-7366
Whether staying at the lodge or not, you can dine by the large, crackling fire on any given night. The menu, somewhat reminiscent of that of a European hunting lodge, spotlights dishes cooked in a sauce, such as Hasenpfeffer (braised rabbit in a hearty hunter's wine sauce), Paupiettes of Beef and osso bucco, to say nothing of the fresh island fish and alternating daily specials.

Volcano House
$20-$30
*every day 7am to 10am,
11am to 2pm and
5:50pm to 9pm
snack bar 8:30am to
4:30pm*
opposite the Visitor Center, in
the park
☎967-7321

The Volcano House
(see p 270) is not re-
nowned for its menu,
but for its location, on
the edge of the Kilauea
crater, of which noth-
ing can be seen at
night or as soon as the
fog rolls in. Breakfast
and lunch are the occa-
sion for a fairly cheap
buffet, while dinner is
based on a truly inter-
national menu featuring
a rather limited choice
of steaks, ribs, pasta
and more. It is better to
eat in the village or,
failing that, at the snack
bar, which offers a
variety of sandwiches
and snacks.

Surt's
$25-$35
every day noon to 9:30pm
at Old Volcano Rd. and
Haunani St.
☎967-8511

Run by a Thai chef,
Surt's offers a double
lunch and dinner
fusion-cuisine menu,
with Asian-inspired
dishes (fairly spicy) on
the one hand, and
Italian-influenced selec-
tions on the other. You
can also opt for a salad
and, at night, fresh fish.
The wine list confines
itself to California
wines.

Ka'u

Mark Twain Café
under $10
Naalehu (Mile 65.3)
☎929-7550

This small shack selling
sandwiches, cookies
and beverages is a very
popular stop on the
way to Kona at Volca-
noes National Park, as
it stands at the foot of
the large monkeypod
tree planted by its
famous namesake in
1866.

Naalehu Fruit Stand
under $10
*Mon to Sat 9am to 6pm,
Sun 9am to 5pm*
Naalehu
☎929-9009

Selling everything from
fruit and beverages to
hearty sandwiches,
pizza and homemade
cookies, as well as
renting out videos and
cylinders of gas, this is
truly the neighbour-
hood convenience
store. The macadamia-
nut pie is quite famous.

Shaka Restaurant
$10-$15
Tue to Sun 8am to 8pm
95-5675 Mamalahoa Hwy.
(Mile 64)
☎929-7404

The only real restaurant
for miles around,
Shaka's offers a stan-
dard menu featuring
steaks, salads, burgers
and fish, all of which
are fairly good and
served in generous
portions. Music on
certain nights. Note that
the establishment
sometimes closes ear-
lier when business is
slow.

Entertainment

Bars and Dance Clubs

The Big Island is hardly
a place with a swinging
nightlife. People here
go to bed early to rise
at dawn. There are no
dance clubs and few
bars to speak of, just a
handful of restaurants
that, after dinner,
loosen up a little – very
little – but only on the
Kona Coast.

Kailua-Kona

Flashbacks Bar & Grill
75-5669 Ali'i Dr.
☎326-2840

With old records and
photographs lining the
walls, the aptly named
Flashbacks Bar & Grill
plunges you into the
1960s in the blink of an
eye. The background
music is in keeping
with the theme, except
for Mondays, when it
gives way to televised
football games. Patrons
can have lunch or
dinner here, but many
come mainly for a beer
or a margarita while
enjoying the harbour
view.

Huggo's
75-5828 Kahakai Rd.
☎329-1493

A popular spot for its
ocean view, this eatery
trips the light fantastic
(so to speak) every
night. Karaoke night is

Pele

Pele, the fire goddess, appeared in Hawaii in the 12th century at the same time as the arrival of the new Tahitian gods. Legends say she first migrated from the far-off Society Islands to Nihoa Island (Hawaii), then she travelled from volcano to volcano and finally made her home in the boiling lava of the Kilauea volcano. Before Pele, an old fire god lived in this pit. But, scared of Pele's power, he fled before she even arrived.

A lower goddess, spirit of the ancestors (*'aumaku'a*) in Tahiti, Pele gradually became central in the Hawaiian pantheon, most probably due to the powerful influence of volcanism on the islands and the fear that it created. Described as daughter of Wakea, the Sky Father, and Haumea, the Earth Mother, she is considered *ka wahine 'ai honua*, "the woman who devours the earth." Legend has it that she appeared sometimes as a young woman, sometimes as an elderly crone – but

she was always fast on her feet and on the go. In many regions of the Big Island, Pele is much more than a myth. If you cross paths with a white dog, for example, you'll definitely know she's present; you must respect and appease her. Each year during the Merrie Monarch *hula* festival, participants discreetly pay homage to her and draw upon her *mana* to perfect songs and dance movements evoking the elements like prayers dedicated to all-powerful Mother Nature.

held every Monday and Tuesday, while local bands and musicians perform throughout the rest of the week, turning the dining room into a dance club of sorts.

Kona Brewing Company
76-5629 Kuakini Hwy.
North Kona Shopping Center
☎334-BREW
The only microbrewery in Kona makes eight home-brewed beers, including the amazing Lilikoi (passion fruit) Wheat Ale. But if swigging it back isn't enough, you can always try the *lilikoi*-beer

cheesecake! You can also dine at the restaurant, which is rather unimaginative, or visit the brewery on weekdays from 10:30am to 3pm. But your best bet remains sipping suds in the pleasant, modern setting while listening to music.

Michaelangelo's
75-5770 Ali'i Dr.
Waterfront Row
This renowned Italian-American restaurant (see p 276) turns into a dance club every night. On sleepy nights in Kona, this place really goes all out to get lo-

cals and tourists on the dance floor. Some of the most popular Hawaiian rock bands perform here.

Verandah
78-6740 Ali'i Dr.
(Mile 5, south of Kona)
Keauhou Beach Resort
(see p 256)
☎322-3441
Located at the very end of the Keauhou Beach Resort, the bar overhangs the water holes formed at low tide, in which small fish frolic. Facing due west, the establishment is just the place to watch the sun go down beneath the

horizon while sipping a cocktail – to the sounds of Hawaiian music from 5pm to 9pm.

Windjammer Lounge
75-5852 Ali'i Dr.
Royal Kona Resort (see p 257)
☎*329-3111, ext. 208*
An excellent place to have a drink while watching the sun set on Kailua Bay, but if you're looking for a little action, come after 8pm, when cocktail hour gives way to dancing. Cha-cha, mambo, samba, salsa, tango, the (short) Latin nights waltz with swing, foxtrot and more. A free 1hr lesson is even given before opening time so that hoofers may brush up on the classics or simply look less awkward.

Events and Festivals

February

Waimea Cherry Blossom Festival
Japanese festival
☎*885-3633*

Hilo Mardi Gras
☎*935-8850*

March

Kona Stampede Rodeo
Honaunau
☎*323-2388*

April

Merrie Monarch Festival
Hilo
☎*935-9168*
The biggest Hawaiian *hula* event of the year.

Moikeha Hawaiian Sailing Canoe Race
Kawaihae
☎*885-7420*

May

Ka Ulu Lauhala o Kona Festival
Keauhou Beach Hotel
☎*325-5592*
Lauhala-weaving demonstrations.

Na Mea Hawaii Hula Kahiko Series
Volcanoes National Park
☎*967-8222*
Old-style *hula* performances.

June

King Kamehameha Day Celebrations
Kohala, Kona, Hilo
☎*935-9338*
Parade on June 12 in Kailua-Kona.

July

Parker Ranch Rodeo
Waimea
July 4

Kilauea Cultural Festival
Volcano
☎*967-8222*

International Barefoot Hula
Hilo
☎*961-8706*
Festival of Pacific cultures.

August

International Festival of the Pacific
Hilo
☎*934-0177*

Aloha Festival's Ka Ho'ola'a'ana
Volcanoes National Park
☎*885-8086*

September

Aloha Festival
☎*885-8086*
Hula contest, parades, sporting events and more.

Queen Lili'uokalani Outrigger Canoe Races
☎*323-2565*

Parker Ranch Round-up Rodeo
Waimea
☎*885-7655*

October

Hamakua Music Festival
Honoka'a
☎*775-0598*

Ironman
Kona
☎*329-0063*

November

Honoka'a Taro Festival
☎*775-9987*

Kona Coffee Festival
throughout the "coffee belt"
☎*326-7820*
Markets, sports competitions, parades and more.

King Kalakaua Hula Festival
Kona
☎*329-1532*

Shows

Luaus

Six major hotels and tourist resorts on the

Kona Coast organize their own *luaus*. The most popular is unquestionably the one held at the **King Kamehameha's Kona Beach Hotel** *(Tue to Thu and Sun 5:30pm to 8:30pm; ☎326-4969)*, which features a torch-bearing ceremony, the traditional opening of the *imu* (underground oven/fire pit), a crafts demonstration, buffet and show. Not only is it the only one held in a genuine historic setting (at the Ahuena *heiau*), but it also allows you to buy a package with cocktail and show (without the buffet) for $28. Also popular is the Legends of the Pacific dinner show, which takes place every Friday night at the **Hilton Waikoloa Village** *(☎886-1234)*. Other options include the Drums of Polynesia, held every Monday, Friday and Saturday at the **Royal Kona Resort** *(☎329-3111)*, as well as the *luaus* at the **Mauna Kea Beach Hotel** *(☎882-7222)* on Tuesdays, the **Kona Village Resort** *(☎325-5555)* on Fridays, and the **Outrigger Waikoloa Beach Hotel** *(☎886-6789)*. Prices range from $50 to $70 per person.

Shopping

Art and Crafts

In Holualoa, on the heights of Kona, don't

fail to drop by **Kimura's Lauhala Shop** *(77-996 Mamalahoa Hwy., ☎324-0053)*, founded in 1914 by the grandfather of the current proprietress, the third generation of Kimuras to ply the noble *lauhala*-weaving trade. It all started during the Great Depression, when Mr. Kimura senior, who ran a grocery store, began supplying coffee pickers with woven baskets. After the war, his daughter decided to devote herself to the craft trade full-time. The reception is unusually warm, and you'll find a wide range of objects woven from pandanus leaves, such as hats, baskets, placemats, wastebaskets and eyeglass cases, as well as a few (wooden) imports from Southeast Asia. The shop is located at the entrance to Holualoa, at the intersection of Hualalai Road and Mamalahoa Highway.

Farther south, at the north entrance to Kealakekua *(Mile 112.2)*, the **Kahanahou** craft co-op *(☎322-3901)*, founded in 1967, specializes in Hawaiian musical instruments for *hula* schools: *pahu, ipu hula* (nasal flute), *uli uli* (maracas) and calabash (gourd). Also available are such items as *tikis* and *kapa* beaters.

As its name indicates, the Bamboo Restaurant & Gallery, in Hawi (Kohala), is also home to a large arts-and-crafts

gallery, **Kohala Koa**, which sells very beautiful objects, including magnificent quilts, sarongs and rare-wood dishes.

In Honoka'a, be sure to drop by **Kama'aina Woods** *(45-469 Lehua St., ☎775-7722)*, a factory that makes fine-quality wooden objects. Some 40 kinds of wood are featured, with a preference for pine, mango-tree, breadfruit-tree, hibiscus and *koa* woods in particular. As it is forbidden to cut down *koa* trees, craftspeople must wait for a storm to pass to be able to gather the precious wood.

Waipi'o Valley Artworks *(☎775-0958)*, located in the village of Kukuiahaele, just before the end of the road leading to the valley, displays a fine selection of carved *koa*- and *kou*-wood artifacts, particularly bowls and boxes.

If you're strolling along Mamo Street in Hilo and happen to come upon Clayton Amemiya's shop, **Rain** *(☎934-9134)*, do not hesitate to venture inside. Born in Hawaii but of Japanese origin, Amemiya learned the techniques of *yakishima*, a very ancient form of superb rustic-looking pottery, in Okinawa.

In the village of Volcano, near the Kilauea General Store, the

Kilauea Kreations souvenir shop (☎967-8090) specializes in quilts. You'll find patterns, fabrics and thread of all colours as well as ready-made pieces for the less enterprising.

Natural Products

In the vicinity of Hilo, many greenhouses grow tropical flowers and orchids. The blooms are available in small bouquets to decorate your hotel room or in arrangements to bring home – some establishments offer to forward them to you. Such is the case with **Akatsuka** (*Mile 22.5*), on the road to Volcanoes National Park, which has the largest orchid hothouses in the region and creates its own hybrids.

Closer to Hilo, in Kurtistown (*Mile 9.4*),

Fuku-Bonsai (☎982-9880) is the inventor of mini bonsais planted on a piece of volcanic rock. They need only be watered regularly – perfect for those with neither time nor a green thumb. On display in the greenhouses are all kinds of bonsais, including Japanese and Chinese (*penjing*) varieties.

Markets

The Hilo market is one of the liveliest in the archipelago. It is held every Wednesday and Saturday as of 6am on Mamo Street, at the corner of Kamehameha Avenue, and ends sometime in the afternoon. All small area producers gather here, offering browsers a profusion of flowers (anthuriums, protea, birds of paradise at $5 a bouquet; orchid branches for only $2 to

$3) as well as an abundance of mostly organic produce, including bananas, papayas, pineapples, oranges and rambutans. Those staying in the area for a few days can stock up on provisions, whereas those just passing through can buy clothing, souvenirs or fish.

In Kona, the Farmer's Market is also held on Wednesdays and Saturdays, from 6am to about 3pm. The stalls are assembled at the Kona Inn Shopping Village, on Ali'i Drive.

Miscellaneous

In Kailua-Kona, at the King Kamehameha Hotel, the **Big Island Outlet** (☎326-4949) specializes in Big Island products, be it coffee, jams, plants, crafts or clothing. You won't find anything "made in Taiwan" here.

Maui is the
only island in the archipelago to have been named after a Hawaiian god.

Actually a demigod, known for his jovial, fun-loving nature, Maui's namesake is said to have hauled the islands up from the ocean floor with his magic fishing line and, from the summit of Hale'a'kala, to have caused the sun to slow its course.

Maui's inhabitants are proud of their beautiful island and are the first to exclaim "Maui no ka o'i!" (Maui is the best!). Smooth, sandy beaches (on the southern and western coasts), rolling breakers that are a paradise for surfers and windsurfers, fields of pineapples and sugar cane, the barren slopes of Hale'a'kala in the central part of the island, and lush pastures and tropical forests in the east: the island flaunts its diversity. Maui is the second in Hawaii's string of islands, with 100,000 inhabitants

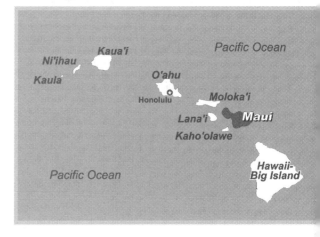

populating its 7,786 sq mi (1,887km²), and is the most popular vacation spot, except for Waikiki. Although 2.5 million tourists visit it each year, only a quarter of its total area is populated.

West Maui was formed by a volcano that erupted some 1.5 to 2 million years ago but has since been eroded. Some distance away, Hale'a'kala broke through the waves at least half a million years later. Eruption

after eruption, the cone grew towards the sky and reached higher than the 10,023ft (3,055m) it measures today. The two volcanoes were eventually linked by an isthmus, which is how Maui got the nickname "The Valley Isle." When the sea level dropped following a glacial period, the island was joined for a while to the neighbouring volcanoes of Kaho'olawe, Lana'i and Moloka'i. This vast terrain, called *Maui Nui*, disappeared when the sea level rose again. It may be in memory of its ancient geological past that Maui is still the head of this group of islands.

The straits separating Maui from Moloka'i and Lana'i are quite shallow, and are used each winter by humpback whales from the North Pacific who come here to mate and give birth. Surprisingly, it was not the humpbacks that the whalers were after when they landed in Lahaina in the 1820s; their interest lay rather in young Hawaiian women and rum toddies. But their frequent visits still made Lahaina the capital of the new kingdom, which had been united 25 years before by Kamehameha, and the whalers and missionaries, who arrived at the same time, led a rather stormy co-existence. However, this aspect of the island's history is long forgotten, and today thousands of visitors stream in to see the majestic whales, who are very well protected.

Finding Your Way Around

By Plane

Kahului Airport

Hawaii's second-largest airport after Honolulu, Kahului has direct flights to destinations throughout the archipelago, as well as numerous cities in the western United States and Canada. There has been talk of expansion for almost 10 years to accommodate direct international flights (from Japan) and enhance Maui's tourism industry. So far, opponents to the project (local residents who are already overwhelmed by the masses of tourists) have managed to prevent this expansion. Flights offered by the small inter-island airlines (such as Aloha Islandair, Pacific Wings, Paragon) leave from the small terminal behind the car rental counters. For more information, call ☎872-3893.

Car rental agencies are located to the right of the exit from the luggage-collection area. A shuttle will take you to the nearby car depot.

Many passengers use the **Airporter Shuttle** (*$13 from the airport, $7 to the airport, $19 return trip; reservations ☎877-7308*) which runs to Lahaina and Ka'anapali every 30min between 9am and 6pm (*last departure from the airport is at 4pm*). The trip lasts between 45 and 90min.

The **Airport Shuttle** (*☎661-6667 or 800-977-2605*) runs only to Kahului (*$6*) and Wailuku (*$9*), while **Speedi Shuttle** (*☎875-8070*) goes almost anywhere on the island, but charges steep fares.

Kapalua Airport

Located in the middle of the last pineapple fields, this tiny airport is used by travellers visiting West Maui. The only airlines that come here are Aloha Island Air, which has flights here from Honolulu and Kona, and Pacific Wings. There are no car rental agencies at the airport.

Hana Airport

Located 4mi (6.5km) west of Hana (*junction at Mile 31.6*), this small airport is used only by Pacific Wings (*with three daily departures for Kahului and two for Honolulu*). This flourishing company hopes to offer flights to Moloka'i in the near future. The airport's only car rental agency is Dollar. There is a shuttle to Hana, where you can pick up your rental car.

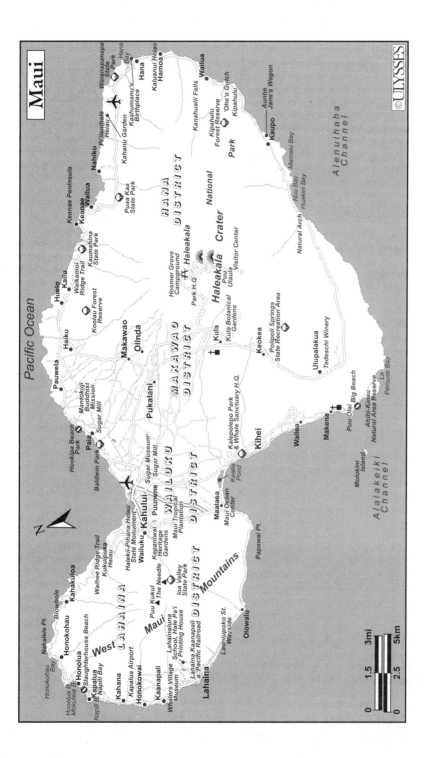

Maui

Pacific Ocean

© ULYSSES

Airlines

Aloha
☎244-9071

Aloha Islandair
☎800-652-6541

American
☎244-5522

Canadian
☎800-426-7000

Delta
☎800-221-1212

Hawaiian
☎871-6132

United
☎800-241-6522

By Car

Car Rental Agencies

Alamo
☎871-6235

Avis
☎800-321-3712 or 871-7575

Budget
☎800-527-0700 or 871-8811

Dollar
☎800-800-4000 or 877-2731

Hertz
☎800-654-3011 or 877-5167

Lahaina

Finding your way around Lahaina couldn't be easier. Front Street runs north-south through the entire town, following the coast. All the shops, restaurants and other busy areas are found along this thoroughfare,

or along the intersecting streets just behind it. There is a large, free parking lot at the corner of Front Street and Prison Street, just south of Banyan Square (there is a 3hr time limit). Most hotels in Lahaina charge for parking *(usually $3 to $5)*. Honoapi'ilani Highway runs parallel to Front Street and takes you through Lahaina, almost without noticing it – be careful not to miss the exit!

The West Maui Tourist Coast

The two-lane Honoapi'ilani Highway (Highway 30) runs along the coast, slightly set back, and gets very busy at rush hour. The Ka'anapali Parkway, a dead-end, leads to Ka'anapali. Further north, Lower Honoapi'ilani Road runs parallel to Highway 30, leading to the hotels and condominiums in Honokowai, Kahana, Napili and Kapalua, where it merges with Highway 30.

Wailuku - Kahului

These two towns are only 3mi (5km) apart. Wailuku, in the west, is an administrative centre, while Kahului, in the east, is a business centre and features the airport and port. The two are linked by Ka'ahumanu Avenue (Highway 32), which is called Main Street in

Wailuku. From the entrance to Kahului, Kahului Beach Drive (Highway 340) follows the coast toward Kahekili Highway, the small road that runs along the northern coast of West Maui. At the eastern edge of town, by the airport, Dairy Road (Highway 380), which later becomes Kuihelani Highway, heads south to Ma'alaea *(by rejoining Highway 30, which runs from Wailuku to Lahaina)* and Kihei. Hale'a'kala Highway (37) also begins at the eastern edge of town, as does the Hana Highway (36), a little further along.

Kihei - Wailea

You can drive right along the coast by crossing Kihei by the South Kihei Road. Intended primarily for local traffic, it moves very slowly. If you go further south, it is better to take the wide, two-lane Pi'ilani Highway (31) which runs parallel but farther away. This road ends south of Kihei, at the outskirts of Wailea, and turns into Wailea Alanui Drive. Further south, the road changes names again to Makena Alanui Drive.

Hale'a'kala

Above all else, make sure you have a full tank of gas if you are heading this way! There are no gas stations beyond the towns on the

Maui

lower slopes of the volcano, nor are there restaurants or snack bars.

Hana

The Chevron gas station is located at the western edge of town, and the one at Hasegawa Store is just behind it. Both close at 5:30pm.

By Taxi

Here are a few of the many companies:

Grand Central Taxi
☎877-7758

Ka'anapali Taxi
☎661-5285

Kihei Taxi
☎879-3000

Sunshine Cabs
☎879-2220 or 667-2220

Yellow Cab of Maui
☎877-7000

By Shuttle

There is no public transportation system on Maui. Several private companies provide transportation for longer distances between tourist sites, but charge very high prices. The **Airport/Activity Shuttle** (☎661-6667 or 800-977-2605) runs from Lahaina and the tourist coast of West Maui to Kapalua, Ma'alaea, Kihei, Wailea and Makena, as well as Kahului's Ka'ahumanu Center. To illustrate

how exorbitant prices can be, a trip from Makena to Ma'alaea (to go on an excursion to Molokini, for example) costs $18 per person. **Speedi Shuttle** (☎875-8070) costs at least as much. At these prices, it is usually better to rent a car.

The **West Maui Shopping Express** ($1; ☎877-7308) runs along three local routes. One links the main shopping centres between Lahaina and Ka'anapali to the two Sugar Cane Train stations. A second route services Ka'anapali's large hotels (*from 10am to 10pm*), while the third stops hourly at the large hotels between Whalers Village in Ka'anapali and the Ritz-Carlton in Kapalua (*from 9am to 9pm*).

By Trolleybus

To reach Ka'anapali from the south coast, one last option is to take the **Whalers Village/Maui Ocean Center Trolley** (☎877-7308). With three trolleys going in either direction each day, this service runs to several hotels between Makena and Kihei, stopping only twice afterwards, at the new Ocean Center in Ma'alaea ($7) and the Whalers Village in Ka'anapali ($15). The prices are for one way, but the return trip is free with proof of purchase.

By Train

Though it is not really a mode of transportation, there is a railway on Maui. The very touristy **Sugar Cane Train** (☎661-0089 or 661-0080) is a replica of an 1890 railway and runs six times a day from Lahaina to Pu'ukolii, across from Ka'anapali (departures approximately every 80min). The toy-like train will bring out the child in you during the 40min trip, running about 6mi (10km) between sugarcane fields and the major coastal road. The fare is $10.50 one way for passengers over 12, and $14.50 for a return ticket. Departures from Lahaina are from the station north of the city centre (*take Hinau St. from the Honoapi'ilani Hwy.*).

By Boat

Expeditions (☎661-3756) has five daily departures from the port of Lahaina to the port of Manele on the island of Lana'i, at $25 per passage. The beach at Hulopo'e is one of the most beautiful in all of Hawaii, and lies only 1,000ft (300m) from the dock. You can also rent a four-wheel-drive vehicle or spend the day in one of the island's two superb golf courses.

Practical Information

Tourist Information Centres

Maui Visitors Bureau
Mon to Fri 8am to 4:30pm
P.O. Box 580
1727 Wili Pa Loop, Wailuku
HI 96793
☎*244-3530 or 800-525-MAUI*
⇌*244-1337*
www.visitmaui.com
The official Maui Visitors Bureau is difficult to find since it is virtually hidden in a remote spot in Wailuku, essentially providing brochures and, if you need them, a few tips.

Lahaina Visitors Center
Mon to Fri 9am to 5pm
648 Wharf St., Lahaina
☎*667-9175*
⇌*661-4779*
www.visitlahaina.com
This visitors centre provides the excellent *Maui Historical Walking Guide*.

State Park Services

Department of Land & Natural Resources Division of State Parks
Mon to Fri 8am to 4pm
54 South High St., no. 101
Wailuku
☎*984-8109*
The State Park Services operates two campgrounds on Maui: one is Polipoli, in the backcountry, and the other is Wai'anapanapa, near Hana. Permits are free, but the stay is limited to five consecutive days. You can also obtain a map of hiking trails here, and permits for camping in Palaau State Park on Moloka'i.

County Parks Services

County of Maui – Permits Office
Mon to Fri 8am to 4pm
1580-C Ka'ahumanu Ave.
Wailuku, HI 96793
☎*270-7389*
The County Parks Services branch is located between Wailuku (1.2mi or 2km away) and Kahului. Turn onto Kanaloa Street, then turn left onto Hali'a Street and continue towards the sports centre. The office is under an awning in front of the gym. Here you can obtain camping permits for Kanaha Beach Park, Maui's only county-run park with a campground. The stay is limited to three consecutive nights, and the cost is $3 per person per night. You can reserve by mail.

Internet

Digital Copy Business Center
Mon to Fri 9am to 5pm
658 Front St., Lahaina
Wharf Cinema Center
(third floor)
☎*667-2679*
This is not a cybercafé but an office store that provides public Internet access. As far as we know, it is the only place in Lahaina to do so. The place makes a tidy profit *(charging $0.20 per minute with a minimum of $3, or $12 an hour)* and the staff is not really helpful.

Aloha Books
Mon to Sat 9am to 9pm, Sun 10am to 10pm
2411 South Kihei Rd., Kihei
☎*874-8070*
This small bookstore is packed with used books in English, Japanese and French. There is a section on travel guides, and the place also provides Internet access. Because it is through WebTV, the connection is a little slower and less efficient, but it only costs $1 for 20 min.

Organized Walks

Several non-profit organizations offer guided walks: the **Hawai'i Nature Center** (see p 314), the **Nature Conservancy** *(81 Makawao Ave., P.O. Box 1716, Makawao, HI 96768, ☎572-7849)* and the **Kapalua Nature Society** *(☎669-0244 or 800-KAPALUA)*, which leaves from the Kapalua Resort. The latter offers various types of excursions, including a hike through the Pu'u Kukui reserve in the higher reaches of West Maui, snorkelling and even a trip to the island of Kaho'olawe.

The **Lahaina Restoration Foundation** (☎*661-3262*) has put out a brochure detailing a complete walking tour of Lahaina that goes to all the historical sites of the ancient Hawaiian capital in 31 stops. Some have completely disappeared and only warrant a short visit. This brochure is available at the tourist centre on Banyan Square or at the Baldwin museum.

Post Offices

Lahaina (city centre)
Mon to Fri 8:15am to 16:15pm
132 Papalaua St.

Lahaina / Ka'anapali
Halfway between the two towns (*1.2mi or 2km to the north*), the main postal outlet of the west coast is located at 1760 Honoapi'ilani Hwy. (*Mon to Fri 8:30am to 5pm, Sat 9am to 1pm*).

Kihei
Mon to Fri 9am to 16:30pm
1254 South Kihei Rd., Azeka I

Laundromats

Kihei

Lipoa Laundry Center
(Lipoa Center)
Mon to Sat 8am to 9pm, Sun to 5pm
41 East Lipoa St.
There are video games while you wait for your laundry.

Kahana

Kahana Koin-Op
every day 6am to 10pm, doors close at 8pm
(Kahana Gateway Shopping Center)
4465 Honoapi'ilani Hwy.
The laundromat is located across from the service station.

Exploring

West Maui

Lahaina

(one day)

Long before the first Europeans set foot in Lahaina, the *ali'i* had made it one of their main residences. In 1802, Kamehameha declared the city capital of the almost-united archipelago, a status it was to enjoy for more than 40 years. The first missionaries landed in the port during this period, followed by a growing number of ships, first carrying cargo, then whalers. After long months at sea, these sailors were looking to enjoy life a little, but their interest in Hawaiian beauties and their penchant for alcohol (which flowed freely) did not mix well with the missionaries' strict religious convictions. Skirmishes between the two groups broke out regularly. Then, with the gradual decline of the whaling industry in the 1860s, Lahaina once again became a mellow tropical town. A plantation town surrounded by sugar-cane fields, Lahaina only reawakened in the 1970s when tourism started booming.

Facing the island of Lana'i, on the western coast of West Maui, Lahaina enjoys a choice location. Protected from the rain-bearing trade winds by the Pu'u Kukui mountain range, the city enjoys radiant days that are perfect for spending at the beach, and especially at one of the nearby resorts north of the city. History is essentially all that remains of its past, since few original buildings have survived. All of the old wooden facades now house galleries, restaurants and souvenir shops.

Front Street runs along the shore and is lined by stores. Banyan Square is located halfway down the street and marks the historic centre.

Begin the tour at **Banyan Square** ★★, with its old banyan tree spreading its branches and air roots like tentacles, and new trunks forming at the ends. Despite the tree's astounding size (the trunk measures nearly 985ft or 300m), it is relatively recent. The tree was planted in 1873 to mark the 50th anniversary of the founding of the first

Protestant mission. Local painters and sculptors exhibit their work in its shade every weekend.

The old **Courthouse**, built in 1859 using stones from Kamehameha III's uncompleted Hale Piula palace, stands across from the banyan. The building once served as Maui's seat of government. Today, it is occupied by the tourism office and the Lahaina Arts Society, whose gallery has been temporarily relocated to 900 Front Street.

Four old Russian cannons stand in front of the building, pointing in the direction of the port. They used to be found on the walls of the old coral stone **fort** which stood guard over the city from 1832 to 1854. Like the other 43 pieces of artillery that were placed there, these were recovered from ships that had sunk in Hawaiian waters. A few vestiges of the fort have also been preserved. Hoapili, then governor of Maui, had ordered its construction following an attack on the mission in 1827 led by English Captain John Palmer, who protested against the rule that forbade women from boarding the vessels. Every morning at dawn a sentinel beat a drum from the top of the walls as a signal to departing sailors that it

was time to return to their ships. If they missed the call, they were likely to spend time in the fort's jail. When it was dismantled, stone blocks from the fort were used to build the new prison.

During the 1840s, the American consul built a canal at the foot of the fort to make it easier for whalers to reach the coast. Lahaina had no proper port to speak of; rather, ships anchored out in the bay. Due to its prosperity, a market was built here, forbidden to women, but in 1913 the entire operation had to be closed because of mosquitoes.

Lahaina's most famous building stands north of Banyan Square. **Pioneer Inn ★** was built in 1901 by George Freeland, a member of the Royal Canadian Mounted Police, who came to Hawaii on the trail of a fugitive he never managed to track down. This was the only hotel here until after the war.

Don't miss the figurehead of a captain with a wooden leg that stands in front of the entrance, facing the port.

Lahaina's port lies across from the hotel, and is crowded with yachts, sailboats and innumerable outlets offering deep-sea fishing, whale-watching or snorkelling excursions. In late afternoon you can see the boats coming back to the harbour and the weighing of their catch. The brig *Carthaginian ★ ($3; every day 10am to 4pm)* is a replica of a typical 19th-century trading vessel. Docked at the quay, it houses a small museum dedicated to whales. The exhibit includes several photographs, a film and an old whaleboat discovered in Alaska in 1973.

Taro fields and the Brick Palace once stood near the present-day location of the Pioneer Inn and the islands' first lighthouse (1840). The Brick Palace was built by Kamehameha in 1798 for Ka'ahumanu, his favourite wife. She never lived here, however, preferring the hut that had been built for her nearby. Today nothing remains of the palace; all that can be barely seen is a stone known as the **Hauola** Stone, on the shore, which the ancient Hawaiians once

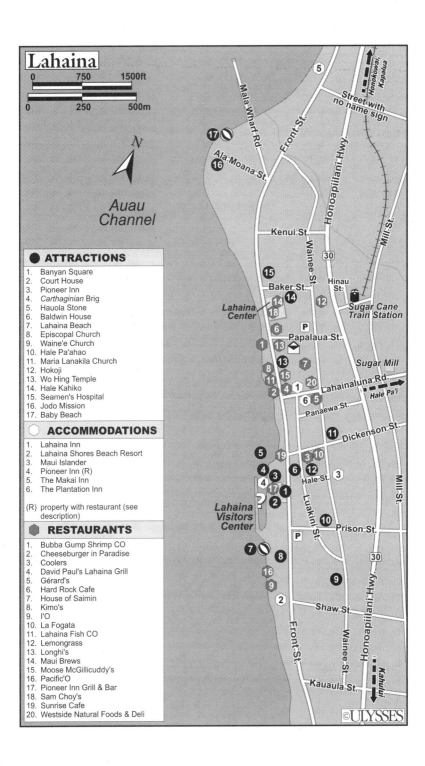

Lahaina

| 0 | 750 | 1500ft |
| 0 | 250 | 500m |

N

Auau Channel

● ATTRACTIONS

1. Banyan Square
2. Court House
3. Pioneer Inn
4. *Carthaginian* Brig
5. Hauola Stone
6. Baldwin House
7. Lahaina Beach
8. Episcopal Church
9. Waine'e Church
10. Hale Pa'ahao
11. Maria Lanakila Church
12. Hokoji
13. Wo Hing Temple
14. Hale Kahiko
15. Seamen's Hospital
16. Jodo Mission
17. Baby Beach

○ ACCOMMODATIONS

1. Lahaina Inn
2. Lahaina Shores Beach Resort
3. Maui Islander
4. Pioneer Inn (R)
5. The Makai Inn
6. The Plantation Inn

(R) property with restaurant (see description)

■ RESTAURANTS

1. Bubba Gump Shrimp CO
2. Cheeseburger in Paradise
3. Coolers
4. David Paul's Lahaina Grill
5. Gérard's
6. Hard Rock Cafe
7. House of Saimin
8. Kimo's
9. I'O
10. La Fogata
11. Lahaina Fish CO
12. Lemongrass
13. Longhi's
14. Maui Brews
15. Moose McGillicuddy's
16. Pacific'O
17. Pioneer Inn Grill & Bar
18. Sam Choy's
19. Sunrise Cafe
20. Westside Natural Foods & Deli

©ULYSSES

believed to be invested with warrior powers. The spot is in the shadow of a large *kiawe* and offers a lovely view of the *Carthaginian*.

East of Banyan Square, on the other side of Front Street, **Baldwin House** ★★ *($3; every day 10am to 4:15pm; Front St., ☎661-3262)* is dedicated to the memory of Lahaina's first missionaries. Built by Reverend Ephraim Spaulding in 1834-1835, the house was occupied by Reverend Dwight Baldwin and his family two years later, when the former died. The Baldwin family lived here for 35 years, and today visitors can see the dining room, bedrooms, bathroom and Baldwin's study. In addition to being a clergyman, Baldwin was a doctor, and the museum displays his intimidating array of medical instruments as well as the venerable doctor's fees, arranged according to the illness: "severe illness" cost $50, "less ill" $40, "much less ill" $30, "slightly ill" $20 and "hardly ill" $10! The neighbouring house is made of lava and coral stone and was built by the missionaries as a warehouse, before becoming the "officers' club" where the ships' captains socialized.

A narrow band of sand called **Lahaina Beach** ★ extends south of the port, wedged between the sea and the low walls of private estates. Here, plenty of budding surfers mill around, patiently waiting for that perfect wave.

Continue your walk by heading south along Front Street.

The **Episcopal Church**, which was only built in 1927, is worth a visit for its altar paintings of a Hawaiian Virgin and Child, and of three scenes from daily life: an *ulu* (breadfruit) harvest, a taro harvest and a fishing scene. Hawaiian birds are painted over the pulpit.

Continue a little further south until you reach the shopping centre at 505 Front Steet. Here, head east by crossing Malu'uluolele Park.

In the old days, this grass-covered area was the site of the royal residence of **Moku'ula**. The structure was built on a small island in the 16th century, in the middle of a fishpond that gradually dried up during the 1860s because of the irrigation of sugar-cane fields. The pool finally ran completely dry in 1918. Legends, which have been well preserved for the chiefs' peace of mind, tell of the *mo'o*, a giant lizard living in its waters. Excavations have unearthed some of the structure, but nothing that is worth seeing. There is apparently a long-term plan to reconstruct the water basin and royal complex.

Built between 1828 and 1832, **Waine'e Church** was the first permanent church in Hawaii, but was destroyed several times. The current building, however, is not particularly interesting. The original bell can barely be seen to the right of the entrance, where in 1858 it was deposited by a whirlwind that destroyed the belfry. The graves of several prominent *ali'i* can be seen in the adjacent cemetery, including that of Ke'opuolani, the first wife of Kamehameha and mother of Kamehameha II and II. She died in Lahaina in 1823. Some of the first missionaries and several of their children are also buried here.

Walk up north along Waine'e Street.

Past the **Hongwanji Buddhist temple** (1927), you will reach the restored **Hale Pa'ahao** ★ (Old Jail) at the corner of Prison Street, which was commissioned by Kamehameha III in 1852. When the fort was dismantled, the prisoners themselves built

their new jail by using its old stones! Towards the back, a wooden building that looks like a chapel was used for the cells. Be sure to stop and read the list of reasons for which people were convicted in

1855-1857 and 1862-1863, posted on the wall of the open cell.

Continue along Waine'e Street to Maria Lanakila Church.

Maria Lanakila Church is located past the Episcopal cemetery. This Catholic church has stood on this site since 1846, although the current edifice only dates back to 1928. The church is frequented by Lahaina's Hispanic community. At one time, sailors were buried in the adjacent cemetery, which is Protestant.

Take Dickenson Street to reach nearby Luakini Street.

Hokoji, Lahaina's Shingon mission, is located just to the left of the junction. A large bell hangs in front of this small, plain wooden Japanese temple, which is painted in tones of yellow and pistachio.

Take Dickenson Street to Front Street, by Baldwin House. Continue north along Front Street.

Several displays and shop windows at the **Crazy Shirt** *(865 Front St.)* store include objects related to whale-hunting, such as pieces of scrimshaw, ivory clothes pegs, whale oil for sewing machines and soaps. Also note the figurehead of the *Loch Loman* schooner (1871-1903) across from

the changing rooms – it depicts a Scot with a sword in a bandolier and a knife in his right sock! The displays are simply a way to lure customers, but that shouldn't stop you from taking a look around without paying an admission fee!

Almost right across the street, the pretty **Wo Hing Temple ★★** *(free admission)*, which dates from 1912, is painted pastel blue. The Wo Hing Society, a Chinese cultural and mutual aid association that is active throughout Hawaii, was established in Lahaina three years earlier (1909). At the time, several hundred Chinese lived in the area, having arrived in

Tiki

1828 when the first sugar mill was established. The building now houses a small museum that contains some magnificent objects, including 19th-century painted wedding chests, a lion used in a dance to celebrate the New Year, and a superb painted parasol with gold leaf dating back to 1858. The kitchen has also been restored, but is located in a different building to reduce the risk of fire. A film shot by Thomas Edison during his trip to Hawaii in 1898 is continually screened.

Continue along Front Street to the Lahaina Center.

Hale Kahiko *(free admission; every day 9am to 6pm, guided tours Mon to Fri 11:30am, 1pm and 4:30pm; ☎667-9216)*, a replica of an ancient Hawaiian village, is incongruously situated in the middle of a parking lot behind the shopping centre. There are three structures standing beside copies of *tiki*, a most inaccurate reconstruction, as the brochure available at the entrance readily concedes! Nevertheless, a visit to the site is quite interesting, and free, including the *hula* shows held on Wednesdays and Fridays at 2pm and 6pm.

North of the shopping centre, a local television network has taken over the old **Seamen's**

Lahaina Jodo Mission's Buddha

Hospital *(1024 Front St.)*, built by Kamehameha in 1833 and made of lava stones and coral. The king found solace here, far from the meddling missionaries who did not approve of his heavy drinking. Beginning in 1844, the building cared for sick and injured sailors. In front of the building is a statue of a weary whaler and a large 4.4 tonne (4,500kg) anchor with pivoting hooks that allowed the ships to remain steady in the strong coastal currents breaking free of their moorings. Workers discovered a skeleton under the northwest pillar during the building's reconstruction in 1982, the remains of a layman who had been killed by a blow of an axe to the head in an ancient pagan ritual that was believed to

make his spirit a "permanent guardian" of the royal residence.

The final section of the tour is best done by car. Continue along Front Street to Ala Moana Street.

Comprising a temple, a three-storey pagoda and the largest Buddhist temple outside of Japan, the **Lahaina Jodo Mission ★★** *(free admission; ☎661-4304)* is a haven of serenity at the foot of the mountains, north of downtown. The temple was built in 1968 to mark the 100th anniversary of the arrival of the first Japanese immigrants in Hawaii. **Baby Beach ★** lies at the foot of the temple. This small, quiet beach is used mainly by locals from this very residential district.

Continue by car to Highway 30 and Lahainaluna Road. Head mauka *from Highway 30, which climbs to the heights of Lahaina passing by the defunct old Pioneer Sugar Mill. The road ends at Lahaina's high school, just over 1mi (2km) farther.*

This was once the site of the Lahainaluna Seminary, founded in 1831. Just beyond the site, visitors can tour the **Hale Pa'i ★**, or House of Printing, *(Mon to Fri 10am to 4pm, but opening hours are rarely respected; ☎661-3262)* where the first Hawaiian bibles and the islands' first newspaper were printed. Period documents and a replica of the original printing press are on display. The bell in front of the entrance once regulated life at the school, ringing out prayer and meal times, as well as classes.

Ka'anapali and the Tourist Coast

(half-day)

The *ali'i* once used the several-mile-long beach at Ka'anapali as a retreat. They came here to surf, bathe and paddle their canoes. The coast was gradually forgotten by subsequent generations, but was rediscovered some time later. Hawaii's first large-scale tourist resort was developed at Ka'anapali in 1959, and

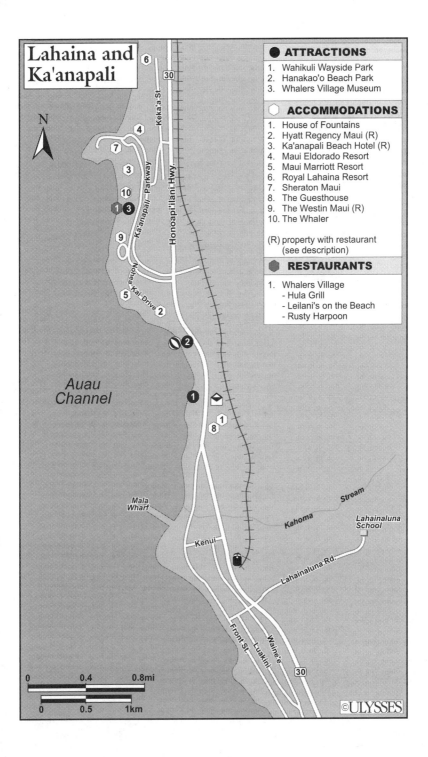

Lahaina and Ka'anapali

N

● ATTRACTIONS
1. Wahikuli Wayside Park
2. Hanakao'o Beach Park
3. Whalers Village Museum

⬡ ACCOMMODATIONS
1. House of Fountains
2. Hyatt Regency Maui (R)
3. Ka'anapali Beach Hotel (R)
4. Maui Eldorado Resort
5. Maui Marriott Resort
6. Royal Lahaina Resort
7. Sheraton Maui
8. The Guesthouse
9. The Westin Maui (R)
10. The Whaler

(R) property with restaurant
(see description)

⬡ RESTAURANTS
1. Whalers Village
   - Hula Grill
   - Leilani's on the Beach
   - Rusty Harpoon

Auau
Channel

Kekaa St.

Honoapi'ilani Hwy.

Ka'anapali Parkway

Nohea Kai Drive

Mala
Wharf

Kenui

Kahoma   Stream

Lahainaluna
School

Lahainaluna Rd.

Front St.

Luakini

Waine'e

30

| 0 | 0.4 | 0.8mi |
| 0 | 0.5 | 1km |

©ULYSSES

today a cluster of luxury hotels is found on this broad band of white sand. Their palm trees, artificial rivers and waterfalls, pink flamingoes and Asian art objects create a fantastic miniature world that coexists parallel to the natural world. Farther north are the more upscale resorts of Honokawi (with its lovely condominiums), Kahana, Napili and Kapalua. Vacationers can while away the hours here without ever coming into contact with the real Maui, or they can use it as a seaside base from which to explore the island. This tour begins in Lahaina and ends in Kapalua.

Leave Lahaina via the Honoapi'ilani Highway.

Wahikuli Wayside Park *(showers, tables, barbecues)* is at Mile 22.8. There is swimming at the grey-sand beach to the north, but the road runs very close. Located past a rocky stretch, just before Ka'anapali's hotels, **Hanakao'o Beach Park** *(washrooms, showers, picnic tables, barbecues, telephone)* is a little farther off the beaten track. The beach here has lifeguards, and is larger and more pleasant.

The largest hotels on Maui's west coast are all located in **Ka'anapali**. The island's first resort lies between two golf courses and a lovely, long beach whose wide sandy expanse is bordered by coconut palms and a number of hotels. The Beach Walk

stretches the length of the strand, almost leading to the Pu'u Keka'a cliffs, at the top of which are some of the facilities of the Sheraton hotel. Visitors gather here each night to watch a torch ceremony and a re-enactment of Grand Chief Kahekili's "leap of death." It is said that this is where the souls of the departed begin their journey to the afterlife. Of course, swimming and water sports are the major attractions at this spot.

Perpendicular to the centre of the beach, the Whalers Village shopping centre has a number of upscale shops and three restaurants. The complex is also home to the fascinating **Whalers Village Museum ★ ★** *(free ad-*

Whales, Oil and Umbrellas

In the 19th century, whales were used for making just about everything. Oil and spermaceti (a substance derived from the head of the whale) were taken from the sperm whale, made famous in *Moby Dick*, and one of the few kinds that have teeth. The oil was obtained by heating the fat, and a single animal could

produce up to 1980gal (7,500l). The oil was used for street and house lights throughout North America, and also to lubricate pendulums and watches. Until the 1970s it was even used in making lunar modules! Spermaceti is the oily substance in the head of the sperm whale (which protects it from the water pressure

when it dives to great depths), and was used primarily to make candles, since it burned without producing smoke. It was also used by the cosmetics industry for a long time. Meanwhile, the whalebones were used to make corsets and crinolines, as well as carriage wheels, umbrellas and other useful items.

Maui

mission; every day 9:30am to 10pm; second floor; ☎661-5992), dedicated to the whaling era. The displays recount the whale hunts as well as the daily life of whalers through a superb collection of old tools and photographs. Visitors will learn the best way to carve up a whale and all about the ceremony of Neptune, an initiation rite for cabin boys on their first voyage south of the equator.

Continue north along the Honoapi'ilani Highway.

Halfway between Ka'anapali and Honokowai, the immaculate, coconut-studded lawn of the **Kahekili Beach Park ★** (*every day 6am to 30min after sunset; showers, washrooms, tables, barbecues, telephones*) is the perfect spot for a picnic. The park borders the northern end of Ka'anapali beach, which provides excellent opportunities for snorkelling or scuba diving, or simply lying on the hot sand and soaking up the sun.

Turn left at the lights just after the car rental lots, onto Lower Honoapi'ilani Road.

Here, **Honokowai** resort stretches along the coast, tucked between the road and the ocean. Less exclusive than Ka'anapali, it is made up entirely of condominiums, most of them of a modest size and more affordably priced.

Of course, the beach is less easily accessible from here. The **Honokowai County Park ★** (*every day 5am to 8pm, washrooms, tables*) is an oasis of greenery in the middle of the built-up area. A rocky barrier delimits a bathing area suitable for young children.

Farther north, Honokowai melds into Kahana at **Pohaku Park**. Many local surfers come to the park's small beach after work to catch some waves. **Kahana Beach ★** lies on the other side of the park, with its large hotels built along the coast. It is not very safe to swim here, and the area is noticeably less built up.

Still very touristy but much more subdued thanks to an ordinance that prohibits the construction of buildings more than two storeys tall, **Napili ★★** enjoys a splendid location on a crescent of golden sand, is a little more exclusive and offers more lush greenery than the other resorts. Motor boats are not allowed into the bay, which is an excellent spot for snorkelling, especially in summer when the water is calmest.

At the northernmost end of the tourist coast, Napili gives way to **Kapalua**, where the coast veers inland, forming the large Oneloa bay between

two long strips of lava (Kapalua means "arms enfolding the sea"). The region, considered sacred by Hawaiians, was first used for cattle-raising, then to grow pineapples. However, many areas are no longer cultivated to make way for the demands of upscale tourism. The Ritz-Carlton now stands on the site of the old Honolua ranch, and is surrounded by three of the island's best golf courses. There is some indication that efforts are being made to preserve the area's heritage and environment. The Ritz (☎669-6200, see p 352) organizes a guided walking tour of Hawaiian tombs once a week. Protected by a reef, **Kapalua Beach ★★** is considered one of the island's loveliest beaches and offers peaceful swimming opportunities in its warm waters in the summer. In the winter, visitors can look for whales from the shore, or hope to see one of the few seals that occasionally hoist themselves onto the white-sand beach.

Take Office Road through Kapalua to rejoin the Hanoapi'ilani Highway. A little farther north, at Mile 31.1, an unmarked turnoff leads to D.T. Flemming Beach Park.

The white-sand beach in **D.T. Flemming Park ★★** (*washrooms, showers, picnic tables, barbecues*) is dominated by the Ritz-Carlton complex. Set against a backdrop of pine, the beach stretches almost as far as the 16th hole of the Kapalua Golf Club. The beach has a lifeguard and is very popular with boogie boarders and with families who flock here on weekends to enjoy a picnic and the beach. Those who go swimming should stay close to shore.

North of Mile 32, the condominiums, large hotels and immaculately groomed golf courses give way to another side of Maui, that of wild coastal regions and the surfers they attract (see tour below).

Tour of West Maui

(one day)

The first of the volcanoes from which the island grew is found at heart of West Maui, one of Maui's least accessible places. Its slopes eroded by rain, Pu'u Kukui stands shrouded in clouds. The higher altitudes are undisturbed by human presence and shelter Hawaiian bats, rare local plants and animals, including the rare 'ohi'a violet that only grows about an inch (2.5cm) tall.

The suggested tour, which takes in all of West Maui, is an extension of the preceding

tour, which is limited to the tourist area. Here, the island displays a different side, as hotel complexes give way to wild coastal regions with myriad bays. The Honoapi'ilani Highway becomes a very narrow coastal road (in fact, some car rental agencies don't allow their vehicles on this road, so check in advance). Those who prefer not to drive in mountains can start in Wailuku and head west so that they are always on the mountain side, rather than along the edge of the road. Return to Lahaina via Highway 30, which runs along the coast.

Slaughterhouse Beach ★, the first beach north of Kapalua (Mile 32.2), was once a nudist beach. This postcardsized patch of sand has attracted a more mainstream clientele since a flight of stairs was built to make it more accessible. The waters off the beach are part of the Honolua-Mokule'ia Marine Life Conservation District, named after the neighbouring bays. Snorkelling is possible here, although the waves can be quite high.

Those looking for a quieter spot can pack their masks and flippers and head to **Honolua Bay ★★** just north of Slaughterhouse Beach. At Mile 32.6, park on the lower side, by the sharp bend. A short path leads to a pebble

beach at the foot of the bay. As at the next beach, don't be deterred by the signs that say "Private Property – Keep Out"; they were posted by the owner to prevent liability in the case of an accident. It is advisable to wear rubber shoes to get to the water. Once in the water, though, the spectacular underwater sites will make it worthwhile.

At Mile 33.4, a trail descends along the edge of a pineapple field to a rocky point that marks the entrance to a bay. In winter, dozens of surfers come here on weekends, as well as the rest of the week. Slippery paths lead down the cliffs to the sea, but many spectators stand at the top of the cliffs to watch the pros take on the waves.

Surfers who prefer a less crowded place to practice their sport can head farther north, to the western end of **Honokohau Bay**. At a sharp bend in the road at Mile 34.6, a path descends to a sand-and-coral beach where surfers hang out. The breakers are impressive along this section of the coast, which is best suited for expert surfers because of the dangerous rocks that crop out of the water along the beach. From here, the road travels through the last pineapple fields before descending into the grand Honokohau

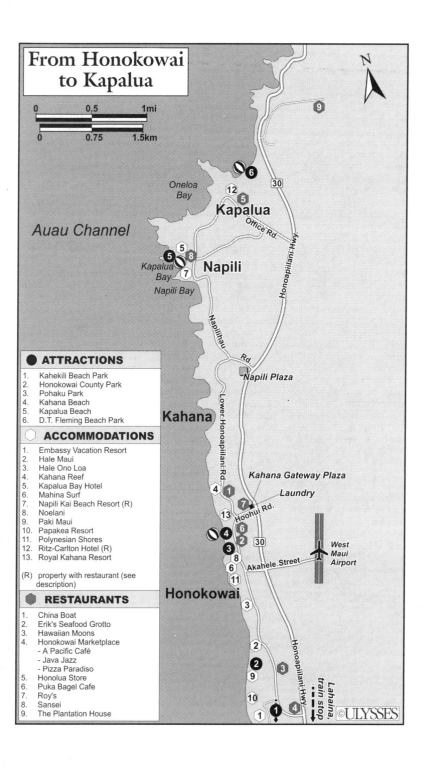

From Honokowai to Kapalua

Oneloa Bay

Kapalua

Auau Channel

Napili

Office Rd.

Kapalua Bay

Napili Bay

Napilihau Rd.

Napili Plaza

Kahana

Lower Honoapiilani Rd.

Honoapiilani Hwy.

Kahana Gateway Plaza

Laundry

Hoohui Rd.

West Maui Airport

Akahele Street

Honokowai

Honoapiilani Hwy.

Lahaina, train stop

© ULYSSES

● ATTRACTIONS

1. Kahekili Beach Park
2. Honokowai County Park
3. Pohaku Park
4. Kahana Beach
5. Kapalua Beach
6. D.T. Fleming Beach Park

⬡ ACCOMMODATIONS

1. Embassy Vacation Resort
2. Hale Maui
3. Hale Ono Loa
4. Kahana Reef
5. Kapalua Bay Hotel
6. Mahina Surf
7. Napili Kai Beach Resort (R)
8. Noelani
9. Paki Maui
10. Papakea Resort
11. Polynesian Shores
12. Ritz-Carlton Hotel (R)
13. Royal Kahana Resort

(R) property with restaurant (see description)

⬢ RESTAURANTS

1. China Boat
2. Erik's Seafood Grotto
3. Hawaiian Moons
4. Honokowai Marketplace
   - A Pacific Café
   - Java Jazz
   - Pizza Paradiso
5. Honolua Store
6. Puka Bagel Cafe
7. Roy's
8. Sansei
9. The Plantation House

Valley, whose lushness stands in marked contrast to the increasingly arid coast, lined with a pebble beach.

Just after Mile 38, the road approaches the island's northernmost tip: **Nakalele Point** ★, with its signal station believed to have been erected to guide fishers. The point also has a view of the barren cliffs so typical of the north coast. Again, pay no heed to the "Private Property" signs. The path is poorly indicated, but begins at the parking area. Descend along this path about 650ft (200m), then turn right at the cairn and skirt the stand of pines to reach the point. The rocky promontory is easy to climb, and on the other side there is a vent hole. You can also reach the vent hole by taking the path from Mile 38.3.

Honoapi'ilani Highway ends a short distance farther, becoming Kajekili Highway (which has a different number). The second highway only has one lane, but there are irregularly spaced bays along the road that allow traffic to pass between Mile 16 and Mile 7.

Just before Mile 16, which is where Kahekili Highway begins, you will see a large rock on the right with round marks. This is the **bellstone**, whose metallic resonance was used by Hawaiians to transmit messages. Un-

less you know just how to hit it, you will probably obtain a mediocre sound at best – and even then, the sound isn't particularly musical.

At Mile 15, a wide curve to the right reveals a sweeping panorama of the lush valley and small hamlet of **Kahakuloa** ★. The clutch of houses and two churches are situated near a small bay with a pebble beach and are bound by an imposing promontory known as Kahakuloa Head. Descending into the valley, you will first pass the Protestant church near the water, with its faded green wooden walls, capped with a red tile roof and a tiny bell tower. On the other side of the river, small terraced taro fields surround the road that leads up to the Catholic Saint Francis-Xavier church, founded in 1846. In the village there are several stands selling fruit, banana bread and sandwiches.

The road climbs back out of the valley to reach the Kaukini Gallery at Mile 13.4. This souvenir shop also displays paintings of questionable quality and taste. You can stop along the way to take in the view of Kahakuloa. Before that, however, at Mile 9.9, you will pass the Turnbull Studios and Sculpture Garden, the studio of Bruce

Turnbull with a small garden of lovely wooden sculptures.

At Mile 7, almost across from the entrance to Mendes Ranch, take the small road to the right indicating Camp Maluhia.

Just before reaching Camp Maluhia (0.8mi or 1.3km), a large embankment marks the head of **Waihe'e Ridge Trail** ★, a lovely path that passes through eucalyptus forests and fields. The trek begins at a steep paved slope that leads to a cistern where the trail actually starts. From here, the path quickly disappears into the forest. The walk is pleasant, although a little muddy when it rains, but is not really worthwhile when the forest is engulfed by clouds since they can obscure the view of the coast and the mountains. At the bottom of the trail a short track leads to a grassy area that on weekends is often used by model-plane enthusiasts. Take the stairs leading off to the left to the restored **Kukuipuka Heiau** ★, which faces a wooded hill. This was once the site of a *pu'uhonua*, a safe place where *kapu* breakers could find refuge, and a *heiau* presided over by the warriors.

Nearing Wailuku, turn right onto Highway 330 which leads to the centre of town, becoming Ka'ahumanu Avenue.

Get back onto Honoapi'ilani Highway (Highway 30) South (for a tour of Wailuku and the central plain, see below). Between here and the port of Ma'alaea, Highway 30 crosses the southern end of the Kealaloloa mountain chain, the spine of West Maui.

At Mile 8.6, **Papawai Scenic Point** presides over the point of the same name, if one looks in the direction of Kaho'olawe. The panoramic view of Ma'alaea Bay and the colossal outline of Hale'a'kala is magnificent. The lookout is very popular in winter, and some visitors spend hours gazing at the ocean in the hopes of spotting the humpback whales that inhabit these waters for several months of the year. Sightings are most common in January and February, but even then are far from guaranteed.

Mile 10.8 marks the head of the **Lahaina Pali Trail** (5mi or 8km) which was once used by Hawaiians to cross the Kealaloloa chain via the road from Wailuku to Lahaina. The trail was widened by the missionaries, and at the beginning of the 20th century was converted to a road for vehicles by prisoners condemned to force la-

bour. The coastal road was not opened until 1951, when a tunnel was dug. There are several petroglyphs and low Hawaiian stone walls along this dry, sunny path.

A little farther along, Highway 30 runs close to the southern coast of West Maui, with intermittent stretches of sand and scrub along the water. Here you will see the island of Lana'i grow closer in front of you. The parks along this stretch are not very enticing because they are so close to the traffic, but the water provides some good

Humpback Whale

snorkelling opportunities, especially around Mile 14 in the cove formed by **Olowalu** point. If you hear tales of shark attacks, rest assured: there was one isolated incident in 1993, and tiger sharks never return to the scene of the crime.

Launiupoko Wayside Park *(washrooms, showers, picnic tables, barbecues)*, located at Mile 18, is the loveliest along this stretch of the coast. The park lies across from

Lana'i island, and is set slightly away from the road. There is a beach and a large square lawn shaded by palm trees. A jetty creates a small, protected basin where young children can frolic in the water.

The Central Plain

★

From Wailuku to Paia

(one day)

Maui's central region has been ruled by two masters: in the past, sugar was the region's staple, and vast fields of cane continue to dominate the plain for which the island was nicknamed "Valley Isle." More recently, however, a new industry has taken over the countryside: water sport. The small towns, which follow one after the other, blend the past and the present into one continuum. Wailuku, the island's political centre, boasts old wooden buildings and cozy restaurants, forming a stark contrast with Kahului, Maui's modern economic centre and home to the island's major airport. Sugar was the sole reason for Kahului's existence when it was founded in the 1950s. Similarly, Spreckelsville and Paia, farther east, currently thrive thanks to the single pursuit of windsurfing.

Ka'ahumanu

Born in Hana in 1768, Ka'ahumanu was the daughter of Maui's chief and of Keaumoko, who herself was chief of Moloka'i and counselor to Kamehameha. At the age of 13, she married Kamehameha and quickly became his favourite wife, though she was not his first. When the king died in 1819, Ka'ahumanu assumed the role of Kuhina Nui, the co-sovereign who ruled alongside Liholiho (Kamehameha II, her stepson), and regent to his young brother, Kamehameha III. This forceful woman persuaded Liholiho to organize a feast and break one of the most sacred of the ancient *kapus*, the one prohibiting men and women from eating together. Ka'ahumanu was baptized soon after the arrival of the first missionaries and devoted her energy to spreading the Christian faith. The famous queen died in 1832 at the age of 64.

The name **Wailuku** means "waters of destruction," likely alluding to the numerous battles that took place in its surroundings. Formerly Maui's political centre, the city today continues to be the administrative centre of the county of Maui. Its downtown area became deserted as soon as many of the offices closed, but new signs of life have appeared in recent years, with restaurants and stores establishing themselves in the wooden buildings.

If you are coming from the west or the south, take Highway 30 into the city, crossing Waikapu.

The **Maui Tropical Plantation** *(every day 9am to 5pm; ☎244-7643)* misleadingly claims that it doesn't charge admission. But the free visit is restricted to a tiny garden, part of an exhibit that provides very general information about the cultivation of sugar cane, coffee and macadamia nuts; a cage that is home to two bored monkeys; and the Tropical Restaurant – not to forget, of course, the main attraction: the gargantuan souvenir shop. Those who wish to visit the fruit trees in the plantation itself must shell out $8.50 for a ticket to take part in an organized tour on a small Disney-style train. This tour lasts 40min, with departures every 45min from 10am to 4pm.

Take Highway 30 into Wailuku.

Built in 1876, the large **Ka'ahumanu Church ★** stands just before the intersection with Main Street (Ka'ahumanu Avenue). The church is dominated by the four-storey bell tower at the back, and was dedicated to the favourite wife of Kamehameha, who was responsible for spreading Christian beliefs. It was she who asked for such a church to be built. To the left of the entrance, note the portrait of the queen by Herb Kawainui Kane, Hawaii's most famous painter, who specialized in historical scenes. A small cemetery contains the tombs of several members of the Kahale family, who were among the first Hawaiians to convert to Christianity. They donated the land for the church.

At the intersection, turn right onto 'Iao Valley Road.

Continue for 650ft (200m) to the **Bailey House Museum ★** *($4; Mon to Sat 10am to 4pm; 2375 Main St., ☎244-3326)* on the left. Reverend Green was the first inhabitant of the house. In 1837, a seminary for young girls was established in the building, with the objective of providing "good Christian wives" to the graduates of the seminary in Lahainaluna. Three

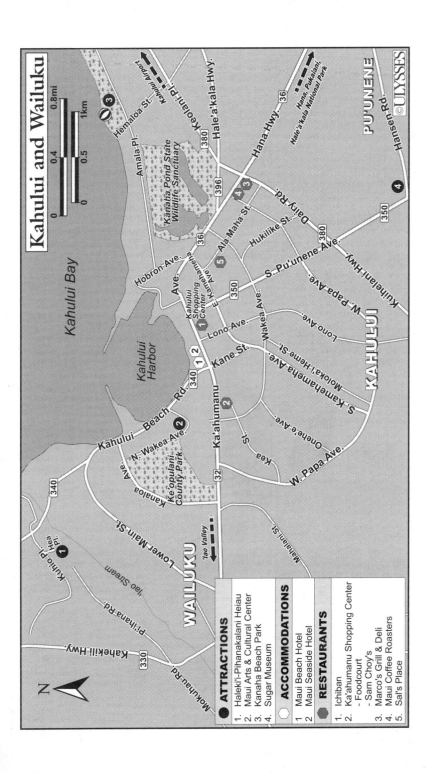

Kahului and Wailuku

© ULYSSES

Kahului Bay

Kahului Harbor

PU'UNENE

KAHULUI

WAILUKU

Kanaha Pond State
Wildlife Sanctuary

Ke'opulani
County Park

'Iao Valley

'Iao Stream

ATTRACTIONS
1. Haleki'i-Pihanakalani Heiau
2. Maui Arts & Cultural Center
3. Kanaha Beach Park
4. Sugar Museum

ACCOMMODATIONS
1 Maui Beach Hotel
2 Maui Seaside Hotel

RESTAURANTS
1. Ichiban
2. Ka'ahumanu Shopping Center
   - Foodcourt
   - Sam Choy's
3. Marco's Grill & Deli
4. Maui Coffee Roasters
5. Sal's Place

years later, the Baileys arrived to assist Green, and eventually took over after his death. The school closed after 12 years due to a lack of funds.

Only two of the 10 original buildings remain, including the house next to the museum, which is where the Baileys lived. The main floor showcases a collection of Hawaiian objects, while the second floor consists of a large furnished room. Don't miss the magnificent canoe outside, under a little roof. Made of *koa* wood, the canoe was carved out of a single tree trunk in 1916. Just below it is a surfboard that once belonged to Duke Kahanamoku (1910).

Less than 0.5mi (1km) from the junction of Highway 30 and Ka'ahumanu Avenue, the road leads to the right into the 'Iao Valley.

The **Tropical Gardens of Maui** *($3 for visitors over 8 years of age; every day 9am to 5pm;* ☎*244-3085)* feature a garden of native plants as well as introduced species, all clearly labeled. You can see the orchids in the greenhouse for free, as long as you look from afar or buy something in the gift shop.

At Mile 2, the road comes to **Heritage**

Gardens ★ *($6; every day 10am to 4pm;* ☎*244-6500),* where houses typical of each of the larger communities making up Hawaii's population are assembled. The dwellings include a Filipino bamboo structure, a Portuguese home with a replica of a bread oven, a Japanese building with a small garden, a wooden pioneer cabin like those found in New England, a Polynesian *hale* built on a platform and surrounded by *ti* plants, and a Chinese pagoda with a bust of Sun Yat-Sen.

Bird of paradise

It was here that Kamehameha vanquished Kalanikupule, the last king of Maui and O'ahu, in 1790. The battle fought here was so bloody that it came to be known as Kepaniwai, or "damming stream," a reference to the corpses that were so numerous that they clogged up the river, which ran red with blood.

Just below the park is the **Hawai'i Nature Center ★★** *($6; every day 10am to 4pm;* ☎*244-*

6500), which provides information about the environment, but also has a small museum with interactive exhibits intended to sensitize the public, both young and old, to the islands' ecology. The exhibits discuss topics such as the colonization of local plants and animals, the importance of maintaining biodiversity and the risk posed by introducing new species of plants, all presented in an engaging manner. Visitors can listen to the call of local birds or even "become" a dragonfly in the flight simulator. The centre also organizes guided rainforest walks along the 'Iao river *($25; weekdays from 1:15pm to 3:30pm; reservations required).*

Some 2,600ft (800m) past the museum is a sign on the right-hand side of the road marking the place that was once known as the *JFK Profile.* However, it is rather difficult to see the rocks resembling the profile of the former U.S. president, or those depicting Kauaka'iwai, a *kahuna* who, according to legend, lived as a hermit in a nearby cave.

The road ends a little further, and with it, **'Iao Valley State Park ★★** *(every day 7am to 7pm),* the "Yosemite of the Pacific" as it was once dubbed by an enthusiastic Mark Twain. The tropical valley is dominated by tall, scrub-

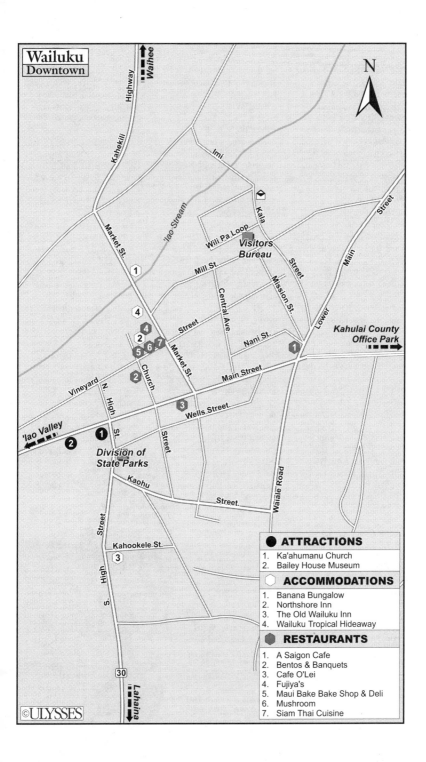

covered cliffs and the Kuka'emoku peak, better known as the 'Iao Needle (2,251ft, 686m). It once belonged to the *ahuapua'a* of Wailuku, the island's political centre, and had great religious significance, as is evident by the large Pihanakalani *heiau* at the mouth of the 'Iao river. Makahiki, a harvest festival dedicated to Lono, was held here, and numerous *ali'i* had themselves walled into caves in the cliffs, a custom that seems to date back to the reign of Kaka'e during the 15th century.

Two short paved circular trails lead into the valley. The upper one leads to a lookout near the 'Iao Needle, while the lower one goes to a garden of Hawaiian plants. Locals come for a dip in the nearby swimming hole. Don't be caught out by nightfall: all parked vehicles are impounded at 7pm.

Retrace your path to the junction with Highway 30, then continue down East Main (Ka'ahumanu Avenue). Turn left on Central Street, then immediately turn right at Nani Street to reach Lower Main, which leads to the coast. Here, turn left at the intersection, onto Kahului Beach Drive (Highway 340), which leads to a major historic site. Just over the bridge across the 'Iao River turn left at Kuhio Place, then left again at Hea Place.

The royal residence of **Haleki'i** once dominated the mouth of the river, along with one of the major *heiau*, **Pihanakalani** ★ *(free admission; every day 7am to 7pm)*. Haleki'i means "house of idols," no doubt alluding to the *tiki* that adorn the complex's terraces. In the 1760s, Grand Chief Kahekili resided here and also used the place to honour the gods during religious festivals. The ruins of the *heiau* at Pihanakalani, the "gathering place of high supernatural beings," have been partially restored with the help of a Hawaiian organization. The temple, which according to legend was constructed by *menehune*, was rededicated by Kahekili to honour Ku'kailimoku. The last human sacrifice was performed here by Kamehameha in 1790, to affirm his control of the island. The site has lost some of its grandeur as a result of the expansion of Wailuku's industrial zone below.

After the visit, return to Kahului.

Stop at the **Maui Arts & Cultural Center** *(One Cameron Way, ☎242-7469)* along the way. This $30-million complex features a cinema, theatres, and a gallery for temporary exhibits *(Tue to Sun 11am to 5pm)*. The quality of the displays varies, but they are usually dedicated to contemporary art.

Perhaps because of its role as a financial centre, Kahului has little interest to visitors, except for its beach. To get there, return via Ka'ahumanu Avenue, take the turnoff marked "Pier 1" just after the Maui Mall, then turn left right away at Hobron Avenue in the direction of the port. The first road to the right (Amala Place) leads there, about 1.5mi (2.5km) farther.

There are several beaches approximately 9mi (15km) east of Kaului that are very popular with windsurfers, and, to a lesser degree, with surfers. The first is **Kanaha Beach Park** *(washrooms, showers, camping, see p 353)*, which is very pretty but is covered in seaweed. Windsurfing schools use the beach to teach novices, but experts also like the spot. There are pleasant shaded picnic tables and a beach volleyball court. To get there, you will pass the Kanaha Pond S.W. Sanctuary, which protects migratory and aquatic birds.

The road ends shortly after the park, near the Kahului airport. At the edge of the city, turn off Ka'ahumanu Avenue onto Dairy Road (380), then take Highway 350 towards Kihei (Mokulele Highway) for a side trip to Pu'unene.

Tucked away amidst fields of sugar cane, the hamlet of Pu'unene once had Hawaii's largest sugar refinery, built in 1900 by Alexander and Baldwin (A&B). The refinery is still in operation, and the adjacent **Sugar Museum ★★** *($4; Mon to Sat 9:30 to 4:30, also Sun in Jul and Aug; 3957 Hansen Rd., ☎871-8058)* will explain all there is to know about $C^{12}H^{22}O^{11}$, or, in layperson's terms, sugar.

Located in what was once the foreman's house, the museum focuses on the creation of A&B, founded by Samuel Alexander and Henry Baldwin, both sons of missionaries. They built the first irrigation canal in 1878, bringing mountain water to the arid, sandy, central plain. The first A&B factory was established in Paia in 1880.

Continue along Hansen Road, which passes between the museum and the refinery. The road passes through fields of sugar cane before joining Hana Highway 3mi (5km) east of Kahului. At Mile 5, Nonohe Street, to the left, leads to the Spreckelsville beach.

To the left, Paami Place has a little beach that can be reached by passing between a condominium and a house. To the right, Kealakai Place ends across from **Spreckelsville Beach ★**, a large, quiet beach lined with pine trees. Partially sheltered by a raised coral reef, a protected basin of water forms at low tide. The beach is always buffeted by winds, and is thus popular with windsurfers who can be seen dancing on the rollers and soaring through the air in summer.

Baldwin Park ★ *(washrooms, showers, picnic tables, telephone)* is one of the most popular parks on the north-central coast, and lies a little farther along the Hana Highway (Mile 6). The large white-sand beach is washed by large waves, and is backed by the same pine forest as Spreckelsville Beach. Swimming is possible in calm weather, but the area is better suited to boogie boarding near the shore, and surfing farther out.

Founded as the sugar industry was emerging,

the town of **Paia ★★** is still nestled under the smokestacks of its refinery, one of the only two still operating on the island. A large *mantokuji* Buddhist temple (1921) and a cemetery next to grave markers of the *kanji* stand at the eastern edge of town, reminders of a bygone era. Every year, descendants of this Japanese community return to celebrate the festival of Obon. In the town centre, history is already long forgotten. Restaurants and boutiques surround the old stores in the old wooden buildings, reflecting Paia's present and future destiny: surfing and windsurfing. Located near some of the best waves on the island, Paia has become a playground for the world's top windsurfers, and the "capital" of the sport.

East of Paia, **Ho'okipa Beach ★★** *(washrooms, showers, barbecues, tables)* forms a lovely contrast to the larger ones. This narrow beach is lined with a rocky strip and does not make for good swimming. People come here to lie on the sand and watch the surfers tango with Maui's famous waves (novices beware!). A lookout built into the small cliff overlooks the sandy stretch to the east, and provides an even better view of the action out in the water. The windsurfers are visible to the west, and include some of the biggest names in the sport, while the surfers catch waves closer to shore. The beach is especially lively when there is a major international event taking place.

From here, you can embark on a tour of the back-country (see p 325) or the tour to Hana (see p 332).

★★

The South Coast

(one day)

Immense Ma'alaea Bay lies south of the isthmus that links Maui's two halves. In summer it is a paradise for surfing fanatics, while in winter humpback whales make the most of the waves. With Hale'a'kala towering over it, keeping the clouds away, the southern coast is Maui's sunniest region. A new series of resorts has developed: the modest Kihei development is joined by the luxurious Wailea and Makena complexes. Offshore lie the small island of Molokini, the remnants of an underwater crater; Kaho'olawe, sacred to Hawaiians; and the shore of West

Maui, almost another island in itself.

Ma'alaea Bay faces south and has almost 3mi (5km) of sand. Its port, which arose near an old fishing village, is now one of the most popular departure points for sea excursions, especially to the islet of Molokini.

Monk Seal

The new **Maui Ocean Center** ★★★ *($17.50, $12 children 3 to 12; $4 for audioguide; every day 9am to 5pm; ☎270-7000)* is said to be the world's largest tropical aquarium. At once educational and entertaining, its focus is the reproduction of green sea turtles and coral reefs. The displays are arranged so that they begin with habitats close to shore and move into progressively deeper waters. Entire sections of reef are reconstructed here, providing habitat for myriad colourful fish. The exhibits show how the species have adapted to their particular environment and their relationship to Hawaiian culture and mythology.

The Ocean Center also houses the Whale Discovery Center, which

provides a good introduction to whales, tracing their migratory path from Alaska to Hawaii through a series of interactive exhibits that capture the interest of people of all ages. There is a lot of interesting information here. In the same building is also a tunnel that travels through a large aquarium filled with sharks who are regularly fed by a diver.

North of Ma'alaea, Highway 31 (North Kihei Road) runs along the bay towards Kihei.

To the east, Ma'alaea Beach turns into **Kealia Beach** ★, where sea turtles reproduce between June and November. The road here is lined by signs that warn: "Turtle X-ing"! The barriers along the beach are not intended to keep people off the beach, but rather to help dunes to form, thereby deterring turtles from heading up to the road. Across the street, inland, is the **Kealia Pond National Wildlife Refuge** *(☎875-1582)*, which protects the large Kealia laguna and more than 690 acres (280ha) of swampland, an important habitat for aquatic and migratory birds. A parking area and observation platform are expected to

Kihei

Ma'alaea Bay

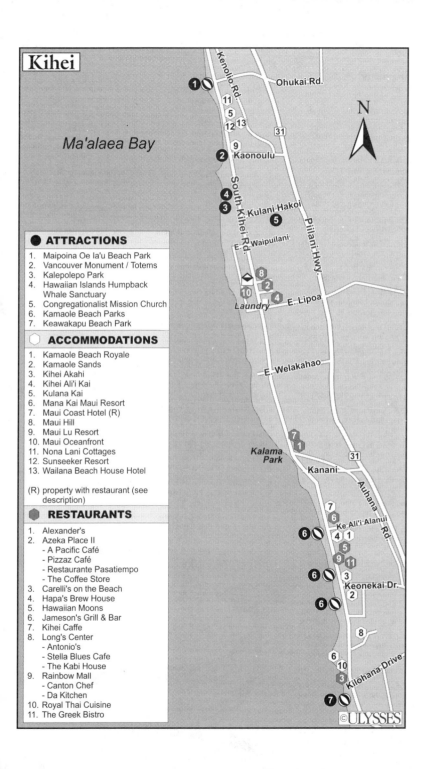

ATTRACTIONS

1. Maipoina Oe la'u Beach Park
2. Vancouver Monument / Totems
3. Kalepolepo Park
4. Hawaiian Islands Humpback Whale Sanctuary
5. Congregationalist Mission Church
6. Kamaole Beach Parks
7. Keawakapu Beach Park

ACCOMMODATIONS

1. Kamaole Beach Royale
2. Kamaole Sands
3. Kihei Akahi
4. Kihei Ali'i Kai
5. Kulana Kai
6. Mana Kai Maui Resort
7. Maui Coast Hotel (R)
8. Maui Hill
9. Maui Lu Resort
10. Maui Oceanfront
11. Nona Lani Cottages
12. Sunseeker Resort
13. Wailana Beach House Hotel

(R) property with restaurant (see description)

RESTAURANTS

1. Alexander's
2. Azeka Place II
   - A Pacific Café
   - Pizzaz Café
   - Restaurante Pasatiempo
   - The Coffee Store
3. Carelli's on the Beach
4. Hapa's Brew House
5. Hawaiian Moons
6. Jameson's Grill & Bar
7. Kihei Caffe
8. Long's Center
   - Antonio's
   - Stella Blues Cafe
   - The Kabi House
9. Rainbow Mall
   - Canton Chef
   - Da Kitchen
10. Royal Thai Cuisine
11. The Greek Bistro

©ULYSSES

be created in the near future.

A little farther on, turn right on South Kihei Road.

You are now heading toward **Kihei**. This sandy coast was practically deserted just 35 years ago, with the exception of a handful of villages scattered in the *kiawe*. Today, Kihei is lined with countless condominiums, making it one of Maui's most popular resorts. Competition between the establishments and the predominantly middle-class clientele have kept the prices here lower than on the rest of the island.

Just past the Kihei Canoe Club, the pretty little **Keolahou church** (1920) is on the left. Across from this green wooden structure, on the sea side, **Maipoina Oe Ia'u Beach Park** *(washrooms, barbecues, telephone)* is popular with windsurfers. The beach is the perfect place to go jogging or for an early-morning dip, and is backed by dunes covered in *naupaka*.

A little farther down, across from the Maui Lu Resort, two colourful totems from Vancouver Island and a dilapidated monument stand on a little outcropping overlooking the sea. They commemorate the arrival of George Vancouver in Ma'alaea Bay in 1792,

and the inscription explains that former prime minister of Canada Pierre Trudeau inaugurated the monument in 1969.

Soon after, you will reach **Kalepolepo Park ★★** *(showers, tables)*, bordered by the Menehune Shores condominiums to the south and Maui's department of marine parks to the north. A Hawaiian village once stood on this site, whose inhabitants tended the royal fishpond Ko'ie'ie which is said to have been built before the fifth century at a spot where water from an underground spring mixed with seawater. Mullets and *awa* were raised here for the *ali'i*. David Malo, a Christian chief, came to Kalepolepo in 1843 to found a church. It was soon followed by a school, a whaling station, and, in the 1850s, a warehouse built by Captain John Halstead from New York. The latter imported products from Asia for the *ali'i*, and sold island-grown potatoes to sailors passing through. Vegetables were sold as far

Humpback Whale

away as California to feed the masses hoping to make their fortune in the gold rush. With the decline of both the gold rush and the whaling industry, the store was shut down. The village disappeared soon after, when sour lime found in the rainwater spelled the end of the fishpool. The latter has now been partially restored, and is a good place to swim or snorkel.

The main office of the **Hawaiian Islands Humpback Whale National Marine Sanctuary ★** *(Mon to Fri 9am to 3pm; ☎800-831-4888)* is located across from Kalepolepo Park. Created in 1992 to protect some 2,000 humpback whales that migrate to Hawaii's waters every winter, this is the newest of the country's 12 marine parks. The reserve encompasses the strait separating Maui from Lana'i and Moloka'i, as well as a large area around the latter island, the Big Island's Kona coast, Oahu's north shore and part of Kaua'i's north shore. All sorts of information about humpback whales is available here, as well as about other marine mammals and turtles found in the reserve. There is a small exhibit on protected species in the small adjoining building.

You can make a little detour by taking Kulanihako'i Street to the ruins of the **Congregationalist Mission Church**, dedicated in 1853 by David Malo, the first Hawaiian to have been ordained into the ministry. Only the foundations remain, although open-air services are still held here. Just behind the church lies the small Lihue Cemetery (1832) with its plain stone markers.

The large **Kalama Park** *(washrooms, telephone, sports equipment)* stretches along the shore, near the centre of Kihei (insofar as one exists). The park is used mainly by locals.

Farther south, **Kamaole Beach Park ★★** *(washrooms, showers, barbecues, picnic tables)* has three sections stretching along the coast between hotels and condominiums. All three sections have supervised beaches that are well suited for swimming and therefore very busy. If we had to choose the best one, it would definitely be Kamaole III, with its large trees. This area was used by the navy during the Second World War to train for landing on the Japanese coast. The whole island was surrounded by barbed-wire fencing

during this time, and those who lived on the beach were forced to move.

At the southern edge of Kihei is **Keawakapu Beach Park ★★** *(every day 7am to 7pm; showers along the main road into the park)* which has one of Maui's most beautiful wide, fine-sand beaches. The park's history is encapsulated in its name: "*Kapu* port" refers to the mooring once found here for the exclusive use of canoes belonging to chiefs. With coconut trees and houses running nearly its entire length, Keawakapu ends at the Mana Kai Maui Resort to the north. Visitors can park for free in the large parking area on the *mauka*, or inland, side of the road: the access point to the beach is across from Kilohana Drive. The

best time to go swimming here is in the morning, before the wind picks up. On calm days, the crystal-clear water is also perfect for snorkelling.

South Kihei Road becomes Okolanio Drive as it turns inland. Turn right onto Wailea Alanui Avenue at the first intersection.

Wailea is located across from Kihei. Its name means "waters of Lea," the goddess of canoemaking who is said to have lived here. The surrounding area was used primarily for ranching in the 19th century, and the first tourist resorts in Wailea appeared in the 1970s. Unlike Kihei, Wailea is a luxury destination, surrounded by beautifully landscaped vegetation. There are five hotels and several condominiums here, set amidst the three renowned golf courses and various beaches.

Tucked away between the Outrigger and the Renaissance, a small park *(every day 7am to 7pm; washrooms, showers, telephone)* leads to two beaches separated by a rocky point: **Mokapu ★** lies to the north, and **Ulua ★** to the south. There is a bunker left over from the war standing on the beach, and it forms a stark contrast with the couples and families strolling along the boardwalk. The beach is often used by diving schools, but be careful if you go swimming: the currents are strong and the drop-off is steep.

Shared by the Four Seasons and the Grand Wailea Resort, **Wailea Beach** ★★ *(every day 7am to 7pm; washrooms, showers)* has recently been designated Most Beautiful Beach in the United States. Even those who don't quite agree will admit that this is a lovely beach. A pleasant promenade runs along it, and a small public park enables the general public to access the warm sand and water.

After Wailea Point, Wailea peters out and **Makena** begins. Makena has thus far been spared massive tourist development and currently has only one resort, the Maui Prince. Makena was a hippie paradise in the 1960s.

Follow the road along the coast then turn right at the Polo Beach Club to reach the beach of the same name. Makena Road begins here.

You will soon come across the first of a series of beaches, each one more peaceful than the last. The pretty, white-sand **Palauea Beach** ★★ is currently being fought over by investors and the public who want to preserve its tranquil atmosphere and free access. Many people camp beneath the *kiawe* despite the

signs forbidding this very activity.

Just to the south, Makena Road rejoins the coastal road (Makena Alanui) at the **Po'olenalena Beach Park** *(no amenities)* by the large beach (Chang's Beach) shaded by *kiawe*.

Keeping right at the first junction (Makena Road), the road leads around the point that shelters Makena Bay, and runs to the small beach at **Makena Landing** ★★ *(washrooms, showers)*. The beach is well known among snorkellers, as it is the perfect place from which to explore the bay's underwater scenery. One of the island's main 19th-century ports was located in the bay, with sailing vessels and steamships docking here. Sugar, pineapples and potatoes were exported, while various supplies and plenty of alcohol were brought ashore. Cattle was also shipped out from here. To reach the big boat anchored off the beach, the cattle had to swim. But to make sure they wouldn't drown or swim away, their horns were secured to longboats by a rope.

Keawala'i Congregational Church ★ *(190 Makena Rd.)* stands by the sea a few hundred yards farther south. Dedicated in 1855, this peaceful spot is

surrounded by palms, and next to it is a small cemetery with graves covered in frangipani. The cement reinforcements on the walls of the church are not very attractive, but the shingled upper portion and bell towers remain unmarred.

Walk some 650ft (200m) up the road to the pretty stretch of sand known as **Malu'aka Beach** ★★. Part of the beach is public, while the other section is dotted with loungechairs belonging to the Maui Prince Hotel, the most southerly large tourist resort on the south coast. The hotel is set back from the beach, which has managed to preserve a relatively natural character that is very difficult to come by on Maui.

Return via the main road.

About 2,600ft (800m) past the Maui Prince Hotel, a decent road on the right leads to **Black Sands Beach** ★ whose sands are more gray than black. The beach is part of Makena State

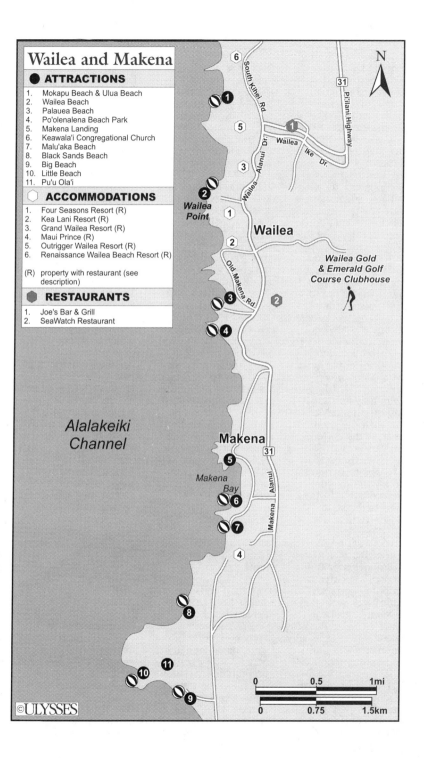

Wailea and Makena

● ATTRACTIONS

1. Mokapu Beach & Ulua Beach
2. Wailea Beach
3. Palauea Beach
4. Po'olenalena Beach Park
5. Makena Landing
6. Keawala'i Congregational Church
7. Malu'aka Beach
8. Black Sands Beach
9. Big Beach
10. Little Beach
11. Pu'u Ola'i

○ ACCOMMODATIONS

1. Four Seasons Resort (R)
2. Kea Lani Resort (R)
3. Grand Wailea Resort (R)
4. Maui Prince (R)
5. Outrigger Wailea Resort (R)
6. Renaissance Wailea Beach Resort (R)

(R) property with restaurant (see description)

● RESTAURANTS

1. Joe's Bar & Grill
2. SeaWatch Restaurant

N

South Kihei Rd.

Pi'ilani Highway
31

Wailea Alanui Dr.

Wailea Ike Dr.

Wailea

Wailea Point

Wailea Gold & Emerald Golf Course Clubhouse

Old Makena Rd.

Alalakeiki Channel

Makena
31

Makena Bay

Makena Alanui

©ULYSSES

| 0 | | 0.5 | | 1mi |
| 0 | | 0.75 | | 1.5km |

Park, and is bordered to the north by the tourist resort's golf course, and to the south by the 360ft (110m) Pu'u Ola'i behind which lie Big Beach and Little Beach. **Big Beach** ★★★ *(every day 5am to 9pm; washrooms)* is exactly what its name suggests: the wide crescent-shaped beach is 0.5mi (1km) long, bordered by thick foliage. One of the park's main features, this is the largest undeveloped beach on Maui. That is not to say that it doesn't draw crowds on weekends, but there is always enough room for everyone, and the sand is so fine that people have even been known to ski here! You can go swimming and snorkelling on calm days, but stay near the shore because the currents are very strong. The beach has several access points: two to the north, with parking areas provided, and a third to the south, closer to the road.

If you walk north to the end of Big Beach, you will notice a path that crosses a rocky outcropping and leads to **Little Beach** ★★. Surprisingly, this beach is more crowded than Big Beach and is especially popular with nudists and young people.

Before the main path reaches Little Beach, a steep, slippery trail branches off to the summit of **Pu'u**

Ola'i ★★ which provides a stunning view of the coast. In the winter, you can even see whales from here. Don't attempt the hike without good shoes, or if you are afraid of heights.

Ahihi-Kina'u Natural Area Reserve ★ is a vast stretch of unspoiled rocky coastline that stretches south of Big Beach to La Pérouse Bay. The road follows the coast from a distance and crosses a flow of *'a'a* lava, Maui's most recent, dating back to 1790. The hollowed crater from which the lava flowed is easy to make out, since the flow is lined by brushwood. Despite its rather hostile environment, the coast is known for its snorkelling. A small, sheltered bay near the last few houses at the end of Makena is a good spot to go, as is the pebble beach that is reached via a short trail (a large parking area marks the beginning of the trail).

The road ends across from **La Pérouse Bay** ★, where the famous French explorer of the same name landed on May 30, 1786, making him the first Westerner to set foot on the island. A progressive thinker, La Pérouse refused to claim the island for France, since

he opposed the way European countries were simply claiming unknown lands for themselves. A memorial commemorates La Pérouse's sojourn here. The Hawaiian village of Keone'e'io was once situated on this rugged lava coast, of which only some house foundations have survived, along with the ruins of a *heiau* (Pa'alua) by the water. The former inhabitants had to bring soil there so that they could grow vegetables. The four settlements La Pérouse discovered were abandoned after a volcanic eruption, which sent a large lava flow down to the ocean. The floor of the bay is very uneven and creates a sheltered basin, protected from the waves and ideal for snorkelling. To reach the best spot, take the path marked by a big sign that says "'Ahihi-Kina'u Natural Area Reserve," some 650ft (200m) before the end of the road. But don't stray from the path; a series of signs

I'iwi

planted in the middle of the lava field reminds visitors that most of the coast is off limits, including the small sandy section.

The **Hoapili Trail** begins a little farther east, near the middle of the bay.

Formerly a royal route along the coast, the sun-baked path now

'Akiapola'au

crosses a lava field, traversing a barren, desolate landscape.

Eastern Maui

★★
The Backcountry

(one day)

Far from the resorts, the lower slopes of Hale'a'kala are covered in lush pastures dotted with clumps of trees, including eucalyptus and cacti that look somewhat out of place. Fields of flowers and vegetables surround some of the towns. At these altitudes, potatoes and carrots flourish, as do Maui's famous onions. So many farmers settled here in the mid-19th century to provide food for the gold rush that the region is called Nu Kaliponi, or New California. There are no big hotels here, only the occasional bed and breakfast set in the peaceful surroundings. Highway 37 runs high up along the middle of the isthmus, affording lovely views of Ma'alaea Bay. The tour begins in Paia, then makes a big loop into the backcountry before ending in Kahului.

Leave downtown Paia via the Baldwin Highway

(Highway 390), heading toward Makawao.

The lovely **Makawao Union Church** ★ is about 2.5mi (4.2km) from Paia. Built in 1917, the stone church has a bell tower reminiscent of one of London's mist-enshrouded steeples. The interior feels like an amphitheatre, with beautiful stained-glass windows that came from an older building.

The road passes through some of the last pineapple plantations on the island. Behind you are lovely views of the sea.

Approximately 2mi (3km) before Makawao, turn right on Hali'imaile Road to reach a small town of the same name 1mi (1.5km) away, lost amidst the pineapple fields. The only reason to stop here is to eat at the restaurant located in the old Hali'imaile General Store (see p 376).

Located 1.4mi (2.2km) from Makawao, the **Hui No'eau Visual Arts Center** ★ *(Mon to Sat 10am to 4pm; 2841 Baldwin Ave., ☎572-6560)* was founded in 1934 and organizes temporary exhibits of

prints, modern painting and sculpture, Japanese paper and more. Courses are also offered here, and visitors are welcome to look around the gift shop.

The village of **Makawao** ★ is quite spread out, but is centred on the junction of highways 390 and 365, the first coming from Paia and the second leading to Hana and the east coast. This small *paniolo* town hosts a popular rodeo every July 4, but has also become something of a centre for New Agers. Yoga schools, centres for Eastern medicine, galleries, natural food stores and "ethnic" crafts make this the California of the tropics. If you are interested in handblown glass, visit the Hot Island Glass studio.

Take Makawao Avenue (Highway 365) back to the road to Kaului at Mile 7.2. Right after, turn left at Mile 7.6, onto the Hale'a'kala Highway (Highway 377 East). Winding up the volcano's lower slopes, the road runs parallel to Highway 37, but at a higher altitude.

The road runs through lush fields, descending the rolling hills dotted with clusters of eucalyptus trees. Here and there, there are pretty views of the central plain with its patchwork fields and the sea on either side. After

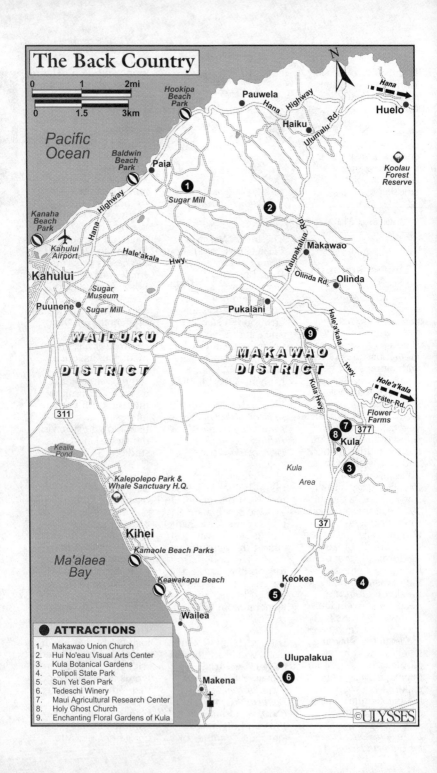

The Back Country

0   1   2mi
0   1.5   3km

N

Pacific Ocean

Hookipa Beach Park

Pauwela

Hana Highway

Haiku

Ulumalu Rd.

Hana

Huelo

Baldwin Beach Park

Paia

Sugar Mill

Koolau Forest Reserve

Kanaha Beach Park

Kahului Airport

Kahului

Hale'akala Hwy.

Hana Highway

Kaupakalua Rd.

Makawao

Olinda Rd.

Olinda

Sugar Museum

Puunene

Sugar Mill

Pukalani

WAILUKU

DISTRICT

MAKAWAO

DISTRICT

Hale'akala Hwy.

Kula Hwy.

Hole'a'kala Crater Rd.

Flower Farms

311

Kealia Pond

Kalepolepo Park & Whale Sanctuary H.Q.

377

Kula

Kula Area

Kihei

Kamaole Beach Parks

37

Ma'alaea Bay

Keawakapu Beach

Keokea

Wailea

Ulupalakua

Makena

● ATTRACTIONS

1. Makawao Union Church
2. Hui No'eau Visual Arts Center
3. Kula Botanical Gardens
4. Polipoli State Park
5. Sun Yet Sen Park
6. Tedeschi Winery
7. Maui Agricultural Research Center
8. Holy Ghost Church
9. Enchanting Floral Gardens of Kula

©ULYSSES

several miles, the road approaches **Kula**, which lies at an altitude of 2,950ft to 3,940ft (900m to 1,200m) between highways 37 and 377. Thanks to its elevation, it has become a major centre for produce and gardening. Vegetables requiring a temperate climate grow alongside fields of poppies and protea with huge blooms. A number of farms in the area are open to visitors.

Pass Kula Lodge (see p 358 and 377) at Mile 6, and keep left at the junction where Hale'a'kala Crater Road begins. This road leads to the top of the volcano (see p 328). Continue along Highway 377 until you reach Kula Botanincal Gardens at Mile 8.5.

Kula Botanical Gardens ★ *($4; every day 9am to 4pm; ☎878-1715)* is located right beside a Christmas-tree nursery and is a pleasant place for a stroll. The small garden is shady and peaceful, with a small stream running through it. It overlooks the central isthmus and the sea, and although it may not have as many flowers as some of the other parks on the island, it has some exquisite species, such as two dracaena from the Canary Islands, which

are located near the entrance.

Just past the garden, Waipoli Road climbs up through pastures to reach **Polipoli State Park ★**. This small road is very windy and passes a launching area for hangliders before entering the Kula Forest Reserve, the remains of an ancient forest of indigenous trees that once grew all the way down to the shores of La Pérouse Bay. When conditions are dry, access is sometimes forbidden to reduce the risk of a forest fire. On the other hand, when it rains the route can be dangerous for regular vehicles: only half the road is paved, and the unpaved section can become muddy and slippery when wet. The road runs 9.6mi (15.5km) from Highway 377, and climbs nearly 6,235ft (1,900m). The forest is often shrouded in a replenishing mist, and is used primarily by hunters and hikers. There is a network of trails as well as campsites and even bungalows for rent (see p 358).

Highway 377 rejoins Highway 30 at Mile 14, just after Waipoli Road forks off. Take Highway 30 heading south.

A little farther, at Mile 16.8, you will reach **Keokea**, a community once known as Chinatown since many of its

inhabitants were Chinese immigrants. The two grocery stores are still run by their descendants.

Sun Yet Sen Park is located by the road at Mile 18.6. The park was created in memory of the "father of the Republic of China," whose bust is found here along with sculptures of Chinese lions. Sun Yat-Sen spent several years in Hawaii because his brother lived here.

Mile 21 marks the end of Highway 37, which turns into Pi'ilani Highway at this point, continuing along the southern coast (see p 338) to complete the tour of the island. A mile or so farther is the **Tedeschi Winery ★** *(every day 9am to 5pm; guided tours every hour from 9:30am to 2:30pm; ☎878-6058)*, a splendid winery that is part of the large Ulupalakua ranch.

The guided tour *(20 to 30min)* takes visitors around the facilities and includes a short lesson on the best way to make champagne... from pineapples! These arrive at the estate in barrels of concentrated juice, ready to be fermented. The ranch also produces 50 tonnes of grapes annually, growing a hybrid of cabernet sauvignon and grenache grapes. Pineapple wine accounts for two thirds of its sales. It is very popular with tourists, despite its lack of wine-like qualities.

Stay on Highway 30 and head in the direction of Wailuku. You will arrive at the lower part of Kula.

At Mile 12.6 take Copp Road followed by Mauna Place to the **Maui Agricultural Research Center** *(free admission; Mon to Thu 7am to 3:30pm)*, the University of Hawaii's agricultural research centre. The experimental gardens are open to the public. It is best to come in December, since this is when the protea begin to bloom.

A little farther, at Mile 11.9, Lower Kula Road climbs to Kula's **Holy Ghost Church** ★★. This Catholic church was built by the Portuguese community in 1894, and has a striking octagonal layout. The high altar is the building's main attraction. The decidedly baroque piece was specially made in Austria. The church's Lusitanian heritage is evident in its rosy colour and the Portuguese-style Stations of the Cross. It is the only one of its kind in Hawaii. There is a replica of Isabelle's crown to the right of the entrance; and most of the graves in the cemetery below the church bear Portuguese surnames.

Just below the road at Mile 10.3 are the **Enchanting Floral Gardens of Kula** ★ *($5; every day*

9am to 5pm; ☎*878-2531)*, a large garden containing some 1,500 types of flowers from the four corners of the world, especially from Asia, the Pacific and the U.S. tropics. There are also fruit trees, including a grapefruit tree bearing gigantic fruit and the stunning "Buddha's Hand Citrus" (*Citrus medica*), whose citrus fruit look like bunches of convoluted carrots. A number of bowers also grace the garden, but the noise of the traffic below takes away from the peace and tranquility of the spot.

★★★
Hale'a'kala

(half-day)

Creator of both parts of the island, the Hale'a'kala volcano, known as the "House of the Sun," emerged from the waters a little more than 900,000 years ago and now reaches a height of 10,023ft (3,055m). The crater at the summit is one of the largest in the world, with a circumference of 21mi (34km) and a depth of 2953ft (900m). People often say that all of Manhattan could fit into the crater. The crater is not only the product of the volcano, but also of erosion. Mountain streams formed around the summit after heavy rainfalls, and gradually hollowed out this huge basin after the volcano had become dormant.

If the volcano were to erupt again, lava would engulf everything. Minor eruptions that occurred relatively recently have formed dozens of residual cones on the floor of this massive open-air furnace, some of them standing up to 590ft (180m) tall. The surrounding countryside, in tones of red, yellow, grey and brown, looks like a lunar landscape, having been repeatedly pounded by lava bombs and covered in ashes.

The volcano has not been active in more than two centuries – if not three or four. The last eruption was long believed to have taken place in 1790, but recent scientific data suggests it occurred near the end of the 16th century. The only thing that is absolutely certain is where this outburst occurred: far from the volcano's summit, near La Pérouse Bay. And volcano experts agree that Hale'a'kala is not yet at rest, with most predicting a renewed period of activity at some point. This is hardly surprising in a place that has seen volcanos erupt after being dormant for three million years!

Originally part of Volcanoes National Park, which also included Mauna Loa and Kilauea on the Big Island, Hale'a'kala became its own national park in 1961, and a UNESCO

Maui

World Biosphere Reserve in 1980. With an area of some 28,700 acres (11,600ha), the park is centred around the crater of the volcano, but stretches east to the humid coast, encompassing Kipahulu Valley, a refuge for rare species (see p 338). There is no road or trail connecting the two areas.

From Kula, go to the junction at Mile 6, and turn left onto Highway 377 which ascends to the Hale'a'kala (378 East).

After several hundred yards you will reach the **Sunrise Protea Farm** *(free admission; every day 8am to 4pm; ☎876-0200)*, a store with a little garden displaying different types of protea grown on the premises. You can buy bouquets (fresh or dried), seeds, and even dolls made of two dried protea. The farm also has a deli and is very popular with Asian tourists.

The road passes the last houses in Kula, then winds up the slopes of Hale'a'kala.

After a 20- to 30min drive, the road reaches **Hale'a'kala National Park** *($10, pass valid for 7 days, Golden Eagle accepted; ☎572-4400; www.nps.gov/hale; mail, P.O. Box 369, Makawao,*

Protea

HI 96768) at Mile 10.1. Just past the entrance, a small road turns off to the left to **Hosmer Grove ★**, a eucalyptus and pine forest with the only camping facilities in Hale'a'kala (see p 359). In 1910, before the national park was created, Ralph Hosmer planted trees from around the world here, attempting to forestall desertification by restoring nutrients to the soil. However, the trees grew too slowly and were not profitable, so the project was abandoned. A small loop trail (30min) runs through the remaining forest.

The northern flank of Hale'a'kala is not part of the national park but is protected by a number of reserves. The walk to **Waikamoi Preserve ★★** begins at Hosmer Grove. This preserve was created in 1983 on more than 4,942 acres (2,000ha) of land belonging to the Hale'a'kala Ranch. It protects one of the last vestiges of the immense old-growth forest that once covered the entire

volcano. Managed by the Nature Conservancy, the public may visit through tours run once a month by the organization *($15; see p 298)*, or twice a week by the national park rangers *(Mon and Thu; ☎572-9306)*. The walk is 3 or 4hrs long, but is not strenuous, covering just over a mile (2km) to the raised path that runs through a magnificent forest of *koa*, *ohia* and *ama'u* ferns. Some native birds have also survived in this corner of the island, including the *'i'iwi*, *'apapane*, *'amakihi* and above all, the famous crested *'akohekohe*, which had long been considered extinct until it was rediscovered in the late 1970s. Your best chance to see this rare bird is in May when it feeds on the nectar of *'ohi'a* flowers, but even then you will likely only get a glimpse.

The park's main **Visitor Center** *(every day 7:30am to 4pm; ☎572-4459)* is located near the entrance, at Mile 11.2. This is also the headquarters for the national park. The centre provides literature on various hikes and the local flora and fauna, and also has a selection of books. A number of silversword are planted right by the entrance.

Mile 14.7 marks the starting point of the **Halemau'u Trail ★★**, one of two trails that lead into the crater. This is the shortest

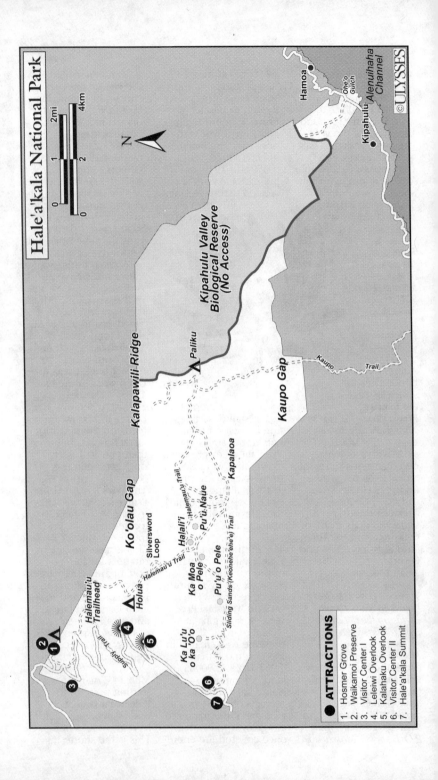

Hale'akala National Park

● ATTRACTIONS

1. Hosmer Grove
2. Waikamoi Preserve
3. Visitor Center I
4. Leleiwi Overlook
5. Kalahaku Overlook
6. Visitor Center II
7. Hale'a'kala Summit

Kipahulu Valley
Biological Reserve
(No Access)

Kalapawili Ridge

Ko'olau Gap

Kaupo Gap

Paliku

Kaupo Trail

Halemau'u Trailhead

Supply Trail

Silversword Loop

Halali'i

Halemau'u Trail

Pu'u Naue

Holua

Halemau'u Trail

Ka Moa o Pele

Pu'u o Pele

Kapalaoa

Sliding Sands (Keonehe'ehe'e) Trail

Ka Lu'u o ka 'O'o

Hamoa

'Ohe'o Gulch

Kipahulu

Alenuihaha Channel

N

0   1   2mi
0   2   4km

© ULYSSES

route to Holua Cabin (3.9mi or 6.3km; one way). The lip of the crater is a 2.2mi (3.5km) trek, while the **Silversword Loop ★** is 5mi (8km), and goes past a "field" of silverswords. The best day hike (if you have two cars at your disposal) is to take the Sliding Sands Trail from the Visitor Center (at the summit), and to drive back.

A 980ft (300m) trail from the parking area at Mile 17.4 leads to **Leleiwi Overlook ★★**, the first lookout with a view of Hale'a'kala's crater (seen from the north). According to an interpretive panel at the site, this is the best place in the park from which to observe a strange phenomenon known as the Brocken effect. In the afternoon when the sun shines at a certain angle it casts human shadows surrounded by a rainbow-coloured halo onto the clouds or mist below. This unique phenomenon is the result of refraction in the water droplets, and is named after Brocken, a waterfall in Austria where the same phenomenon occurs.

A turnoff at Mile 18.8 (unmarked since it is prohibited to turn up-hill due to a dangerous curve) leads 980ft (300m) to **Kalahaku Overlook ★★**, another lookout over the crater. There is a

sign that explains how Maui was formed, and silverswords of various sizes (mainly small) can be seen below the parking area.

The road ends its long climb at the parking area of the second **Visitor Center** (*every day 6am to 3pm in winter, 5:30am to 3pm in summer*) at Mile 20.8. The visitor centre provides all kinds of information about hiking and other activities offered at the park, as well as information about local geology, plants and animals. A lookout is located nearby, offering a view straight down into Hale'a'kala's **crater ★★★**. Below you will see cones and lava needles that have been eroded into various shapes on a barren red, grey, black and sometimes olive-green expanse of ground.

Every day, hundreds of people get up in the middle of the night to reach the top of the volcano in time to see the sun rise – an experience that has gradually become very popular with tourists.

If the weather is good (which it generally is at dawn), the surrounding scenery is bathed in incredible rosy hues. After a quick breakfast, entire groups of people take to their mountain bikes for the second part of the experience: coasting down the volcano's summit. Agencies organizing these packages were so successful that there are now at least a dozen offering this type of excursion (see p298).

The more popular of the two trails leading into the crater is **Sliding Sands Trail ★★**, which begins at the entrance to the parking area. Most people who hike this trail arrange to be picked up at the head of the Halemau'u Trail (Mile 14.7, see below). This way, much of the 11mi (18km) trek is downhill, except for the steep climb to the higher plateau right at the end. Leave yourself 6 to 9hrs for the hike, depending on your level of fitness. The small detour to **Pele's Paint Pot ★★** on the edge of Halali'i crater is worthwhile. The bright colours are the result of mineral deposits.

A small road leads to the true **summit** of Hale'a'kala (Mile 21.2), known as the *'Ula'ula* ("red hill"), which reaches an altitude of about 10,020ft (3,055m). The peaks of Mauna Kea and Mauna Loa on the Big Island are visible to the east from the observation tower overlooking the crater, while West Maui and Lana'i can be seen in the opposite direction. The U.S. military occupied this strategic spot during the Second World War, and built (a little too late) a radar station to detect Japanese planes. The white buildings of Science City are closed to the public since they are still used by the U.S. Air Force. A radar beam continually measures the position of the Earth in relation to the moon. Some silverswords have been planted in the middle of the base.

The drive back to Kahului takes about 1hr, but many people visit the backcountry the same day.

★★
The Road to Hana and Tour of the Island

(one to two days)

As inescapable as it is spectacular, the Road to Hana winds along the luxuriant northern coast, going from one valley to the next, cooled by the refreshing wind from the northeast. Steep cliffs dominate some sections of the road, while others are battered by the powerful ocean waves or bordered by sheer drops that give way to deep valleys harbour-

ing humid jungles. Streams and waterfalls break up the deep-green countryside, their white torrents leading to natural pools of cool, clear water. Trails have run along this wild coast for generations, linking the ancient Hawaiian villages tucked away in the valleys. The first semblance of a road

Petrel

was built in 1877 to allow for the construction of Hamakua Ditch, a major part of the irrigation system. It was not until 1926 that Hana was finally linked by a road, which was carved out through the hard labour of prisoners. The road was only paved in 1962.

All the island's tourist shops sell T-shirts that brag "I survived the Hana Highway," but don't take this to heart. Sure, the road has many curves (600 in all!) and bridges (54), but is not particularly treacherous. Just relax, leave yourself plenty of time, avoid driving along the road at night, let the locals pass you and remember that the whole point of the drive is to enjoy the scenery along the way. Count on 2.5 to 3hrs from Wailuku to Hana.

The Hana Highway actually begins at Mile 0, where it meets Ulumalu Road which leads to Makawao.

At Mile 3.7, take Dora Faith Road and descend *makai* to Huelo, a scattered village in a pretty, tropical setting. The impressive **Kaulanapueo Church** (1853) stands on the left side of the road. This large coral church has a small bell tower with green shingles and is surrounded by *ti* plants.

All along the way, you will come across sections of the **Ko'olau Ditch ★**, built by Alexander & Baldwin in 1878 to irrigate their sugar-cane plantations. Approximately 50 of the canal's 75 miles (80 of 120km) were carved out of rock, and many of the pipelines had to cross deep ravines. At Mile 8.1, just after the bridge, is the opening of a dark, narrow tunnel that pierces the mountain. The massive amount of rock that had to be removed gives an idea of the magnitude of the undertaking. Some 985ft (300m) farther, at the foot of a large tulip-tree whose orange-coloured blooms strew the ground, is the exit of a second tunnel and the entrance to a third.

At Mile 9.5, in Ko'olau State Forest Reserve, a parking area marks the beginning of **Waikamoi Nature Trail** ★. The trail runs through a lovely forest of eucalyptus, bamboo, pandanus and *ti* plants. The walk takes about 30min and has two partially obscured views of the Waikamo Valley, with the Hana Highway winding along the bottom. There is a small picnic area right at the top, in a clearing surrounded by cypresses.

At the bottom of the valley (Mile 9.9), the road passes a long series of small **waterfalls** that, like most other in Hawaii, cascade into natural pools surrounded by lush vegetation.

At Mile 10.5, the **Garden of Eden** ★ (*$5; every day 9am to 2pm; ☎280-1912*) is a large private garden of just over 25 acres (10ha). Crisscrossed by footpaths, the garden is a little corner of jungle that has been landscaped and tamed. Some of the plants are labeled, and in fair weather there is a lovely view of the sea. The most striking view, however, is of the **Puohokamoa Falls** ★, which can be seen even more clearly (and for free) from the Hana Highway. The garden has an area for picnics. It is closed on very rainy days.

At the bottom of Puohokamoa Valley (Mile 11), a small path leads close to the falls. It is very hard to miss

since there are usually a large number of cars parked here. You can bathe in the pool below the waterfall, which is only a few yards high, but be careful on the slippery rocks. About 2,625ft (800m) farther, another small waterfall cascades into another small pool which for some reason is rarely visited by tourists.

At Mile 12.2, **Kaumahina State Wayside Park** (*washrooms, picnic tables*) provides the first view (if somewhat distant) of the Keanae Peninsula. From here, the road becomes even more winding, and gradually descends to the verdant cliffs of large **Honomanu Bay** ★★. Having crossed the river after Mile 14, a small road quickly descends to the horseshoe bay. Lined luxuriant vegetation around a pebble beach, this pristine bay shows the serene side of Hawaii, which is too often overshadowed by the massive tourist developments. Returning to the east side of the bay, there are several lovely viewpoints.

The next section is one of the most beautiful on the north coast: the long lava finger of the **Kaenae Peninsula** ★★ gradually becomes visible between the branches of mango- and tulip-trees.

Just before reaching the peninsula (Mile 16.6), take a short stroll

through the **Kaenae Arboretum** (*free admission*), which was built in 1971. A path, which becomes increasingly unkempt, runs along the Piinaau through a park of more than 5 acres (2ha), which is unfortunately quite badly maintained. *Ti* plants, breadfruit, palm trees, ginger, bamboo and banana trees lead up to a small field of taro. From here, a path leads along an irrigation canal that looks exactly like one of the *levadas* in Madeira. The path becomes increasingly narrow and slippery before disappearing completely into the forest, the hunters' domain.

Don't miss the turnoff to Keanae at Mile 16.7.

A small road makes a steep descent, offering beautiful views of the patchwork fields of carefully tended taro. A dozen houses are scattered here and there, and there is a small **church** (1860), Ihiihi o Iehowa o na Kaua, made of lava rock and capped by a tiny bell tower. The road ends under the pandanus, by the sea.

At Mile 16.9 the main road crosses a small river with a small pool that is very popular with local families who come here to swim. Cars parked nearby will help you find the spot.

Park in the *makai* parking area approximately

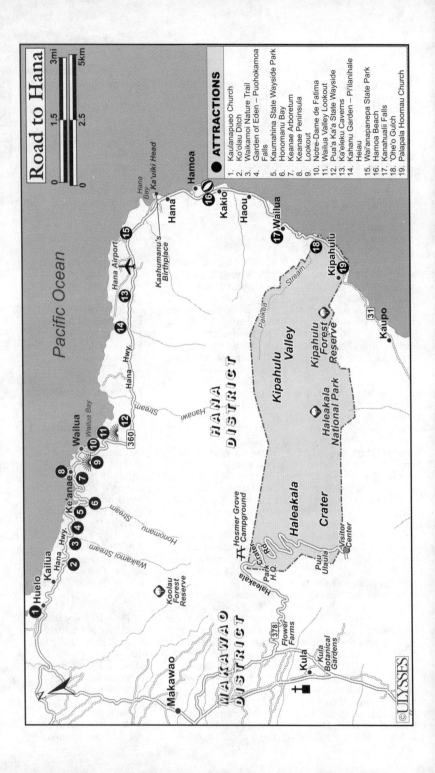

Road to Hana

Scale:
0 — 1.5 — 3mi
0 — 2.5 — 5km

Pacific Ocean

ATTRACTIONS

1. Kaulanapueo Church
2. Ko'olau Ditch
3. Waikamoi Nature Trail
4. Garden of Eden — Puohokamoa Falls
5. Kaumahina State Wayside Park
6. Honomanu Bay
7. Keanae Arboretum
8. Keanae Peninsula
9. Lookout
10. Notre-Dame de Fatima
11. Wailua Valley Lookout
12. Pua'a Ka'a State Wayside
13. Ka'eleku Caverns
14. Kahanu Garden — Pi'ilanihale Heiau
15. Wai'anapanepa State Park
16. Hamoa Beach
17. Kanahualii Falls
18. 'Ohe'o Gulch
19. Palapala Hoomau Church

Huelo
Kailua
Ke'anae
Wailua
Wailua Bay
Hana Hwy.
360
Waikamoi Stream
Honomanu Stream
Hana Hwy.
Hana Airport
Kaahumanu's Birthplace
Ka'uiki Head
Hana Bay
Hana
Hamoa
Kakio'
Haou
Wailua
Kipahulu
Hanawi Stream
Palikea Stream

HANA DISTRICT

Kipahulu Valley
Kipahulu Forest Reserve
Haleakala Crater
Haleakala National Park

Hosmer Grove Campground
Haleakala Crater Rd.
Park H.Q.
Puu Ulaula
Visitor Center

31
Kaupo

MAKAWAO DISTRICT

Koolau Forest Reserve

378
Flower Farms
Kula Botanical Gardens
Makawao
Kula

© ULYSSES

650ft (200m) farther. There is a magnificent **view ★★** of Keanae Point and the checkered taro fields. You can also see the small pebble beach nestled in the hollow of the bay.

Just past the Uncle Harry's stand at Mile 18.3, a turnoff leads to the village of Wailua, built on a large coastal platform. To the left, the **Notre-Dame de Fatima ★** Catholic church, a white building capped by a short bell tower, stands beside a flower-filled cemetery. The church is known as "coral miracle church" because of the circumstances surrounding its construction in 1860. When the faithful had to dive for pieces of coral reef, a storm blew up and washed ashore more coral than they could use. The following day, when people had harvested this gift of God, another storm came and washed the leftover pieces from the beach.

At Mile 19.2 on Hana Highway, a lookout offers a beautiful panoramic **view** of the houses of nearby Wailua, which dot the patchwork of taro fields. You can make out the white edifice of Notre-Dame de Fatima. A short distance away, by the single-lane bridge, the road passes a lovely **waterfall** that is a little higher than the previous ones.

Those who enjoy refreshing, and we do mean refreshing, swims, have several pools to choose from: one at Mile 20.9 (right below the bridge, with relatively easy access compared with other spots) and in **Pua'a Ka'a State Park** (at Mile 22.7).

The number of stands selling fruit and flowers grows as you approach Hana. Some are self-service and payment is left in a box according to the honour system.

Turn left on Ulaino Road at Mile 31.1.

The road quickly approaches the departure point for tours of the **Ka'eleku Caverns** *($25 to $175 depending on the duration of the excursion, which ranges from 1 to 6hrs; ☎248-7308, www.hanacave.com)*, a network of underground lava tunnels that was created by a volcanic eruption some 3,000 years ago. The ceiling is often at least a dozen yards high, and the corridors open into large cathedral-like chambers, some of which are illuminated by light shafts. There are all kinds of rock formations here, both volcanic and otherwise. The longer visits can be trying, especially for people who are somewhat claustrophobic (in some parts you have to crawl on your hands and knees), but most people will enjoy the shorter visits.

From here, Ulaino Road passes close to the **Kaia Ranch Tropical Botanical Gardens** *($3; every day 9am to 5pm)*, created for people who forgot to make reservations at the **Kahanu Garden ★★** *($10; Mon to Fri 11am and 1pm; ☎248-8912)*, located a little farther along. The "little sister" of the National Tropical Botanical Garden, this huge garden was created on former pastures in 1972, and contains a major ethnobotanical collection. There are more than 120 varieties of breadfruit trees and other species brought over by Polynesian immigrants, or used by them, as well as a section on vegetables indigenous to Maui. The restored remains of **Pi'ilanihale Heiau ★★**, the largest *heiau* in Hawaii, are located within the premises. Some claim it was built in the 14th century, while others maintain it was at a later date, after Maui had been unified by the great Chief Pi'ilani, who come to this place regularly. The temple's name means "House of Pi'ilani." The platform measures 338ft by 413ft (103m by 126m), and is spread over several terraces, a little like the foundations of pre-Columbian temples. The *heiau's* highest point reaches 49ft (15m).

Slightly more than 1.2mi (2km) past the garden, the road crosses several fords that are usually dry.

Maui

Cross the stream at the end of the road and head about 492ft (150m) north. Behind the rocky outcrop is the lovely **Blue Pool** ★★, a natural basin fed by a waterfall that truly is like a little piece of paradise on earth.

Return to Hana Highway.

At Mile 32, a small road leads to a lovely tropical setting, right by the ocean. **Wai'anapanapa State Park** ★★ *(washrooms, picnic tables, barbecues, camping – see p 359)* is one of Maui's most beautiful natural areas. Along a rocky coast, waves ruffle the surface of a deep bay studded with large eroded rocks in jagged formations, pierced, arched or punctured by other types of holes. The coast is bedecked in pandanus and tender green *naupaka* which form a striking contrast with the black lava. There is a lovely little black-sand beach at the end of the bay where you can swim, as long as you stay close to shore.

Two sections of the old Hawaiian coastal road, which once ran all around the island, lead north to an old pre-colonial cemetery (0.5mi or 1km) and south (in the direction of Hana) to a major *heiau* (0.5mi or 1km). The walk to Hana is lovely, but is best done in the morning to avoid the heat.

At Mile 33.8 turn left onto Uakea Road and head to the waterfront in Hana.

A major population centre in ancient times, **Hana** ★ is now just a sleepy little town with 2,000 inhabitants, overlooking a quiet bay bordered by a brown-sand beach and dense vegetation that attests to the heavy rainfall it receives. The first sugar-cane plantation was established here in 1849. Because of the growth of the sugar industry, there were six of them by 1883. During that time, the little town doubled in population and boasted 154 stores and two movie theatres. Production, which was already jeopardized by escalating costs, came to an abrupt halt in 1946, when a tsunami (tidal wave) destroyed a significant amount of infrastructure and claimed 12 lives. Following this disaster, Hana turned to agriculture, which, along with tourism, is still the major industry. It may be its isolation or its large Hawaiian population (50%), but Hana seems to live a little in the past.

The **Hana Cultural Center & Museum** ★ *($2; every day 10am to 4pm but opening hours vary;* ☎*248-8622)* is located just before the bay. A local initiative, it houses a small collection of Hawaiian objects, shells and old bottles. There is infor-

mation about fishing techniques, the cultivation of taro, and the production of *kapa* and quilts. The small wooden building beside the museum served as Hana's prison and courthouse from 1871 until as recently as 1978. In 1990 the courthouse began to operate once again on the first Tuesday of each month. Made of palm *hale* and *ti* leaves and surrounded by an ethnobotanical garden, the Kauhale o Hana is a replicated Hawaiian village from pre-European times.

Although it is hardly enticing for swimmers, **Hana Bay** ★ has a long brown-sand beach (Hana Beach Park). The bay is bound to the east by **Ka'uiki Head**, a mass of rock created by a late volcanic eruption. The volcanic cone has been eroded, exposing the crater's red, iron-rich core. Pine trees were planted on the peninsula in the 1930s. There is a small path that runs along the rocky coast from the base of the quay at the eastern end of the beach. A short walk along the path leads to a plaque that commemorates the birth of Ka'ahumanu here in 1768. The parents of Kamehameha's future wife sought refuge here during the war between Maui's Chief Kahekili and the Big Island's

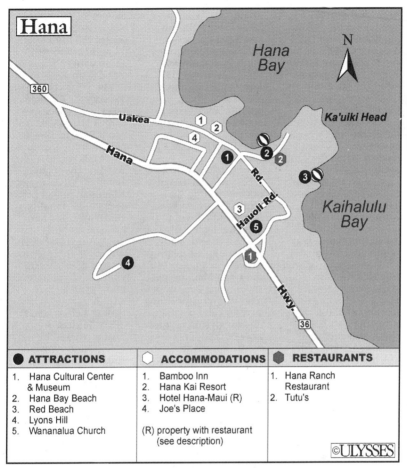

Chief Kalaniopu'u. Two massive rocks have blocked the entrance of the path since a landslide occurred, but you can still access it by climbing over some uprooted tree trunks. Along the way, you will discover a tiny beach with brick-coloured sand, created by the erosion of the cliffs that tower above it. The trail ends at the point, off of which lies an islet with a lighthouse.

Red Beach ★★ unfurls on the other side of the point. Frequented by nudists and people looking for some solitude, the simplest way to get there is to take the path from the Hana Community Center. The trail runs along the property of the Hana-Maui hotel, and then along the coast. An abandoned Buddhist cemetery lies just below. Red Beach lies just beyond the point, and stretches along a bay

dominated by an impressive red cliff and protected from large waves by a barrier of rocks facing the waves. The barrier makes it safe to go swimming and snorkelling in calm weather, as long as you stay in the sheltered area.

You can obtain the key to access **Lyons Hill ★** at the reception of the Hana-Maui hotel, which lies right across from it. A small road crosses fields before reaching a large cross erected in memory of Paul Fagan. A buyer for Hana's sugar company in 1930, Fagan became interested in cultivation and turned the town into a *paniolo* city. He also opened the first hotel, the Hana-Maui's predecessor. Access is restricted when the cattle are in the field. It is best to go by car since the walk takes 30min. The key is available from sunrise to sunset.

Wananalua Church was originally constructed on Hana Bay in 1838, built haphazardly with what materials were on hand. It was moved to its present site in 1842 and built as a coral stone structure that took 22 years to complete. This enormous church was entirely renovated in 1989 and has lost its original charm.

At the southern edge of town is **Hasegawa General Store**, the most popular store in Hana, which was immortalized in a song by local musician Paul Weston in 1965. The store was founded at the turn of the 20th century by the great-grandparents of its current owner. This is an exact replica of the original building, erected after the original store burnt down in 1990.

South of Hana the road runs through huge fields.

At Mile 51.7 Haneoo Road turns right toward **Koki Beach**, a grey-sand beach bordered to the north by a large red cliff. The strong currents make it impossible to swim here, and only the most experienced surfers brave the waves. A little farther, past a big bend in the road, the road opens onto **Hamoa Bay ★★**, where the Polynesians once landed in their large canoes. A set of stairs leads down to the beach, which is also of gray sand and shaded by large *kukui*. The beach is managed by the Hana-Maui hotel, but anyone can use it. You can go snorkelling here in calm weather, and "bodysurfers" and boogie boarders come from all over the island in winter.

Haneoo Road rejoins the peripheral road at Mile 49.1.

After Hamoa, the fields along the Pi'ilani Highway are gradually replaced by more tropical scenery. Huge mango, breadfruit and *kukui* trees cast their branches over the road. Surprisingly, quite a few people live along this part of the coast. So look out for children on the road, and also for "baby pig crossings"!

The **Kanahualii Falls ★★** (or Wailua Falls) are right near the road, at Mile 44.7. Surrounded by tropical vegetation, the waterfall plummets 95ft (29m) like a fine veil, and is one of the most beautiful and easy to reach in all of Maui.

At Mile 41.8 you reach the edge of **Kipahulu Valley**, which became part of Hale'a'kala National Park in 1969 to protect its near-pristine forests, home to *'ohi'a* and *loa*. The higher altitudes thrive on the abundant rainfall (250in or 6,350mm) and provide shelter for rare indigenous birds like the Maui parrotbill and *nukupu'u*. In order to protect their habitat, visitors are not allowed into the area.

Farther below lies **'Ohe'o Gulch ★★**, a ravine crossed by the Palikea and Pipiwai streams. Just before the mouth of the ravine, the current branches into a dozen mini-waterfalls that link pools of various sizes. Although they have long been known as the Seven Sacred Pools, they are not in fact sacred, nor are there seven of them. The water crashing to the foot of the waterfalls has gradually hollowed out the pools, with the deepest one being 40ft (12m) deep. A number of fish live in the water, the most interesting of which is the *'o'opu*. Like salmon, this little fish is born in fresh water but spends its life out at sea before returning to the place of its birth to lay its eggs. To help it with the difficult task of

Kaho'olawe

At a mere 50 sq mi (116.5km²), Kaho'olawe is the smallest of the main islands of the archipelago, and the only one that is uninhabited. Located about 6mi (10km) west of Maui in the shadow of the majestic Hale'a'kala that blocks the rain clouds, Kaho'olawe is an arid island buffeted by strong winds. It has high cliffs in the south and east, and is dominated by a high plateau that culminates at 1410ft (430m), at Pu'u Mao'ulanui. There is a series of bays to the north and west.

Though it appears not to have changed in millenia, this inhospitable landscape was not always deserted. In fact, Hawaiians did live on the island for about 1,000 years. Believed to be sacred, the island was called Kohemalamalama 'o Kanaloa, in honour of the god of the oceans and the earth. Before relations with Tahiti were severed in the 15th century, *kahuna*

and navigators set out on long voyages to the South Pacific from here. Research indicates that most of the small bays along the coast show signs of permanent habitation. Close to 1,000 archaeological sites have been found on the island, many of which had altars dedicated to fisher-protecting gods. Some of Hawaii's largest *heiaus* are found here. Kaho'olawe also has a basalt quarry at Pu'u Moiwi, where rock was used to make axes.

Several thousands of the island's inhabitants died of diseases brought over by the early explorers and European colonists, and the island's terrain was devastated by the introduction of goats and sheep who ravaged the sparse vegetation. Subsequent erosion has stripped away about 5in (12cm) of soil. The last Hawaiian farm disappeared in 1830, and with it, the island's inhabitants. Several attempts were made in the early 20th century to restore crop

farming to Kaho'olawe, but they were unsuccessful.

After the attack at Pearl Harbor, the U.S. Navy took complete control of Kaho'olawe. Despite a written promise by President Eisenhower in 1953 to make the island habitable once more after the military had left, the world's largest non-nuclear bomb exploded here in 1965, leaving a crater nearly 164ft (50m) in diameter.

Since Kaho'olawe was taken over by the military, Native Hawaiians have protested the occupation of this sacred ground. Their struggle went on for years, and led to a resurgence of Hawaiian culture. The foundation of the non-profit Protect Kaho'olawe 'Ohana in 1976 was the first concrete step taken in this struggle. "Illegal" occupation of the island by activists who risked imprisonment were among the acts of political resistance. 'Ohana brought forth a lawsuit accusing the military of infringing on religious liberty and laws protecting the environment and historic sites, which resulted in their obtaining the right for members of the organization, as well as their guests, to visit the island. An archaeological inventory was conducted and the island was cleared of non-detonated munition and other abandoned military refuse. At the same time, programs were introduced to rid the island of goats, control soil erosion and reintroduce indigenous plants. In 1981, the island was added to the registry of historic sites and monuments – even as the navy continued its destructive maneuvers!

Several years and various studies later, the U.S. Congress finally voted to end all military operations on the island in November 1993, and to return it to the jurisdiction of the state of Hawaii, which had already taken steps toward turning it into a natural reserve. A budget was drafted for the full restoration of the island's environment. Until this project is completed, the island and surrounding waters are still dangerously polluted and access continues to be restricted.

Visiting Kaho'olawe

'Ohana organizes monthly work excursions to the island where participants can help in restoring it. Those who are interested in such visits can join the group, which is mostly made up of Hawaiians in search of their roots, though anyone is welcome. This is not a tourist excursion, but a true collective effort that is in many ways a memorable cultural experience.

For more information, contact:

Protect Kaho'olawe 'Ohana
P.O. Box 152
Honolulu, HI 96810
www.kahoolawe.org

To go to Kaho'olawe:
Davianna McGregor
☎*956-7068 (office)*
☎*847-3840 (home)*

The Kapalua Nature Society (☎*800-KAPALUA*) has recently begun organizing day trips to Kaho'olawe.

swimming back up the waterfalls, the *'o'opu* has a suction-cup-like appendage on the front of its neck.

The circular **Kuloa Point Loop Trail** is a scant 2,625ft (800m) long, but runs near the stream where it forms four basins and a number of little waterfalls, just before emptying into the ocean. Some

people dive right into the chilly waters, but if you do, mind the slippery rocks and strong current. Do not go into the water when it is stormy since flash floods are quite common and very dangerous. A safer option is to picnic on Kuloa Point, on the site of an ancient altar erected by Hawaiian fishers.

Those who don't mind wading up to their knees in mud generally enjoy the 2,625ft (800m) walk along the Pipiwai Trail to the 184ft (56m) **Makahiku ★** waterfall. In dry weather, the path is much better but the waterfall dwindles to a mere trickle. Further upstream, having crossed the river at two different points, the

Maui

trail heads back about 2mi (3km) along the Pipiwai to a second, much higher (400ft, 122m) waterfall called **Waimoku ★★**. This forested area is quite magnificent, and has been planted with *ti* plants, bamboo and mangoes. Be prepared for the mosquitoes! The Ranger Station *(every day 9am to 5pm; ☎248-7375)* organizes a guided walk to Makahiku Falls every morning at 9:30 (and to Waimoku Falls on Saturdays).

Just west of the park, the village of **Kipahulu ★** is shaded by large trees and features the ruins of a sugar mill and two churches. Saint Paul, the Catholic church, is a wooden structure, while the Protestant **Palapala Hoomau** (1864) is made of lava stone and has a small pointed bell tower. The large, plain lava-stone tomb in the cemetery behind this church is that of Charles Lindbergh, Atlantic explorer (1927), who died on Maui in 1974. The neighbouring Kipahulu Point Park, which looks out on the coast from above, has a pleasant picnic area.

Unless you have a four-wheel-drive vehicle, Kipahulu is as far as most car rental agencies allow you to go, which means you have to return to the central isthmus the same way you came. Many people either don't know

The Sugar Cane

Hawaiians cultivated several different varieties of sugar cane, which they call *ko*. Having originated in Papua New Guinea some 10,000 years ago, the crop was no doubt imported during the course of various migrations. Chinese immigrants planted the archipelago's first family plantations at the end of the 18th century. Large-scale cultivation of the crop began in 1835 in Koloa, on Kaua'i. Production increased again during the U.S. civil war, which cut off the northern states from southern products on which they depended. It was during this time that the islands attracted settlers from all over the world: Hawaii's ethnic blend is actually the result of its sugar industry. The king of Hawaii signed a reciprocity treaty in 1876, allowing the United States to import sugar, duty free. The industry gradually became monopolized by five large companies, which had taken a gamble by installing irrigation systems on their land. The famous "Big Five" that emerged at the time still today control a large portion of the industry and commerce in Hawaii. Sugar-cane production fuelled the Hawaiian economy until the advent of tourism in the 1970s. Generating one tonne of refined sugar per acre, the archipelago still produces one third of the total amount of sugar produced in the United States, and one tenth of the country's domestically consumed sugar.

of this restriction or choose to ignore it, and continue on their tour of the island. And it's hard to blame them: from here to Kaupo only 5mi (8km) of the road is unpaved (and even then it's only small sections). Although the road is narrow, it is no more difficult than some parts of the Hana Highway. And despite the small inconveniences, returning via the south coast is the faster alternative.

West of Kipahulu, the road leaves behind the tropical forest and returns to the coast which it more or less follows. Sheltered from rain by Hale'a'kala's bulk, the landscape becomes increasingly dry, and eventually becomes a hostile wasteland covered in scrub.

This is the setting for **Kaupo** *(Mile 34.5)*, the last town on the south coast before Keokea, some 30mi (50km) farther west. The surrounding landscape is dotted with only a few scattered ranches, while the town is centred around the Kaupo Store (1920), the only source of life in this ghost-town-like place. Saint Joseph's church is nothing but a ruin, and Auntie Jane's truck (see p 377) has hardly fared better.

Just after Kaupo, the road is paved again. However, it is old and patched in many places, and still quite rough. At Mile 29 there is a good view of a large arch hollowed from a rock, and after Mile 20 the road is newly paved. Just before the Ulupalakua ranch is a lookout with a view of Kaho'olawe Island.

From Ulupalakua, return to Kahului via Kula.

Outdoor Activities

Swimming

With 81 accessible beaches to choose from, no one can say that Maui is lacking in spots to enjoy the ocean! Generally speaking, the two tourist coasts, between Lahaina and Kapalua and between Kihei and Makena, are the most protected from the strong ocean currents and are best for swimming.

On the west coast is **Na'anapali**, offering the best swimming possibilities at its northern end, at the foot of the cliffs of Pu'u Keka'a (in front of the Sheraton). Farther north is the attractive **Napili Bay** and **Kapalua Beach**, known as the most beautiful beach in the United States (watch out for the currents in winter at those two places). Two other beaches are especially good if you are travelling with young children: **Launiupoko Wayside Park**, 3mi (5km) south of Lahaina, has a very well-protected swimming area, and **Honokowai County Park**, at the centre of Honokowai.

On the southern coast, **Kalepolepo Park** in Kihei is also a great place for children, boasting a former fishpond with a sandy floor. Adults will probably prefer the three white-sand beaches further south at **Kamaole** (especially II and III), all of which have lifeguards. There are a number of coves near Makena, including **Ulua** and the shallow **Keawakapu Beach**.

The water tends to be rougher on the east coast. The exception is **Hana Beach Park**, but it's hardly worth mentioning. **Hamoa Beach**, several kilometres further south, is quite lovely in summer.

Surfing and Boogie Boarding

Most beginners stick to the smaller waves in **Lahaina** where most of the island's surf schools are located, concentrated near the port as well as Launipoko Wayside Park and Puamana Beach Park. On the west coast, the pros head to **Thousand Peaks** *(near Olowalu, Mile 12)*, Ka'anapali, Pohaku Park (north of Honokowai) and, above all, the famous **Honolua Bay**, north of Kapalua. Serious surfers come here on weekends to catch the waves, or head to nearby D.T. Flemming Park, Slaughterhouse

Maui

Beach, or the bay at Honokohau, even further west. **Ma'alea Bay**, on the south shore, is very famous: in autumn, the seaswell from the southwest creates colossal breakers here, nicknamed Freight Trains by some – and *Fright* Trains by other! Other popular places for surfing are **Big Beach**, **La Pérouse Bay** and, in winter, the famous **Ho'okipa Beach Park** on the north coast (east of the beach).

Boogie boarders mainly congregate at **Ka'anapali**, **Napili** and **Baldwin Park** and, on the south coast, at **Kamaole Park III** near Kihei as well as the popular **Ulua**, at **Big Beach** and at **La Pérouse Bay**. **Hamoa Beach** near Hana is considered one of the best places to go bodysurfing or boogie boarding in winter.

Windsurfing

The central part of Maui's northern coast is to windsurfers what the North Shore of O'ahu is to surfers: paradise. People flock here every summer to enjoy the big waves and the constant wind. **Kanaha Beach Park** in the west gives way to **Spreckelsville Beach**, **Baldwin Park** and **Ho'okipa Beach Park**. The top windsurfers gather

here several times a year to square off in international competitions. **Ma'alaea Beach** has really taken off in the last few years. Located at the southern end of the central isthmus, the bay enjoys constant wind, creating ideal conditions. Beginners prefer the (relative) safety of **Ka'anapali** and **Kanaha**, where most windsurfing schools are found.

The newly fashionable sport of kitesurfing is becoming more and more popular on Maui, especially at Kahana and Spreckelsville, but also at Ho'opika. The first competition in this sport was held on Maui in 1999.

Scuba Diving and Snorkelling

Maui has no fewer than three marine parks, namely Honolua-Mokule'ia, 'Ahihi-Kina'u and La Pérouse Bay, in addition to the island of Molokini. Just like the beaches, the coast of West Maui, facing Lana'i, and the south coast are the best places for snorkelling and scuba diving. You can explore the waters near the

shore, or head farther out in a catamaran, sailboat or rubber raft with one of the various agencies. For something a little different, you might want to try "snuba," a blend between snorkelling and scuba diving, which can also be practiced close to shore or from a boat farther from land.

A reef with a fairly constant depth of about 40ft (12m) runs along virtually the entire west coast. There are excellent snorkelling opportunities near **Black Rock**, north of Ka'anapali Beach, and in **Napili Bay**, where turtles can often be seen in the morning. **Kahekili Beach Park** and **Kapalua Beach** are also popular, but nothing can match the underwater splendour of the Honolua-Mokule'ia marine park, particularly in the well-protected **Honolua Bay**. Summer is the best time for snorkelling off this coast, since the water is calmer.

The stretch of coast that runs south of Lahaina to Olowalu is well suited for snorkelling. The most popular spot is at Mile 14, in the calm waters of the cove near the entrance to the **Olowalu** campground.

The entire south coast, from Kihei to La Pérouse Bay, also presents excellent snorkelling and scuba-diving opportunities. Those who prefer very calm waters will love

Kalepolepo Park near Kihei. Several coral reefs have formed inside an old fishpond, attracting all sorts of fish, including moonfish, and sometimes even turtles.

Further south, you can explore the underwater scenery in the shadow of condominiums and large hotels at the **Kamaole** parks (especially II and III), and in the clear waters of **Keawakapu Beach**. You can also head to the beach at **Ulua** or the neighbouring **Polo Beach**. As you go further south, the water becomes increasingly clearer. The small bay at **Makena** (by Makena Landing) and Big and Little Beaches (be careful of the currents) offer superb underwater scenery. Although it looks dangerous, the rocky coast of **'Ahihi-Kina'u Reserve**, which stretches up to La Pérouse Bay, has an abundance of tropical fish.

There are plenty of spots for snorkelling throughout the rest of the island. **Hamoa Beach**, south of Hana, is highly recommended in summer.

With a multitude of different species (underwater visibility here is 100 to 130ft or 30 to 40m), the ancient underwater crater off the shore of **Molokini Island** is probably *the* site for diving in Maui, and perhaps all of Hawaii.

Simply don a diving mask and stick your head underwater at Reef's End to experience a stunning display: Manta rays, yellow butterfly fish, octopi, *humuhumu-nukunukuapua'a* and even sometimes small white-tipped reef sharks can all be seen here. Scuba divers can stay in the crater or venture beyond it. At Black Wall, the rock face drops vertically about 330ft (100m). The Edge of the World, meanwhile, is a platform anchored some 50ft (15m) out on the side of a slope and is populated with large fish and sharks.

Many excursion agencies offer combination packages featuring a dive off Molokini and a stop at the aptly named **Turtle Town** (Kalaeloa). In addition to its large population of Hawaiian green turtles, there are some beautiful underwater rock formations and caves.

In addition to the sites described above, certified divers can explore the spellbinding coast off the island of **Lana'i**, with its stunning lava formations, including the famous Cathedrals. A number of organizations in Maui offer tours, and night diving is also available. The cost is generally $55 for a dive near the beach and $105 further offshore by boat. Prices are higher on Molokini.

Other Water Sports

On the west coast, **Ka'anapali** offers the largest choice of water sports. There is **waterskiing** and **jet-skiing** from mid-May to mid-December, when the whales are gone. You can also go parasailing during these months. Most of these airborne adventures last between seven and 10min and cost between $30 and $50, depending on the altitude and length of the flight. **Sea kayaks** are also for rent here and in the Kamaole parks. Enticing day trips to Makena and La Pérouse Bay are available from **Kihei** (*$50 to $60*). Kayaking is also popular in Honolua Bay in West Maui, and in Hana.

Deep-Sea Fishing

Because the waters between Maui and Kaho'olawe, Lana'i and Moloka'i are quite shallow, you must head out a little farther, south of Kaho'olawe or Lana'i, if you are hoping for a big catch. Like elsewhere in Hawaii, blue marlin is the main attraction, but people also come for such species as swordfish, *'ahi, mahi-mahi, ono, ulua* and bonita. Most boats leave from

Lahaina or Ma'alaea. The captains usually fillet the fish for their passengers and keep the remainder.

Cruises

Many companies offer sea excursions by sailboat (you can even venture out in a vessel that once participated in the Americas Cup race!), catamaran, glass-bottomed boat, canoe, and even submarine. Some people simply enjoy a day on the water, while others set out to snorkel, explore deserted parts of the coast, or watch whales (in winter) and dolphins. There is sure to be a package that offers what you are looking for, with excursions running from 2hrs to a full day.

Molokini Island is the preferred destination for many. Prices vary *(approximately $30 to $70)*, depending largely on the length of the trip and whether meals are included or not. The trip to Molokini is often combined with a stop in Turtle Town (Kalaeloa). All companies leave from Ma'alaea and Kihei, with only one offering departures from Lahaina.

Whale-watching expeditions take place from late November to May, and depart almost

exclusively from **Lahaina** since most whales are found in the channel between Maui and Lana'i. Maui is the best island for watching whales, but don't expect to have a close encounter with these majestic animals since boats have to keep a distance of at least 330ft (100m). Unless the whales themselves choose to come up alongside the boat, visitors must content themselves with viewing them from afar. The best time to see whales is from late December to late March.

The **Pacific Whale Foundation** (*☎879-8811*) organizes whale- and dolphin-watching tours as well as snorkelling on Molokini and Lana'i. All profits go towards protecting the environment.

While some visitors have their heart set on whales, others come in search of dolphins. **Dolphin-watching** is much more popular in summer, when the whales have left. The island of Lana'i is the most popular place for this activity, and the Kanaio coast, east of La Pérouse Bay, is also one of the best places to see dolphins in a setting of lava arches and grottos.

Other sea excursions include a day trip to **Lana'i** (go to Trilogy rather than Club Lana'i, which stands alone on the east coast), an un-

derwater adventure aboard the submarine Atlantis *($80)*, and dinner cruises with music *($60 to $90 for 1.5 to 2hrs; some have shows or a dance floor)*.

Cycling

The island's most popular cycling tour has become so popular that a dozen agencies organize mountain-bike excursions from the top of **Hale'a'kala**. The adventure begins just after sunrise at the Visitor Center at the top of the volcano, and ends 36mi (60km), 3.5hrs later, by the sea. Cyclists coast down the slopes at a leisurely speed (for safety), donning helmets and other safety gear in bright yellow, blue and red. The price ranges from $50 to $110, depending on whether the excursion includes breakfast and transportation to the summit. You can also choose to hike down the volcano on a guided walk (you must stay with the group), but these excursions begin at the border of the national park, as opposed to the summit. Hardier cyclists can even choose to continue on to the Tedeschi Winery for refreshments. If you have two vehicles at your disposal, you can rent bicycles and transport them yourself *($30)*.

Mountain biking is also popular on the road leading to **Polipoli State Park**. The most convenient rental agencies are **Maui Rental Center** *(☎875-7368)* in West Maui (they deliver to your hotel), **Maui Sports & Cycle** *(☎875-2882 or 875-8448, Dolphin Plaza and Long's Center)* in Kihei, or **West Maui Bicycles** *(Lahaina ☎661-9005, Kahana ☎669-1169)*. The latter is the only one that specializes in bicycles.

Golf

Maui boasts some 15 golf courses, most of which are located along the touristic coast of West Maui and around Kihei and Wailea. Two of the courses host international tournaments each year. Set in natural surroundings, **Kapalua** is Maui's golfing mecca, with one green running along the sea, another in a valley, and a third between the two. The newest of the three is Plantation Course, which is especially popular both because of its beauty and its level of difficulty. Although they are surrounded by hotels and condominiums, the two golf courses at **Ka'anapali** are just as impressive. The 18th hole of the North Course lies across a stretch of water, and is reputed to be one of

the most difficult on the island. At **Wailea**, the Blue Course and the newer Emerald Course are among the most pleasant. And if financial considerations are a factor, try the Waiehu Golf Course, a municipal green set between the sea and the mountains, and the least expensive option at $35. The larger golf courses charge between $130 to $160 per day.

Tennis

While some of the hotels offer their own tennis courts, public facilities are also available. There are 11 of these on the island, free of charge and available on a first-come, first-served basis. There is a time limit to ensure that everyone gets a turn *(45min singles, 1hr doubles)*. The Wailea Tennis Club is the island's largest paying club. Located on the south shore, this huge complex has 11 courts, three of which are lit up at night.

Hiking

With 27mi (43km) of trails, **Hale'a'kala** is ideal for leisurely walks or more ambitious several-day treks. If you plan to cross the crater, bear in mind that while the

hike begins with a descent, there is an uphill climb waiting at the end! Among the easier walks are Hosmer Grove (30min) and the half-mile (1km) Sliding Sands Trail which leads to a lookout over the volcanic cones and lava flows covering the bottom of the crater. The most popular day-long hike starts at the Visitor Center at the summit to Leleiwi Overlook (11mi or 17.5km), reached by descending along the Sliding Sands Trail and returning via the Halemau'u Trail. If you have two days, you can combine this hike with the Silversword Loop and its many silversword plants. This trail can also be a day-long excursion, leaving from Leleiwi Overlook (10mi or 16km return). Much less frequented, the Kaupo Trail leaves from Paliku, east of the caldera, and descends to the small town of Kaupo (8.4mi or 13.5km), on the coast. The path leaves the crater and runs through a forest before following a blistering road for four-wheel-drive vehicles. You don't need a permit if you are only coming for the day, but must obtain one if you plan to camp inside the crater (see p 359).

Still in the park but on the eastern side of the island, hikes in the **Kipahulu Valley** to the Makahiku (1mi or 1.6km return) and Waimoku (3.7mi or 6km) waterfalls are very popular, despite the mud and mosquitoes.

Sections of the old King's Highway, which once circled the entire island, still exist today, and some have been fixed up for hiking. The **Lahaina Pali Trail** crosses Kealaloa Ridge, using 5mi (8km) of the old road linking Maui's Central Plain with Lahaina. The trail climbs almost 1640ft (500m) before descending to sea level. The Hoapili Trail runs along a bleak, blistering section of the southern coast from La Pérouse Bay, and is also part of the old road network used by the ancient Hawaiians. As is the case elsewhere, the road linking Hana, from Kainalimu Bay, to **Wai'anapanapa** passes the ruins of a *heiau*. The seaside setting is superb, with lush vegetation and lava rocks covered in ocean spray.

Waihe'e Ridge Trail is located on West Maui's north coast, and climbs 2.5mi (4km) through a cloud-filled eucalyptus forest, eventually reaching a crest with a view of the ocean far below and Wailuku in the distance. On the Road to Hana, the **Waikamoi Nature Trail** makes a short loop through a beautiful forest.

If you are planning a lengthier hike, consult the weather service at ☎*877-5111* (☎*871-5054 for the Hale'a'kala crater*).

Horseback Riding

Horseback riding is immensely popular on Maui, and there are numerous stables from which to choose. One of the most popular horseback excursions is into **Hale'a'Kala's crater** (*$130 to $160; PonyExpress*, ☎*667-2200*), but there are also rides through the fields on the slopes of the volcano (*Adventures on Horseback in Ha'iku*, ☎*242-7445; Thompson Ranch near Keokea*, ☎*878-1910*). You can also ride from **'Ohe'o Gulch** (*Ohe'o Stables*, ☎*667-2222*) to Waimoku Falls and the edge of the Kipahulu preserve.

Horseback riding is also possible on the south coast, where **Makena Stables** (☎*879-0244*) organizes excursions that last two to 6hrs, with the longest going to La Pérouse Bay. In **West Maui**, contact **Mendes Ranch** (☎*871-5222*) on the road to Kahakaloa or **Ironwood Ranch** in Napili (☎*669-4991 or 669-4702*). Prices vary depending on the duration of the ride (*from $40 for 1hr to $120*).

Flying and Aerial Sports

Helicopter tours of the island all leave from the airport in Kahului (Commuter Terminal). The most popular excursion costs about $150 for 45 to 60min ($200 with a short stopover in Hana), and takes in the coast around Hana, 'Ohe'u Gulch and Hale'a'kala's crater. Five helicopter companies operate on Maui. Alex Air (☎*871-0792*) is one of the smallest and offers the lowest fares with the "West Maui Special" costing $69 for 20min. The other four are Air Maui (☎*877-7005*), Blue Hawaiian (☎*871-8844*), Hawaii (☎*877-3900*) and Sunshine (☎*871-0722*). All start at about $150 for the same 30min excursion, and offer a package that includes West Maui and Moloka'i for about $200. Hawaii Helicopters is the only to offer a package that includes Hale'a'kala and the volcanoes on the Big Island (*3hrs, $420*), and one that takes in Maui, Kaho'olaw, Lana'i and Moloka'i (*1hr 45min, $240*). In addition, Pacific Wings (☎*873-0877*), Paragon Air (☎*244-3356*) and Maui Air (☎*877-5500*) offer flights in small **planes** over Maui and the neighbouring islands.

You can go **paragliding** from the small road to **Polipoli State Park**, above Kula, with **Pro Flight Paragliding** (☎874-5433 or 877-GO-FLY-HIGH). Solo and tandem jumps are available, and the descent lasts from 15 to 40min, depending on weather conditions.

Accommodations

Lahaina

The Makai Inn
$65-$95
laundry, K, ⊗
1415 Front St.
☎662-3200
⇌661-9027
makai@maui.net
Available on a long- or short-term basis, The Makai Inn's 12 apartments offer some of the best quality accommodations for that price range in Lahaina. Some are more like studios while others are one-bedroom suites, but all have a well-equipped kitchen and living area. The building is located near the sea, north of the city centre.

House of Fountains
$95-$145 bkfst incl.
≡, *laundry,* ℝ, ◙, *ctv,* ♁
1579 Lokia St.
☎667-2121 or 800-789-6865
⇌667-2120
private@maui.net
Managed by Daniela Clément, a German woman of French origin, this large bed and breakfast is located in a residential area on the northern outskirts of Lahaina *(just above Highway 30)*. At the time of our visit the rooms were being redecorated in a Hawaiian theme, with furniture made of *koa, tapas* and the like. The rooms are comfortable and well equipped, but rather expensive. Daniela has a friend who is a Hawaiian healer and arranges traditional Hawaiian wedding ceremonies – guaranteed to be exotic!

Lahaina Inn
$109-$169 bkfst incl.
ℜ, ≡, ♁
127 Lahainaluna Rd.
☎661-0577 or 800-669-3444
⇌677-9480
www.lahainainn.com
This hotel used to be a store and was recently completely renovated by Rick Ralston, owner of Crazy Shirts. The 19 small rooms have been converted into 12 more spacious units (including three suites), furnished in high Victorian style. Parquet floors, quilts, old carpets and classical music create an atmosphere that is very much rooted in the past. Half the rooms have a view of the sea. A calm atmosphere pervades the inn despite its very central location (there are no televisions and no children under 15). There is a minimum stay of two nights. The David Paul Lahaina Grill (see p 363) is located on the main floor.

Maui Islander
$99-$299
≈, ≡, ℝ, ◙, *ctv*
660 Waine'e St.
☎667-9766 or 800-92-ASTON
⇌667-2792
www.aston-hotels.com
This Aston property has 327 rooms and has been a Lahaina institution for years. The establishment comprises several buildings linked together, forming a rather sprawling complex. Still, the hotel provides good quality for the price, especially given its central location – just a few steps from Banyan Square. Standard hotel rooms, studios, and apartments with one, two or three bedrooms are available.

Pioneer Inn
$100-$165
≈, ≡, ℝ, 🛇, *ctv*
658 Wharf St.
☎661-3636 or 800-457-5457
⇌667-5708
www.pioneerinnmaui.com
The distinctive Pioneer Inn (see p 300) dates back to the turn of the century and is now part of the Best Western hotel chain. The 45 recently renovated rooms are rather small for standard units. Those facing Front Street are the noisiest, but those looking out onto Hotel Street are also quite loud. The quietest rooms are those with an even number (except 36), which look out onto the small swimming pool in the lovely courtyard. If you are prone to romantic whims, ask for the

"Tracy-Hepburn Suite" where the two actors stayed during the filming of *Devil at Four O'Clock* in 1961.

Lahaina Shores Beach Resort
$140-$260
≈, K, ≡, ctv, ☂
475 Front St.
☎*661-4835 or 800-628-6699*
⇌*661-4696*
This large resort is located just south of the city centre, and is the only one in Lahaina with direct access to the beach. Studios and one-bedroom apartments are available. All have different owners but most are decorated in the same pleasant pastel tones. Some studios have a foldaway bed, creating extra space.

The Plantation Inn
$135-$215 bkfst incl.
≈, ≡, tv
174 Lahainaluna Rd.
☎*667-9225 or 800-433-6815*
⇌*667-9293*
inn@maui.net
With parquet floors, canopy beds and antique furniture, the Plantation Inn's 19 rooms exude character. They also have all the modern comforts (air conditioning, soundproof walls) and look out over the swimming pool and whirlpool, surrounded by tropical vegetation. Hotel guests enjoy discounts at Gérard's restaurant (see p 364) which is located in the main house of the old plantation.

The Guesthouse
$115 bkfst incl.
≈, laundry, ≡, ℝ, ctv
1620 Ainakea Rd.
☎*661-8085 or 800-621-8942*
⇌*661-1896*
www.mauiguesthouse.com
This bed and breakfast is located in a large house in a residential area, above Highway 30, on the northern outskirts of Lahaina. The four charming rooms all have their own bathroom, and three come with whirlpools. The owners do not live on the premises, so guests have greater privacy. Despite these advantages, the prices are still very high.

Puamana Condos
$110-$160
≈, △, laundry, K, ctv, ☂
☎*661-3500 or 888-661-7200*
⇌*661-5210*
www.mauibeachfront.com
This cluster of small houses is located just south of Lahaina on a large oceanfront property dotted with coconut palms. A precursor to gated communities, this self-enclosed compound has its own private network of streets. Guests can choose from apartments with one to four bedrooms, with the latter occupying an entire house. Apartments near the water are more expensive. The entrance is at the southern end of Front Street, just before it rejoins Highway 30.

Ka'anapali

Ka'anapali Beach Hotel
$170-$265
≈, laundry, ≡, ℝ, ◙, ctv, ☂
2525 Ka'anapali Pkwy.
☎*661-0011 or 800-262-8450*
⇌*667-5978*
www.kaanapalibeachhotel.com
This large hotel is located along Ka'anapali Beach, between the Whaler and the Sheraton, but is less luxurious than its neighbours, and also less expensive. Still, the rooms are comfortable and quite spacious. The hotel initiated a program to preserve Hawaiian culture, and offers all sorts of traditional activities including *hula*, *lei* and *lauhala*.

Maui Eldorado Resort
$195-$375
≈, ⊘, K, laundry, ≡, ctv, ☂
2661 Keka'a Dr.
☎*661-0021*
☎*800-OUTRIGGER*
⇌*667-7039*
www.outrigger.com
Located north of Ka'anapali along the golf course rather than by the beach, this resort belongs to the Outrigger chain and rents studios and one- or two-bedroom apartments. The prices are rather high given the location and the age of some of the units, which are comfortable but a little too "1970s." Guests who prefer to be by the sea will enjoy the hotel's beach cabanas.

Royal Lahaina Resort
$185-$450
≈, ≡, ℝ, ◙, *ctv*, ☂
2780 Keka'a Dr.
☎*661-3611 or 800-447-6925*
⇌*661-6150*
The oldest hotel in Ka'anapali, the Royal Lahaina was built in the 1960s on the less busy northern part of the beach. Originally the resort consisted only of cottages, but now most rooms are found in a large, uninter- esting 10-storey building. Al- though they were renovated in 1996, the rooms are rather small and most only have a shower and no bath. Many services cost ex- tra, including parking.

The Whaler
$195-$510
≈, ◔, △, *laundry, K,* ◙, *ctv*, ☂
2481 Ka'anapali Pkwy.
☎*661-4861 or 800-367-7052*
⇌*(435) 647-3822*
www.ten-io.com/vri
This luxury resort is located near Whalers Village at the centre of Ka'anapali's beach, and has comfortable, airy studios and apartments with one or two bed- rooms. The bathrooms are decorated in mar- ble, and the exception- ally large balconies allow guests to enjoy a view of the beach 24hrs a day. A minimum stay of two nights is re- quired.

Hyatt Regency Maui
$275-$425
ℜ, ≈, ◔, ≡, ℝ, ◙, *ctv*
200 Nohea Kai Dr.
☎*661-1234 or 800-233-1234*
⇌*667-4498*
www.hyatt.com
One of Ka'anapali's premier hotels, the Hyatt is built around a central courtyard planted with orchids and palms, comple- mented with works of Asian art. Hawaiian tourist complex *par excel- lence*, this hotel has 815 very comfortable rooms, four restaurants, tennis courts, plenty of shops, a beach where all sorts of water sports are orga- nized, and a veritable maze of artificial streams and waterfalls with caves, suspended bridges and other high- lights.

The Westin Maui
$265-$495
ℜ, ≈, ◔, *ctv*
2365 Ka'anapali Pkwy.
☎*667-2525 or 800-WESTIN-1*
⇌*661-5764*
www.westin.com
Similar to the Hyatt Regency, the Westin is also decorated with Asian art. The hotel is built around a huge network of five swim- ming pools and basins tucked away amid the palms, where flamin- goes and crested cranes frolic. The rooms are comfortable, but could be better. Most have a view of the beach.

Sheraton Maui
$320-$500
≈, ◔, ℜ, ≡, ℝ, ◙, *ctv*, ☂
2605 Ka'anapali Pkwy.
☎*661-0031 or 800-782-9488*
⇌*661-0458*
www.sheraton-hawaii.com
This massive Sheraton complex is the most expensive hotel in Ka'anapali and stretches from the sum- mit to the foot of Pu'u Keka'a, the black rock cliff that delimits the main beach at the north. The site is well chosen since this is the best place for swim- ming and snorkelling. In front of the hotel is a swimming pool in the shape of a river that winds its way between palms and artificial rocks – or, if you pre- fer, an artificial river that is also used as a pool. The rooms are luxurious and there are plenty of activities.

From Honokowai to Kapalua

Hale Maui
$75-$95
laundry, K, ctv, ☂
3711 Lower Honoapi'ilani Rd. Honokowai
☎*669-6312*
⇌*669-1302*
This small, modest "apart-hotel" has 12 studios, each with a well-equipped kitchen and some with a Japanese-style sliding screen that partitions off one section of the room. The owner is German, and the prop- erty is impeccably maintained. The beach is easy to reach, only 65ft (20m) away. There

Maui

is a minimum stay of three nights.

Hale Ono Loa
$95
laundry, K, ctv, vcr, ⊗
3823 Lower Honoapi'ilani Rd. Honokowai
☎*669-0525 or 800-300-5399*
⇌*669-0631*
This complex rents large, well-maintained studios, each with a kitchen and large living room. The prices are reduced by about 20% from mid-April to mid-December for stays of two nights or more.

Mahina Surf
$120-$170
≈, *laundry, K, ctv,* ⊗, ♨
4057 Lower Honoapi'ilani Rd. Honokowai
☎*669-6068 or 800-367-6086*
⇌*669-4534*
www.mahinasurf.com
Here, guests in all of the one- or two-bedroom units can enjoy the soothing sound of the waves. There is no beach, but you can swim in the pool, and the hotel provides an adequate level of comfort. There is a minimum stay of three nights.

Noelani
$117-$257
≈, *laundry, ctv,* ⊗, ♨
4095 Lower Honoapi'ilani Rd. Honokowai
☎*669-8374 or 800-367-6030*
⇌*669-7904*
www.noelani-condo-resort.com
The studios and apartments (with one, two or three bedrooms) in this resort are spread over three two-storey buildings situated between the ocean and the road. Their proxim-

ity to the latter means you may be woken up in a less-than-ideal fashion, but on a positive note, the hotel offers access to a small beach. There is a minimum stay of three nights.

Polynesian Shores
$110-$200
≈, *laundry, K,* ⊗, ♨
3975 Lower Honoapi'ilani Rd. Honokowai
☎*669-6065 or 800-433-MAUI (800-488-2179 from Canada)*
⇌*669-0909*
www.polynesianshores.com
All of the apartments, with one, two, or three bedrooms, look out onto the swimming pool and the sea. Although they have different owners, most units are bright and decorated in a pleasant tropical style. There is a minimum stay of three nights.

Kahana Reef
$160-$180
≈, *laundry, K,* ◙, *ctv,* ⊗, ♨
4471 Lower Honoapi'ilani Rd. Kahana
☎*669-6491 or 800-253-3773*
⇌*669-2192*
www.aston-hotels.com
Member of the Aston chain, this complex was undergoing renovations at the beginning of the year 2000. All of the apartments are privately owned and therefore slightly differ from one another. Some are decorated in a lovely tropical style.

Napili Kai Beach Resort
$185-$600
≈, ⊘, ℜ, *laundry, K,* ≡/⊗, ◙, *ctv,* ♨
5900 Honoapi'ilani Rd., Napili
☎*669-6271 or 800-367-5030*
⇌*669-5740*
www.napilikai.com
Founded in 1962 on a superb sandy bay, the Napili Kay was the Napili's first hotel establishment, and has grown from one building to 11, spread over a 10 acre (4ha) property. Nevertheless, the sprawling resort still feels intimate rather than overwhelming and caters to a clientele in search of peace and quiet. All units have a more or less direct view of the ocean. Studios and two- or three-room apartments are available, all of them very comfortable (only half have air-conditioning, however). The hotel organizes numerous cultural activities, rents out snorkelling equipment and serves cocktails every Wednesday. With all these little extras as well as a friendly staff, it is no surprise that each year, returning guests make up 70% of this hotel's clientele.

Paki Maui
$179-$299
≈, *laundry, K,* ◙, ⊗, *ctv,* ♨
3615 Lower Honoapi'ilani Rd. Honokowai
☎*669-8235 or 800-535-0085*
⇌*800-633-5085*
www.marcresorts.com
The 112 units of this resort are fanned out near the sea, with 72 overlooking the waves

and the other 40 facing the parking lot. The studios and one- or two-bedroom apartments are well maintained, but rather small and without air conditioning.

Papakea Resort
$140-$300
≈, ⌂, K, laundry, ◘, ⊗, ctv
3543 Lower Honoapi'ilani Rd.
Honokowai
☎669-4848
☎800-92-ASTON
⇄665-0662
www.aston-hotels.com
This member of the Aston hotel chain is located right on the water, although there is no beach. The apartments, all equipped with kitchens, are slightly older, but have been well maintained. Guests can choose from a studio or a one- or two-bedroom apartment.

Royal Kahana Resort
$179-$389
≈, ⏲, ⌂, K, laundry, ctv, ⊗
4365 Lower Honoapi'ilani Rd.
Kahana
☎800-447-7783
☎800-535-0085
www.marcresorts.com
This upscale resort rents out studios and one- or two-bedroom apartments, all located in a 12-storey building that is right on Kahana Beach. The beach is narrow and the drop-off makes it better for surfing than for swimming.

Embassy Vacation Resort
$290-$560 bkfst incl.
≈, ⏲, K, ≡, ◘, ctv
104 Ka'anapali Shores
Honokowai
☎661-2000 or 800-EMBASSY
⇄800-633-5085
www.marcresorts.com
This massive pink building is easy to see from afar. It provides all the services of a hotel, but also resembles a resort, because of its size. The apartments were renovated in 1998, and come with one or two bedrooms. Despite the many services available, the prices seem high and the hotel's beach is quite narrow and steep.

Kapalua Bay Hotel
$295-$525
≈, ⏲, ℜ, ≡, ℝ, ◘, ctv
1 Bay Dr., Kapalua
☎669-5656 or 800-325-3589
⇄669-4605
www.luxurycollectionhawaii.com
During our last visit, this tourist complex was finishing renovating its common areas. Now that peace and quiet have returned, you will find an atmosphere of calm and luxury once more. In addition to the villa suites, there are only 191 rooms (very tropical in style), which is significantly less than most of its competitors. There is a hotel shuttle service to Kapalua's three golf courses, tennis courts and beach.

Ritz-Carlton Hotel
$265-$395
≈, ⏲, ℜ, ◘, ⩗, ctv, ⛉
1 Ritz-Carlton Dr., Kapalua
☎669-6200 or 800-262-8440
⇄665-0026
www.ritzcarlton.com
The northernmost tourist complex on the east coast and also one of the most stylish, the Ritz Carlton is built around a three-tiered swimming pool overlooking the ocean. The hotel was supposed to have been built closer to the coast, but plans had to be changed when architects discovered a Hawaiian cemetery. The 548 rooms provide the level of comfort one expects from this type of hotel, and come with marble bathrooms. There is also a host of services, as well as a croquet lawn – that meets "regulation" standards, if you please!

Around West Maui

Camp Pecusa
camping $5
bungalow up to $140
showers, chemical toilets, picnic tables, barbecues
800 Olowalu Village (Mile 14.6)
☎661-4303
norm@maui.net
linda@maui.net
A small sign, half-hidden in the trees, indicates the campground of the Episcopal church. It is located along a small beach 40ft (12km) south of Lahaina, and has become more shady as the surrounding trees have matured. The campground works on

The hotels on Waikiki, "the most famous beach on the Pacific," offer a great view of Honolulu.
- *Claude Hervé-Bazin*

Built in 1842, Honolulu's Kawaiaha'o Church is located on the same spot where the first missionaries, shortly after their arrival, chose to erect their church.
- *Claude Hervé-Bazin*

At the end of the day, the palm trees at the Kapuaiwa Coconut Grove on Moloka'i seem to stretch above the waves to admire the sunset. - *Tibor Bognàr*

Like other beaches on the archipelago, Lydgate Park Beach reveals a charming crescent of golden sand, embraced by both the forest and the sea. - *Claude Hervé-Bazin*

Hawaii, perhaps more than any other place on Earth, evokes this unusual dance in which humans must yield to Mother Nature to become her ally...
- *M. Raget*

Surfboards, longboards and Boogie Boards add a touch of colour to almost all of the archipelago's beaches.
- *Claude Hervé-Bazin*

a first-come, first-served basis, and guests are restricted to a maximum stay of seven nights per month. Large bungalows can also be rented, but these are usually reserved months, if not years, in advance by schools and local groups. The beach is good for swimming and excellent for snorkelling.

Wailuku, Kahului and Paia

Many establishments in Wailuku offer rooms at reasonable prices, and cater mainly to a local clientele. Usually, accommodations are rented by the week, but you might be lucky and find a place that rents by the day.

Molina's Sports Bar *(Wailuku Tropical Hideaway, 197 North Main St., ☎244-4100)* is a good bet, offering single rooms with television and refrigerator at $35 for one person, and $45 for two.

In Paia, consult the board posted in front of the Mana Foods store, which lists various rooms and apartments available for rent, shared or not. Prices range from about $45 to $60 for studios, with a minimum stay of several nights.

Kanaha Beach County Park
$3/pers.
washrooms, showers, picnic tables
Here you can camp beneath scattered young trees, slightly away from Kanaha beach. The campground itself, however, is somewhat poorly maintained. From Ka'ahumanu Avenue, turn in the direction of "Pier 1" at the bend after Maui Mall, then make an immediate left turn onto Hobron Avenue, heading toward the port. Take the first right (Amala Place) and continue 1.5mi (2.5km) to the park. The campground is closed for five or six days each month (for permits, see p 298).

Adventure Maui Rooms
Starting at $60/week, $180/month
sb, laundry, K
151 Hana Hwy., Paia
☎*579-8000*
Although the place only has dormitories, the prices are unbeatable. In addition to a kitchen and common living room, there is free unlimited Internet access.

Banana Bungalow Maui
dormitory $16
room $40
sb, laundry, K
310 North Market St., Wailuku
☎*244-5090 or 800-8-HOSTEL*
⇄*244-3678*
home1.gte.net/bungalow
Part of the Banana Bungalow network, this rather worn-out youth hostel has dormitories for four to six people, as well as private rooms. The large communal kitchen is a little too camping-style, but the place is popular for its whirlpool in the adjacent garden and for the free guided walks offered each morning around the island. There is also free Internet access.

Northshore Inn (Hotel & Hostel)
dormitory $15
room $38
sb, K, ℝ
2080 Vineyard St., Wailuku
☎*242-8999 or 800-647-6284*
www.hostelhawaii.com
Wailuku's other youth hostel is also a little dilapidated, but enjoys continued popularity with an international set. It offers similar types of lodging: dormitories for four or six, and very small private rooms. There is a communal kitchen and a common room with a giant-screen television, as well as free Internet access. In summer, most of the clientele consists of European windsurfers. The establishment rents out windsurfers and surfboards.

Rainbow's End Windsurf Hostel
dormitory $80/week, $250/month
private room $160/week, $550/month
sb, K
221 Baldwin Ave., Paia
☎*579-9957*
home1.gte.net/surfpaia/
The name practically says it all. In summer, this place houses windsurfers on tight budgets, including many from Europe who come for the very attractive rates. Guests can stay in dormitories (four beds each) or simple private rooms

that have a pleasant tropical touch.

Maui Beach Hotel
$65-$125
≡, ℝ, ctv/tv
170 West Ka'ahumanu Ave. Kahului
☎877-0051 or 888-649-3222
⇄871-5797

Even though the Maui Beach Hotel is located by the ocean, right on the beach, this does not mean that the spot is especially good for swimming; development on Kahului Bay is more industrial than recreational in nature. The establishment has motel-style rooms in two different wings. The first is newer and most of its rooms have two beds, and some are quite noisy since they look out onto Highway 340 where it meets Ka'ahumanu Avenue. Only the more expensive oceanfront rooms are quieter. The second wing is quiet, but in need of renovations (it used to be, in fact, the neighbouring Palm Hotel). Although they are well maintained, the rooms have a distinct "1970s" feel.

Maui Seaside Hotel
$98-$135
≈, ≡, ℝ, ctv
100 West Ka'ahumanu Ave. Kahului
☎877-3311 or 800-560-5552
⇄877-4618
www.sand-seaside.com/maui.htm

Part of a Hawaiian mid-budget chain, the Maui Seaside stands beside the Beach Hotel. The quality of the rooms depends on the build-ing they are in. The deluxe rooms around the pool are the most pleasant. Some might find the others a little noisy, since Ka'ahumanu Avenue goes by within 65ft (20m) of the place.

Mama's Beachfront Cottages
$135-$300
K, laundry, ≡, tv, vcr
799 Poho Pl., Paia
☎579-9764
☎800-860-HULA
⇄579-8594
www.mamasfishhouse.com

Surrounded by palms, these cottages are located only a few steps from Mama's Fish House restaurant, on the eastern outskirts of Paia. Some look out over the bay of Kuau and the ocean, while others are set farther back. The former have two windows and a pleasant covered patio, while the one-room units in the latter are two to a cottage.

The Old Wailuku Inn at Ulupono
$120-$180 bkfst incl.
≡, ctv
2199 Kaho'okele St., Wailuku
☎244-5897 or 800-305-4899
⇄242-9600

This residential district of Wailuku is a surprising location for a bed and breakfast. The seven rooms in this old 1924 house have been arranged in accordance with the principles of Feng Shui, a traditional Chinese practice (here interpreted through American culture), which seeks to bring about well-being by achieving a balance between all material and spiritual entities. The bed and breakfast was even officially dedicated to cleanse it of negative energy. But don't conclude that Janice and Tom Fairbanks are fanatical New Agers. Quite the contrary; with parquet floors, quilts and an Oriental decor, their house evokes a nostalgic atmosphere of Hawaii as it used to be. Each room has a floral theme inspired by poet Dan Blanding's book *My Hawaiian Garden* (it was Blanding who promoted Lei Day in Hawaii). There is a minimum stay of two nights.

Kihei

Most condominiums and rented accommodations in Kihei tend to be less expensive than other resorts on the island.

Kulana Kai
$45
K, ctv, ⊗
531 South Kihei Rd.
☎897-2806

North of Kihei, Earl Shelton rents out two small but well-equipped studios. The price is unbeatable (taxes are included!), and remains the same throughout the year. At these rates, guests do not even complain about the noise from the street that runs right in front of the house. Rather, they simply cross it to reach the

Maui

beach on Ma'alaea Bay. They also know to reserve far in advance.

Nona Lani Cottages
$75-$88
laundry, K, ≡, tv/ctv
455 South Kihei Rd.
☎*879-2497 or 800-733-2688*
www.nonalanicottages.com
Located on South Kihei Road across from the beach, this establishment rents out three large rooms and eight cottages with small living room, bathroom, bedroom and kitchen. The cottages are set on an open property of a little less than 2.5 acres (1ha). When you reserve, ask for one of the cottages farthest from the road. The minimum required stay varies between two nights in low season to one week for cottages in winter. Credit cards are not accepted.

Sunseeker Resort
$70-$275
laundry, K, ≡/⊗, ctv
551 South Kihei Rd.
☎*879-1261*
☎*800-532-MAUI*
↩*874-3877*
Don't trust the name of this establishment: this is not a large tourist resort but rather a small family hotel with two studios and three apartments. The reception is very friendly, and the two studios (less expensive than the apartments, they cost $60 in low season) offer good quality for the price. The proximity of the road, however, can be somewhat disturbing at night. The large two-bedroom units are not

as good a deal. There is a minimum stay of three nights; credit cards are not accepted.

Wailana Beach House Hotel
$60-$75
K, ℝ, ≡, ctv
14 Wailana Pl.
☎*874-3131 or 800-399-3885 (only from the U.S.)*
↩*874-0454*
This modest hotel has 10 newly renovated rooms on two storeys, and provides excellent quality for the price. The rooms on the main floor all have an outdoor barbecue.

Kihei Akahi
$87-$152
≈, K, ≡/⊗, laundry, ctv, ⛱
2531 South Kihei Rd.
☎*879-2778 or 800-367-5242 (800-663-2101 from Canada)*
↩*879-7825*
www.crhmaui.com
The quality of the apartments found in this complex, located across from the Kamaole III beach, varies considerably depending on the owner. Here, guests can rent a studio or a one- or two-bedroom apartment, all with the same amenities, except for air conditioning which is rarely provided. If you are only staying four to six nights, the rates go up $10 to $15 per night.

Kamaole Beach Royale
$105-$130
≈, K, laundry, ctv, ⊗
2385 South Kihei Rd.
☎*879-3131 or 800-421-3661*
↩*879-9163*
davi@aloha.net
This large seven-storey building contains one-, two- and three-bedroom apartments owned by different individuals. Generally, the place offers quite good quality for the price, especially in summer (-20%). The units on the fifth and sixth floors are a little more expensive since they have a view of the sea. Reservations can be made directly or through an agent. The minimum stay is five nights, and credit cards are not accepted.

Kamaole Sands
$134-$350
≈, ℜ, K, laundry, ≡, ◨, ctv, ⛱
2695 South Kihei Rd.
☎*874-8700 or 800-367-5004 (800-272-5275 from the other islands)*
↩*879-3273*
www.castle-group.com
This huge resort contains 315 apartments (from studios to four-bedrooms) in 10 buildings, and is located across from Kamaole Park III and its attractive beach. Rather upscale, this place works like a hotel (with daily room service), and offers a swimming pool, tennis courts, whirlpool and barbecue area.

Mana Kai Maui Resort
$120-$290
room ≈, ≡, ℝ, *ctv*
condo ≈, *K*, ⊗, ♨
2960 South Kihei Rd.
☎*879-2778 or 800-367-5242*
(800-663-2101 from
Canada)
⇄*879-7825*
www.crhmaui.com
This tourist re-
sort enjoys a
magnificent
location on
an out-
crop-
ping at
the
north-
ern end of
the lovely
Keawakapu
beach. It rents
out both hotel
rooms and
condominium-style
apartments. The former
are quite small, but
otherwise impeccable.
The latter are also very
pleasant, and most
have a large balcony
that looks out over the
beach. They are, how-
ever, quite expensive.

Maui Lu Resort
$110-$185
≈, *laundry*, ≡, ℝ, *ctv*
575 South Kihei Rd.
☎*879-5881 or 800-922-7866*
⇄*879-4627*
Part of the Aston chain,
this large hotel is com-
prised of several build-
ings and has comfort-
able rooms, whose
prices vary according to
their location. Ocean-
front rooms are located
on the seaside of the
road, while the others
are *mauka* (facing the
mountains).

Maui Oceanfront
$100-$179
laundry, ≡, *ctv*, ℝ, ◙
2980 South Kihei Rd.
☎*879-7744 or 800-367-5004*
(800-272-5275 from the
other islands)
⇄*874-0145*
www.castle-group.com
This small 85-room
hotel is part of the Cas-
tle Resorts chain,
and is perpen-
dicular to
Keawakapau
beach, with only
a small access
area. The
rooms are
well maintained
but rather small,
and only have showers.

🦐 **Maui Coast Hotel**
$145-$349
≈, *laundry*, ≡, ℝ, ◙, *ctv*, ♨
2259 South Kihei Rd.
☎*874-6284 or 800-895-6284*
⇄*875-4731*
www.westcoasthotels.com/
mauicoast
Kihei does not have
many hotels, but this is
undoubtedly the best
one of all. It features
265 rooms, half of
which are comfortable,
spacious one- or two-
bedroom suites. The
swimming pool and
two whirlpools are
pleasant, the two tennis
courts are lit up at
night (you can borrow
rackets and balls), and
the laundry machines
are free. Near the hotel
is Jameson's Bar & Grill
(see p 373). You can
also keep your room
until 6pm by paying a
supplement.

Maui Hill
$230-$400
≈, *K*, *laundry*, ≡, *ctv*, ♨
2881 South Kihei Rd.
☎*879-6321 or 800-92-*
ASTON
⇄*922-8785*
The two-storey build-
ings of this large com-
plex belonging to the
Aston chain stretch
along the slope of a hill
overlooking the ocean,
on the southern out-
skirts of Kihei. The
units belong to individ-
ual owners and thus
are slightly different,
but they do have some
common traits: all are
really large, with giant
bathrooms and balco-
nies, one, two or three
bedrooms and at least
two bathrooms. There
is a swimming pool,
whirlpool, tennis
courts, a putting green
and a barbecue area.

Wailea to Makena

Outrigger Wailea Resort
$229-$399
≈, *laundry*, ≡, ℝ, *ctv*, ♨
3700 Wailea Alanui
☎*879-1922*
☎*800-OUTRIGGER*
⇄*875-4878*
www.outrigger.com
Located on a rocky
outcropping along the
coast, near the pretty
Ulua beach, this estab-
lishment was recently
bought by the Outrig-
ger chain. It is slowly
being renovated and its
facilities are being
improved. Less extrava-
gant than most neigh-
bouring resorts, it is
less overwhelming,
with 516 comfortable
rooms spread out in
several smaller build-

ings. Guests have not two, or even three, but *four* whirlpools at the their disposal, so they are never too crowded. The additional charges for various services are unfortunate for a hotel in this price category.

Maui Prince Hotel
$280-$430
≈, ⊙, ℜ, ⑭, ctv
5400 Makena Alanui
☎874-1111 or 800-WESTIN1
⇌879-8763
www.westin.com
Makena's only resort, this large hotel is built around a huge atrium filled with tropical vegetation and turns its back to the ocean, despite the pretty beach nearby. The two swimming pools are rather small, and the prices are high. Luckily, guests enjoy a number of special deals, including unlimited access to the golf course, making the price somewhat more reasonable. Stargazing sessions take place on Monday and Thursday nights.

Kea Lani Hotel
$295-$1,600
≈, ⊙, ℜ, ≡, ℝ, ctv, ⑮
4100 Wailea Alanui
☎875-4100 or 800-882-4100
⇌875-1200
www.kealani.com
This ultra-luxurious resort is located near a lovely sandy bay and features one-bedroom suites with marble bathrooms. Great attention has been paid to detail, and the resort has all the little extras. Young honeymooning couples, or those who can afford it, may pre-

fer to rent one of the 37 villas with two to four bedrooms, patios and private swimming pools with a lovely view of the ocean. Unfortunately, the hotel's main building is a little further from the shore. In low season, the fifth night is free.

Four Seasons Resort
$305-$725
≈, ⊙, ℜ, ≡, ℝ, ◙, ctv, ⑮
3900 Wailea Alanui
☎874-8000
☎800-334-MAUI
⇌874-2222
www.fourseasons.com
Very pleasant and with a good location, the Four Seasons looks out over a lovely beach and is set around a huge swimming pool guarded by royal palms and surrounded by pools of water and tropical vegetation. Decorated with an orchid motif, the hotel has large, luxurious rooms with marble bathrooms, as well as a number of suites. The room rates on the Club Floor, the highest level, include breakfast, afternoon tea, cocktails, desserts and digestifs.

Renaissance Wailea Beach Resort
$320-$550
≈, ⊙, ℜ, ≡, ℝ, ctv
3550 Wailea Alanui
☎879-4900 or 800-992-4532
⇌874-5370
www.renaissancehotels.com
The northernmost of Wailea's large tourist resorts is only a few miles from Kihei, but in a countryside that is much more open and green. This establish-

ment distinguishes itself because it is directly on Mokapu beach. The 345 rooms and suites are comfortable but not exceptional for the price.

Grand Wailea Resort
Starting at $380
≈, ⊙, △, ℜ, ≡, ◙, ⑭, ctv, ⑮
3850 Wailea Alanui
☎875-1234 or 800-888-6100
⇌874-2442
www.grandwailea.com
The Grand Wailea offers all the attributes of a large luxury resort and more. The complex includes five restaurants, the most distinguished nightclub on this part of the island (see p 381), swimming pools set in the middle of a garden landscaped with palm trees and artificial rocks, not to forget a small artificial beach and pool for children on days when the ocean current is too strong – and all just a few steps from the superb Wailua Beach. Add to this list a gym, wedding chapel, squash court and a stunning collection of Botero sculptures, original bas-reliefs by Fernand Léger and several Picassos... There is even an elevator to go from the lower to the upper level of the swimming pool! The rooms are very comfortable and large, with marble bathrooms. Of course, none of this comes without a price: the rates rise quickly, and at $10,000 per night, the "Grand Suite" is the most

Maui

expensive in all of Hawaii!

The Backcountry

Polipoli State Recreation Area
free camping
bungalow $45
(up to 4 people.)
Rarely visited by tourists, this high-altitude park must be reached by a trail and has a campground in the forest. Nights are cool here (in winter, it often freezes!). The amenities are minimal, with picnic tables and washrooms but no showers. You can rent a 10-person bungalow with no electricity, but equipped with a wood stove and gas lanterns. To obtain a permit, see p 298.

Golden Bamboo
$85-$95 bkfst incl.
K, ctv
422 Kaupakalua Rd. (Mile 7.8) between Makawao and Ha'iku
☎/≈ 572-7824
☎ 800-344-1238
www.goldenbamboo.com
This old plantation house from the 1920s is surrounded by almost 7.5 acres (3ha) of magnificent tropical and fruit trees. Guests can choose between a cottage, two suites and a large studio. All are comfortable, with separate bathrooms and kitchens, and all are immaculately clean.

🌿 Olinda Country Cottages
$120-$195 bkfst incl.
laundry, K, tv
2660 Olinda Rd., Olinda
☎ 572-1453 or 800-932-3435
≈ 573-5326
www.mauibnbcottages.com
Below Makawao, Olinda Road climbs upward to the high slopes of Hale'a'kala, and seems as though it were trying to touch the clouds. The maple at the entrance to this bed and breakfast may be the only tree on Maui to turn red in winter. Set in the heart of a protea plantation, this establishment really feels much more like a lodge than anything else. With a shingle roof and rosebushes, all in the calm, cool mountain air, it has a certain English elegance, especially on misty evenings. In addition to the two cottages (the most popular choice), there are three guestrooms in the main house. The balcony of Hidden Cottage is very pleasant, despite its sloping roof, and has a whirlpool that commands a lovely view of Maui's central isthmus and the ocean in the distance. Breakfasts are delectable, consisting of fruit plates and fresh pastries.

🌿 Silver Cloud Guest Ranch B&B
$85-$150 bkfst incl.
K, tv, ☆
RR2 Box 201, Kula, HI 96790
☎ 878-6101 or 800-532-1111
≈ 878-2132
www.SilverCloudRanch.com
Set amid verdant fields on the lower slopes of Hale'a'kala, this old ranch was built in the early 19th century and was later converted into a tasteful bed and breakfast. The location is ideal for those who prefer the peacefulness and cool air of the higher altitudes. The main house has five guestrooms, and there are an additional five studios in another building (all with their own kitchen). There is also an adjacent cottage with a stove. The King Kamehameha Room on the second floor is very bright and has a balcony overlooking the central isthmus and neighbouring islands. The ranch also organizes horseback excursions. The hosts are very friendly and children are welcome.

Kula Lodge
$110-$165
☆
RR1, Box 475, Kula, HI 96790
Highway 377 (Mile 5.3)
☎ 878-1535 or 800-233-1535
≈ 878-2518
www.kulalodge.com
Located just before the junction on the road to Hale'a'kala at an altitude of 3,280ft (1,000m), Kula Lodge cannot be surpassed, both for its restaurant (see p 377) and its panoramic view of the central isthmus and the ocean. Several chalets offer pleasant rooms, the best of which have a sunny terrace and wood stoves (if possible, ask for chalet 1).

Maui

Pilialoha
$120 bkfst incl.
laundry, K, ctv
2512 Kaupakalua Rd. (Mile 3.9)
between Makawao et Ha'iku
☎ *572-1440*
↝ *572-4612*
www.pilialoha.com
Japanese-American
couple Bill and
Machiko Heyde live in
a house near this large,
bright apartment with
wooden floors. The
place is more than well
equipped: guests not
only have videos,
beach towels, a boogie
board and snorkelling
gear at their disposal,
but the apartment is
also stocked with choc-
olate and postage
stamps. The hosts re-
ceive their guests in the
most pleasant fashion,
and breakfast is served
à la carte. In short, if
you are looking for a
bed and breakfast with
a personal touch, this is
it. There is a minimum
stay of three nights,
and credit cards are not
accepted.

Hale'a'kala

**Camping and shelters in
the crater**
free camping
**Shelters $40 for up to six
people, $80 for up to 12**
Hale'a'kala National Park
P.O. Box 369, Makawao, HI
96768
☎ *572-9306 (8am to 3pm)*
There are two undevel-
oped sites in the crater
where people can
camp: Holua, on the
Halemau'u Trail (at an
altitude of 6,939ft or
2,115m), and Paliku,
further east, at the edge
of the Kipahulu reserve

(6,381ft or 1,945m).
You should know that
temperatures can drop
to freezing here at
night. You can get a
permit at the Visitor
Center between 8am
and 3pm on the day
you set out, since there
are no reservations.
The shelters at both of
these locations and at
Kapalaoa (7,251ft or
2,210m) on the Sliding
Sands Trail through the
desert landscape are so
much in demand that
they are awarded
through a lottery. Ap-
plications must be sub-
mitted three months
before the desired date
of the stay. Each shelter
has a wood stove,
kitchen utensils, 12
bunk beds and a lim-
ited water supply (there
is no drinking water).
There are occasional
cancellations during the
low season: for more
information, call be-
tween 1pm and 3pm.

Hosmer Grove
Campground
free
*washrooms, picnic tables,
barbecues, drinking water*
This campground is
located in a lovely rural
setting with forests of
pine and eucalyptus,
just past the park en-
trance (6,890ft or
2,100m in altitude).
Campers do not need a
permit, but are limited
to a maximum stay of
three nights. Be sure to
bring along warm
clothes for the eve-
nings, since tempera-
tures can be cool.
Campsites are available
on a first-come, first-
served basis.

The Road to Hana
and Tour of the
Island

Kipahulu Campground
free
*portable washrooms,
picnic tables, barbecues,
no water*
☎ *248-7375*
Located in the Kipahulu
section of Hale'a'kala
National Park, this
campground is just a
short distance from the
shore, on the site of an
ancient Hawaiian vil-
lage. Half the campsites
are shaded, the others
are in a vast grassy
expanse, and each has
a picnic table and a
barbecue. The two best
campsites are under the
two padanus trees
facing the sea. All
campsites are available
on a first-come, first-
served basis, and may
be used for three con-
secutive nights (camp-
ing permits required).

Wai'anapanapa State
Park
free camping
*bungalows $45 (up to 4
people)*
*washrooms, showers,
picnic tables, barbecues*
The campground at
Wai'anapanapa is very
pleasant, located on a
large grassy area a
short distance from the
coast, but far enough
from the beach and the
parking area to avoid
daytrippers from wan-
dering through the
campground. Be sure
to obtain the required
permit, since the atten-
dant here is quite strict.
Follow the road to the
right after the park

entrance to reach 12 green wooden bungalows that are for rent. Surrounded by pandanus trees, set slightly away from the coast, they are in quite good condition and very popular. Each bungalow has a kitchen (including a refrigerator) with a dining area, a bedroom and a bathroom. For permits, see p 298.

YMCA – Camp Keanae
dormitory/camping $10
sb, K, laundry
Hana Hwy. (Mile 16.4)
☎248-7202
The campground is located on a promontory overlooking the peninsula, just before you reach Keanae itself. Undergoing renovations at the time of our visit, this establishment is used mainly by groups who stay in the dormitories, as well as some individual travellers (*maximum two days*). For the same price, you can pitch your tent in the large grassy area below the road.

Joe's Place
$45-$65
sb/pb, K
4870 Uakea Rd. (Mile 0.4)
☎248-7659 or 248-7033
The best (and only) option in the budget hotel category, Joe's Place has eight rooms with or without private bathrooms, most with twin beds. Families often rent the house in its entirety since it has a communal kitchen and a TV room.

Bamboo Inn
$130-$175 bkfst incl.
K, ctv, ☂
Uakea Rd. (Mile 0.4)
☎248-7718
⇄248-7429
Recently opened by the owner of the Hana Hale Malamalama (see below), the Bamboo Inn lives up to its name since it is entirely decorated with bamboo. Studios and small two-storey houses with one bedroom can be rented. The reception is somewhat impersonal.

Hana Hale Malamalama
$110-$165 bkfst incl.
K, ctv, ☂
P.O. Box 374, Hana HI 96713
☎248-7718
⇄248-7429
www.hanahale.com
The Hana Hale Malamalama is a bed and breakfast that can also be rented as a house, with three units grouped around an old restored Hawaiian fishpond. Two of the suites are in the same building, with one located on the main floor and the other, more expensive, on the second floor. The latter is surrounded on all sides by a balcony that has a series of openings that let in plenty of light. The other unit is the Tree House Cottage, a room perched among tree branches (with an outdoor shower).

Hana Kai Resort
$125-$195
K, ⊗, ☂
1533 Uakea Rd., Hana
(Mile 0.6)
☎248-8426 or 800-346-2772
(only from the U.S.)
⇄248-7482
www.hanakai.com
The 10 studios and seven one-bedroom apartments of the Hana Kai Resort are located in two wooden buildings that blend in well with the surrounding countryside, on the west coast of Hana Bay. There is a small black-sand and Popolona-pebble beach below. Don't be discouraged by the rusty patches on the exterior caused by the ocean spray: the interior is immaculate. The units are comfortable and airy, although they do not have telephones, television or air conditioning.

Heavenly Hana Inn
$100-$250 bkfst incl.
4155 Hana Hwy. (Mile 32.9)
☎/⇄248-8442
hanainn@maui.net
To enter this establishment, guests must go through a garden with bamboo and a statue of Buddha, and an old wooden door with creaking hinges. The bed and breakfast lies just behind this entrance, with three superb, newly renovated rooms decorated in a streamlined Japanese style, as well as an older studio. The raised beds are hidden under

a mountain of cushions. There is a minimum stay of two nights.

Huelo Point B&B
$125-$350 bkfst incl.
K, tv
P.O. Box 1195, Paia HI 96779
☎/≈*572-1850*
huelopt@maui.net
Located at the end of Dora Faith Road, just past the village of Huelo, this upscale bed and breakfast looks out over Waipi'o Bay from the top of a small cliff. The three cottages and main house *(rented as a whole with three bedrooms, two bathrooms and a living room with fireplace)* bask amid the palms, elephant ears, banana trees and ginger. The design is modern, and all units have high ceilings and large bay windows that let in plenty of light. The "Guest House" and the main house come with private whirlpools built into the edge of the cliff.

Hotel Hana-Maui
$425-$795
≈, ☉, ℛ, *laundry*, ℝ, ⊗, ☂
Hana Hwy.
☎*248-8211*
☎*800-321-HANA*
≈*248-7202*
Maui's most exclusive hotel, the Hotel Hana-Maui is located in the centre of the peaceful town of Hana, with a view of Kaihalulu Bay. The establishment is luxurious, tropical, and rents out rooms in several small one-storey buildings that are spread over the large grassy property. There

is no television or air conditioning, but the rooms are still very comfortable and have huge bathrooms. The cottages are set closer to the sea and have the same exotic touches, with bamboo bedframes, straw mats on the floor, and rattan furniture. The property is quite large, so people drive around in golf carts. The hotel offers a host of services and amenities.

Restaurants

Lahaina

House of Saimin
under $10
Mon 5pm to 2am, Tue to Thu 3:30pm to 2am, Fri to Sat 3:30pm to 3am
Lahaina Shopping Center (building 5)
☎*667-7572*
The name says it all: this restaurant serves nothing but *saimin*, accompanied by various sauces. The price depends on the size of the bowl, and you can add wonton or Portuguese soup to the meal. The jazz or classical music in the background creates a mellow atmosphere that draws in a loyal clientele of frazzled employees from nearby businesses.

Sunrise Cafe
under $10
every day 6am to 6pm
693 Front St.
(corner of Market St.)
☎*661-8558*
The bagels on the menu seem a tad pricey, especially the "Lux" with salmon and cream cheese, but they are served on proper plates and are as pleasant to look at as they are to eat. Breakfast is the best meal of the day at the Sunrise Cafe. There are some shaded tables, set back from the street, with a view of the Pioneer Inn.

Westside Natural Foods & Deli
under $10
Mon to Sat 7:30am to 9pm and Sun 8:30am to 8pm
193 Lahainaluna Rd.
☎*667-2855*
This centrally located grocery store sells organic products and has a small deli with displays of cold appetizers (salads) and warm ones (stuffed peppers, lasagna, vegetarian chili and vegetarian quiche). It also has a tempting selection of fruit and pastries and all kinds of juice, including carrot, beet, celery and wheat juice. You can eat in or take out.

Bubba Gump Shrimp Company
$10-$20
every day 11am to 10:30pm
889 Front St.
☎*661-3111*
One of the many theme restaurants that have popped up over the

last several years, Bubba is based on the movie *Forrest Gump*, with photos, all kinds of souvenirs and the original soundtrack contributing to the atmosphere. The menu is hardly more original than that of its neighbour, the Hard Rock Cafe, except that it features a lot of shrimp, served in a variety of ways. The clientele of this family restaurant appreciate the terrace overlooking the ocean.

Cheeseburger in Paradise
$10-$20
every day 8am to midnight
811 Front St.
☎661-4855
The first Cheeseburger in Paradise was established right here in Lahaina, not in Waikiki (see p 173). The hamburgers are the same, as are the tasteless jokes of how to rip off tourists, but at least this place has a terrace with a view of the ocean. Vegetarians can opt for the tofu burger. See also p 380.

Coolers
$10-$20
every day 8am to midnight
180 Dickenson St.
☎661-7082
Both a restaurant and a bar, Coolers serves the standard *pupus*, salads, hamburgers, pasta and daily fish special for dinner, complemented by such original touches as Moroccan chicken enchiladas, *kalua* pork and chocolate tacos with straw-

berry sauce for dessert. There are some quiet tables outside, and live music on Wednesdays.

Hard Rock Cafe
$10-$20
every day from 11:30am
900 Front St.
☎667-7400
Maui's Hard Rock Cafe holds no surprises, with the decor centered on the inevitable Cadillac carrying a load of surfboards. The menu is equally predictable: calorie-laden steaks, ribs and hamburgers, with a few salads for health-conscious diners. There is live music several times a month.

La Fogata
$10-$15
every day 10am to 10pm
180 Dickenson St.
☎661-5391
This is the real thing, a true Mexican *donde se habla espanol*, serving quality meals at reasonable prices. You can order fajitas, nachos, quesadillas and tacos, accompanied with every kind of sauce imaginable. In addition, there are various *tortas* filled with pork, ham and *chorizo*, beef, vegetarian or Cuban-style with sausages, and traditional soups, including *pozole* with corn and pork, *birria* with kid and *menudo* (tripe). To round out the meal, don't pass up the *ceviche* (marinated fish), Mexican sodas and Latin music!

Lahaina Fish Company
$10-$25
every day from 11am to 10pm
831 Front St.
☎661-3472
It only stands to reason that the Fish Company would specialize in fish and seafood. If you want to know exactly what to order, check the insert that describes the various fish on the menu, including *'ahi, shutome* (swordfish), *mahi-mahi, ono, poakapaka* and *onaga* (all available depending on the daily catch). Adventurous gourmets might spring for the *mako* shark, while others may stick with the Louis crab, house pasta or meat dishes.

Lemongrass
$10-$20
Mon to Sat 11am to 9pm, Sun 5pm to 9pm
930 Waine'e St.
Behind the Lahaina Center
☎667-6888
Run by two sisters, one in the kitchen while the other waits on tables, Lemongrass is the only Vietnamese restaurant in West Maui, and certainly does justice to this type of cuisine. True to the name of the establishment, many of the dishes are flavoured with lemongrass, accompanying chicken, *pho*, and beef *ragout*, the latter being a delicious dish inspired by French cuisine and inherited from the sisters' mother, Mrs. Nguyen, who was a renowned chef in Vietnam in the 1960s. There is also a large

selection of vegetarian dishes. The decor is not unpleasant, but the reception could be improved.

Moose McGillicuddy's
$10-$20
every day 7:30am to 2am
844 Front St.
☎667-7758

The little brother of Moose in Waikiki (see p 172), this restaurant and bar has an almost identical menu: various breakfast choices, North-American-style tacos, quesadillas and fajitas, as well as steaks and fish for dinner, at prices that are only a little higher. In a concession to local cuisine, you can also order "Maui onion rings." Wednesday is steak night, with hearty servings accompanied with baked potatoes, vegetables, soup and salad. See also p 380.

Pioneer Inn Grill & Bar
$10-$25
every day 6:30am to 10pm
658 Wharf St.
☎661-3636

This is a lovely spot to grab a bite or have a drink with pleasant music in the background, while seated under the impassive gaze of a figurehead. The menu is more elaborate at night, featuring such dishes as steak, Thai chicken curry and pasta. Be sure to take a look at the collection of harpoons along the wall.

Kimo's
$15-$25
every day 11am to 3pm and 5pm to 10:30pm, bar open until 1:30am
845 Front St.
☎661-4811

With a view of the ocean and the island of Lana'i, Kimo's owes its popularity to its sunny terrace where people come especially at night to enjoy tender meat dishes and steaks. There are also dishes with local flavours, such as "Polynesian" chicken with teriyaki sauce, or pork ribs in a prune sauce. The selection is more limited at lunchtime, consisting of hamburgers, salads, sandwiches and a daily fish special, but the prices are much lower. You may also wish to indulge in a cocktail here before or after dinner.

Longhi's
$15-$25
every day 7:30am to 10pm
888 Front St.
☎667-2288

Voted several times as Best Breakfast on Maui, and ranking as one of the top 100 independent restaurants in the United States, Longhi's creates delicious dishes that combine fresh ingredients and northern Italian flavours. What cannot be grown or raised in Hawaii is flown in from Europe and North America. The olive oil and Parmesan cheese come from Italy, the pasta (not homemade) comes from Abruzzia, the

mozzarella from New York, the salmon from Alaska and the china from Hong Kong. The service is impeccable and the decor is simple and airy, but not at all tropical. Prices are very reasonable given the work that goes into preparing the food.

Sam Choy's
$15-$30
every day 5pm to 9:30pm
900 Front St. (Lahaina Center)
☎661-3800

This chain has now opened a location on Maui. Here, as in other locations, you will find Sam's famous regional Hawaiian cuisine, combining generations of culinary traditions in a single plate. Those on a budget can still enjoy the Louis crab salad, Sam-Choy-style (served in a papaya). A little more expensive, the macadamia-nut-encrusted island fish in a butter, garlic and soy sauce is prepared with the catch of the day. The place also brews its own beer, and the vats can be seen in the adjoining room.

David Paul's Lahaina Grill
$20-$45
every day 5:30pm to 9:45pm (bar open until 1am)
127 Lahainaluna Rd.
☎667-5117

This restaurant is certainly not lacking in credentials: it was voted Maui's best establishment six years in a row! Leaning more towards "Pacific Rim" flavours than Hawaiian nouvelle cuisine, the

Grill only uses ingredients from the island. As an appetizer, try the smoked-duck salad with macadamia nuts and arugula, a blend of cashew nuts and goat cheese, or opt for the *foie gras*, the sashimi platter or the Mediterranean platter with pita, hummus, artichoke hearts and *tapenade*. This is but a small sample of the breadth of international flavours the chef draws on. The *plat de resistance* is the leg of mutton with Kona coffee. The ambiance is refined, the service is attentive, and the wine list is impressive.

Pacific'O
$25-$40
*every day 11am to 4pm
and 5:30pm to 10pm*
505 Front St.
☎667-4341

The large terrace of the Pacific'O is situated beneath coconut palms, directly on the beach. It is easy to find in the evening since it's lit up by torches. Chef James McDonald moved here from Philadelphia and is now one of the rising stars of Hawaiian regional cuisine. As an appetizer, try the delicious Chinese wonton with basil and shrimp, or sample the fried sashimi or fresh *'ahi*. The establishment has been called the best seafood restaurant in Lahaina, and is also quite original with its hint of Indian influence. There is jazz in the evenings from Thursday to Saturday.

Gérard's
$30-$60
open from 6pm
174 Lahainaluna Rd.
☎661-8939 or 877-661-8939

Born in Gascogne, Gérard Reversade established himself in Maui in the early 1980s. Gradually, his restaurant, set in the romantic Plantation Inn, has become one of the best on the island. The secret of his success is as simple as his dishes are elaborate: he prepares them with the best ingredients from the archipelago, using the principles of French cuisine. With a very few exceptions, everything that is served here comes from the islands. For some real French specialties try the *terrine de foie gras de canard* steeped in Banyul wine, or "*la bonne gabure*," white-bean soup with cabbage, ham and conserve of duck. The mango *tarte Tatin* is a spectacular way to finish the evening.

I'O
$30-$40
every day 5:30pm to 10pm
505 Front St.
☎665-4646

Located next to the Pacific'O and also run by James McDonald, I'O has a decidedly modern decor, with a subdued designer bistro look, and centered on an open kitchen area. The menu is representative of Hawaiian nouvelle cuisine, with some original dishes like jellyfish salad and fern shoots (*pohole*) with papaya. The presentation is sophisticated, the service is attentive, and the large selection of wines is reasonably priced.

Ka'anapali

Hula Grill
$15-$30
every day 11am to 9:30pm
2435 Ka'anapali Pkwy.
Whalers Village
☎667-6636

The Hula Grill is popular for its pleasant terrace right on the beach, with a view of Lana'i and Moloka'i. The menu lists a large selection of American, Hawaiian and international dishes, with sandwiches and pizza as well as seafood and "raw fish" from Tahiti, and the local variation of *dim sum*.

Spatts Trattoria
$15-$30
every day 6pm to 9:30pm
200 Nohea Kai Dr.
Hyatt Regency Maui (see p 350)
☎667-4727

This Italian restaurant offers refined surroundings at prices that are barely higher than at some mediocre restaurants along the ocean in Lahaina. The menu has the standard fish, pasta and meat dishes, but also lists some house specialties such as the appetizer of papaya wrapped in *prosciutto*.

Maui

🌺 The Tiki Terrace
$15-$30
every day 7am to 11am and 5:30pm to 9pm brunch Sun 9am to 1pm
2525 Ka'anapali Pkwy.
Ka'anapali Beach Hotel
(see p 349)
☎667-0124
Under the (distant) gaze of Ku'kailimoku, god of war, Tiki Terrace serves more authentic Hawaiian fare than other restaurants in Ka'anapali. Try the fern salad with calamari, the vegetable *laulau* with tofu, the sweet potato from Moloka'i with coconut milk or stuffed *lawalu* fish wrapped in a *ti* leaf. The tempting Hawaiian fixed-price menu is very exotic, with fern salad, chicken breast or filet of fish with grilled bananas, sweet potato, taro and *poi*, and papaya with lemon for dessert. There is music every night, followed by a *hula* show. The champagne brunch on Sundays features Hawaiian and American specialties.

Leilani's on the Beach
$20-$30
grill every day 11am to 11pm, restaurant 5am to 10pm
2435 Ka'anapali Pkwy.
Whalers Village
☎661-4495
Located across from the Hula Grill, near Ka'anapali's beach, Lailani's has the same magnificent setting, and the menu is also quite similar. Dishes prepared on the grill on the main floor are the

most popular, while the upstairs restaurant specializes in steak and seafood, with good fresh fish and grilled dishes cooked on *kiawe* wood.

Rusty Harpoon
$20-$40
every day 8am to 10pm (bistro open until midnight)
2435 Ka'anapali Pkwy.
Whalers Village
☎661-3123
The Rusty Harpoon is slightly set back from Ka'anapali's beach. While neighbouring restaurants provide views of the sea, people come here to get a good view of the television screens. The results of sporting matches roll across the screens like the figures of the Wall Street stock market. The food is nothing out of the ordinary but rather expensive.

Sound of the Falls
$30
Sun 9:30am to 1:30pm
2365 Ka'anapali Pkwy.
The Westin Maui (see p 350)
☎667-2525
The atmosphere is somewhat similar to the romantic Swan Court (see below), and the Westin's Sunday brunch is served against a backdrop of artificial waterways, with a view of the sea. The brunch is famous for its large selection of baked treats and fresh fruit, as well as omelets and waffles, salads, various appetizers, seafood and hot dishes prepared on the spot. Champagne

adds the finishing touch to the experience. Reservations are required.

🌺 Swan Court
$30-$60
Mon to Sat 6:30am to 11:30am, Sun until noon, every day 6pm to 10pm
200 Nohea Kai Dr.
Hyatt Regency Maui
(see p 350)
☎667-4727
Beneath the high roof of a covered courtyard, tables are nestled by the side of an artificial lake surrounded by tropical greenery. Swans glide across the water, and there is a gently cascading waterfall. No wonder Swan Court was chosen as one of the 10 most romantic restaurants in the United States! The dishes have more "Pacific Rim" flavours than Hawaiian influences, but manage to form a coherent style even though the menu lists foods as diverse as bison pepper steak, *opakapaka* sautéed in ginger dressing and wonton Napoleon with seafood.

Villa Terrace
$30
every day 5:30pm to 9pm
2365 Ka'anapali Pkwy.
The Westin Maui (see p 350)
☎667-2525
Located on the boardwalk that runs along the Ka'anapali beach, the Villa Terrace offers a buffet every night, with crab, pasta, steak, ribs, fresh fish, sashimi, seafood and assorted desserts. There is a $5 discount between

5:30pm and 6pm, and between 8:30pm and 9pm.

From Honokowai to Kapalua

Hawaiian Moons
under $10
Mon to Fri 7am to 8pm, Sat to Sun 8am to 8pm
3636 Lower Honoapi'ilani Rd.
Honokowai
☎665-1339
This large organic food shop has a deli that sells appetizers at $5 per pound (salads, taboule, guacamole), as well as various sandwiches and freshly squeezed fruit and vegetable juices. There are also warm daily specials such as vegetable curry and vegetarian chili. Some tables are available, but it is more pleasant to have a picnic on the benches of Honokowai County Park, just across the street.

Honolua Store
under $10
every day 6am to 3pm
Office Rd., Kapalua
☎669-6128
This is the only place in Kapalua still offering affordable plate lunches, hamburgers, fish & chips and sandwiches, just a few steps from the Ritz and right near the golf course. It's almost a miracle the place still exists! Breakfast is served until 10am, and includes eggs, pancakes, bagels,

biscuits and gravy. The store also sells chips, drinks, fruit, pastries and basic provisions.

Java Jazz
under $10
every day 6am to 8pm or 10pm depending on the day
3350 Lower Honoapi'ilani Rd.
Honokowai Marketplace
☎667-0787
After a brief sojourn in Sweden and several years in California, Farzad has finally settled down for good in Maui, where he opened this charming little café. Though he now has U.S. citizenship, he has kept alive the tradition of hospitality from his native Iran. Sip your cappuccino or espresso on the pillow-strewn sofas, listening to easy jazz. Farzad plays guitar himself, and on some weekends jazz-lovers come to jam at the café.

Pizza Paradiso
under $10
every day 11am to 10pm
3350 Lower Honoapi'ilani Rd.
Honokowai Marketplace
☎667-2929
Both fast-food counter and Italian restaurant, Pizza Paradiso prepares pizza (also sold by the slice) that is a hit with everyone who lives and works nearby. You can also order panini, crostini, pasta or one of the many salads without breaking the bank – something all too rare in these parts.

Puka Bagel Cafe
under $10
Mon to Fri 6:30am to 5pm, Sat to Sun 7am to 3pm
4310 Lower Honoapi'ilani Rd.
Kahana
☎871-1453
This chain has locations only on Maui, and is a good place to go for a quick breakfast or to grab a bite to eat. The menu lists pastries, sandwiches, ham croissants and various bagels with cream cheese, including the half-pound smoked salmon (approx. 250g).

China Boat
$10-$50
Mon to Sat 11:30am to 2pm, every day 5pm to 10pm
4474 Lower Honoapi'ilani Rd.
Kahana
☎669-5089
Located north of Kahana, across from the Aston Kahana Reef, this Chinese restaurant specializes in fish and seafood, serving everything from crab to oysters and abalone. With the exception of vegetarians, who have very limited options, there is something for everyone: there are no less than 93 items on the menu! You can dine inside or on the terrace by the street.

A Pacific Café – Honokowai
$20-$40
every day 5:30pm to 9:30pm
3350 Lower Honoapi'ilani Rd.
Honokowai Marketplace
☎667-2800
Jean-Marie Josselin has done it again! The French chef who has

become one of the leading figures in regional Hawaiian cuisine recently opened his new restaurant in Hawaii, this time on Maui. The last we heard, there were some difficulties in getting this establishment off the ground, but it is sure to find its niche soon since the menu is the same as Josselin's other restaurants throughout the archipelago. There is live Hawaiian music on Saturdays, and live jazz on Sundays.

Erik's Seafood Grotto
$20-$30
every day 11:30am to 2pm and 5pm to 10pm
4242 Lower Honoapi'ilani Rd.
Kahana
☎ **669-4806**
Erik Jakobsen, a chef of Danish origin, has established a reputation as a master of fish and seafood preparation over the years. The menu lists no fewer than 12 Hawaiian fish, with nine guaranteed to be available on any given day. The long list of tantalizing dishes includes *bouillabaisse, cioppino, coquilles Saint-Jacques,* lobster and Alaskan crab. There are also some meat dishes, and a more limited selection of sandwiches and salads at lunch. There is also an early-bird discount on some dishes between 5pm and 6pm.

Roy's
$20-$40
every day 5:30pm to 10pm
4405 Honoapi'ilani Hwy.
Kahana
Kahana Gateway Shopping Center
☎ **669-6999 or 669-5000**
These two establishments stand side by side on the second floor of the shopping centre in Kahana. Because the first of the two, Roy's Kahana Bar & Grill, was always full, owner Roy Yamaguchi decided to open a second establishment, Roy's Nicolina. The menus are similar, with an emphasis on the island's finest fish, meat, poultry and vegetables prepared with various flavours, such as ginger and lemongrass.

Sea House Restaurant
$20-$35
every day 8am to 11am, noon to 2pm and 6pm to 9pm (from 5:30pm in winter)
5900 Honoapi'ilani Rd., Napili
Napili Kai Resort (see p 351)
☎ **669-1500**
Looking out over the very pretty Napili beach, this restaurant serves high-quality Hawaiian cuisine with a heavy emphasis on fresh local ingredients, although it is not nouvelle cuisine. Dishes consist of freshly caught tuna, served with Maui-grown onions, or pork cutlet with ginger, papaya and banana. There is a Polynesian Dinner Show every Friday, featuring the employ-

ees' children who are enrolled in courses with the Napili Kai Foundation, an organization dedicated to preserving Hawaiian culture.

Sansei
$20-$35
every day from 5:30pm, to 10pm Sat to Wed and 1:30am Thu to Fri
115 Bay Dr., Kapalua
Kapalua Shops
☎ **669-6286**
Sansei ("master") is the unlikely combination of a sushi bar and a North American seafood restaurant. The result is so popular that it is full to the point of bursting in the evenings every weekend. The crab cakes are excellent, and classic sushi is served along with more innovative varieties such as the "caterpillar" made with eel and avocado, or the mango-and-crab salad roll with spicy Thai dressing. The rest of the menu is similarly multi-ethnic. You will therefore find beef cutlet with udon, glazed duck and herbed lamb. See also p 380.

The Plantation House
$20-$35
every day 8am to 3pm and from 5:30pm
2000 Plantation Club Dr.
Kapalua
☎ **669-6299**
The airy interior of the clubhouse restaurant of the Kapalua golf course has a lovely view of the green and the ocean. The menu is not as Mediterranean as you might think, but rather emphasizes "Pacific

Rim" cuisine with a strong regional flavour, especially evident in the appetizers and the heavy use of macadamia nuts. Breakfast and lunch are served throughout the day, regardless of the time. Unfortunately, the service is equally oblivious to the clock and is quite slow, and the finished plates are cleared away very quickly.

Anuenue Room
$30-$60
Tue to Sat 6pm to 9:30pm
1 Ritz-Carlton Dr., Kapalua
Ritz-Carlton Hotel (see p 352)
☎669-1665
The name of this restaurant, set in the Ritz, translates as "rainbow," and the establishment is known as one of the best in Hawaii. The original cuisine could be called regional except for the Provencal influence. The sea-urchin appetizer, pork in *kalua* milk with *o'helo* berries or the *ulu* (breadfruit) soup with coconut milk and seaweed are distinctly Hawaiian, while the *confit de canard* and *raviolini à la provençale*, cheese and olive oil are certainly French.

Tour of West Maui

Chez Paul
$30-$80
dinner served in two sittings: 6:30pm and 8:30pm
Highway 30 (Mile 15)
Across from the Olowalu General Store
☎661-3843
This is a surprising place for a restaurant that is undeniably fashionable and French to the core. Belgian owner Lucien Charbonnier definitively settled the question by putting up posters of *"Les Routiers"* in the dining room. Not that the cuisine here has anything in common with the type found in roadside eateries in France. People have always come to Chez Paul to celebrate big occasions, especially since the arrival of chef Patrick Callarec who trained at Martinez in Cannes. The house motto sets the tone at this establishment: There is no such thing as nouvelle cuisine, there is no such thing as traditional cuisine; there is only good cuisine! The food at Chez Paul is 100% French, with distinctive Provencal overtones that are evident in everything from the salad of mixed greens with warm goat cheese, *bouillabaisse marseillaise*, lobster with *foie gras* and grilled endives. The desserts are equally delicious, especially the mango *tarte Tatin* with coconut ice cream.

Wailuku, Kahului and Paia

Bentos & Banquets
under $10
Mon to Fri 10am to 2pm
85 North Church St., Wailuku
☎244-1124 or 232-0023
You are sure to encounter the delivery trucks of this establishment along the highways at least once during your trip. While he caters banquets on much of the island, Bernard also offers a variety of reasonably priced plate lunches to eat in or take out. The emphasis is on traditional Hawaiian fare.

Cafe O'Lei
under $10
Mon to Fri 10:30am to 2:30pm
Ka'ahumanu Ave., Wailuku
just before the corner of Market St.
☎244-6816
The brand new Cafe O'Lei (*olé* or *au lait?*!) has quickly become one of the preferred lunch stops for many people working in Wailuku. There is a selection of sandwiches, salads, plate lunches and several good warm dishes (fettuccini, *mahi-mahi*). Orders are taken on one side of the establishment, and you can eat on the other in a small room with lots of windows.

Ichiban
under $10 to $15
Mon to Fri 10am to 5pm,
Sat 8am to noon
Sushi bar 6:30am to 2pm
and 5pm to 9pm, Sat
10:30am to 2pm and
5pm to 9pm
47 Ka'ahumanu Ave., Kahului
Kahului Shopping Plaza
☎871-6977
This small, quality Japanese restaurant has two sections specializing in different types of food. One serves *donburi*, udon, teriyaki and even sandwiches at lunch. Meanwhile, the sushi bar serves only that. There are very copious fixed-price menus with two main dishes (tempura and teriyaki), miso soup, rice and a salad.

Ka'ahumanu Center Foodcourt
under $10
275 Ka'ahumanu Ave., Kahului
Ka'ahumanu Center, second floor
Local and national chains representing various ethnic origins, like Panda Express, Maui Tacos, McDonald's, Mixed Plate, Gyros Greek Food and Tepanyaki are found in the concourse in the middle of the shopping centre.

Maui Bake Shop & Deli
under $10
Mon to Fri 6am to 4pm,
Sat 7am to 2pm
2092 Vineyard St., Wailuku
☎242-0064
This excellent little pastry shop was established by a Frenchman who married a woman from Maui. Cakes and croissants, marzipan mice, pigs and rabbits

are all sold here. You can also order sandwiches, salads or the soup of the day.

Maui Coffee Roasters
Under $10
Mon to Fri 7:30am to 6pm, Sat 8am to 5pm, Sun 8am to 2:30pm
444 Hana Hwy., Kahului
☎877-2877
This large coffeehouse is located at the corner of Dairy Road, and roasts a range of local and more exotic types of coffee. The decor is very Californian, with retro posters and images of surfers gracing the walls. They serve pastries, bagels and sandwiches all day long.

Mushroom
under $10
every day 11am to 2pm and 5pm to 8pm
2080 Vineyard St., Wailuku
☎244-7117
This place is hard to miss, with smiling mushrooms cavorting around the doorframe. Located just below the Northshore Inn, the restaurant is the perfect place for an inexpensive meal. The menu lists all the mainstays of traditional Hawaiian cuisine, including *saimin*, wonton, chicken curry, fresh tuna and *shoyu* pork. The restaurant prides itself in preparing everything from scratch, so be patient – and take the owner's advice: phone 15 to 20min ahead. Rice and a soup or salad accompany all main dishes.

Pic-Nics Restaurant
under $10 (except picnic baskets)
every day 7am to 7pm
30 Baldwin Ave., Paia
☎579-8021
As its name indicates, this local fast-food counter specializes in preparing picnic baskets that people can take along on day trips to Hana or Hale'a'kala. You can also get sandwiches and hamburgers here. The house special is the spinach nut burger.

Siam Thai Cuisine
under $10
123 North Market St., Wailuku
☎244-3817
Siam is the place to enjoy Thai food at a reasonable price. There is a complete selection of traditional dishes including soups, red, yellow and green curries, noodles, fish and seafood, not to mention vegetarian options. Curries can be ordered spicy or mild. If you're feeling very daring, ask for your food "Thai hot" – it really sets your mouth on fire!

The Vegan Restaurant
under $10
every day noon to 9pm
115 Baldwin Ave., Paia
☎579-9144
True to its name, Vegan is Maui's only all-vegetarian restaurant. More lightweight than true-blue New Age, the place mainly draws a younger clientele. Salads obviously feature prominently on the menu, but there are also tempting Mexican-inspired dishes, vegan

hamburgers, fried vegetables and Asian-style noodles.

🌴 A Saigon Cafe
$10-$15
Mon to Sat 10am to 10pm, Sun 10am to 9pm
1792 Main St., Wailuku
☎243-9560

The name won't be of much use, unless you get lost coming here. The restaurant's owner, Jennifer Nguyen, stopped putting out the lovely sign she ordered from the continent since regulars are worried about too many tourists finding out about the place. But that doesn't stop people from coming here, though, and the place is always full to the point of bursting. The menu contains a thousand and one flavours, with homegrown lemongrass, mint and basil being the dominant aromas in many of the dishes. Try the delicious spring rolls or summer rolls as an appetizer before launching into the main courses, which include *pho* (traditional Vietnamese soup with a beef broth base) rice or egg noodles, succulent vegetables, tofu, meat and seafood (there are more than 70 choices in all). No doubt one of Maui's best ethnic restaurants.

Charley's
$10-$20
every day 7am to 10pm
142 Hana Hwy., Paia
☎579-9453

Very popular for its breakfasts, Charley's is

a typical North American restaurant, serving pizza, calzones, pasta, soup and salad for dinner, and chili and hamburgers for lunch. The house specialty is barbecue ribs smoked on *kiawe* wood. The walls are decorated with photographs of turn-of-the-century Paia.

Fujiya's
$10-$15
Mon to Fri 11am to 2pm, Mon to Sat 5pm to 10pm
133 North Market St., Wailuku
☎244-0206

Don't be put off by the rather worn exterior; the inside is more dapper. This rather standard Japanese restaurant is known for its *tepanyaki* (sautéed meat and vegetables with rice) and sushi (sushi bar at night). The service is a little slow.

Milagros
$10-$20
every day 8am to 9:30pm
Corner of Hana Hwy. & Baldwin Ave., Paia
☎579-8755

Of all the restaurants in Paia, Milagros may be the most popular, especially with surfers and windsurfers. There is a good selection of Mexican dishes (burritos, enchiladas, tacos) that often feature fresh fish, as well as a small array of Hawaiian regional food (especially pasta).

Moana Bakery & Café
$10-$20
every day 7am to 9pm
71 Baldwin Ave., Paia
☎579-9999

The decor of this pastry-shop-tea-house

is somewhat kitschy, with fake Greek columns and plastic palm trees, but there is a good selection of tarts, *palmiers*, apple turnovers, chocolate eclairs and blueberry strudels made by a French pastry chef. You can come here for breakfast or have a big salad, pasta or a sandwich for lunch. The dinner selection is a little more limited, inspired by regional cooking. Choices include lemongrass shrimp, vegetable Napoleon, *'opakapaka ahi* or *laulau* and filet mignon.

Marco's Grill & Deli
$15-$25
every day 7:30am to 10pm
444 Hana Hwy., Kahului
☎877-4446

Located right near the airport at the edge of Kahului, Marco's is a family affair and is a cross between an Italian eatery (the chef's homeland) and a sports bar with mounted television screens and fake leather booths. The menu is very predictable but the food is well prepared. The choices are salad, pizza (you choose the toppings), different kinds of sandwiches and a huge selection of pasta and desserts. The prosciutto, vodka rigatoni and tiramisu are house specialties.

Paia Fishmarket Restaurant
$15
every day 11am to 9:30pm
110 Hana Hwy., Paia
corner of Baldwin Ave.
☎*579-8030*
This small restaurant with large tables and wooden benches is the family restaurant *par excellence*. Fish is prepared in every way imaginable: grilled, sautéed, in sashimi, in tacos, with pasta, shrimp and fries, calamari and fries and more. You can also opt for a salad. Guests order at the counter, then take a seat and wait for the food. The setting is pleasant, with bamboo mats and a large tuna hanging from the ceiling.

Sam Choy's
$15-$30
Mon to Fri 8am to 9pm, Sat to Sun from 7am
275 Ka'ahumanu Ave., Kahului
Ka'ahumanu Center
☎*893-0366*
True to his values, Sam Choy built his newest restaurant in a busy everyday commercial area rather than in a tourist district. As in his other restaurants, the food is influenced by nouvelle cuisine and by the culinary traditions of the various islands. The lunch menu is simple and affordable, with hamburgers, sandwiches, salads, noodles, teriyaki and plate lunches, all distinctly "Sam Choy." To better appreciate the distinct style, come here in the evening to try such

dishes as *laulau*, Ka'u orange duck and *ono* with macadamia nuts. The portions are gigantic, but the restaurant is a little noisy.

Mama's Fish House Restaurant
$20-$40
every day 11am to 2:30pm and 5pm to 9:30pm
799 Poho Pl., Paia (Mile 8)
☎*579-8488*
This famous seafood restaurant is located across from a little beach just west of Ho'okipa Beach, a windsurfing haven. The fish is as fresh as ever, though the relaxed atmosphere has become somewhat more formal over the years and the prices have risen considerably. The menu has become more heavily influenced by Hawaiian cuisine. The *moi* is served with a salad of hearts of palm and *po'hole* ferns, and the sesame *'ahi* comes with a papaya sauce and sweet-potato fries.

Kihei

Offering the same quality of food, restaurants located in the shopping centres are often half as expensive as those along the coast.

Alexander's
under $10 to $20
every day 11am to 9pm
1913 South Kihei Rd.
☎*874-0788*
Kihei's king of fish & chips is located across

from Kalama Park, and is always completely full. *Mahi-mahi, ono* and *'ahi* are served along with oysters, shrimp, chicken and ribs. All meals come with coleslaw and fries (or rice). You can eat outside on the terrace.

Canton Chef
under $10 to $20
every day 11am to 2pm and 5pm to 9pm
2463 South Kihei Rd.
Kamaole Shopping Center
☎*879-1988*
The food is Cantonese, but Szechwan as well (with varying degrees of spiciness), with a large selection of fish and seafood. Like other establishments in the area, the restaurant offers inexpensive plate lunches with a choice of beef teriyaki, lemon chicken or chicken with barbecue sauce, ribs and wontons. Rice and salad are included. Unique house specialties, such as abalone with black mushrooms, are more expensive.

Da Kitchen
under $10
every day 8am to 9pm
2439 South Kihei Rd.
Rainbow Mall
☎*875-7782*
This mini-chain also has locations in Wailuku and Kahului, and is very popular with locals for its simple, inexpensive Hawaiian cuisine. Here, *saimin, kalua* pork, *loco moco* and chicken teriyaki are featured.

El Restaurante Pasatiempo
under $10
Mon to Sat 11am to 9pm
1279 South Kihei Rd.
Azeka Place II
☎*879-1089*
The decor is a little cold for a Mexican restaurant, but the menu brings a touch of warmth and the live music on Friday and Saturday nights stirs things up even more. The *chimichangas* tamales and *enchiladas verdes* are very reasonably priced. The combo platter with *taquitos*, tacos, quesadillas and guacamole is easily an entire day's worth of food.

Hawaiian Moons
under $10
Mon to Sat 8am to 9pm,
Sun 8am to 7pm
2411 South Kihei Rd.
☎*875-4356*
This popular organic food store has a small deli with appetizers at $5 per pound (potato salad, noodle salad, taboule, marinated vegetables). You can also buy sushi, cookies and freshly squeezed fruit and vegetable juice.

Kihei Caffe
under $10
Mon to Sat 5am to 3pm,
Sun 6am to 3pm
1945 South Kihei Rd.
☎*879-2230*
This is the best breakfast place in Kihei. Of course, you'll have to be assertive to order your eggs, bagels and pancakes since it's always very busy. Fruit salad and papaya with yogurt and granola are also an excellent treat

on a hot morning. In addition to breakfast, the place has a good selection of reasonably priced sandwiches and salads.

The Coffee Store
under $10
every day 6am to 10pm,
Fri to Sat until 11pm
1279 South Kihei Rd.
Azeka Place II
☎*871-6860*
This coffeehouse is located in a shopping centre, but is a pleasant place to enjoy a coffee or a frappé (various flavours) along with a salad, bagel, pastry or fruit salad.

The Kalbi House
under $10
Mon to Sat 9:30am to
9:30pm, Sun 11am to
9pm
1215 South Kihei Rd.
Long's Center
☎*874-8454*
A local establishment through and through, the specialties at Kalbi House are Korean barbecue, reasonably priced plate lunches, fish and teriyaki or *katsu* meats (fried in a batter), not to mention the large selection of noodles (*saimin*, *udon*, and Korean *kook soo* with or without meat). You can also order *bulgoki*, cooked meat sliced at your table in a ceramic stewpot, served with rice and vegetables.

Antonio's
$10-$25
Tue to Sun 5pm to
9:30pm
1215 South Kihei Rd.
Long's Center
☎*875-8800*
Chef Antonio Fontana is 100% Sicilian, so obviously the cuisine has a strong Italian influence. Fontana always dons a pirate's kerchief, and the food gives off the heady aromas of southern Italy. Try the *pasta al salmone* with a creamy vodka and tomato sauce, or the excellent *osso buco*. The tiramisu is a big hit for dessert. If money is an object, there is an early-bird special discount on the spaghetti *a la bolognese*.

Royal Thai Cuisine
$10-$15
breakfast Mon to Fri
11am to 3pm, dinner
every day 4:45pm to
9:30pm
1280 South Kihei Rd.
Azeka Place
☎*874-0813*
With more than 90 dishes to choose from, a good third of which are vegetarian, this restaurant serves food in the grand Thai tradition: noodles with tofu, curries, meat and fish in peanut sauce. All dishes can be ordered spicy or mild, depending on how you prefer them.

Stella Blues Cafe
$10-$15
every day 8am to 9pm
1215 South Kihei Rd.
Long's Center
☎874-3779
This place is popular with tourists and locals alike, offering a large selection of inexpensive sandwiches, hamburgers, bagels and gigantic salads for lunch, as well as Hebrew National hot dogs with sauerkraut. The dinner selections are slightly more elaborate and the prices a little higher.

Jameson's Grill & Bar
$20-$30
every day 8am to 3pm and 5pm to 10pm
2259 South Kihei Rd.
☎891-8860
The menu here has lots of variety, blending local specialties (*paniolo* for breakfast with Portuguese sausages and even *saimin*) with international and modern Hawaiian foods (pepper tuna steak, catch of the day). The calamari salad with spinach, tomatoes and Maui-grown onions is an enjoyable take on the classic Caesar salad. The wine list is extensive, with 425 kinds sold by the bottle and 25 by the glass.

Pizazz Café
$20-$25
Tue to Sun 11am to midnight (Sun until 11pm)
1279 South Kihei Rd.
Azeka Place II
☎891-2123
Don't be misguided by the name; Pizazz Café makes few pizzas. The name is just a bad play on words to indicate that owner Yorman Williams takes to his double bass on weekend evenings (*Thursday to Sunday*) and fills the room with jazz along with his band. Music is certainly the theme here: even the bar is in the shape of a violin. The restaurant is still in the process of establishing itself, and is one of the few places in Hawaii that specialize in Cajun cuisine. You can order a *po'boy* sandwich for lunch (fried sheat-fish), and *jambalaya* (a sort of paella), *gumbo* and fried okra for dinner. It's basically Louisiana served on a plate!

The Greek Bistro
$20-$25
every day 5pm to 10pm
2511 South Kihei Rd.
Ke Nani Village
☎879-9330
For a change of taste or to evoke memories of the Aegean, head to The Greek Bistro to savour souvlaki, leg of mutton or kebabs. You can enjoy a "feast fit for the gods" with *sirtaki* in the background on the lovely terrace across from Kamaole Beach Park II, dining on *moussaka, pastichio,* lamb and *spanakopita.*

Carelli's on the Beach
$25-$40
every day 6pm to 10pm
2980 South Kihei Rd.
☎875-0001
Located behind the Maui Oceanfront Inn, Carelli's is right on Keawakapu's lovely little beach. The menu is pricey, and mainly features adapted Italian cuisine and some international dishes. Don't plan to come and enjoy this refined setting and only order a pizza; there is a minimum charge of $25 per person. Talk about exclusive!

A Pacific Café
$30-$40
every day 5:30pm to 9:30pm
1279 South Kihei Rd.
Azeka Place II
☎879-0069
This is a return to his roots for Jean-Marie Josselin, one of the leading figures in regional Hawaiian cuisine. Josselin brought his nouvelle cuisine to Maui when he took over the kitchen at the renowned restaurant of the Hana-Maui hotel. Of course, with all the new restaurants under his direction he hardly ever toils over the stove anymore. Chef George Gomes puts together delightful meals worthy of the Pacific Café's reputation, using local ingredients and culinary influences from the other islands.

Wailea to Makena

Caffe Ciao
under $10 to $30
deli every day 6:30am to 10pm, restaurant 11am to 10pm
4100 Wailea Alanui
Kea Lani Hotel (see p 357)
☎875-4100
The restaurant in the Kea Lani Hotel is part

Maui

restaurant, part deli, specializing in northern Italian cuisine. With a lovely decor reminiscent of a fine Italian grocer, the deli serves all sorts of dishes including pizza and sandwiches, as well as delicious smooth ice cream (the strawberry is especially good!). The restaurant serves more elaborate meals, and the menu includes minestrone, veal scallop with mushrooms, salmon *carpaccio* and seafood linguine with olives and capers.

Hakone
$20-$50
Mon (buffet) 6pm to 9pm,
Tue to Sat 6pm to 9:30pm
5400 Makena Alanui
Maui Prince Hotel (see p 357)
☎875-5888
The Japanese restaurant in the Maui Prince Hotel has an excellent reputation, and showcases different types of Japanese cuisine, enhanced by unique tropical touches evident in the "aloha rolls" adorned with edible flowers and the taro tempura ice cream with mandarin sauce. Those who prefer more traditional fare won't be disappointed either. The cost of the meal depends on how exotic your tastes are and how much you eat. The

three fixed-price menus are more affordable.

Hula Moons
$15-$40
every day 11am to 10pm
3700 Wailea Alanui
Outrigger Wailea Resort
(see p 356)
☎879-1922
Hula Moons is named after the book of poetry by Hawaii's bard, Don Blanding, to whom the decorations on the wall pay tribute. Located by the swimming pool, the restaurant serves local-style hamburgers and sandwiches as well as salad with onion rings made from onions grown on Maui. Dinner is more formal, with meat and seafood dishes. Be sure to leave room for the stunning all-you-can-eat "Chocoholic dessert bar" laden with brownies, mousse, pies and cakes. The buffet alone is worth the trip!

Joe's Bar & Grill
$20-$40
every day 5:30pm to 10pm
131 Wailea Ike Pl.
☎875-7767
Surprisingly, since it is located in Wailea's tennis club, this restaurant is open only in the evenings. The place is named after the husband of Beverly Gannon, chef of the famous Hali'imaile Store (see p 376). This place also uses fresh ingredients but in a more refined, continental manner, to create such delights as

meatloaf, leg of mutton, veal cutlet, freshly caught fish and seafood ragout.

Prince Court
$20-$40
every day 6pm to 9:30pm
5400 Makena Alanui
Maui Prince Hotel (see p 357)
☎875-5888
The Prince Court strikes a delicate balance between traditional Hawaiian cuisine and regional nouvelle cuisine, with strong Asian influences. The menu lists items as diverse as *laulau*, *kalua* duck, lobster cakes, spring rolls and salmon prepared in innovative ways, as well as quail salad with a mandarin dressing and marinated roast pheasant with lemongrass and ginger served on a bed of Thai noodles. There is a seafood and rib buffet on Fridays, and a champagne brunch on Sundays.

SeaWatch Restaurant
$25-$40
every day 8am to 10pm
100 Wailea Golf Club Dr.
☎875-8080
Located on Wailea's Gold and Emerald Golf Courses, the SeaWatch is run by the same trio as the Plantation House in Kapalua. Like the other establishment, it has a lovely view of the sea, facing Molokini and Kaho'olawe islands. The Hawaiian emphasis is evident in everything from the salads with meat toppings to the sandwiches. Breakfast and lunch are served all day

from 8am to 3pm. The dinner menu has a good selection of fish.

Humuhumunukunukuapua'a
$30-$50
every day 5:30pm to 10pm
3850 Wailea Alanui
Grand Wailea Resort
(see p 357)
☎ *875-1234*

Surrounded by an artificial lagoon just a few steps from the beach, this restaurant prides itself for its large aquarium filled with fish from the reef, including the incredible *humuhumunukunukuapua'a*, Hawaii's "national" fish. The Polynesian theme is reflected in the large *tikis* and in the food, which is regional Hawaiian cuisine with an emphasis on fish and seafood, thought there are also some meat dishes. Few can resist the delicious desserts, especially the "Picasso plate" composed of raspberry, mango and lychee sorbets topped with macadamia nuts.

Kincha
$30-$65
every day 6pm to 10pm
3850 Wailea Alanui
Grand Wailea Resort (see p 357)
☎ *875-1234*

Here, guests are plunged into an archaic setting as soon as they step off the elevator, which is the only way of getting to the restaurant. The decor evokes a traditional Japanese country house. The restaurant features a bar, small rooms with tatami mats and a sushi bar with tables looking out into the gardens with a small artificial waterfall. Sushi, sashimi and tempura are served along with salmon in a sake and teriyaki sauce, *wafu* steak, Japanese fish soup and seven-spice *opakapaka*. The most expensive fixed-price menu is the *omakase*, which comes with nine dishes. Kincha is located on the fourth floor, just below the hotel reception.

Nick's Fishmarket
$30-$50
every day 5:30pm to 10pm
4100 Wailea Alanui
Kea Lani Hotel (see p 357)
☎ *875-4100, ext. 290*

As its name indicates, Nick's specializes in fish and seafood prepared in classic "Pacific Rim" style. There are also some good meat dishes and, if money is no object, caviar shipped directly from Russia. You can eat indoors or on the poolside terrace from which you can almost see the ocean.

Seasons
$75-$95
Tue to Sat 6pm to 9:30pm
3900 Wailea Alanui
Four Seasons Resort
(see p 357)
☎ *874-8000*

The Four Seasons' most upscale restaurant has an elegant yet airy atmosphere and overlooks the pool and the ocean. Designated Best Restaurant in Maui, it serves refined "Pacific Rim" cuisine that highlights fresh local ingredients and betrays some strong French influences. The fixed-price menus do not include wine, and it goes without saying that Seasons is reserved for the (very) wealthy, or for special occasions.

The Backcountry

Casanova Deli
under $10
Mon to Sat 7:30am to 6pm, Sun 8:30am to 5pm
1188 Makawao Ave., Makawao
at the intersection of highways 365 and 390
☎ *572-0220*

This place serves some of the best croissants on Maui, and maybe even in all of Hawaii! This is a cheaper option than the adjacent Casanova restaurant (see p 376). The deli was established by a real Italian, and serves pastries and baked goods, eggs and coffee in the morning, and sandwiches, pizza, soup, bagels and other items the rest of the day. Gourmets will notice some Italian specialties, as well as Swiss chocolate. You can eat inside in a small corner with Mediterranean colours, or at the counters looking out at the street.

Maui

Duncan's Coffee Company
under $10
every day 7:30am to about 5pm
3647 Baldwin Ave., Makawao
☎573-9075
This place is rare because it still serves tea (many varieties) in real teapots. You can also enjoy a good coffee, pastries or a mango or pineapple smoothie, or cool off with a Lappert's ice cream.

Grandma's Coffee House Cafe
under $10
every day 7am to 5pm
153 Kula Hwy., Keokea
☎878-2140
Whether you prefer black coffee, a *mocha* or a *latte*, this place is sure to win you over. Originally from Puerto Rico, the Franco family has grown coffee on the slopes of Hale'a'kala for four generations. There are also some snacks like salads, sandwiches and pastries. Credit cards are not accepted.

Ulupalakua Ranch Store
under $10
every day 9am to 5pm
Ulupalakua Ranch
Pi'ilani Hwy.
☎878-2561
Located at the end of the wine-tasting room at the Tedeschi Winery, this souvenir store is also a deli that serves hamburgers, pizza, sandwiches, some prepared dishes and pie. This is the last stop before Auntie Jane's truck in Kaupo, 1hr away.

Casanova Restaurant
$10-$20
Mon to Tue 5:30am to 12:30pm, Wed to Sat until 1am
1188 Makawao Ave., Makawao
at the intersection of highways 365 and 390
☎572-0220
This Italian-owned place has a bistro feel, with portraits of *paniolos* donning hats hanging on the walls, and serves excellent pasta. Be sure to try the pizza since the wood oven was actually brought over from Italy. With names like *margherita*, *romana*, *napolia* and *fiorentina* appearing on the menu, this place is sure to transport you to the old country. Those who insist on a tropical twist will find a pineapple *makawao*, but this is really more the place to enjoy *linguini primavera* and *carpese* salad with homemade mozzarella. Wine is available by the glass, and there is a large selection of beer. After dinner, the restaurant comes alive with dancing (see p 381).

Polli's
$10-$15
every day 10am to 10pm
1202 Makawao Ave., Makawao
at the intersection of highways 365 and 390
☎572-7808
The poster at the entrance declares "Say No to Drugs – Say Yes to Tacos." Filled with chicken, *mahi-mahi*, beef, pork, vegetables and even chocolate, tacos certainly run the show here. Polli's also serves other Mexican mainstays such as nachos, burritos and *chiles rellenos* (the name alone makes your mouth water!). The walls and ceiling are covered in Mexican decorations, like wooden chili peppers. The restaurant opens before 10am, but it quickly fills with cyclists who come here for breakfast before their long descent down the slopes of Hale'a'kala.

Hali'imaile General Store
$20-$40
breakfast Mon to Fri 11am to 2:30pm, dinner every day from 5:30pm to 9:30pm
900 Hali'imaile Rd., Hali'imaile
☎572-2666
Run by Beverly Gannon, the old grocery store of the town of Hali'maile has become one of the island's most preferred restaurants. Very new Hawaiian nouvelle cuisine is served in a decor of carved wood and modern ceramics. There are dishes with flavours from around the world, such as fish cakes with Japanese cucumber salad and Peking duck tacos with dried cranberries and *nashi* (Asian pear), seafood coconut curry and barbecued Szechwan salmon with caramelized onions, orange zest, ginger and lemongrass. There are also meat dishes reflecting the *panioli* heritage of this region. People either love it… or hate it.

Kula Lodge Restaurant
$20-$40
every day 6:30am to 9pm
Highway 377 (Mile 5.3), Kula
Kula Lodge (see p 358)
☎*878-1535*
The warm atmosphere of the lodge is carried through to the restaurant, which is built into a hillside with bay windows that provide a superb view of Maui's central plain, the western mountains and the island of Lana'i. The menu is less elaborate at lunch than in the evening, but both have Hawaiian-style dishes with meat and seafood. There are also organic salads and vegetarian options. Try the chocolate macadamia pie if it's available, served with flavourful vanilla ice cream.

The Road to Hana and Tour of the Island

Auntie Jane's Café
under $10
generally Mon to Sat 10am to 2 or 3pm
Pi'ilani Hwy., Kaupo (Mile 34.5)
Located in an old delivery truck, this is a real institution, and the only place along the highway along the south coast with a sign that announces "Just Like Mom's" in big capital letters! For just a few dollars, Auntie Jane serves locals and tourists her famous rice plate and a seriously fierce coffee that she roasts herself.

Hana Ranch Restaurant
Under $10 to $15
restaurants every day 11am to 2:45pm, Tue 5:30pm to 10pm, Fri to Sat 6pm to 10:30pm
Hana Hwy., Hana
☎*248-8255*
The only real alternative to the ultra-chic and expensive restaurant at the Hana-Maui hotel, the Hana Ranch has a lunch buffet as well as a limited number of à la carte choices ("deluxe" sandwiches, penne, hamburgers). You can add the appetizer buffet for only a few dollars more. The restaurant is open only three nights a week, and reservations are required. You can also order plate lunches, *saimin*, fish & chips, fried chicken, hot dogs, salads and ice cream at the counter to the right of the entrance.

Keanae Landing Stand
under $10
every day 8am to 3pm
Keanae
Located to your right as you arrive on the peninsula, this simple snack stand sells some of the best banana bread around. There are a few other stands at the eastern outskirts of Hana (Half Way to Hana, Uncle Harry's).

Tutu's
under $10
every day 8am to 4pm
Hana Bay Rd., Hana
☎*248-8224*
The food is as mediocre as the reception, but in Hana there aren't many choices when it comes to cheap sandwiches, hot dogs, plate lunches and hamburgers. You can also grab an ice cream to keep you cool on the beach that lies right next to this place.

Hotel Hana-Maui Restaurant
$30-$50
every day 7:30am to 10pm, 11:30am to 2pm and 6pm to 9pm
Hana Hwy., Hana
☎*248-8211*
The restaurant of the Hana-Maui hotel (see p 361) is the only one of its calibre within over an hour's drive. The establishment is obliging to its guests, and serves regional Hawaiian cuisine (*ono* with *po'hole* fern salad, *'ahi* with papaya and date chutney) and more traditional dishes that will appeal to most people (seafood *penne*, steak with french fries and beans). There is an all-you-can-eat buffet on Sundays with a *hula* show and Hawaiian music.
There is also a *hula* show on Thursdays.

Entertainment

Holidays and Festivals

January

Hula Fest Week

Hula competition
at the Lahaina Cannery Mall
☎661-5304

February

Chinese New Year
in Lahaina
☎667-9194
(with the Lion Dance
on Front Street)

Whale Week
in Wailea
☎879-8860

March

**Queen Ka'ahumanu
Festival**
at the Ka'ahumanu Shopping
Center in Kahului
☎877-3369
(with exhibits, games
and more)

Whale Fest
in Lahaina
☎667-9194

East Maui Taro Festival
in Hana
☎248-8972

April

David Malo Day
at Lahainaluna High School in
Lahaina
☎662-4000
(with a *hula* competi-
tion)

Buddha Day
at the Lahaina Jodo Mission
☎661-4304

**Banyan Tree Birthday
Party**
in Lahaina
☎667-9194

May

May Day
May 1
at the Outrigger Wailea Resort
☎879-1922
(a *lei* and Hawaiian
music competition)

In Celebration of Canoes
in Lahaina
☎667-9194
(with a flotilla of ca-
noes from around the
Pacific)

June

**King Kamehameha Parade
and Day Celebration**
in Lahaina
☎667-9194

Upcountry Fair
in Makawao
(with a cattle auction,
market, music and
more)

**Bankoh Ki Ho'alu Guitar
Festival**
☎242-7469
(featuring the best Ha-
waiian guitar players –
slack key guitar)

July

**Lantern Boat Ceremony
and Dances**
at the Lahaina Jodo Mission
☎661-4304
(honouring the souls of
the deceased)

**Makawao Parade and Ro-
deo**
July 4
☎572-2076

Keiki Hula Festival
at the Lahaina Cannery Mall
☎661-5304

Maui Onion Festival
at the Ka'anapali Resort
☎661-4567

August

Tahiti Festival
in Wailuku
☎244-5831

Pineapple Festival
at the Ka'ahumanu Shopping
Center in Kahului
☎877-3369, ext. 25

September

**International Cultural
Festival in Lahaina**
☎661-5304

Aloha Festival
☎800-852-7690

October

Aloha Festival
(continued)

Halloween
in Lahaina
☎667-9175
(the "Mardi Gras of the
Pacific")

November

Hula o Na Keiki
at the Ka'anapali Beach Hotel
☎661-0011
(children's *hula* competition)

International Film Festival
at the Maui Arts and Cultural
Center in Kahului
☎800-752-8193

December

Christmas and **New Year**

Theatre and Performances

Free Shows

Several hotels and shopping centres on the island host free *hula* performances, many of them in West Maui. Among these locations are **Hale Kahiko**, a reconstructed Hawaiian village behind the Lahaina Center *(Wed and Fri 2pm to 6pm)*, the **Lahaina Cannery Mall** *(Tue and Thu 7pm, Sat and Sun 1pm)*, **Whalers Village** *(Mon, Wed, Fri 7pm)*, **Kapaula Shops** *(Fri 11:30am)* and the **Ka'anapali Beach Hotel** *(every day 6:30pm)*. Consult the free brochures to confirm the times.

Most large hotels organize a ceremony featuring torches at sunset. By far the most impressive of these is held at the **Sheraton Maui** in Pu'u Keka'a

(Ka'anapali) where there is also a reenacted "death plunge" from the cliffs.

Many hotels and resorts have craft demonstrations on Fridays.

Theatres and Performance Halls

Surprisingly, for such a small island, 50% of the financing for the **Maui Arts & Cultural Center** *(☎242-SHOW)* in Kahului comes from the donations of island residents. The centre is home to the Maui Symphonic Orchestra, the Academy of Performing Arts and the Philharmonic Society. Three theatres, seating from 300 to 1,200 people, are used for theatre performances, concerts, festivals and, occasionally, big music stars on tour.

Lahaina's **Maui Myth and Magic Theater** *(878 Front St.)* presents *'Ulalena*, a popular extravaganza that integrates dance, flamboyant costumes, history and Hawaiian mythology *(Tue to Sun 6:30pm and 9pm)*.

The Lahaina Center's new magic show, **Warren & Annabelle's** *($36; Mon to Sat 7pm; ☎667-6244)*, has already made a name for itself, thanks to its special effects and the intimate setting in a space that seats only 80 spectators. You can have dinner here before the show.

The **Hawai'i Experience Domed Theater** *($7; every hour 10am to 10pm; 824 Front St., ☎661-8314)* offers an entirely different type of entertainment. Here, 40min films about Hawaii are screened every hour on a 360° screen.

Luaus

The **Old Lahaina Lu'au** *($65; ☎667-1998)* is one of the most popular on the island, thanks to its proximity to downtown Lahaina, its seaside location and its (relative) authenticity. The *lu'aus* are held every day near the Lahaina Cannery Mall, north of downtown.

Many tourist resorts on the west coast organize their own *lu'aus*. The **Maui Marriott** in Ka'anapali *(every day; ☎661-5828)* arranges Hawaiian games and cultural activities before bringing out the pig for the *imu* ceremony, the buffet and Polynesian entertainment. The **Royal Lahaina Resort** *(☎661-9119)* also hosts a daily *lu'au* that can be enjoyed with or without the buffet *($62 with buffet, $35 with dessert only)*. The **Hyatt Regency** *(☎667-4727)* also organizes *lu'aus*. The Polynesian Hula Show held every Friday at the **Sea House Restaurant** *(Napili Kai Beach Resort, ☎669-1500)* is also worth noting, and features the employees' children.

The best *lu'au* on the south coast is organized by the **Outrigger Wailea Resort** *($62; Mon, Tue, Thu and Fri;* ☎*879-1922)*. Every show features Ifi So'o, a Samoan Fire and Knife dancer (the world champion in this dance!). The **Renaissance Wailea Beach Resort** *(Tue, Thu and Sat;* ☎*879-4900)* also has *lu'aus*.

Feast at Lele *(Tue, Thu and Sat; 505 Front St.,* ☎*667-5353)* is somewhere between a restaurant and a *lu'au*. The dinner menu (not a buffet) is the creation of James MacDonald, chef of the Pacific'O and the I'O, and integrates the cuisine of the four Pacific archipelagos, namely Hawaii, Tahiti, Tonga and Samoa. The meal is followed by a music and dance performance.

Bars and Nightclubs

Lahaina

Cheeseburger in Paradise
(see p 362)
811 Front St.
☎*661-4855*
Home of the Mauian hamburger, this joint fills with crowds of locals every night and moves to the rhythms of rock music.

Longhi's
(see p 363)
888 Front St.
☎*667-2288*
Featuring live music, Longhi's is the place for after-dinner dancing on Friday nights. There is a cover charge for those who do not dine here.

Maui Brews
900 Front St. (Lahaina Center)
☎*667-7794*
Maui Brews consists of a rather humdrum restaurant, a well-stocked bar and a nightclub. With a selection of 22 bottled beers and 16 on tap, it is unlikely you will leave this place disappointed, except maybe with the outcome of the soccer game on TV. The nightclub grooves to different kinds of music almost every night, featuring touring various bands. Styles range from reggae, salsa, rock and "oldies" to Hawaiian music. On weekends, a DJ spins the tunes.

Moose McGillicuddy's
(see p 363)
844 Front St.
☎*667-7758*
At Moose McGillicuddy's, drinks go for rock-bottom prices during Happy Hour, from 3pm to 6pm. After dinner, music takes over from the restaurant with its kitschy decor and walls covered with old posters and yellowed photographs. Live bands play here every night, starting at 9:30pm.

Ka'anapali and the Tourist Coast

Sansei
(see p 367)
Kapalua Shops
115 Bay Dr., Kapalua
☎*669-6286*
Karaoke fans take over this Japanese-American restaurant every Thursday and Friday after 10pm.

Weeping Banyan Bar
Hyatt Regency Maui (see p 350)
200 Nohea Kai Dr.
☎*667-4727*
Don't expect a banyan tree here, because you won't find one. Still, this bar is the perfect place to relax and watch the sunset at the end of a day, as it is situated between a courtyard and gardens planted with coconut trees. Surrounded by water, the bar feels like a floating island and is decorated in a tropical theme. There is a ceremony of torches every evening at 6:15pm, followed by Hawaiian music.

Kahului to Wailuku

Sal's Place
162 Alamaha St., Kahului
☎*893-0609*
Sal's has it all: an Italian restaurant and a sushi bar, both with a sports-bar ambiance, as well as a nightclub. There is live music on Thursday, Friday and Saturday nights.

The South Coast (Kihei to Makena)

Hapa's Brew House
41 East Lipoa St., Kihei
☎879-9001
This place is so successful it has no need to create any hype. In addition to a restaurant (standard and rather pricey), a bar and a nightclub, the establishment is in the process of adding a sushi bar to the premises. Local bands play here on some nights (*mainly Mondays and Fridays*), and DJs are also featured. The "Sonic Party" on Sundays is targeted to 13- to 18-year-olds from 6pm to 10pm, and 18 and over after 10pm.

Molokini Lounge
5400 Makena Alanui, Makena
Maui Prince Hotel (see p 357)
☎874-1111
A good place to go for a drink, with one of two Hawaiian singers providing the entertainment every night, alternating every other week.

Sunset Terrace
3550 Wailea Alanui, Wailea
Renaissance Wailea Beach Resort (see p 357)
☎879-4900
The terrace has a view not of the beach, but of the sea (!) which lies behind the screen of coconut trees. If you look carefully between the palms you might see a whale in the winter, as you sip a colourful cocktail. They even tell you exactly when the sun will set, to make sure you don't miss the sight, with

Hawaiian music playing in the background.

Tsunami
3850 Wailea Alanui, Wailea
Grand Wailea Resort (see p 357)
☎875-1234
A large, chic establishment (no T-shirts allowed), the isthmus's most fashionable nightclub is open only from Thursday to Saturday.

The Backcountry

Casanova Restaurant
1188 Makawao Ave., at the intersection of highways 365 and 390
☎572-0220
This very popular Italian restaurant on the Makawao strip (see p 376) becomes a nightclub after dinner from Wednesday to Saturday nights. People dance as bands play modern Hawaiian music, funk and reggae, making Casanova one of the favourite local nightspots on Maui. Internationally known groups have played here.

The Road to Hana and a Tour of the Island

Paniolo Bar
Hotel Hana-Maui
Hana Hwy., Hana
☎248-8211
The Paniolo Bar opens onto the gardens next to the hotel's restaurant. Simple dishes are served here during the day, and in the evening it becomes Hana's liveliest nightspot. Live Hawaiian music is

featured on Thursday and Sunday nights.

Shopping

Shopping Centres

Lahaina is not short on shopping centres! Right downtown, across from Banyan Square, is the **Wharf Cinema Center**, with some 50 shops and restaurants on three floors, as well as a cinema. Farther south along the shore is **505 Front Street**. To the north is the **Lahaina Center** (*900 Front St.,* **☎667-9216**), with a large Hilo Hattie, a store specializing in Hawaiian products. The large **Cannery Mall** (*1221 Honoapi'ilani Hwy.,* **☎661-5304**) is located in an old cannery, and resembles the average North American shopping mall (with air conditioning guaranteed!).

Whaler's Village (*2435 Ka'anapali Pkwy.,* **☎661-4567**) is one of Maui's most popular shopping centres, both because of its numerous shops and restaurants and because of its museum showcasing the history of whaling. It is located near the beach by the Ka'anapali resort.

The island's largest shopping centre, the **Ka'ahumanu Center** (*275 Ka'ahumanu Ave.,* **☎877-4325**), is located at the western edge of Kahului. There are more than 100 shops, as well as several restaurants and cinemas.

Kihei's main shopping centres, **Kama'ole Shopping Center**, **Azeka** (Plaza I and II) *(1279 and 1280 South Kihei Rd., ☎879-5000)*, are smaller and more widely scattered. **The Shops at Wailea** were still under construction in early 2000, but should open during the year, perhaps even in summer. Most of the stores here sell clothing.

Local Merchandise

Local items associated with Maui are available in shopping centres and in souvenir stores. These include island-grown onions, cookies of various kinds but always containing macadamia nuts, *manju* (a type of Japanese cake made with red beans) and protea sold individually or in bouquets and which can last weeks without drying or losing their colour. In addition to the Hilo Hattie store in Lahaina, the Maui Tropical Plantation, on the outskirts of Wailuku, sells all sorts of Hawaiian souvenirs, including clothing, natural products and jams.

Arts and Crafts

Lahaina alone has some 20 **galleries** that sell paintings (of varying quality), antiques (ranging from very old to fairly recent), and sculptures (both modern and traditional). Seascapes are especially well represented, having been popularized in Hawaii by Wyland more than 20 years ago. Some appreciate this style of art while others find it affected or contrived... to each their own. Every Friday is **Art Night** *(6pm to 10pm)* in Lahaina, when the galleries open their doors and invite art afficionados – and others – to step in for wine and appetizers, while music plays in the background. The **Martin Lawrence Gallery** at the corner of Front Street and Lahainaluna Road *(☎661-1788)* is one of the best, and usually has interesting lithographs by well-known artists.

Lahaina is also the *scrimshaw* capital. Although old ivory can no longer be found and sperm whales are not hunted anymore, some sculptors carve fossilized bones or those of Alaskan walrus (which can still be legally hunted). This type of craftsmanship has undergone significant

change over the years, and is now often done in conjunction with goldsmithing. The more elaborate, multicoloured pieces can be worth a fortune.

Markets

Maui has two **Farmer's Markets**: one is in Kihei *(north of the city, near Suda's Store; Mon, Wed and Fri 1:30pm to 5:30pm)*, the other in Honokowai *(in the parking lot of the Hawaiian Moons organic supermarket, across from Honokowai Park; Mon, Wed and Fri 7am to 11am)*. Both markets sell the same variety of organic fruits and vegetables, flowers, cheeses, pastries and freshly baked bread.

Markets are also held at the Kahului Shopping Center on Wednesdays *(7am to noon)*, in Hana on Thursdays *(9:30am to 3:30pm)* and at the K'ahumanu Shopping Center on Fridays *(9am to 5pm)*.

The **Maui Swap Meet** is held at the Kahului Fairgrounds every Saturday from 7am to 1pm. You can find everything and anything in its many little stands: clothing, souvenirs, knick-knacks old and new, fruits, vegetables and much more.

L ana'i, which means
"bump" in Hawaiian, gets its name from its shape. Indeed, from Maui, the island looks like a diving whale.

Formed 1.2 to 1.4 million years ago, Lana'i is not as high as its neighbouring islands. With Lana'ihale peaking at over 3,300ft (1,026m), the mountain cradles Palawai Basin, the crater of its ancient volcano. The rest of the island is quite flat.

Lana'i is quite significant in Hawaiian mythology. Legend says that it is here, in a place called Kumoku (island of Ku) that the four main gods landed in Hawaii: Ku and his wife Hina, then Kane and Kanaloa. The island was uninhabited for a long time, since the ancient Hawaiians believed the island was haunted by the *ka polo*, or evil spirits. But one day, Kualula'au, the tempermental but courageous son of a Maui chief, was exiled to Lana'i and he succeeded in banishing the *ka polo* from the island,

which finally allowed settlers to come there.

Farming land in the 19th century, a Mormon colony and an equally short-lived sugar-cane plantation, the island of Lana'i came together under a single banner at the turn of the 20th century. In 1904, Charles Gay began buying land on the island and four years later owned in its entirety. Gay set up one of Hawaii's largest ranches in Ko'ele, on the central plateau, and in 1922, he sold Lana'i

to James Dole, the "pineapple king" and inventor of the fruit-packing machine. The entrepreneur then founded what was to become the world's biggest pineapple plantation (19,027 acres or 7,700ha) in the central crater where fields of pineapple flourished for three generations and later gave Lana'i its nickname: "The Pineapple Island."

The unthinkable happened in 1993 when, victim of international competition, the

Dole company – purchased by Castle & Cooke, one of Hawaii's "Big Five" – harvested its last crop. The ambitious consortium had launched Lana'i into a new venture that many considered risky: tourism. Instead of growing pineapples, Lana'i would cater to luxury. Under the iron fist of the Lana'i Company and with the help of hundreds of millions of dollars, the island saw the birth of two prestigious resorts: the mountain Lodge at Ko'ele and the seaside Manele Bay Hotel. Former pineapple-industry employees became tour guides, receptionists, porters or even bellboys. The rural exodus came to a halt and, despite the protest of a minority, the construction of new luxury accommodations promised better days for Lana'i.

Hawaiians who never previously set foot on Lana'i are coming to the island in increasingly greater numbers. Today, the island welcomes around 100,000 visitors a year – 25% more than Moloka'i – including many celebrities. Red

from laterite and dry with the exception of the mountains, the island is not picture-perfect Hawaii; Lana'i is 141 sq mi (365km²) of quasi-desert, a village island where everybody knows and greets each other. Its new promotional slogan, "Hawaii's Most Secluded Island," is no overstatement. Despite new projects, wide-open spaces remain and virtually all of the island's 2,800 residents still live in Lana'i City, which has the unmistakable feel of a plantation village. Here, there are neither shopping centres nor traffic lights.

Finding Your Way Around

Airport

Located 3mi (5km) west of Lana'i City, the island's small airport was entirely renovated after the Lodge at Ko'ele and the Manele Bay Hotel opened. It receives flights from Honolulu (two daily flights on Hawaiian, flights every 2hrs on Aloha Islandair from 6am to 6pm), but also from Kahului (three daily flights on Islandair), Kona (one daily flight on Islandair) and weekends from Moloka'i.

Shuttles from the Lodge at Ko'ele and Manele Bay Hotel pick up guests for $10. If you are staying at the Lana'i Hotel, you can also take the shuttle and be dropped off at the hotel.

Transportation

Airlines

Aloha Islandair
☎565-6744 or 800-652-6541

Hawaiian
☎565-6977 or 800-367-5320

Maritime Shuttles

Shuttles (☎661-3756 or 800-695-2624) travel to Lana'i five times a day

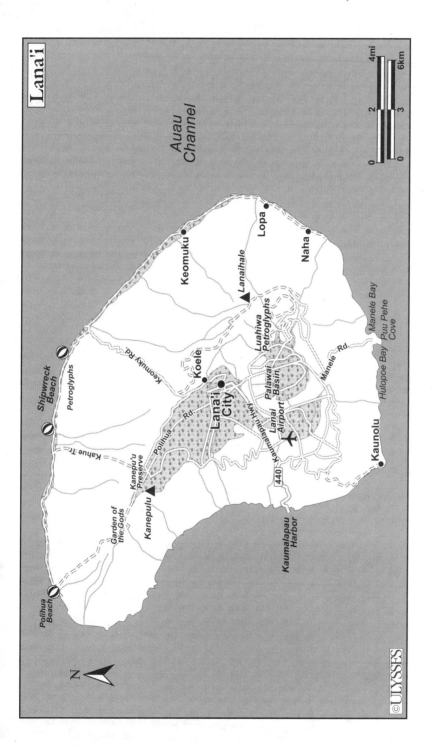

from the port of Manele, at Lahaina on the island of Maui. The crossing *($25, $20 from two to 11 years of age)* takes a little less than 1hr. The first departure is at 8am and the last return trip leaves at 6:45pm. With a bit of luck, in winter you might even catch a glimpse of some whales. The agency also offers day packages, including course fees for Experience at Ko'ele or Challenge at Manele (see p 394), and even trips of several days.

Roads

Only three of the island's roads (covering a total of 31mi or 50km) are paved, beginning in Lana'i City. The most popular, Manele Road, crosses through Palawai Basin to the port of Manele and Hulopo'e Beach. Westward, Kaumalapa'u Highway serves the airport and the commercial harbour of Kaumalapa'u. The third road, Keomuku

Road, leads to Shipwreck Beach on the northeast coast. The rest of the island (east and north coasts) is only accessible by trails, which are for the most part easily managed by four-wheel-drive vehicles (except after heavy rain), though unreachable by car.

Car Rental Agencies

The island only has one car rental agency, **Lana'i City Service** *(1036 Lana'i Ave., ☎565-7227 or 800-JEEP-808, ≈565-7087)*, which is affiliated with the Dollar Company. The business, which takes advantage of its unique position, charges $60 a day for a tourist car and $129 for the least expensive of its four-wheel-drive vehicles. Renting a standard vehicle is useless: without a four-wheel-drive vehicle, you won't be able to reach most of the island's intriguing spots, with the exception of Hulopo'e Beach. Making a reservation is recommended since there is only a limited number of vehicles available. Once behind the wheel, be careful not to overestimate your vehicle's capabilities. In addition to the risk of getting into a quarrel with your travelling companion, getting stuck in the mud (the Munro Trail becomes really muddy after heavy rain) will

cost you a long walk and... $145 for towing. This does not mean that the only suitable trails are those you will be pointed out when you sign the contract. Stay clear of the Kaunolu Trail, which is really bad, even in a four-wheel-drive vehicle. If you are leaving the island by boat, you can leave the car at the port *($20 more)*.

Lana'i City Service also has the only service station on the island.

Red Rover *(☎565-7722)* also rents four-wheel-drive vehicles, but only has a few cars available. Similar price range.

Shuttles

There is no public transportation on the island. **Lana'i City Service** *(☎565-7227)*, obviously unavoidable, offers a shuttle service to and from the airport, port, hotels and golf courses. If you are a guest at one of the two major hotels, the round trip to and from the airport will cost you $10, with all other shuttles being free. There are shuttles every hour, Monday to Thursday, and every 30min Friday to Sunday. A day trip will cost you $20 for the round trip between the port and Lana'i City. The Lana'i EcoAdventure Centre *(☎565-7737)* also offers transportation to hikers, cyclists and kayakers throughout the island.

Practical Information

Tourist Information

Destination Lana'i
P.O. Box 700, Lana'i City
HI 96763
☎ *565-7600 or 800-947-4774*
≈565-9316

Post Office

The island's only post office is located on Lana'i Avenue, next to Dole Park *(Mon to Fri, 9am to 4:30pm, Sat 10am to noon)*.

Bank

The only ATM is located in front of the First Hawaiian Bank *(644 Lana'i Ave., ☎ 565-6969)*, east of Dole Park.

Laundromat

Lana'i City's laundromat *(every day, 6am to 9pm)* is located on Seventh Street, on Dole Park, two doors from the Blue Ginger Café.

Grocery Shopping

The city has two small food stores, both located near Dole Park: **Richard's Shopping Center** *(every day, 8:30am to 6:30pm; 434 Eighth St.,*

☎ *565-6047)* and **Pine Isle Supermarket** *(Mon to Sat, 8am to 7pm; 356 Eighth St., ☎ 565-6488)*.

Exploring

The Mountains and the South Coast

(one day)

This first tour between Lana'i City and Hulopo'e Beach, between the Lodge at Ko'ele and the Manele Bay Hotel, mainly features roads that are accessible to all vehicles. If you do not plan on renting a four-wheel-drive vehicle, forget the Munro Trail (or tackle it on foot) and take Manele Road instead.

Located on the central plateau, Lana'i City is home to virtually the entire population, who enjoys the crisp, fresh air at 1,690ft (520m) above sea level. Lanes with rows of small, colourful, and practically identical wooden houses are set up in a grid pattern in the village. Set amongst papaya and banana trees, some homes are bedecked with trophies such as buck antlers or Japanese glass floats. Built in the 1920s when Dole set up the base of his pineapple plantation, the houses are a stone's throw from the headquarters of the

Lana'i Ranch at Ko'ele. Intended for Filipino workers, most of the homes initially had no electricity, bathroom or kitchen. Meals were served in a canteen and bathrooms were shared. Despite significant improvements over the years, housing remains a serious problem on Lana'i, whose population has grown considerably – today, the city numbers nearly 2,800 residents. After having purchased the island, the Lana'i Company launched an extensive construction and renovation program.

Dole Park, at the heart of Lana'i City, consists of a big rectangular lawn with pine trees. Nearly all of the island's businesses and popular restaurants, banks, churches, the police station and post office are located here, on the two streets that delimit the park: Seventh and Eighth.

Past the Lodge at Ko'ele, at the northern exit of Lana'i City, begins Keomuku Highway, the paved road that leads to Shipwreck Beach (see p 392). After 1mi (1.5km), Cemetery Road appears to your right. The paved road comes to an end just past the cemetery, where a clay trail begins with three forks begins. A sign, which changes depending on the season, indicates which trail travellers should take to reach the start of the Munro Trail.

Named after the director of the Lana'i Ranch in the 1930s, who initiated the first reforestation attempt on the island, the **Munro Trail ★** climbs to the highest peak of Lana'ihale, Lana'i's highest point at 3,335ft (1,026m). The mountain is the legendary domain of Hina, goddess of the moon, and is frequently veiled by clouds. It is best not to make the trip if the weather is bad, as you will not be able to enjoy Lana'ihale's greatest feature – the view of the island and neighbouring islands.

The trail is steep and narrow at times, with just enough space for a car to pass, and is only accessible by foot or by four-wheel-drive vehicle. It is 7mi (11.2km) long and is a good hiking challenge – provided that you will be picked up at Palawai Basin (*ask at the Lana'i EcoAdventure Centre,* ☎*565-7737*). While driving, keep an eye open for other vehicles travelling in the opposite direction, and occasionally horses or bicycles. After it rains, the trail is extremely muddy and there is a high risk of getting stuck.

The trail winds through the pine trees and after approximately 1.9mi (3km), you will come to a fork in the trail. Take the wide climbing

curve to the right (there is a dead-end to the left). The forest, nourished by persistent mist, becomes increasingly humid as you drive up. Ferns, *iliau* and *'ohi'a* dominate the scenery. The trail runs along ridges covered with Cook's pines whose silhouettes stand out against the backdrop. When the thick cloud clears up, the peak become visible, as do Moloka'i, Kaho'olawe and Maui off in the distance. The most stunning views from atop Lana'i and neighbouring islands span around 6mi (10km).

The trail leads down to **Palawai Basin**, a vestige of the ancient crater that originally formed Lana'i. For years, the basin held nearly all of the island's pineapple fields. But since the last harvest in 1993, its only regular visitors are grazing cattle. The former boundaries of the cultivated rectangular fields are still easily recognizable from the top of the Munroe Trail and from the airplane, as you land at the airport.

The Munro Trail ends at the Palawai Basin.

The maze of criss-crossing trails will lead you back to Manele Bay Road, but before you reach it, take a short detour through the **Luahiwa Petroglyphs ★★**. It is not easy to find your

The Pineapple

Originally from Paraguay, the pineapple was discovered by the first conquistadors at the dawn of the 16th century, who then presented it to the royal courts of Europe. From there, the fruit conquered the world several times over. The first plants were introduced in Hawaii as early as the start of the 19th century. Islanders, who likened the pineapple to the pandanus (*hala*), named the fruit *hala kahiki* ("foreign *hala*"). Despite the development of several plantations, the impossibility of exporting the fruit without it rotting on the lengthy voyage limited its expansion for a time. At the turn of the 20th century, however, James Dole solved this problem by inventing a pineapple-packaging machine. The archipelago's industry harvested two thirds of the world's pineapple crops during its peak years, between 1930 and 1950.

way between the different trails, but it is important to always keep Lana'ihale to your right. If you are coming

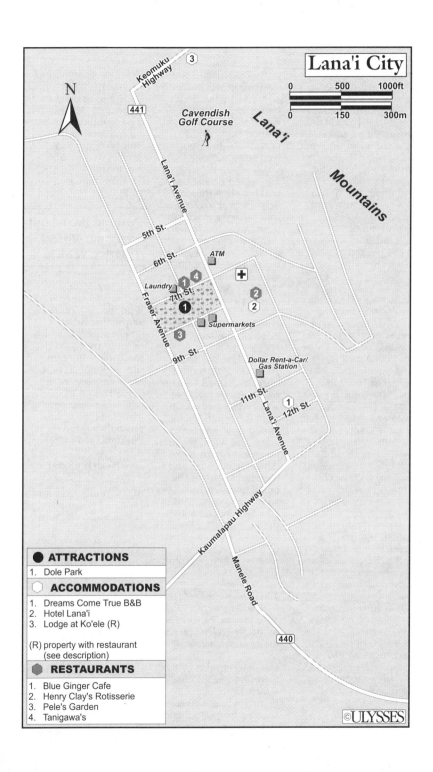

Lana'i City

N

| 0 | 500 | 1000ft |
| 0 | 150 | 300m |

Keomuku Highway
3
441
Cavendish Golf Course
Lana'i
Mountains
Lana'i Avenue
5th St.
6th St.
ATM
Laundry
Fraser Avenue
7th St.
1 4
1
2
2
Supermarkets
3
9th St.
Dollar Rent-a-Car/ Gas Station
11th St.
Lana'i Avenue
1
12th St.
Kaumalapau Highway
Manele Road
440

● **ATTRACTIONS**
1. Dole Park

◯ **ACCOMMODATIONS**
1. Dreams Come True B&B
2. Hotel Lana'i
3. Lodge at Ko'ele (R)

(R) property with restaurant
   (see description)

⬡ **RESTAURANTS**
1. Blue Ginger Cafe
2. Henry Clay's Rotisserie
3. Pele's Garden
4. Tanigawa's

©ULYSSES

directly from Lana'i City, which may be somewhat easier, around 1.5mi (2.5km) south of the city, take the large trail marked by a clump of trees and a stop sign. At the end of the right lane, the trail curves to the right and immediately climbs to a crossroads. Turn left. After 2,625ft (800m), an old wooden sign indicates the way to the petroglyphs. The rocks are a little farther to your right.

The lower side of the crater once featured an *heiau* dedicated to Ku and Hina, the god and goddess of rain. Those who cultivated the fields made their way here to receive the gods' blessing. Some of the big black rocks scattered over the steep slope, to which ancestors attributed the *mana* of gods, are engraved with some 400 drawings. Only 1% were drawn before the 17th century. Many date from the 18th century and mainly feature human figures. The depiction of cows, dogs on leashes, canoes and cavalrymen are for the most part attributed to students of the Lalainaluna seminary vacationing on the island in the 1870s. The presence of these later drawings seriously complicates the work of archaeologists and historians.

Manele Road crosses Palawai Basin before it leads down in tight

turns towards the south coast. You will come to a fork just past the entrance to the Manele Bay Hotel: the left branch leads to the port, while the right leads to the beach.

The island's most beautiful beach is **Hulopo'e Beach ★ ★ ★** *(equipped with washrooms, showers, picnic tables, barbecues, telephones and a campground – see p 396)*, which is also one of Hawaii's finest. It stretches between a public park and the Manele Bay Hotel, which towers over the beach to the west. A Hawaiian village founded between the 10th and 13th centuries once stood here. Historians believe that long ago, navigators coming from the South Pacific ended their journey here. The wide, white fine-sand beach is bordered by coconut and pine trees. This is the only beach on Lana'i where you can swim in complete peace and is the best spot for snorkelling – the bay is part of a marine reserve where fishing is prohibited.

You can take the old path that runs westward along the coast and explore the basins formed in between the rocks at low tide.

Delimited to the east by towering black cliffs, **Manele Bay** shelters a marina where maritime shuttles from Maui and sightseeing boats dock. Up until 1926 and the

creation of the port of Kaumalapa'u, merchant ships also docked in the marina. Manele Bay is part of the same maritime reserve as Hulopo'e, but swimming is not possible due to the marine traffic, even though it is quite light.

Around the Island by Four-Wheel-Drive Vehicle

(one day)

With the exception of Shipwreck Beach, whose shores may be reached by a paved road, all of the other sites mentioned here are accessible by dirt road. The order in which you visit sites matters little, as you must always travel through Lana'i City.

North Coast

At the northern exit of Lana'i City, just past the Lodge at Ko'ele, turn left on a wide trail heading towards the stables, then turn right at the next intersection, onto Polihua Road. You can often see herds of deer late in the day.

When you reach an enclosed area, ignore the sign pointing left to Kanepu'u and go through the surrounding wall protecting the **Kanepu'u Preserve** from intruding deer and moufflon, which used to graze on the young growths and seeds of

Asian Axis Deer

You will have plenty of opportunity to run into Asian axis deer during your strolls throughout the island, and even on the lawn of your hotel. Deer outnumber people two to one here. Travelling in herds, they particularly venture out at dawn and at dusk.

the few endemic plants that still grow here.

Kanepu'u, which can be translated as "kane in the shape of a hill," alludes to the *heiau* that once stood at its peak, where the god was revered. All of the territory between Lana'ihale and the northwest coast was once forested. Today, Kanepu'u holds one of the last vestiges of the island's dry woodland, where you can still see *olopua* and *lama*, typical regional trees. Hawaii has 48 endemic species in all. A few hundred feet from the gate begins a small looped path that takes barely 10min to walk. A kind of "trail game" leads you from one sign to the next, emphasizing the degradation of Lana'i's natural environment. Groups of five or more can contact the Nature Conservancy (☎537-

4508 on O'ahu, ☎565-7430 on Lana'i), which manages the island's only reserve, for a guided tour. Unless you are a botany expert, however, you might not find the place that interesting.

The trail becomes increasingly difficult for vehicles past the reserve. If you are not driving a four-wheel-drive vehicle, it might be better to park your car and continue on foot to the Garden of the Gods (15-20min).

Around 1.2mi (2km) north, the trail leads to the **Garden of the Gods ★★**, a stunning bare little plateau strewn with thousands of rocks. The colour of the laterite and the strange shapes of some piles of stone – more or less assembled by Lana'i residents – are reminiscent of the desolate and chaotic surface of Mars. Lights are most spectacular at sunrise and sunset: yellow, ochre, brown, sienna... an entire sea of colours!

Past the Garden of the Gods, the trail, reserved for four-wheel-drive vehicles from this point on, leads down towards the north coast. You'll reach the grand **Polihua Beach ★★** in 15min. Legend says that Pele used to come here to gather turtle eggs, hence its name, "The Bay of Eggs." Moloka'i towers before you and red, grainy sand swirls, whipping your skin as

waves crash. Polihua is one of Hawaii's few empty beaches; solitude reigns in this place devoid of accommodations and tourists. Currents are violent (their nickname, The Tahitian Express, says it all...) and swimming is absolutely impossible here.

East Coast

From Lana'i City, Keomuku Road climbs a small crest before it winds down towards the extremely dry east coast.

At the end of the paved road, take the trail immediately to your left, which will lead you directly to the littoral.

You will then pass a cluster of old worn-out huts, known as Federation Camp. Dating from the 1930s, they are still used by some residents who come to fish on weekends. The trail ends a little farther, marked by a clump of *kiawe* whose branches bend towards the ground when whipped by the wind. Those who are not in a four-wheel-drive vehicle usually park at the end of the paved road and climb along the edge of the littoral or trail on foot, which adds around 1.5mi (2.5km) to your excursion. This may not be the most attractive section of the trail, but it is pleasant just the same.

At the end of the trail at Po'aiwa, a fairly well-

Lana'i

marked path climbs above the bay of Kaiolohia towards the aptly named **Shipwreck Beach ★★**. Stretching more than 8mi (13km) towards the northern tip of the island, this pretty, deserted beach reveals a series of successive coves. You will soon notice the rusty shipwreck that gave the beach its name. This old U.S. Navy liberty ship must have sunk after the Second World War in the Kalohi Channel, which separates Lana'i from Moloka'i, but ended up washing up near the coast. Parts of the beach are littered with debris washed ashore by storms. If you're really lucky, you just might find a Japanese glass float or some other sea-going treasure. Those who love to take walks can stroll along the shore all the way to Polihua Beach. The foundation of the former lighthouse, which is no longer standing today, lies above the end of the trail. A path between two veils of brushwood leads *mauka* to a huge rock featuring **petroglyphs**, mostly anthropomorphical depictions and animals. To make sure you don't get lost, despite following the short path (around 984ft, 300m), walk between two cairns. The beginning of the path is marked by traces of white paint, but they have almost completely faded. You will know

you are on the right path when you see "Do not deface" written on a rock.

Head back to the end of the paved road.

A long dirt road picks up where the paved road left off and leads down along the island's eastern littoral to Naha, 12mi (20km) away. Easily accessible by four-wheel-drive vehicle during dry weather and flanked by *kiawes*, the trail runs along the coast and offers glimpses of the sea and the island of Maui. The scenery is not particularly spectacular, but the stroll is rather pleasant. Do not believe locals, who rarely trek this far, when they tell you that the trail is one of the worst on the island. With the exception of a short rocky passage after Lopa, the trail is in fact better than the one leading to Polihua Beach, on the north coast. Plan between 45min to 1hr for getting from Shipwreck Beach to Naha.

Malamalama, the ruins of a small wooden church that is being restored in the village of **Keomuku ★**, appears to your right after about 5.7mi (9km). An old sign behind the pulpit reveals that it was opened on October 4, 1903. Seashell *leis*, flowers and a stuffed teddy bear are displayed on what used to be the altar.

The Maunalei Sugar Company, which sought to exploit the eastern side of the island, was founded in Keomuku in 1898. Sugar cane was planted, a small plantation train was set up and the population quadrupled. Soon after, a large proportion of Lana'i's residents was living here. Nevertheless, after falling victim to a series of misfortunes, the company had to close its doors a few years later. Islanders attributed the company's collapse to the destruction of a *heiau* during the construction of the railway. The village, eventually converted to ranching, was abandoned for good in 1954.

Just before you get to the dried-palm fence of the Club Lana'i at Kahalepalaoa, where there used to be a quay, you will come across vestiges of the *heiau*, with a small **Buddhist altar**. For its part, the Club Lana'i is an enclave reserved for those who signed up for an excursion from Maui and is not very interesting.

A little further stretches the lovely beach of **Lopa ★**, where a table shaded by a *kiawe* is the perfect spot to have a picnic. As it directly faces Maui, the beach is rarely littered; swimming, however, is not recommended. The area features four fishponds, only one of which is still above water level.

Just past Lopa, the trail crosses a somewhat difficult, steep and gravelly passage, but quickly leads back to the coast.

The trail ends in **Naha**, whose small beach is protected by two stretches of rock, which hold the vestiges of a former Hawaiian fishpond discovered at low tide. Breathtaking cliffs crown the south and west coasts of the island. Swimming is strongly discouraged, even if some surfers don't think twice about braving the waves formed in Kealaikahiki Channel.

Towards the West

Kaumalapa'u Highway leads westward from Lana'i City to the airport and farther still to the port of the same name, which remains the island's main economic artery. There is nothing to see but the cliffs marking the west coast of Lana'i, stretching north.

Pandanus

Before reaching the port, located 4.1mi (6.5km) from Lana'i City, a path leads to the Hawaiian site of Kaunolu. It is the second to the left past the airport on a right bend. Partially paved, it quickly reverts back to dirt and heads west around the airport. After 2.1mi (3.3km), turn right towards the sea. Gullied by rain, the trail is strictly reserved for four-wheeldrive vehicles and deteriorates rapidly. The last mile is terribly bumpy.

Finally, a sign indicates the entrance to **Kaunolu Interpretive Park ★**. A path dotted with signs takes you around the site in about 1hr and leads down to the seaside.

Research carried out by archaeologists at the Bishop Museum led to the discovery a fishing village, dating from 1500, which expanded little by little under the influence of Maui's *ali'i*. It even appears that Kaunolu, extremely important in Hawaiian myths and legends, eventually became Lana'i's main religious centre. The *heiau* of Halulu featured a rare *pu'uhonua*. In the 18th century, a young Kamehameha sought rest and relaxation here in the summer months. But it is another Maui chief, Kahekili, with whom the place is most often associated. From atop the cliffs, to the west of the village, Kahekili dared his men to practise the little-

known sport of cliff jumping – an 60ft (18m) leap here! Despite the historical significance of the site, the few vestiges scattered over the hillside of the dried-up valley do little justice to its past. The visit may not be worth the bumpy ride...

Outdoor Activities

Swimming and Surfing

Swimming in Lana'i is essentially limited to the pools at the major hotels and the magnificent **Hulopo'e Beach** on the south coast. Forming a marine reserve with neighbouring Manele Bay, this vast playground attracts sunbathers, boogieboard enthusiasts, surfers, snorkellers and divers from all over the island and Maui. The bay is home to a rainbow of tropical fish, the occasional turtle, and even dolphins in summer. Whales splash about a few hundred feet away in wintertime. The most experienced surfers enjoy the breaks of Polihua, Lopa and Naha in summertime.

Lana'i

Scuba Diving and Snorkelling

Lana'i was recently voted among the top ten diving spots by a U.S. magazine. In addition to Hulopo'e Bay, all knowledgeable diving enthusiasts appreciate the beauty of the **Cathedrals** of the superb lava formations of Kaunolu Bay or even those of **Three Stones Bay**. While most diving excursions off the coast of the island are organized in Maui, you can contact Lana'i's Trilogy (☎565-7700 or 888-MAUI-800), the best represented company on the island. Guests at the two resorts have a choice between a snorkelling expedition by catamaran ($95, 4hrs) and deep-sea diving ($140, 4hrs), including underwater caves, lava tunnels, moray eels and reef sharks.

Kayaking

The Lana'i EcoAdventure Centre (☎565-7737) offers a morning kayak/snorkelling package ($70) off the coast of Shipwreck Beach. You can also rent single or tandem kayaks ($30/$55).

Cruises and Fishing

Among the activities offered by Trilogy (☎565-7700 or 888-MAUI-800) from the port of Manele are a 3hr excursion around the island in a zodiac for $95 and a whale-watching excursion for $75 between December and April. Several activities are also available from Maui, particularly dolphin watching; in summertime, these mammals are present in great numbers off the southern coast of the island (by catamaran and, extremely popular, by zodiac). Spinning Dolphin Charters (☎565-6613) also offers excursions from Lana'i to catch the blue marlin of your dreams.

Golf

Golf is Lana'i's best feature. Up high, **Experience at Ko'ele** (☎565-4604) combines the refreshing mountain setting and the charm of an English-style lodge. It was created by Greg Norman and Ted Robinson. The eighth hole is the course's most original, and is located 245ft (75m) below the previous hole at the edge of a small, narrow valley.

The seaside **Challenge at Manele** (☎565-2222) was voted one of the world's top ten new golf courses. Its famous twelfth hole is located on the other side of a cliff nearly 164ft (50m) high...warning to lost-ball experts! This is where Bill Gates got married in 1994. Course fees are high: $175; $125 if you are a guest at one of the two hotels.

There is also a third option, the **Cavendish Golf Course**, a nine-hole course in Lana'i City built between the two world wars. Locals can play for free and visitors can play for a small donation.

Hiking

The island's wilderness makes Lana'i a good place for hiking, as long as you don't mind the monotonous, bland scenery. The first choice of hikers is the **Munro Trail** (see p 388), which climbs to the peak of Lana'ihale. You may encounter four-wheel-drive vehicles, but remember, this isn't rush-hour traffic, either. The trail offers a good day's hike (7mi or 11km). **Shipwreck Beach** offers a similar distance without the climb; the stroll from Kaiolohia Bay to Polihua Beach is 8mi (13km). All kinds of other treks are possible along the trails, which are most often deserted. The Lodge at Ko'ele also offers guided hiking tours.

Cycling

Island trails provide endless playgrounds for **mountain-biking** enthusiasts. Once again, the Munro Trail is the perfect spot. As the bicycles rented by the Lodge at Ko'ele are forbidden on the Munro Trail, it is preferable to ask at the Lana'i EcoAdventure Centre (☎565-7737), which rents mountain bikes for $25 to $30 a day. They also offer excursions.

Horseback Riding

The lodge offers both expert and novice riders a selection of **cavalcades** from its stables (☎565-7300). You can choose a simple 1 to 2hr ride in the hills towering over Lana'i City.

Tennis and Recreational Shooting

You can play **tennis** at both the Lodge at Ko'ele and the Manele Bay Hotel, which has a specialized tennis centre (☎565-2072).

Another option is **clay pigeon shooting**, which no doubt appeared as an alternative to deer hunting and is very popular among islanders. Again, depending on the lodge, the Lana'i Pine Sporting Clays (☎563-4600) is the only one of its kind in a Hawaiian resort. The lot is located in a pine forest, right above Lana'i City. An annual competition is even organized in the fall.

Accommodations

Lana'i City

Dreams Come True Bed and Breakfast
$110-$250 bkfst incl.
sb/pb
547 12th St.
☎565-6961 or 800-566-6961
Located on a small street at the entrance to Lana'i City, this bed and breakfast's three reasonably comfortable rooms are not exceptional for the price. Two are equipped with their own bathroom and the third should have one shortly. The owner, who lived with his family in Bali for six years and in Sri Lanka for seven, also rents three houses with two or three rooms. Either way, the seventh night is free.

Hotel Lana'i
$95-$140 bkfst incl.
ℜ, ⊗, ☂
☎565-7211
☎877-ON-LANAI
≈565-6450
www.onlanai.com
Lana'i's oldest, and for a long time only hotel, was built in 1923 by Dole to house the company's directors and guests. Ten single rooms of various sizes are available, and the best rooms feature a *lanai*. Equipped with only a shower, the rooms nevertheless have an old-world decor: quilted bedspread, antique furniture and old pictures. You might prefer a separate cottage, with private entrance and bath. The hotel belongs to the Lana'i Company (like just about everything else), and offers free shuttle service between the Lodge at Ko'ele and the Manele Bay Hotel.

Lodge at Ko'ele
from $350
≈, ⊙, ℜ, ≡, ▣ *tv*
Keomuku Hwy.
☎565-7300 or 800-321-4666
≈565-4561
www.lanai-resorts.com
Located in the middle of a pine forest high up in the mountains of Lana'i, the Lodge at Ko'ele offers a world of elegance and luxury: a large lounge adorned with columns and two chimneys, stunning gardens and just enough European flair. The furniture and profuse art collection are also of Asian origin. Voted North America's best resort, the lodge

Lana'i

offers an almost endless variety of services (free for the most part) such as afternoon tea in the library between 2pm and 5pm. Guests can take part in all kinds of activities, including croquet, lawn bowling on the artificial turf around the pool, horseback riding, clay pigeon shooting and archery. Let us not forget Experience at Ko'ele, the first golf course designed by Greg Norman. The lodge shares the Manele Bay Hotel's Hulopo'e Beach, its golf course (designed by Jack Nicklaus) and its fitness centre. Free hourly shuttle service links the two establishments via Lana'i City.

South Coast

Hulopo'e Beach Park
$5/pers. + $5 registration fee
washrooms, showers, picnic tables, barbecues
Lana'i Company
P.O. Box 310, Lana'i City
HI 96763
☎ *565-3978*
It's a miracle that the Lana'i Company, despite the presence of the Manele Bay Hotel on Hulopo'e Beach, still allows camping. Even though this activity is particularly geared towards islanders, anybody can camp here. The six sites stretch to the edge of the sand under *kiawes* and feature everything campers

might need. The simplest way to get your permit is on site in a small white building in the middle of the beach. If you do not visit on a weekend, you are almost guaranteed a spot. Campers can stay for up to two weeks.

Manele Bay Hotel
from $325
≈, ⊙, △, ℜ, ≡, ◻ *tv*
☎ *565-7700 or 800-321-4666*
⇌ *565-2483*
www.lanai-resorts.com
This seaside alter ego of the Lodge at Ko'ele towers magnificently over Lana'i's most beautiful beach, Hulopo'e. The luxurious Manele Bay Hotel features extensive oriental and tropical decor and is adorned with orchids, just like the lodge. The hotel offers 250 of the most comfortable, stylish rooms. Guests can enjoy a wide variety of activities and services such as tennis, a massage centre, water sports, billiards and a game room. The hotel's superb golf course hugs the coast. Guests can also take advantage of all of the services offered by the Lodge at Ko'ele and the free shuttle service to both the Lodge and Lana'i City.

Restaurants

Lana'i City

Pele's Garden
less than $10
Mon to Fri, 11am to 7pm, Sat 11am to 2:30pm
811 Houston St. (in Dole Park)
☎ *565-9629*
Somewhere between an organic food store and a deli, Pele's Garden is the closest thing to a gourmet eatery in Lana'i. It offers a variety of sandwiches and soups as well as a small selection of quesadillas, hamburgers and pizzas. You can even buy mascarpone and Boursin cheese.

Tanigawa's
less than $10
Thu to Tue, 6:30am to 1pm
Seventh St.
The most local of local restaurants, Tanigawa's offers a huge choice of hamburgers, omelets, mix plates, sandwiches, *saimin* and other beef stews at very low prices. This isn't high-class cuisine, but it does the trick. No credit cards.

Blue Ginger Café
$10
every day, 6am to 9pm
409 Seventh St.
☎ *565-6363*
Blue like its name, Lana'i City's most popular restaurant stands on the northern side of Dole Park. From breakfast to dinner, you will

find hamburgers, fish or chicken dishes, fish & chips, salads and even pizza – nothing too exotic. No credit cards.

Henry Clay's Rotisserie
$20-$30
every day, 5:30pm to 9pm
828 Lana'i Ave.
Hotel Lana'i
☎*565-7211*
In the rural setting of the Hotel Lana'i, Henry Clay's Rotisserie offers quality cuisine with probably the best quality/price ratio on the island. The relatively eclectic menu features both meat and fish, and all dishes feature a surprising Cajun twist – courtesy of the restaurant's chef, who hails from New Orleans.

The Terrace
$20-$40
every day, 6am to 9:30pm
Lodge at Ko'ele
Keomuku Hwy.
☎*565-7300*
Not quite a terrace, but located next to a spacious lounge, The Terrace is the most affordable restaurant at the Lodge at Ko'ele. Its large bay windows open onto the garden. The classic cuisine features both gifts from the sea and land, sometimes offering a regional Hawaiian twist: salmon on a bed of spinach and onions, cold grilled shrimp ratatouille, venison sandwiches, 'ahi hamburgers and pineapple gazpacho.

Formal Dining Room
$50-$60
every day, 6pm to 9:30pm
Lodge at Ko'ele
Keomuku Hwy.
☎*565-7300*
The lighthouse restaurant at the Lodge at Ko'ele is a tad formal, as its name indicates (jacket and shirt required for men), but not overly so. If you do not have a jacket, they will lend you one. Between the Pacific and North America, between ocean and continent, the restaurant offers quality cuisine that features local ingredients including, of course, seafood (*mahimahi, 'ahi* foie gras), but also leg of mutton and venison. The desserts are especially delicious, though servings are somewhat small.

South Coast

Pool Grille
$10-$15
every day, 11am to 5pm
Manele Bay Hotel
☎*565-7700*
Only open for lunch (with the exception of the golf clubhouse), the Pool Grille offers a basic choice of salads, sandwiches, pizzas and hamburgers. You can order wine by the glass, enjoy a cocktail by the pool at the end of the day, or even indulge in homemade ice cream or sorbet in the afternoon.

Hulopo'e Court
$25-$50
every day, 7am to 11am and 6pm to 9:30pm
Manele Bay Hotel
☎*565-7700*
Fancy, though a little less posh than 'Ihilani (see below), Hulopo'e Court opens onto a terrace overlooking the ocean. Specialized in regional Hawaiian cuisine, it offers a rather limited selection of meat and fish, in addition to a buffet featuring 12 different dishes.

'Ihilani
Tue to Sat, 6pm to 9:30pm
Manele Bay Hotel
☎*565-7700*
'Ihilani means "heavenly splendour" in Hawaiian. In a refined setting, on the terrace overlooking the pool and ocean, the fanciest restaurant at the Manele Bay Hotel offers cuisine that is not surprisingly exquisite. The menu features enough variety and notable French influence (rather, Mediterranean) including a cheese platter, which is attributed to a French chef now living in Honolulu. A jacket is recommended, though not required.

Entertainment

Lana'i's nightlife is not extensive and is essentially limited to the bars at the two hotels: the Music Room/Bar at the Lodge at Ko'ele, where tea is served between

3pm and 5pm – an event not to be missed – and Hale Aheahe at the Manele Bay Hotel with music every night except for Sundays. Those who want to mingle with locals will opt for the movie theatre *(Lana'i Theatre, 456 Seventh St., ☎ 565-7500)*.

The Lodge at Ko'ele and the Manele Bay Hotel run the Lana'i Visiting Artist Program, through which renowned writers, musicians, actors and chefs visit the island regularly to give conferences and meet hotel guests.

Shopping

Pineapples are only produced for local consumption and souvenir shops are few and far between. Professional shoppers will have to settle for the boutiques at the two major hotels, with an assortment of Lana'i caps, clothes and crafts. Lana'i City has only one souvenir shop, **Gifts with Aloha** *(☎ 565-6589)*.

Moloka'i

Nearing the ripe old age of two million, Moloka'i has a surface area of 260 sq mi (673km²) and is the fifth largest island in the archipelago.

Stretching itself over 37mi (60km), the island is formed by two volcanoes separated by a central plain, which, in times ancient, was a plateau of lava created by ongoing eruptions. In the west, Maunaloa, the "long mountain," is the oldest and most eroded. Virtually the entire volcano, arid and overspread with *kiawe*, belongs to the second biggest ranch in Hawaii, the immense Moloka'i Ranch. In the east, Kamakou is three times as high. Poking into the moisture-laden clouds, it serves as Maunaloa's umbrella. Troughed by deep valleys in the north, it tapers into the world's highest cliffs. Across 15mi (24km), the northern coast (backside) between Halawa Valley and Kalaupapa Peninsula is a flat protrusion of lava that was used to isolate a leprosy colony

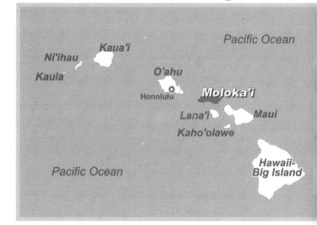

in the 19th century, featuring a string of natural defenses. The cliff at Umilehi Point, for example, is nearly 2,624ft high (800m)! A little more to the east, Kahiwa, the highest waterfall in the islands, boldly rushes down 1,748ft (533m).

A long time ago, scraggly paths led Hawaiians to these remote valleys, the first to be populated. Today, however, only a handful of hunters and hikers make their way here. The flatter south-ern coast, shielded by a barrier reef, is where the elders created the greatest number of fishponds in the archi-pelago. For a long time, Moloka'i's powerful *kahuna* protected the island from the territo-rial ambitions of chiefs on neighbouring is-lands, but on one fate-ful day in 1795, Kamehameha, on his way to conquer O'ahu, took control of the island.

Only 22mi (35km) east of the capital island, Moloka'i seems

like another world. It belongs to the county of Maui, yet it prefers the east to the west and country living to city life; no traffic light, shopping mall or night-club troubles its haunting peacefulness. Here, life unfolds at a slower rhythm, functioning according to Hawaiian time. Furthermore, the island is definitely not a seaside resort destination since strong currents sweep most of its beaches. Maybe this explains why Moloka'i, with 30 times less tourists than Maui, is the least visited island in Hawaii. Not very commercial by nature, it is the most traditional of the islands and the closest to the old way of living. Nearly half of its 6,800 inhabitants are Hawaiian by birth and will greet you with a smile, hence its double nickname: "The Most Hawaiian Island" and "The Friendly Island."

Finding Your Way Around

By Plane

The major airport on the island is located next to the village of Ho'olehua, approximately 6.2mi (10km) west of Kaunakakai, the county seat. Only three airlines fly to this tiny airport: Aloha Islandair (nine flights to Honolulu, three to Kahului), Hawaiian (one morning flight and one afternoon flight to Honolulu via Lana'i) and Pacific Wings (13 flights to Kahului, Honolulu and Kalaupapa, Hana and Kapalua). Moloka'i Air Shuttle also flies to Honolulu. There are only two car rental agencies on the island: Budget and Dollar. There is no public transportation to Kaunakakai or anywhere else on the island.

Only residents and members of excursions organized by Damien Tours are authorized to touch ground on the Kalaupapa airfield. Aloha Islandair and Moloka'i Air Shuttle fly from Honolulu and Ho'olehua, and Aloha Islandair and Paragon fly from Maui.

Airlines

Aloha Islandair
☎*800-652-6541 or 484-2222 (O'ahu)*

Hawaiian
☎*800-367-5320 or 882-8811*

Pacific Wings
☎*873-0877 or 888-575-4546*

Paragon Air
☎*800-428-123189079*

Moloka'i Air Shuttle (☎*567-6847 on Moloka'i,* ☎*545-4988 in Honolulu*) operates in the same manner as shared taxis: flights are based on demand, so planes only take off when full. The rates, however, are unbeatable: $35 one-way, $60 return trip. You simply call and give your desired time of departure, a few days in advance if possible, and they will call you back to confirm. (As long as it's not within 2hrs, since there are several flights to Honolulu per day). The airline also flies to Kalaupapa and Lana'i but tickets are more expensive.

By Boat

The **Maui Princess** (☎*667-6165*) sails from Lahaina to Moloka'i (*Sat in the winter, several times per week in the summer*). Prices start at $69 for return trip and walking tour of Kaunakakai, $198 for two including car rental, and $129 with excursion. The boat leaves Lahaina at 6:30am and returns at 3:30pm (*the trip lasts about 90min*).

By Car

Because there is no public transportation on Moloka'i, renting a car is strongly recommended.

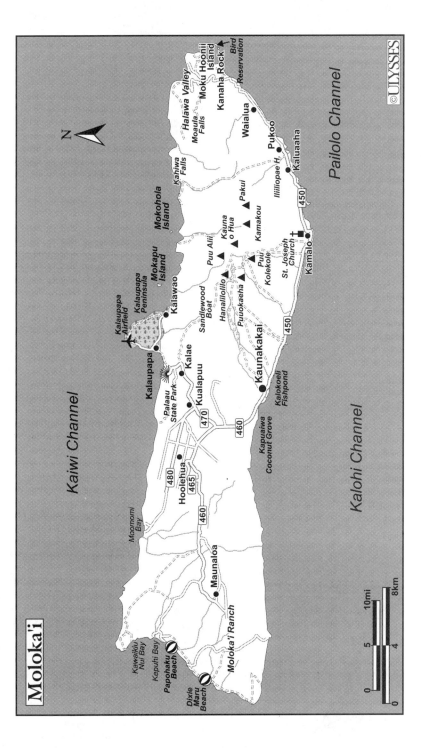

Moloka'i

Kaiwi Channel

Pailolo Channel

Kalohi Channel

N

Moomomi Bay

Kawaikiu Nui Bay

Kepuhi Bay

Papohaku Beach

Dixie Maru Beach

Moloka'i Ranch

Maunaloa

480
465
460
470

Hoolehua

Palaau State Park

Kalaupapa Airfield

Kalaupapa Peninsula

Kalaupapa

Kalae

Kualapuu

Kapuaiwa Coconut Grove

460

Kalokoeli Fishpond

Kaunakakai

450

Mokapu Island

Kalaupapa

Kalawao

Sandlewood Boat

Hanalilolilo

Puu Alii

Puuokaeha

Puu Kolekole

Kauna o Hua

Kamakou

St. Joseph Church

Kamalo

450

Mokohola Island

Kahiwa Falls

Halawa Valley

Moaula Falls

Pakui

Ililiopae H.

Kaluaaha

Pukoo

Waialua

Moku Hoonii Island

Kanaha Rock

Bird Reservation

© ULYSSES

0   5   10mi
0   4   8km

Car Rental Agencies

Budget
☎800-451-3600 or 567-6877

Dollar
☎800-367-7006 or 567-6156

Island Kine Auto Rentals
☎553-5242
cars@molokai-aloha.com
Established in 1999, this company is currently the only one to rent four-wheel-drive vehicles. In the Kamakou Preserve, vehicles are not authorized beyond the first lookout.

By Taxi

Kukui Tours (☎553-5133) This company offers island excursions and transfers from the airport to Kaunakakai ($9) and Kaluako'i ($18).

Moloka'i Off-Road Tours and Taxi (☎553-3369) operates four-wheel-drive excursions and taxi service for hikers, cyclists and canoeists wanting to reach isolated areas.

Practical Information

Tourist Information Offices

Moloka'i Visitors Association
Mon to Fri 8:30am to 4:30pm, Sat 8am to noon
P.O. Box 960, Kaunakakai HI 96748
☎553-3876 or 800-800-6367
⇄553-5288
www.molokai-hawaii.com
The highly informative Moloka'i Visitors Association is located at the corner of Kamehameha V Highway and Wharf Road.

State Park Service

Department of Land and Natural Resources Division of State Parks
Mon to Fri 8am to 4pm
54 South High St., Wailuku (Maui)
☎984-8109
Palaau is the only state park on Moloka'i. The maximum stay is five consecutive nights, and the permit is free.

County Park Service

City & County Parks
Mon to Fri 8am to 4pm
beside the Mitchell Pau'ole Center
☎553-3204
County park offices are located right behind the police station. This service manages two campgrounds, Papohaku Beach Park and One Ali'i Park. Reservations are not accepted. Sites are assigned on a first-come, first-served basis (*$3 per adult per night*).

Mail

The Kaunakakai post office is at the corner of Kamo'i Street and Ala Malama Street (*Mon to Fri 9am to 4:30pm, Sat 9am to 11:30am*). There is also a tiny post office in Maunaloa.

Internet

The Moloka'i Visitors Association now offers free Internet service to visitors. This welcome addition is the only one currently available on the island.

Laundromat

Located at the corner of Kamehameha V Highway and Kamo'i Street, the Ohana Launderette is open every day from 6am to 9pm.

Gas Stations

There are only four gas stations on the island. Two are in Kaunakakai: Chevron (*every day 6:30am to 8:30pm, corner of Wharf St. and Kamehameha Hwy.*) and Kalama's (*Mon to Thu 6:30am to 8pm, Fri and Sat until 9pm, Sun 7am* to 6pm, 656ft or 200m away from the first). The other two stations are in Maunaloa (Mon to Fri 7am to 5pm, Sat 9am to 5pm, Sun 12pm to 6pm) and in Kualapu'u.

Walking Tours

The Nature Conservancy (P.O. Box 220, Kualapu'u HI 96957; ☎553-5236) oversees three preserves on the island: Mo'omomi, Kamakou and Pelekunu. Only the first two are open to the public, provided you have your own means of transportation (four-wheel-drive vehicles obligatory for Kamakou) or join a walking tour conducted by Nature Conservancy volunteers. As in the rest of the archipelago, these walks are organized once a month and cost $25. If you call ahead of time, you will be picked up at the airport. For Kamakou, reservations must be made months in advance.

The Nature Conservancy offices (Mon to Fri 8am to 3pm) are located at the western exit of Kaunakakai, on the left just past the Plumeria Farm, in the industrial sector. If you've reached the bridge, you've gone too far.

Exploring

The Centre of the Island

(half-day)

Located in the centre of the island on the southern coast, **Kaunakakai ★** looks more like a village than a county seat. Its only commercial street, Ala Malama Street, is lined with old shops with Western-style wooden facades, including some small stores and family restaurants... most of the island's businesses, in fact. Wharf Street leads to the port which, despite its appearance, is the most important in the island since this is where all merchandise is unloaded. A pier stretches nearly a mile into the ocean; a few deep-sea fishing boats and sailboats are docked at its extremity. Once a week, the Maui Princess offloads its cargo of excursionists from Maui.

Kaunakakai is not so much a city to visit as it is a place to stop and relax for a while as you soak in the daily lives of its residents. If you insist on finding something to do, you can explore the thin border of sand on the southern shoreline or visit the remains of Kamehameha V's residence, at the base of the pier.

As you head out of Kaunakakai west on Highway 460 (Maunaloa Highway), you'll pass by the **Kapuaiwa Coconut Grove ★**. This is one of the last royal coconut groves in Hawaii, planted by Kamehameha V at the end of the 19th century. Nearly a million trees are squeezed between the road and the ocean on a piece of land fed by a spring. Watch your head if it's very windy! Across the street, **Church Row** encompasses several small, wooden churches such as the lovely mustard-coloured Pomakai Church, situated slightly off the road. Soon after, on the right side of the road (Mile 2.7), you'll see the **Plumeria Farm** framed by a field of frangipani trees.

At Mile 4.4, turn right on Highway 470.

Formerly devoted to pineapple-growing, the small town of Kualapu'u is located at the junction of Highways 480 and 470 (Farrington Avenue). Nowadays, **Coffees of Hawaii** (☎567-9241 or 800-709-BEAN) grows coffee. The establishment produces two types of arabica, Malulani Estate and Moloka'i Muleskinner, which can be sampled at the espresso bar (see p 422xx).

see p 422xx

Moloka'i

At the junction, turn left on Farrington Highway and on Lihi Pali Road at Mile 1.

About 0.3mi away (500m), a large blue sign with a rainbow marks the entrance to the **Purdy Macadamia Farm ★** *(free admission; Mon to Fri 9:30am to 3:30pm, Sat and holidays 10am to 2pm; ☎567-6601).* Founded in 1982 by Kammy and Tuddie Purdy on lands granted under the Hawaiian Home Lands program, this farm, the only one of its kind on Moloka'i, has 53 trees that are about 80 years old. Tuddie has recently planted another 250, but it will be another four or five years before they produce any nuts. Here, quality takes precedence over productivity. Everything is done naturally, without chemical fertilizers or products, allowing visitors to walk through the trees without any health risks. Tuddie will explain the life cycle of the tree, from the flower to the nut – which is fairly easy given that all the various stages happen simultaneously. What's more, Tuddie will let you sample as much as you want before you decide to buy, or not, their macadamia nuts or honey.

Return to Farrington Highway.

The road crosses the sprawling village of **Ho'olehua**, established on Hawaiian Home Lands. Numerous families live here in difficult conditions, as shown by the ramshackle homes and old trailers.

After 5.3mi (8.6km), the tar road gives way to a dirt trail, which becomes very slippery when it rains.

Approximately 1.5mi further (2.5km), the dirt trail leads to the **Mo'omomi Recreational & Cultural Park** managed by the Department of Hawaiian Home Lands *(washrooms and tables).* Right on the eastern bank of Mo'omomi Bay, composed of two large coves separated by a rocky advance, the park includes a small beach and is a good place to start discovering the island's northwestern coast. As you head west, you'll come across a second beach littered with refuse as a result of storms, and then a third, a most beautiful beach that is definitely not to be missed, on **Kawa'aloa Bay ★★**. This wild and deserted beach can be reached in 20 to 30min by following the shoreline. Or you can get there directly by driving along the access road and taking the road which starts 0.5mi (800m) before the park. Note that this junction is not indicated and access is controlled by the Nature Conservancy. You can obtain the key to the gate at the association's offices or, even simpler, walk 10 to 15min to the beach.

The entire area is part of the **Mo'omomi Preserve** that was created in 1988 to protect one of the last natural beaches of Hawaii. Stretching over 922 acres (373ha) of plump sand dunes, this preserve shelters a record number of endemic species (especially plants); every year, it becomes the nesting site of the rare Hawaiian green sea turtle. Occasionally, timid monk seals are also sighted. Archaeological excavations have revealed the existence of numerous bird species that are now extinct. Today, only the *pueo*, Hawaiian falcon, Pacific plover and frigate bird inhabit the area. Every month, the Nature Conservancy organizes guided tours of the preserve; usually conducted by the person who is in charge of counting the turtles, these tours provide a wealth of information on the subject (see p 418).

Return to Highway 470 (Kala'e Highway) and head north.

Highway 470 climbs sharply, past the Ironwood Hills Gold Club, before coming to the **Moloka'i Museum and Cultural Center ★★** *($5; Mon to Thu 10am to 4pm, Fri and Sat 10am to 2pm; ☎567-6436).* It features an interesting exhibit on the history of Moloka'i in addition

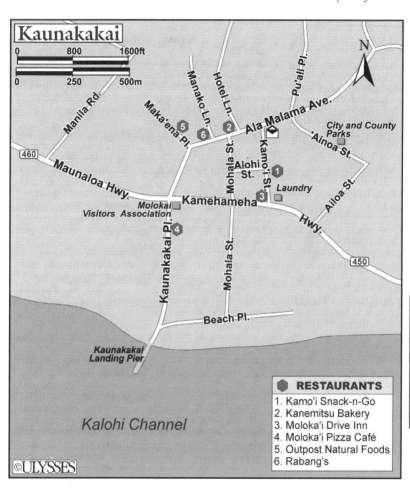

Kaunakakai

0   800   1600ft
0   250   500m

Manila Rd.

Maunaloa Hwy.

460

Maka'ena Pl.

Manako Ln.

Hotel Ln.

Pu'ali Pl.

Ala Malama Ave.

City and County Parks

'Ainoa St.

Mohala St.

Kamo'i St.

Alohi St.

Laundry

Ailoa St.

Kamehameha

Molokai Visitors Association

Kaunakakai Pl.

Mohala St.

Hwy.

450

Beach Pl.

Kaunakakai Landing Pier

Kalohi Channel

N

RESTAURANTS
1. Kamo'i Snack-n-Go
2. Kanemitsu Bakery
3. Moloka'i Drive Inn
4. Moloka'i Pizza Café
5. Outpost Natural Foods
6. Rabang's

Moloka'i

©ULYSSES

to an old sugar mill founded in 1878 by a German settler. Rudolph Wilhelm Meyer, a trained engineer, arrived in the archipelago in 1850 and was employed by the government to record lands in the island cadastre. The following year, he married chieftainess Kalama Waha and became a Hawaiian citizen. He and his family settled on a farm in Kala'e and grew sugar cane in the more protected areas, taro, and even peach trees. Patriarch and father of 11 children, Meyer had six of them trained in various fields to ensure his family's self-sufficiency. He was able to establish a sheep-breeding station in 1859 on lands that would one day form the Moloka'i Ranch.

Built in 1878 but abandoned in 1889 because of weak market prices and a prolonged drought, the **sugar mill** was meticulously restored with the help of Meyer's descendants, who now manage the vast Meyer Ranch. In fact, it is in such good condition that it could almost be put to work again! Instead of using steam, Meyer preferred the traditional press run by steer. Hence only a ton of sugar cane could be processed per day. In the museum, a short film shows its operation and gradual reconditioning.

At the Mile 5.3 marker, the stables of **Moloka'i Mule Rides** are right before the beginning of the Kalaupaga Trail, which is about 656ft further (200m) on the right. This trail leads down to the peninsula (see p 409).

The road ends in the **Palaau State Park**. From the parking lot, a very short path winds its way between pine trees to the **Kalaupapa Lookout ★★**. This overlooks the peninsula where, for over a century, victims of leprosy were forced to live in complete isolation. From this viewpoint, you can clearly see the village and the small airport at the tip of the peninsula. Information panels recount the colony's terrible history (see below).

A second path from the parking lot leads to the top of a small hill, **Pu'u Lua**, in a matter of minutes. Poking through the pines, the Phallic Rock is a natural rock formation that was partly sculpted by Ancient Hawaiians and known as Kauleonanahoa. According to legend, Nanahoa and his wife Kawahuna once lived here. One day, a beautiful young girl appeared and Nanahoa caught her gazing at herself in a small pool of water. He smiled and the young girl's reflection smiled back at him. At the sight of this, Kawahuna flew

into a fit of jealousy and yanked the young girl by the hair. Nanahoa became furious and hit his wife, accidentally causing her to fall off the cliff – where she turned to stone. Nanahoa was also petrified, and his virility was preserved in the shape of this rock. According to tradition, by spending the night here, women who are sterile or want to become pregnant will be pregnant the next day.

Since this is the end of the road, turn around and return to Highway 460.

Kalaupapa

(One day)

The Kalaupapa Peninsula was formed by Kauhako, a small volcano that was formed under water off the cliffs of the north coast. By continuously spewing lava, it gradually attached itself to the much bigger and much older mass constituting the island of Moloka'i. Isolated from the rest of the island and often hit by strong storms, the area seemed perfect when King Kamehameha V decided to banish all islanders who were seriously affected by leprosy in 1865. The first instance of the illness had been detected 30 years earlier on Kaua'i. It is thought that Chinese immigrants introduced this illness to Hawaii, hence its

Hawaiian name *mai pake*, meaning Chinese sickness. Its dramatic propagation throughout the archipelago created a wind of panic.

As early as 1866, the first lepers, as they were called, were mercilessly shipped to the peninsula and thrown overboard as the boats neared the coast. Not everyone knew how to swim and of those who did, some were too weak to make it to shore.

The survivors settled down in makeshift huts in Kalawao, at the eastern base of the peninsula, with no help or food other than what they managed to grow. Without any sanitary, administrative or police authorities, Kalaupapa had to deal with the worst kinds of atrocities. Children, whether they were contaminated or not, were forced into slavery or prostitution.

Little by little, a microsociety began to form. Most of the residents were Hawaiian, yet small communities, such as Chinese and Japanese, slowly began to emerge.

Men were more prone to leprosy and died at a faster rate, the majority dying of untreated pneumonia or gangrene. Because leprosy caused the loss of sensation in body parts, many accidents became fatal injuries because of

lack of treatment. Many victims also became blind. Only those who had the financial means were buried; the remaining bodies were left out in the open and eaten by pigs. Approximately 8,000 people succumbed to leprosy in the peninsula.

During this period, Hawaiian officials doubled their efforts to quarantine the sick. It was under such dismal circumstances that Father Damien arrived in Kalaupapa on May 10, 1873, at the age of 33. After having met leprosy victims in the course of his work on the Big Island, this Belgian priest told his superiors that he was willing to live full-time on the peninsula. Others had gone before him, but had rarely stayed for more than a few days. Upon his arrival, nearly 800 people lived in Kalaupapa. One of his first initiatives was to grow sweet potatoes and trade them with passing ships for goods needed by the colony. Houses and dispensaries were then built by the stronger residents. Coffins were also made, and graves were dug.

In 1885, after 12 years of backbreaking work, Father Damien himself was diagnosed with leprosy. Isolated and abandoned by his superiors, who condemned his independent ways, he was luckily joined the following

year by a former soldier, Joseph Dutton. During this time, a Home for Boys was built and, two years later, a Home for Girls; up until then, children had lived in huts surrounding the priest's hut. In 1888, three nuns came to assist Father Damien. Very ill, he died of pneumonia the following year.

Although not as known as Father Damien, "Brother" Dutton continued his work for 44 years. A patriotic man, he instituted a daily flag ceremony (American) even before Hawaii's annexation to the United States. Under his direction, the Kalawao colony on the eastern side of the peninsula was progressively abandoned for Kalaupapa, located in the west, where the air was drier and warmer and the ocean was less fierce. During this period, the first treatments for leprosy emerged... and failed.

In 1909, a research hospital was founded in Kalawao. However, tests failed because the few patients who accepted to collaborate, accustomed to being wary of strangers, eventually stopped coming. The establishment closed down in 1913. It wasn't until 1941 that an efficient treatment was discovered, and it took another five years before it was offered to residents of Kalaupapa. Finally, the walls built

Moloka'i

Father Damien

Born in 1840 in Tremeloo, Belgium, Joseph DeVeuster grew up in a strict Catholic family in the countryside; three of his brothers also became priests. As a theology student, he left for Hawaii in 1863 with 15 other missionaries. Under the name of Damien, he was ordained two months after arriving in the archipelago. Initially posted on the Big Island, he asked to be transferred to Kalaupapa in 1873; until that moment, priests had only made brief visits to the peninsula. He was eventually diagnosed with leprosy and died 16 years later in Kalaupapa. During his lifetime, his devotion to the sick drew the attention of the media, and the repatriation of his body to Belgium in 1936 was marked by a grand and solemn celebration. He was buried in the crypt of the cathedral in Louvain. Declared Venerable in 1977 by Pope Paul VI and beatified in 1995 by Pope John Paul II, Father Damien might obtain sainthood, a "reward" that many in Moloka'i and elsewhere in the world hope is bestowed upon him. In memory of his attachment to Kalaupapa, a relic was brought back from Belgium and placed in his original tomb.

to isolate the sick were torn down. Leprosy sufferers were authorized to leave Kalaupapa if they so desired. Ever since 1969, when the policy on isolating victims of leprosy was finally abandoned, no one has been allowed to live on the peninsula. In 1980, it officially became the **Kalaupapa National Historical Park** *(Kalaupapa, HI 96742, ☎567-6802)*.

In 1905, the maximum population of the colony was 1,262 inhabitants. Today, 125 people live on the peninsula, including 49 former patients who did not wish to leave. The youngest are in their 60s. Other residents are park employees or administrators.

With the exception of residents' guests, visitors are not allowed to stay overnight in Kalaupapa, nor to walk around alone. To visit the peninsula, you have to register for a guided tour with Kalaupapa's only agency, **Damien Tours** *(☎567-6171)*. You can choose how you wish to go down to the peninsula: along a narrow trail down the cliff or by plane. This second option *($199 from Honolulu or Maui)* is not recommended since the visit loses all its meaning. Hiking down the trail or riding a mule to the peninsula, in addition to providing a succession of unobstructed views, is the only way to really feel the absolute isolation of the peninsula.

Probably retracing an old Hawaiian footpath, the Kalaupapa trail was created right along the cliff in 1886-87 by a Portuguese immigrant from Madeira. It takes about 1.5hrs to hike down this ragged, 3mi (5km) path that descends from the topside to the peninsula, with a variation in level of 1,640ft (500m) and exactly 26 bends (they are numbered!).

The National Park Service refurbished the trail in 1992-95 and added several steps. You can either hike down at your own pace or ride a mule with **Moloka'i Mule Rides** (☎ *567-6088 or 800-567-7550; www.muleride.com)*. In the first case, you have to reserve with Damien Tours *($40)*. Because of an old law, children under 16 are not allowed in Kalaupapa.

You might have seen the bumper sticker with the slogan "Wouldn't you rather be riding a mule on Moloka'i?" or a T-shirt saying "I survived the Kalaupapa Trail." Part tourism, part folklore, the descent on mule back has become the ultimate attraction on Moloka'i. Lasting about 7.5hrs, it costs $135, including permit and bus tour of the peninsula. You can choose package deals from Honolulu or Maui for $259 including flight to Moloka'i and tour. For practical reasons, mule rides are not available to people weighing over 242lb (110kg).

The excursion begins at 8am with a brief riding lesson. You are even giving a mini-stairway to climb onto your mule! The mules are very accustomed to riding down the trail and follow each other closely in single file, in automatic-pilot mode. The path descends along the edge of a precipice, which can be daunting, but the thin border of vegetation provides some psychological comfort. After the 26th turn, the path runs alongside a lovely grey-sand beach before joining the base of the peninsula. There is no swimming here since you are not allowed to stop. After getting off your proud mount, you are invited aboard Damien Tours' old school bus for an in-depth tour of Kalaupapa. The same applies for those who hiked down. And if you arrived by plane, you will be the first to be picked up.

The tour begins with a list of things to do (i.e. follow without flinching) and things not to do (virtually everything else). Obviously, leaving the group is not permitted. You will slowly ride through the **village** and pass by the hospital, Kalaupapa's unique bar called Elaine's Place, the fairly decrepit Saint-François-Xavier Church (1904) as well as the Mormon church, which includes a proud congregation of three! Next is the "industrial" zone, featuring the plumber, the carpenter and Dock no. 1 where, twice a year, new furniture and appliances arrive by barge. The tour of the hamlet ends with the Kalaupapa Store; the Visitor Quarters, where residents' guests stay for $10 per night; and finally the gas pump, which is less expensive than topside since the peninsula is exempt from state taxes.

Still in the village, the first stop is in front of the **grave** and monument of Mother Marianne Cope (1838-1918) who was in charge of the first nuns who came to Kalaupapa in late 1888 to manage the "boarding school for young girls" that was created to house single women. Right next to it, a stunning Celtic cross **monument** was erected in memory of Father Damien in 1893. The second stop of the tour is the small **bookstore ★**. You will have about 15min to look at a collection of old photos taken between 1880 and 1930 as well as a series of articles adapted by Kalaupapa residents, revealing their daily challenges: shoes with bands instead of laces, pants with strips instead of zippers, and pieces of silverware with large handles.

After the village, the bus heads out to **Kalawao**, on the east end of the peninsula, where the first colony was founded. It is also the home of the **Siloama Church**, a Protestant church founded by the residents in 1871; the current building dates back to the 1930s. Close by is the famous pastel-coloured **Saint-Philomena Church ★**. Built in Honolulu in 1872, it was conse-

Moloka'i

crated by Brother Victorin Bertrant. The very small, original building now corresponds to the wing situated to the left of the entrance. Four years later, with the help of residents, Father Damien extended the chapel and made it into a church. Its actual layout, which includes a stone tower, dates back to its second reconstruction in 1888 prior to the priest's death. Your guide will point out the holes made in the floor to allow the sick to spit during masses. To the right of the entrance are the graves of Father Damien and his successor, Brother Dutton.

The last stop is a picnic in Judd Park at the base of the peninsula. Beyond the large rocky islets of Mokapu and Okala, you will see the impressive outline of the **cliffs** ★★ on the north shore of Moloka'i, considered the highest in the world.

The West

(half-day)

West of Kaunakakai, past the junction with Highway 470, the 460 gently climbs through an arid landscape of barren hills and desert lowlands. Erosion is clearly visible, revealing laterite. The entire region is sheltered from rain by the massive Kamakou that looms in

the east. Here lies the second volcano that formed the island, the Maunaloa. Christened the "long mountain," this volcano is no higher than 1,312ft (400m). In fact, it's so low that it's difficult to distinguish its shape.

Just before Mile 15, a fork in the road leads to the **Kaluako'i Resort**, the only hotel complex on the sunny coast of Moloka'i. In the 1970s, this area was destined to welcome a vast residential project designed by the Moloka'i Ranch: thousands of residences were to be built to create a remote suburb of Honolulu, linked by a sea shuttle. However, local opposition to this controversial project was so strong that in the end, only a golf course, hotel and three condominiums ever saw the light of day, north of **Kepuhi Bay** ★. Strong currents and rocky outcrops make swimming dangerous at this beach, which is covered in pale sand. The end of the road that crosses the golf course (Kaiaka Road) affords a lovely view of the beach and shoreline, in the northern direction.

Right before reaching the entrance to the Kaluako'i Resort, turn right on Kakaako Road which leads to the Paniolo Hale condominiums. At the intersection, continue straight (don't turn left) all the way to hole 14 on the golf course.

Just beyond the fairway, the **Make Horse Beach** ★ is a long stretch of sand rarely frequented by more than a handful of people, perhaps because swimming is forbidden. Access is free.

From the golf course, four-wheel-drive vehicles can follow the road north to the deserted **Kawakiu Beach** ★★. On foot, it takes between 20 to 30min to get there, through dry savanna covered with *kiawe*. Don't hesitate to climb over the fence that prevents livestock from escaping. The path then leads down to the beach, skirting a well-shaped cove. Carpeted with fine sand, with rocks here and there, this beach is often deserted.

South of the hotel complex, the **Papohaku Beach Park** ★★ *(washrooms, showers, barbecues, camping – see p 418)* features the most beautiful beach on Moloka'i, one of the longest and largest in all of Hawaii. Almost 3mi long (5km), Papohaku is free of development. Most of the time, you'll be alone to enjoy it, accompanied only by strong gusts of wind sweeping the sand. Papohaku has only one fault: the strong currents make swimming impossible.

Kaluako'i Road continues alongside the coast and crosses the lots that were supposed to accommodate a residential project elaborated in the 1970s. Only a few dozens homes are scattered here and there. After 1.2mi (2km), a small road with no name other than "Dead End" leads to the southern tip of Papohaku Beach, which is perhaps even more deserted.

Turn right at the stop sign about 0.5mi further (800m).

You'll see two accesses to the shoreline: the first, 0.5mi away (800m), leads to a rocky creek with a sandbank; the second goes to a shore strewn with big lava rocks and interrupted by a few tidal pools; the third and last access, 0.5mi further (800m), leads to Kapukaheku Beach, better known as **Dixie Maru ★★** *(shower)*,

which is the site of a shipwreck. Much smaller than Papohaku and covered in coarser sand, this beach is much more popular since it surrounds a well-protected bay that is perfect for swimming and snorkelling. Children in need of a break from building sand castles can play on an old swing hanging from the branches of a *kiawe*.

Return to Highway 340.

After 17mi (27km), Highway 460 reaches **Maunaloa ★** and the **Moloka'i Ranch**. As the second largest ranch in Hawaii, it covers one third of the island, almost all of western Moloka'i. After the Mahele was signed, the first owner was none other than the great chief Kapuaiwa, the future Kamehameha V. The king enjoyed

Moloka'i and came here often. Upon his death, Princess Ruth inherited the ranch, then Princess Bernice Pauahi Bishop. In 1898, a group of businessmen from Honolulu bought over 69,188 acres (28,000ha) from the Bishop Estate, created after the princess's death, and leased another 29,652 acres (12,000ha) from the new territorial government. The Moloka'i Ranch was born. A first attempt at cultivating sugar cane failed because of a water shortage. In 1908, one of the partners, Charles Cooke, bought out all of the other partners. His son George was put in charge of the ranch, which was devoted to breeding, as well as growing potatoes, oats and... honey. In fact, from 1910 to 1937, Moloka'i was the largest honey producer in the world. In the early 1920s, the "king pine" pineapple made its appearance. This led to the creation of the small town of Maunaloa in 1923 to house all of the newly arrived farm workers. In this period of economic euphoria, the village had as many as four movie theatres and 10 restaurants.

In 1986, the last pineapple-growing business left the island and the Cooke family sold its ranch to an investment company from New Zealand. Under its rule, the ranch and the village

The Birth of the *hula*

The young goddess Laka was taught the secrets of the *hula* by her sister Kopo in Ka'ana, a sacred site near Maunaloa. She spread her knowledge of the *hula* around the islands before finally withdrawing to Ka'ana, depicted in myths as a wooded

area despite its actual barrenness. Every year, on the third Saturday of May, the birth of the *hula* is celebrated here before sunrise and preludes the Moloka'i Ka Hula Piko Festival, held on Papohaku Beach Park.

Moloka'i Hoe

Every year in early October, the Hale o Lono port on Moloka'i is the departure point of the most famous outrigger canoe race in Hawaii. Teams of nine people – six paddlers per canoe – compete in this 40mi (65km) race to Fort DeRussy Beach in Waikiki. The event is made all the more difficult by strong currents in the Kaiwi Channel. The race begins at 7:30am, and the fastest arrive as early as 1pm.

were completely remodeled. The old quarters of the town were razed to the ground and redesigned. Only a few old wooden houses in the downtown area were saved to form the **Maunaloa Museum & Cultural Park** (☎533-9804) which was still under construction in early 2000.

Determined to continue breeding livestock, at least for the time being, the new owners have invested a lot in tourism. They sold the zebras and giraffes that used to be part of the Cookes' private zoo and put up three cloth tents, destined for luxury camping amateurs (see p 419), across the

southwestern tip of the island. More recently, they inaugurated a lodge in the village. A variety of sports activities are now provided, but the recent wave of tourism overtaking Maunaloa is really due to one thing: the discovery of the rich heritage of the *paniolo*, formerly reserved for the initiated only. Today about 135 Hawaiian cowboys maintain their traditional lifestyle, transmitted from generation to generation, and share it with visitors thanks to horseback outings, lasso lessons as well as herding, triage and livestock-branding.

The East

(half-day)

East of Kaunakakai, the Kamehameha V Highway travels nearly 22mi (35km) alongside the south shore towards the island's eastern tip before suddenly veering towards the Halawa Valley on the north coast.

Very shallow and sheltered from the currents by the longest barrier reef in Hawaii, the meridional coast was ideal for aquaculture, as the Hawaiians of yesteryear soon discovered. According to historians, there are 62 fishponds on the island, the greatest concentration in the archipelago, and most probably date back to the 13th century.

Kaloko'eli is the first fishpond east of Kaunakakai. For a closer look, the simplest way is to cut across the Moloka'i Shores condominiums. The fishpond lies next to a small beach and is partly covered in vegetation.

A little more to the east *(Mile 3.3-3.4)*, another fishpond is next to the two parks called **One Ali'i Park** *(washrooms, tables, barbecue, camping – see p 420)*. Families flock to these parks on weekends to picnic under the shade of coconut and *kiawe* trees.

At Mile 4.3, a paddock fenced in black wire and plastic and two barn-like wooden houses indicate the **Nene Bird Preservation** ★★ *(free admission; ☎553-5992)*, which protects and breeds the Hawaiian goose. The *nene* disappeared from Moloka'i in the late 19th century. However, the first *nenes* raised in captivity here will soon be set free. Visits are by appointment only and start at 9am (you are requested to confirm on the eve of your visit). In addition to the *nene*, you can see stilts (*ae'o*) and colourful migratory ducks from North America.

The place named **Kawela** marks the site of a bloody battle where Kamehameha vanquished over the forces of Moloka'i. The great king was en route to conquer O'ahu. In former times, there was a *pu'uhonua* here.

A little further *(Mile 5.6-5.8)* along the road, the seaside **Kakaha'ia Beach Park** is very popular with fishers. As you head upcountry, you'll come across a wildlife reserve built around an old pond that has been converted into a fishpond. Several endemic species, such as Hawaiian stilts and moorhens, gambol in swamps with dense scrub. You must obtain authorization (☎875-1582) to gain access.

More to the east, the small village of **Kamalo**, with its few citrus and exotic fruit plantations, was for a long time the most important port of the island. At Mile 10.6, the small **St. Joseph Church ★**, in white wood surmounted by a tall steeple, symbolizes Father Damien's presence topside as well as in

Kalaupapa. The Belgian priest oversaw the building of four churches on the island; two still stand today. This church dates back to 1876. In front of it, the bronze statue of Father Damien in his cassock is often adorned with *lei*.

At Mile 11.8, a wooden sign overgrown with vegetation marks the spot where, on July 15, 1927, Ernest Smith and Emory Bronte had to make an emergency landing during the first trans-Pacific flight. An old monument at the foot of the signpost indicates that they had left Oakland, California 25hrs and 2min earlier. The sign is easier to see in the opposite direction.

Soon after is Moloka'i's largest fishpond, **Keawa'nui ★**, which assumes the shape of a bay formed by a small peninsula. Classified as a historical monument, it extends over 54 acres (22ha) and is circumscribed by a wall that is 1,968ft long (600m). It slightly

precedes the 'Ualapu'e fishpond that faces the other remaining church built by Father Damien, **Our Lady of the Sorrows Church**. Built two years before St. Joseph's, to which it is similar but larger, it was rebuilt in 1966.

At Mile 15.3 in **Mapulehu**, a sign announces the Moloka'i Horse & Wagon Ride. This small family-owned business, established on an immense plantation of old mango trees, operates amusing carriage and horse rides to the impressive **'Ili'ili'opa'e Heiau ★★**. One of the largest in the archipelago and composed of four terraces, this *heiau* is a platform that is 22ft (6.7m) high and as big as a football field. According to legend, its stones were carried in at night by an uninterrupted chain of *menehune* from the Waiau Valley on the north shore. Ancient Hawaiians are said to have performed human sacrifices here.

This historical monument is located in

Our Lady of the Sorrows Church

the Mapulehu Valley, approximately 0.3mi (500m) from the road. If you prefer to visit on your own, you should first stop and ask Moloka'i Horse & Wagon Ride permission to get there on foot – it is rarely refused. Otherwise, you can contact Pearl Petro at ☎558-8113. A Visitors Bureau sign indicates the beginning of a wide road which leads, in less than 10min, to a residence. The *heiau* is close by, on the left. If you want to get a real feel for the work carried out by the *menehune*, you can hike all the way to Wailau Valley. Destined for hardy hikers, it is a long and difficult hike and the trail is often not well marked; it is recommended to be accompanied by a guide *(contact Walter Naki, Ma'a Adventures, ☎558-8184, or the Department of Forestry, ☎553-5019 for more information)*.

Puko'o features the remains of the Kalua'aha Church, the first church built on Moloka'i in 1844, as well as two beaches. Snorkelling is good on the eastern beach near the reef. Past Waialua, where you can also swim, the Mile 20 marker along the road indicates the **Mile Twenty Beach** ★, also called Murphy's Beach Park. This long strand of fair sand adorned with a bouquet of coconut trees is protected by the barrier reef and is an excellent place for swimming and snorkelling.

From Mile 20, the road narrows and meanders along the coastline. It passes by **Rock Point**, a renowned surfing spot which faces a rocky advance of land, then travels along a small sandy beach before it begins to climb. There are lovely views of Mokuho'oniki Isle, used during the Second World War as a target practice by the marines, as well as Kanaha Rock and Lana'i in the background. At Mile 24, the roadway strays from the coast and reaches into the interior of the island, through the green pastures of the large Pu'u O Hoku Ranch ("hill of the stars"), which encompasses nearly 9,019 acres (3,650ha).

At this point, the tar ribbon of the road, which looks like it's slowly melting under the warm sun, begins its descent, in sharp turns, to **Halawa Valley** ★★, the only easily accessible valley on the northern coast. One of the first valleys on Moloka'i to be inhabited (around AD 650), it had a large population until a tidal wave hit in 1946. Here, taro was widely cultivated. The plunging view reveals the valley's vast amphitheatre streaked by waterfalls and the bay guarded by formidable cliffs. A little before it ends at Mile 27.3, the road snakes by the **Ierusalema Hou Church** ★ (1948), a pretty church built in green wood and crowned with a small bell tower. The road finally stops by a small beach park with shabby installations; here, the Halawa River flows into the bay, forming a sandspit. To feel the grey-sand underfoot, you must walk across the water. When conditions are good, surfers flock to this horseshoe-shaped bay.

Unless you penetrate into the heart of the valley, you will merely brush past it. For many years, the 2mi (3km) trail to the beautiful 246ft (75m) **Moa'ula Falls** was the object of controversy between landowners and hikers. Between marginal Hawaiian activists who elected to live in the valley and clandestine marijuana growers, the hike was more of an obstacle course than a quiet walk in the woods. Today, it is again possible to hike to the falls accompanied by a guide who was born and raised in the valley, Pilipo Solatorio *($25; ☎553-4355)*. In this magnificent forest setting, you will discover the remains of terraces where taro used to be cultivated as well as ancient homes and *heiau*. You will have to cross two torrents to reach the falls. If you don't mind cold water, you can swim in the basin at the foot of the falls.

The only way to return to Kaunakakai from Halawa Valley is to turn around on the Kamehameha V Highway.

The Central Mountains

(half-day to full day)

The higher slopes of the Kamakou, the culminating point of the island at 4,969ft (1,515m), are covered with the remnants of a rainforest that used to cloak the eastern side of the island. Created in 1982 on lands belonging to the Moloka'i Ranch, the **Kamakou Preserve** ★★ includes over 2,718 acres (1,100ha) of protected land managed by the Nature Conservancy (see p 403). A hunting program has been put in place to control the wild boars that destroy the forest and rare species of plants and birds such as the *'amakihi*, *'apapane* and *pueo*. It was in this area that the very rare *oloma'o* and *kakawahie* were seen for the last time; it is not known for sure whether they have disappeared or not.

The preserve can be visited during monthly guided walks organized by the Nature Conservancy, or at your own leisure in a four-wheel-drive vehicle. The only company that rents

them on the island (see p 402), however, does not allow its vehicles to go beyond the first lookout since the road is almost always muddy and there is too much of a risk of getting stuck or having an accident. For information on road conditions, stop at the Nature Conservancy offices located 3.7mi (6km) west of Kaunakakai on the Maunaloa Highway. The trail begins a few hundred of metres further, behind the Homelani Cemetery.

Hawaiian Falcon

The access to the preserve is found right before a bridge. Any type of car can manage the first 3.4mi (5.5km) but as soon as the road starts to climb it becomes necessary to have a four-wheel-drive vehicle.

The trail begins in the Moloka'i Forest Reserve. After 9mi (14.5km), it passes by the **Sandalwood Pit** (Lua Moku 'Iliahi), a trench that is 98ft (30m) long, 39ft (12m) wide and 23ft (7m) deep – the exact dimensions of the hold of an early 19th-century ship. In those days, the sandalwood commerce thrived and the population was forced by its chiefs,

indebted to occidental merchants, to cut down trees. This is where they measured the cargo before transporting it down to the shores so that it could be shipped to China.

About 1mi or so further (1.5km), the trail arrives at the **Waikolu Lookout** ★★, which affords a majestic view of its namesake valley and the infinite blue sea some 3,280ft (1,000m) below. During heavy rains, the sides of the valleys are streaked with spirited water cascades. In front of the lookout is a campground with no facilities (see p 421) and a picnic area. Unless you are an expert at driving four-wheel-drive vehicles and it is inordinately dry, this is where you will have to leave your vehicle to penetrate by foot into the rainforest of the Kamakou Preserve.

The most popular footpath of the preserve, the **Pepe'opae Trail** ★★, begins 2.5mi (4km) from the Waikolu Lookout. Created so that hikers will not disturb the natural habitat, the trail is constituted of a narrow platform above the spongy ground. Through clouds and fog, rain and wind,

Moloka'i

you'll discover a world where survival is a daily struggle. Some plants suffer from giantism, others from dwarfism. This is where you will have the most opportunity to observe certain rare species of endemic birds – in fact, this path is featured in walks organized by the Nature Conservancy. After about 1mi (2km), the Pepe'opae Trail ends at a spot with a marvelous view of the inaccessible Pelekunu Valley.

Since 1987, the Nature Conservancy manages another protected area on the north shore: the **Pelekunu Preserve**, encompassing the entire valley of the same name, approximately 5,683 acres (2,300ha). One of the most pristine valleys on the island, it is protected to the east by the highest cliffs in the world. Slightly to the east, the cliffs at Umilehi Point

drop over 3,280ft (1,000m). The valley can only be accessed by boat, and is reserved for park employees only.

Outdoor Activities

Swimming

Moloka'i is clearly not ideal for swimming. Not only does the island count less than a dozen or so beaches, but the water is often too rough to swim in. Protected by a barrier reef, the southern shores are safer but mostly quite shallow. However, you can swim at One Ali'i Park and Kakaha'ia Beach Park. The best places are in the east: **Puko'o**, **Waialua** and especially **Mile Twenty Beach**, which is very popular with families. On calm days, you can also take a dip in the Halawa Bay. On the Kaluaco'i coast, the Kawakiu Beach is fine when the sea is quiet, but your only safe bet is **Dixie Maru**.

Scuba Diving and Snorkelling

Like swimming, snorkelling options around the island are limited

and are concentrated on the southern coastline. In addition to **Puko'o**, one the most popular places is the **Mile 20 Beach**. Moloka'i Outdoor Activities, in the lobby of the Moloka'i Hotel, rents masks and flippers *($6 per day, $24 per week)*. Bill Kapuni's Snorkel and Dive Adventure (☎553-9867) offers snorkelling and diving excursions to various sites around the island *($45 to $85)*. Bill is the president of the Moloka'i Voyaging Canoe Society and provides an impassioned perspective on the great Hawaiian voyages of the past and present.

Surfing and Windsurfing

Surfers generally gather on the southeast coast of the island. Favourite areas are Rock Point and the edge of the Halawa Valley. In the winter, beautiful rollers crash on the western coast and are for experienced surfers only, in Kepuhi Beach, Kawakiu, Dixie Maru. **Windsurfing** amateurs enjoy their favourite sport on the south shore. Moloka'i Outdoor Activities, in the lobby of the Moloka'i Hotel, rents surf boards and Boogie Boards.

Kayaking

Kayaking is becoming more and more popular along the southeastern littoral or at the Moloka'i Ranch – in Hale o Lono, for example, which is the departure point every year of the great canoe races between Moloka'i and O'ahu. Lani's Kayak Tours (☎558-8563) organizes day trips (*$45 to $65*) to the northern shores of the island, at the foot of the world's highest cliffs. When the sea is too rough, which isn't uncommon, excursions go to the eastern shore instead. Moloka'i Outdoor Activities, in the lobby of the Moloka'i Hotel, rents kayaks (*$25 to $30*).

Deep-Sea Fishing

The waters off Moloka'i are bountiful, particularly around Penguin Banks. From the Kaunakakai port, you can take a seafaring excursion of 2hrs, half-day, or full day of deep-sea fishing. Moloka'i Outdoor Activities, in the lobby of the Moloka'i Hotel, rents fishing rods to those who prefer to try their luck fishing from the shore. For the best spots, watch the locals. Moloka'i Action Adventures (☎558-8184)

conducts underwater fishing expeditions.

Cruises

Like deep-sea fishing, all ocean cruises get under way in the port of Kaunakakai. In the winter, the most popular boat excursions are the **whale-watching** trips in the straits between Moloka'i, Maui and Lana'i. Ma'a Moloka'i Action Adventures (☎558-8184) organizes day trips or camping excursions for several days in the valleys of the north shore. Note that the ocean is rarely clement.

Cycling

Mountain bikers can practice their favourite sport along a number of biking paths on the island as well as at the Moloka'i Ranch, which offers an incredible network of paths, albeit a slightly monotonous landscape. There are several places to rent bikes: the ranch (*$20 to $30 without guide*), Moloka'i Outdoor Activities, in the lobby of the Moloka'i Hotel (*$15 to $23 per day, $65 to $105 per week*), as well as Moloka'i Bicycle in Kaunakakai.

Golf

The only 18-hole golf course is located on the western coast of the island at the **Kaluako'i Resort**. Designed by Ted Robinson, this fairway stretches out by the sea. Hotel guests can play for free. There is also a local nine-hole course, the Ironwood Hills Course, in **Kala'e**.

Tennis

The Kaluako'i Resort and a number of condominiums have tennis courts. There are also public courts in Kaunakakai.

Hiking

The relatively pristine nature of Moloka'i makes it a lovely place for hiking. However, because the land is often private and secluded, you will have to pay to hike in most destinations. One of the most popular walks is down the **Kalaupapa Trail** (*90min of walking*). You must reserve with Damien Tours to obtain authorization. Another appreciated stroll is to the Moa'ula falls in **Halawa Valley**, accompanied by guide Pilipo

Moloka'i

Solatorio *($25; ☎553-4355 between 5:30pm and 9:30pm)*. Valleys on the northern seaboard form an immense playground for hardy hikers. The **Kamakou Preserve** is the most accessible, particularly if you join a guided walk organized by the Nature Conservancy along a superb path through the rainforest, the Pepe'opae Trail. For people who love to hike, the **Wailau Trail** is longer and more difficult *(two to three days)*, and leads through the central mountains all the way to its namesake valley. It is preferable to be accompanied by a guide. Moloka'i Off-Road Tours *(☎553-3369)* can drop hikers off at the beginning of the trail and pick them up later. The Nature Conservancy also offers tours to **Mo'omomi**, which is fairly easy to visit on your own. The vast lands of the Moloka'i Ranch also provide myriad hiking opportunities for guests.

Horseback Riding

The most memorable mule ride you'll ever take is probably to **Kalaupapa** *($135, ☎567-7550)*. Despite the change in altitude and the thrilling slope, the excursion is available to people over 16 years of age and weighing under 242 lb (110kg).

Or you can take a short horseback ride through an immense plantation of old mango trees to the great **'Ili'ili'opa'e heiau** with Moloka'i Horse & Wagon Ride *($40; ☎558-8132 or 558-8380)*. But when it comes to horseback riding, the **Moloka'i Ranch** is the best: from simple tours to diverse activities (lasso, triage and counting of livestock, mini-rodeos), the horse is king, and here you'll feel like a real *paniolo*!

Accommodations

The Centre of the Island

Palaau State Park
free
washrooms, showers, tables, barbecues, no drinking water
Situated on the left, approximately 656ft (200m) before the·end of the Kala'e Highway, this campground occupies a clearing shaded by tall pines and eucalyptus trees. The site is rather enjoyable during dry weather and you probably won't be bothered by noisy neighbours – except perhaps on weekends.

Hotel Moloka'i
$75-$130
≈, ℜ, laundry, K, ℝ, ctv, ⊗
Kamehameha V Hwy. (Mile 1.9)
☎553-5347 or 800-367-5004
⇰553-5047
East of Kaunakakai along Kamiloloa Beach,

this old hotel composed of bungalows (each divided into three rooms), one of the most popular on the island, was recently bought and renovated by Castle Resorts. All traces of its age have not disappeared but the fresh coat of paint certainly did some good. The less expensive rooms are dark, while rooms located near the bar can be noisy.

Moloka'i Shores
$144-$189
≈, laundry, K, ⊗, ctv, ☼
Kamehameha V Hwy. (Mile 1.5)
☎/⇰553-5954
☎800-535-0085
www.marcresorts.com
To the east as you exit Kaunakakai, this condominium stretches out by the sea, next to the large Kaloko'eli fishpond. Reaching a certain age, it is nonetheless well kept and offers apartments with one or two bedrooms, all with a living room and oceanfront *lanai*. The three buildings surround a large lawn and swimming pool. Rates apply to four and six people, respectively.

The West

🌴 **Papohaku Beach County Park**
$3/person
washrooms, showers, barbecues
This pleasant shady site is set back from the immense Papohaku Beach. Egrets are often sighted here and it is not rare to see a herd

of deer at the end of the day. Make sure your tent is secured tightly on windy days.

Kaluako'i Hotel
$105-$220

≈, *laundry*, ℜ, ⊗, *tv*, ⏣
Kepuhi Beach, Kaluako'i
☎ *552-2555 or 888-552-2550*
⇄ *552-2821*
www.kaluakoi.com
Bordered by the golf course, the Kaluako'i Hotel faces Kepuhi Beach. Units vary from rather small but reasonably comfortable rooms to more pleasant suites. In some rooms, the cracks between the door and the walls will make you feel like you're in a mountain cabin, especially on windy days. The hotel also manages 20 or so apartments (studios, two-room apartments and cottages) that have been converted into condominiums (see below).

Kaluako'i Villas
$125-$200

≈, *laundry*, K, ⊗, *tv*, ⏣
1131 Kaluako'i Rd.
☎ *552-2721 or 800-367-5004*
⇄ *552-2201*
www.castle-group.com
Managed by Castle Resorts, these villas are set in the aging but still comfortable buildings of the Kaluako'i Hotel, a little ways from the seaside. Built to compensate for the hotel's low occupancy rate, these condos feature studios that are similar but larger, with kitchenette. The fourth night is free.

Ke Nani Kai
$149-$199

≈, *laundry*, K, ⊗, *ctv*, ⏣
Kepuhi Beach Dr., Kaluako'i
☎ *552-2761 or 800-535-0085*
⇄ *552-0045 or 800-633-5085*
www.marcresorts.com
Slightly set back from Kepuhi Beach, beyond the Kaluako'i Hotel and Villas, the Ke Nani Kai lies between holes 8, 16 and 17 of the golf course, a sure guarantee of tranquillity. Managed by Marc Resorts, this hotel complex includes 120 apartments with one or two bedrooms, all belonging to different owners. The quality/price ratio is better than the Kaluako'i Villas and Hotel. Residents have access to tennis courts.

Paniolo Hale
$115-$265

≈, K, *laundry*, ⊗, *tv*, ⏣
Kakaako Rd., Kaluako'i
☎ *552-2731 or 800-367-2984*
⇄ *552-2288*
www.lava.net/paniolo
This rather luxurious condominium, located between holes 10 and 18 of the golf course, rents over 20 studios and apartments with one or two bedrooms. Spacious and generally well kept, they all include a large airy balcony. The closest ones to the ocean are twice as expensive than those facing the garden. Minimum stay is three nights. To reach the Paniolo Hale Resort, follow the Kakaako Road to the entrance of the Kaluako'i Resort then turn left at the first fork in the road.

Moloka'i Ranch
camps $145-$245 bkfst incl. lodge $295-$350

camps ≈, ℜ, ⊗
lodge ≈, ⊘, △, ℜ, ≡, ▣, ℝ, *ctv*
Moloka'i Ranch Outfitters Center, P.O. Box 259 Maunaloa HI 96770
☎ *552-2791 or 877-PANIOLO*
www.molokai-ranch.com
Without abandoning its breeding activities, the ranch has considerably invested in tourism by creating three outdoor campsites, a lodge and a host of sports facilities. There are various package deals including horseback riding, mountain biking, kayaking and snorkelling, among others. All kinds of activities are also organized, such as fishing and whale-watching expeditions on rafts during the winter months and dolphins-watching during the rest of the year. However, the most exciting activities are undoubtedly those related to the fascinating lifestyle of the *paniolos*. All activities are coordinated by the Outfitters Center (*every day 6am to 7pm*) located in the heart of Maunaloa. This centre also houses the reception, the bike rental shop, a small exhibit retracing the history of the ranch as well as a large souvenir shop.

Located in the village and despite its rather dull architecture, the lodge is an indisputable success. Inaugurated in the autumn of 1999, it includes 22 extremely luxurious and comfortable rooms. The six rooms in the main building are all decorated differently. However, rooms in the adjoining cottages are even more pleasant: very warm and cozy, they include a refrigerator and a large sofa-bed that is perfect to laze around and watch TV. The building includes a lounge with fireplace, a view of the ranch's property and the ocean in the distance, a restaurant, a bar with pool table, a massage centre, work-out equipment and heated pool.

The campsites are spread out on an immense territory. They include between 20 and 40 *tentalows* that resemble, but in a more rustic version, the luxurious camps of eastern Africa. Mounted on a wooden platform, each has a bed and a separate bathroom, partially open and solar-powered. The Paniolo Camp, the closest to the village, is designed for families and is situated in a bushy area far from the ocean. The smaller Kolo Camp is more than a 30min shuttle ride away, lost on the southern shore along a long deserted beach. It is designed for honeymooning couples, maybe because the rickety cloth canopies, often blown by strong winds, would keep them up all night anyway... The third camp, the Kaupoa Beach Village, is found on a beach on the western coast of the island.

The major inconvenience of these campsites is the isolation and the necessity of having to use the shuttles to get around *(every hour between 6:45am and 8:45pm from the Outfitters Center, last departure 10pm)*. Another inconvenience is the very high price, even though it includes a number of activities. For the time being, this type of package seems to attract mostly Hawaiian residents who benefit from reduced rates.

The East

One Ali'i County Park I
$3/pers.
washrooms, showers, picnic tables, barbecues
Here you can camp under coconut trees (the nuts have been removed) right by the sea, next to two monuments commemorating Japanese immigrants. This campground, with shaded tables and games for kids, is especially popular with local families. It is pleasant but somewhat lacking in privacy. It can also be quite windy at times.

Waialua Pavilion and Campground
washrooms, showers, picnic tables
HC 01 Box 780, Kaunakakai
HI 96748
☎ 558-8150
≈ 558-8520
vacate@aloha.net
Adjacent to the church of Waialua, this small campground is squeezed between the quiet road and the seaside. You can set up your tent under one of the awnings that form a circle around a central pavilion. Local families mostly frequent this site on weekends.

Country Cottage
$85
≈, K
HC 01 Box 900, Kaunakai
HI 96748
☎ 558-8109
≈ 558-8100
Situated on land owned by the large Pu'u O Hoku Ranch, just before the road winds its way back down to Halawa Valley *(Mile 25)*, this large and rustic old-fashioned cottage includes a living room, a large *lanai*/patio converted into a dining room, two bedrooms and two bathrooms (television by request only).

Ka Hale Mala
$70 (no bkfst)
$80 (bkst incl.)
K, ⊗, tv, ☞
Kamehameha V Hwy. (Mile 4.7)
P.O. Box 1582, Kaunakakai
HI 96748
☎/⇌ *553-9009*
www.molokai-bnb.com
Halfway between a
regular hotel room and
a bed and breakfast,
here you will find a
rather large apartment
occupying the ground
floor of a private home
in a residential neigh-
bourhood. The recep-
tion is friendly, beach
and snorkelling equip-
ment is available, and
you can even be
picked up at the air-
port. From the
Kamehameha V High-
way, turn left on
Kamakana Place; the
house is at the end of
the road, on the left.

🌺 Kamalo Plantation
Bed and Breakfast
$85 bkfst incl.
K, ⊗
Kamehameha V Hwy.
(Mile 10.6)
☎/⇌ *558-8236*
kamaloplantation@aloha.net
In front of Saint-Jo-
seph's Church, a road
leads to a tropical-fruit
plantation located on a
heiau (Puili) where a
kahuna healer used to
live. In the heart of the
vegetation, far from the
main residence, you'll
find a very comfortable
cottage equipped with
a kitchen, small bath-
room (with shower)
and bedroom/living
room, all decorated in a
pleasing Polynesian
style. Breakfast awaits
you in the refrigerator.
The minimum stay is

two days, and it is pref-
erable to reserve a long
time in advance, espe-
cially during the winter.

Dunbar Cottages
$125
K, laundry, tv, ☞
Kamehameha V Hwy.
(Mile 18.5-18.6)
☎ *553-3273 or 800-673-0520*
⇌ *558-8153*
*www.molokai-
aloha.com/kainalu*
The two very popular
greenwood cottages
rented out by Kip and
Leslie Dunbar are situ-
ated between the road
and the shore, about
656ft (200m) apart.
Both cottages feature
two rooms and a large
lanai overlooking the
ocean. In the winter, it
is best to reserve sev-
eral months in advance.
There is also an addi-
tional $70 cleaning fee.

🌺 Kumu'eli Farms B&B
$100 bkfst incl.
≈, ℝ, tv
Kamehameha V Hwy.
(Mile 10.5)
☎ *558-8284*
*www.visitmolokai.com/kum
ueli/*
This big wooden house
stands in the midst of a
citrus-fruit plantation
just before Saint-Jo-
seph's Church. Divided
in two, one section of
the house is a pleasant
and well-furnished stu-
dio; large picture win-
dows in the bedroom
open onto the garden
and long pool in the
backyard. Dorothy
Curtis is the author of a
book on ancient Ha-
waiian trails and knows
the island like the back
of her hand; she and
her husband are gold-

mines of information.
Take heart if you don't
like dogs: although
they are endearing,
their two Labradors are
a little overwhelming.

Wavecrest Resort
$119-$189
K, laundry, ⊗, tv, ☞
Kamehameha V Hwy. (Mile 13)
☎ *558-8103 or 800-367-2980*
⇌ *558-8102*
This aging condomin-
ium is composed of
three three-storey
buildings built along-
side a vegetation-cov-
ered Hawaiian fish-
pond. It includes a
variety of apartments,
well kept for the most
part, with one or two
bedrooms. Only 10 or
so are available for
rent. Rooms with gar-
den view are a bit dark.

The Central
Mountains

Waikolu Lookout
Campground
free
washrooms, picnic tables
Department of Forestry and
Wildlife
P.O. Box 347, Kaunakakai
HI 96748
☎ *553-5019*
Although camping is
prohibited in the
Kamakou Preserve,
hikers can camp right
outside the preserve on
this piece of land man-
aged by the State Park
Service. Be aware that
it generally gets pretty
cold at night and that it
often rains.

MOLOKA'I

Restaurants

The Centre of the Island

Note that none of the restaurants in the $10 or less category accept credit cards.

Coffees of Hawai'i Espresso Bar
less than $10
Mon to Fri 7am to 5pm, Sat 8:30am to 5pm, Sun 10am to 4:30pm
junction of Highways 470 and 480, Kualapu'u
☎567-9241
Attracting more and more tourists for no other apparent reason than the possibility of visiting the establishment's coffee plantation, this snackbar offers light meals and, of course, a variety of coffees. Try the iced Mocha Mamma served with chocolate and Chantilly cream.

Kamo'i Snack-n-Go
less than $10
Mon to Sat 9am to 9pm, Sun 12pm to 9pm
Kamo'i Professional Center Kaunakakai
☎553-3742
For a quick stop on the road, Kamo'i offers a selection of snacks to nibble on (chips, candy, etc.) as well as all kinds of ice cream: sundaes, floats, milk shakes, with apple pie...

Kanemitsu Bakery
less than $10
Wed to Mon 5:30am to 6:30pm (restaurant until 1pm)
79 Ala Malama St., Kaunakakai
☎553-5855
Located right in the centre of town, Kanemitsu has provided the island with fresh bread since 1936. Baked in a *kiawe* wood-burning oven, this famous bread comes in many varieties: white, bran, cheese, onion, banana, apricot, pineapple, mango, strawberry, coconut and more. On weekend and holiday mornings, all of Moloka'i stops by to stock up on donuts and croissants or to pick up the pie or cake that was ordered. You can also ask for a sandwich made with the famous homemade bread or enjoy an omelet, hamburger or any other light meal in the "restaurant" section of the bakery.

Moloka'i Drive Inn
less than $10
every day 6am to 10pm, Fri and Sat until 10:30pm
Corner of Kamehameha V Hwy. and Kamo'i St.
☎553-5655
The Moloka'i Drive Inn is one of Kaunakakai's oldest establishments. Since its creation in 1960, practically nothing has changed. Here you'll find the usual classics available in this type of restaurant: hamburgers, hot dogs, sandwiches, salads and plate lunches that are a

good deal, and of course, ice cream.

Moloka'i Pizza Café
$10 to $15
Mon to Thu 10am to 10pm, Fri and Sat until 11pm, Sun 11am to 10pm
Wharf Rd. Kaunakakai
(behind the Visitors Association)
☎553-3288
Very popular with islanders, the Moloka'i Pizza Café is the most fashionable of the family-style restaurants in Kaunakakai. Of course, it specializes in pizza: there are seven kinds to choose from (whole or by the slice), named after each of the islands in the archipelago. Molokini is obviously the smallest! There are also salads, sandwiches, linguini and grilled chicken, among others. Wednesdays are Mexican Night, Thursdays feature *laulau* pork and Sundays are for rib-lovers.

Outpost Natural Foods
less than $10
deli Mon to Sat 11am to 3pm
behind Kalama's gas station Kaunakakai
☎553-3377
The only one of its kind on Moloka'i, this tiny organic-food store includes a small deli selling a variety of sandwiches, salads,

burritos and hamburgers. Lunch specials include the Mushroom Mountain, a baked potato covered in onions, mushrooms, sour cream and cheese, served with a small salad. The juice bar opens 1hr earlier (open on Sunday but closed on Saturday).

Rabang's
less than $10
every day 7am to 9pm
67 Ala Malama St., Kaunakakai
It is so rarely crowded at Rabang's that if you show up for breakfast, you'll probably be the first customer of the day to get the ovens fired up. That being said, the eggs with bacon or Portuguese sausages are as good as anywhere else. You might even get a smile if you ask about the house specialties, which are as Filipino as the owners, such as *loko* (pork tripe), *adobo* turkey and *dinardaraan* (a kind of blood pudding). Or you can opt for a more traditional lunch plate like beef or pork *teriyaki* or *mahimahi*. The choice for desert is simple: ice cream or *halo halo* (ice cream with coconut, fruit and Chantilly cream).

Hotel Moloka'i Restaurant
$10 to $25
Sat and Sun 7am to 10:30pm, every day 11am to 2pm and 5pm to 9pm
Kamehameha V Hwy. (Mile 1.9), Kaunakakai
☎ 553-5347
Residents of Kaunakakai and the rest of the island come to the Hotel Moloka'i Restaurant for all kinds of special occasions, such as romantic dinners, birthdays and business lunches. The menu isn't particularly exciting (steak, fish, salads, etc.) but the proximity of the ocean and the live Hawaiian music on Friday and Saturday evenings make it a pleasant setting.

The West

'Ohi'a Lodge
$15-$30
every day 6:30am to 10:30am and 6pm to 8:45pm
Kaluako'i Hotel
☎ 552-2555
The Kaluako'i Hotel's only restaurant presents a rather typical menu of salads, fish of the day, steak, chicken and ribs, as well as one or two vegetarian dishes with Asian hints. Dinner reservations are obligatory. For lunch, you will have to content yourself with chili or hamburgers at the hotel snackbar *(every day 11am to 3pm)*.

The Village Grill
$20-$25
every day 11:30am to 2pm and 6pm to 9pm
Maunaloa
☎ 552-0012
Recently opened by the owners of the Moloka'i Ranch, the Village Grill is the first restaurant in the archipelago to feature hot-stone cooking: fish of the day, steak, seafood or other combinations are brought directly to your table and it is up to you to cook each ingredient using the hot stone as a cooking plate. For the same price as most of the dishes, the stone menu includes a soup or salad and desert. The *lilikoi*-and-macadamia-nut pie is delicious! The lunch menu is limited to a few daily specials and slices of pizza. In keeping with the ranch style of the village, the restaurant has a *paniolo* decor.

Maunaloa Room
$20-$40
every day 6:30am to 10am, 11am to 1:30pm and 6pm to 9pm
Maunaloa Lodge
☎ 552-2741
The large picture windows in this country-style dining room look out to the arid slopes of the ranch and the far-off ocean. Halfway between regional Hawaiian cooking and the continental classics, the Maunaloa Room's menu features fresh produce from Moloka'i and generous portions. You can pick from a vast array of salads, sand-

Moloka'i

wiches, hamburgers, steak, chicken and seafood, as well as innovative dishes such as venison pie or ribs with coffee sauce.

The East

Neighbourhood Store N Counter
less than $10
Thu to Tue 8am to 6pm
Kamehameha V Hwy.
(Mile 15.8)
☎*558-8498*
A local favourite, the one and only restaurant east of Kaunakakai is simple, good and inexpensive. There is a large choice of sandwiches, *bentos* and hamburgers (including one for vegetarians) as well as plate lunches featuring chicken or beef *teriyaki*, chicken *katsu* or roast pork. Top off your meal with ice cream or a *malassada*. Most of the regulars order take-out, but there is a sitting area right outside the restaurant. You can't be in too much of a hurry though: there is only one cook and many hungry customers!

Entertainment

Nightlife in Molokai is virtually nonexistent. At 9pm (10pm at the very latest) the last restaurants close up for the night. The only place to go out is to the movies (in Maunaloa).

Festivals

January

Ka Moloka'i Makahiki Festival
In Kaunakakai
☎*553-3673*
(various Hawaiian games such as javelin throwing and wrestling)

March

Moloka'i Ranch Rodeo

May

Commemoration of the Death of Father Damien
May 10
☎*553-5220*

Moloka'i Ka Hula Piko Festival
third Saturday of the month
Papohaku Beach Park
☎*672-3220 or 553-3876*
(birth of *hula* on the island: performances by *halau*, historical tours, craft demonstrations)

The festival often occurs at the same time as the **Starbuck's Kayak Challenge**, the world sea-kayaking championship.

June

King Kamehameha Celebration
☎*567-6361*

July

Moloka'i Sea Fest Ho'olaulea o Ke Kai
fourth and fifth
Kaunakakai pier
☎*553-5071*
(Hawaiian musicians, canoe and kayak races, fishing tournament and other sports events)

September

Na Wahine O Ke Kai
end of the month
☎*541-5323*
(canoe race)

October

Aloha Festivals
(*hula*, Kaunakakai parade, Moloka'i mule run, canoe races, concerts, etc.)

Moloka'i Hoe
mid-October
(men's canoe race)

Shopping

If you wish to shop in Kaunakakai, you can visit the **Friendly Market Center**, the largest, as well as **Misaki's**. There are only a couple of grocery stores on the island: the **Kualapu'u Market** and the **Maunaloa General Store**. On the eastern side of the island, you will have to content yourself with the rather limited choice of the Wavecrest General Store situated at Mile 13.

Moloka'i is about as rich in souvenir shops as it is in places to go out in the evening. In Kaunakakai, **Moloka'i Island Creations** sells knick-knacks, clothes, books and postcards. In Maunaloa, the **Plantation Gallery** displays crafts made in Hawaii and elsewhere in the world, especially Indonesia. Next door, owned by the same couple, the **Big Wind Kite Factory** specializes in kites.

Their flying creations come in original shapes such as fish, whales, jungle animals and dancers. You can watch Jonathan and his wife Daphne as they work on the latest models, and they will even give you free flying lessons.

Other souvenir ideas include bringing back bags of macadamia nuts (without additives) from **Purdy's** in Ho'olehua or making an appointment to visit some of the island's artisans who create a wide variety of items (jewellery, feather *lei*, bedspreads, wood sculptures, etc.) For addresses, stop in at the Visitors Association.

Fruits, vegetables and crafts are sold at the **Moloka'i Market Place** (☎*553-9075)* which is held twice a month in different locations.

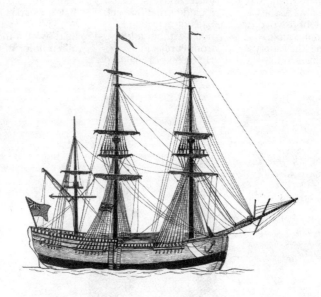

Kaua'i

Kaua'i is an island
that truly stands out in the Hawaiian scenery.

It is the northernmost and westernmost island of the main archipelago, located 68mi (110km) from O'ahu, and it is the most free-spirited. Some claim that Kaua'i was the first island to be inhabited – a role that is also claimed by the Big Island. But here, such assertions are anchored in dreams: the *menehune*, small male workers who live in the island's legends, are said to have inhabited Kaua'i. Today, an increasing number of specialists claim that they were actually the first Marquisian colonizers, thus bridging the gap between myth and reality.

One thing is certain, though: one fateful day in 1778, Kaua'i was indeed the first island to be discovered by Westerners, thanks to Captain Cook. Always looking to set itself apart, it was also the last island to join the united archipelago. As

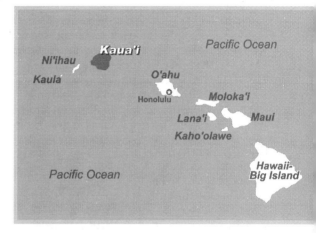

a first attempt in 1796, Kamehameha gathered more than 1,200 canoes and 10,000 soldiers to launch an assault, but a storm ruined his plans. A second expedition was prepared in 1804, but was curbed by a typhoid epidemic. In 1820, King Kaumuali'i finally, albeit grudgingly, accepted that Kaua'i join the unified kingdom upon his death, which only happened in 1824. In the meantime, the island was nearly invaded by Russia, but that's another story, one that is

as gripping as it is astonishing.

The fourth largest island of the archipelago (554 sq mi or 1,435km²), Kaua'i is also the oldest of the main islands, having emerged from the water at least five million years ago. Suffering from erosion on all sides, its formative volcano has been melting for years, leaving what is now Wai'ale'ale, reaching 5,145ft (1,569m) above sea level. Its unaccessible peaks are pounded each year by 472in

(12m) of rain, making Kaua'i the most watered island on Earth. Sculpting the rock, the rains have produced the most beautiful, greenest and most luxurious Hawaiian island, aptly nicknamed "the Garden Island."

Almost a perfect circle on paper, Kaua'i in fact features a marvelous succession of unique and sinuous landscapes. To the north, deep valleys shape the Na Pali coast, with its unbelievable number of cliffs. To the west, Waimea Canyon, nearly 2,950ft (900m) deep, engulfs the heart of the island. The marshy plateau of Alaka'i, which is protected by the highest peaks and showered by mist and waterfalls, feature some of the archipelago's rarest flower and animal species, sheltered from the outside world.

Abundant rainfalls led Kaua'i to develop Hawaii's first sugar-cane plantation as early as 1835. Though many sugar-cane fields remain, guava and papaya orchards as well as coffee-tree groves have

also been planted. The least populated of the large islands, with a little more than 50,000 residents, Kaua'i preserves a rural charm that is becoming increasingly uncommon in Hawaii. However, tourism has made its mark here, especially in the last decade, but the three main tourist resorts – one in the east, one in the south and one in the north – remain limited to very specific areas.

Finding Your Way Around

By Plane

Located just a few miles from Lihu'e, Kaua'i's main airport receives flights on Aloha and Hawaiian airlines from Honolulu every 30min between 6:30am and 9pm. Nearly all flights to other islands include a stop or changeover on O'ahu. United also offers direct flights from Los Angeles.

At the airport, you will find an information booth in the tiny baggage-handling hall. For information, dial ☎*333* on site and ☎*245-2831* from outside the airport.

Car rental agencies are located across from the entrance. You pick up your car on site, but most of the agencies ask that you return your car at a depot located at the airport's exit, 3min away (a shuttle will bring you back).

It will cost you between $16 and $20 to get to Wailua/Kapa'a by taxi, around $35 to get to Po'ipu and over $60 to get to Princeville. Located less than 2mi (3km) east of Princeville, the island's second airport is now used by helicopter tour companies.

Airlines

Aloha
☎*245-3691 or 800-367-5250*

Hawaiian
☎*835-1555* (O'ahu)
☎*800-367-5320*

United
☎*800-241-6522*

By Car

Car Rental Agencies

Alamo
☎*246-0645 or 800-327-9633*

Avis
☎*245-3512 or 800-321-3712*

Budget
☎*245-1901 or 800-527-0700*

Dollar
☎*245-3651 or 800-800-4000*

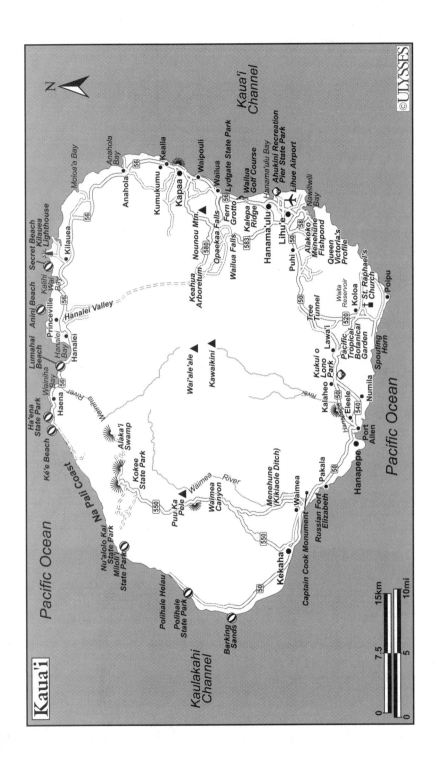

Hertz
☎ 800-654-3011

National
☎ 245-5636
☎ 800-CAR-RENT

Lihu'e

Located on Kaua'i's eastern coast near the airport, the village of Lihu'e is located at the island's nerve centre. The Na Pali coast bars the western side of the island with its murals, making it impossible to go around the entire island. Visitors must therefore pass through Lihu'e when travelling north to south.

At the heart of the city is Rice Street, linking the village to the port of Nawiliwili, the island's most important port. To the west, the artery joins the road that leads to the northern and southern coasts: the Kuhio Highway (56) begins in the north and the Kaumuali'i Highway (50) begins in the south.

North of Lihu'e

You head north of Lihu'e by taking the Kuhio Highway or Kapule Highway, which begins on Rice Street between the centre of town and the port, and links up with the Kuhio Highway at the Hanama'ulu exit, past the airport.

Further north, covering some 3mi (5km) from Wailua to Waipouli and Kapa'a, the eastern coast seems to stretch endlessly. Following the coastal road to get here is often fastidious, and traffic jams are common at quitting time (yes, even here!). Every morning, one of the two lanes climbing northward is reserved for traffic travelling in the opposite direction, heading to Lihu'e. To win some time at rush hour, it might be wise to take the alternate route, which, from Wailua, circles Waipouli through the interior to join the 56 at the heart of Kapa'a. This bypass road begins at Mile 6.7 when travelling south.

After a little more than 18mi (30km), the Kuhio Highway reaches Princeville (change in mile numbering). Beyond that point, towards Hanalei and Ha'ena, the highway comes to an end as it narrows and crosses several one-way bridges (priority goes to the first one there).

South of Lihu'e

Less than a dozen miles south of Lihu'e, Maluhis Road leaves the Kaumuali'i Highway (50) heading towards Koloa and ends facing Po'ipu. Here, on the edge of the seaside resort, you have two options: you can either take Po'ipu Road to the left, which leads to most beaches and establishments, or Lawa'i Road to the right, which leads to a smaller tourist area and the vent hole of the Spouting Horn. Both roads finish in dead ends.

From Koloa, Koloa Road joins up with the 50 near Lawa'i.

The Kaumuali'i Highway crosses through Kalaheo, Hanapepe, then Waimea. It ends 9mi (15km) westward at Polihale Park.

Two roads, which meet halfway up the mountain, lead to Waimea Canyon and Koke'e Park. Waimea Canyon Drive, the less clearly indicated of the two, begins at the western exit of Waimea and quickly climbs along the canyon's edge. Koke'e Road leaves from Kekaha, further west. It does not feature as many breathtaking views, but it is a little wider, which can be reassuring.

By Taxi

Here are a few of the main taxi companies:

ABC Taxi of Kaua'i
☎ 822-7641

Ace Kaua'i Taxi Service
☎ 639-4310

Akiko's Taxi
☎ 822-7588

Kaua'i Cab Service
☎ 821-1222

By Bus

Kaua'i is one of the only islands in the archipelago with public transportation. **The Kaua'i Bus** *($1; ☎241-6410)* offers two lines serving the northern part of the island, starting from Lihu'e. The 500 goes to Hanalei seven times daily during the work-week *(between 6:45am and 6pm)* and four times on Saturday *(between 6:45am and 6pm)*. There is no service on Sundays or holidays. Large bags, bicycles, surfboards and Boogie Boards are not allowed on the bus.

By Trolley

The **Coconut Coast Trolley** *(☎245-5108)* serves the eastern coast between Wailua *(from the Holiday Inn Sunspree Resort)* and the heart of Kapa'a, from 10am to 10pm, every day *($2 one way, $5 per day)*.

By Motorbike and Moped

Hawaiian Riders *(4-776 Kuhio Hwy in Kapa'a; ☎822-5409)* rents scooters at $50 for 24hrs, and $39 per 8hr-day *(minimum of 21 years of age)*. A car will cost you about the same.

Practical Information

Tourist Information Offices

Kaua'i Visitors Bureau
Mon to Fri 8am to 4:30pm
4334 Rice St., Lihu'e
Watumull Plaza
☎*245-3971 or 800-262-1400*
⊷*246-9235*
www.kauaivisitorsbureau.org
The bureau essentially provides pamphlets.

State Parks Department

Department of Land & Natural Resources Division of State Parks
Mon to Fri 8am to 4pm
3060 Eiwa St., Lihu'e
(suite 306)
☎*274-3444 or 274-3445*
It is here that you can obtain permits for camping in state parks, as well as in the interior wilderness of Koke'e Park and on the Kalalau Trail. In the summer, a third of these permits are held for reservations of up to four weeks in advance. Mountain trips are limited to five consecutive nights – only one night at Hanakapi'ai on the way there and one night on the return leg, and a maximum of three nights at Milo'li *(from May to September only)*.

County Parks Department

Department of Public Works
Division of Parks & Recreation
Mon to Fri 7:45am to 4:15pm
4444 Rice St., Lihu'e
Mo'ikeha Bldg. (150)
☎*241-6660 or 241-6670*
The County Parks Department maintains about 20 parks throughout the island, nine of which are open to camping (although some are not exactly spectacular). No reservations are needed and stays are limited to seven days on each site. Each lot is generally closed one day a week for maintenance. Permits cost $3 per day per person and are granted at the parks' bureau, just right of the entrance to the new Lihu'e Civic Center, located in the heart of town. You can also get permits from rangers on site for $5 per person.

Post Office

Lihu'e
Mon to Fri, 8am to 4:30pm, Sat 9am to 1pm
4441 Rice St.

Internet Access

Atomic Clock Cafe
3897 Hanapepe Rd.
Hanapepe
☎*335-5121*
Housed in the same building as Hawaii Helicopters, this mini

Kaua'i

Internet café is one of the few on the island. The coffee is there mostly to keep you company as you browse the Web. Access costs $7.50 for 30min.

Bubba Burgers in Kapa'a (see p 479) and Hanalei (see p 480) offers free Internet access on Web TV to customers who want to check their E-mail.

Organized Tours

The **Kikiaola Foundation** (☎338-0006), based in Waimea, organizes sugar-cane history tours. The Plantation Lifestyle Tour *(Tue and Sat 9am, duration 1.5hrs)* lets visitors discover the former Waimea Mill Camp, where employees of the city's sugar refinery used to live. Most of the volunteer guides have ties to the sugar industry, which helps shed light on the everyday life of workers.

From June to September, the **Koke'e Natural History Museum** (☎335-9975) organizes Sunday walks led by tour guides *($3 with reservation)*. You can even sign up to help rid the area of invasive plants (☎335-0924), which is not easy work.

Exploring

Lihu'e

(half-day to full day)

Lihu'e, Kaua'i's commercial and political centre, was founded on the eastern coast of the island near the large port of Nawiliwili. Like the island's other villages, Lihu'e was born as a result of the sugar industry and grew around the Lihu'e Plantation, founded in the mid-19th century. The Rice family, missionaries who became planters, and the Isenbergs, who came here from Germany, played an important role in the village's development. Despite suffering the wrath of time, the refinery, which is set up at the foot of German Hill at the city's entrance, is still in operation. Other than that, the town has few other tourist attractions but does indulge in tropical indolence.

The village is based around Rice Street, which links the town centre to the port. Across from the post office, at no. 4428, the **Kaua'i Museum ★★** *($5, free the first Saturday of every month; Mon to Fri 9am to 4pm, Sat 10am to 4pm; ☎245-6931)* has preserved the history of the island. The Wilcox Building, its main building, is named after

Abner and Lucy Wilcox, who were among the first missionaries to settle on Kaua'i. The main floor features a Hawaiian section displaying a beautiful canoe, a few examples of *tapa* cloth, *poi* pylons made with volcanic rock and beautiful *koa* bowls, some of which are quite large. Based on a principle adopted by most of the archipelago's museums, a small section upstairs is devoted to objects illustrating the everyday life and beliefs of the different ethnic communities.

The adjacent Rice Building, which is the most interesting, features a review of all of the major fields of knowledge concerning the archipelago: geology, ecology (wildlife and flora), Hawaiian culture (the art of ancestral voyage, agricultural techniques, *tapa*-cloth making) and history (Cook's discovery of the archipelago, the Russian presence, the sugar industry and the missionary influence). The magnificent costumes, including an *i'iwi* and *mamo* feather ceremonial helmet, will catch your eye. A 30min video set up at the building's entrance lets you experience the island from the perspective of a helicopter.

Go down Rice Street towards Nawiliwili.

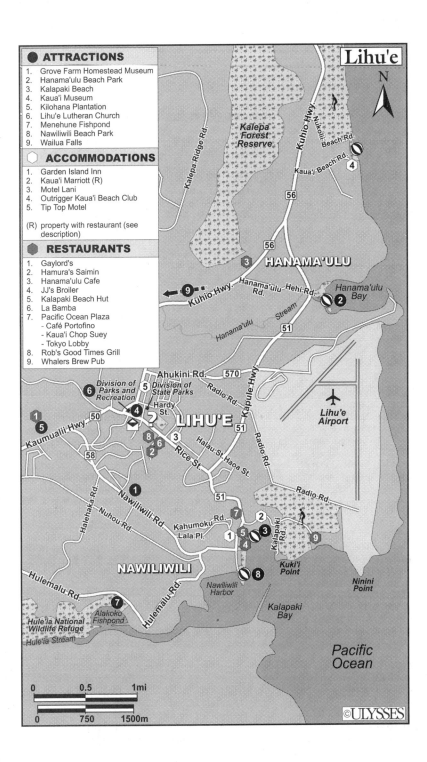

Lihu'e

N

● ATTRACTIONS

1. Grove Farm Homestead Museum
2. Hanama'ulu Beach Park
3. Kalapaki Beach
4. Kaua'i Museum
5. Kilohana Plantation
6. Lihu'e Lutheran Church
7. Menehune Fishpond
8. Nawiliwili Beach Park
9. Wailua Falls

◻ ACCOMMODATIONS

1. Garden Island Inn
2. Kaua'i Marriott (R)
3. Motel Lani
4. Outrigger Kaua'i Beach Club
5. Tip Top Motel

(R) property with restaurant (see description)

◼ RESTAURANTS

1. Gaylord's
2. Hamura's Saimin
3. Hanama'ulu Cafe
4. JJ's Broiler
5. Kalapaki Beach Hut
6. La Bamba
7. Pacific Ocean Plaza
   - Café Portofino
   - Kaua'i Chop Suey
   - Tokyo Lobby
8. Rob's Good Times Grill
9. Whalers Brew Pub

Kalepa Forest Reserve

Kuhio Hwy

Nukolii

Beach Rd.

Kaua'i Beach Rd.

56

56

HANAMA'ULU

Hanama'ulu Bay

Kuhio Hwy

Hanama'ulu-Hehi-Rd.

Hanama'ulu Rd.

Hanama'ulu Stream

51

Ahukini Rd. 570

Division of Parks and Recreation

Division of State Parks

Radio Rd.

Kapule Hwy

Lihu'e Airport

Kalepa Ridge Rd.

Hardy St.

LIHU'E

51

Halau St.

Haoa St.

Rice St.

Radio Rd.

Kaumualii Hwy 50

58

Nawiliwili Rd.

Halehaka Rd.

Nuhou Rd.

Kahumoku Rd.

Lala Pl.

51

Kalapaki Rd.

Kuki'i Point

Ninini Point

NAWILIWILI

Hulemalu Rd.

Hule'ia National Wildlife Refuge

Hule'ia Stream

Alakoko Fishpond

Nawiliwili Harbor

Kalapaki Bay

Pacific Ocean

| 0 | 0.5 | 1mi |

| 0 | 750 | 1500m |

© ULYSSES

Movies on Kaua'i

Kaua'i is well known among movie directors and producers, and Steven Spielberg in particular seems to have a weakness for the island. Of the 50 or so big movies that have been shot here, three have been Spielberg productions: *Jurassic Park, Raiders of the Lost Arc* and *Indiana Jones and the Temple of Doom.*

Kaua'i's movie fame began in 1933 with the filming of *White Heat.* Some of the better-known movies that followed include *South Pacific* in 1958, starring Joshua Logan and Mitzi Gaylor, whose famous singing scene was shot on Lumaha'i Beach; *Blue Hawaii*, in 1962, starring Elvis Presley as the rebel son of a

pineapple-growing family; and the second version of *King Kong*, shot in 1976, in which Jessica Lange and Jeff Bridges hunt the giant ape in the Kalalau Valley. Kaua'i's filmography is so diverse and plentiful that **Hawaii Movie Tours** (☎822-1192 *or 800-628-8432*) offers tours to the various movie sites.

Deeply curved, the large Kalapaki Bay features the beautiful **Kalapaki Beach** ★★, bordered by coconut trees and boasting a Marriott Hotel. Perfect for swimming because it is well sheltered, the bay is also a favourite of surfers who take advantage of the great waves that form at its mouth. **Nawiliwili Beach Park** (*washrooms, showers, picnic tables*), occupying the western side of the bay, is a popular meeting place. The other side, which is rocky and hilly, is home to houses on stilts and in the backdrop, the Kaua'i Lagoons Golf Course. The beach is easily reached by the Marriott Hotel or by the footbridge crossing Naliwiliwili's torrent between Kalapaki

Beach and Duke's Canoe Club.

Wa'apa Road leads to the port from Nawiliwili Beach Park.

Past the tip that closes off the bay to the west lies **Nawiliwili Port**, the island's most important port, where cargo and cruise ships, as well as small sea-excursion boats, can dock. The marina is further west, facing Niumalu Beach Park, at the mouth of the Hule'ia River.

Cross the bridge at Pu'ali's torrent and take Hulemalu Road to the right.

The small road climbs above the **Hule'ia River** ★, a vast humid area where rice and taro were once culti-

vated. The entire area is part of the Hule'ia National **Wildlife Refuge** ★ (☎828-1413), to which entrance is forbidden. It is possible, however, to go up the river by kayak from Niumalu Park, in Nawiliwili. This is a great opportunity to see some endemic bird species that live there, such as *ae'o* (stilt) and especially *koloa*, the Hawaiian duck.

It is also a great time to take advantage of the view of the valley, into which the river runs, from a viewpoint located a little more than a mile from the beginning of the road. Just below lies Alekoko's fishpond, known as **Menehune Fishpond** ★. Legend says that this large fishpond was built in one night by a mythical tribe of small people. Parallel to the river, it is separated by a long stone wall, 820ft (250m) long and 5ft (1.5m) wide, which has been blanketed by vegetation for a long time. Its designers in fact cut one of the loops of the Hule'ia River. Mullet is still bred here.

Head back to Niumalu Road, then take Nawiliwili Road (58) travelling west.

The Wilcox family, descendants of the first missionaries that settled on Kaua'i, founded the Grove Farm plantation in 1864. The residence became the **Grove Farm Homestead Museum** ★ *($5; guided tours Mon, Wed and Thu at 10am and 1pm with reservation; ☎245-3202).* Following a rather slow tour of the gardens, the visit moves on to the main residence, which is surrounded by a shaded porch where you can take a breath of fresh air. Despite a tropical touch and several pieces of Asian furniture, you cannot help but notice, through the decor, the 19th-century moral rectitude of its founders. Windows display a small collection of Hawaiian items. After a visit to George Wilcox's office, the tour ends in the kitchens, which date somewhere between the 19th century and the 1940s. Homemade cookies and iced tea are served. Despite

all of this, the visit is unjustifiably long (2.5hrs).

Nawiliwili Road joins up with Highway 50 at the southern exit of Lihu'e, by the Kukui Grove Shopping Center.

The **Kilihana Plantation** *(free admission, Mon to Sat 9:30am to 9:30pm, Sun 9:30am to 5pm; ☎245-5608)* lies south of the crossroads. Despite being classified as a museum, the Tudor-style planter's residence primarily houses luxury and craft shops, as well as Gaylord's restaurant (see p 478). It was built in 1935 by another Wilcox family member, who cultivated approximately 24,710 acres (10,000ha) of sugar cane in the surrounding area. The furniture was brought from San Francisco and the art comes from Asia and the entire Pacific. At the end of your visit, you can window-shop or take a carriage ride through the park *(Mon to Sat 11am to 6:30pm, Sun until 5pm)* or the fields *($21; Mon to Thu at 11am and 2pm).*

Go back up Highway 50 towards Lihu'e's town centre. Just before the turn, at the foot of the sugar refinery, take Ho'omana Road to the left.

Across from the refinery stands German Hill, whose name is a reminder of the German immigrants who settled here at the end of the

19th century and in 1885 founded the **Lihu'e Lutheran Church** ★, which is dominated by a slender church bell tower. Rebuilt in 1982 after Hurricane Iwa, the church rediscovered the vitality of its youth. It was designed in the image of the boat aboard which the community arrived to the island after a long trip by Cape Horn. The floor thus slightly bulges, like the bridge of a ship, and the altar is lit by sea lanterns. The tribune is supposed to remind you of the upper deck where the captain usually stands. Not long ago, German Hill was home to the community's German school.

Continue to trek back to the centre of town. Turn left at the lights onto Kuhio Highway. At the northern exit of Lihu'e (Mile 1.2), take Ma'alo Road (583) after a steep descent.

Crossing through the sugar-cane fields, you will reach **Wailua Falls** ★ ★ ★ after 4mi (6.5km). About 80ft high (25m), the twin falls (Wailua means "two waters") pour into a vast basin surrounded by rich vegetation. After heavy rains, they form a single silvery waterfall. Signs warn against climbing to the top of the falls, as many people have lost their lives after slipping on wet rocks.

Kaua'i

Three paths lead down to the foot of the falls, the best path being the farthest. It starts in a large unpaved parking lot, around 1,640ft (500m) before the end of the road. Steep and slippery when it rains, the path is interspersed with tree roots, but is manageable if you're careful. The other two paths, which are closer to the belvedere, are even steeper and more slippery as they cut through the forest. The most popular path, beginning right next to the crash barrier bordering the road, is lined with ropes to make the path easier to tackle. The third path, the closest, begins behind the Emergency Call Box. It does not have ropes and is as dangerous as the second path; trekkers have to hang on to trees to keep from sliding down faster than they might want to... The reward is worth the effort, though. From the river bank, which is blanketed by wild grass, you will see the two falls flowing majestically into the circus, which is closed off by towering cliffs. Phaetons (white tropicbirds with long tails) circle overhead.

Back onto Highway 56, you will reach Hanama'ulu. Turn right onto Hanama'ulu Road near the Hanama'ulu Cafe and the 7-Eleven. The road eventually turns into Hehi Road. Follow it to the end.

Hanama'ulu Beach Park *(washrooms, showers, picnic tables, camping)* lies on the deep Hanama'ulu Bay at the mouth of the Hanama'ulu River. It especially attracts locals who come to camp on weekends. Swimming is not really on the agenda due to the alluvions pouring from the river.

Wailua – Kapa'a

(one day)

Along with the Po'ipu's eastern coast to the south, the island's eastern coast is the most touristic, nicknamed **Coconut Coast** in memory of the vast coconut groves that once grew here. Wailua was then the heart of Kaua'i's temporal and spiritual power, as can attest the many vestiges of temples and sacred sites. Today, only a few clumps of trees remain. During the past 20 years, the entire coast, which features a few less-than-spectacular beaches, has however not been spared the invasion of condominiums and shopping centres.

North of Hanama'ulu, past the intersection of Routes 50 (coming from Lihu'e) and 51 (coming from the airport), the paved road runs along the Wailua Golf Course (Mile 4.3), one of Hawaii's most popular public golf courses. The entire

length of the course if bordered by a beach that is quite lovely, known as **Wailua Golf Course Beach ★**.

At Mile 5.1, a road leading to Lydgate Park comes up on the right. After 1,640ft (500m), turn right again onto Nalu Road.

The extremely popular and vast **Lydgate Park ★★** *(washrooms, showers, picnic tables)* stretches along a beautiful beach near the mouth of the Wailea River. It has a huge playground that is ideal for children. To make up for the rather strong currents that sweep the coast, two closed-off lava stone basins were built, one for children, and one where you can even snorkel. The extremely popular site is packed during the day, which can make underwater swimming rather difficult. For better visibility, go in the morning. A sign near the bathrooms lists the different species of fish that swim in the waters here.

The area located on the summits of Mount Kalepa and Mount Nounou, parallel to the coast of Wailua Bay, was once part of a sacred territory known as Wailuanuiahu'ano. Long ago, it was the religious and political centre of Kaua'i, confirmed by the *mana* (spiritual force) of several great *heiaus*, especially in Holoholoku, where great chiefs were

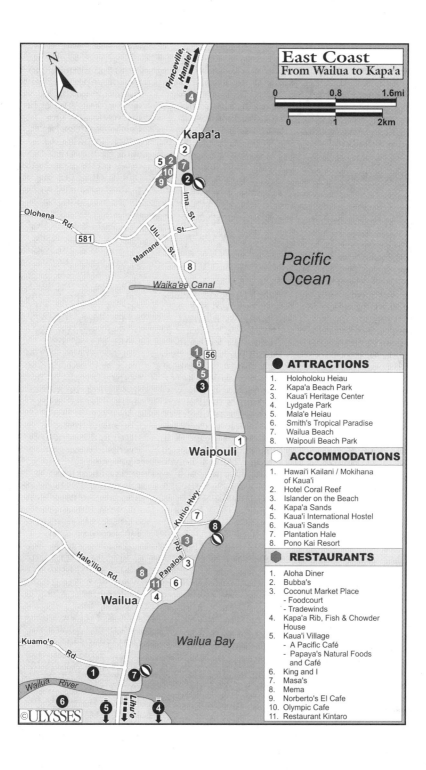

East Coast
From Wailua to Kapa'a

Princeville, Hanalei

Kapa'a

Olohena Rd.

581

Ulu St.

Mamane St.

Ima St.

St.

Waika'ea Canal

56

Waipouli

Pacific Ocean

Kuhio Hwy.

Papaloa Rd.

Hale'ilio Rd.

Wailua

Kuamo'o Rd.

Wailua Bay

Wailua River

Lihu'e

©ULYSSES

● ATTRACTIONS
1. Holoholoku Heiau
2. Kapa'a Beach Park
3. Kaua'i Heritage Center
4. Lydgate Park
5. Mala'e Heiau
6. Smith's Tropical Paradise
7. Wailua Beach
8. Waipouli Beach Park

○ ACCOMMODATIONS
1. Hawai'i Kailani / Mokihana of Kaua'i
2. Hotel Coral Reef
3. Islander on the Beach
4. Kapa'a Sands
5. Kaua'i International Hostel
6. Kaua'i Sands
7. Plantation Hale
8. Pono Kai Resort

■ RESTAURANTS
1. Aloha Diner
2. Bubba's
3. Coconut Market Place
    - Foodcourt
    - Tradewinds
4. Kapa'a Rib, Fish & Chowder House
5. Kaua'i Village
    - A Pacific Café
    - Papaya's Natural Foods and Café
6. King and I
7. Masa's
8. Mema
9. Norberto's El Cafe
10. Olympic Cafe
11. Restaurant Kintaro

born. Today, the same area makes up the **Wailua River State Park** ★★.

North of Lydgate Park, at the mouth of the Wailua River, stands one such temple, the **Hikinaakala Heiau** ★, religious centre of the *pu'uhonua* of Hauola, where *kapu*-breakers could take refuge. The massive 605ft (2m) high and 11.5ft (3.5m) thick walls once protected the sacred grounds that were guarded by a row of *tikis*, facing the river. After the abolition of that religion in 1819, a residence was built on the site, and towards 1850, sweet potatoes and coconut trees were planted within the walls of the *heiau*. Offerings wrapped in *ti* leaves are still laid at the base of the walls.

On the other side of the Kuhio Highway, across from the Holiday Inn Sunspree Resort, the thick blanket of vegetation makes it difficult to see the ruins of another *heiau* (Mala'e), once Kaua'i's largest.

Right next to it, just before the bridge over the Wailua, a small road leads down towards the left to the river. From the pier, Smith's Tropical Paradise (☎821-6895) and Wai'ale'ale Boat Tours (☎822-4908) provide maritime shuttles to the **Fern Grotto** ★. Located upstream, this lovely grotto draped with

ferns is the most popular destination of organized tours and towers over the river. Though it is extremely well kept, particularly for "tropical" weddings, the $15 asked by both companies might not be worth the visit. If you decide to go anyway, you should know that Smith's and Wai'ale'ale boats take turns every 30min from 9am to 11:30am and 12:30pm to 3pm.

Beyond the pier stands **Smith's Tropical Paradise** *($5; every day 8:30am to 4pm; 174 Wailua Rd., ☎821-6895)*, a tropical theme garden on the south bank of the river. It features, in a rather kitschy fashion, its (extremely) scaled-down version of the Polynesian Cultural Center of O'ahu. Here, every islet is devoted to one of the main communities that people Hawaii: Polynesians, Japanese and Filipinos. Even though the gardens can be visited all day long, they are in fact the setting for the *lu'au* that is organized here every day (see p 489).

Once you have crossed the Wailua River, (Mile 6), turn left onto Kuamo'o Road (Highway 580).

Kuamo'o Road climbs above the river, following the path of the ancient Road of the King, which linked the island's seven most sacred sites.

Almost immediately to the left appears a launching ramp, and 655ft (200m) further lie the vestiges of the **Holoholoku Heiau** ★, which according to some, is the oldest *heiau* on the island. All that is left of this important royal site are the surrounding walls and a terrace. The ancient temple is located at the foot of a small hill blanketed in vegetation, Ka Lae O Ka Manu. To the right, stairs lead to its summit, where queens and princesses gave birth to future chiefs of Kaua'i by leaning against a birthing stone, or *pohaku ho'ohanau.* The umbilical cords of newborns were placed in the cleft of the rock marked by the inscription "Pohaku Piko." The *mana* freed through this series of events is what gave this place such religious and political importance in the eyes of the ancestors in the valley of the Wailua River. The stairs lead to the Japanese cemetary.

A little less than 1.2mi (2km) away, Kuamo'o Road leads to a parking lot to the left, which offers a superb **view** ★★ of the valley and river. Originally devoted to taro, it was used for rice at the end of the 19th century by Chinese and Japanese immigrants. The rice fields eventually became grazing lands, which remain to this day. Information signs retrace the site's historical importance.

Right above lie the vestiges of the **Poli'ahu Heiau ★**, a four-sided building built with stones taken from the river bed. Kaua'i's last king, Kaumuali'i, kept it for his own personal use.

A trail below the viewpoint leads to a bellstone, which is a "musical stone." At the end of the trail, a short path overrun by vegetation leads down to a site that majestically towers over the Wailua River on one side, and remaining taro fields on the other. From here, the bellstone is easily recognizable by the marks left by repeated hits.

Just past the *heiau*, a second parking lot offers a panoramic view of the **'Opaeka'a Falls ★★**, formed by a river that is more or less parallel to the Wailua River, joining it just before its mouth to form two big lovely chutes. It is impossible to get much closer.

At the top of the falls, a small narrow road to the left leads down into the Wailua Valley to **Kamokila Hawaiian Village ★★** *($5; Mon to Sat 8:30am to 4:30pm; ☎823-0559)*. This family reconstruction of a Hawaiian hamlet, where several movies have been filmed, is quite well done. It features *hale*, a stone with

petroglyphs, an altar dedicated to Lono where offerings were made, and an authentic bellstone whose metallic resonance was used to communicate messages to other villages. But it is the commentary of the Hawaii-born tour guide that is the most interesting: it opens a window on the ancient culture and daily lives of the Hawaiian ancestors, which is rarely this accessible.

Past the starting point of the path of Kuamo'o-Nounou, and further than that of Kuilau Ridge, the paved road ends in front of a ford. The Keahua Arboretum stretches further on. A path crosses a vast stretch of grass scattered with clumps of eucalyptus with multicoloured trunks. The trail, reserved for four-wheel-drive vehicles, continues deep into the Wailua Valley to the foot of Kawaikini.

Head back on Kuamo'o Road to get to the coastal road.

North of the mouth of the Wailua River stretches **Wailua Beach ★** *(no infrastructure)*, which is quite lovely, though somewhat close to the road. The waters that surround it are fed by the river and quickly become muddy when it rains, which explains why the beach is especially popular with a

few local boogie-board enthusiasts.

At Mile 6.5, near the Sizzler restaurant, Hale'ilio Road (left side) leads to the beginning of the path that climbs up Mount Nounou, better known as the **Sleeping Giant**. This nickname refers to the flat mountain that towers over the agglomeration and stretches from Wailua to Kapa'a, and which looks like a giant resting on his back with his head pointing south. It is an important part of island legends. A tourism-bureau sign indicates the mountain further north on the Kuhio Highway (Mile 7.7), but you can see it from anywhere in the region, with its profile being more visible in the south. The beginning of the path is easy and is marked on the right side of the road, 1.2mi (2km) away (near telephone pole no. 38). The path reaches the giant's chest in only 1.7mi (2.8km).

Kaua'i's main tourist district begins at the Wailua River. Only 3mi (5km) away and developed at a furious pace over the last decade, from Wailua in the south, to Waipouli, to Kapa'a in the north, it is an endless stretch of hotels, condominiums, restaurants and both small and large shopping centres, the largest of which is the Coconut Market Place. The Kaua'i Village features

Kaua'i

the **Kaua'i Heritage Center of Hawaiian Culture & the Arts** *(Mon to Fri 10am to 6pm, Sat 10am to 5pm; ☎821-0802)*, a cultural centre with family atmosphere devoted to Hawaiian crafts and traditions. Add to this a few acres of sand that aren't really ideal for swimming... One of the loveliest beaches is **Waipouli Beach Park ★**, a stone's throw from the Coconut Market Place. Here, the rocky barrier marking the coast forms a natural basin at high tide where it is fun to take a dip. The park itself is nothing but a vast grassy stretch, where greater golden-plovers prance about in wintertime. Further north, the tucked-away beach of the **Kapa'a Beach Park** *(washrooms, picnic tables)*, next to a football field, offers nothing exceptional.

It is at the heart of **Kapa'a** (Mile 8.4), a former plantation village that was converted for tourism, where you find what looks most like a living centre. The old, fixed-up wooden shop fronts feature a variety of restaurants and boutiques, as well as a few craft shops.

The tour continues northward.

The North Coast

(one to two days)

North of Kapa'a stretches Kaua'i's final frontier. Despite the Princeville condominiums, less than 19mi (30km) away, the north coast remains the island's most rural and authentic coast. Drenched in almost constant torrential rain in winter, it features rich vegetation, a big part of its particular charm. Its coast features an infinite number of sandy coves that are more or less known, and either deserted or popular.

At the northern exit of Kapa'a near **Kealia Beach** lies a simple stretch of sand protected by a reef and bordered by shallow waters (viewpoint at Mile 9.2). Boogie boarders gather further north, where lie the vestiges of a popular 19th-century quay. A little past Kealia, you will reach Kumukumu, better known as **Donkey's Beach** (Mile 10). This vast, tucked-away stretch of red sand, located at the mouth of a small river, is especially popular with surfers. Swimming here is impossible.

At Mile 13, to the right, Kukuihale Road leads down to Anahola Beach Park (you can also take Anahola Road at Mile 13.5).

On the eastern side of the large Anahola Bay, over which tower the mountains of the same name, **Anahola Beach Park ★** *(washrooms, showers, picnic tables, camping)* is marked by a pretty beach shaded by pine trees. Popular with surfers and boogie-board enthusiasts, the beach is less popular among swimmers, depending on the day.

At the southern end of the beach, a natural basin protected by a reef is accessible to children. Camping, however, is not ideal, since many families live here year-round.

The hamlet of **Anahola**, stretching along the Kuhio Highway, only consists of a few houses, two businesses and the small, wooden Anahola Baptist Church, located on the mountainside.

At the exit of the hamlet (Mile 14.1), just before the climb, Aliomanu Road cuts through mango trees and wooden homes to reach another **beach ★** that closes off Anahola Bay to the west. Rarely visited, if only by local residents who come to fish or surf, the beach stretches along the mouth of the Anahola torrent.

Even though a Scenic Overlook is located at Mile 14.8, you in fact have to trek 1,640ft (500m) farther to see the "hole in the mountain" marked on a tourism bureau sign, just below the highest peak of the Anahola mountain chain. Partially filled by a rock slide, it

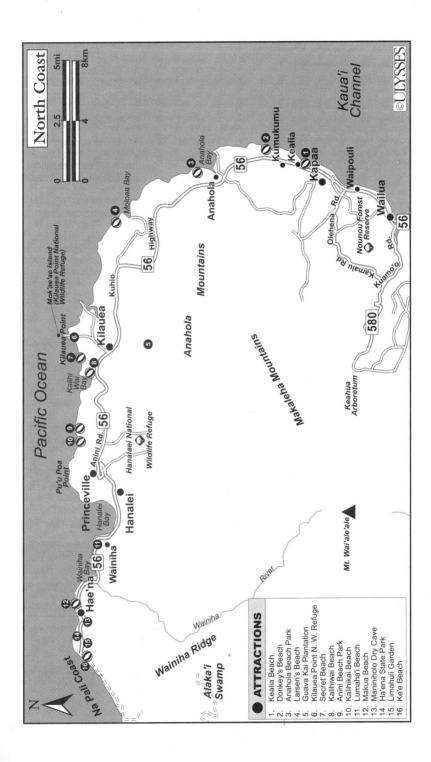

North Coast

Pacific Ocean

Na Pali Coast

Kaua'i Channel

Mountains

Anahola Mountains

Makaleha Mountains

Mt. Wai'ale'ale ▲

Wainiha Ridge

Alaka'i Swamp

Wainiha River

Wainiha

Ha'ena

Hanalei

Hanalei Bay

Princeville

Pu'u Poa Point

Wainiha Bay

Kalihi Wai Bay

Kilauea

Kilauea Point
Mok'ae'ae Island
(Kilauea Point National
Wildlife Refuge)

Hanalaei National
Wildlife Refuge

Anini Rd.

Moloaa Bay

Anahola Bay

Anahola

Kuhio

Highway

56

56

Kumukumu

Kealia

Kapaa

Waipouli

Wailua

Olehena Rd.

Kamalu Rd.

Nounou Forest
Reserve

Kuamo'o Rd.

Keahua Arboretum

580

56

© ULYSSES

● ATTRACTIONS

1. Kealia Beach
2. Donkey's Beach
3. Anahola Beach Park
4. Larsen's Beach
5. Guava Kai Plantation
6. Kilauea Point N. W. Refuge
7. Secret Beach
8. Kalihiwai Beach
9. Anini Beach Park
10. Kalihikai Beach
11. Lumaha'i Beach
12. Makua Beach
13. Maniniholo Dry Cave
14. Ha'ena State Park
15. Limahuli Garden
16. Ke'e Beach

Scale: 0 — 2.5 — 5mi / 0 — 4 — 8km

is not as impressive as it once was.

At Mile 16.7, take a small detour on Ko'olau Road.

Parallel to Highway 56, **Ko'olau Road** ★ leads down to the Moloa'a River. Just before reaching the water, the road of the same name cuts through thick vegetation and leads to a lovely cove marked by a stretch of sand and pine trees. A few residents and fishers enjoying the peaceful area can be found here, and this is also a great spot for camping. Less than 1mi up Ko'olau Road, just before the cemetery, a white vertical Beach Access marker indicates the start of the path that leads to Kaakaaniu Beach – better known by surfers as **Larsen's Beach**.

From the end of the road, it will only take you 5min to walk down a path to get to the beach. Narrow, solitary and sometimes strewn with black rocks, it stretches at the foot of the hill. Swimming is possible although the water is shallow.

Ko'olau Road joins Highway 56 a little before Mile 20.

At the entrance to Kilauea (Mile 23.2), Guava Man, with a yellow guava head smiling and sporting glasses, welcomes you to the **Guava Kai Planta-**

tion *(free admission; every day 9am to 5pm;* ☎*828-6121)*, located less than 1mi away on Kuawa Road. With nearly 494 acres (200ha) of guava trees, it is the biggest of its kind in Hawaii. Fruit trees frame the road as soon as you enter the property. The visit is à la carte: you can take a look at the unloading and sorting of fruit and enjoy a (short) tour of the tropical garden, where there is actually little to see. The goal of this tour, however, is quite obviously to lure tourists to the souvenir shop, which is generously stocked. Visitors can pick fruit for free, within reasonable limits, during harvest season.

At Mile 23.4, turn right on Kilauea Road.

Just past the fork stands the **Christ Memorial Episcopal Church** ★, an odd little church made of lava stones. The road just past the church turns left and climbs towards **Kilauea Point National Wildlife Refuge** ★★ *($2; every day 10am to 4pm;* ☎*828-1413)*, at the northern tip of the island. The most important Hawaiian nesting site of seabirds, it stretches over 30 acres (12ha) of cliffs and rocky peninsulas,

with the main one being crowned by a lighthouse. Its primary role is to protect the reproduction of red-footed boobies and petrels. Petrels nest in trees, while red-footed boobies nest in burrows on the side of precipice. Along the cleared path leading to the lighthouse, you can catch a glimpse of such nests behind the "Birds only beyond this sign" signs. They can be up to 6.5ft (2m) deep and it is common to see young petrels stick their feathered heads out. Unless you make it out to Midway, this is your best chance to see big species of seabirds found on the islands, such as large frigatebirds, brown boobies and white- or red-tailed phaetons. The magnificent Laysan albatross has only been on the island since the 1970s. In winter, these birds set up on grassy slopes overlooking the sea, from where their rather awkward take-off is made easier. Here, it is also possible to spot bold *nenes*. Every morning at 10:15am, rangers organize guided 2hr tours towards Crater Hill. The visitors reception centre also features a small exhibition dedicated to Hawaii's natural environment, flora and wildlife.

Nene

The small **lighthouse** on the very tip of the island was built in May 1913 to help guide ships travelling between Hawaii and Asia. Until it was automated in 1976, the lighthouse, barely 50ft (16m) high, was equipped with a French Fresnel lens. The view from the tip overlooks cliffs chiselled by waves and the islet of Mokuaeae, where many birds nest. To the west lies the magnificent Secret Beach. With a little luck in winter, you might see a humpback whale, since the neighbouring waters are part of Hawaii's marine sanctuary.

Get back onto Kuhio Highway. At Mile 23.9, Kalihiwai Road comes up on the right.

Just past the first turn, a trail leads to **Secret Beach ★ ★**, which is not that secret anymore but beautiful just the same. Indeed, the beach, which was reserved for nudists for a long time and also goes by the Hawaiian name of Kauapea, has now been discovered by tourists. From the parking lot, a good path (though a tad slippery) is 5min away from the blanket of sand. If you want to be alone, keep to your left at the bottom of the path; another beach lies behind the rocks. Basins formed by the tide and warmed by the sun are a swimmer's delight. To the east is the silhou-

ette of Kilauea's lighthouse.

Just before this point, Kalihiwai Road leads to the large **Kalihawai Beach ★**, which opens onto the bay that shares its name. Beaten by strong waves, it is perfect for surfers (experienced only) and boogie-board enthusiasts. The road ends here, right by the Kalihiwai River, since the bridge that once crossed it was destroyed by a tsunami in the late 1950s. The river's mouth forms a wide basin, but swimming is not recommended due to the risk of leptospirosis. Kayak outings in this tropical setting are very popular, though.

Get back onto Highway 56.

Once back on the highway, the **Scenic Overlook** lies at Mile 25. From there, if you climb around 655ft (200m) on foot, you will discover a small waterfall that flows quite discreetly between the trees, depending on the season. By crossing the bridge over the Kahihiwai River, you'll see a larger waterfall that is formed upstream.

The second branch of Kalihiwai Road, which once led to the beach before it was cut by a tsunami, lies at Mile 25.5. Once on the road, immediately turn left onto Anini Road.

The road runs along the coast up to **Anini Beach Park ★ ★** *(washrooms, showers, picnic tables, camping – see p 472)*, which includes one of the few beaches on the northern coast that are ideal for swimming, thanks to the great Anini Reef, the archipelago's most important reef, which stretches 655ft (200m) off the coast. The access road is flanked by luxurious residences, and their affluent owners meet at the Polo Club.

The long, straight beach is bordered by shade-providing trees. In addition to snorkelling, beach-goers can enjoy windsurfing. Most locals prefer to fish. Despite its popularity, 'Anini remains relatively quiet, but this peacefulness is threatened by the prospect of a road directly linking the beach to Princeville – this project has been discussed for several years and many riverside residents are fiercely opposed to it. If you follow the road to the end, you will reach **Kalihikai Beach ★**, which is quite calm since it is protected by the same barrier. Princeville's first condominiums stand in the distance.

A little past **Princeville**'s airport, the road reaches the seaside resort at Mile 28. It is named after a plantation founded on the

Kaua'i

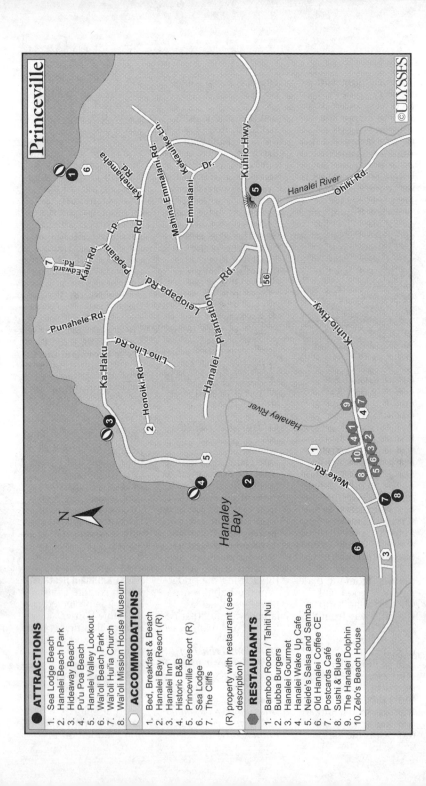

Princeville

© ULYSSES

N

Hanaley Bay

Hanalei River

Hanalei River

Kuhio Hwy.

Ohiki Rd.

Hanalei Plantation Rd.

Leiopapa Rd.

Punahele Rd.

Ka-Haku

Liho-Liho Rd.

Honoiki Rd.

Kamehameha Rd.

Pepelani Lp.

Kaiui Rd.

Edward Rd.

Mahina Emmalani Rd.

Kekekaiike Ln.

Emmalani Dr.

Weke Rd.

56

banks of the Hanalei River in the early 1860s by Scotsman Robert Crichton Wyllie. He shipped a sugar refinery in pieces from England and named his domain Princeville after young Prince Albert, Kamehameha V and Queen Emma's only son. The kingdom's most influential people visited Wyllie, who for 20 years was the minister of foreign affairs. Today, this sugar refinery's past is buried, and the present is strictly devoted to tourism. Princeville is not actually a city but rather a huge complex of condominiums, hotels and holiday cottages, also featuring a 36-hole golf course. With the exception of a few stores in the Princeville Center, businesses and activities are few and far between.

Princeville lies on a coastal plateau delimited by cliffs and towers over the Hanalei River, and the magnificent bay of the same name to the east. The rocky surroundings feature many trails (slippery when wet) that lead down to three sandy creeks. Nothing spectacular, they are almost completely submersed by waves in winter, but you can practice snorkelling here in summer. Stretching from east to west are the **Sea Lodge Beach** (which can be reached by the condominium complex of the same name), Pali Ke Kua Beach (idem),

Taro

Legend says that the first child born to the ancestral gods Wakea and Ho'ohokukalani died at a young age. A foot of taro grew where the child was buried. A second child was born, Haloa, who gave birth to the human race. Since these immemorial times, man continues to respect the taro as an older brother. As the cornerstone of ancestral agriculture, the taro defined social organization. Even the word *o'hana*, referring to the extended family who worked together in the fields, is derived from *oha*, describing the taro sprouts from

which the plant reproduces itself. Hawaiians grow nearly 300 species of taro, each having a different name. Several species were named after reef fish, whose colours resembled those of the taro stem.

better known as **Hideaway Beach** ★, and finally, at the foot of the Princeville Hotel, towards the mouth of the Hanalei River, **Pu'u Poa Beach**, the largest of the three. It is near here that Schaeffer, an employee of the Russian-American Company of Alaska, attempted to build one of his three forts in 1816 (see p 456).

At Mile 28, mile counting begins at zero, so reset your odometer!

Shortly thereafter to the left, the **Hanalei Valley Lookout** ★★ magnificently overlooks the valley's irrigated checkered taro fields, which form marroon, green and grey patches depending on whether the fields have been cultivated or flooded. The chiselled summits of Wai'ale'ale and Kawaikini, the island's

Kaua'i

highest peak, tower in the backdrop. On rainy days, waterfalls gush down their jagged slopes, forming the large, gleaming Hanalei River in the Hanalei Valley. Over 60% of Hawaiian taro is grown on these banks – a tradition that can be traced back 1,000 years. Since the early 20th century and because of the increasing Americanization of Hawaii, the archipelago's production has plummeted 95%. The entire valley is protected by the **Hanalei National Wildlife Refuge** (☎828-1413), which shelters some of Hawaii's rarest bird species, including gallinules, *koloa* (duck), *ae'o* (stilts) and migrating birds. It is forbidden to enter the reserve, but wildlife can be observed from Ohiki Road, which cuts through the valley just past Hanalei River Bridge (at Mile 1.2), or by kayak. Despite numerous expansion projects, which have yet to be approved, the old metal bridge, the first of seven one-way bridges, still holds up. Trucks are currently forbidden from entering Hanalei and the rest of the northern coast, thus ensuring peace and quiet for the locals.

At Mile 2.4, you will cross into **Hanalei**, which lies on the edge of the bay of the same name, with pastures in the background and located at the foot of the rounded, clouded

summits of Mamalaha and Hihimaku. Younger and livelier than Princeville, Hanalei attracts surfers who come to challenge the bay's colossal waves in winter. Kayak enthusiasts paddle up the river or head for the Na Pali coast, as do day-trippers. Hanalei flanks the Kuhio Highway, which runs parallel to the coast, though always a fair distance away. Two neighbouring shopping centres mark its boundaries: the Ching Young Village and the Hanalei Centre.

Take Aku Road makai.

Hanalei Bay forms a perfect crescent and features a 2mi (3km) beach stretching from the mouth of the Hanalei River in the east to Makahoa Point in the west. The beach is broken up into different sections: Hanalei Beach Park to the east, Wai'oli Beach Park in the middle, and Waipa Beach in the west, past the bridge at the village's exit. Weke Road, a residential road that runs parallel to the Kuhio Highway, leads to the first two parks. Houses for rent line its entire length and are a stone's throw from the beach.

At the mouth of the Hanalei River, the **Hanalei Beach Park** ★ *(washrooms, showers, picnic tables, camping on weekends)* is popular in summer with swimmers and boogie-board en-

thusiasts. In winter, this long pier stretching out to sea is frequented by surfers and fishers. It was built in the 1910s, when the city's economy was booming, and enabled the exportation of rice to neighbouring areas.

On weekends, local families come to camp at the few campgrounds amidst the pine trees further east, at a place known as Black Pot Beach – named in memory of the community cauldron used by fishers that was once kept here. Equipped with longboards, most surfers gather at **Wai'oli Beach Park** *(washrooms, beach volleyball court)*, also known as Pinetrees and Toilet Bowl. In wintertime, the beach becomes a hot spot for the best of the best in this sport.

Take Mahimahi Road to get back onto the Kuhio Highway.

One of the island's loveliest churches stands at Mile 3. Set against a mountain backdrop and cutting through palm trees, the **Wai'oli Hui'ia Church** ★★ is bedecked with green shingles. A mission, the island's second, was established here as early as 1834, but the church only dates from 1912. Built in American Gothic style, it features stained glass. Mass is held in both English and Hawaiian. The

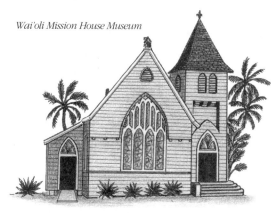

Wai'oli Mission House Museum

neighbouring building (Mission Hall), which serves as a meeting room, is Kaua'i's oldest religious building. Standing in a vast tropical garden behind the church, the residence of Hanalei's first missionaries houses the **Wai'oli Mission House Museum** ★ *(Tue, Thu and Sat, 9am to 3pm; ☎245-3202)*. The museum perfectly reproduces the austere ambiance of the everyday lives of the Alexanders and their successors, the Wilcoxes, who lived here from 1846 to 1869. The house was originally constructed in New England and shipped in pieces to Hawaii.

After Hanalei, you will come across one-way bridges and virtually empty beaches. Perfect for swimming and surfing, the first, **Waikoko Beach** ★, borders the large Hanalei Bay to the west. At Mile 4.7, a parking lot on the right side of the road gives

you access to a short path leading to **Lumaha'i Beach** ★★, one of the island's most striking beaches. Golden sand stretching alongside rampant vegetation contrasts magnificently with the black rocks and foaming waves. When the sea is calm in summer, it is possible to swim in the cove to the east formed by a small rocky tip, but be careful of currents and the strength of the waves. At Mile 5.8, just before the new bridge, a second access path leads to Lumaha'i where the beach is larger and bordered by pine trees.

At Mile 6.4, the road reaches **Wainiha Bay**, on the outskirts of the valley of the same name. Now deserted, it was once inhabited by Hawaiians for a long time, and it is even said that *menehune* lived here. When a census was taken at the end of the 19th century, dozens of people residing here unexpectedly de-

clared themselves of *menehune* descent…

At Mile 8.4, 985ft (300m) past Ha'ena Place, near the sign for Narrow Bridge, lies the access path to **Makua Beach** ★, better known by surfers as Tunnels for its winter rollers. Cars parked on the lower side should help indicate the way. Among divers, the place is well known for its underwater caves. In summer, when the sea is calm, its reefs swarm with a rainbow of fish.

At Mile 8.8, after a small ford passage, the **Maniniholo Dry Cave** is 80 to 100ft (35 to 30m) deep into the rock, and attests to the time around 4,000 years ago, when the coast was further back. Just across from the cave lies **Ha'ena State Park** *(washrooms, showers, picnic tables, camping – see p 472)*. Swimming is not advised, especially in winter.

Located shortly after, the **Limahuli Garden** *($10; Tue to Fri and Sun, 9:30am to 4pm; ☎826-1053)* depends on the National Tropical Botanical Garden, which manages the other two botanical gardens near Po'ipu on the southern coast. Limahuli Garden is completely devoted to Hawaiian flora and plants introduced by the Polynesians. A stroll through the garden, which takes between one and 1.5hrs (a little more than 0.5mi or

Kaua'i

about 1km) climbs the side of the valley. Every species is identified. You can even see vestiges of a *heiau* and terraces used to cultivate taro. You can either visit the garden on your own – with the help of a detailed guide – or choose the guided tour *($15, 10am and 2pm)*.

The Kuhio Highway ends at Mile 10, in a sea of cars. Here lies the gorgeous **Ke'e Beach** ★★ (Makana in Hawaiian), which is protected by a reef designed for snorkelling. Those who are not fond of swimming can sunbathe on the beach all day long. The eastern part of the beach is the best.

Westward of Ke'e Beach, a small path leads up to the *heiau* of **Kaulu a Pa'oa**. Carefully restored, it is easy to identify its three terraces and upper floor, Kaula o Laka, where a well-known *hula* school was once housed. A place dedicated to the *hula* goddess Laka, some legends claim that Hawaii's sacred dance originated here, though this is disputed by Moloka'i. Some *halau* still come sometimes to dance on the terrace in honour of Pele, their protector.

To the west towers the **Na Pali coast** ★★, which is partially protected by a state park. From Ke'e Beach to Polihale (see

p 458), covering around 19mi (30km), this coast offers some of the archipelago's most spectacular views. Shaped over millions of years, the cliffs are chiselled by the sea into a staggering series of peaks and rocky ridges. After it rains, the gaps between the eroded fortified tower, reaching towards the central mountains, trickle with hundreds of bountiful cascades, sharpening the stone to the point of wearing it down. Though the peaks are bare, the lower part of the mountain is covered with vegetation and is home to an endless series of isolated valleys that seem straight out of the imagination of Arthur Conan Doyle. Inhabited for many years by Hawaiians, who found security in the inaccessibility and abundance of the tropical climate, several Na Pali valleys remained populated until the beginning of the 20th century. Some families cultivated taro fields, others coffee-tree orchards. Residences and schools were built and are today completely blanketed by vegetation and drenched in torrential rains. In the 1960s, the hippie trend made its way to Kalalau. Up until recently, it was not uncommon to cross paths with a few buck-naked draft dodgers!

As docking was impossible for part of the year, men and mer-

chandise alike used to travel on a single path. Cleared above the drop by Hawaiian ancestors, the **Kalalau Trail** ★★★ runs over 11mi (18km) along the Na Pali coast until it reaches the valley of the same name – even though you also overlook it from the end of the road at Koke'e Park (see p 460). This rather arduous hike can be done in no less than two days, though more likely in three. Revealing valley after valley, the views from the trail are each worth the sweat and effort it takes to get there. As the trail has become extremely popular, especially in the summer when there is less rain, the demand for permits is high and it can be difficult to get your hands on one (see p 431). A permit for hiking beyond Hanakapi'ai is also mandatory, but no permit is necessary if you stop there.

The trail leaves the parking lot of Ke'e Beach and quickly climbs above it to offer a superb view of the reef and turquoise waters. Muddy at the start, as well as slippery and narrow, it is still easy enough to trek the first 2mi (3km) to the **Hanakapi'ai Valley** ★★, which is marked by a pleasant beach in the summer (currents sweep over it in winter). Swimming is nonetheless strongly discouraged. Stretching between pandanus and candlenut trees whose nuts cover the ground, this section makes for a great day trip. Some jump at the chance to climb along the torrent to the lovely **Hanakapi'ai Falls ★★**, a good hour's walk from the beach (2mi or 3km). The waterfall flows in three stages for 295ft (90m) into a small basin where you can take a dip, but be careful of falling rocks. Steeper and more difficult than the previous path and strewn with dead trees, especially in its upper part, the path features several ford passages. Never attempt to cross when water levels rise or during stormy weather. Camping at the mouth of the torrent at Hanakapi'ai is an option for some hikers, so they can leave for Kalalau early the following morning.

The path departs from the Hanakapi'ai Valley by tightly winding up 820ft (250m) to splendidly overlook the beach. It then leads through a series of forgotten valleys: Ho'olulu, Waiahuakua, and after 4mi (6.5km), **Hanakoa**. After around 1,640ft (500m), a poor path leading along the eastern branch of the torrent (not indicated) reaches the pretty **Hanakoa Falls ★**. The last section of the path, between Hanakoa and Kalalau, is the most difficult. The trail steepens dramatically every now and then, but never to a point of

making it dangerous. The natural shelter gets thinner and thinner, making it preferrable not to trek through this section during the hottest hours of the day. Little by little, the chiselled cliffs that frame the **Kalalau Valley ★★** and neighbouring valleys come into view. After a final ford passage, a wide beach and the ruins of a *heiau* appear. For a few years now, the Kalalau has been visited by an increasing number of day-trippers who come by boat, and the cleanliness and tranquility of the valley is left to suffer the consequences. If you plan on spending the night, you should know that rangers strictly enforce permits. You can camp by the beach or, in summer, in westward caves. Climbing around 2mi (3km) to the valley's interior, a path leads to a natural basin formed by Kalalau's torrent. On the way, you will come across terraces and former sites of ancient homes, now overtaken by the jungle.

Those who prefer water to land can explore the Na Pali coast by boat. Miloli'i Beach, where you can camp from May to September, is only accessible by sea, which is rarely calm. Though the helicopter flight is expensive, it is an unforgettable experience, especially at sunset, when the shadows of the cliffs create the illusion

of an endless accordeon.

The South Coast

(one to two days)

The entire southern part of the island, from Lihu'e to Waimea and beyond, is covered in sugar-cane fields. Charging up the low hills of the central mountains, this green carpet is crisscrossed by a network of private dirt trails. All of the local villages developed around sugar refining, beginning with Hawaii's first plantation, founded in Koloa in 1835. Most of the population descends from immigrants who came to work here in the second half of the 19th century. The Zen temples, *jodo* and *hongwanji* missions and who succeeded them, attest to this.

On the Po'ipu coast, the sun is usually out even when it's raining to the north or east. This, in addition to a few beaches, is what makes the south coast a favourite of vacationers.

Leave Lihu'e by taking the Kuhio Highway (50).

A little past the Kilohana Plantation, a Visitors Bureau sign indicates a viewpoint on Hoary Head Mountain, better known by its nickname, **Queen Victoria's Profile**. You'll need a vivid imagination to recognize the

Kaua'i

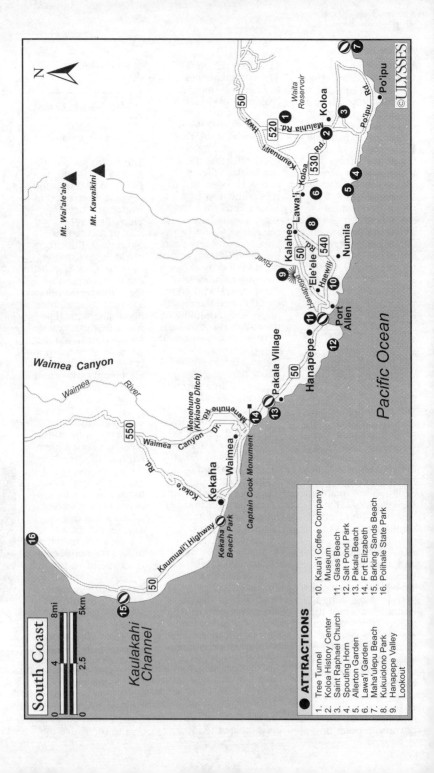

South Coast

N

0   4   8mi
0 2.5 5km

Kaulakahi Channel

Pacific Ocean

Waimea Canyon

Waimea River

Mt. Wai'ale'ale
Mt. Kawaikini

Waita Reservoir

Koloa
Po'ipu
Po'ipu Rd.

Kaumuali'i Hwy

520
Maluhia Rd.

530 Rd.
Koloa

Kaumuali'i

Lawa'i

Koloa Rd.

Kalaheo
Ele'ele Rd.
540
Haewili

Numila

50

Hanapepe Rd.

River

Port Allen

Hanapepe

Pakala Village

50

Menehune (Kikiaole Ditch)
Menehune Rd.

Waimea Canyon Dr.

550

Kohe'e Rd.

Kekaha

Waimea

Captain Cook Monument

Kaumuali'i Highway

Kekaha Beach Park

50

①
②
③
④
⑤
⑥
⑦
⑧
⑨
⑩
⑪
⑫
⑬
⑭
⑮
⑯

●ATTRACTIONS

1. Tree Tunnel
2. Koloa History Center
3. Saint Raphaël Church
4. Spouting Horn
5. Allerton Garden
6. Lawa'i Garden
7. Maha'ulepu Beach
8. Kukuiolono Park
9. Hanapepe Valley Lookout
10. Kaua'i Coffee Company Museum
11. Glass Beach
12. Salt Pond Park
13. Pakala Beach
14. Fort Elizabeth
15. Barking Sands Beach
16. Polihale State Park

©ULYSSES

queen's chin, especially when, more often than not, clouds have swallowed her head!

At Mile 6.7, keep left at the fork (Highway 520) to reach Koloa and Po'ipu.

The road travels through the **Tree Tunnel ★**, formed by eucalyptus foliage. Severely damaged by Hurricane Iniki, it has already partially restored itself. The trees were planted in the 19th century by a grower in Koloa.

Still lost amidst the fields of sugar cane, **Koloa ★** was born at the dawn of the sugar-refining era. Like the first Chinese immigrants, Hawaiians already cultivated sugar cane, but on a very small scale. In 1835, the archipelago's first plantation was created under the initiative of William Hooper. It comprised nearly 988 acres (400ha) of land, rented to Kamehameha III by his Honolulu employer, Ladd and Company. The first mill was completed in 1836, inaugurating a long period of growth and immigration.

At the crossroads of the 520 and Koloa Road, near the vestiges of a refinery chimney that dates back to 1841, lies a small park dedicated to the memory of all sugar workers. A lovely collection of **sculptures ★** represents the main people in-

volved in the industry: Hawaiian, Chinese, Japanese, Portuguese, Puerto Rican, Korean and Filipino. These various peoples landed in large numbers from the 19th century to the Second World War. A nearby sugar-cane grove features the different varieties of cane that are sold on the market.

Right next to the park, old wooden houses line Koloa's main street, Koloa Road. Though sugar cane remains in the area, old stores have long since given way to souvenir shops and restaurants. History buffs can have a look at old photographs at the **Koloa History Center**.

The fruit of its long immigration history, Koloa also features several religious buildings. Among the most important is the **Church at Koloa** (1859) in the centre of town, a charming white wooden church with three belltowers, as well as a *hongwanji* temple (1910). Weliweli Road, and then Hapa Road, lead to the **Saint Raphael Church**, founded in 1841. Built from coral stones whitened with limestone, it is Kaua'i's oldest Catholic church, and is associated with the Portugese community. The building dates from 1856 and has been entirely renovated.

From Koloa, Highway 520 leads farther south to Po'ipu.

The island's main seaside resort, **Po'ipu ★**, stretches the length of the often rocky coast, which harbours coves and a few pretty beaches. Its appeal can be summed up in a single word: sun. When it rains or is windy on other parts of the island, the sun still shines here. The resort is primarily visited by retirees and families who stay in one of its many condominiums. Upon arrival at Po'ipu, a crossroads offers two roads leading to both parts of the resort, located around the torrent of Waikomo – at the mouth of which once stood the Koloa Landing Port. Most condominiums and hotels can be reached by Po'ipu Road and are located on the eastern side. Lawa'i Road leads westward to a smaller number of establishments and runs along the coast until it reaches Spouting Horn.

Turn right on Lawa'i Road.

Around 1,640ft (500m) from the fork in the road, **Prince Kuhio Park** pays tribute to the birthplace of the revered prince Jonah Kuhio Kalaniana'ole Pi'ikoi, who represented Hawaii in the U.S. Congress from 1902 to 1922 and founded the Hawaiian Home Lands. In addi-

Kaua'i

tion to a commemorative monument, you can see vestiges of a *heiau*, the foundations of a home and a fishpond.

A little further, the road passes **Beachhouse Beach**, a narrow stretch of sand across from the Lawa'i Beach Resort.

Powerfully surging through a hole in the volcanic plateau that borders the coast and is dug between two layers, **Spouting Horn** ★★ is a kind of geyser that spouts to the rythym of the waves. Legend says that what you hear is the breathing of a *mo'o* (giant lizard), trapped in the orifice. The site is spectacular, especially at the end of the day when the sun is setting. Nevertheless, you may be nostalgic for a time not so long ago when there were no barriers or souvenir stands. The sea's strength determines how interesting the show will be.

Almost directly across from Spouting Horn, a 1920s planter's house holds the reception centre of the **National Tropical Botanical Garden** *(every day 8:30am to 5:30pm; ☎ 742-2623, www.ntbg.org)*. This centre maintains three gardens in Kaua'i, two of which are located nearby and can be reached by shuttles. The landscaped **Allerton Garden** ★★ *($25; Tue to Sat, 9am, 10am, 1pm and 2pm, duration*

2.5hrs), featuring ponds and statues, and shelters some 75 different kinds of fruit trees. The section of the **Lawa'i** ★★ *($25; Mon 9am and 1pm)* valley, which is much more overgrown, holds a significant number of rare endemic species, medicinal plants, orchids and palm trees. When she wanted to get away, Queen Emma used to come here; today her cottage can be visited. The tour also includes a stop on Lawa'i Kai Beach, where green turtles lay their eggs. In both cases, it is recommended to make reservations ahead of time.

Trek back to the crossroads of Lawa'i Road and Po'ipu Road, then take Po'ipu Road travelling east. The fourth road to your right, Ho'owili Road, leads down to the sea.

You are now east of **Po'ipu Beach** ★ which, despite its inclusive name, is really made up of several sandy coves between the Sheraton to the west and Nukumoi Point to the east. You can only enjoy the beach if you walk up the it or if you are staying at one of the large hotels spanning the entire coastline.

Most day-trippers head east of Nukumoi Point towards **Po'ipu Beach Park** ★★ *(washrooms, showers, picnic tables)*. The beach, protected by the tip's rocks, is

one of the few beaches on this coast that is ideal for swimming. Next to it is **Brennecke's Beach**, which is more rocky than sandy and is perfect for boogieboarding.

The golden **Shipwreck Beach** ★★ stretches eastward along the Hyatt, up to a rocky headland. Currents and waves limit the beach to experienced boogie boarders and the monk seals that sometimes come here to bask in the afternoon sun.

Past the Hyatt, Po'ipu Road becomes a trail. Follow it for about 2mi (3km) beyond the golf course to a stop sign. Turn right. After 985ft (300m), you will come across a barrier that gives access to the lands of the Grove Farm Company (every day 7:30am to 6pm).

Still farther, the trail joins up with the long **Maha'ulepu Beach** ★, which runs along a coral reef for 2mi (3km). In 1795, Kamehameha's troops sent to conquer Kawa'i landed here after losing most of the royal fleet in a storm. Nearly all were massacred shortly thereafter by Kaumuali'i soldiers. Forming something of a double *S*, Maha'ulepu is in fact a series of three beaches. Two parking lots neighbour each other: the first leads to Kawailoa Bay the most rapidly by a short path cutting through high dunes that are covered with

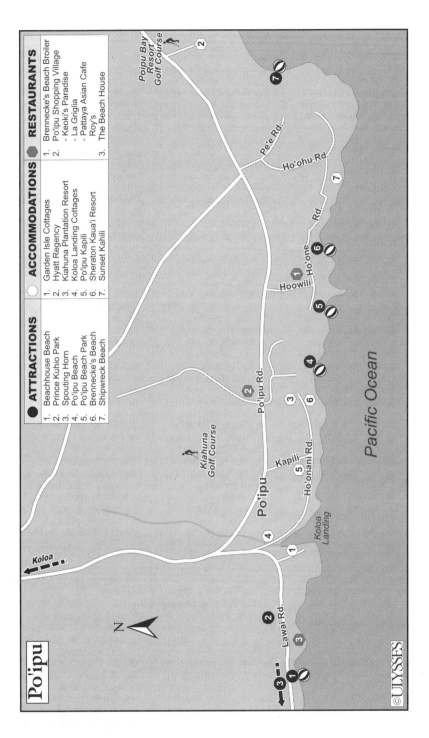

Po'ipu

● ATTRACTIONS

1. Beachhouse Beach
2. Prince Kuhio Park
3. Spouting Horn
4. Po'ipu Beach
5. Po'ipu Beach Park
6. Brennecke's Beach
7. Shipwreck Beach

⬡ ACCOMMODATIONS

1. Garden Isle Cottages
2. Hyatt Regency
3. Kiahuna Plantation Resort
4. Koloa Landing Cottages
5. Po'ipu Kapili
6. Sheraton Kaua'i Resort
7. Sunset Kahili

● RESTAURANTS

1. Brennecke's Beach Broiler
2. Po'ipu Shopping Village
   - Keoki's Paradise
   - La Griglia
   - Pattaya Asian Cafe
   - Roy's
3. The Beach House

Poipu Bay Resort Golf Course

Pe'e Rd.

Ho'ohu Rd.

Ho'one Rd.

Hoowili

Kiahuna Golf Course

Po'ipu Rd.

Po'ipu

Kapili

Ho'onani Rd.

Koloa Landing

Pacific Ocean

Koloa

Lawai Rd.

N

© ULYSSES

undergrowth and pine trees. If you want to swim or go snorkelling, it is better to continue to the next cove, which harbours Gillin's Beach. From there, the path leads to another beach that is empty, though unfortunately littered with debris brought in by the tides.

Walk back towards Koloa. From there, Koloa Road cuts through the sugar-cane fields to join Highway 50 in Lawa'i, at Mile 10.1.

At Mile 11.5, the road runs through the village of **Kalaheo** which, like all other villages in the area, owes its existence to the sugar refinery. The pastel-coloured Iglesia ni Cristo is a witness the large Portugese population that immigrated here.

From the heart of Kalaheo, the small Papalina Road leads up towards **Kukuiolono Park ★** *(every day 6:30am to 6:30pm; ☎332-9151),* where a tropical park, small Zen-inspired Japanese garden and a nine-hole public golf course are found next to each other. The site's name means "light of Lono," since it was here that fires marking the coast were once kept going for longboats out at sea. At the park, you can observe some ancient utensils made from lava stone or simply enjoy the peaceful surroundings and have a picnic. Leave the park by turn-

ing right onto **Pu'u Road ★**, a small narrow road that winds its way over the mountainside. Cutting through mango, papaya and eucalyptus trees at the end of the road, between sugar-cane and coffee-bush fields, great views of the island's eastern coast await you. Papalina Road is just up Highway 50.

At Mile 12.4, at the exit of Kalaheo, you will cross Halewili Road (540), which leads to Numila. Parallel to Route 50, it joins up with it just before Port Allen by travelling through the coffee plantations of the Kaua'i Coffee Company (see below). Stay on the main road, which quickly heads back down towards the coast, crossing through coffee fields. At Mile 14.1, there is a parking lot that offers a great view of the **Hanapepe Valley ★**, dug by the river of the same name – one of the island's seven main rivers.

At Mile 15.6, turn left onto Route 540 towards Numila.

You will soon come to the **Kaua'i Coffee Company Museum ★** *(free admission; every day 9am to 5pm; ☎335-3237),* set right in the middle of the coffee trees. In the early 1980s, due to the success of Kona coffee, more than 3,950 acres (1,600ha) of sugar cane were reconverted. To-

day, it is the archipelago's most important coffee grove. The museum provides explanations on processing and fruit-drying. Red when ripe, the beans are machine-harvested in early winter. For those who have never seen coffee trees up close, this is your chance: they grow right next to the parking lot. You can taste their different coffees for free.

Come back onto Highway 50. At the end of the descent (Mile 16), Route 541 to the left leads towards Port Allen's oil-handling terminal.

On the last road to the left before the port, just past the Red Dirt T-shirt factory, stands the refinery. At the yellow barrier, a suitable path to the right leads quickly to **Glass Beach**, which is worth a detour for curiosity's sake. The beach consists of a blend of black sand and millions of glass splinters rolled by the waves, vestiges of a former dumping ground. The cove is closed off by a Japanese cemetary.

Get back onto Kaumuali'i Highway.

At Mile 16.3, a small road leads to the centre of **Hanapepe ★**, "Kaua'i's biggest little town." This sleepy village is based around the Hanapepe River, crossed by the Swinging Bridge, a suspension bridge that doesn't really swing too much. Sugar, and later the Marines, who stationed thousands of soldiers here during the Second World War, represent the good old days, but the good times eventually came to an end. A local church and a row of wooden houses reconverted for peaceful tourism still line the main road. Today, they house cafés, several art galleries and Dr. Ding's surfboard clinic, where you can have your damaged board repaired.

You will come to Route 543 (Lele Road) at the exit of Hanapepe (Mile 17.1). After 2,625ft (800m), turn right onto Lolo Kai Road.

Less than a mile away lies **Salt Pond Park ★ ★** *(washrooms, showers, picnic tables, camping – see p 476)*, which harbours a long tucked-away beach guarded by tall coconut trees. Swimming and snorkelling are excellent here. East of the park, next to the Port Allen aerodrome, which was once Kaua'i's largest, are Hawaiian salt ponds that are still being exploited. In summertime, the salt has been harvested in laterite basins by generations of families for culinary and medicinal use. After it rains, Hawaiian seabirds, including stilts, come out to play.

The hamlet of **Makaweli** is so small that it could easily go unnoticed. It

Bellstones

Pohaku stones are found throughout the entire archipelago and were once used to communicate messages from a distance. Their size does not matter; only their resonance is important. When the stone is struck accurately with a pebble, the extremely metallic sound that resonates is reminiscent of a hammer hitting iron.

is nevertheless the main quarters of the Robinson family, who own a large part of Kaua'i's sugar-cane land and the entire island of Ni'hau. It is from here that the barge that goes irregularly to the Forbidden Isle departs. **Gay & Robinson Plantation Tours** *(Mon to Fri 8:45am and 12:45pm; ☎335-2824)* has recently begun offering tours of an operational sugar refinery. Visits through the fields and cane-processing plant last 2hrs, and the best time to visit is between April and October. At Mile 19.1, go down Kaumakani Avenue, which is bordered by large trees, until you reach the offices to the left.

A little past Makeli lies a lovely beach that is not visible from the road: **Pakala ★**, better known by surfers as Infinities. To get there, park on the lower side at Mile 21.1, just after a little bridge. A path,

whose beginning is marked by an opening in the wire fencing, cuts through the brush and leads to the crescent-shaped **Aakuhui Beach**, situated 1,640ft (500m) away. Pakala is located south from here. To get there, surfers and boogie-board enthusiasts don't think twice about going through the fence.

At Mile 22.5 lie the few remains of one of the most unexpected witnesses of Hawaiian history: **Fort Elizabeth ★** *(free admission)*, one of the three Russian forts built between 1815 and 1817 on Kaua'i under the aegis of an expedition. It all began in 1815 when Anton Georg Schaeffer, a German representative of the Russian-American Company of Alaska, landed on the island. His mandate was twofold: to recover the cargo of pelts on the Bering, a Russian ship that shipwrecked at Waimea a few months

Kaua'i

earlier and was seized by Kaumuali'i, the king of the island; and to try to establish a monopoly on the export of sandalwood. Then a czarist land, Alaska was entirely devoted to trade between North American and Asian ports. Schaeffer first sought the assistance of Kamehameha, but the king refused. He then turned to Kaumuali'i. The circumstances that brought the two men together remain somewhat troublesome: was it a political agreement, with the Kaua'i's king, a few years earlier, reluctantly agreeing to submit to Kamehameha? Or was it a gesture of friendship, to thank Schaeffer for healing the king's wife? Whichever the case, the monopoly was granted, the cargo was returned and vast lands were handed over to Waimea. In exchange, Russia agreed to provide Kaumuali'i with military support to conquer O'ahu, Moloka'i, Lana'i and Maui.

Three sites were selected for their solid ground and strategic sea positions. Thus began the construction of two forts at the mouth of the Hanalei River and, starting in 1816, of Fort Elizabeth in Waimea. It was named after the czarina, wife of Alexander I. Made aware of these projects, Kamehameha requested that Kaumuali'i expel Schaeffer, which he did

in 1817. Fort Elizabeth, not yet completed, was occupied and completed by Hawaiian troops, who renamed it Fort Hipo. It was attacked in 1824 by chiefs opposed to Kaua'i's integration into the kingdom of Hawaii, and was later dismantled in 1864. All that is left are its surrounding lava-stone walls and part of the building's interior foundation – nothing worth mentioning.

Back on the Kaumuali'i Highway, you will cross the Waimea River, Hawaii's longest at 19mi (31km). The main agglomeration of the southern coast, the large and charmless village of **Waimea** was established in 1844 around the Waimea Sugar Mill Company. It is here that James Cook landed in Hawaii, 66 years earlier ,on January 19, 1778. A village had already been constructed near the taro fields of the Waimea Valley. The gracious island hosts were more than ready to trade with the English who, coming from the Bering Strait, were in dire need of replenishing their provisions and water supplies. Perfectly aware of the potential danger he and his men represented to a people who had never come into contact with Westerners or the diseases they carried, Cook did his best to minimize the impact of his discovery by forbidding his men

from mingling with locals. After three days on Kaua'i, the English set sail. Strong winds, however, forced them to stop on "Oneeheow" (the isle of Ni'hau) for four more days. Two boats then set sail once more on a one-year trip in search of the Northwest passage, with no plans to return. Less than half a century later, the first missionaries had already settled in Waimea.

Immediately past the bridge over the Waimea River, Ala Wai Road leads left to **Lucy Wright Park** ★, located at the mouth of the river, across from the ruins of the Russian fort. Swimming is not recommended since the river ceaselessly pours unappealing, earthy alluvium into the sea. Between the canoes of the Hanama'ulu Canoe Club and the grey-sand beach, a poorly indicated sign commemorates Cook's visit to the island. Around 655ft (200m) away, at the heart of Waimea, a **statue** of the navigator stands in the shade of palm trees on the grassy stretch of Hofgaard Park, which has picnic tables. It is a replica of the work of Sir John Tweed, the original of which is in Whitby, England.

Just before the police station, Menehune Road runs along the Waimea River and leads up to **Menehune Ditch**. This huge stone and earth trench, once 25mi (40km) long, aided with the irrigation of the taro fields next to the water. According to its Hawaiian name, Kiki a Loa, it was built for Waimea's grand chief, Ola. The workmanship of the *menehune* is obvious. One thing is certain: when Cook landed at Waimea, the Hawaiians he met had lost the know-how to build such a structure. A plaque indicates the location of a section unearthed near a suspension bridge, less than 1mi from the centre of town. Across Menehune Road, along the Kaumuali'i Highway, stands **Waimea Hawaiian Church**, built in 1870 after the split from the Foreign Mission Church. In this building, made of white wood and adorned with a short, pointy belltower, mass is still held in Hawaiian. Two roads down, Pokole Road leads to **Waimea Pier**, an old quay that was built in 1865 for boats importing sugar and rice products to dock. Abandoned since 1930, the pier cuts the beach in half and is popular with fishers. A few shaded tables make this a good place for a picnic.

Turn right on Makeke Road, just before the fork of Route 550.

Built between 1848 and 1853, the former **Waimea Foreign Church** ★ today belongs to the United Church. The building was largely rebuilt after suffering the wrath of Hurricane Iniki in 1992. With a belltower truncated with shingles, this attractive stone church is neighboured by a Japanese cemetary whose tombs are scattered between sweet-smelling frangipani trees.

At the intersection of the Kaumuali'i Highway and Waimea Canyon Drive, stands the brand-new **West Kaua'i Technology and Visitor Center** *(free admission; every day 8am to 5pm; 9565 Kaumuali'i Highway; ☎338-1332).* This center is devoted to humankind's conquest and domestication of the world, with a Hawaiian twist: Polynesian navigation, ancient aquaculture and sugarcane irrigation techniques are some of the topics covered here and illustrated by old photographs and interactive screens.

To visit Waimea Canyon and Koke'e Park, take the following route (see p 460).

At the city's exit (Mile 23.3) is Waimea Plantation Cottages, a tourist resort featuring the old wooden cottages of plantation employees (see p 476). The resort also houses the **Fayé Museum** ★ *(free admission)*, devoted to Waimea's history of sugar refining and the Norwegian family that founded Kekaha's refinery.

At Mile 24.6 to the left, near an Asian cemetary, stands the **Kikialoa Small Boat Harbor**, from where certain tours depart for the Na Pali coast.

The beach, which stretches more than 2mi (3km) and faces **Kekaha**'s sugar refinery (Mile 25-27), was greatly damaged by Hurricane Iniki. Only the middle section of the beach, where fishers and boogie-board enthusiasts meet, is still relatively wide. Swimming is reserved for strong swimmers, as currents are quite powerful. Kekaha, for its part, is still dominated by an enormous sugarcane processing plant (Mile 25.9), founded in 1898 and continuously sustained by a fleet of dump trucks. The identical wooden homes of workers surround the plantation.

Past Kekaha, the scenery becomes more monotonous and the plain widens. At Mile 30, Tartar Drive leads to the control point of the Pacific Missile Range army base. Except on days when military exercises are held, civilians are allowed to go through the base to get to Major's Bay, better known as **Barking Sands Beach** ★, which takes its name from the sound the sand sometimes makes when it slides down the highest dunes. You will have to

Kaua'i

present your driver's licence and car rental contract at the control point to obtain a pass. After 1,310ft (400m), turn right at the first intersection, onto Nohili Road, which will lead after a little less than 1.5mi (2.5km) to a sign announcing Major's Bay.

Extremely wide and long, the beach stretches all the way to the isle of Ni'hau and is swept by large waves that are thoroughly enjoyed by surfers and boogie boarders. Swimming is impossible due to the strong currents, but sun worshippers will find paradise here: not a tree in sight to cast shade.

At Mile 32.5, a little before the road leading to military complexes, lies a bumpy road that cuts through the sugar-cane fields. After 3.5mi (5.5km), a large tree marks a hidden fork.

To the right appears **Polihale State Park ★★**. The largest beach on the island and bordered by large dunes covered by *naupaka*, Polihale marks the end of the sandy coast and the beginning of Na Pali, which is crowned with cliffs. Ancestral Hawaiians built a *heiau* here, where the souls of the dead left the island. Blanketed in vegetation, the *heiau* is difficult to spot and is in very poor condition. Dangerous currents and viscious waves limit the

waters to experienced surfers. The only protected site on the coast is **Queen's Pond**, a little further south, and is reached by taking the left branch of the fork in the road. When the sea is calm, it is possible to swim.

The road comes to an end here, so you can only head back.

Waimea Canyon and Koke'e State Park

(half-day to full day)

West of Kaua'i, a sinewy paved road climbs between ravines and forests towards the central mountains, offering a unique opportunity to discover the secret heart of the island. In around 19mi (30km), you will come to two of Hawaii's most beautiful spots: Waimea Canyon and Koke'e State Park, which are located at the foot of the highest peaks, towering over stunning cliffs and the Na Pali coast's impregnable valleys.

Two roads charge up the mountains to meet halfway. Though more winding, Waimea Canyon Drive, which splits from Kaumuali'i Highway at Mile 23.2 at the Waimea exit, offers the most stunning views of the canyon it runs along, closely at first, and then from a greater distance. Koke'e Road leaves Kaumuali'i High-

way further west at Mile 26.1, near Kekaha.

If you decide to take Waimea Canyon Drive, turn right at Waimea, past the movie theatre and small church.

The road rapidly climbs and after a couple of turns, the first views of **Waimea Canyon ★★★** are revealed, split between Waimea Canyon State Park to the south and Koke'e State Park to the north. Legend has it that Mark Twain, the bard of the wild U.S., nicknamed it the Grand Canyon of the Pacific. Twain never actually visited Kaua'i, but the name is nonetheless fitting. Not as deep, though much younger than the original and completely unexpected on such a small island, the Waimea Canyon cuts the western part of Kaua'i with a north-south fissure, stretching 9mi (15km) and nearly 2,625ft (800m) deep. Carved by rain and excavated by the Waimea River, the rock is new and exposes laterite that contrasts sharply with the green vegetation. Permanent or temporary waterfalls cascade in tributary valleys and cause frequent rainbows. The most beautiful pictures are taken after a rainfall, when the colours are most intense – in the middle of the day, haze slightly shrouds the view.

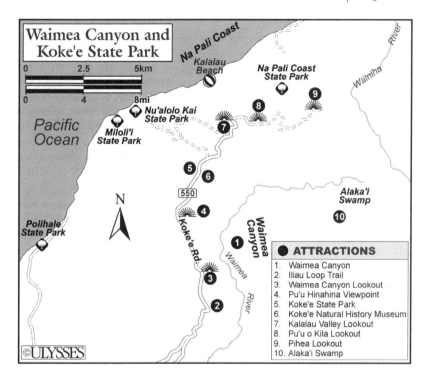

Waimea Canyon and Koke'e State Park

Pacific Ocean

Na Pali Coast

Kalalau Beach

Na Pali Coast State Park

Nu'alolo Kai State Park

Miloli'i State Park

550

Koke'e Rd.

Polihale State Park

Waimea Canyon

Waimea River

Alaka'i Swamp

Wainiha River

N

0   2.5   5km
0   4   8mi

© ULYSSES

● ATTRACTIONS

1. Waimea Canyon
2. Iliau Loop Trail
3. Waimea Canyon Lookout
4. Pu'u Hinahina Viewpoint
5. Koke'e State Park
6. Koke'e Natural History Museum
7. Kalalau Valley Lookout
8. Pu'u o Kila Lookout
9. Pihea Lookout
10. Alaka'i Swamp

At Mile 6.9, the two roads meet to form one.

The sugar-cane fields that blanket the low hills give way to forest: as you climb, *koa, 'ohi'a* and eucalyptus gradually replace the cane. Take a last look back – as serene as it is inaccessible, Ni'hau, the Forbidden Isle, lies off the coast on the other side of the Kaulakahi Channel.

Beginning at Mile 8.8, the **Iliau Loop Trail ★★** is a short loop path (1,310ft or 400m) that offers an incredible panoramic view of Waimea Canyon. Waterfalls flow abundantly, depending on

the season, into Wai'alae, a neighbouring valley. The names of endemic plants are clearly marked on the path. The steep **Kukui Trail**, dropping 1,970ft (600m) in altitude after 2.5mi (4km), leads down to the canyon's floor. Plan at least 1.5 to 2hrs for the trek down, and 2.5 to 3hrs for the climb back up. The hike is far from easy, but the views are worth the effort. You can spend the night at Wiliwili Camp, on the canyon floor.

The **Waimea Canyon Lookout ★★**, which offers the most gorgeous panoramic views of the canyon, is located at

Mile 10.3. On the other side, steep valleys stand out by the Koaie River to the left and the Wai'alae River to the right. Often in the afternoon, rainbows hook onto the mountainside when the sun plays hide-and-seek behind the heavy rainclouds.

There are other viewpoints between Miles 10.9 and 12, from which the white trail of the Waipo'o Falls can be seen in the distance. You can sometimes stop on the lower side. The **Pu'u Hinahina Viewpoint ★**, located at Mile 13.7, is the highest viewpoint towering over Waimea Canyon. White-tailed phaetons

Kaua'i

often glide overhead and Hawaiian forest birds can also be seen sometimes. To the north lies the Koke'e plateau and its *koa* forest.

Mile 14.1 marks both the entrance to Koke'e State Park and the end of the Halemanu Valley trail, which leads to a network of several interconnected paths, all the way from the Waimea Canyon to the Koke'e Forest.

If you just want to stretch your legs, the **Climb Trail ★** leads 655ft (200m) to a panoramic view of the canyon. If you are looking for a bigger challenge, you can opt for different trails that feature several paths, including the **Canyon Trail ★**, which brings you close to Waipo'o Falls, at 785ft (240m).

Shadowed on all sides by a screen of four forest reserves, **Koke'e State Park ★★★**, spanning across a plateau between 3,280ft (1,000m) and 4,265ft (1,300m) high, includes 4,345 acres (1,759ha) of *'ohi'a* and *koa* forest. The only true gateway to the wild interior of the Garden Isle, the park is crisscrossed by a multitude of trails enabling visitors to discover partially preserved flora and fauna. More endemic birds thrive here than anywhere, including the *'i'iwi*, *'apapane*,

'anianiau and *'elepaio*. But even more than providing the opportunity to explore the island's summital area, which is left to hikers, Koke'e State Park offers clear, unrestricted views of valleys slashing the sides of the plateau to the north, including those of Honopu and Kalalau.

Just before reaching Kanaloahuluhulu Meadow and the museum, Mile 15.8 marks

I'iwi

the starting point of one of the most beautiful hiking trails of Koke'e, the 4mi-long (6km) **Nu'alolo Trail ★★**. It travels through a *koa* forest and drops 1,575ft (480m) between Mahanaloa Valley to the west and Nu'alolo Valley to the east. Just before it ends, it reaches the junction of the Nu'alolo Cliff Trail, which leads to the Awa'awapuhi Trail further east. In total, this hike is 10mi (16.6km) long and takes one day. The trek is not easy, but is worth the effort. From the junction, the last mile to the Lolo Vista Point, which offers breathtaking views, is the the most

overgrown part of the trail.

The vast clearing of Kanaloahuluhulu, where *moas* (roosters) peck in freedom, shelters the **Koke'e Natural History Museum ★★** *(suggested donation $1; every day 10am to 4pm; ☎335-9975, ⚐335-6131)*. This museum is devoted to the ecology and geology of Kaua'i, to endemic plants and birds and to hunting, and has paths that let visitors explore the park. Featured here are old Hawaiian tools, a meteorology section that focuses on damage caused by Hurricane Iniki in 1992, as well as a short movie showing the natural mechanisms that made and shaped Kaua'i. The museum houses a small shop selling crafts, cards and works depicting Hawaii's nature and wildlife, hiking and history. Every year, two important cultural festivals take place here: the Banana Poka Festival in late May, devoted to public sensitization of natural balances, while the Eo E Emalani I Alaka'i Festival is a *hula* contest held in memory of Queen Emma's visit to Koke'e in 1871.

Right beside the museum, the extremely short **Nature Trail ★** (656ft or 200m) is a good introduction to endemic plant species. For $1, you can obtain a museum brochure that describes the

Ni'ihau

Around 17mi (28km) southwest of Kaua'i, on the other side of the Kaulakahi Channel, lies an island that stands out in the Hawaiian scenery. Often referred to as "The Forbidden Isle," Ni'ihau is the smallest inhabited island in the archipelago and the only one that cannot be visited. No visitors, residents of other islands, ethnologists or Hawaiians are authorized to visit without an invitation, which is rarely given. Some journalists are tolerated, as is, inevitably, the tax collector.

It all began in 1833 when the Sinclairs, a Scottish family in search of new land, set sail for New Zealand. Thirty years later, the extended family decided to leave their adopted homeland for Hawaii, where they met Robert Crichton Wyllie, a fellow countryman who was a minister under Kamehameha V. With his help, the family was offered land on Lana'i, in

Waikiki and in other spots on O'ahu, as well as the entire island of Ni'ihau. Refusing to separate themselves from Ni'ihau, the Sinclair-Robinsons withdrew after the annexation of Hawaii to the United States in 1898 and adopted a paternalistic management style, restricting access to the island – a policy that is still valid today.

Approximately 18mi (29km) long and 8mi (13km) wide at its widest point, Ni'ihau, which is officially part of the county of Kaua'i, covers an area of 69 sq mi (180km²). The vestige of an eroded 4.9-million-year-old volcano, it is quite flat, with its caldera having broken off during a landslide on the eastern part of the island. Ni'ihau features several lakes that are an important source of drinking water, including Halali'i (865 acres or 350ha), Hawaii's largest lake, parts of which are often dry. Coves, rocky hea-

dlands and light-sand beaches stretch along its western coast. At nearly 3.5mi (5.5km) long, Keawanui Beach is Hawaii's second longest beach. The islet of Lehua, the remains of an ancient crater, lies at the island's northern tip.

Still 230 residents strong in 1990, Ni'ihau's population has declined and fluctuated in recent years between 150 and 200 people, depending on the period. In 1860, the island counted 647 residents. Most people on the island today live in small wooden houses in the hamlet of Pu'uwai. Telephones, sewers, alcohol and firearms are unknown to the island and are forbidden. Generators have been installed and solar-energy captors were recently set up to enable those with televisions to get a clear picture, to run a refrigeration system and to provide power to run the school's two computers. Classes are given in Hawaiian,

Kaua'i

which remains the mother tongue. Many of the archipelago's singers and composers have come from Ni'ihau.

Though free to leave the island when a barge is available, residents are nonetheless subject to a number of restrictions that reflect the moral values of the Robinsons. They are bound to a "reasonably honest, serious and moral lifestyle" and are forbidden from criticizing the Robinsons' management of the island. Should a resident not respect either of these two precepts, he or she would be exiled from the island and would never be allowed to return. Should they marry a non-island native, the sanction is the same. It is for such steadfast rules that the Robinsons are most often criticized.

When asked, Ni'ihau residents admit that first and foremost, they seek to maintain their peaceful way of life.

For generations, nearly the entire population, which was exclusively employed by the

Robinson family, lived off breeding and supplemented their income by producing charcoal, honey and seashell *lei*. This ancestral tradition, which everywhere else has disappeared, requires extreme detail: the tiny seashells are collected on the western coast where they are deposited by currents, then threaded depending on their colour and according to complex designs. Necklaces take weeks to make, which is why they cost so much.

In 1997, the Robinsons decided to close their ranch, which had been suffering from financial problems for quite a while. The 15 or so residents who worked there suddenly found themselves on welfare. Relying on a financial argument, the Robinsons threatened to pull out of the islands for good.

The navy had an automatic radar station on the island for some time, and its generators and technical equipment were managed by the Robinsons. In 1997, it announced plans to develop a anti-air defense testing centre for short-range

ballistic missiles around the Barking Sands base, in Kaua'i, and thus required three launching sites: one on Ni'ihau and the other two on Northwest islands, a natural reserve. The Ni'ihau launching site would double as a 5,900ft (1,800m) long landing strip and would feature new roads and a launching pad for atmospheric missiles – quite a revolution! Supported by certain elected local officials and faced with a gloomy economy following Hurricane Iniki in 1992, the announcement nevertheless led to protests from ecological organizations and sovereignists who had never been in the Robinsons' good graces. The family affirmed their inalienable right to do as they wished with their property. Despite a few bad experiences with the navy in the past, residents in need of work approved the project in April 1998. Ni'ihau entered a new era.

Though it is true that island residents, who are devout followers of the brand of Christianity professed by the Robinsons, have little in common with Hawaiians of yesteryear, they must now develop the know-how to preserve this unique heritage, this place frozen in time, for the future.

Visiting Ni'ihau

Legally, the Robinsons are not permitted to bar access to the island's beaches, which, like all beaches in the archipelago, are part of public domain. The family, though, does not recognize the notion of law passed by the state, and believes it should not apply to land acquired under the kingdom.

In the early 1990s, a first window was opened: to raise money for a helicopter for health emergencies, flights over the island were organized (Ni'ihau Safaris, $250; Mon to Sat 9am to 1:30pm, minimum of four or five people; ☎335-3500). Though expensive, after a 15min crossing of the Kaulakahi Channel the excursion brings you close to the uninhabited parts of the island, with the helicopter landing on an isolated beach (generally Nanina, in the north), where you can sunbathe and swim, collect seashells and have a picnic. The village of

Pu'uwai is carefully avoided. Hunting trips are also organized (Mon to Sat 6:30am to 5pm) at the cost of... $1,650 per person!

The only other way to get close to Ni'ihau is to sign up for a catamaran tour, which includes snorkelling near the island's reefs (HoloHolo Charters ☎246-4656). But don't even think of setting foot on the island. Dolphins are often seen swimming in the waters, as are whales sometimes in winter, but be careful because the channel crossing is usually turbulent.

30 species that can be observed here.

Beyond the museum, the road continues to climb in tight turns. Offering one of Kaua'i's most beautiful hikes, the **Awa'awapuhi Trail** ★★ begins at Mile 17. Hooked onto the towering slopes of the valley of the same name and accessible only by sea, the trail quickly drops 1,640ft (500m) in altitude. It ends after 3.2mi (5.2km), a little past the fork of the Nu'alolo Cliff Trail (which leads to the Nu'alolo Trail).

From there, you can enjoy the exquisite views of the Awa'awapuhi and Nu'alolo Valleys. Although the descent is not too difficult (just muddy on rainy days), this hike is no cakewalk either: remember that you have to climb back up what you've just come down!

Below a military base (Mile 18), the **Kalalau Valley Lookout** ★★★, which is accessible to all, offers the most striking view of Koke'e. The valley and entire Na Pali coast, whose

sharply edged, draped cliffs unravel at your feet. With a little luck at the end of the day, a rainbow will slip in front of your camera lens. If clouds veil your view, do not despair, as the weather quickly changes and the sun might soon return. At the end of the road, the **Pu'u Kila Lookout** ★★ overlooks the Kalalau Valley, offering a more central view. At both places, 'i'iwi, 'apapane and 'amakihi are common. A forgotten path once led Hawaiians down into the valley.

Kaua'i

Today, only goats roam the slopes.

The end of the paved road marks the beginning of the **Pihea Trail ★★**, which runs along the crest looming over the Kalalau Valley. The path once outlined the circular road that was to join Ha'ena on the northern coast. Thankfully for the plants and wildlife, the project was abandoned due to obvious technical difficulties. Wide and easy, the Pihea Trail narrows as it approaches the **Pihea Lookout ★★** (1mi or 1.6km), a steep headland that is slippery to climb, and that reveals another view of Kalalau.

At this level, the path leads up towards **Alaka'i Swamp ★★**, which is surrounded by a distant arena of mountains. A multitude of cascades, formed when grey clouds tear open over the rocky, sharp peaks, run down the rock face. The 2mi (3km) wide and 10mi (16km) long swamp is one of the last refuges for endemic bird species that have become very rare, including the 'akepa, 'akiki (Kaua'i creeper), 'anianiau and nukupu'u. Ancestral Hawaiians used to come here to gather bird feathers. The dense vegetation, which is shrivelled elsewhere, is also unique: here where the wind blows the strongest and the sun never shines, a

great number of species have adapted and stunted their growth in order to survive.

Most hikers take the Alaka'i Swamp Trail, which crosses the Pihea trail after a descent. Once known for its difficulty, when hikers had to literally wade in mud up to their knees, a raised, narrow platform was added, making the trail easier to manage. This does not mean that you won't have to grapple with mud, but reaching the **Kilihana Lookout ★**, perched above a crest overlooking the Wainiha Valley, will be easier. When the clouds deign to drift away and the haze lifts, which is not all that often, the view is simply breathtaking. You can also choose to hike the entire Alaka'i Swamp Trail from its official starting point located on the path that passes by the YMCA Camp Sloggett. The first part is still the muddiest, however, and the least interesting.

Outdoor Activities

Swimming

With its 40 or so beaches, Kaua'i is ahead in the hot-sand

race. Those located on the southern coast are wider and longer and are generally your best bet, but be careful of currents in certain spots – especially in summer. **Po'ipu Beach Park** as well as **Salt Pond Park**, near Hanapepe feature ideal beaches, with a natural protected basin for children.

On the eastern coast, the beautiful and well-protected **Kalapaki Beach** at Nawiliwili should be your first choice, and further north, the basins of **Lydgate Park** are perfect for swimmers of all ages and are great for snorkelling.

The northern coast harbours a series of coves, but only a few are good for swimming: **Anini Beach Park**'s beach, facing a reef, is the most popular; **Hanalei Pier**, on the eastern side of the bay and **Secret Beach** are both great in summer; and **Ke'e Beach**, at the end of the road, is wonderful. Currents are dangerous in winter and it is best to postpone your swim for another spot or time.

Surfing and Boogie Boarding

Kaua'i is not as famous as O'ahu or Maui when it comes to wave sports, but nevertheless offers some places that are perfect for surfing and boogie boarding.

Here too, surfers pick their beach according to their level. Beginners can check out **Po'ipu Beach Park** or **Kalapaki Beach** at Nawiliwili. More experienced surfers should head to the northern coast in wintertime, when the waves form; to **Donkey's Beach** past Kapa'a on **Kalihiwai Bay**, known for its Killer Kalihiwai breaker; and also to **Hanalei Bay** (Wai'oli Beach Park) and **Makua Beach**, renamed "Tunnels" for its perfect rollers. Waves abound at the southern tip of the island in summer, and surfers gather at **Shipwreck Beach** in Po'ipu, at **Pakala**, one of the island's wildest beaches, and at the mouth of the Waimea River – at **Lucy Wright Park** – at **Major's Bay** and at **Polihale**.

The best boogie-board spots are at the edge of **Kalapaki Beach**, **Kealia Beach**, at the exit of Kapa'a (currents), **Kalihiwai** and many coves on the northern coast. **Brennecke's Beach** at Po'ipu and **Shipwreck Beach** are the most popular beaches in the southern part of the island.

To find out the strength of the waves ahead of time, you can contact the National Weather Service (surf advisory) at ☎*245-3564*.

Windsurfing

One place stands out for this sport: **Anini Beach**, ideal for both novices, thanks to its sandy and shallow depths, and experienced windsurfers. You can take courses or rent boards (*Windsurf Kaua'i*, ☎*828-6838*). Beginners also windsurf at **Kalapaki Beach**. Other possible sites that are better suited to experienced windsurfers include **Makua Beach** in the north, **Maha'ulepu** and **Shipwreck Beaches** in the south, as well as **Salt Pond Park**.

Scuba Diving and Snorkelling

Kaua'i's best beaches are also those that are perfect for snorkelling: **Kalapaki Beach** on Nawiliwili Bay, **Lydgate Park**, on the biggest of the two basins, **Anini Beach Park** (at high tide), **Hideaway Beach** at the foot of the Princeville Hotel, and further west (but only in summer) **Makua Beach** (be careful of currents; it is best to pick a day when the water is calm). **Ke'e Beach** is also an excellent snorkelling spot. South of the island, **Po'ipu Beach**, where you can observe different fish, as well as **Koloa Landing** and **Salt Pond Park** (at both ends of the beach) are ideal. Along the Na Pali coast, boat excursions bring you to the **Nu'alolo Kai Reef**, across from the beach, which stretches along the edge of the valley.

Some of these sites are also great for diving: **'Anini** (away from the reef), **Koloa Landing**, where you can find items thrown in the water by ships who came to load their boats with sugar in the 19th century, rocky arches and... curious eels. Being the oldest of the eight main islands, erosion has had more than enough time to create a good number of underwater rock formations. The **Sheraton Caves**, Po'ipu's parallel lava tunnels, are one of the most popular diving sites. They feature turtles and sometimes reef sharks. Nearby, **Brennecke's Ledge**, right across the beach that shares its name, also often shelters turtles that come to sleep in the crevices of cliffs. Other intriguing sites located around the island include **Aqauriums** at Nawiliwili and **Oasis Reef** off the tip of Kaulala. Both sites are home to lobsters and other marine life. Shipwreck dives and spots off the coast of **Ni'hau**, the Forbidden Isle, should also be mentioned for the bravest of novices. With its reef 131ft (40m) below the sea, Ni'hau's coast is considered one of the best diving spots in the archipelago (especially in summer). Divers can see rays, sharks and sometimes even monk seals.

The island boasts a great number of diving centres. Dives begin at $85 and can reach $200 for a trip to Ni'hau. For an original approach, Sunrise Diving Adventures (☎822-REEF) offers diving with an underwater thruster enabling you to cover a greater distance. You can enjoy snorkelling (at Po'ipu) here as well.

Kayaking

The only navigable rivers of the archipelago are on Kaua'i: you can paddle up several of them, including **Hule'ia River**, from its mouth in Nawiliwili Bay. The Menehune Fishpond lies upstream and a vast natural reserve stretches along its banks. Outfitters Kaua'i offers an organized tour combining a paddle up the river and a short hike in the Hidden Valley to the Kipu Falls. An excursion along the desert coast of **Kipu Kai**, marked by high peaks, is also offered; the coast can only be reached by sea.

Without a doubt, the **Wailua River** is the most popular for kayaking, whether you decide to

venture out on your own or take part in an organized tour. Wide and calm, it runs deep into the superb valley of the same name. Upstream from the pier, the river forks: the left branch leads to the Fern Grotto (you can reach it, but it is forbidden to dock at the quay) and, 10min later, a bathing area with ropes; the right branch leads to a trail (around 30min) that goes to the Secret Falls. The Kayak Kaua'i Company (☎822-3574) and Kayak Wailua (☎822-3388) both rent kayaks ($20 to $40) and can provide maps to help you find your way. The same excursion, when organized, costs $80 for half a day. The family that opened the Kamokila Hawaiian Village (☎823-0559) in the valley also organizes outings. Lasting 3hrs, it gives you the most for your money. This is an opportunity to kill two birds with one stone by exploring the valley and taking advantage of your Hawaiian guide's cultural perspective on everything.

The less popular **Kalihawai River** is bordered by luxuriant vegetation and can be navigated for close to 2mi (3km). As the second most popular kayak excursion after the Wailua, the **Hanalei River** is also very calm. Renters are found at Hanalei, where the river flows. The bravest kayakers can paddle up

to the nature reserve that covers all of the taro fields nestled deep in the valley.

The last option is reserved for experienced kayakers only: travelling along the **Na Pali** coast from Ha'ena to Polihale, and camping overnight at Kalalau and Miloli'i. As the water is usually rough, this excursion, which is more of an expedition, is only authorized from June to August, when the waters are less powerful. The safest bet is to sign up for an organized trip. If you are alone, arrange to at least be picked up at Polihale; the return leg towards Ha'ena is against the current. A permit issued by the State Parks office is required.

Water Sports

The Wailua River is also ideal for **water skiing** and wakeboarding. **Sailing** is popular as well, especially at Kalapaki where you can rent a Hobie Cat for an outing in Nawiliwili Bay.

Fishing

Waters are extremely deep not far off the coasts of Kaua'i, making it almost a sure bet for catching a large fish, such as a blue marlin, *mahi-mahi*, tuna (*aku*, but also *'ahi*), *ono*, and shark. Outings last four, six or 8hrs. Fresh-water fishers can try their luck in the Waita reservoir, near Koloa. All fish must be released.

Cruises

Around 15 companies in Kaua'i offer a variety of sea excursions, some departing from Nawiliwili Port and others from the northern (Hanalei) or southern (Po'ipu, Port Allen, Kikialoa Port) coasts.

The **Na Pali** coast is, without a doubt, the most popular destination by zodiac or mini catamaran, whether you dock at one of its isolated beaches or not. This is truly one of the best ways to enjoy the spectacular cascading cliffs. Be warned though that the sea is often stormy. Depending on the season and weather conditions, the outing may be combined with snorkelling (at Nu'alolo Kai), whale- or dolphin-watching, or even underwater cave exploration. Excursions from the northern coasts are generally less expensive since they are closer (*$90 to $100, southern coast $110 to $125*).

Some of the same companies also offer short outings out to sea with cocktails and Hawaiian music to add to your enjoyment of the sunset on the southern coast, as well as snorkelling excursions or trips to the southeast coast (Kipu Kai, from Nawiliwili). Whale-watching excursions are offered between December and April (*$50 to $60 and more for 2 to 3hrs*).

Cycling

Having begun in Maui, where it is extremely popular on Hale'a'kala, free-wheeling down mountains is now all the rage on Kaua'i. Several companies today offer a trip from Koke'e State Park to the sourthern coast along the **Waimea Canyon**, without you having to break a sweat pedalling... or almost! The guided excursion lasts all morning and costs around $60 to $70.

Those who love wide-open spaces will no doubt prefer the wild paths of the **Koke'e State Park** (*only some are open to mountain bikes*) or the even hardier **Powerline Trail**, which links Princeville to Wailua and crosses through the central mountains. Outfitters Kaua'i rents bicycles from $20 per day and also offers guided tours. However, there are also a great many other renters throughout the entire island.

Golf

Kaua'i has nine golf courses. Though at first this number may be less impressive than on the other islands, four of Kaua'i's courses are among Hawaii's best.

The **Prince Course** at the Princeville Resort (☎800-826-1105), designed by Robert Trent Jones Jr., wins top prize. Embracing the jolts of the coast, it is known as one of the archipelago's most difficult courses.

The **Po'ipu Bay Resort Golf Course** (☎800-858-6300), also designed by Robert Trent Jones Jr., reaches along the southern coast, east of Po'ipu. Here, it is very windy all the time, which helps spice up the game. The course also has no fewer than 86 sandpits. At the 16th hole, be careful not to send your ball towards a former altar of Hawaiian fishers, as it apparently brings bad luck.

The Kaua'i Lagoons lie next to the Marriott at Nawiliwili. The 16th hole of the **Kiele Course** is the most magnificent, located on a rocky tip that closes off Kalapaki Bay.

Kaua'i

These great courses are rather pricy ($90 to $150), except during the warmest hours of the day, but a package for all three courses is available.

Those travelling on a tight budget can stick to the **Wailua Golf Course** (*$25 Mon to Fri, $35 Sat to Sun;* ☎*241-6666*), one of the most famous public golf courses in the United States. It stretches along the ocean on the eastern side of the island. The **Grove Farm Golf Course** (*$35, $60 for 20 holes;* ☎*245-8756*), located at the exit of Lihu'e, is a 10-hole course and is among golfers' favourites. The least expensive of all is the **Kukuiolono Golf Course** (☎*332-9151*), which offers nine holes for only $7. Reservations are not accepted.

Hiking

Along with the Big Island, Kaua'i doubtlessly offers the most trails. Its wild scenery and dense vegetation make it the favourite destination of hikers.

Sharp cliffs tower over turquoise waves, deep and humid valleys, waterfalls, pandanus, candlenut trees, *ti* plants and passion fruit covering the ground – this is all part of a lost paradise that will make

the **Kalalau Trail** the hiking excursion of your dreams. With your fantasies all figured out, all that is left to do is tackle 11mi (18km) of climbs and descents, from valley to valley, through heat and moisture... and mosquitoes. You can also opt for a one-day stroll to **Hanakapi'ai Beach**, with an eventual climb to the waterfalls. It is also possible, to save time or energy, to be dropped off or picked up by boat at Kalalau. Be careful – it is imperative that you treat the water you drink along the entire trail.

Pandanus

Other hiking alternatives that are quite close as the crow flies are at the other end of the island, in the **Waimea Canyon** and **Koke'e State Park**. The latter has no less than 45mi (70km) of trails, with the most stunning being those that slice through crests and cliffs at the foot of the humid central mountains. **Nu'alolo**, **Awa'awapuhi**, and the **Alaka'i Swamp Trail** penetrate one of Hawaii's best-preserved forests. Here and there, incredible views overlook isolated, unreachable valleys. Each one can consist of a day's

hike, but there are shorter trails: the **Nature Trail** near the museum and the **Iliau Nature Loop**. Both feature the names of plants. The Koke'e Museum organizes guided walks in summer and also provides information on the latest trail conditions.

Asides from these two unavoidable sets of trails, you can enjoy trekking the **Sleeping Giant** (1.7mi or 2.8km), which looms over the eastern coast, or the **Powerline Trail** that cuts through the interior valleys of the northeastern part of the island, between Waihua and Princeville (13mi or 21km). As its name suggests, the trail follows an electrical powerline. It starts at the end of Kuamo'o Road, past the Keahua Arboretum. This trail is strictly for experienced hikers.

Horseback Riding

The **Silver Falls Ranch** (☎*828-6718*) at **Kalihiwai** on the northeast coast offers horseback rides in a lovely setting, as do the Princeville Ranch Stables (☎826-6777 or 826-7473) in **Princeville**, which offer rides ranging from 1.5 to 4hrs. You can take a simple ride in the surrounding area to a waterfall and you can even tag along with *paniolos*. On the southern part of the island, CJM Country Stables (☎742-6096) offers rides to **Maha'ulepu Beach**. Prices range between $50 and $70 for 2hrs. Those who prefer to watch from the sidelines can enjoy **polo matches** held in 'Anini on Sunday afternoons from April to August.

Flying and Aerial Sports

If you want to treat yourself to at least one flight over a Hawaiian island, this is the place to do it. From the airports of Lihu'e, Port Allen or Princeville, no fewer than 10 companies offer flights ranging from 20min to 1hr. Among the better known are Air Kaua'i (☎246-4666 or 800-972-4666), Island Helicopters (☎245-8588 or 800-829-5999), Jack Harter Helicopters (☎245-3774 or 888-245-2001), Safari (☎246-0136 or 800-326-3356) and Will Squyers Helicopter Tours (☎245-8881 or 245-7541).

The lowest rates begin at $60 to $80 for 20min flights from Port Allen over the Waimea Canyon. Rates climb to $100 to $150 for a complete tour of the island in approximately 50min.

Fly Kaua'i and Kumulani Air (☎246-9123) offer less expensive flights on small **planes** leaving from Lihu'e, starting at $49 for 45min. Thrill seekers can also choose to fly by ULM with the Birds of Paradise ($95 for 30min, $165 for 1hr; ☎822-5309).

Accommodations

A complete list of agents is available at the Visitors Bureau.

Aloha Rental Management
P.O. Box 1109, Hanalei HI 96174
☎826-7288 or 800-487-9833
⇌826-7280
www.hanalei-vacations.com
Specializing in the northern coast, this agency rents out apartments in a dozen Princeville condominiums, as well as studios, cottages and houses, all at a good price.

Paradise Adventures
Kuhio Highway, Hanalei
☎826-9999 or 888-886-4969
⇌826-9998
www.paradise-adventures.com/bungalow
This agency offers a reservation service and has contacts with 75

bed and breakfasts and owners of houses for rent on the northern coast. Prices begin at around $50.

Prosser Realty
4379 Rice Street, Lihu'e
☎245-4711 or 800-767-4707
⇌245-8115
www.prosser-realty.com
Covering the entire island, Prosser is especially well established on the eastern and southern coasts. You couldn't have a wider selection: houses, studios, and condominiums, all at very reasonable prices.

Suite Paradise
1941 Po'ipu Road, Po'ipu
☎367-8020 or 742-7400 or 800-367-8020
⇌742-9121 or 742-7865
suite-paradise.com
This agency manages six similar condominiums in Po'ipu. Prices, which are high for a single night, drop quickly for longer stays. The agency also offers car rental packages.

Lihu'e

Motel Lana'i
$34-$50
ℝ, ⊗
4240 Rice Street
☎245-2965
Those travelling on a tight budget will find sparsely-furnished dim rooms, but at this price... Nawiliwili Road passes right in front of the motel and soundproof walls are obviously lacking.

Tip Top Motel
$45
℞, ⊗, tv
3173 Akahi St.
☎245-2333
The Tip Top Motel
houses a restaurant,
bakery (which doubles
as reception) and mo-
tel. It offers nothing
luxurious: rooms are
basic and rather dark
but clean and equipped
with new TVs. The "re-
ception" is only open
from 6:30am to 3pm.

Garden Island Inn
$75-$125
K, ⊗, ≡, ℝ, ⏱
3445 Wilcox Rd.
☎245-7227 or 800-648-0154
⇌245-7603
www.gardenislandinn.com
A stone's throw from
Kalapahi Beach in
Nawiliwili, the Garden
Island Inn offers rooms
at quite a good qual-
ity/price ratio. Located
on the first floor, the
less expensive rooms
are somewhat lacking
in light and do not
have air conditioning.
The second- and third-
floor rooms are better
ventilated and feature a
tropical decor. Some
include a kitchenette.
Beach towels, Boogie
Boards and diving
equipment are available
for clients and many of
the regulars to use. The
only real downside is
the proximity of the
road leading to the
port, which is ex-
tremely busy.

**Outrigger Kaua'i Beach
Hotel**
$180-$290
≈, ℞, ≡, ℝ, ctv, ⏱
4331 Kaua'i Beach Dr.
☎245-1955 or 888-805-3843
⇌246-9085
Located right next to
the ocean, just north of
Lihu'e, this reasonably
large tourist resort fea-
tures a set of pools
surrounded by palm
trees. The recently ren-
ovated rooms are com-
fortable, and offered at
a good quality/price
ratio by Hawaiian stan-
dards. Canadian guests
enjoy the "Canadian
Dollar at Par" program:
rates are the same in
Canadian as in US dol-
lars. The hotel houses
one of the island's most
popular nightclubs,
Gilligan's (see p 486).
To get there, take the
first road to your right,
past the Highway 50
crossroads and the road
leading from the air-
port.

Kaua'i Marriott
$259-$369
≈, ℞, ≡, ctv, ⏱
3610 Rice St.
☎245-5050 or 800-220-2925
⇌245-5049
www.marriott.com
Kalapahi Beach, one of
the island's best,
stretches to the foot of
this tourist resort.
Though its beach fa-
cade is not exceptional,
the hotel is radiant
once you step through
the main doors. The
hotel is built around a
large basin that resem-
bles an artificial river,
surrounded by tropical
plants. The refined
decor of the common
areas features a great

deal of Hawaiian and
Asian art and crafts. Do
not miss the magnifi-
cent *koa* outrigger that
once belonged to
Prince Kuhio, displayed
in the reception. The
345 rooms and 11
suites are obviously
comfortable.

Wailua – Kapa'a

Kaua'i International Hostel
dormitory $16
room $40
sb, laundry, K
4532 Lehua St., Kapa'a
☎823-6142
Located just behind
Bubba's Burgers near
the Kapa'a Beach Park's
football field, the is-
land's only youth hostel
offers both beds in
dormitories and private
rooms. Guests share a
common kitchen and
lounge, as well as a
pool table. Hikes are
organized to different
spots on the island.

House of Aleva B&B
$40-$55 bkfst incl.
sb/pb, ℝ
5509 Kuamo'o Rd., Wailua
☎822-4606
Located near Wailua,
the House of Aleva
offers no-frills rooms,
but good enough for
the price. The single
room has its own bath-
room (separate), and
the other two share
one. Guests are mainly
European – German,
especially. Beach and
snorkelling equipment
is lent out without fuss.
No credit cards are
accepted.

Hawaii Kailani / Mokihana of Kaua'i
$65-$75
K, ⊗
796 Kuhio Hwy., Wailua
☎*822-3971 or 800-640-4786*
⇄*822-7387*
The two names refer to two establishments managed by the same agency: Mokihana studios and two-bedroom apartments in Kailani. The former are a little worn out and poorly organized, but include a kitchen, making them popular with retirees travelling on a tight budget. The latter are much more spacious and offer a better quality/price ratio (the rate is good for four), which explains why they are booked up in winter. The two seaside condominiums are located side by side. To get here, take Kamoa Road near the McDonald's restaurant.

Hotel Coral Reef
$59-89
ℝ, *tv/ctv, ♨*
1516 Kuhio Hwy., Kapa'a
☎*822-4481 or 800-843-4659*
⇄*822-7705*
More of a motel than a hotel, the Coral Reef is located at the northern exit of Kapa'a. The first of its two buildings, at the seaside, is the most pleasant; the second, perpendicular, stretches towards the road. Its rooms are smaller and noisier, but very good for the price – just make sure you're as close to the reception as possible.

Kapa'a Sands
$85-$129
≈, *laundry, K, tv*
380 Papaloa Rd., Wailua
☎*822-4901 or 800-222-4901*
⇄*822-1556*
www.kapaasands.com
This small, seaside condominium located north of Wailua Bay offers one of the best quality/price ratios on the island's eastern coast. Its 15 studios and four apartments are reserved months, sometimes even years in advance for the winter season. All are equipped with a kitchen, dishwasher and shower. The minimum stay is three days (one week from mid-December to mid-March). To get here, take Papaloa Street just past Wailua Beach.

Kaua'i Sands
$98-$135
≈, *K, ≡, ℝ, ctv*
420 Papaloa Rd., Waipouli
☎*822-4951 or 800-560-5553*
⇄*822-0978*
www.sandseaside.com/kauai.html
The fourth Sands Hotel, part of a local chain belonging to a Hawaiian family, is located at the entrance of the Coconut Market Place. It offers some 200 recently renovated rooms in two seaside two-storey buildings with that unmistakable motel feel.

Royal Drive Cottage
$80-$120
K, ⊗, tv
147 Royal Dr., Wailua
☎*822-2321*
www.royaldrive.com
The two cottages near Wailua are overgrown with vegetation and stand between coconut and canna trees. Simple but comfortable, they include a small kitchen and chairs in the garden where you can enjoy the fresh air. The only downside is the corrugated iron roof; when it rains, it's very noisy. You can also rent a house with one bedroom, two bathrooms, a kitchen and a living room. Royal Drive is located right before the intersection of Routes 580 and 581 coming from Wailua.

🌺 Islander on the Beach
$110-$195
≈, *laundry, ≡, 🔲, ℝ, ctv*
484 Kuhio Hwy., Waipouli
☎*822-7417 or 800-847-7417*
⇄*822-1947*
www.islander-kauai.com
Recently renovated, the Islander offers extremely comfortable, charming rooms at a good price. Rooms are located in eight wooden buildings near the beach and around the pool, a stone's throw from the Coconut Market Place.

Kaua'i

Plantation Hale
$135-$165
≈, *laundry, K,* 🔲 ⊗, *ctv*
484 Kuhio Hwy., Waipouli
☎*822-4941 or 800-775-4253*
⇄*822-5599*
www.plantation-hale.com
Part of the Best Western chain, this 10-building condominium complex houses comfortable one-bedroom apartments (most with two beds) that have recently been renovated. It is located at the entrance to the Coconut Market Place, around 655ft (200m) from the sea, through the parking lot.

Pono Kai Resort
$139-$269
≈, △, *laundry, K,* 🔲 ≡, ⊗, *ctv,* ☂
1250 Kuhio Hwy., Kapa'a
Pono Kai & Pacific Fantasy:
☎*822-9831 or 800-438-6493*
⇄*822-7212*
www.ponokai-resort.com
Marc Resorts:
☎*823-8427 or 800-535-0085*
⇄*823-8526*
www.marcresorts.com
This vast 10-building resort, located between the Waikaea Canal and Kapa'a Beach Park, is partly managed by Pono Kai & Pacific Fantasy and Marc Resorts. Reservations can be made with either company, but the second offers a better quality/price ratio. Four of the buildings are located by the sea and two by the canal. All apartments belong to different owners and therefore vary in terms of category and decor, though all share the same infrastructure. Pono Kai also offers

mini-suites equipped with a kitchen and apartments without air conditioning.

Aston Kaha Lani
$175-$460
≈, ☂, *K,* 🔲 ⊗, *ctv, laundry*
4460 Nehe Rd., Wailua
☎*822-9331 or 800-92-ASTON or 800-321-2558 (in Hawaii)*
⇄*922-8785*
www.aston-hotels.com
They may not be brand-new, but the Kaha Lani ("heavenly place") apartments are well equipped and located on a gorgeous beach, between Wailua's public golf course and Lydgate Beach Park. You can choose from one-, two- or three-bedroom apartments that can comfortably house up to four, six or eight people. Shared amenities include pool, lit tennis courts and barbecue area.

Holiday Inn Sunspree Resort
$150-$275
≈, ⊘, ℜ, *K, laundry,* ≡, 🔲 ℝ, *ctv,* ☂
3-5920 Kuhio Hwy. (Mile 5.6), Wailua
☎*823-6000 or 888-823-5111*
www.holidayinn-kauai.com
Located between Lydgate Park and the mouth of the Wailua River and offering a view of the Hikina A Ka La *heiau*, this tourist resort caters essentially to families and retirees. Its 196 recently renovated rooms are well equipped *(with showers only)* and all of its 26 cottages include a kitchen and a *lanai* on

the ocean. Tennis enthusiasts can borrow rackets and tennis balls. Children up to 19 who share their parents' room stay for free.

The North Coast

Most of Princeville's condominiums are managed by intermediary rental agencies. Few establishments take reservations directly.

🌴 **'Anini County Beach Park**
$3/pers.
washrooms, showers, picnic tables, ☎
'Anini Rd.
This is one of the best spots on the island to pitch your tent: a vast grassy lot stretches along 'Anini Beach, where you can swim and take part in all kinds of sports in complete safety. If you set up camp facing the sea, just make sure your pegs are well into the ground, since the wind can sometimes be violent.

Ha'ena State Park
free
washrooms, showers, picnic tables
Kuhio Hwy., Ha'ena (Mile 8.8)
The seaside campground is located just before the end of the Kuhio Highway, at the tip of the northern coast. A logical choice if you plan on hiking the Kalalau Trail the following day. Otherwise, the site lacks intimacy and its infrastructure needs repairs.

There is no camping here on Monday.

YMCA – Camp Naue
camping $10
dormitory $12
sb, K
Kuhio Hwy., Ha'ena
☎826-6419
The rustic dormitories are located no less than 30ft (10m) from the waves. The YMCA (also open to women) offers only 36 places, but it is uncommon for anyone to be turned away. Reservations are not possible: first come, first served.

(Classic Old 1920s) Plantation Manager's Home
$50-$60 bkfst incl.
sb
4481 Malulani St., Kilauea
☎828-1693
Laurie and Paul Goodrich rent two basic rooms in their home, located in a residential area east of Kilauea. Their rates are among the least expensive on the island. From Kolo Road, ignore the lighthouse road and drive straight to Malulani Street (second to the right).

Hale Ho'o Maha B&B
$55-$80 bkfst incl.
sb/pb
2883-A Kalahiwai Rd., Kalihiwai
☎828-1341 or 800-851-0291
⇥828-2046
hoomaha@aloha.net
This simple bed and breakfast, whose Hawaiian name means "the home of rest," has four rooms, two of which share the same bathroom. The biggest room is also the most

fun: it is entirely decorated in a pineapple theme – even the bed is round! Toby, the owner, loves classic cars and spends his days fixing them up. The minimum stay is three days.

Hanalei Inn
$55-$65
K, laundry
5-5468 Kuhio Hwy., Hanalei
☎826-9333
Located at the northern exit of Hanalei, this simple hotel offers five studios with kitchens. It does not have a reception; everything is self-serve. All you have to do is write your name on the sign located in the covered courtyard marked "Office" and phone to announce your arrival. The owners also rent three rooms at 5404 Weke Road – parallel to Kuhio, by the sea.

Historic B&B
$68-$85 bkfst incl.
sb/pb, ℝ
Kuhio Hwy., Hanalei
☎826-4622
bubbaburger.com/bnb/for.html
The setting here couldn't be more original: this bed and breakfast was set up in an old Buddhist temple that was built in 1901 and remained in use until 1986. The three rooms on the main floor, with shared bathroom, parquet floors and bamboo canopy beds, are quite simple, though. The most pleasant one is on the upper floor, which also features a subtle tropical twist. The house is located at

the entrance to Hanalei on the left, next to the Postcards Café. Young children are not allowed and the minimum stay is two nights.

Bed, Breakfast & Beach
$70-$125 bkfst incl.
ℝ, ⊗, *tv*
5095 Pilikoa St., Hanalei
☎826-6111 or 826-1212
bestofhawaii.com/hanalei/
Located a fair distance from beach-hugging Hanalei Bay, this bed and breakfast houses two studios on the main floor, each with private bathroom and entrance, an upstairs room and a "honeymoon" suite on the second – the loveliest of the four. Credit cards are not accepted. From the Kuhio Highway, take Ahu Road just past the Hanalei Wake Up Café, then turn right again on Pilikoa Street. It's the big grey house on the left, past the crossroads of Opelu Street.

Jungle Cabana / Jungle Bungalow
$95-$115
K
Paradise Adventures, Hanalei
☎826-999 or 888-886-4969
These two small wooden houses are located right in the middle of the forest along the Hanalei River and one of the last traditional squares on the northern coast. Both offer a tropical setting, and some of their walls are covered with braided rattan. Furnishings are simple. Both properties belong to the managers of

Kaua'i

Paradise Adventures, based in Hanalei and housed in a green roadside stand across from the Ching Young Village.

Sea Lodge
$105-$139
K, laundry, ⊗, ctv, ☗
Kamehameha Rd., Princeville
☎*826-6751 or 800-585-6101*
(East Coast Time)
Do not judge the Sea Lodge by its bungalows' exterior, whose wood has been ravaged by the salt air and frequent rain on the northern coast; its interior is much snazzier. One- or two-bedroom rooms are offered (the two-bedroom being on the mezzanine) as well as one or two bathrooms. Cleaning fees are charged.

Hanalei Colony Resort
$130-$240
≈, laundry, K, ☗
Kuhio Hwy., Ha'ena (Mile 7.4)
☎*826-6235 or 800-628-3004*
⇄*826-9893*
www.hcr.com
The rest of the world fades away at the Colony Resort. The most isolated resort on the island, located at the tip of the northern coast, it lies on a long, almost empty beach. Pleasant and well-ventilated, the condominium is rocked by the rhythm of the waves; 15 of the 52 apartments *(one- or two-bedroom)* overlook the ocean. Though the resort's wooden exterior has been damaged by the salt air, the interior of the place is immaculate. No air conditioning, television or tele-

phone is available, but the resort offers a plethora of daily activities.

🌴 Mahina Kai B&B
$125-$150 bkfst incl.
≈, K, tv, laundry
4933 Aliomanu Rd., Anahola
☎/⇄*822-9451*
☎*800-337-1134*
Hard to find anything as Japanese less than 3,700mi (6,000km) away! This superb house with a blue thatched roof is built around a reception area in a basin where a few *koi* swim. Paper walls, decorative objects, a tea house with a view of the sea and open for yoga or meditation sessions – everything here evokes the Empire of the Rising Sun. The owner, a Californian photographer who fell in love with Japan, has marvelously recreated the decor. This bed and breakfast offers three rooms and a studio. Credit cards are not accepted. As you exit Anahola, turn right onto Aliomanu Road at the bottom of the hill, and drive along for around 2,625ft (800m). You are just a short distance from the sea.

The Cliffs
$155-$225
≈, △, laundry, K, ⊗, ☗
3811 Edward Rd., Princeville
☎*826-6219 or 800-367-7032*
⇄*(435) 647-3822*
www.cliffs-princeville.com
These comfortable apartments, which are for the most part well decorated, include a bedroom, living room, kitchen, two bathrooms

and sometimes a mezzanine. While some have a great view of the sea, others are obviously farther away.

Hanalei Bay Resort
$170-$1,061
≈, K, laundry, ≡, ℝ, ◎, ctv
5380 Honoiki Rd. Princeville
☎*826-6522 or 800-827-4427*
⇄*826-6680*
www.quintusresorts.com
Located a bit back from the sea, the Hanalei Bay Resort offers both hotel rooms and apartments, as well as a four-room studio. The hotel rooms, which are dimly lit, seem sparse for the price. The apartments, differing slightly depending on their owner, are also too expensive. The resort is surrounded by two golf courses, two pools and eight tennis courts.

🌴 Princeville Resort
$380-$625
≈, ⊘, ℜ, ◎, ctv
5220 Ka Haku Rd.
☎*826-9644*
☎*800-325-DLUX*
⇄*826-1166*
www.princeville.com
Famous for its pool in which the bay and mountains of Hanalei are reflected, the mountainside Princeville Resort consists of three-storey buildings that overlook the small Pu'u Poa Beach. Part of the prestigious "Luxury Collection," it offers all of the services of a renowned hotel: extremely comfortable rooms complete with marble bathroom, a ballroom, a tennis court, a golf course, and a thousand

daily attractions to guarantee an unforgettable stay. In short, it makes a visit to Princeville worthwhile all on its own.

Po'ipu

🏝 Koloa Landing Cottages
$60-$110
K, laundry, ⊗, ctv
2704-B Ho'onani Rd.
☎*332-6326 or 742-1470 or 800-779-8773*
⇌*332-9584*
planet-hawaii.com/koloa
Fed up of rain in their native Netherlands, the Zeevats came here to retire under the Hawaiian sun. They rent five units of various sizes, from the studio to the main house (which can accommodate up to six people), at excellent rates for Po'ipu. There is a minimum stay of four days, however, and cleaning fees are charged for all rentals. The reception is excellent and reservations are recommended several weeks in advance. From Lawa'i Road, take the new bridge to the left, to Ho'onani Road. Cottages are 655ft (200m) on the left.

Garden Isle Cottages
$102, $199
K, laundry, ctv, ♨
2666 Pu'uholo Rd.
☎*742-6717 or 800-742-6711*
⇌*742-1933*
www.oceancottages.com
The Sea Cliff Cottages tower over the mouth of the Waikomo torrent, where the Koloa Landing used to be and

from where sugar produced in the region was exported. Managed by Sharon and Robert Flynn, a sculptor, the one- or two-bedroom studios and units are relatively comfortable. Some face the ocean, while others look onto the mountain. From Lawa'i Road, turn left onto Pu'uholo Road a little after leaving Highway 50.

Sunset Kahili
$125-$155
≈, K, laundry, ctv, ♨
1763 Pee Rd.
☎*742-7434 or 800-82-POIPU*
⇌*742-6058*
www.sunsetkahili.com
This five-storey mountainside condominium overlooking the sea is popular with retirees. It offers 36 somewhat worn-down apartments, with a choice of one or two bedrooms and baths. The minimum stay here is three days.

Kiahuna Plantation Resort
$190-$470
≈, ℜ, K, laundry, ⊗, ◙, ctv, ♨
2553 Po'ipu Rd.
☎*742-6411 or 800-688-7444*
⇌*742-1698*
Part of the Outrigger chain, this large tourist resort stretches from Po'ipu Road in the north, across from the Po'ipu Shopping Center, and Po'ipu Beach in the south. Its many buildings stand at the heart of a vast tropical garden. You can opt for an attractively-decorated apartment with one or two rooms. The minimum stay is two days.

🏝 Po'ipu Kapili
$170-$370
≈, K, laundry, ⊗, tv
2221 Kapili Rd.
☎*742-6449 or 800-443-7714*
⇌*742-9162*
www.poipukapili.com
This luxury condominium is a few steps from the beach and offers 60 apartments housed in several buildings surrounding a central pool. Featuring one or two bedrooms, they are extremely comfortable and all are equipped with a full kitchen and a living room with a tropical decor. Rooms with a view of the sea are the most expensive. From Po'ipu Road, turn right onto Kapili Road and keep driving for 655ft (200m).

Gloria's Bed and Breakfast
$250 bkfst incl.
≈, ⊗, tv
4464 Lawa'i Rd.
☎/⇌*742-6995*
Completely rebuilt after it was levelled by Hurricane Iniki in 1992, this house is located next to the sea, near a small beach – waves crash less than 16ft (5m) away from the terrace and the hammock set up at the foot of a clump of palm trees. One of the archipelago's classiest bed and breakfasts, Gloria's caters primarily to young couples; not only can they come and spend their honeymoon here, but can get married here as well: Gloria's husband is a retired minister and still has the right to perform marriages. The house holds only three rooms,

two upstairs with very high ceilings, and the third on the main floor. The wood decor is refined and comfortable. Credit cards are not accepted and it is recommended to make reservations quite far in advance. Despite the luxury of the place, it is still a tad expensive.

Sheraton Kaua'i Resort
$265-$740
≈, ⊙, ℜ, ≡, ℝ, ◙, *ctv*, ✧
2440 Ho'onani Rd.
☎*742-1661 or 800-782-9488*
≈*742-9777*
www.sheraton-hawaii.com
One of Po'ipu's most exquisite resorts, the Sheraton crowns a small rocky peak, bordered on both sides by beautiful beaches with coconut trees. It is no surprise that the 413 rooms are very comfortable, and their price essentially depends on the view. Guests have a variety of amenities at their disposal, including a massage centre, shops, tennis courts and video games in their room.

Hyatt Regency
from $310
≈, ⊙, ℜ, ≡, *ctv*, ✧
1571 Po'ipu Rd.
☎*742-1234*
☎*800-55-HYATT*
≈*742-1557*
www.kauai-hyatt.com
The extensive Hyatt borders Shipwreck Beach, Po'ipu's most beautiful. Its 600 rooms are housed over some 50 acres (20ha) of scenic tropical gardens with lakes, palm trees, exotic flowers, pools, water toboggans and

artificial beaches bordering a lagoon that is just as pleasant. Add to this a beauty salon, tennis courts and a golf course designed by Robert Trent Jones Jr.

The South Coast

Salt Pond County Park
$3/pers.
washrooms, showers, picnic tables, drinking water
Utterly charming, this campground borders the tucked-away Salt Pond Beach, which is adorned with tall palm trees. You can pitch your tent just about anywhere on the grass on the left side, provided that you stay away from the sand and do not set up camp under a coconut tree. If you don't respect these rules, a ranger might wake you up at dawn. On weekends, families come to camp and unfortunately take away some of the serenity of the place. Swimming and snorkelling conditions are excellent.

Kahili Mountain Park
$30-$125
sb/pb, K
P.O. Box 298, Koloa HI 96756
Kaumuali'i Hwy. (Mile 7)
☎*742-9921*
At the foot of Mount Kukui on a very safe site, the Adventist Church manages 40 or so rustic bungalows, varying in size and comfort. The least expensive are rather

worn down and share a bathroom. Up in the mountain and isolated between the trees, the newest all-wood bungalows (no. 31 to no. 35) are the most pleasant. They can easily accommodate an entire family. From the camp, a path leads up the Kahili (2hr walk), which offers a panoramic view on the meridional coast of the island. Just past Mile 7, take the dirt trail on the right and follow it around 1mi (1.5km) to the campground.

Kalaheo Inn
$55-$75
ℜ, *laundry, K*, ⊛, *tv*
4444 Papalina Rd., Kalaheo
☎*332-6023 or 888-332-6023*
www.kalaheoinn.com
Located on a road that climbs towards the Kukui o Lono Park, this small family hotel has 14 different rooms, ranging from studio to three-room unit. Units are small, but impeccable and all include a kitchen. The Kalaheo Steak House (see p 486) is managed by the same owners. A good place to keep in mind to stay for a good price.

Waimea Plantation Cottages
$175-$515
≈, ℜ, *laundry, K*, ⊛, *ctv*, ✧
9400 Kaumuali'i Hwy., Waimea (Mile 23.3)
☎*338-1625 or 800-321-2558*
≈*338-2338*
www.waimea-plantation.com
At the western exit of Waimea, 50 or so wooden houses dating

from the 1920s and 1930s stand at the heart of a vast coconut grove. Each is named after one of the former employees of the Fayé family, Norwegian immigrants who founded the sugar refinery in Kekaha. Completely modernized, you have a choice of bungalows with one to five bedrooms. Featuring an old-style plantation decor with wooden furniture, foot baths, fans and Hawaiian decorations, they exude wonderful charm.

Waimea Canyon and Koke'e

Koke'e State Park
free
washrooms, showers, picnic tables
You can pitch your tent beyond the museum, but the infrastructure is rather basic. For a few extra dollars, you'd be better off at Camp Sloggett.

YWCA Camp Sloggett
camping $10
dormitory $20
sb, K
☎/⇌335-6060
Serenaded by the song of forest birds in a massive isolated glade, the YWCA camp, founded in 1930, is open to everyone year-round. You can pitch you tent on the grass or opt for the dormitories. Only groups can make reservations, but the camp is so quiet that it is uncommon to see two guests arrive on the same day, except in

summer. This means that you have a good chance of getting a bed in the smallest dormitory, which is basically like a private room. Showers are hot, but you must provide your own sheets and sleeping bag in wintertime, when it can get quite cold in Koke'e. Just past the fork leading to the museum, take the dirt trail on the other side. After approximately 2,625 ft (800m), turn right onto a sloped path; the camp is just past a house.

Koke'e Lodge
$35-$45
K
3600 Koke'e Rd.
P.O. Box 819, Waimea HI 96796
☎335-6061
office: every day 9am to 3:45pm
Located below the Koke'e Natural History Museum, the lodge's 12 wooden cabins are rather rustic, but all are equipped with their own kitchenette and bathroom, as well as a stove – wood is extra. One-bedroom cabins can accommodate three people, the others up to seven. Be aware that, theoretically, you cannot arrive after 4pm when the reception closes (located in the restaurant). Even though the lodge relies on State Parks, it is recommended to make reservations through the agency ahead of time.

Restaurants

Lihu'e

Several restaurants are located in the Pacific Ocean Plaza, across from the entrance to the Marriott, in Nawiliwili.

☛ Hamura's Saimin
under $10
Mon to Fri 10am to 11pm, Sat 10am to 1pm, Sun 10am to 9:30pm
2956 Kress St.
☎245-3271
Located on a small street behind the Lihu'e Shopping Center, this must-see Kaua'i restaurant has served its simple, excellent *saimin* (noodle soups) to workers in the region for generations. It simmers and boils, and when customers arrive, it's ready to serve. The menu does not change, only the size of portions varies. The only exception to the rule is the passion-fruit pie for dessert.

Kalapaki Beach Hut
under $10
every day 7am to 7pm
3474 Rice Street
☎246-6330
The Kalapaki Beach Hut offers crepes and eggs for breakfast, as well as hamburgers, sandwiches, fish & chips the rest of the day for you to satisfy your hunger pangs between swims on the neighbouring Kalapaki

Kaua'i

Beach. Adventurous eaters will try the ostrich or buffalo burgers, as both animals are bred on Kaua'i.

Kaua'i Chop Suey
under $10
Tue to Sun 4:30pm to 9pm
3501 Rice St.
Pacific Ocean Plaza
☎245-8790
This no-frills Chinese restaurant offers a large variety of mainly Cantonese dishes, at a good quality/price ratio.

La Bamba
under $10
Mon to Sat 11am to 9pm, Sun 4pm tp 9pm
4261 Rice St.
☎245-5972
Don't be scared off by the large kitchen door that is kept wide open. If you have a craving for Mexican, you won't find anything better. The decor features Mexican colours, naive frescoes of the gardens of Xochimilco, thorny cacti and siesta-indulging Mexicans, dolls and a small, kitschy donkey with a sombrero on its head. The cuisine is excellent, of course, and portions are generous. Everything here is truly Mexican, except for the owner, Omar Muñoz, who is Salvadoran. Shhh... don't tell anyone, because the enchiladas, tacos and quesadillas don't know.

Hanama'ulu Cafe (Tea House and Sushi Bar)
$10-$25
Tue to Fri 10am to 1pm, Tue to Sun 4:30pm to 8:30pm
3-4291 Kuhio Hwy.
Hanama'ulu (Mile 2)
☎245-2511 or 245-3225
The Hanama'ulu Cafe is located at the northern exit of Lihu'e. Its traditional Japanese cuisine is enjoyed by locals and tourists alike. The sushi counter is open every night, except Sundays, when the café offers a buffet.

Café Portofino
$15-$30
every day 5pm to 10pm
3501 Rive St.
Pacific Ocean Plaza (first floor)
☎245-2121
This quality Italian restaurant managed by Giuseppe Avocadi is appreciated by couples for a romantic dinner or weekend date. A harpist performs here every night. The food served is more specifically from northern Italy: pasta, escalope, osso buco, lobster, etc. To finish your meal, indulge in a "Caffe d'Amore," with Grand Marnier, Kahlua and whipped cream.

Duke's Canoe Club
$15-$25
every day 11:30am to 11:30pm (bar until midnight)
3610 Rice St.
Kaua'i Marriott (see p 470)
☎246-9599
Duke's Waikiki (see p 173) has expanded. The Kaua'i club, which is just as tropical, surf-style and nostalgic, is not located on the "world's most famous beach," but on Kalapaki Beach, which has little to be envied for. The grill, with sandwiches, hamburgers and other fast-food items, is open all day for a few bites between swims. The upstairs restaurant, with a more varied menu geared towards seafood, is open at night only. Catches of the day are recommended. Also see p 486.

Tokyo Lobby
$15-$20
Mon to Fri 11am to 2pm, every day 4:30pm to 9:30pm
3501 Rice St.
Pacific Ocean Plaza
☎245-8989
In a family setting that is both simple and pleasant, the Tokyo Lobby will satisfy any craving for sushi, sashimi, *udon* and tempura. At night, don't hesitate to try the " love boat," a miniature Japanese boat featuring miso soup, rice, a main dish and salad.

Gaylord's
$20-$25
Mon to Sat 11am to 3pm, Sun 9:30am to 3pm, every day from 5pm
3-2087 Kaumuali'i Hwy.
☎245-9593
Located in the inner courtyard of the Kilohana plantation, Gaylord's is one of Kaua'i's poshest restaurants. The ratan furniture, dining room overlooking the park and soft lighting make it a perfect spot for roman-

tics at heart. The wine list is one of the best on the island.

JJ's Broiler
$20-$25
every day 11am to 10pm
3416 Rice St.
☎246-4422
If, at lunchtime, customers on the main floor satisfy themselves with regatta, sandwiches, hamburgers and salads, they can enjoy a more serene setting upstairs in the evening. Sheltered by three enormous sailboat models suspended from the ceiling, you can enjoy a panoramic view of Kalapaki Beach and savour a wide variety of seafood. Meatlovers have not been forgotten: the restaurant is renown for its Slavonic steak in butter, white wine and garlic sauce. On Sundays and Mondays, American football games are broadcast, creating a different ambiance.

Wailua – Kapa'a

Aloha Diner
under $10
971 Kuhio Hwy., Waipouli
Waipouli Complex
☎822-3851
The most local of greasy spoons on the eastern coast offers a choice of basic, popular dishes, prominently featuring Hawaiian specialties. You can eat at the restaurant, but since there are only six seats, most people order take-out.

Bubba's
under $10
every day 10:30am to 8pm
4-1421 Kuhio Hwy., Kapa'a
(across from Kapa'a Beach Park)
☎823-0069
Founded here in Kapa'a, this mini local chain has expanded all the way to Maui. It offers hamburgers ranging in size and price, as well as chili, fish & chips and other dishes. The restaurant's motto, "We cheat tourists, drunks and attorneys" reveals an American spirit, in keeping with the menu... Internet access by Web-TV is free.

Coconut Market Place
under $10 to $25
Mon to Sat 9am to 9pm, Sun 10am to 6pm
4-484 Kuhio Hwy., Waipouli
☎822-3641
Located between two shops, you will find a variety of restaurants here, none of which particularly stand out.

King and I
under $10 to $15
every day 11am to 2pm and 4:30pm to 9:30pm (10pm Fri-Sat)
4-901 Kuhio Hwy. (Mile 7.1)
Waipouli Plaza
☎822-1642
You will not regret your foray into the land of a thousand smiles if you are looking for something different or a taste of another continent. Spring rolls, curries and vegetarian dishes all evoke the flavours of Thai cuisine. The green-papaya salad

is one of the house specialties.

Masa's
under $10 to $20
Tue to Sat 11am to 2pm and 5pm to 9pm, Sun 2pm to 9pm
1384 Kuhio Hwy., Kapa'a
☎821-6933
This authentic little sushi counter, located at the heart of old Kapa'a, offers a good choice of traditional and Hawaiian-style sushi. You might prefer a plate lunch at a good price for breakfast or a combination with sashimi.

Olympic Cafe
under $10
every day 6:30am or 7am to 7pm or 8pm
4-1387 Kuhio Hwy., Kapa'a
☎822-5825
The Olympic Cafe is a breakfast option offering an assortment of omelets and hot dishes, fruit, muffins and crepes. The rest of the day features nothing special: hamburgers, sandwiches, salads and a few Mexican snacks, to which pasta and fish are added at night. The restaurant could use a little cleaning up.

Papaya's Natural Foods and Café
under $10
Mon to Sat 9am to 8pm
4-831 Kuhip Hwy. (Mile 7.3)
Kaua'i Village
☎823-0190
This café is first and foremost an organic-food (and food supplement) store, which also offers a choice of 100% natural snacks including salads, tacos and

sandwiches (grilled fish) for breakfast and lunch. You can take in the sun's early rays on outdoor tables.

Mema
$10-$25
Mon to Fri 11am to 2pm, every day 5pm to 9:30pm
361 Kuhio Hwy., Wailua
Wailua Shopping Plaza
☎823-0899

Among the archipelago's most renown Thai restaurants, Mema is managed by the same couple as the Po'ipu's Pattaya Asian Cafe (see p 483). The decor is rather chic and the service is courteous. You can order any of the great Thai classics, with a large choice of curries, vegetarian dishes (stir-fried vegetables) and noodles. Coconut milk, ginger and peanuts enhance the flavours.

Norberto's El Cafe
$10-$15
Mon to Sat 5:30pm to 9pm
4-1373 Kuhio Hwy., Kapa'a
☎822-3362

Located in the heart of Kapa'a for over 20 years, this Mexican restaurant offers a good choice of traditional dishes à la carte such as burritos, enchiladas and fajitas, and six menus at reasonable prices, featuring soup, vegetables, rice, *frijole* and corn chips.

Restaurant Kintaro
$15-$25
every day 5:30pm to 9:30pm
4-370 Kuhio Hwy., Wailua
☎822-3341

Kintaro is the name of a Japanese hero, an ancestor of Superman armed with his magic ax, known for his good deeds. Despite its anonymous exterior, the restaurant's interior is rather quaint. The varied cuisine is completely traditional: sushi prepared in front of you, complete meals, *sukiyaki*, *nabemono* (a seafood vegetable casserole) and *tepanyaki* – oysters, chicken, steak, shrimp, fish or even lobster prepared in front of you on a large hot plate. If you want to see a moray eel up close, ask to be seated next to the aquarium.

Kapa'a Rib, Fish & Chowder House
$20-$40
every day from 4pm
4-1639 Kuhio Hwy., Kapa'a
☎822-7488

This big wooden building painted in ocean tones stands at the northern exit of Kapa'a, near Kealia Beach. Shrimp, squid, lobster, crab, *cioppino*, clams, oysters... this is heaven for seafood-lovers. Its wood decor is more reminiscent of New England than Hawaii, though. Meat enthusiasts can satisfy their appetite with a choice of steaks and ribs.

A Pacific Café
$30-$40
every day 5:30pm to 9:30pm
4-831 Kuhio Hwy. (Mile 7.3)
Kaua'i Village
☎822-0013

As in all of his establishments, Jean-Marie Josselin offers Hawaiian nouvelle cuisine combining the flavours of all continents: from the ancestral *foie gras* (panfried with mango!) to Peking duck served with shrimp tacos to grilled tuna smoked with *kiawe* wood with Japanese mushrooms. The posted menu is just as long as in the French chef's other restaurants. The setting is airy and you can wait for a table at the bar.

The North Coast

Banana Joe's
under $10
every day 9am to 6pm
5-2719 Kuhio Hwy., Kilauea
☎828-1092

This is neither a restaurant nor a café, but rather a simple roadside counter at the northern exit of Kilauea. You can buy food such as tropical fruit grown in the neighbouring plantation, ice cream and sorbet, and *poi*. In short, this is a picnic stop on the way to the beach.

Bubba Burgers
under $10
every day 10:30am to 8pm
5-5183 Kuhio Hwy., Hanalei
☎826-7839

The baby brother of Bubba's in Kapa'a (see p 479) offers the same high-calorie menu and has the same silly motto. Here too, Internet access is free by Web TV (for E-mail only).

Duane's Ono Char-Burger
under $10
Mon to Sat 10am to 6pm,
Sun 11am to 6pm
Kuhio Hwy., Anahola
(Mile 13.9)
☎*822-9181*
A few roadside tables scattered amongst the palm trees await customers travelling to the northern coast. At the counter, you can order a good choice of hamburgers, sandwiches or milk shakes. Garnishings are so generous that you'll have to open wide to take a bite.

Hanalei Wake Up Cafe
under $10 to $15
Mon to Sat 5:30am to 11:30am, Sun 5:30am to 1pm, every day 5:30pm to 9pm
Kuhio Hwy., Hanalei
☎*826-5551*
All surfing enthusiasts on the north coast and a good number of tourists gather for breakfast on the roadside terrace. The café's walls are covered with autographed pictures of the greatest surfers and boards hang from the ceiling. Don't miss the picture taken in Waimea in late 1967 of a pro surfing a 40ft (12m) wave! In the morning, the Hanalei Bowl (half a papaya with homemade yogurt and granola) is excellent. Famished customers will also find breakfast classics. The rest of the day, the menu varies between Hawaiian and Mexican dishes such as chicken or tuna tacos, the Big Wave enchilada plate and

grilled tuna filet. Credit cards are not accepted.

Kilauea Farmers Market
under $10
every day 8:30am to 8:30pm
adjacent to the Kong Lung Center, in Kilauea
☎*828-1512*
This small organic-food shop also offers healthy sandwiches, such as salad and tuna or mango and tofu, and a dish of the day, most often with a macro-organic twist. You can also opt for soup or tropical fruit picked right off the tree.

Old Hanalei Coffee Company
under $10
every day 7am to 7pm
5-5183 C Kuhio Hwy., Hanalei
☎*826-6717*
It isn't as popular as the Wake Up Cafe, but the Old Hanalei Coffee Company has its regulars and not as many tourists. For breakfast, you can choose from a (limited) selection of waffles, fruits and bagels, as well as a few house pastries. Orange juice is squeezed fresh – a rare treat!

Kilauea Bakery and Pau Hana Pizza
$10-$30
Mon to Sat 6:30am to 9pm
Kong Lung Center, Kilauea
☎*828-2020*
Kilauea residents stop here on their way to work for a bagel, Viennese bun and fresh bread. Pizza is just as popular and can be ordered whole or by the slice. The Big Blue,

featuring smoked *ono*, capers, mozzarella and parsley, is worth a try. Large pizzas are quite expensive, but are really big. Take-out is available, or you can sit indoors or under a parasol between the trees if it's sunny.

Neide's Salsa and Samba
$10-$20
from 11am
5-5161 Kuhio Hwy., Hanalei
☎*826-1851*
Founded by an exiled Brazilian, this small, simple restaurant also offers a variety of Mexican dishes to which local palates are accustomed. Don't let that keep you from trying the *muqueca*, a catch of the day in a shrimp and coconut sauce, or *panquecas*, crepes stuffed with a choice of vegetables and pumpkin or chicken and covered in a house sauce that is excellent, though spicy. Neide is known in Hanalei for its dancing.

Postcards Café
$10-$25
every day 8am to 11am (Sun until noon) and 6pm to 9pm
Kuhio Hwy., Hanalei
☎*826-1191*
Simple and featuring a tropical decor, the green wooden house is located at the entrance to Hanalei. No meat or poultry is served here: the credo is all organic, all vegetable, all fish. At night, you can taste the Hanalei Valley's taro and polenta. The menu has an Asian twist, and vegetarians will even

find desserts especially prepared for them.

Roadrunner Café & Bakery
$10-$15
Mon to Fri 7am to 8pm, Sat 7am to 8:30pm, Sun 7am to 1:30pm
2430 Oka St., Kilauea
☎826-6360
The Roadrunner Café & Bakery features two establishments in one: a bakery where you can buy all kinds of Viennese buns and breads, and an American-Mexican cantina. The dining-room walls are covered with naive frescoes that spice up the room and evoke the good life south of the American border. The combination plate will satisfy your appetite.

Bamboo Room / Tahiti Nui
$15-$20
every day from 11:30am
5-5134 Kuhio Hwy.
☎826-1078
Renown for its *lu'au* organized by Louise Marston, a former Tahitian, the Tahiti Nui also houses a bar and a restaurant. Unpretentious and serving generous portions, it offers cuisine with a strong Asian twist, including Thai, Vietnamese, curry, soup and noodle dishes. The restaurant also offers a large variety of vegetarian dishes. Weekend evenings usually feature live music.

Surt's on the Beach
$15-$25
Kuhio Hwy., Ha'ena (Mile 7.4)
Adjacent to the Hanalei Colony Resort, Surt's on the Beach, as its name suggests, is right on the beach. Under the leadership of chef Surt Thammoutha, who is both Thai and Laotian, Asian and French influences join together to offer a menu often described with concupiscence. Don't miss the desserts, especially the mango or passion-fruit tiramisu.

The Hanalei Dolphin
$15-$30
every day 11am to 10pm
Kuhio Hwy., Hanalei
☎826-6113
Located at the entrance of Hanalei next to the river, the Dolphin specializes in seafood, as can attest the squid, tuna and swordfish hung from the walls and ceilling. The restaurant doubles as a fish market. At lunchtime, you can enjoy rich fish & chips, a hamburger with anything and everthing (fish, squid, vegetables and even meat) or a salad. At night, the selection grows, with lobster and meat making their appearance. The grill would benefit from more scrubbing, but no one seems to complain.

Zelo's Beach House
$15-$25
11am to 9pm
5-5156 Kuhio Hwy., Hanalei
☎826-9700
Zelo's is not located on the beach, as its name might suggest, but roadside, at the heart of Hanalei. It offers good hamburgers, sandwiches, pasta (all-you-can-eat marinara spaghetti), ribs and classic catches of the day. At night, the influence of regional Hawaiian cuisine can be enjoyed with a few more complex dishes. The dining room is quite pleasant and features a patio.

Bali Hai Restaurant
$20-$50
every day 7am to 11pm, 11:30am to 2pm and 5:30pmto 9:30pm
5380 Honoiki Rd., Princeville
Hanalei Bay Resort
☎826-6522
The dining area, shaped like an over-sized Polynesian hut, overlooks Hanalei Bay from afar. The menu highlights the Pacific Rim and marks a preference for seafood hors d'oeuvres and meats and poultry as main dishes. The catch of the day can be prepared with crab cakes and sweet potatoes, vegetables sautéed in a shiitake-mushroom or fruit sauce, etc.

Cafe Hanalei
$25-$50
every day 6:30am to 9:30pm
5220 Ka Huka Rd., Princeville
Princeville Resort
☎826-2760
The Princeville Resort's main restaurant features a dining room in a refined setting overlooking the pool and Hanalei Bay. It offers a varied menu for all tastes and includes soups, salads, Thai curry, steaks, bouillabaisse, lamb chops, a catch of the day and even a few Japanese

dishes. Buffets are quite pricy and are served at breakfast, as well as Friday and Sunday.

La Cascata
$25-$50
every day 6pm to 10pm
5220 Ka Huka Rd., Princeville
Princeville Resort
☎ *826-2761*
La Cascata's tablecloths are pink, just like its fake columns and wrought-iron doors, somewhat reminiscent of Italy. The Princeville Resort's second restaurant offers a large choice of salads such as Caesar and fresh tuna *niçoise*, as well as a dozen Mediterranean-influenced Hawaiian dishes.

Po'ipu and Koloa

The **Po'ipu Shopping Village** *(2360 Kiahuna Plantation Dr.)* is a real gold mine for restaurants and snack bars.

Koloa Fish Market
under $10
Mon to Fri 10am to 6pm, Sat 10am to 5pm
5482 Koloa Rd., Koloa
☎ *742-6199*
This tiny fish caterer will seduce fish-lovers with Hawaiian and Japanese dishes such as sashimi tuna and seaweed salads, sushi, *poi*, smoked marlin and fresh fish depending on delivery. Customers, who are mostly locals, swear only by him. Only take-out is available, but the plastic containers are perfect for a picnic.

La Griglia
$10-$25
every day 7am to 10pm
2360 Kiahuna Plantation Dr.
Po'ipu Shopping Village
☎ *742-2147*
In a simple but classy setting, with Ital-European music playing in the background, La Griglia is set up around a white wooden stand next to a shopping centre. The Sicilian-born chef's menu incorporates all of the influences she has picked up in her career: New York, Louisiana and Hawaii. Italy, however, is always featured, with a generous use of olive oil, pasta and pizza. Salads are delicious and hearty. You can also order wine by the glass.

Pattaya Asian Cafe
$10-$25
Mon to Sat 11:30am to 2:30pm, every day 5pm to 9:30pm
2360 Kiahuna Plantation Dr.
Po'ipu Shopping Village
☎ *742-8818*
The decor is simple and relaxed, but the Thai cuisine of chef Choy is exceptional – he also owns the Mema, in Kapa'a (see p 480). The menu features Thai dishes such as summer rolls, green papaya salad, *tom yum* (citronelle soup with a choice of fish, seafood or chicken) and spicy curries.

Pizzetta
$10-$25
every day 11am to 10pm
5408 Koloa Rd., Koloa
☎ *742-8881*
Established by the son of the Sicilian owner of La Griglia, the Pizzetta is housed in the old wooden Asahi Soda Building, built in the 1920s where a former *poi* plant once stood. The dining room is ventilated. Pizzas take centre stage of course, but you can also order pasta and salads, as well as a large variety of local and European beer.

Keoki's Paradise
$15-$20
every day 11am to 11:30pm
2360 Kiahuna Plantation Dr.
Po'ipu Shopping Village
☎ *742-7535*
Bamboo decor, rich vegetation, tropical flowers and fountains make for a very "South Seas" setting. The café menu, served all day, is quite classic and features sandwiches, hamburgers, salads, *pupus* and a few Hawaiian dishes. Fresh fish are added to the menu at night, including *ono*, *'ahi*, *a'u* (swordfish), *mahi-mahi* and *ulua*, and are served with a *ponzu* sauce, made with lemon, soy and sesame sauce. Shrimp with Macadamia nuts and steak are also available.

Kaua'i

Roy's Po'ipu Bar & Grill
$15-$30
every day 5:30pm to 9:30pm
2360 Kiahuna Plantation Dr.
Po'ipu Shopping Village
☎742-5000
This Kaua'i restaurant owned by renowned chef Roy Yamaguchi, a leader in tropical Hawaiian nouvelle cuisine, is no exception to the rule: its menu features all the flavours brought to the island by immigrants. Presentation is impeccable, as always, and the wine list is worthy of Bacchus himself, but the huge dining room feels like a tourist factory.

Brenneke's Beach Broiler
$20-$25
every day 11am to 10pm
2100 Ho'one Rd.
☎742-7588
Located across from the Po'ipu Beach Park, Brenneke's is reminiscent of tropical California. Under fans on the terrace, you can enjoy the charcoal-grilled catch of the day and large salads, such as crab Louis, shrimp Louis, and such. The evening menu features a larger selection, offering more land products. Desserts are good; and the restaurant's bar livens up at sunset.

Piatti Italian Restaurant
$20-$25
every day 5:30pm to 10pm
Kiahuna Plantation Resort
(see p 475)
2253 Po'ipu Road
☎742-2216
Set up in the charming setting of a former 1930s planter's house with cherrywood parquets, the Piatti specializes in northern Italian cuisine. You can enjoy an excellent wood-stove pizza or a pasta dish that is just as delicious, indoors or on the veranda that has a view of the gardens. The wine list is just as good. Reservations are recommended.

The Beach House
$25-$30
every day 11:30am to 2pm and 6pm to 9:30pm
5022 Lawa'i Rd.
☎742-1424
Housed under the same roof and overlooking Beachhouse Beach are a French café and fine-cuisine restaurant. Both are the creations of chef Jean-Marie Josselin, who switched from his native Hexagone to regional Hawaiian cuisine. Based on fresh products, the menu combines the ingredients and know-how of the four corners of the world and features such dishes as Thai fried-tuna rice nachos with *lilikoi* sauce, New Zealand mussels in a balsamic vinegar sauce, Pacific salmon prepared with soy and sesame served with Japanese noodles. The café is more reasonable in both taste and price and offers salads, sandwiches, hamburgers and other such dishes.

Ilima Terrace
$30
every day 6am to 2:30pm and 6pm to 9pm
1571 Po'ipu Rd.
Hyatt Regency (see p 476)
☎742-1234
Known for its excellent buffets at both breakfast and dinner, the restaurant overlooks the hotel gardens and Keoneloa Bay. At its feet runs an artificial river in which *koi* and swans swim. Buffet themes are different every night, featuring Italian, Hawaiian, ribs, and champagne brunch on Sunday. You can still order a pizza or salad, and at lunchtime, you can order "natural cuisine" dishes à la carte.

Tidepools
$30-$40
every day 6pm tp 10pm
1571 Po'ipu Road
Hyatt Regency (see p 476)
☎742-1234
Tables are located in several bungalows on stilts with palm roofs and are wide open on the hotel's artificial lagoon. Polynesian cuisine makes way for regional Hawaiian cuisine, though less adventurous eaters can order traditional American dishes. The catch of the day, such as the *mahi-mahi* in sesame and sake, is excellent, but you might also want to try the guava chicken.

The South Coast

Hanapepe Café (& Espresso Bar)
under $10 to $20
Tue to Sat 8am to 2pm,
Thu to Sat 6pm tp 9pm
3830 Hanapepe Rd., Hanapepe
☎*335-5011*

Despite its plastic tables and chairs, the large dining room, which is abundantly decorated with flowers and objects featuring cows and cats, is pleasant and fun. Located right in the heart of town across from the church, the Hanapepe Café offers an Italian-influenced menu featuring soups, salads, hamburgers and sandwiches at breakfast, and lasagna, fettucini and other pasta dishes at dinnertime. The café is also a bookstore and souvenir shop.

John's Place
under $10
9875 Waimea Rd., Waimea
☎*338-0330*

If thirst gets the best of you, John's Place is a good place for a quick stop. Located at the heart of Waimea, across from Cook's statue, its specialties include shaved ice and tropical-fruit smoothies. The number of bottles lined up on the shelf gives you a good idea of the variety of flavours. You can also have breakfast, fish & chips, grilled tuna sandwich, coffee and other treats.

Kalaheo Coffee Company & Café
under $10
Mon to Fri 6am to 4pm,
Sat 6:30am to 4pm, Sun
7am to 2pm
2-2436 Kaumuali'i Hwy.
Kalaheo
☎*332-5858*

Let your nose lead the way... past the "Order here" sign up to the "Odor here" sign, where the coffee steeps in large pots lined up along the wall. Perfect for a quick stop on the way to Waimea, the Kalaheo Café offers 25 coffees, six of which are Hawaiian blends. You can also indulge in a variety of teas, pastries, big breakfasts and all kinds of sandwiches. The café is on the left side of the road, just past Papalina Street.

Mustard's Last Stand
under $10
every day 10am to
5:30pm
crossroads of Routes 50 and 530, Lawa'i
☎*332-7245*

Right next to the parking lot of the Hawaiian Trading Post, Mustard's is quaintly framed by two traveller's trees. Its motto says it all: "World-Famous Hot Dogs!" For more details, just read the menu posted on a surfboard. You can also try the fish & chips, which are not exactly low-calorie but are quite good.

Green Garden Restaurant
$10-$20
Mon to Fri 8:30am to
2pm, Sat 8am to 2pm,
Sun 7:30am to 2pm; every
day 5pm to 9pm
Kaumuali'i Hwy., Hanapepe
☎*335-5422*

True to its name, the large dining room of the Green Garden Restaurant is pleasantly adorned with green plants. Popular with locals and tourists alike, the restaurant, which has been an institution for over 50 years and was founded by Japanese immigrants, is particularly busy in the morning. Breakfast has a tropical twist, with fresh papaya, guava or pineapple juice. The rest of the day, you can choose between sandwiches, fresh fish (such as *'ahi, ono, mahi-mahi*) grilled over a fire of *kiawe* wood, and a whole selection of Japanese-inspired dishes. For dessert, let yourself indulge in a passion-fruit tart, worthy of its fame.

Kalaheo & Brick Oven Pizza
$10-$20
Tue to Sun 11am to 10pm
2-2555 Kaumuali'i Hwy.
Kalaheo
☎*332-8561*

Its brick-oven pizzas, plain or all-dressed, are more American than Italian, but the large wooden dining room with tables covered with checkered tablecloths is rather quaint. Regulars take out or nibble on a salad or sandwich on site. The restaurant is located at the entrance of Kalaheo.

Pomodoro
$10-$20
every day 5:30pm to 10pm
Rainbow Plaza, Kalaheo
☎*332-5945*

Located upstairs from the Rainbow Plaza in a well-ventilated room, Pomodoro was voted Hawaii's best Italian restaurant. It offers authentic cuisine where pasta, veal (*parmigiana, pizzaiola,* etc.) and chicken take centre stage. Squid and lobster are also offered. All dishes feature side orders of farfalle and vegetables.

Toi's Thai Kitchen
$10-$15
Mon to Fri 10:30am to 2pm, Sat 11am to 2pm; Mon-Sat 5:30pm to 9:30pm
'Ele'ele Shopping Center 'Ele'ele
☎*335-3111*

Sitting on their thrones behind the cash, King Bhumipol and Queen Sirikit welcomes you to Toi's Thai Kitchen. This small, simple restaurant, located in a shopping centre, offers delicious Thai specialties such as fried rice, chicken with cashews, *pad thai* (fried noodles with soy sprouts) and tofu soup. All dishes feature side orders of green-papaya salad, rice and dessert. You can also choose from a variety of *pupus* at a good price.

Kalaheo Steak House
$15-$30
every day 6pm to 10pm
4444 Papalina Rd., Kalaheo
☎*332-9780*

Belonging to the same owners as the Kalaheo Inn (see p 476) and true to its name, this steakhouse offers a variety of beef, pork, chicken, and seafood. The wooden dining room is pleasant and its tables are decorated with candles. Good reception.

Wranglers Steakhouse
$15-$25
Mon to Fri 11am to 4pm and 5pm to 8:30pm, Sat 5pm to 9pm
9852 Kaumuali'i Hwy., Waimea
☎*338-1218*

Wranglers cultivates its Western decor: the terrace is bedecked with comfortable ratan-like braided-leather armchairs and the dining room features stools and a mechanical bull. You may also choose to dine on the wooden patio, which is decorated with saddles. Steaks share the bill with fish and seafood, as well as a few Mexican dishes, including a soup and salad all-you-can-eat buffet.

Waimea Canyon and Koke'e

Koke'e Lodge
under $10
every day 9am to 3:30pm
3600 Koke'e Rd.
☎*335-6061*

Despite its name, you won't find a lodge here but a rather simple souvenir shop doubling

as a snack stand. You can choose between breakfast dishes, sandwiches, salads, hot dogs and even a few desserts.

Entertainment

Bars and Nightclubs

Lihu'e

Duke's Canoe Club
3610 Rice St.
Kaua'i Marriott (see p 470)
☎*246-9599*

Every Thursday and Friday nights, Duke's features local bands. The Kalapaki Beach setting makes it one of the most popular spots in Lihu'e.

Gilligan's
4331 Kaua'i Beach Dr.
Outrigger Kaua'i Beach Hotel (see p 470)
☎*245-1955*

Kaua'i's most popular bar rocks each night to a different beat: country music on Thursdays, 1970s and 1980s music on Fridays and the latest Top 40 hits on Saturdays.

Rob's Good Times Grill
4303 Rice St.
Rice Shopping Center
☎*246-0311*

Rob's Good Times Grill has football days and disco nights hosted by a DJ *(Thu to Sun).*

Whether you're looking for a hearty hamburger, pool, karaoke or a local outing, you'll find it all here.

Whalers Brew Pub

3132 Ninini Point St.
Kaua'i Lagoons Resort
☎245-2000

A blue whale holding a beer glass with its fin welcomes you to the Whalers Brew Pub. Overlooking the sea and golf course, the pub brews eight beers. Try the Da Kine, which is light and popular, or the more exotic Tutu's Guavam, made with guava. You can also have breakfast and dinner here, but most regulars come at night to knock back a few beers and play a game of pool or cheer on their favourite American football team. Local bands perform here on weekends. To get to the Whalers Brew Pub, cross the Marriott golf course until Ninini Point. You can park in the large parking lot, then cross through the abandoned shopping centre to the pub.

Wailua – Kapa'a

Tradewinds

4-484 Kuhio Hwy., Waipouli
Coconut Market Place

Everything goes in this place! You can either enjoy a cocktail or knock back a beer at dusk, go dancing on Wednesdays and Saturdays, show off your talent at karaoke or play electronic darts on other nights.

The North Coast

Hanalei Gourmet

Hanalei Center, Hanalei
☎826-2524

Every night, this rather simple restaurant comes to life to rock, R&B or jazz. Sundays are reserved for Hawaiian music improvisation.

Happy Talk Lounge

5380 Honoiki Rd., Princeville
Hanalei Bay Resort (see p 474)
☎826-6522

This bar overlooks an artificial waterfall and offers a lovely, though distant view of Hanalei Bay. Hawaiian musicians and local bands perform every night (jazz on Sunday from 3pm tp 7pm). The movie South Pacific, which was shot in Hanalei, is shown on Friday, when pupus are free and drinks are offered at a good price.

Sushi & Blues

5-5190 Kuhio Hwy., Hanalei
☎826-9701

Between America and Asia, this sushi and Thai-style restaurant features jazz musicians on Wednesdays and Sundays. Fridays and Saturdays, the room is turned into a dance floor.

The Living Room

5220 Ka Haku Rd., Princeville
Princeville Resort (see p 474)
☎826-9644

You don't have to be a guest at the hotel to enjoy this place's charm. Enjoy some tea as you take in the view of Hanalei Bay. Traditional and contemporary musicians perform here every night. You can even take part in hula kuhiko demonstrations.

Po'ipu

Stevenson's Library

1571 Po'ipu Rd.
Hyatt Regency (see p 476)
☎742-1234

This chic, English-style bar features an tropical decor with a colonial twist: wooden frames, large leather armchairs, pool tables and a library. Cigar smokers meet to have a glass of cognac or port while listening to jazz musicians performing every night (8pm to 11pm). Proper attire is required.

The South Coast

Waimea Brewing Company

Waimea Plantation Cottages
(see p 476)
9400 Kaumuali'i Hwy., Waimea
(Mile 23.3)
☎338-9733

"The world's most Western bar" offers three house beers: Wai'ale'ale Golden, Waimea Red and Pakala Porter. To help you enjoy your beer, choose one of the dishes on the pub-like menu and enjoy it on the pleasant lanai. Modern Hawaiian musicians perform on Wednesday night, while Friday and Saturday nights feature jazz.

Kaua'i

Holidays and Festivals

February

Waimea Town Celebration
(games, canoe races, etc.)

March

Prince Kuhio Celebration
(*lu'au*, canoe races, etc.)

May

May Day Lei Contest
May 5
(*lei* contest at the Kaua'i Museum)

Banana Poka Festival
late May
organized by the (Koke'e Museum: traditional activities, Hawaiian music to celebrate a day to educate the public on forest ecology)

Prince Albert Music Festival in Princeville
(classical concerts featuring internationally renown musicians, *hula*, etc.)

June

Kamehameha Day
Ho'olaulea Festival at Kekaha
(crafts)

Obon feasts
in Buddhist temples
(dances, music, etc.)

July

Koloa Plantation Days
(celebrated in honour of the former sugar refinery)

Na Holo Kai
between O'ahu and Po'ipu Beach Park
(canoe race)

August

Tahiti Fête
Every year, celebrates Kaua'i's Polynesian heritage, as well as its historical and cultural ties to the South Pacific. Around 50 dancers and musicians come from Tahiti for this event.

September

Mokihana Festival
☎822-2166
(Hawaiian music, popular arts and *hula*)

October

Kaua'i Paniolo Ranch Rodeo
in Po'pui
☎742-6096

Aloha Festival
(various cultural demonstrations, including the **Eo E Emalani I Alaka'i**, a *hula* festival held in Koke'e)

Coconut Festival
at Kapa'a Beach Park
☎639-8080

Kaua'i Taro Festival

November

Bankoh Ki Ho' Alu Slack Key Festival
Hawaiian guitar festival attracting the most popular musicians of the archipelago.

December

Christmas
(parades)

Shows

Free shows

You can attend free dance shows at several shopping centres and hotels, such as the **Coconut Market Place** *(Mon, Tue, Fri and Sat at 5pm;* ☎822-3641*)*, which features Tahitian dancing, *hula*, *auana* and *kahiko*; the **Po'ipu Shopping Village** *(Mon and Thu at 5pm;* ☎742-2831*)* which features the same Tahitian dances; the **Hyatt Po'ipu** *(every day 6pm to 8pm)*; the **Coconut Beach Resort** in Kapa'a *(every day at 7pm)*; the **Marriott** *(Wed and Sat 6:30pm to 8pm)* on Kalapaki Beach and even the **Princeville Hotel** *(Tue, Thu and Sun at 6:30pm)*, where the show is followed by contemporary music. Every Friday at 6pm, the **Kukui Grove Center** *(*☎245-7784*)* also organizes quite a large Polynesian show featuring *hula*, Tahitian dances and Samoan fire-knife dances.

Days and times of performances change regularly, so the best thing to do is to consult the latest edition of *This Week Kaua'i*.

Luaus

Like all the tourist islands, several large hotels on Kaua'i organize their own *lu'aus*. The **Kaua'i Coconut Beach Resort**'s *lu'au (every day 6pm; ☎822-3455, ext. 651)* is most famous for keeping it as traditional as possible. It devotes itself exclusively to legends and dances specific to Kaua'i. The *lu'au* of the **Hyatt** regency in Po'ipu *(Thu and Sun 6pm; ☎742-1234)*, "Drums of Paradise," is preceded by cultural activities and devotes itself to the entire Pacific, as does the **Princeville Resort**'s *lu'au (Mon and Thu 6:30pm; ☎826-9644)*, which is held in a evocative setting overlooking Hanalei Bay. Other options include **Gaylord's**, at the Kilohana Plantation *("Reflections of Paradise," Mon and Thu 6:30pm; ☎245-9593)*, the **Tahiti Nui restaurant** *(Wed 6pm; ☎826-6277)* in Hanalei, or even **Smith's Tropical Paradise** *(daily)*. This last option is, without a doubt, rather kitsch: the traditional Polynesian show includes dances borrowed from Asian communities who immigrated to the archipelago. It is possible to only attend the show and not the buffet ($14). All *lu'aus* gener-

ally cost slightly over $50.

Shopping

Shopping Centres

Unlike the other islands, where shopping facilities are grouped together in a few places, almost every village on Kaua'i has at least one small shopping centre or grocery store. You therefore don't have to do your groceries in Lihu'e, thinking there won't be anything beyond that point. The shopping centres listed here with phone numbers provide free shuttles that go to certain hotels upon request.

The island's biggest shopping centre, the **Kukui Grove Center** *(☎245-7784)*, is located at the southern exit of Lihu'e. It features 50 boutiques, restaurants, a movie theatre, minigolf and much more.

Almost directly across from it stands the **Kilohana Plantation**, which has luxury boutiques, art galleries and craft shops. Prices are high, but they offer beautiful items.

In Lihu'e, souvenir hunters can also stop at **Hilo Hattie** *(3252 Kuhio Hwy.; ☎245-3404)*.

The vast assembly of shops in the **Coconut Market Place** *(☎822-3641)* is Kaua'i's second largest shopping centre after Kukui Grove. The ambiance is somewhat dismal during the day. It houses a movie theatre, restaurants and 70 shops in total. A number of other shopping centres of various sizes can also be found between Wailua and Kapa'a, of which the biggest are the Waipouli Town Center *(Mile 7.1)* and the Kaua'i Village *(Mile 7.3)*.

More to the south, the **Po'ipu Shopping Village** *(☎742-2831)* houses restaurants and boutiques.

Crafts and Souvenirs

Kapaia Stitchery *(☎245-2281)*, located on the road to the Wailua Falls at the northern exit of Lihu'e, specializes in quilts. You can buy one already made or pick up some patterns and flowered fabric to make one yourself.

Further north, Kapa'a features some arts-and-crafts galleries. The **Kia Gallery** *(1388 Kuhio Hwy.; ☎823-8725)* offers beautiful Hawaiian objects, and its window is decorated with Japanese glass floats found on the island's beaches. The **Lemongrass Gallery** *(4-871 Kuhio Hwy.; ☎822-1221)* specializes in Oriental art. The extremely popular *koa-*

wood furniture of **William and Zimmer** is extremely pricy, but you can easily be satisfied by the less expensive utensils.

Further north, in Kilauea, on the road to the lighthouse, the **Kong Lung Company** *(at the Kong Lung Center;* ☎*828-1822)* has a large variety of exotic objects, especially Asian, such as Chinese furniture, ceramics, kimonos, natural products and less expensive decorative items.

On the southern part of the island, Hawaiian crafts and products are superbly featured at the **National Tropical Botanical Garden shop** in Po'ipu, with such objects as Ni'hau necklaces, *koa*-wood utensils, wickerwork, jams, Macadamia oil, etc. The **Hawaiian Trading Post** in Lawa'i *(*☎*332-7404)*, however offers the largest selection of Ni'hau necklaces, which are true works of art made with thousands of tiny seashells and featured alongside such items as

Tahitian black pearls and eel-leather products. Prices are high.

If you haven't had your fill of shopping, try the galleries of Hanapepe, such as **Kaua'i Fine Arts**, which is specialized in the reproductions of old engravings of the first explorers, or even one of the shops selling **Red Dirt Shirt** T-shirts that are dyed with Kaua'i's brick-red laterite. The company set up its plant at Port Allen.

Markets and Natural Products

The travelling **Sunshine Markets** offer the opportunity to meet small fruit and vegetable producers, and to buy flowers, crafts and other items. They are held on Mondays in Koloa, Tuesdays in Kalaheo, Wednesdays in Kapa'a, Thursdays in Kilauea, Fridays in Lihu'e and Saturdays in Kekaha, as of 9am. With the exception of the latter, the others

open in the afternoon. Private markets are also open: Saturday mornings at the Long Lung Center in Kilauea or at Anahola, Thursday afternoons in Hanapepe, etc.

Kaua'i Island Products Store has two stores that specialize in products made on Kaua'i. One of them is located next to the Red Dirt Shirt store, at the northern exit of Kapa'a, and the other is in the Kukui Grove Center. You will find beauty products, but also sauces, jams and a variety of other items. If you prefer to go to the production plants, the **Guava Kai Plantation**, at the entrance of Kilauea, is not lacking in guava products. The **Kukui** plant *(during the week)*, located at Mile 11.2 on the Kaumuali'i Highway, offers famous tropical-fruit jams such as pineapple, mango, papaya, guava and strawberry, which are sold throughout the archipelago, but can also be purchased here.

Midway

Although Kaua'i is
often considered the westernmost Hawaiian island, beyond it is actually a long string of islets that stretch nearly 1,056mi (1,700km).

A wildlife refuge, these islands are uninhabited and not accessible to the public, with the recent exception of Midway.

One of the first islands to appear more than 25 million years ago above the hot spot that created the rest of the Hawaiian archipelago, the island has succumbed to the forces of erosion. Its volcano gradually vanished, swallowed up by the sea, and its summit now lies 515ft (157m) beneath the surface of a lagoon! But at the same time, in accordance with a typical process of all volcanic islands, a coral crown appeared around the mountain, on which eventually formed sandbars forming the three islands that today make up the Midway atoll: Sand Island, the

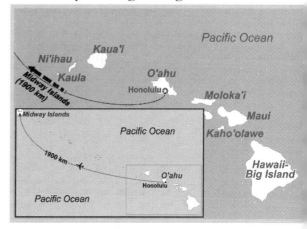

largest and only inhabited island, with an area of 3 sq mi (4.9 km²); tiny Spit Island, with an area of 6 acres (2.4ha); and Eastern Island, with an area of 0.8 sq mi (1.3 km²). Except for Kure, which is located 93mi (150km) away, Midway is the most westerly Hawaiian island, situated about 1,180mi (1,900km) from Honolulu and only 137mi (220km) from the International Date Line. Midway is even a bit closer to Japan, at a distance of 2,175mi (3,500km), than to the

western coast of the United States, which is 2,796mi (4,500km) away. This halfway position between the two countries is, in fact, how the island got its name.

History

The Early Years

Midway is one of the last spots on Earth to have been discovered, on July 5, 1859, by Captain Brooks who gave it his name (Middlebrooks Islands). At the time, the atoll was merely a low expanse of white sand covered with *naupaka*, so the main island was appropriately named Sand Island and the future Eastern Island was named Green Island. Claimed under the Guano Act, which allowed the uninhabited islands of the Pacific to be mined for guano, the atoll nevertheless remained uninhabited. The United States officially took possession of Midway in August 1876, but it remained uninhabited until 1903, when U.S. President Theodore Roosevelt handed control of it over to the U.S. Navy. A contingent of 20 soldiers was sent here to prevent Japanese albatross hunters from taking eggs and feathers from the birds – as well as to prevent the Japanese from encroaching upon Uncle Sam's new territory. That same year, the Commercial Pacific Cable Company built a telegraph relay station, which was run by 30 employees. To improve living conditions, 9,000 tonnes of earth were brought here from O'ahu and Guam to plant a vegetable garden and pine trees. Midway was annexed by the United States in 1908 and became its first overseas territory.

The Interwar Period

In 1935, Pan American World Airways built an operations base and a 45-room hotel, soon nicknamed "Gooneyville Lodge," so that travellers heading from San Francisco to China on its trans-Pacific clippers could rest the night. Their journey to Macao, China, included stopovers in Honolulu, Midway, Wake and Manila, and a one-way ticket cost over three times the annual salary of the average American! The last flight from Asia landed here on December 8, 1941, the day *after* the Japanese had attacked Pearl Harbor and Midway. The passengers had not even been informed. An attempt was made to revive the clippers after the war, but with the new aircraft technology developed during the Second World War, its days were over.

The U.S. Navy

The Navy was responsible for dredging the channel between Sand and Eastern islands in 1938, and soon after began construction of its base, which was finally opened on Sand Island in August of 1941, only four months before Japan's attack on Pearl Harbor. Midway was attacked the same day by two Japanese destroyers, resulting in four deaths and the destruction of the naval base. Other than 17min of combat, the atoll escaped the worst of it. On June 4, 1942,

the pivotal Battle of Midway took place in the seas to the north of the atoll. The U.S. Navy broke the Japanese code and sent out disinformation regarding Midway's freshwater supply. The Japanese decided to attack, but the U.S. Navy was well prepared for them. Taken by surprise, the Japanese lost four aircraft carriers and 3,500 men (the Americans lost 300 men) and Japan never recovered from this devastating defeat. After the Second World War, Midway came under the jurisdiction of the U.S. Navy, which established the headquarters for the DEW line (Distant Early Warning). During the Cold War, radar planes flew off night and day from Midway to Adak Island (Aleutian Islands), Alaska, drawing a symbolic surveillance line between the U.S. mainland and the Soviet enemy. A top-secret underwater listening post was established, and access to the island was strictly limited to military personnel. By the height of the Cold War at the end of the 1950s, the island had nearly 5,000 residents. During the Vietnam War, Midway served as a military outpost. After the Iron Curtain collapsed, Midway's significance to national security began to diminish, and finally, in 1988, the Midway Atoll National Wildlife Refuge was established.

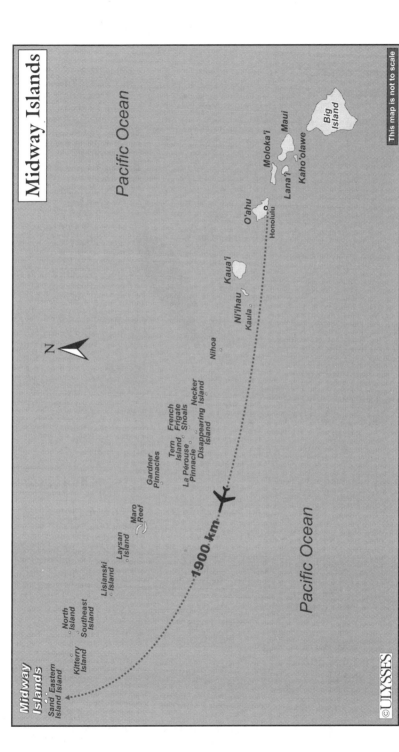

Midway Islands

Pacific Ocean

Pacific Ocean

N

Midway Islands

Sand Eastern
Island Island

Kitterry
Island

North
Island

Southeast
Island

Lisianski
Island

Laysan
Island

Maro
Reef

Gardner
Pinnacles

Tern
Island

French
Frigate
Shoals

La Pérouse
Pinnacle

Necker
Island

Disappearing Island

Nihoa

Kaula

Ni'ihau

Kaua'i

O'ahu

Honolulu

Moloka'i

Lana'i

Maui

Kaho'olawe

Big
Island

1900 km

© ULYSSES

This map is not to scale

The Military Withdrawal

In June 1997, the U.S. Navy officially transferred jurisdiction of Midway to the United States Fish and Wildlife Service (F&WS) and began an intense environmental cleanup of munitions, destroyed military buildings and rubble, which were all taken away by plane. Midway's landscape reverted to its original look. Worried about the cost of maintaining a F&WS station on the island, the U.S. government entered a 30-year agreement with Midway Phoenix Corporation, which was authorized to look after Midway's infrastructure and develop the island for low-impact tourism. The co-management agreement gives the Fish and Wildlife Service the final say in matters concerning the environment, while Midway Phoenix is responsible for ecotourism. In order to minimize disturbance to the wildlife, the number of visitors is limited to 100 at any time.

Flora and Fauna

Midway Atoll National Wildlife Refuge

Ever since it took over control of the island, the Fish and Wildlife Service has implemented a drastic plan to eliminate imported plant and animal species in order to return the island to its natural state. All the rats, which were destroying birds' nests, were exterminated in 1997, and the pine trees on Eastern Island are scheduled to be removed in the near future. In the end, only shade-providing trees sheltering in the "village" will be preserved. The only nature refuge in the Pacific that is accessible to the general public, Midway is *Laysan Albatross* definitely well off the beaten path. Just like the famous Galápagos Islands, time is measured according to natural cycles, storms and the arrival and departure of the 15 species of birds that nest here. Over two million birds nest here every year. They are actually quite tame, and you can walk right up to them.

The Laysan Albatross

Over 750,000 Laysan albatrosses (*Diomedea immutabilis*) stop here at the end of autumn every year. During nesting season, they're everywhere: sometimes right in the middle of the airfield (they think it's *their* landing strip!), along roads, perched on shacks – they literally blanket the ground in a vast sea of hundreds, thousands and tens of thousands of white bodies topped with grey heads. Also known as "gooney birds" because of their clumsy walk, the Laysan Albatros is remarkably graceful once it takes flight after its long run-up. F&WS volunteers spend several months on the island tagging and monitoring the albatrosses in the well-defined observation areas (outlined with orange markers).

Other Bird Species

The island is home to two other albatross species: the black-footed albatross, with its magnificent smoky brown plumage, and the golden-feathered albatross, which is the rarest albatross; there are only 600 to 800 left in the North Pacific. There are also graceful tropicbirds (with red or white tails); white terns, who flutter above your head and lay eggs anywhere (in the crook of a branch, on a roof, on top of an air conditioner – you name it);

short-legged black and brown noddies; and Bonin petrels, which nest in 8.2ft (2.5m) high burrows.

There are also over 200 frigate birds, masked boobies, the first hatching of which was observed in 1999, as well as many red-footed boobies. Migratory species, such as the bristle-thighed curlew and the golden plover, come here in winter from Alaska. You can also see canaries, which

Albatrosses

The best time of year to see albatrosses on Midway is between late of November and June. The first birds return to the island at the beginning of winter, and nearly all of them arrive by December. After finding their partner, they begin a courtship ritual; the birds then mate and a single egg is laid a few days later. The egg usually hatches at the beginning of February after an incubation period of about 63 days. It takes five months for the chicks to reach maturity, after which time they are able to fend for themselves. In the summertime, albatrosses stay at sea and do not return to the island.

were set free by employees of the Pacific Cable Company during the 1930s.

Marine Life

The Midway lagoon is remarkably pristine – an absolute paradise for scuba divers. Soldiers here spent most of their time on land and did not have the opportunity, like in many other places, to inflict much damage to the water. There are more than 258 species of fish here, as well as over 100 dolphins, Hawaiian green sea turtles and some 45 endangered monk seals, which bask in the sun on the beaches. In 1999, a record 12 seal pups were born. Midway is in fact the only place in the world where the monk-seal population is growing. There are also white- and black-tip sharks, hammerheads, Galápagos sharks, as well as dangerous tiger sharks, which eat their fill of young albatrosses along the coast. The fishing in both the lagoon and the open sea is excellent. The sea is teeming with a variety of species, including tuna, *ono* and marlins, many of which grow to considerable sizes.

Population

The animals share the atoll with a population of about 200 permanent

residents on Midway. In one way or another, everyone is affiliated with either Midway Phoenix Corporation or the Fish and Wildlife Service. While the training posts and visitor centres are staffed by personnel from Hawaii and the U.S. mainland, all of the island's operations are run by about 150 Asian employees from the Philippines, Thailand and Sri Lanka. Although residents enjoy an exceptional environment, the isolation, the small size of the island and its status as a nature reserve severely restrict their lives. Pets are forbidden, as are children, since there are no schools on the island. Everyone therefore tries to make the best of their free time: some spend hours surfing on the Internet, while others prefer to play cricket, which is only possible in summer when the albatrosses are gone.

Finding Your Way Around

By Plane

The first flights to Midway, just after it was opened to the public, left from Kaua'i and took more than 5hrs to get here. Today, it takes only 3hrs on an Aloha Airlines Boeing 737 (two weekly flights). The schedules vary according to the presence or absence of albatrosses on the island and according to the time of dusk. The large number of birds prevent the planes from landing during the day, as much to protect their natural cycle as to prevent collisions. Because the birds do not generally fly at night, arrivals and departures are scheduled after 11pm. In the year 2000, a return economy-class ticket from Honolulu to Midway cost $496 and a first-class ticket cost $696 plus tax (Aloha, ☎888-477-7010). In Honolulu, flights depart from the Inter-Island Terminal. On the return trip, planes land at the international terminal so that passengers can clear customs and immigration.

Upon arriving in Midway, a minibus picks up passengers and drives them to their lodgings. If you've reserved a car or a golf cart, you can pick it up the next day after attending the compulsory information session at the Fish and Wildlife Service.

Transportation

Since the island is so small, you'll quickly find your way around. For the first day, you can consult the map given to visitors. Midway has 10mi (16km) of paved roads, 2mi (3km) of tracks, as well

as a few trails. With the exception of commercial vehicles, you get around on foot, by bike or golf cart. Bicycle rentals cost $5 per day and golf carts cost $30 per day. If you're coming here in summer, the busiest time of year, it's best to reserve them at the time of booking.

Practical Information

Customs

Although Midway's location makes it a thoroughly Hawaiian island, it doesn't officially belong to the State of Hawaii (probably due to the island's former military status). This may seem strange, however, especially since all of the other Northwestern Hawaiian Islands come under the political jurisdiction of the City and County of Honolulu. Midway Atoll is considered to be outside the United States by U.S. customs and immigration, therefore proper identification is needed when you return to Honolulu – even if you're a U.S. citizen. Canadians and Europeans must present their passport. There are no formalities upon arriving in Midway, but just before your departure, your passport will be stamped with the Midway emblem, a

pretty tropicbird in flight.

Midway Phoenix

Midway Phoenix Corporation
100 Phoenix Air Dr.
Cartersville, GA 30120
☎770-387-2942
☎888-MIDWAY-1
≈770-387-1327
www.midwayisland.com
Midway Phoenix Corporation operates the infrastructure needed to keep a small town functioning. If you simply plan to walk on the island and relax a while, you can contact the company directly to reserve a plane ticket and hotel package. However, if you want to take part in a particular activity, such as fishing or diving, it's best to contact directly Destination: Midway (☎808-325-5000 or 888-BIG-ULUA, 808-325-7023, *www.fishdive.com*). Ecotours are run by Oceanic Society Expeditions (see below). Most packages are for three, four or seven days, but you can also decide to stay 10 days or longer. The services offered by Midway Phoenix Corporation are excellent. If you have any questions while you're on the island, whether you want to sign up for an activity or obtain information, you can inquire at Guest Services, situated inside Ships Store in the Midway Mall. To learn more about the island, you can also consult the information

signs located in front of the entrance to Guest Services.

Oceanic Expeditions
☎*(415) 441-1106*
☎*800-326-7491*
(Mon to Fri 9am to 5pm, Pacific Time)
(415) 474-3395
www.oceanic-society.org
Located in San Francisco, Oceanic Society is a non-profit organization dedicated to the preservation of marine life and offers expeditions to the four corners of the globe. One of their tours, run in co-operation with Midway Phoenix, heads to Midway for a seven-day visit *($1,890 from Honolulu with shared bathroom)*. You can sign up for two types of excursions: guided tours in small groups with a naturalist or historian, or research expeditions. The volunteer research programs require no prior knowledge or scientific training. You participate in activities like tagging albatrosses and monitoring the spinner dolphin population. Note that the majority of the participants are elderly.

Fish and Wildlife Service

Midway Atoll National Wildlife Refuge
Midway Island Station #4
P.O. Box 29460
Honolulu, HI 96820-1860
☎*808-599-5888 then after the beep dial 808-421-3363 (don't dial 1 before)*
www.rl.fws.gov/midway

The morning after arriving on the island, all visitors must attend a compulsory orientation and information session given by the F&WS to learn about Midway's history and natural habitat, the day-to-day operations of the refuge, as well as the wildlife areas, which are off-limits. Visitors must pay a $5 per day tax *(up to a maximum of $35)*, which goes towards the F&WS. This fee is included in the price of organized tours.

After the meeting, you can obtain more information about the atoll's flora and fauna at the F&WS, or you can participate in a free guided walking tour with a ranger to various places on the island (see below). Several nights a week, the F&WS also offers films at the Station Theatre, situated in Midway Mall (see p 506). Biologists sometimes give lectures here.

Organized Walking Tours

The Fish and Wildlife service organizes four different walking tours, all of which are free. Two of them begin alternately right after the information session. The first tour is dedicated to Midway's history and leads through the "industrial" area of the town, from the greenhouse, where endemic species are

reintroduced, to the memorial, erected in memory of the Battle of Midway, to the seaplane hangars. The second tour is devoted to the long-term plan to return the island's habitat to its natural state. You can also participate in an easy hike on West Beach Trail, which takes place on Saturdays. The tour to Eastern Island is usually on Tuesdays or Fridays, but the schedule can change. All visitors, on a package tour or not, are invited to participate.

Those who prefer a tailor-made excursion can contact resident biologist Heidi Auman *(☎808-599-5400, 808-599-2922, hjauman@yahoo.com)*. The visits *($25 for one or two people)*, which last one to 2hrs, allow you to discover some of the most beautiful spots on the island as well as places where the wildlife is most abundant.

Climate

Situated farther north than the rest of the Hawaiian archipelago, Midway has two distinct seasons. Summer *(May to Oct)* is the most pleasant time of year, with average temperature of about 77°F (25-26°C) and usually sunny weather. This is the best time of year for fishing and scuba diving. Winter *(Nov to Mar)* is marked by windy and rainy

Midway

Marine Pollution

Even an island as isolated as Midway – a nature paradise without any industries – is affected by pollution. The figures, which clearly illustrate the seriousness of marine pollution on a global scale, are quite alarming: in 1998, more than 10 tonnes of waste, washed up by the tides and currents, were collected. Thousands of animals die each year after becoming entangled in abandoned fishing nets or after eating plastic materials. At the Fish and Wildlife Service, a chart lists the stomach contents of an albatross chick that was found dead: 13% squid, its main source of food, 4.7% various materials (wood, polystyrene) and more than 50% plastic materials.

weather with the occasional violent storm. However, there can be week-long stretches of gorgeous weather during this period. In February, nighttime temperatures drop to 53°F (12°C). Although it's generally less advisable to come here in winter, this is the best time of year to see the thousands of albatrosses that nest on Midway.

Time Difference

Midway is 1hr behind Honolulu time year-round. There's a 6hr time difference between the Eastern United States in winter and a 7hr difference in summer.

Emergencies

A different doctor comes to Midway by plane from Honolulu every week. In return for a free vacation, they treat those in need of medical attention. This service, which is common in remote regions, unfortunately does not always take the doctor's speciality into account – you can't ask a dentist or an ophthalmologist to do an appendix operation. However, this has never presented a problem. If the case is serious, the patient can be taken away by air ambulance. To contact the doctor for emergencies, dial ☎*911* (the same number throughout Hawaii).

Post Offices

The Midway post office is located in the airport terminal. It's only open 1hr per day (*Mon to Fri 11:30am to 12:30pm*). If you have stamps, you can drop your mail off here at any time of day. You can also buy stamps at the Gift Shop in the Midway Mall.

Telecommunications

Local telephone calls on the island are free and can be made from your hotel room. There is, of course, a charge for long-distance calls. Most residents use portable phones and visitors can also rent one for $5 per day. Internet access is limited to local residents. The only way you'll be able to connect to the Internet is if you bring your own laptop computer. If you expect an urgent message, you can give out the island fax number, ☎*599-2922* ("Attention Mr./Ms. X").

Laundromat

The Charlie and Bravo buildings have their own washing machines. Only use these ancient machines if you have to, though, as your laundry may end up coming out dirtier than when you put it in.

Grocery Store

The Ships Store, located in the Midway Mall, is the only grocery store on Midway. It's poorly stocked with only the bare necessities and sometimes not even that. Local residents occasionally have to go without toothpaste, shampoo – or worse yet, Coca-Cola – for weeks on end! However, you'll find drinks, soap, cookies and the like here. Credit cards are not accepted. The adjacent Midway Island Gift Shop has postcards and a small supply of film.

Since you can pay for nearly everything at the end of your stay right before taking the plane, you don't have to keep much cash on you – just enough for tips and small purchases. There are no banks or ATM machines on the island.

Exploring

Buildings and the long landing strip take up a large portion of Sand Island's surface area. The "town" stands to the north, halfway between the port and the only accessible beach. Although the island is tiny, you can spend several days exploring it, combined with the activities offered by the Fish and Wildlife Service and tour operators.

You'll discover absolutely sublime places on the island, which are not necessarily indicated on the map.

Midway City

(half-day)

Rather spread out, the town has buildings and pretty wooden homes facing the beach, as well as administrative and technical buildings closer to the port. There are a few Second World War relics scattered here and there, including dilapidated military buildings awaiting repairs. Across the atoll, 63 relics have been listed has "historic" monuments, but they don't hold much interest for visitors.

After the information session at the Fish and Wildlife Service ★, you can spend some time at the centre, which has a small interesting exhibit devoted to wildlife and the island's ecology. An information panel describes the different species of birds found on Midway, the periods when they're present on the island and the location of the main colonies. The small section dedicated to marine pollution speaks volumes. There's also a collection of shells and pretty Japanese glass floats.

On the other side of Morrel Street, just a few steps from the F&WS, is

a **monument** dedicated to the American soldiers killed during the Second World War. If you come in winter, you'll soon notice that the nearby fields, the red and white water tower, as well as the airfield are all covered with literally thousands of tame albatrosses.

Go back in front of the F&WS and head down Peters Avenue towards the east.

At the corner of Nimitz Avenue stands another memorial, consisting of a 11mm anti-aircraft cannon and a large **statue of a giant albatross ★★** – a perfect spot to take a picture.

To the left is the Midway Mall, which houses the Ships Store and Guest Services, the Midway Island Gift Shop and All Hands Club. During the Second World War, it welcomed movie stars who came to visit the troops.

Opposite the mall, at the corner of Cannon Avenue, a Japanese stela commemorates Sakurai Matagora and four other Japanese fishers who disappeared at sea off Midway in 1911. Surprisingly, the gravestones were left untouched during the Second World War.

Across from the stela stands the large Seaplane Hangar, which was chopped in half during the Japanese bomb raids on the island in December 1941. It is the only structure that still bears impact marks from the Battle of Midway. Today, the building is used as a storage facility.

The surrounding area contains most of the industrial- and military-style buildings, including the **Command Post**, which was supposed to be bombproof, but was destroyed during the attack of 1941. Records confirm that the Japanese in fact hit the adjacent laundromat and a bomb ricocheted off the open window! Lieutenant George Cannon was killed and became the first U.S. marine to be decorated in the Second World War. A school for the children of military and civilian personnel was later named after him. The F&WS guided historic walking tour examines the past and present uses of all the buildings in the area.

Cannon Avenue heads behind the seaplane hangar to the port, where the aircraft used to take off. The Midway Sport Diving and Midway Sport Fishing headquarters stand side by side at the end of Hennessy Avenue. Twice a week, barges depart from Tug Pier and head to Eastern Island (see p 503xx). Right at the end of the port, a plaque at the foot of a white wooden cross reminds visitors that the last Easter mass in the world is celebrated every year at this very spot – 137mi (220km) from the International Date Line. If you approach the cross, be careful where you walk, as the ground is covered with burrows dug by petrels.

Head straight up Hennessy Avenue towards the Fuel Farm. Before arriving at the farm (access is forbidden for security reasons), you'll walk along a small white-sand beach. Return towards the town centre via Nimitz Avenue, then turn right on Halsey Drive.

Halsey Drive soon crosses Commodore Avenue, which heads to the north towards Charlie and Bravo (Guest Quarters). Just before reaching these buildings, on the right-hand side of the road, you'll see **Midway House** (*every day 9am to 4pm*), a pretty, white wooden home which was once the residence of the superior officer in charge of Midway. Built in 1941, it was the place where U.S. President Nixon and South-Vietnamese General Thieu held negotiations in 1969. The main floor is open to visitors during the day. There are a few old photographs, some documents related to the Second World War and Midway's mark in history – but nothing of particular interest.

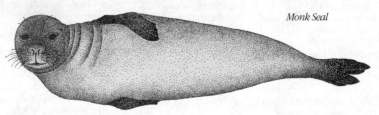

Monk Seal

Past Charlie and Bravo, Commodore Avenue ends a short distance from superb **North Beach ★★★**. The Clipper House restaurant and Captain Brooks Tavern stand side by side here. Bathed by the turquoise sea, the white coral-sand beach stretches about 0.6mi (1km) west to Rusty Bucket. The reef here extends far north. An ideal swimming spot, North Beach is also a great spot to sunbathe – and you'll be joined by monk seals that often bask in the sun here, especially towards the west. If you encounter any, try to stay at least 98ft

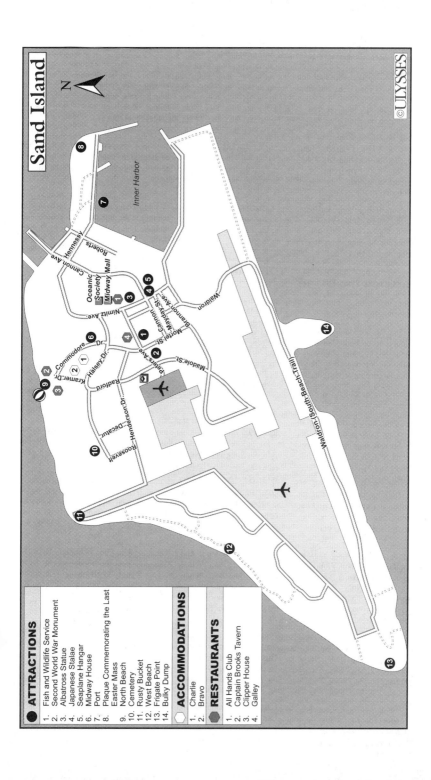

Sand Island

N

© ULYSSES

ATTRACTIONS

1. Fish and Wildlife Service
2. Second World War Monument
3. Albatross Statue
4. Japanese Statue
5. Seaplane Hangar
6. Midway House
7. Port
8. Plaque Commemorating the Last
   Easter Mass
9. Cemetery
10. Rusty Bucket
11. West Beach
12. Frigate Point
13. Bulky Dump

ACCOMMODATIONS

1. Charlie
2. Bravo

RESTAURANTS

1. All Hands Club
2. Captain Brooks Tavern
3. Clipper House
4. Galley

Oceanic
Society
Midway Mall

Cannon Ave.
Hennessy
Roberts

Inner Harbor

Nimitz Ave.
Commodore Dr.
Kramer Dr.
Halsey Dr.
Radford
Henderson Dr.
Decatur
Roosevelt

Peters Ave.
Morell St.
Cannon St.
Midway St.
Brannon Ave.
Waldron
Madole St.

Waldron / South Beach Trail

(30m) away in order to avoid disturbing them.

Behind the restaurant and the Bravo Barracks stand the oldest buildings on the island, built between 1904 and 1905 by the Commercial Pacific Cable Company to house its employees. The cable carried the first round-the-world message from President Theodore Roosevelt on July 4, 1903.

Around the Island

(one to two days)

The most remote spots on Midway are scattered on the edge of the airfield, which occupies a large part of the island. Most of these places can be reached by bike or golf cart, while others, such as the West Beach Trail, can only be reached on foot. In order to avoid disturbing the wildlife, note that all beaches outside North Beach are off-limits, although you can get close to them in several places. This restrictive policy, which can sometimes be frustrating for visitors and especially residents, has had a very positive effect, as the monk seals are now returning to give birth on Sand Island, something they haven't done since the 1940s.

Exit the town via Henderson Drive (the gravel road that passes through the pine trees

The Green Flash

Jules Verne was the first person to refer to "the green flash," and his discovery, in 1890, became all the rage during the Belle Époque. At the precise moment when the sun disappears below the horizon, a flash of green light sometimes appears within a fraction of a second. To see it, there you must be no haze or pollution, and you have to be at the same level as the sun – and be very lucky! In 20 to 30% of cases, the flash lasts less than one second and produces a bright emerald-green light. This phenomenon is due to the refraction of slightly curved rays as they pass through the densest layers of the atmosphere at sunrise or sunset. Midway is an ideal spot to see the green flash.

from the foot of the water tower).

After the small hill (one of the only hills on the island), Decatur Street on the right soon leads to the old **Midway cemetery ★**, which has five graves. The surrounding area, which used to be occupied by an anti-artillery battery, is now home to thousands of albatrosses.

The road heads down to the airfield access road. Take this road towards the sea up to **Rusty Bucket ★★**. This is the northwestern tip of the island, right between North Beach to the east and West beach to the west. An observation tower, which has a steep

wooden staircase, offers a wonderful view overlooking the beach. Monk seals often bask in the sun towards the east, near an enormous tree trunk that washed up on the beach.

Heading down the opposite side of the runway, you'll soon notice the start of the **West Beach Trail ★★**, which disappears into a pine forest where the most timid albatrosses – including many black-footed albatrosses – settle every winter. The trail runs beside pretty West Beach for about 1.2mi (2km). A pleasant bike and golf cart path runs parallel to the trail behind the beach. The F&WS offers organized tours (see p 497) of this area.

West Beach Trail ends near the beginning of the main runway, only 984ft (300m) from **Frigate Point ★★★**, the western tip of Midway. You can safely walk along the landing strip provided that a plane isn't approaching. Situated on the windy coast, Frigate Point is reached by two short trails that pass between soft, green *naupaka* (an endemic plant) on the wide blanket of sand surrounding the point. During the winter, albatrosses flock here by the thousands, soaring with the air currents in single file. Facing the setting sun, this peaceful spot is absolutely breathtaking.

Rather than turning back, head towards the town on **South Beach Trail ★** (Waldron), which follows the edge of the airstrip for almost its entire length. Near an airplane hangar is a sign forbidding you to stop. This is the spot where a female golden albatross usually comes every year. If she's here, you'll see one of the rarest birds in the world. Birding enthusiasts travel thousands of kilometres to witness this event.

A little farther, another short trail leads to a different viewpoint. The beach stretches out below the slope, above which a tidal wave of albatrosses soars each year from November to June.

Thousands of black-footed albatrosses gather along South Beach Trail. About 1.2mi (2km) farther, past a pretty beach where monk seals rest, is the Bulky Dump base, an artificial peninsula that was created by the military. The coral reef, where many Pacific steam ships ran aground, is only about 33ft (38m) away.

South Beach soon crosses the end of the airfield and then heads to the town. Once again, make sure the road is clear. If you're on foot, you can end the island tour by walking along the coast, which is protected from storms by a stone wall.

Eastern Island

(half-day)

Twice a week (except during bad weather) the Fish and Wildlife Service organizes a morning tour of **Eastern Island ★★**. The trip departs from the port at 8am and the crossing by barge only takes about 15min. Along the way, you will pass tiny Spit Island, which is a nature reserve. The visit to Eastern Island, accompanied from start to finish by a ranger, ends with a short trip *(90min to 2hrs)* along the edge of the old landing strip (which is listed as an historic monument!). Depending on the sea-son, you could see different species of birds, some of which are not found on Sand Island, including albatrosses, large frigates, red-footed boobies, masked boobies, terns in the springtime and brown noddies. While the visit does not approach the coast, you might nevertheless be lucky enough to see a monk seal on the beach near the pier where the barge docks.

Outdoor Activities

Most people who come to Midway to dive or fish (the main activities on the atoll) sign up for a package with specialized tour operators. You can also enroll in one of these activities on site. Simply contact Guest Services.

Swimming

Swimming is possible and actually quite pleasant along the only beach open to the public, situated below the Clipper House restaurant. Because it is so long, you will definitely have all the privacy you need. Note that you should avoid swimming when the baby albatrosses take flight *(Jun to Jul)*, as the tiger sharks can come right up to the beach – in water less than 7ft (2m) deep – to snatch up some unlucky birds. It's not a very pleasant site to see.

Scuba Diving and Snorkelling

Relatively unexplored until 1996, the Midway lagoon is home to a variety of different species of fish, many of which are rarely seen in the rest of the Hawaiian archipelago. The most harmless ones, including parrotfish, butterflies and surgeonfish, swim about with large Schleigel's grouper and Japanese and masked angelfish, as well as the striking Galápagos sharks and even tiger sharks. Outside the reef, at depths of about 50 to 65ft (15 to 20m), there are caves, shoals and shelves where manta rays often hide. Ship and plane wrecks from the Battle of Midway lie on the bottom – to the delight of daring divers. The best time to come here is between the end of spring and the beginning of fall, when the sea is calm and clear. Most of the dive sites, which include several caves, are situated just outside the reef, south of Sand Island and near the channel.

Destination: Midway (☎888-BIG-ULUA), which represents Midway Sport Fishing and Diving, offers one-week packages ranging from $10 to $650 and $15 to $800, depending on the number of tanks. If you simply want to take a dive or two, the cost is $85 for a one-tank dive and $125 for a two-tank dive. A night dive costs an extra $65. Snorkelling is also possible three days a week (usually Tue, Thu and Sun) at a cost of $25 per person.

Water Sports

Since Midway is an atoll, its reef is pounded by waves. Surfing and boogie boarding are therefore out of the question. Nor is windsurfing permitted, as it disturbs the wildlife.

Fishing

Within a few years, Midway has become a first-rate fishing destination. Its pristine waters are home to some incredibly large species found nowhere else in the Hawaiian archipelago. Since the island opened to the public in 1996, 18 world records have been broken, particularly the *ulua*

(giant trevally). From the shore, you can fly fish, and, outside the lagoon, you can try to reel in tuna (including six different species), *mahi-mahi*, swordfish, *ono* and blue marlins. Except for record catches, all fish are tagged and released. This is all the more necessary since the lagoon fish have contracted *ciguatera*, a disease caused by the ingestion of bad coral, which can be deadly for humans. The deep-sea-fishing season is between April and November.

Destination: Midway (☎888-BIG-ULUA), representing Midway Sport Fishing and Diving, offers excursions on boats of five different sizes, with prices ranging from $450 (three people) to $790 (for six people). The trips usually last from 8am to 4:30pm (depending on the weather). Night fishing is also possible, as well as mini-expeditions for a few days to Kure Island and the Pearl and Hermes atolls.

Cycling

Except for a few short trails that border Frigate Point and West Beach Trail, which runs along the beach, the entire island is accessible by bike. It's not a long bike ride, but quite enjoyable nevertheless, with the wind blowing through your hair and the occasional white tern accompanying you along the way.

Other Activities

Visitors have free access to a variety of sports equipment on the island, including a gymnasium, exercise room, and tennis, basketball and handball courts.

Accommodations

Every package offered by Midway Phoenix includes accommodation and all meals. Breakfast and lunch are served in the Clipper House, and dinner is served in the Galley (see below). The same goes for the packages offered by Destination: Midway. Plans for a new hotel near the Clipper House were announced in early 2000.

Midway City

Charlie and Bravo
$122-$195/person
sb/pb, laundry, ≡, ℝ, ctv
For the time being, accommodation on the island consists of two former military barracks that have been renovated into hotels. A few pipes have been impossible to hide (especially the ones in the bath-

rooms), but the ambiance nonetheless is that of a decent motel rather than a military camp. Charlie offers more upscale accommodations, with two large suites that have kitchenettes, and smaller suites with identical rooms and living rooms. Most of Bravo's rooms have two single beds and although the bathrooms are shared, you probably won't have to worry about your neighbours bothering you, except during the summer when the hotel is usually full. You can keep the room until 5pm on your final day.

Restaurants

Midway City

Galley
Mon to Sat 6am to 7:30am, Sun to 10am, every day 11:30am to 1pm and 5pm to 7pm
All of the employees on the island have their meal in this large dining hall, the former military base mess hall. Since the Clipper House is closed at lunchtime, you can have lunch with the employees. Although it's a cafeteria, it offers a large selection of decent meals. In addition to usual fare like hot dogs and hamburgers, there are many hot dishes, including Thai and Filipino special-

ities. There's also an hors-d'oeuvre buffet, soups, ice cream, drinks – and everything is all-you-can-eat.

Clipper House
every day except Wed and Sat 7am to 9am and 6pm to 8:30pm
Picture this: an authentic French restaurant, offering a selection of high quality cuisine, in a pretty white wooden building nestled between a white-sand beach and a cluster of pine trees, located on one of the most isolated islands in the world. The Clipper House was named after the Pan Am seaplanes that made the trip to Midway during the interwar period. It was a fortunate series of events that led Alain and Laure, originally from southwestern France, to come to Midway.

Thanks to their fierce determination, they prepare crispy hot croissants and a variety of freshly baked pastries every morning – a miracle considering the limited supplies at the island's only store! Dinner is so divine that you won't want to leave a morsel: there's chicken and truffle mousse, *ono* carpaccio as an hors d'oeuvre, linguini with shrimp, as well as a selection of incredible desserts, including homemade ice cream, flambéed pineapple, pears poached in wine with cinnamon – the list is

Midway

endless and reflects Alain's vivid imagination. The restaurant's reputation is growing and guests now come all the way from Honolulu just to taste his cuisine. Alcoholic beverages and tips are not included in the table d'hôte. You can also ask them to prepare a picnic basket for you.

Entertainment

Movies are presented several nights a week at 7:30 or 8pm at the Station Theatre (Midway Mall). There's often a documentary on the Battle of Midway on Thursday and another one on the albatross on Sunday, but the schedule can change. You can also watch Filipino or Sri Lankan films, which are shown for staff members, but visitors are also welcome.

Bars

All Hands Club
Midway Mall
The only nightlife on Midway, All Hands Club has an American-style ambiance right out of *Top Gun*. You can meet all of the local residents, sip a beer, a

Japanese Glass Floats

Throughout the Hawaiian Islands, inhabitants are crazy about an unusual kind of treasure hunt: glass ball hunting. Replaced by plastic floats, these glass-balls came from Japanese fishing nets and have found their way to Hawaii via the Kuroshio Current. The balls come in all shapes and sizes, depending upon what they were used for. The largest ones are round balls up to 17in (44cm) in diameter, while the smallest ones are smaller than a golf ball. Although they have no monetary value, collectors are fascinated by their incredible journey at sea – sometimes as long as several decades – which makes these glass floats an extremely popular collector's item. But the true pleasure is finding one.

glass of wine or cocktail, or have a hamburger, pizza or fries. Regulars come here to enjoy the music, friendly atmosphere, dartboards and pool tables. On some evenings, the local residents take to the stage. Note that this is the only establishment that's not included in packages.

Captain Brooks Tavern
Situated next to the Clipper House, in a tiny white wooden house on the edge of the beach, this bar is a pleasant place to have a drink.

Shopping

You won't be able to spend a fortune on souvenirs on Midway. The **Midway Island Gift Shop**, situated in the Midway Mall, and the **airport boutique** (only open before flight departures) offers a limited selection of postcards, books, T-shirts, designer Midway bags, as well as adorable, cuddly albatross toys.

Glossary

A Few Tips on Hawaiian Pronunciation

As the official language of the archipelago along with English, Hawaiian is melodious and features a rich vocabulary. The alphabet, introduced in the 1820s by missionaries in order to translate the Bible, only has 12 letters. The pronunciation isn't very difficult, except perhaps for the glottal stop (*'u'ina*, marked as ') which is present in numerous words. In Hawaiian, this linguistic specificity corresponds to a brief pause exhaled between two letters, usually two vowels; a commonly cited example is the English expression "oh-oh!" A glottal stop that is not well placed can completely change the meaning of a word. In addition to the length of many Hawaiian words, the limited number of letters and the frequent repetition of syllables, the other main difficulty resides in the art and manner of pronouncing continuous sounds that are fairly similar without getting confused...

Consonants

p, k	Pronounced as in English but with less aspiration
h, l, m, n	Pronounced as in English
w	In most cases, pronounced as in English, as in *wahine* (wa-hi-nay). After *e* or *i*, it is frequently pronounced as the letter *v*, as in Hale'iwa (Haleiva). Following the letter *a*, it can be pronounced as *v* or *w*.

Vowels

They're everywhere! Each consonant is separated by at least one vowel and every word ends with a vowel. As in most languages, short and long vowels are used in Hawaiian; to indicate elongated vowels, a straight line or a macron might appear over the vowel (called *kahako*). However, this sign is often omitted, especially for Hawaiian words that have been integrated into local English. As for the diphthong, which is common in English, it is rare in Hawaiian. Contiguous vowels are pronounced separately, adding a barely perceptible link between the two vowels when necessary. In most cases, syllables containing diphthongs are stressed.

e	Almost always pronounced as "ay."
u	Always pronounced as "oo" like "pool."

List of Hawaiian Terms

Here is a list of Hawaiian terms used along with English on the islands.

Ahupua'a	In the past, because of their uneven topography, islands were divided into chiefdoms. These territories were delimited by the summits of mountains and cut like a cake; each "slice" was named *ahupua'a*.

'Aina	The earth, sacred to Hawaiians, who themselves are *malama 'aina*: children of the earth.
Ali'i	A Hawaiian chief, and by extension, royalty and nobility of which priests were descendants; superior caste who, in ancient times, had power over life and death.
'Aumakua	Guardian spirit, associated to one place; spirit of the ancestors.
Hala	The pandanus tree, whose leaves (*lau*) are braided (See *lauhala*).
Halau	*Hula* school
Hale	House. This noun is used to form all kinds of words, such as Hale'a'kala, "house of the sun."
Haole	White person; formerly used for "stranger."
Heiau	Ancient Hawaiian temple. Some were dedicated to protective gods, where *kapu* breakers could seek solace (*pu'uhonua*); others were dedicated to warrior gods and used for human sacrifices (*luakini heiau*). Temples reserved for healing purposes were called *heiau ho'ola*.
Hula	Traditional Hawaiian dance, formerly a form of prayer. The *hula kahiko* (old) is different from the *hula auana* (modern).
Imu	Natural stone-carved oven where pigs and other dishes wrapped in banana-tree leaves are cooked with hot stones.
Kahili	Royal insignia depicting a sceptre and topped with a large feather. It is found in some churches.
Kahuna	The priest who presided over ritual ceremonies and human sacrifices; also a sorcerer. *Kahuna* were sometimes specialized in different types of art.
Kalua	Verb meaning "to cook in earth" (see *imu*). The *kalua* pig is a popular dish.
Kama'aina	"Child of the earth"; Hawaiian by birth, as opposed to strangers and immigrants. Also used for residents.
Kane	Man
Kapa	*Tapa*, a fabric made from flattened tree bark.
Kapu	Taboo. Priests used to impose hundreds of *kapu* to regulate daily life. Often used to designate private property.
Keiki	Child; baby
Kiawe	Tree found in dry regions, introduced in Hawaii in the 19th century; it is now found throughout the archipelago.

Ki'i	Divine image sculpted in wood or stone.
Kipuka	Islet of vegetation untouched by a lava flow. Fauna often seeks refuge there and certain subspecies are even created.
Koa	Hawaiian acacia, highly popular for the beauty of its wood. Chopped down in great numbers in the 19th century, it is now protected.
Kona	Leeward coast
Ko'olau	Windward coast
Kukui	Tree whose large nuts were used to make necklaces that possessed a strong *mana*, as well as oil (for lighting purposes).
Kumu	Professor
Lanai	Veranda; balcony. Not to be confused with the island of Lana'i.
Lauhala	Thorny leaves (*lau*) of the pandanus (*hala*), dried, cut into fine strips and braided.
Laulau	Fish or meat (usually pork) cooked in *ti* or banana-tree leaves.
Lei	Flower or fern necklace made according to an established tradition. There are also *lei* made of seashells, feathers, pig's teeth, etc.
Lele	Simple wooden altar in a *heiau* where offerings were placed.
Lomilomi	Traditional massage. Also the name of a marinated salmon-based dish.
Lu'au	Banquet that usually gathered the *'ohana* (family); made popular for tourists by large hotels.
Makai	Towards the sea (as opposed to *mauka*)
Malihini	Stranger, tourist
Mana	Spiritual or divine power that emanates from something. It is the spirit of humans, animals and things, and can be good or evil. Certain *kapu* areas still have a dangerous *mana*.
Mauka	Towards the mountain (as opposed to *makai*).
Mele	Song; poem
Menehune	This colony of small men that lives in Hawaiian legends is said to have built many fishponds, *heiau* and other buildings in one night.

Mu'u mu'u	Hawaiian dress derived from the long robes introduced by missionaries.
Nene	Hawaiian goose; state bird.
'Ohana	Family; brothers, sisters, uncles and aunts, but also close friends, more or less distant cousins, etc. Sort of a familial clan.
'Ohia	Small tree belonging to the myrtle family, with lovely red flowers. It is the first one to grow after a lava flow.
Paepae	Lava-stone platform
Pahu	Drum, traditionally made from shark skin
Paniolo	Hawaiian cowboy, derived from the word *español*, after the first cowboys came from Mexico in 1830.
Pupu	Snack served with beer, cocktail or wine
Pu'uhonua	Sacred area where *kapu* breakers and defeated warriors could find refuge and escape death. They could only go back home after an absolution ceremony.
'Ukulele	"Jumping flea"; small four-stringed guitar whose use was popularized by Portuguese immigrants.
Vog	Kind of sulfurous fog formed by emissions from the Kilauea and covering the region of Ka'u on the Big Island.
Wahine	Woman

A Few Hawaiian Expressions

Hello	*Aloha*
Goodbye, see you soon	*Aloha, a hui hou*
How are you?	*Pehea'oe?*
Well	*Maika'i*
Very well	*Maika'i no*
Not well	*Maikai*
And you?	*A'o'oe?*
What is your name?	*'O wai kou inoa*
My name is...	*'O ... ko'u inoa*
Excuse me, I'm sorry	*E kala mai ia'u*
Where are you from?	*No hea mai 'oe?*
Thank you	*Mahalo*
Thank you very much	*Mahalo nui loa*
You're welcome	*'A'ole pilikia*
No	*'A'ole*
Yes	*'Ae*
OK	*Hiki*
Please	*'Olu 'olu*

Vocabulary

A number of words designating objects that were unknown to Hawaiians before 1778 were borrowed from English. It is frequent to double adjectives to add emphasis.

Big	*nui*
Book	*puke*
Car	*ka'a*
Cliff	*pali*
Fire	*ahi*
God	*akua*
Happy	*hau'oli*
Hospitality	*ho'okipa*
Mountain, hill	*pu'u*
New	*hou*
Newspaper	*nupepa*
Old	*kahiko*
Paper	*pepa*
Pen	*peni*
Shark	*mano*
Small	*li'i*
Very small	*li'ili'i*
Spider	*nananana*
Star	*hoku'*
Street	*alanui*
To help	*kokua*
To love	*aloha*
Wave, to surf	*nalu*

Food and Drink

Beer	*pia*
Coffee	*kope*
Feast	*'aha'aina*
Good, delicious	*ono*
Restaurant	*hale'aina*
Tea	*ki*
To eat	*'ai*
To drink	*inu*
Tuna	*'ahi*
Water	*wai*

Expressions

Darn!	*'Aue!*
Great!	*Kamaha'o!*
Happy Birthday!	*Hau'oli la hanau!*
Happy New Year!	*Hau'oli Makahiki hou!*
I love you	*Aloha au ia 'oe*
Idiot!	*Lolo!*
Merry Christmas!	*Mele Kalikimaka!*
Super!	*Kupaianaha!*
To make love	*Ho'alohaloha*
(or to thank!)	

Index

Index

Index

Order Form

Ulysses Travel Guides

☐ Atlantic Canada .... $24.95 CAN
$17.95 US
☐ Bahamas .... $24.95 CAN
$17.95 US
☐ Beaches of Maine .... $12.95 CAN
$9.95 US
☐ Bed & Breakfasts .... $14.95 CAN
in Québec $10.95 US
☐ Belize .... $16.95 CAN
$12.95 US
☐ Calgary .... $17.95 CAN
$12.95 US
☐ Canada .... $29.95 CAN
$21.95 US
☐ Chicago .... $19.95 CAN
$14.95 US
☐ Chile .... $27.95 CAN
$17.95 US
☐ Colombia .... $29.95 CAN
$21.95 US
☐ Costa Rica .... $27.95 CAN
$19.95 US
☐ Cuba .... $24.95 CAN
$17.95 US
☐ Dominican .... $24.95 CAN
Republic $17.95 US
☐ Ecuador and .... $24.95 CAN
Galapagos Islands $17.95 US
☐ El Salvador .... $22.95 CAN
$14.95 US
☐ Guadeloupe .... $24.95 CAN
$17.95 US
☐ Guatemala .... $24.95 CAN
$17.95 US
☐ Honduras .... $24.95 CAN
$17.95 US
☐ Las Vegas $17.95
$12.95
☐ Lisbon .... $18.95 CAN
$13.95 US

☐ Louisiana .... $29.95 CAN
$21.95 US
☐ Martinique .... $24.95 CAN
$17.95 US
☐ Montréal .... $19.95 CAN
$14.95 US
☐ New Orleans .... $17.95 CAN
$12.95 US
☐ New York City .... $19.95 CAN
$14.95 US
☐ Nicaragua .... $24.95 CAN
$16.95 US
☐ Ontario .... $27.95 CAN
$19.95US
☐ Ottawa .... $17.95 CAN
$12.95 US
☐ Panamá .... $24.95 CAN
$17.95 US
☐ Peru .... $27.95 CAN
$19.95 US
☐ Portugal .... $24.95 CAN
$16.95 US
☐ Provence - .... $29.95 CAN
Côte d'Azur $21.95US
☐ Puerto Rico .... $24.95 CAN
$17.95 US
☐ Québec .... $29.95 CAN
$21.95 US
☐ Québec and Ontario ...... $9.95 CAN
with Via $7.95 US
☐ Seattle .... $17.95 CAN
$12.95 US
☐ Toronto .... $18.95 CAN
$13.95 US
☐ Vancouver .... $17.95 CAN
$12.95 US
☐ Washington D.C. .... $18.95 CAN
$13.95 US
☐ Western Canada .... $29.95 CAN
$21.95 US

Ulysses Due South

☐ Acapulco .... $14.95 CAN
$9.95 US
☐ Belize .... $16.95 CAN
$12.95 US
☐ Cartagena .... $12.95 CAN
(Colombia) $9.95 US
☐ Cancun Cozumel .... $17.95 CAN
$12.95 US
☐ Huatulco - .... $17.95 CAN
Puerto Escondido $12.95 US

☐ Los Cabos and La Paz .... $14.95 CAN
$7.99 US
☐ Puerto Plata - Sosua ..... $14.95 CAN
$9.95 US
☐ Puerto Vallarta .... $14.95 CAN
$9.95 US
☐ St. Martin and .... $16.95 CAN
St. Barts $12.95 US

Ulysses Travel Journals

☐ Ulysses Travel Journal ... $9.95 CAN
(Blue, Red, Green, Yellow, Sextant)
$7.95 US

☐ Ulysses Travel Journal ... $14.95 CAN
(80 Days) $9.95 US

Ulysses Green Escapes

☐ Cycling in France .... $22.95 CAN
$16.95 US
☐ Cycling in Ontario ...... $22.95 CAN
$16.95 US

☐ Hiking in the .... $19.95 CAN
Northeastern U.S. $13.95 US
☐ Hiking in Québec .... $19.95 CAN
$13.95 US

Ulysses Conversation Guides

☐ French for Better Travel .. $9.95 CAN
$6.50 US

☐ Spanish for Better Travel .. $9.95 CAN
in Latin America $6.50 US

Title	Qty	Price	Total
Name:		Subtotal	
		Shipping	$4 CAN
Address:		Subtotal	
		GST in Canada 7%	
		Total	

Tel: _____ Fax: _____

E-mail: _____

Payment: ☐ Cheque ☐ Visa ☐ MasterCard

Card number_____ Expiry date_____

Signature_____

ULYSSES TRAVEL GUIDES

4176 St-Denis,
Montréal, Québec, H2W 2M5
(514) 843-9447
fax (514) 843-9448

305 Madison Avenue,
Suite 1166,
New York, NY 10165

Toll free: 1-877-542-7247
www.ulyssesguides.com
info@ulysses.ca